THE HANDBOOK OF ELECTION NEWS COVERAGE AROUND THE WORLD

The Handbook of Election News Coverage Around the World provides an in-depth analysis of the journalistic coverage of national elections in democracies around the globe. The volume develops a framework for analyzing and comparing the news coverage of elections, providing information about how the news media cover national elections in various democracies, and how that news coverage is related to and affected by system- and culture-specific factors in each country. In addition to focusing on the history, culture, media and political structures, and the importance of, as well as the content of, news coverage of national elections, the volume also provides a comparative overview and analysis of similarities and differences among the countries discussed.

Presenting original research from contributors with particular expertise in the countries they cover, each contribution includes an overview of the political and media systems in the country under discussion; lays out the regulations and laws that apply to the media coverage of elections; and highlights the importance of the news coverage of elections in relation to other forms of political communication, such as paid advertising. Each chapter also includes an overview of previous research regarding the news coverage of national elections, and, with a focus on the most recent elections, reports on recent research about the content of the news coverage of the national elections.

As a comprehensive examination of media coverage of elections, this volume provides important insights into the relationships between the democratic processes around the world and the media reporting on them. It will appeal to scholars, researchers, and graduate students in political communication, political science, mass media and society, international media, and to anyone considering elections and media coverage from a global perspective.

A Volume in the ICA Handbook Series

THE HANDBOOK OF ELECTION NEWS COVERAGE AROUND THE WORLD

Edited by

Jesper Strömbäck
and
Lynda Lee Kaid

Routledge
Taylor & Francis Group

NEW YORK AND LONDON

First published 2008
by Routledge
270 Madison Ave, New York, NY 10016

Simultaneously published in the UK
by Routledge
2 Park Square, Milton Park, Abingdon, Oxon OX14 4RN

Routledge is an imprint of the Taylor & Francis Group, an informa business

© 2008 ICA
The Handbook of Election News Coverage Around the World by Jesper Strömbäck and Lynda Lee Kaid is the first volume in the ICA Handbook Series.

Typeset in Times and Helvetica by EvS Communication Networx, Inc.
Printed and bound in the United States of America on acid-free paper by Edwards Brothers, Inc.

Library of Congress Cataloging in Publication Data
The handbook of election news coverage around the world / [edited] by Jesper Stromback and Lynda Lee Kaid.
p. cm.
ISBN 978-0-8058-6037-5 — ISBN 978-0-8058-6036-8 — ISBN 978-0-203-88717-2 1. Communication in politics.
2. Elections—Press coverage. 3. Press and politics. I. Strömbäck, Jesper. II. Kaid, Lynda Lee.
JA85.H35 2008
070.4'43249—dc22
2007041875

ISBN10: 0-8058-6036-3 HB
ISBN10: 0-8058-6037-1 PB
ISBN10: 0-203-88717-4 EB

ISBN13: 978-0-8058-6036-8 HB
ISBN13: 978-0-8058-6037-5 PB
ISBN13: 978-0-203-88717-2 EB

Contents

PART II: ELECTION NEWS COVERAGE IN COUNTRIES WITH PROPORTIONAL ELECTIONS

PART III: ELECTION NEWS COVERAGE IN COUNTRIES WITH COMBINED SYSTEMS

**PART IV: ELECTION NEWS COVERAGE
IN A COMPARATIVE PERSPECTIVE**

List of Figures

Series Editor's Foreword

Robert T. Craig

With this volume we inaugurate the ICA Handbook Series, an ongoing series of scholarly handbooks jointly sponsored by the International Communication Association and Routledge.

The goal of this series is to advance communication theory and research internationally, reflecting the interests of ICA members. Volumes in the series will provide benchmark summaries of current scholarship and set the agenda for future work on problems of broad potential interest among scholars in communication and media studies and related fields. Scholarly excellence, timeliness, international scope, relevance to significant normative and empirical questions, and integration across disciplinary and national boundaries to open new prospects for collaborative investigation are among the qualities we hope to achieve with each volume.

The Handbook of Election News Coverage Around the World exemplifies our best hopes for the series. Jesper Strömbäck and Lynda Lee Kaid have assembled a stellar, international group of contributing authors to summarize and assess the current state of knowledge on media coverage of national elections in each of 22 countries across five continents and the European Parliament. Country-based chapters examine not only the content and effects of election news coverage but also the historical context and structural characteristics of electoral systems, media systems, regulatory environments, and the complex relations among political actors, media, and audiences, all factors that influence election coverage. Complementing this parallel assessment of election coverage in each country from multiple disciplinary perspectives, the editors' introductory and concluding chapters unify the volume by placing this large and often quite fascinating body of information in a comparative framework.

The result of this collaborative effort is a rich contribution to our understanding of political communication in the contemporary world and, we may hope, a spur to further empirical and critical inquiry on problems of democratic communication.

THE ICA HANDBOOK SERIES

The ICA Handbook series is a joint venture between the International Communication Association and Routledge. It will be a series of scholarly handbooks that represent the interests of ICA members and help to further the Association's goals of promoting theory and research across the discipline. These handbooks will provide benchmark assessments of current scholarship and set the agenda for future work. The series will include handbooks that focus on content areas, methodological approaches, and theoretical lenses for communication research.

We seek proposals from prospective editors of handbooks. We especially seek proposals that cross the boundaries of established disciplines and fields to address timely problems of international scope, not just representing different specialties but bringing them together collaboratively to address intersecting interests and research problems of broad interest. For example, such problems might be formulated as topical concerns (e.g., globalization, virtual environments), theoretical approaches (e.g., social cognition, critical studies), or matters pertaining to communication or communication research in general (e.g., methodological innovations, communication theory across cultures).

For more information about this series, contact:

Robert T. Craig
ICA Handbook Series Editor
Department of Communication
University of Colorado at Boulder
270 UCB
Boulder, CO 80309-0270
303-492-6498 voice
303-492-8411 fax
Robert.Craig@colorado.edu

or

Linda Bathgate
Senior Editor, Communication Studies
Routledge
270 Madison Avenue
New York, NY 10016
212-216-7854 phone
212-643-1430 fax
linda.bathgate@taylorandfrancis.com

Acknowledgements

The idea of this book was born during discussions in the fall of 2004, when Jesper Strömbäck was a visiting scholar at the University of Florida for the purpose of studying the media coverage of the U.S. presidential campaign. Most of the editing was done in the spring of 2007 when Jesper Strömbäck returned to the University of Florida for six months as a visiting professor. Thus, he would like to thank The Swedish Foundation for International Cooperation in Research and Higher Education (STINT), which provided the funding for his visit to the University of Florida in 2004, and Sundsvalls kommun/Mid Sweden University and Karl Staaffs fond för frisinnade ändamål, which provided the funding for his visit to the University of Florida in 2007. The importance of the support from these agencies cannot be overestimated. Jesper Strömbäck would also like to thank the College of Journalism and Communications at the University of Florida for their hospitality and for providing support during his visits there.

Lynda Lee Kaid would like to acknowledge the support of the Fulbright Commission/CIES whose support in the spring of 2007 made it possible for her to devote time to this project while pursuing comparative political communication research in Germany, Switzerland, and France. This support provided opportunities to meet with several of the contributors and to coordinate the completion of several chapters.

The editors would also like to thank Linda Bathgate and the staff at Lawrence Erlbaum Associates/Taylor and Francis, and Robert T. Craig at the International Communication Association, for their support during this project.

Finally, the editors would like to thank all the authors for their efforts and contributions to this book, which we feel is an important contribution to the understanding of the antecedents, content, and effects of the election news coverage in democracies around the world.

Contributors

Annette J. Aw, Ph.D. is Adjunct Associate Professor in the Department of Communication at the University of Maryland University College. She is also an independent research consultant in Washington, D.C., where she conducts media-related studies for private businesses, trade associations, and government agencies. Before working in the United States, she taught at Nanyang Technological University in Singapore between 1995 and 2001. Her research and teaching interests focus on public relations and intercultural communication in Asia and the United States. Professor Aw received her Ph.D. in Intercultural Communication from the University of Oklahoma in 1994.

Arnold S. de Beer is Professor Extraordinary, Department of Journalism, Stellenbosch University, South Africa. He is the managing, editor of *Ecquid Nov: African Journalism Studies* and research director of the Institute for Media Analysis in South Africa (iMasa). He has published on media and democracy in Africa, news flow and journalism education, and is the editor of *Global Journalism – Topical Issues and Media Systems* (Pearson, 2008).

Eric Darras is the Research Director of the Toulouse School of Political Science, University of Toulouse. He is a former staff advisor to the Conseil Supérieur de l'Audiovisuel (CSA), the French counterpart to the U.S. Federal Communications Commission. His recent publications include "Media Consecration of the Political Order" in Benson & Neveu (Eds.), *Bourdieu and the Journalistic Field* (Polity Press, 2004), "Le pouvoir de la télévision? Sornettes, vieilles lunes et nouvelles approches," in Lacroix & Riutord (Eds.), *Les formes de l'activité politique: Eléments d'analyse sociologique (18è–20è siècles)* (Paris, PUF, 2005), and "Permanences et mutations des émissions politiques en France," *Recherches en communication, 24*, 2005, Louvain: UCL.

Nicolas Demertzis is Professor at the Faculty of Communication and Media Studies, Athens University. He has taken part in numerous conferences and has published extensively in Greek and English journals and volumes. His current academic and research interests include political sociology, political communication, and the sociology of emotions. His major works are: *Cultural Theory and Political Culture: New Directions and Proposals; Culture, Modernity, Political Culture* (co-authored with Thanos Lipowatz); *Essay on Ideology: A Dialogue between Social Theory and Psychoanalysis; Local Publicity and the Press in Greece; The Nationalist Discourse: Ambivalent Semantic Field and Contemporary Tendencies; Political Communication: Risk, Publicity and the Internet* (with Thanos Lipowatz); *Envy, Ressentiment: The Passions of the Soul and the Closed Society*. In 1994 he edited the book *The Greek Political Culture Today* and in 2002 the collective volume *Political Communication in Greece*. Also, in 2002 he co-edited the book *Religions and Politics in Modernity*.

Claes H. de Vreese is Professor and Chair of Political Communication and Scientific Director of The Amsterdam School of Communications Research (*ASCoR*) at the Department of Communication Science at the University of Amsterdam. He is also Director of the Netherlands School of Communications Research (*NESCoR*), and Adjunct Professor of Political Science and Journalism at the University of Southern Denmark. His research interests include comparative journalism research, the effects of news, public opinion and European integration, and effects of information and campaigning on elections and referendums. He has authored more than 30 articles in international journals such as *Communication Research, Journalism Studies, Political Communication, International Journal of Public Opinion Research, Scandinavian Political Studies, European Journal of Communication, West European Politics, EU Politics, Journalism & Mass Communication Quarterly, Mass Communication & Society*, and *European Journal of Political Research*.

Daniela V. Dimitrova, Ph.D. is an Assistant Professor in the Greenlee School of Journalism and Communication at Iowa State University. Her research interests include new media technologies, news framing, and international coverage of conflict events. She has published several articles in refereed journals such as *The Harvard International Journal of Press/Politics, Social Science Computer Review, Gazette: The International Journal for Communication Studies*, and the *Journal of Computer-Mediated Communication*. Currently Dr. Dimitrova serves as the Head of the Communication Technology division of AEJMC, the premier association for journalism educators in the United States.

Bogusława Dobek-Ostrowska is Professor of Communication and Head of the Department of Social Communication and Journalism at the University of Wroclaw, Poland. She is General Editor of the Series on Mass Media and Communication, published by the University of Wroclaw Press. Her research interests are mass media in Poland and other post-communist countries, and political communication with particular attention to the role of the media in politics. Among her major publications are: *Komunikowanie polityczne i publiczne* (2006), *Media masowe i aktorzy polityczni w świetle badań nad komunikowaniem politycznym* (2004), and *Podstawy komunikowania społecznego* (1999).

Frank Esser, Ph.D. is Professor and Chair of Comparative Media Research in the Department of Mass Communication and Media Research at the University of Zurich. He was assistant professor of mass communication at the University of Mainz and the University of Missouri-Columbia, and visiting professor at the University of Oklahoma. His research centers on cross-national studies of news journalism and political communication. He has published five books, including *Comparing Political Communication: Theories, Cases, and Challenges* (2004), and sixty book chapters and journal articles. He is on the board of directors of both the Swiss Centre for Studies on the Global Information Society and the NCCR Democracy, a national center of competence launched by the Swiss National Science Foundation.

Stephen J. Farnsworth is Assistant Professor of Communication at George Mason University, where he teaches courses in political communication and journalism. He is the author or coauthor of three books, including most recently *The Nightly News Nightmare: Television's Coverage of U.S. Presidential Elections, 1988–2004* (2nd edition, and is a former daily newspaper journalist. A former associate professor of political science at the University of Mary Washington, he was also the 2006–2007 Fulbright Research Chair in Public Policy at McGill University, Montreal, Canada, where he completed the U.S. elections chapter for this volume.

Elisabeth Gidengil is a Hiram Mills Professor of Political Science at McGill University. Her research focuses on public opinion and voting behavior, with particular interests in gender and the media. She is a former Shorenstein Fellow in the Press, Politics and Public Policy at Harvard University and has been a member of the Canadian Election Study team since 1992. Her books include *Making Representative Democracy Work* (1991), *The Challenge of Direct Democracy* (1996), *Unsteady State: The 1997 Canadian Election* (2000), *Anatomy of a Liberal Victory* (2002), and *Citizens* (2004). She recently co-edited *Gender and Social Capital* (2006) with Brenda O'Neill.

Amanda Gouws is Professor of Political Science and chair of the department at the University of Stellenbosch. She teaches Political Behavior, South African Politics and Gender Politics. She has done extensive research on the South African electoral system. She is co-author with Professor Jim Gibson of Washington University, St Louis of *Overcoming Intolerance in South Africa: Experiments in Democratic Persuasion* that received the Alexander George Book Award from the International Society of Political Psychology for the best book in Political Psychology in 2004. She engages regularly with the media by writing op-ed articles in *Die Burger*, an Afrikaans newspaper. Her articles deal with contemporary political issues in South Africa.

Katharina Hemmer, M.A. is a doctoral student and research associate in the Department of Mass Communication and Media Research at the University of Zurich. Her research interests are in international and comparative mass communication.

Lynda Lee Kaid is Professor of Telecommunication in the College of Journalism and Communications at the University of Florida. She previously was a George Lynn Cross Research Professor at the University of Oklahoma, where she also served as the director of the Political Communication Center and supervised the Political Commercial Archive. Her research specialties include political advertising and news coverage of political events. A Fulbright Scholar, she has also done work on political television in several Western European countries. She is the author/editor of more than 25 books, including *The Encyclopedia of Political Communication, The Handbook of Political Communication Research, The Sage Handbook of Political Advertising, The Millennium Election, Political Television in Evolving European Democracies, Civic Dialogue in the 1996 Presidential Campaign, Videostyle in Presidential Campaigns, The Electronic Election, New Perspectives on Political Advertising, Mediated Politics in Two Cultures,* and *Political Advertising in Western Democracies.* She has also written more than 150 journal articles and book chapters and numerous convention papers on various aspects of political communication. She has received more than $2 million in external grant funds for her research efforts, including support from the U.S. Election Assistance Commission, the U.S. Department of Commerce, the U.S. Department of Education, the National Endowment for the Humanities, and the National Science Foundation.

Chappell Lawson is an Associate Professor of Political Science at MIT. His recent books include *Building the Fourth Estate: Democratization and Media Opening in Mexico* (University of California Press, 2002) and *Mexico's Pivotal Democratic Election* (Stanford University Press, 2003), co-edited with Jorge Domínguez. He is the Principal Investigator for the Mexico 2000 Panel Study and the Mexico 2006 Panel Study.

S. Robert Lichter is Professor of Communications at George Mason University, where he also directs the Center for Media and Public Affairs, which conducts scientific studies of the news and entertainment media, and the Statistical Assessment Service (STATS), which works to improve the quality of statistical and scientific information in the news. He has authored or co-authored fourteen books and over a hundred scholarly articles and monographs, including *The Nightly News Nightmare: Television Coverage of Presidential Elections* (2006, 2nd ed.); and *The Mediated Presidency: Television News and Presidential Governance* (2005).

Bartłomiej Łódzki is a doctoral student at the University of Wroclaw. He graduated from the faculty of Political and Communication Science in 2004. His research primarily concerns agenda-setting, mass media influence, political communication, and development of new media. He is author of the article *Agresja, przemoc i terror w telewizyjnych programach telewizyjnych,* and other articles published in *Studia Medioznawcze.*

Esteban López-Escobar, LLD is Professor of Public Opinion at the School of Communication, University of Navarra (Spain). He holds a doctoral degree in Law (University of Sevilla), and he also graduated in Communication and Journalism (University of Navarra). He has been WAPOR president (2005–2006), is a Joan Shorenstein Center Fellow (Harvard University), and has been a trustee of the International Institute of Communications (London), a member of the board of the European Media Institute (Manchester and Düsseldorf), and a member of the European Communication Council (Berlin). He has published many books (among them the pioneering study *Análisis del "nuevo orden" internacional de la información*, 1978) and articles that have appeared in a number of journals.

Jürgen Maier is a Professor at the Department of Methods of Empirical Social Research at the University of Kaiserslautern, Germany. His research focuses on public opinion and voting behavior, political communication, and quantitative methods of social research. He has published several articles in scholarly journals such as *European Journal of Political Research, International Journal of Public Opinion Research, Communications*, and *German Politics*.

Michaela Maier is a Professor at the Department of Communication Psychology, Media Pedagogics and Speech at the University of Koblenz-Landau, Germany. Her research focuses on organizational and political communication as well as journalism. She has co-edited the volume *Campaigning for Europe: Parties, Campaigns, Mass Media and the European Parliamentary Elections 2004* (Münster: LIT 2006) as well as guest-edited an issue of the *Journal of Political Marketing* on the 2004 European Election.

Jack McLeod is Professor Emeritus at the University of Wisconsin-Madison. He was Maier-Bascom Professor of Journalism and Mass Communication and Director of the Mass Communications Research Center at the University of Wisconsin-Madison. His research has focused on the effects of news media use and interpersonal communication patterns on democracy, most recently on knowledge acquisition, civic and political participation, political socialization of adolescents and young adults, and macro influences across levels in communication research.

Misha Nedeljkovich, Ph.D. is Associate Professor of Film and Video Studies at the College of Journalism and Mass Communication, University of Oklahoma. He received his M.F.A. from UCLA, Film & Television Department, did post-graduate work at Kenkysei Tokyo University; and completed his Ph.D. at Ohio University. He has worked professionally with CBS (Los Angeles); Japan Cable Television; TV and National Theater in Belgrade; and the International Festival (Monte Carlo). He received Fulbright grants in 1983 and in 2003 and a Mombusho, Japanese Ministry of Education grant in 1986. He publishes on film and mass media in former communist countries, and his publications include *Aesthetics of Film Noir* (2005).

Sarah Oates is a Senior Lecturer in the Politics Department at the University of Glasgow. She studies the potential of television to constrain political choice and signal fear. She has been Principal Investigator on three British Economic and Social Research Council grants to examine the political role of the media in Russia, the United States, and Great Britain. She is the author or co-author of *Television, Democracy and Elections in Russia* (2006), *The Internet and Politics: Citizens, Voters and Activists* (2005), and *Introduction to Media and Politics* (Sage, in press). She currently is a co-investigator on a major grant to develop more effective measures for communicating counter-terrorism messages to the public.

George Pleios is Associate Professor and Director of the Laboratory for Social Research on Mass Media, at the Department of Communication and Mass Media, University of Athens, Greece. He has published three books (*Moving Pictures and Artistic Communication, The Discourse of the*

Image: Ideology and Politics, The Image Culture and Education) and many articles in Greek and international reviews and collected volumes. He has also participated in many international conferences on mass media and currently is carrying out research on TV newscasts.

Mauro P. Porto, Ph.D. is Assistant Professor in the Department of Communication at Tulane University, New Orleans. He holds a Ph.D. in Communication from the University of California, San Diego. In 2002, he received the Best Doctoral Dissertation Award by the Brazilian Society of Interdisciplinary Communication Studies (INTERCOM). His research and teaching interests focus on media and democratization in Brazil and in Latin America. Porto has published widely in several academic journals around the world, including *Political Communication*, *Journalism*, *Television and New Media*, *The Communication Review*, and *Journal of Health Communication*. He is currently working on a book about television and politics in Brazil.

Lilia Raycheva is a member of the Council for Electronic Media (the regulatory authority for radio and television broadcasting in Bulgaria) and a member of the Standing Committee on Transfrontier Television of the Council of Europe. She has been a Vice-Dean for Scientific Research and International Affairs and Head of Radio and Television Department at the Faculty of Journalism and Mass Communication of the St. Kliment Ohridski University of Sofia. She has lectured in both Bulgaria and other countries. Her work has been extensively published, and she has successfully participated in a number of international research and administrative projects on mass media issues.

Jolán Róka, Ph.D. has been Associate Professor of Speech Communication in the Department of Modern Hungarian, Eötvös Loránd University (Budapest), since 1978. She is the author or editor of five books and 70 journal articles and book chapters, and has received several awards from the Hungarian Scholarship Board to do research in England, Finland, Italy, Turkey, Israel, Sweden, Netherlands, Germany, France, Luxemburg, Turkey, India, Greece, a George Soros Grant to the School of Communication at the Pennsylvania State University, an IREX Grant to the Annenberg School for Communication, University of Pennsylvania, a TEMPUS Grant to the University of Wales, Cardiff, and a Fulbright Grant to Texas A&M University, Faculty of Journalism.

Franca Roncarolo is Associate Professor of Political Science at the University of Turin. She has written on the changes that have occurred in the political communication systems of American and Italian democracy and has been monitoring the Italian electoral campaigns in the media since the 1990s.

Teresa Sádaba is Associate Professor of Political Communication at the School of Communication, University of Navarra, Spain. She is also Associate Director of the University of Navarra's Master's program on political and corporate communication, a program in collaboration with George Washington University, Washington, D.C. She has been visiting scholar at the University of Austin, Texas; research scholar at the London School of Economics and Political Science; and Fulbright fellow at George Washington University. She has written several books and papers on political communication in Spain, framing theory, and communication and terrorism.

Shinichi Saito, Ph.D. is a Professor of Communication at Tokyo Woman's Christian University. He received his Ph.D. from the Annenberg School for Communication, University of Pennsylvania. His research interests include the contents and effects of mass communication, the social impact of new communication technologies, and quantitative research methods. Besides many articles in Japanese, his recent publications in English include chapters in *Images of the U.S. around the World* (1999), *Handbook of the Media in Asia* (2000), and *News Media and New Media* (2003), as well as articles in journals such as *Journal of Communication*, *Disability & Society*, and *Gazette*.

Margaret Scammell is senior lecturer in Media and Communications at the London School of Economics. She has published widely on politics, communication, and political marketing and is the author of *Designer Politics* (Macmillan, 1995), *On Message: Communicating the Campaign* (Sage, 1999) with Pippa Norris, John Curtice, David Sanders and Holli Semetko, and *Media Journalism and Democracy* (Ashgate, 2000) with Holli Semetko.

Holli A. Semetko is vice provost for International Affairs and director of Office of International Affairs and The Claus M. Halle Institute for Global Learning at Emory University, where she is also a professor of political science. Dr. Semetko was previously professor and chair of Audience and Public Opinion Research in the Faculty of Social and Behavioral Sciences at the University of Amsterdam, the Netherlands. Recognized internationally for her research on news contents, uses and effects in a comparative context, she has received numerous grants, honors and awards including the Samuel H. Beer Prize for the best dissertation on British politics and the ICA's article of the year for "The Divided Electorate: Effects of Media Use on Political Involvement" in *The Journal of Politics*. With more than 80 publications, including five books and 35-plus peer-reviewed journal articles, her most recent book, co-authored with Claes de Vreese, is *Political Campaigning in Referendums: Framing the Referendum Issue* (Routledge, 2004).

Tamir Sheafer, Ph.D. studied communication at the University of California, Berkeley and received his Ph.D. from the Hebrew University in 2001. He is now Assistant Professor at the Departments of Political Science and Communication, the Hebrew University of Jerusalem, Israel. His main area of research is political communication. Two specific areas to which he has mostly contributed include the "actor-centered" approach to the study of the competition of political actors over the political communication arena, and the study of media effects on electoral behavior. His research has been published in leading journals, such as *Political Communication, Journal of Communication, Communication Research, Public Opinion Quarterly, Legislative Studies Quarterly,* and *Harvard International Journal of Press/Politics*.

Mira Sotirovic, Ph.D. is Associate Professor at the University of Illinois at Urbana-Champaign. Her research interests are in media effects and democracy. Most recently she has co-authored the chapter "Knowledge as Understanding: The Information Processing Approach to Political Learning" in the *Handbook of Political Communication Research*, edited by L. L. Kaid (2004). She teaches reporting, public opinion, and research methods courses. Before receiving her Ph.D. from the University of Wisconsin-Madison, she was a reporter and editor in Yugoslavia.

Jesper Strömbäck is Professor in Media and Communication and Lubbe Nordström Professor and Chair in Journalism at Mid-Sweden University, Sundsvall, Sweden. He is also Director of the Centre for Political Communication Research at Mid-Sweden University, and has been a visiting professor at the College of Journalism and Communications at the University of Florida. His research specialties include political news coverage, political campaigning and political marketing, and the news coverage of wars and crises. He has published more than ten books in Swedish, and articles in scholarly journals such as the *European Journal of Communication*, the *Harvard International Journal of Press/Politics*, *Journal of Political Marketing*, *Journalism Studies*, and *Scandinavian Political Studies*.

Toshio Takeshita, Ph.D. is a Professor of Mass Communication at Meiji University, Tokyo. His research interests include the uses and effects of mediated communication and the media's role in public opinion processes. He has been especially engaged in agenda-setting research in Japan. Besides the books and papers published in Japanese, his papers have appeared in such volumes as *Media and Politics in Japan* (Pharr & Kraus, Eds., 1996) and *Communication and Democracy*

(McCombs, Shaw, & Weaver, Eds., 1997), as well as in journals such as the *International Journal of Public Opinion Research*.

Rodney Tiffen is Professor of Government and International Relations at the University of Sydney. He has written widely on Australian media and politics. His books include *News and Power* (1989), *Scandals: Media, Politics and Corruption in Contemporary Australia* (1999), and (with Ross Gittins) *How Australia Compares* (2004).

Yariv Tsfati, Ph.D. is a Senior Lecturer in the Department of Communication, University of Haifa, Israel, and a research associate at the Chaim Hertzog Institute for Media, Society and Politics at Tel Aviv University. His areas of interest include media and politics, audience trust in news media, and audience perceptions of media influence. His research has been funded by the Israeli Science Foundation, the Edelstine Foundation, the Burda Center for Innovative Communication, and the Israeli Democracy Institute. His articles have appeared in academic journals including *Communication Research, Journal of Communication, Journal of Broadcasting & Electronic Media,* and *Journalism & Mass Communication Quarterly*.

Gabriel Weimann is a Professor of Communication at the Department of Communication at Haifa University, Israel. His research interests include the study of media effects, political campaigns, persuasion and influence, media and public opinion, modern terrorism and the mass media. He has published six books: *Communicating Unreality* (2000), *The Influentials: People Who Influence People* (1995), *The Theater of Terror* (1994), *Hate on Trial* (1986), *The Singaporean Enigma* (2001) and *Terror on the Internet* (2006). He has published more than 110 publications in various journals, books, and research reports. He has been a Visiting Professor at various universities including University of Pennsylvania, Stanford University, Hofstra University, Lehigh University (USA), University of Mainz (Germany), Carleton University (Canada), and the National University of Singapore.

Lars Willnat is Associate Professor at the School of Media & Public Affairs at the George Washington University in Washington, D.C. Before joining GWU in 1996, he taught at the Chinese University of Hong Kong and was a MacArthur Foundation Fellow at the Indiana Center on Global Change and World Peace. His teaching and research interests include media effects on political attitudes, theoretical aspects of public opinion formation, and international communication. He has published book chapters and articles in journals such as *Journalism & Mass Communication Quarterly*, *International Journal of Public Opinion Research*, *Political Communication*, *Journalism*, and *International Communication Gazette*. Professor Willnat received his Ph.D. in Mass Communication from Indiana University in 1992.

Ricardo Zugasti, Ph.D. is Lecturer in the Spanish Political System and Spanish Journalism History at the School of Public Communication, San Jorge University, Spain. In his doctoral dissertation he examined the political characterization which the Spanish press attributed to King Juan Carlos and his monarchy during the transition to democracy. He has been Lecturer at the University of Navarra (Spain) and at the Istmo University (Guatemala), and Visiting Research Fellow at the Department of Journalism Studies at the University of Sheffield (United Kingdom). His most recent book is *La forja de una complicidad. Monarquía y prensa en la transición española (1975–1978)*.

1

A Framework for Comparing Election News Coverage Around the World

Jesper Strömbäck and Lynda Lee Kaid

The histories of election research and political communication research have been closely inter-twined ever since the end of World War II. According to Blumler and McQuail (2001, pp. 216–218), six reasons for this state of affairs can be identified. First, elections are spurring "continual innovation and development in the strategic organization and conduct of political communica-tion" by political parties and candidates. Second, elections are convenient benchmarks for chart-ing trends over time, not least with regards to how the media cover elections. Third, "elections provide opportunities to study the roles in political communication of major innovations in media formats," such as political debates and political advertising. Fourth, election campaigns are very suitable with regards to cross-national and comparative political communication research. Fifth, new theories can and often have been pioneered in the context of election campaigns. Finally, empirical data collected during election campaigns contribute to the debate surrounding different notions of citizenship and the quality of democracy. This is not surprising when one considers how important elections are from both a practical and a normative point of view.

Underlying these reasons for the close intertwining of election research and political com-munication research is the fact that modern politics is *mediated politics* (Bennett & Entman, 2001). This might seem self-evident to most readers of this book. Still, even today, much research on democracy and democratic theory lacks a coherent discussion, or any discussion at all, of the importance of communication and the media. As noted by Thompson (1995, p. 3): "in the writ-ings of social theorists, a concern with communication media is most noticable for its absence."

However, there is not only a lack of discussion on the importance of communication media in much of the literature on democracy and democratic theory. Despite the fact that elections are very suitable for cross-national studies in political communication, there is also a noticeable lack of comparative research on how the news media in different countries cover national elections (De Vreese, 2003). There are some important exceptions (Gerstlé, Davis, & Duhamel, 1991; Lange & Ward, 2004; Semetko, Blumler, Gurevitch, & Weaver,1991), but the overall picture is clear: there is a decided deficit in comparative studies on national election news coverage in dif-ferent countries.

Moreover, the literature in this area is dominated by research conducted in countries such as the United States and Britain. Thus, most research and theory on election news coverage (its antecedents, content, and effects) suffer from an Anglo-American bias. This does not, of course, mean that they are not valid or applicable in other countries. Gerstlé et al. (1991) found striking similarities in news coverage of candidates, issues, and themes when comparing news coverage of the 1988 French and U.S. presidential elections. Frank Esser and colleagues have made comparisons between the United States, Britain, and Germany in regard to "tabloidization" of news and metacommunication trends (Esser, 2000; Esser & D'Angelo, 2003; Esser, Reinemann, & Fan, 2001). On the other hand, comparative research on the election news coverage in countries such as the United States, Sweden, Spain, and Britain indicates that there are significant variations across countries (Strömbäck & Dimitrova, 2006; Strömbäck & Luengo, 2006; Strömbäck & Shehata, 2007). What is more important, however, is that we can never know what trends or characteristics are cross-nationally valid in the absence of comparative research. Hence, it is easy to agree with Blumler and Gurevitch (1995, p. 75) when they state that "Comparative research is an essential antidote to naive universalism."

These observations suggested a need for a *Handbook of Election News Coverage around the World.* In this chapter, we outline a framework for thinking about and comparing the election news coverage in different democracies around the world. The following chapters will present detailed analyses of the election news coverage within a number of countries. Revisiting this framework in the concluding chapter, we consider similarities as well as differences in order to deepen our understanding of the causes for the patterns observed.

MEDIATED AND MEDIATIZED POLITICS

On the most general level, the concept of *mediated politics* is often used to denote a situation in which the mass media constitute the main channel for political information for most people. In such a situation, not only do people depend upon the mass media for information; political parties and candidates, as well as all other actors with a need to reach out to people, also depend upon the mass media. Put differently, the mass media *mediate* between the electorate on the one hand and the institutions involved in government, electoral processes, or, more generally, opinion formation of any kind on the other. Politics could thus be described as mediated whenever the mass media are the main channels through which politics is communicated and when, as a consequence, the depictions of "reality" that are conveyed through the mass media presumably have an impact on how people perceive "reality."

From this perspective, it does not matter whether the media landscape is dominated by radio, newspapers, or television. Nor does it matter whether the mass media are independent from or controlled by government or political actors, such as parties or interest groups. What matters is whether the mass media constitute the most important channels for information exchange and communication between the people and political actors. Mediated politics is thus something fundamentally different from politics experienced through interpersonal communication or directly by the people.

From a descriptive point of view, the concept of mediated politics is obviously important, and it does capture a very important aspect of politics in advanced, postindustrial societies. However, it is also a rather static concept that largely fails to capture the dynamics of modern political communication processes and how they have evolved over the last decades. Thus, there is a need for a concept that is better suited for capturing changes over time and the dynamics of the relationship between citizens, the mass media, and politics. One such concept is the concept of *mediatized politics.* Sometimes, this process of mediatization is also referred to as the *medialization* or the *mediazation* of politics.

Broadly speaking, the concept of the mediatization of politics refers to a process through which the mass media have gained increased influence and independence from the political system. Four different phases of mediatization could, theoretically, be identified (Strömbäck, 2007; see also Asp & Esaiasson, 1996).

1. The first phase of mediatization is reached when the mass media constitute the most important communication channels between those who are governed and those who govern. This is also when politics can be described as mediated, as noted above.

2. The second phase of mediatization is reached when the mass media have become largely independent from governmental or other political bodies. This is not to say that the mass media are ever totally independent from outside political influence. From a social system perspective, the relationship between the mass media, politics, and other groups in society should be perceived as interactive, dynamic, and characterized by interdependence. Rather, the second phase of mediatization means that the mass media have become semi-independent and that they largely control their own content as well as the necessary resources that can be put to use in what Cook (2005) has termed "the negotiation of newsworthiness" with those trying to influence the news. The political system or political actors might still have the upper hand, but they cannot control the media or unconditionally use them to further their own interests.

3. The third phase of mediatization is reached when the mass media have become so independent and important that political actors and others begin to adapt to the predominant notion of newsworthiness and the so-called *media logic*, in order to influence the news, gain visibility, and use the news to send "signals" to other political actors as part of the governing process (Cook, 2005). At this stage, not only is the social or political system affected by the media. The social system also adapts itself to the mass media, their news values, and the media logic; the media logic becomes the logic that sets out the boundaries for all parts of society which have a need to communicate through the mass media or at times risk finding themselves at the center of the mass media´s attention. This is what Altheide and Snow (1991, p. ix) refer to when they state that: "Today all social institutions are media institutions. As more experiences are influenced by media logic, our worlds are totally media."

One need not, however, agree that all social institutions today are media institutions to see that the media in many countries operate according to their own logic, and that it has become more important than it used to be for political actors to adapt to the media logic. Media logic means "a form of communication, the process through which media present and transmit information. Elements of this form include the various media and the formats used by these media. Format consists, in part, of how material is organized, the style in which is presented, the focus or emphasis on particular characteristics of behavior, and the grammar of media communication" (Altheide & Snow, 1991, p. ix). On a less abstract level, this means adaption to the predominant news values and the storytelling techniques the media make use of in order to be competitive in the struggle to capture people´s attention. These storytelling techniques include simplification, polarization, personalization, stereotyping, and visualization (Asp, 1986; Gans, 1980; Hernes, 1978; Strömbäck, 2000). The more a potential news story can be told using these storytelling techniques, the more likely it is that it will be reported. And the more political actors can offer stories that can be reported using these storytelling techniques, the more likely it is that these political actors gain visibility in the news.

The adaption to media logic can be made more or less reluctantly, however. As political parties and candidates also operate and need to be successful within the political system, they also have to take what might be called a "political logic" into consideration (Meyer, 2002). Such a political logic operates differently in different countries, depending on a number of factors related to, for example, the electoral system, the number of parties, and the need to be successful while governing. Political decision making is a time-consuming, complex process, and political actors always have to consider that they might be held responsible for their actions or inactions. This arguably creates a very real tension between the media logic and the political logic, or the demands of the media system versus the demands of the political system.

4. The fourth phase of mediatization is reached when political or other social actors not only adapt to the media logic and the predominant news values, but also *internalize* these values and, more or less consciously, allow the media logic and the standards of newsworthiness to become a built-in part of the governing process. If political actors in the third phase *adapt* to the the media logic and the predominant news values, they *adopt* the same media logic and the standards of newsworthiness in the fourth phase. Thus, in the fourth phase, the media and their logic can be said to colonize politics (Meyer, 2002), with political or social actors perhaps not even recognizing the distinction between a political logic and a media logic. As noted by Cook (2005, p. 163): "Politicians may then win the daily battles with the news media, by getting into the news as they wish, but end up losing the war, as standards of newsworthiness begin to become prime criteria to evaluate issues, policies, and politics."

This is not to say that the process of mediatization has reached phase 4. Which phase the process has reached is ultimately an empirical question, and the answer most likely differs among countries. Moreover, the process must not necessarily be linear. It is also likely that the degree of mediatization differs between periods when parties and politicians focus on campaigning and when they focus on governing—although permanent campaigning appears to have become more common (Ornstein & Mann, 2000).

However, it is safe to conclude that politics in modern postindustrial democracies is mediated and also, to varying degrees, mediatized. Thus, it is also safe to conclude that the election news coverage is very important in all modern postindustrial democracies.

The question then is: how can we understand the antecedents and the content of the election news coverage in different countries around the world? What factors shape the election news coverage, with particular emphasis on: (1) the amount of news space devoted to covering elections; (2) the usage of issue frames versus strategy or game frames; (3) descriptive versus interpretive journalism; (4) the publication of opinion polls and other aspects of horserace coverage; and (5) degree of political bias?

Election campaigns, including the election news coverage, are complicated subjects to study and understand, as they reflect a coming together of system characteristics, semistructural factors, contextual factors, and the dynamics of the relationship between political actors, news media actors, and people as voters and media consumers. The important factors can be located at a macro-, meso-, or microlevel. To structure this discussion, however, we will take as our starting point that political and media systems, as well as the patterns of relationship between these systems and their characteristics, ultimately is what matters most.

DIFFERENT MODELS OF MEDIA AND POLITICAL SYSTEMS

On a very general level the political system in any country includes the constitution and the legal framework, all institutions with political relevance, and the configuration of politically relevant organizations and actors. The media system, while partly shaped by the political system, similarly includes all media institutions and the configuration of media organizations. At any point in time the political system and the media system should be perceived as shaped by history and a dynamic and culturally entrenched relationship between the citizenry, media actors, and political actors. In no country is the political system and the media system at a particular point the result of conscious and deliberative decision making only. Rather, it is the result of intended and unintended effects or countless more or less conscious and deliberate, formal as well as informal, decisions taken by politicians, media owners, editors and journalists, and ordinary people, to mention just some of the most important actors from a political communication perspective.

This seemingly chaotic process of system formation does not, however, mean that it is not possible to identify patterns in system characteristics which can be useful in comparative analyses. One of the first such attempts was presented in the classic book *Four Theories of the Press* by Siebert, Peterson, and Schramm (1956/1984). More relevant in this context, however, is the analysis by Blumler and Gurevitch (1995, pp. 60–67) in which they proposed four dimensions of particular importance along which the connections between political institutions and media institutions can vary: degree of state control over mass media organizations, degree of mass media partisanship, degree of media-political élite integration, and the nature of the legitimizing creed of media institutions. More recently, Hallin and Mancini (2004) identified three different models of media and politics among Western democracies: a Liberal Model, a Democratic Corporatist Model, and a Polarized Pluralism Model. With regards to media systems they emphasized four dimensions: (1) the development of media markets, with particular emphasis on the development of a mass circulation press; (2) political parallelism, which refers to the degree and nature of the links between the media on the one hand and political parties or major political and social divisions in society on the other; (3) the development of journalistic professionalism; and (4) the degree and nature of state intervention in the media system. With regards to political system characteristics they emphasized (1) the political history, more specifically patterns of conflict and consensus; (2) consensus or majoritarian government; (3) individual or organized pluralism; (4) the role of the state and state intervention in society; and (5) the development of rational legal authority as opposed to clientilism. In short, they argue (p. 11) that:

> The Liberal Model is characterized by a relative dominance of market mechanisms and of commercial media; the Democratic Corporatist Model by a historical coexistence of commercial media and media tied to organized social and political groups, and by a relatively active but legally limited role of the state; and the Polarized Pluralist Model by integration of the media into party politics, weaker historical development of commercial media, and a strong role of the state.

The countries represented in this book, Greece, Spain, Italy, and to a lesser extent France, can be said to illustrate the characteristics of the polarized pluralist model, with Greece as the prototypical example of this model. Sweden, the Netherlands, and Germany belong mainly to the Democratic Corporatist Model, with Sweden as a prototypical example; whereas especially the United States but also the United Kingdom belong mainly to the Liberal Model. The other countries included in this book are not classified by Hallin and Mancini.

This kind of analysis and classification is very useful and important in furthering our understanding of the importance of media system and political system characteristics. It is also very useful for an analysis of the antecedents of the election news coverage in different countries. Still, it was not developed primarily for a cross-cultural analysis of the election news coverage in general or the five areas of particular interest mentioned above. In this context, some features of political systems and media systems, respectively, might be more imporant than others. Of particular importance with regards to the political system might be the electoral system, whether the system is party-centered or candidate-centered, the number of political parties, the type of government, and the political culture.

POLITICAL SYSTEMS MATTER

One important feature of the political system is the electoral system. That is, whether a country has a proportional, majoritarian, or combined type of system (Lijphart, 1999; Norris, 2004). In proportional systems people vote for party lists (closed or open) or rank their preferences among the candidates as in the single-transferable vote (STV) system. Majoritarian systems can make use of a first-past-the-post (FPTP) or a second ballot system, whereas different combinations are used in combined systems. On a global level, approximately one third of the countries in the world make use of a proportional system, whereas about half of the countries make use of a majoritarian system, and the remainder combine them (Norris, 2004, p. 40). The aim of majoritarian systems is to create a parliamentary majority in order to produce an effective one-party government and thus government accountability, whereas the aim of proportional systems is to include as many voices as possible, emphasizing the need for bargaining and compromise within parliament, government, and the policy-making process. Majoritarian systems are often called adversarial systems, whereas proportional systems are called consensus systems (Lijphart, 1999, Norris, 2004). As noted above, this is one of the dimensions emphasized by Hallin and Mancini (2004) in their analysis of political systems.

One important aspect of the electoral system is that it shapes the party system and affects the number of political parties in a particular country. Generally speaking, a majoritarian system fosters a two- or few-party system, whereas proportional elections foster a multi-party system. The mean number of political parties in the former system is thus significantly lower than in the latter system (Norris, 2004, p. 85). Voter turnout is also higher in proportional systems than in majoritarian and combined systems, indicating that the incentives for supporters of smaller parties or minority viewpoints to vote might be higher in proportional systems; that is, those voters not represented by the two or three major parties that dominate the party landscape in majoritarian systems. In proportional systems every vote counts, in contrast to majoritarian systems where it often might be common knowledge long before the election which party is likely to win, either nationally or in different voting districts.

This might have implications for the election news coverage in different countries. In proportional systems where turnout is high and the election outcome is an open affair there are incentives for the media to devote a considerable amount of news space to the election, as more people in such cases are looking for political information. This kind of incentive might not exist to the same extent in majoritarian systems, especially in cases where one party or one candidate has a significant lead in the polls and thus is very likely to win the election.

The higher number of political parties in proportional systems as compared to majoritarian systems might also have consequences for the election news coverage, especially if the system is party-centered rather than candidate-centered. In party-centered systems with many parties the issues, often linked to different social or political cleavages in society, tend to be more important than the individual candidates (Holmberg & Oscarsson, 2004; see also King, 2002). Political parties in such systems are also likely to be more product- and sales oriented rather than market oriented (Lilleker & Lees-Marshment, 2005; Strömbäck, 2007a), which also encourages an emphasis on issues rather than personalities and images. The larger parties might have the character of a catch-all party, but mid-sized and smaller parties are more likely to focus on particular cleavages or segments in society and the issues they think are the most important. Taken together, this issue orientation might be reflected in the political culture while simultaneously encouraging the news media to frame politics as issues rather than as a game (Cappella & Jamieson, 1997; Patterson, 1993).

In terms of the different models identified by Hallin and Mancini (2004), this suggests that the news media in countries that form part of the polarized pluralist model and the Democratic Corporatist Model are more likely to devote significant news space to national elections and to frame politics as issues, than the news media in countries that form part of the Liberal Model—if the former have proportional elections and multi-party systems. However, if Polarized Pluralist or Democratic Corporatist countries have majoritarian electoral systems, or a presidential system, then this might not be the case. News media in majoritarian and presidential systems with single-member districts are those most likely to frame politics as a game.

There is also a connection between the type of electoral system and party and the question about political parallellism.. In countries with proportional elections and multiple parties which are connected to particular social or political divisions in society, there has been a historical connection between the political parties and the news media, especially newspapers. In such countries the news media in general, and the newspapers in particular, were or still are a part of the party-political system rather than independent organizations with their own—commercial—agenda. This might encourage the news media to think of elections as important, but it might also encourage them to cover the elections in a partisan way for both ideological and commercial reasons. Thus, ideologically or politically biased election news coverage is more likely in such countries, especially Polarized Pluralist countries, than in countries that form part of the Liberal Model. However, it might also be the case that the issue about partisan bias is considered as more important, while also more hotly debated, in countries that form part of the Liberal Model, simply because partisan bias is not considered as legitimate in such countries. This issue appears to generate the most controversy in the United States (Farnsworth & Lichter, 2006; Niven, 2002), despite evidence showing that partisan bias is rather uncommon in the U.S. news media (Graber, 2006; Gulati, Just & Crigler, 2004), which indicates that this is the case. Stated differently, one tentative conclusion is that partisan bias will be more common but also less controversial in party-centered countries with multiple parties, proportional elections, and which belong to the Polarized Pluralist Model, while partisan bias will be less common, but also more controversial and hotly discussed, in countries with fewer parties, majoritarian electoral systems, and which belong to the Liberal Model.

MEDIA SYSTEMS MATTER

However, not only the political system matters, but also characteristics of the media system in different countries. During the last decades these have gone through major transformations in a number of countries around the world (Campbell, 2004). Technological advances have been a major impetus for deregulation of broadcast media as well as for the innovation and growth of the Internet as a major new medium (Norris, 2001; Pavlik, 2001). While there were only a couple of television stations in many countries worldwide in the late 1970s, cable and satellite technology has caused this number to multiply in most advanced democracies. In many countries consumers can choose between 50 to 60 channels and in some between more than 100 channels. This has put increased pressure on public service media in countries where they used to have a monopoly, not least in European countries. A simultaneous process is the process of globalization, spurred by large global media conglomerates, with the end result that there is less concentration in terms of media products as compared with 20 or 30 years ago, but also more concentration in terms of ownership (Bagdikian, 2000; Croteau & Hoynes, 2001; Demers, 1999). Media systems worldwide have also become more commercialized, as a consequence of the increased competition, the rise of major media conglomerates, the breakdown of public service monopolies, and because of a breakdown of the traditional legitimizing creed of news media; namely, that they have a moral obligation to serve the common good and people as citizens rather as consumers. As the freedom of choice between different news media has increased, people increasingly behave as consumers on the media markets and are thus treated as consumers by media companies that need to be competitive in the struggle for attention in order to thrive economically (Hamilton, 2004; McManus, 1994). Traditionally speaking many news media were once ruled by people with journalistic values and a journalistic background. Today many news companies are publicly traded, valued as investments rather than from the perspective of societal needs, and MBAs have increasingly taken over the role of publicists in many newsrooms (Underwood, 1995). The public service ethos has weakened whereas the profit-making motive has become more important (Hamilton, 2004; Picard, 2005). This might especially be the case in countries which form part of the Liberal Model of media and politics, but all countries and their media systems are affected by the technological revolution, the globalization processes, the increasing competition for people's attention, and the ongoing process of commercialization. Thus, it can also be said that there is less room for significant variation between media systems in different countries because there is a trend toward convergence not only with regards to different media formats (TV, Internet, newspapers, radio) but also with regard to media systems as such.

However, less room for variation does not equal no room for variation. Public service media still play a major role in many countries, such as Britain and Norway. Media systems are not shaped by technology and economy only, but also by history, traditionally rooted expectations, values and patterns of media consumption, as well as by political decisions. Some countries are more television-centric whereas others are newspaper-centric (Hallin & Mancini, 2004). In some countries many news media companies are still owned by foundations, family companies, or organizations that are not interested in financial return only. The extent to which media companies are publicly traded or form part of large global media conglomerates also varies across countries, as does the degree of regulation of the media system. Furthermore, the extent to which the news media are expected to serve the common good and perceive of people as citizens and not only consumers varies across countries. The degree of journalistic professionalism, and how journalists in different countries understand the notion of journalistic objectivity, also varies across countries (Donsbach & Patterson, 2004; Patterson, 1998). Finally, in some countries, most notably those which form part of the Polarized Pluralist Model, the news media are considered by both media actors themselves, the citizenry, and political actors as part of the party-political system rather than as totally external and independent.

Differences such as these might have implications for the form and content of the news coverage of national elections. To start with, the more commercialized a particular media system is, the more likely it is that politics will be framed as a game rather than as issues (Patterson, 2000). This is because a frame of this kind requires less interest and knowledge from the audience. Furthermore, it requires less knowledge from and is less time-consuming for the journalists, while it also lends itself more easily to dramatic and thus attention-grabbing storytelling. Stories about winners and losers are widely known from other areas in society; thus, they are often culturally congruent and lend themselves to complexity-reducing stereotyping. Yet another reason is that the framing of politics as a game allows journalists to distance themselves from the political candidates and parties. Hence, the framing of politics as a game allows journalists to be critical without necessarily being accused of partisan bias. In this case polls are also very helpful because they feed the framing of politics as a game and allow journalists "a quasi-objective, proactive role in the news-making process" (Lavrakas & Traugott, 2000, p. 4). The use of opinion polls and the framing of politics as a game is thus closely connected, providing that there are no rules restricting the publication of opinion polls.

While the framing of politics as a game and the publication of opinion polls generally speaking can be expected to be more common the more commercialized a particular media system is, the opposite is likely true with regards to the existence of partisan bias. Although there might be exceptions in countries where the news media form part of the political system, generally speaking partisan bias would restrict the opportunities for the news media to reach out to as many people as possible. Thus, from a commercial standpoint it would be unwise. It would also be unwise for news media in highly commercialized media systems to devote a lot of news space to an election—if a particular election is not considered especially important or exciting. News media in less commercialized media systems can hence be expected to give a higher priority to the election news coverage than news media in highly commercialized media systems. The same is true of news media which aim at a highly educated and politically interested part of the public, as constrasted to media which target a mass audience or less educated and politically less interested people.

However, this tendency might be moderated by the political and the journalistic culture, or more specifically the extent to which politics and elections are valued as such. In some societies and in some media organizations, politics and elections might be considered important and newsworthy as such, reflecting what Blumler and Gurevitch (1995) have labeled a "sacerdotal" rather than a "pragmatic" approach. In the former case, political news is regarded "as an intrinsically important service that must be provided as of right, and in the latter insisting that political material should fight its way into print and programmes on its news values alone" (Blumler & Gurevitch, 1995, p. 68). Such a sacerdotal approach is, however, less likely in highly commercialized media systems and in political systems where political parties play a less dominant role. Thus, it is less likely in countries with majoritarian electoral systems and few political parties, and more likely in countries with proportional representation and many political parties. Hence, a sacerdotal approach is less likely in countries which form part of the Liberal Model than in countries which form part of the Democratic Corporatist or the Polarized Pluralist Model. At the same time it should be noted that increased commercialization and competitiveness has made a sacerdotal approach less likely even in countries belonging to these models.

Another part of the political and media systems of importance is whether televised political advertising—in particular paid political advertisning—is allowed or not and whether it constitutes an important channel for political information and political communication (Kaid & Holtz-Bacha, 2006). The less important televised advertising is—paid or provided free through regulation—the more important the election news coverage becomes. Similarly, the more important televised advertising is, the less important the election news coverage becomes, although the latter will probably be perceived as more trustworthy by the people, but also as significantly less controllable by the political actors. The existence and importance of paid political advertising might also give rise to specific journalistic features such as ad-watches. It might also have the indirect effect that news media actors feel less responsible for providing people with political information and news, as the political actors in such cases have other means for the communication with people.

JOURNALISTIC NORMS AND VALUES MATTER

This brings us to the question of journalistic norms and values. On the surface journalists in different countries might seem to share journalistic norms and values, but a closer look reveals significant differences. Partly these differences can be related to the different models of media and politics and to different levels of journalistic professionalism (Hallin & Mancini, 2004; Waisbord, 2000), but these are not the only precurors. Journalists, both across and within the same model of media and politics and across different media formats within countries, tend to interpret fundamental concepts such as journalistic objectivity differently, they have different job motivations, and they occupy different roles vis-à-vis the political system (Donsbach & Patterson, 2004; Patterson, 1998). Stated differently, the journalistic field and its relationship with the political field varies across countries (Benson, 2005), as do news room cultures. In some countries, for example, the United States and Sweden, journalists tend to hold a critical and adversarial position vis-à-vis politicians; whereas, in countries such as Italy and Britain, they tend to take a more supportive and mediating position vis-à-vis politicians. Similarly, in some countries journalists prefer an advocacy type of reporting whereas in other countries they prefer a more detached style. However, in some countries there are significant differences between print and broadcast journalists; for example, in Britain where broadcast journalists are more neutral and less partisan than print journalists (Donsbach & Patterson, 2004, p. 266). Thus, in some countries and some media there is a stronger emphasis on neutral and descriptive reporting, whereas in other countries there is a stronger emphasis on a literary style of journalism, allowing more interpretation and analysis than in the former countries (Benson & Hallin, 2007). This might have implications for the extent to which the election news coverage in a particular country is interpretive rather than descriptive. One tentative conclusion here might be that interpretive journalism is more common in countries which belong to the Polarized Pluralist Model than to the Liberal Model, with countries belonging to the Democratic Corporatist Model falling in between.

However, there are indications that an interpretive or even assertive style of journalism and journalistic commentary has become more common over the last decades in different countries (Kovach & Rosenstiel, 2001; McNair, 2000; Strömbäck, 2004). Views have in many cases replaced news. This is an indication that the norm of journalistic objectivity and impartiality might have weakened even in countries where it used to be fairly strong. The rise of the Fox News Channel is another indication of ongoing changes of journalistic norms and values, which is particularly interesting as such a news channel would have been much more likely in a country belonging to the Polarized Pluralist Model. Thus, if there is a process of convergence of media systems going on (Hallin & Mancini, 2004), it is not necessarily the case that countries which (used to) belong to the Democratic Corporatist or the Polarized Pluralist Models are moving toward the Liberal Model. The opposite might also be(come) true, at least in certain respects.

STYLE AND CHARACTER OF POLITICAL CAMPAIGNING MATTER

The rise of a more interpretive and assertive style of journalism has many explanations, but one of them is the increasing professionalization of political advocacy and campaigning worldwide (Plasser & Plasser, 2002). Broadly, professionalized political campaigning is characterized by being permanent, although with varying intensity; by the central campaign headquarters being able to coordinate the messages and the management of the campaign; and by using expertise in analyzing and reaching out to members, target groups, and stakeholders, in analyzing its own and the competitors´ weaknesses and strengths and making use of that knowledge, and in news management (Farrell & Webb, 2000; Gibson & Römmele, 2001; Strömbäck, 2007b). In this context this is important, because the increasing efforts and skills in the packaging of politics, in news management, and the spinning of the news (Franklin, 2004; McNair, 2000) appears to trigger a journalistic self-defense, as noted by Blumler and Kavanagh (1999, p. 215): "journalists do not relish having their news choices severely narrowed by those whose activities they are supposed to cover. Their sense of their own professionalism—in which autonomy and independence figure prominently—leads them to seek ways to stamp their marks on political stories." Similarly, evidence from the United States suggests a "rule of product substitution" according to which "the more strenuously politicians challenge journalists for control of a news jurisdiction, the more journalists will seek to develop substitute information that the mass audience is willing to accept as news and that gives expression to journalistic voice" (Zaller, 2001, p. 255).

This is probably particularly true in countries where journalistic professionalism is highly developed and where journalists thus consider themselves as independent from the political systems, in particular countries with the characteristics of the Liberal Model. Interpretive, assertive, or critical reporting is therefore more likely in countries where political actors have become more professionalized in their advocacy and campaigning than in countries where they have become less professionalized, although this tendency might be moderated by country-specific traditions of a literary style of journalism. The framing of politics as a strategic game is also more likely in countries with the characteristics of the Liberal Model, and for the same reasons. Even the news media's use of opinion polls could be perceived as a means to counterbalance the political actors and their use of often confidential polling results.

To some extent the character and style of political campaigning and news management could be perceived as a semi-structural factor, but it also varies between parties within countries, and across time. Although the long-term trend is towards increased professionalization of political campaigning, there are important variations across countries—in important respects due to variations in political systems and media systems (Plasser & Plasser, 2002)—and the trend need not be linear. The style and character of political campaigning reflect, just as they do with regard to the election news coverage, a coming together of system characteristics, semi-structural factors, contextual factors, and the dynamics of the relationship between political actors, news media, and the citizenry. Changes in people's behavior as voters and media consumers have spurred both the changes in political campaigning and news media coverage in general and in political news reporting in particular.

PEOPLE AS VOTERS AND MEDIA CONSUMERS MATTER

When Lazarsfeld and colleagues conducted their classic study of the American presidential campaign in 1940, most voters had decided on their party long before election day. Most voters tended to vote for the same party in successive elections, often the same party as their parents and grandparents had chosen. Only 8% of the voters in the *People's Choice* study changed party allegiance; the main effect discovered in this study was an activation effect: "while people hesitate and mediate and imagine that they decide rationally on the better road to take, it would often have been possible to predict at the outset what they would decide to do in the end. Knowing a few of their personal characteristics, we can tell with fair certainty how they will finally vote: they joined the fold to which they belong. What the campaign does is to activate their political predispositions" (Lazarsfeld, Berelson, & Gaudet, 1948, p. 73).

However, much has changed since then. During the last few decades people have changed their behavior considerably with regards to both politics and media. Some significant trends in many though not all countries worldwide is: decreasing voter turnout (Norris, 2001), decreasing party identification (Dalton, 2000), and participation through traditional means, such as being a member of a political party (Scarrow, 2000; Dalton, 2002), increasing distrust of politicians and political institutions (Norris, 1999), increasing electoral volatility, and more people waiting until late during a campaign before deciding which party to vote for (Dalton McAllister, & Wattenberg, 2000), and decreasing class identification and voting (Oskarson, 2005; Thomassen, 2005). Thus, campaigns and the election news coverage matter more than they used to do, as the share of undecided or wavering voters has increased.

All this also indicates that people's cognitive need for orientation has increased, which has implications for the effects of the mass media. As shown by McCombs (2004, p. 54), "an individual's need for orientation (Weaver, 1977) is defined in terms of two lower-order concepts, relevance and uncertainty, whose roles occur sequentially. Relevance is the initial defining condition of need for orientation." People who experience something as relevant will want to understand the phenomenon, thus seeking information about it. This is particularly true among those who experience uncertainty about the same issue or topic. As people rely on the mass media for information about things beyond their own experiences, this means that they will likely search for mass mediated information to reduce the uncertainty. This, in turn, makes it likely that the strongest agenda-setting effects—and perhaps also framing effects—will be found among people with a high need for orientation.

The trends in political behavior noted above certainly indicate that the level of uncertainty has increased during the last decades, implicating a higher need for orientation today than in earlier times. Research also indicates that the levels of political information, interest and sophistication has increased (Dalton, 2002), indicating that the experienced relevance of politics has not decreased. It might even have increased, leaving people even more susceptible to the power of the news media in the opinion formation processes. This is no less true with regards to the news coverage of election campaigns.

On the other hand there is also clear evidence of changes in how people consume and attend to the news media. As the number of mediated channels of information has increased, both with regards to magazines, television channels, and the Internet, the patterns of news consumption has become more fragmented (Campbell, 2004; Graber, 2006; Kovach & Rosenstiel, 1999). No longer can it be assumed that people watch the same news shows or read the same newspapers or magazines: the size of the mass public has shrunk while the numbers of niche media and niche audiences have multiplied. This has made it less likely that any particular single medium will reach and set the agenda or the frames for the public. However, the media as a collectivity can still have a profound effect upon which issues or frames people experience as most salient, especially if different media focus on approximately the same issues and actors while also framing them similarly. An individual single news medium might have lost power, while the media collectively have gained power in the opinion formation processes.

In any case, the trends with regards to both political behavior and media consumption are similar in the sense that stability, uniformity, and trust to a significant extent have been replaced by volatility, plurality, and distrust. Both political actors and the news media must fight harder than before to reach out to and connect with the citizenry. Both political actors and the news media must thus become more attuned to the wants and needs of their target groups; that is, there is a pressure towards increased market orientation. While political actors try to adapt to this situation by attempting to professionalize their campaigning and advocacy, the news media adapt to this situation partly by focusing more on soft news and less on hard news, more on easy accessible framing such as the framing of politics as a game, and less on framing that demands higher cognitive efforts on the part of the audiences. However, the chain of causality is difficult to establish, as people as well as political actors and the news media are always involved in an ongoing interdependent relationship where changes in demand trigger changes in supply and vice versa. What appears clear is that everyone—individuals as well as organizations and institutions—both shape and are shaped by the processes of modernization, individualization, instrumentalization, globalization, and mediatization that are taking place worldwide, although at a different pace and with different patterns of adaption and reaction. Thus, it matters how people behave as individuals and in their roles as citizens and media consumers, not only to themselves but also for its effect on the behavior of political actors and the news media. Hence, it also matters for how democracy works.

ELECTION NEWS COVERAGE AND DEMOCRACY

In the introduction to this chapter we noted the lack of discussion on the importance of communication media in much of the literature on democracy and democratic theory. From both a practical and theoretical point of view this deficit is unsatisfactory, as the way democracy works can never be fully comprehended without also understanding the role of the communication media and the complex interdependencies which shape the political communication system and its outputs, including the election news coverage. This is true as soon as politics in a particular country has reached the first phase of mediatization, and it should be even more obvious with regards to countries, including most advanced postindustrial democracies, which have reached successive phases of mediatization.

The importance of the election news coverage for the way democracy works originates from the simple fact that people rely mainly on the news media for information that might help them decide how to vote, and that the news media thus can exert considerable power with regards to which issues, attributes, and frames people consider important and salient. Thus, if we believe that it is important from a democratic point of view that people are at least reasonably well informed with regards to politics on Election Day, then it is imperative that the election news coverage provides people with the information they need to make enlighted judgments and decisions.

This is not to deny a lack of consensus about exactly what kind of information people need to make informed judgments (Delli Carpini & Keeter, 1996; Page, 1996; Popkin, 1994). As shown elsewhere (Strömbäck, 2005) this dissensus stems from the fact that there exist several different models of democacy with different normative implications for citizens and political actors as well as for news media in general and journalism in particular. For example, whereas it is important for proponents of competitive democracy that the news media focus mainly on the record and behavior of current office-holders and the platforms of political parties and candidates, it is more important from the perspective of participatory democracy that the news media mobilize the citizens' interest, engagement, and participation in public life. From the perspective of deliberative democracy, it is furthermore imperative that the news media foster public discussions that is deliberative, that are characterized by rationality, impartiality, intellectual honesty, and equality. None of these normative demands matter from the perspective of procedural democracy, however. From such a perspective the only thing that really matters is that the news media act as a watchdog or as a burglar alarm exposing wrong-doing (see further Bennett, 2003; Patterson, 2003; Strömbäck, 2005; Zaller, 2003).

In the context of election news coverage, this dissensus is illuminating because it illustrates not only that the news media and how they cover national elections on a general level are essential to how democracy works. The election news coverage is important also because it helps or undermines efforts to reform democracy in different countries so that it becomes more attuned to procedural, competitive, participatory, or deliberative visions of democracy. It would, for example, be almost impossible to make a democracy more deliberative or participatory without a news media system in which journalism and the election news coverage contributes to such a change by living up to the normative demands of these models of democracy. Thus, the debate and controversies surrounding public journalism can be perceived as a debate which essentially is about different models of democracy (Glasser, 1999; Merritt, 1998; Rosen, 1999), although few have made this explicit.

In sum, the election news coverage matters because it is a prerequisite for an informed electorate and because it contributes to how democracy works and what normative model of democracy different countries resemble. Beyond disagreements rooted in different normative models of democracy there is also a rather wide consensus regarding the importance of election news journalism providing factually correct information, at least some basic information about how society and the political system work, and about the electorally relevant issues and actors. At the same time we have seen that the election news coverage reflects a complex coming together of system characteristics, semi-structural factors, contextual factors, and the dynamics of the relationship between political actors, news media actors, and people in their roles as voters and media consumers. The complex interdependencies between the different parts of the political communication system both restrict and enable the news media in their efforts to both be profitable and considered as performing a public service, thus shaping the way the media in different countries cover national elections both directly and indirectly.

These complex interdependencies also make it difficult on this broad level of analysis to state particular hypotheses with regards to similarities and differences in the election news coverage across countries, especially considering the lack of systematic comparative research in this area thus far.

The framework discussed in this chapter should thus be considered a first step towards a deeper understanding of the election news coverage and its antecedents and content in different countries. The country chapters which will follow will provide a more detailed description and analysis of the situation in each country. We revisit this framework, consider the methodological concerns raised by current election news coverage research, and offer our conclusions in the final chapter.

BRIEF OUTLINE OF THE BOOK

This book is organized in four parts. Following from the notion that the electoral system in any country is crucial in shaping the dynamics of electoral communication, and hence also the election news coverage, we have chosen to use different electoral systems as the main organizing principle.

The first part focuses on the election news coverage in countries with majoritarian elections, and it includes chapters on the United States, Canada, Britain, France, Australia and India. With respect to the United States, the section includes two chapters. The vast amount of research on election news in the United States, coupled with the importance of this research in guiding studies in other countries, made it useful to include two chapters: one focused on the U.S. election news coverage in general and one focused on the election news coverage in television network news.

The second part focuses on the election news coverage in countries with proportional elections and includes chapters on the Netherlands, Sweden, Spain, Greece, Israel, Poland, Serbia, Brazil, and South Africa. The third part of the book focuses on the election news coverage in countries with combined electoral systems, including chapters on Germany, Italy, Hungary, Bulgaria, Russia, Mexico, and Japan.

The fourth and final part focuses on election news coverage in a comparative perspective, and it includes two chapters. The first of these summarizes research on the news coverage of European Union Parliamentary elections, while the second and final chapter provides comments and conclusions from a revisit of the framework that guided the volume.

REFERENCES

Altheide, D. L., & Snow, R. P. (1991). *Media worlds in the postjournalism era*. New York: Aldine de Gruyter.

Asp, K. (1986). *Mäktiga massmedier: Studier i politisk opinionsbildning* [*Powerful mass media. Studies in political opinion formation*]. Stockholm: Akademilitteratur.

Asp, K., & Esaiasson, P. (1996): The modernization of Swedish campaigns: Individualization, professionalization, and medialization. In D. L. Swanson & P. Mancini (Eds.), *Politics, media, and modern democracy: An international study of innovations in electoral campaigning and their consequences* (pp. 73–90). Westport: Praeger.

Bagdikian, B. H. (2000). *The media monopoly* (6th ed.). Boston: Beacon Press.

Bennett, L. W. (2003). The burglar alarm that just keeps ringing: A response to Zaller. *Political Communication 20*(2), 131–139.

Bennett, W. L., & Entman, R. M. (Eds.) (2001). *Mediated politics: Communication in the future of democracy*. Cambridge, UK: Cambridge University Press.

Benson, R. (2005). Mapping field variation: Journalism in France and the United States. In R. Benson & E. Neveu (Eds.), *Bourdieu and the journalistic field* (pp. 85–112). Cambridge, UK: Polity Press.

Benson, R., & Hallin, D. C. (2007). How states, markets and globalization shape the news. The French and U.S. national press, 1965–97. *European Journal of Communication, 22*(1), 27–48.

Blumler, J. G., & Gurevitch, M. (1995). *The crisis of public communication*. London: Routledge.

Blumler, J. G., & Kavanagh, D. (1999). The third age of political communication: Influences and features. *Political Communication, 16*(3), 209–230.

Blumler, J. G., & McQuail, D. (2001). Political communication scholarship: The uses of election research. In E. Katz & Y. Warshel (Eds.), *Election studies: What's their use?* (pp. 219–246). Boulder, CO: Westview Press.

Campbell, V. (2004). *Information age journalism: Journalism in an international context*. London: Arnold.

Cappella, J. N., & Jamieson, K. H. (1997). *Spiral of cynicism: The press and the public good*. Chicago: University of Chicago Press.

Cook, T. E. (2005). *Governing with the news: The news media as a political institution* (2nd ed.). Chicago: University of Chicago Press.

Croteau, D., & Hoynes, W. (2001). *The business of media: Corporate media and the public interest*. Thousand Oaks, CA: Pine Forge Press.

Dalton, R. J. (2000). The decline of party identifications. In R. J. Dalton & M. P. Wattenberg (Eds.), *Parties without partisans: political change in advanced industrial democracies* (pp. 19–36). New York: Oxford University Press.

Dalton, R. J. (2002). *Citizen politics: Public opinion and political parties in advanced industrial democracies*. New York: Chatham House.

Dalton, R. J., McAllister, I., & Wattenberg, M. P. (2000). The consequences of partisan dealignment. In R. J. Dalton & M. P. Wattenberg (Eds.), *Parties without partisans: Political change in advanced industrial democracies* (pp. 37–63). New York: Oxford University Press.

Delli Carpini, M. X., & Keeter, S. (1996). *What Americans know about politics and why it matters*. New Haven, CT: Yale University Press.

Demers, D. (1999). *Global media. Menace or messiah?* Cresskill, NJ: Hampton Press.

De Vreese, C. H. (2003). Television reporting of second-order elections. *Journalism Studies, 4*(2), 183–198.

Donsbach, W., & Patterson, T. E. (2004). Political news journalists: Partisanship, professionalism, and political roles in five countries. In F. Esser & B. Pfetsch (Eds.), *Comparing political communication: Theories, cases, and challenges* (pp. 251–270). New York: Cambridge University Press.

Esser, F. (2000). Tabloidization of news: A comparative analysis of Anglo-American and German press journalism. *European Journal of Communication, 14*(3), 291–324.

Esser, F., & D'Angelo, P. (2003*). Framing the press and publicity process in German, British and U.S. general election campaigns: A comparative study of metacoverage*. Paper Presented to the Political Communications Division, International Communication Association, San Diego, CA.

Esser, F., Reinemann, C., & Fan, D. (2001). Spin doctors in the United States, Great Britain, and Germany: Metacommunication about media manipulation. *The Harvard International Journal of Press/Politics, 6*(1), 16–45.

Farnsworth, S. J., & Lichter, S. R. (2006). *The mediated presidency: Television news and presidential governance.* Lanham, MD: Rowman & Littlefield.

Farrell, D. M., & Webb, P. (2000). Political parties as campaign organisations. In R. J. Dalton & M. P. Wattenberg (Eds.), *Parties without partisans:Political change in advanced industrial democracies* (pp. 102–128). New York: Oxford University Press.

Franklin, B. (2004). *Packaging politics: Political communications in Britain's media democracy.* London: Arnold.

Gans, H. J. (1980). *Deciding what´s news: A study of CBS Evening News, NBC Nightly News, Newsweek and Time.* New York: Vintage.

Gerstlé, J., Davis, D. K., & Duhamel, O. (1991). Television news and the construction of political reality in France and the United States. In L. L. Kaid, J. Gerstlé, & K. R. Sanders (Eds.), *Mediated politics in two cultures: Presidential campaigning in the United States and France* (pp. 119–144). Westport, CT: Praeger.

Gibson, R., & Römmele, A. (2001). Changing campaign communications: A party-centered theory of professionalized campaigning. *Harvard International Journal of Press/Politics, 6*(4), 31–43.

Glasser, T. L. (Ed.) (1999). *The idea of public journalism.* New York: Guilford.

Graber, D. A. (2006). *Mass media & American politics* (7th ed.). Washington, D.C.: CQ Press.

Gulati, G. J., Just, M. R., & Crigler, A. N. (2004). News coverage of political campaigns. In L. L. Kaid (Ed.), *Handbook of political communication research* (pp. 237–256). Mahwah, NJ: Erlbaum.

Hallin, D. C., & Mancini, P. (2004). *Comparing media systems: Three models of media and Politics.* New York: Cambridge University Press.

Hamilton, J. T. (2004). *All the news that's fit to sell: How the market transforms information into news.* Princeton, NJ: Princeton University Press.

Hernes, G. (1978). Det mediavridde samfunn [The mediatized society]. In G. Hernes (Ed.), *Forhandlingsøkonomi og blandadministrasjon* [*Bargaining economy and mixed administration*] (pp. 181–195). Oslo: Universitetsførlaget.

Holmberg, S., & Oscarsson, H. (2004). *Väljare. Svenskt väljarbeteende under 50 år* [*Voters. Swedish voter behavior during 50 years*]. Stockholm: Norstedts juridik.

Kaid, L. L., & Holtz-Bacha, C. (Eds.). (2006). *The Sage handbook of political advertising.* London: Sage.

King, A. (Ed.). (2002). *Leaders' personalities and the outcomes of democratic elections.* Oxford: Oxford University Press.

Kovach, B., & Rosenstiel, T. (1999). *Warp speed: America in the age of mixed media.* New York: Century Foundation.

Kovach, B., & Rosenstiel, T. (2001). *The elements of journalism: What newspeople should know and the public should expect.* New York: Crown.

Lange, B-P., & Ward, D. (Eds.) (2004). *The media and elections: A handbook and comparative study.* Mahwah, NJ: Erlbaum.

Lavrakas, P. J., & Traugott, M. W. (2000). Why election polls are important to a democracy: An American perspective. In P. J. Lavrakas & M. W. Traugott (Eds), *Election polls, the news media, and democracy* (pp. 3–19). New York: Seven Bridges Press.

Lazarsfeld, P. F., Berelson, B., & Gaudet, H. (1948). *The people's choice: How the voter makes up his mind in a presidential campaign.* New York: Columbia University Press.

Lijphart, A. (1999). *Patterns of democracy: Government forms and performance in thirty-six countries.* New Haven, CT: Yale University Press.

Lilleker, D. G., & Lees-Marshment, J. (2005). Conclusion: Towards a comparative model of party marketing. In D. G. Lilleker & J. Lees-Marshment (Eds), *Political marketing: A comparative perspective* (pp. 205–228). Manchester, UK: Manchester University Press.

McCombs, M. (2004). *Setting the agenda. The mass media and public opinion.* Cambridge, UK: Polity Press.

McManus, J. H. (1994). *Market-driven journalism. Let the citizen beware?* Thousand Oaks, CA: Sage.

McNair, B. (2000). *Journalism and democracy. An evaluation of the political public sphere.* London: Routledge.

Merritt, D. (1998). *Public journalism and public life: Why telling the news is not enough.* Mahwah, NJ: Erlbaum.

Meyer, T. (2002). *Media democracy: How the media colonize politics.* Cambridge, UK: Polity Press.

Niven, D. (2002). *Tilt? The search for media bias.* Westport, CT: Praeger.

Norris, P. (Ed.) (1999). *Critical citizens: Global support for democratic governance.* New York: Oxford University Press.

Norris, P. (2001). *Digital divide: Civic engagement, information poverty, and the Internet worldwide.* New York: Cambridge University Press.

Norris, P. (2004). *Electoral engineering: Voting rules and political behavior.* New York: Cambridge University Press.

Ornstein, N., & Mann, T. (Eds.). (2000). *The permanent campaign and its future.* Washington, D.C.: AEI Press.

Oskarson, M. (2005). Social structure and party choice. In J. Thomassen (Ed.), *The European voter: A comparative study of modern democracies* (pp. 84–105). New York: Oxford University Press.

Page, B. I. (1996). *Who deliberates? Mass media in modern democracy.* Chicago: University of Chicago Press.

Patterson, T. E. (1993). *Out of order.* New York: Vintage.

Patterson, T. E. (1998). Political roles of the journalists. In D. A. Graber, D. McQuail, & P. Norris (Eds.), *The politics of news, the news of politics* (pp. 17–32). Washington, D.C.: CQ Press.

Patterson, T. E. (2000). The United States: News in a free-market society. In R. Gunther & A. Mughan (Eds.), *Democracy and the media: A comparative perspective* (pp. 241–265). New York: Cambridge University Press.

Patterson, T. E. (2003). The search for a standard: Markets and media. *Political Communication, 20*(2), 139–145.

Pavlik, J. V. (2001). *Journalism and new media.* New York: Columbia University Press.

Picard, R. G. (2005). Money, media, and the public interest. In G. Overholser & K. H.. Jamieson (Eds.), *Institutions of American democracy: The press* (pp. 337–350). New York: Oxford University Press .

Plasser, F., & Plasser, G. (2002). *Global political campaigning: A worldwide analysis of campaign professionals and their practices.* Westport, CT: Praeger.

Popkin, S. L. (1994). *The reasoning voter: Communication and persuasion in presidential campaigns* (2nd ed.). Chicago: University of Chicago Press.

Rosen, J. (1999). *What are journalists for?* New Haven, CT: Yale University Press.

Scarrow, S. E. (2000). Parties without members? Party organization in a changing electoral environment. In R. J. Dalton & M. P. Wattenberg (Eds.), *Parties without partisans: Political change in advanced industrial democracies* (pp. 79–101). New York: Oxford University Press.

Semetko, H. A., Blumler, J. G., Gurevitch, M., & Weaver, D. H. (1991). *The formation of campaign agendas: A comparative analysis of party and media roles in recent American and British elections.* Hillsdale, NJ: Erlbaum.

Siebert, F. S., Peterson, T., & Schramm, W. (1963). *Four theories of the press: The authoritarian, libertarian, social responsibility and Soviet Communist concepts of what the press should be and do.* Urbana: University of Illinois Press.

Strömbäck, J. (2000). *Makt och medier* [*Power and the media*]. Lund: Studentlitteratur.

Strömbäck, J. (2004). *Den medialiserade demokratin. Om journalistikens ideal, verklighet och makt* [*The mediatized democracy. On the ideals, reality and power of journalism*]. Stockholm: SNS Förlag.

Strömbäck, J. (2005). In search of a standard: Four models of democracy and their normative implications for journalism. *Journalism Studies, 6*(3), 331–345.

Strömbäck, J. (2007a). Antecedents of political market orientation in Britain and Sweden: Analysis and future research propositions. *Journal of Public Affairs, 7,* 1–11.

Strömbäck, J. (2007b). Political marketing and professionalized campaigning: A conceptual analysis. *Journal of Political Marketing, 6*(2/3), 49–67.

Strömbäck, J. (2007, May). Four phases of mediatization. An analysis of the mediatization of politics. Paper presented to the International Communication Association, San Francisco, CA, USA.

Strömbäck, J., & Dimitrova, D. V. (2006). Political and media systems matter: A comparison of election news coverage in Sweden and the United States. *Harvard International Journal of Press/Politics, 11*(4), 131–147.

Strömbäck, J., & Luengo, Ó. G. (2006, June). Framing and election news coverage in Spain and Sweden. Paper presented to the 4th International Symposium Communication in the Millenium, Eskisehir, Turkey.

Strömbäck, J., & Shehata, A. (2007). Structural bias in British and Swedish election news coverage: A comparative study. *Journalism Studies, 8*(5), 798–812.

Thomassen, J. (2005). Modernization of politics. In J. Thomassen (Ed.), *The European voter: A comparative study of modern democracies* (pp. 254–266). New York: Oxford University Press.

Thompson, J. B. (1995). *The media and modernity: A social theory of the media.* Stanford, CA: Stanford University Press.

Underwood, D. (1995). *When MBAs rule the newsroom.* New York: Columbia University Press.

Waisbord, S. (2000). *Watchdog journalism in South America: News, accountability, and democracy.* New York: Columbia University Press.

Weaver, D. H. (1977). Political issues and voter need for orientation. In D. L. Shaw & M. E. McCombs (Eds.), *The emergence of American political issues: The agenda-setting function of the press* (pp. 107–119). St. Paul, MN: West.

Zaller, J. R. (2001). The rule of product substitution in presidential campaign news. In E. Katz & Y. Warshel (Eds.), *Election studies: What´s their use?* (pp. 247–270). Boulder, CO: Westview Press.

Zaller, J. R. (2003). A new standard of news quality: Burglar alarms for the monitorial citizen. *Political Communication, 20*(2), 109–131.

I

ELECTION NEWS COVERAGE IN COUNTRIES WITH MAJORITARIAN ELECTIONS

2

Media Coverage of U.S. Elections: Persistence of Tradition

Mira Sotirovic and Jack McLeod

During the last seven months of the 2004 American presidential election, public support for candidates in polls resembled three waves rolling gently between three percentage points advantage for each candidate. The tops and bottoms closely followed the publication of the Abu Ghraib prison photos, the two party conventions, the Swift Boat attack ads against Kerry, and the debates.[1] The campaign attracted levels of attention rivaled over the last fifty years only by the 1992 election. About 84% of Americans reported being at least somewhat interested in the campaign (American National Election Studies, 2007). The election ended with the winning margin of 2.46 percentage points, the fifth smallest in post World War II elections, and the 60.7% turnout, the largest since the sixties.

Most Americans first become aware of the top national events by watching local news or reading local newspapers. About two-thirds of Americans habitually watch local television news and about 60% read local newspapers at least several times a week (Gallup, 2004). Television is also the main source of election news and information for 76% of Americans, followed by newspapers at 46%, radio at 22 %, Internet at 21 %, and magazines at 6 % (Pew Research Center for the People & the Press, 2005). Since 1952 when the national party conventions were televised for the first time, mass media and especially television have played dominant roles in national elections. It has become clear that candidates' television appearances, even when reduced to only a sentence or two of a sound bite, reach more voters and create more potential for influence than all the in-person campaigning. Without media competing for audience attention, levels of public participation in presidential campaigns and preferences toward candidates would be much more static and more closely resemble a flat line.

The roles media play in election campaigns, how they cover the issues and candidates, and their potential influence on the electorate, are fundamentally functions of constraints imposed by the political system and the rules that system sets for media operations. The United States political system is a representative democracy with three separate branches of government—legislative, executive, and judicial—represented by Congress, the President, and the Supreme Court. Based upon the constitutional protection of a free press, the American news media have established themselves as an independent estate "a fourth institution outside the government as an additional check on the three official branches" (Stewart, 1975, p. 633). In that role, they serve the interests of the public and operate as a watchdog of government and governmental officials. The American news media system exemplifies a liberal model characterized by commercialism, relative independence from the state, and journalistic professionalism (Hallin & Giles, 2005).

ORIGINS OF THE U.S. ELECTORAL SYSTEM

U.S. Constitution of 1787 and the First Amendment

In a *representative democracy* the people elect a certain number of their fellow citizens to represent them in making laws and other decisions. The election system emanates from the U.S. Constitution developed in 1787. In seven Articles and only about 5,000 words, the document specifies a federal system with three branches of government. Article I establishes the selection procedures and powers of the two legislative branches—the House of Representatives and the Senate—together known as Congress. Members of the House of Representatives are elected every two years, and their number is determined by a decennial Census with a minimum of one member for each state. Each state is also represented by two Senators elected for six year terms. In the U.S. presidential system legislators are elected to represent their state or district. In contrast, parliamentary system members elected in particular constituencies represent the parliament at large. This helps to account for the relative weakness of party discipline over legislators in the United States.

Article II set the term of office of the President at four years and created an institution, later called the Electoral College, which continues to be a powerful constraint on how presidential elections are conducted. Each state is given the number of electoral votes according to its number of House and Senate seats. Electors in each state meet to vote shortly after the popular vote in November. Formally, then, presidents are selected by the Electoral College and only indirectly by popular vote. In current practice, all electors vote for the winning candidate in their state. The Electoral College thus affects presidential elections by constituting a winner-take-all system within each state and gives smaller states a lower population-to-electoral vote ratio: today each electoral vote in the least populated state, Wyoming, represents only 165,000 people in contrast to California, the most populous, with 616,000 people per electoral vote.

Beyond guaranteeing regular elections and specifying their procedures, the Constitution has little to say about elections. It makes no mention of political parties, primaries, nominating conventions, or more recent campaign procedures. Nor does that most revered and contestable term "democracy" appear in its pages. The phrase "We, the People" in the Preamble of the Constitution can be considered as an assertion, innovative and radical for its time, that the rights of the government derive from the people rather than the people's rights emanating from the ruling authorities as had been the prevailing view for centuries (Wood, 1993). On the other hand, the framers' concept of "people" can be seen as limited to propertied white men. Broad enfranchisement took almost two centuries to achieve what we consider today as government by "the people." Women gained the right to vote in 1920, Native Americans in 1940, and African-Americans effectively in the 1960s.

Article V provided for amending the Constitution. The First Amendment, adopted in 1791 along with nine other Amendments, states: "Congress shall make no law respecting an establishment of *religion*, or prohibiting the free exercise thereof; or abridging the freedom of *speech* or of the *press*; or the right of the people peaceably to *assemble* and to *petition* the Government for a redress of grievances." The wording of the First Amendment has been criticized for its ambiguity that has resulted in highly varied interpretations. It was not until the first half of the 20th Century that the U.S. Supreme Court for the first time applied the First Amendment to state laws. This markedly increased the volume of free speech cases reaching the Court. Today, the First Amendment serves as a legal as well as a symbolic bulwark against suppression of speech and prior restraint of media content. It also serves as a positive incentive to use media to expand the ideals of electoral democracy.

Emerging Features of the Electoral System

Two-Party System.   Parties are not mentioned in the Constitution, and there are no limits to be found on the number of parties allowed to contest Presidential elections in any subsequent legislation. *Factions,* a term for the forerunner of parties, were seen as collections of private interests opposed to the public good. Parties with three distinct labels first appeared in the election of 1832, and third parties have contested virtually all elections since that time. The complete official list of 2004 candidates indicates 15 candidates with 11 different party names. Together they managed to garner less than 1% of the popular vote. The question becomes, do third parties matter at all in American politics?

Third parties have played at least four roles at various times in American history: (1) as a viable force contending for power; (2) as a spoiler to punish or move candidates or parties away from mainstream or outworn positions; (3) as a source of innovative ideas and policies to influence those in power; and (4) as a creator of diversity to provide expression for citizens whose perspectives lie outside the mainstream.

Electoral College margins of the winning major party candidates have usually been sufficient to prevent third parties from playing a spoiler role. In the 2000 election, third party candidate Ralph Nader, who received 2.7% of the popular vote, may have spoiled an election in that George W. Bush lost the popular vote but became President by receiving a majority of Electoral College votes. If in New Hampshire only half of Nader's 22,198 votes had gone to Al Gore, the state's three electoral votes and the Electoral College would have gone to Gore. The unimpressive performance by third parties justifies the description of the United States as a *de facto two-party* system. If third party candidates have little chance to gain power, their chances to be a spoiler are not much greater.

As for their serving as a "source of innovative ideas and policy to influence those in power," there is some historical evidence that they sometimes do so. The Socialist parties, which fielded candidates from 1904 to 1944 and received as much as 6% of the popular vote in 1912, proposed policies that ended up in somewhat modified form in the New Deal and legislation enacted by later Democratic administrations. The Prohibition party, with only 1.2% of the vote in the previous election, helped the passage of the 1919 18th Amendment that prohibited the sale of liquor. The repeal of Prohibition in 1933 did not deter the Prohibition party from fielding candidates in four later campaigns, most recently in 2004 when they garnered exactly 140 popular votes.

To the extent that the third party obtains sufficient visibility, it can play a role of "a creator of diversity to provide expression for citizens whose perspectives lie outside the mainstream." In that role the party may become effectively a social movement to promote its causes and attract new converts. Present media campaign coverage practices are not likely to be helpful to third parties to play any of the four roles. The news media use the perceptions of candidate and party viability—the likelihood of success—as important criteria for how much coverage they are willing to allocate. For third parties this means a vicious circle of lack of visibility and coverage. Further, the news media and sponsors of candidate debates tend to be strongly opposed to participation of multiple candidates, which reduces audience exposure to diverse viewpoints.

Presidential Primary Elections.   The presidential primary is a 20th Century innovation used to select the candidates that will represent each party in the November election. It was developed in an attempt to give power to ordinary citizens rather than party bosses to select their candidates. Starting in January of each presidential year, seven months before the parties hold conventions where they formally nominate their presidential candidates, candidates must compete within their own party in a series of state *presidential primary* elections contests. Primary elections are regulated by the individual states, and candidates must qualify for appearance on the ballot for each of 50 states according to the requirements of that state. Primary voting may be *closed* to all but registered adherents of a given party, or *open* to all citizens of the state. Some states have opted for a *caucus* system where preferences are openly indicated, though most states have opted for primaries with a secret ballot. A few states have both caucuses and primaries.

Primary campaigns have attracted heavy media attention since their inception. Competing candidates from each party have traditionally traveled from state to state making personal contact with citizens and giving standard stump speeches. They are followed closely by reporters who seek to construct fresh daily stories from these largely repetitious events. They have found the most interesting stories in conflicts between famous people.

REGULATIONS OF MEDIA AND CAMPAIGN FINANCE

Political reporting in the United States is protected by the First Amendment rights of free press and speech. Therefore, the government cannot prohibit any campaign coverage by media organizations regardless of how objectionable or irresponsible it may appear to someone. The only content limitation is imposed by libel laws that discourage publishing false and defamatory information and protect individual privacy. The first modern restrictive governmental interventions started with the necessity to control the distribution of limited radio frequencies. The Federal Communications Commission (FCC), established in 1934, was charged with the oversight of broadcasting. The FCC regulations were devoted to setting up structural rules that would prevent the consolidation of communication industry and cross-ownership, perceived as the main threats to public interest in hearing diverse views. The FCC stated that in the interest of informing the public the carriers of broadcast licenses issued by the Commission were required to present a balanced treatment of controversial issues of public importance. This policy statement is usually referred to as the "Fairness Doctrine." The FCC was also given the right to revoke licenses of broadcasters who fail to allow reasonable access or purchase of time to legally qualified candidates for federal elective office.

Since the late 1970s, as a result of growth of media, technological changes, and the prominence of conservative ideologies that favored deregulation and unbridled competition, many of the regulations were eliminated or relaxed (Horwitz, 2005). In 1987 the FCC abolished the Fairness Doctrine on the grounds that with so many media voices in the marketplace, the doctrine inhibits rather than enhances debate. As a result, the industry moved toward concentration of ownership and homogenization of content. For example, from 1996 to 2001, the last time the FCC published the data, the number of radio stations in the country increased by about 7% to almost 11,000 but the number of owners fell by 25% to fewer than 4,000. In 2006, more than 90% of about 800 TV stations were affiliates of one of the four biggest television networks—ABC, CBS, Fox Television, and NBC. They carry national news and programming produced by those networks.

After the repeal of the Fairness Doctrine, the number of radio stations that carry talk shows tripled, to about 1,400 (Project for Excellence in Journalism, 2007a). About 20% of Americans who say that they listen to political radio talk shows regularly are likely to receive a steady diet of conservative views and abrasive remarks. According to talk personality listenership data, only about 10% of top talk show hosts are liberal ("Top Talk Personalities," 2006; *Talkers* magazine list of top hosts). Without the Fairness Doctrine it was possible for the Sinclair Broadcast Groups to air daily on 62 local television stations it owns across the country a one-minute conservative, pro-Bush administration commentary by Sinclair vice president Mark Hyman. This incident is one of the starkest examples of how concentrated ownership may trump the fairness principles and restrict the availability of diverse ideas.

Without being able to rely on regulations, free time, or news organizations' sense of public service to inform citizens about candidates, American political campaigns increasingly rely on advertisements to both control and distribute their messages (Kaid, 2004). Candidates, parties, and independent groups spent more than $2.3 billion on political advertising in 2004 elections, and the spending in the 2008 elections is expected to reach another record $3 billion. Television advertising typically accounts for almost 60% of political campaign media spending.

The campaigns pay for ads from the money received as donations from supporters, gifts from organizations, and from fund-raising events. With the primary goals of limiting the influence of well-funded special interests and wealthy individuals on electoral outcomes. The Federal Election Commission, an independent governmental agency established in 1974, regulates campaign spending and mandates public disclosure of campaign finances by candidates and parties. In 2003, the U.S. Supreme Court upheld the provision of McCain-Feingold's campaign finance reform bill that bans soft money (unlimited campaign contributions to political parties) and prevents special interest groups from spending corporate or labor union money on broadcast ads that mention a candidate just prior to an election.

The Freedom of Information Act (FOIA), established by Congress in 1966, made federal records available to the public and became an invaluable resource for journalists in collecting information. The documents that journalists have received using the FOIA have led to major investigative stories, many of them uncovering wrongdoings of governmental officials. At the heart of the Act and its uses are the ideas of transparency and accountability of government to citizens, which are essential for maintaining a free and democratic society. Every year Americans file more than a million requests using the FOIA. However, the news media requests constitute only a small fraction of FOIA petitions—6%, according to research by the Coalition of Journalists for Open Government. In light of the downsizing of American newsrooms and decreasing managerial tolerance toward reporters who explore time consuming investigative leads that may not materialize as daily stories, public benefits from the FOIA may not be fully realized.

History and Development of Political News Coverage

The press and political parties, the two key institutions of campaign coverage, developed together humbly and uncertainly in the early 19th Century. The press was led not by editors but by entrepreneurial printers whose contribution to campaign history came as much from printing of campaign pamphlets and posters as from newspapers. The early newspapers were small commercial enterprises with advertising filling more than half the space leaving limited room for news. Nonetheless newspapers proved to be highly successful overall. Between 1790 and 1835 the number of newspapers in the United States grew from 106 to 1,258, more than three times the population growth during that period (Starr, 2004). Newspapers were more common in the United States than anywhere else in the world, an advantage that held until late in the 19th Century when European nations caught up.

The financial success and popularity of U.S. newspapers in the 19th Century was due to increasing literacy, federal postal subsidies, advertising revenues, and financial support from political parties. Local support for common schools cut illiteracy by 1850 to 23% of the whole population, half of that in Europe at the time (Starr, 2004). Newspapers benefited from wise decisions of the early political leaders to eliminate restrictions on the press and to subsidize postal rates that kept newspaper prices low and permitted exchange of news between papers. Revenues from business and government advertising and financial support from their affiliation with political parties also helped. However, the common characterization of a *press* totally subordinate to parties is misleading. The first parties had so little organization and sense of campaigning that newspapers were the organizational base on which modern party politics began to take shape (Starr, 2004).

As a result of the Constitutional separation of powers of the presidency from those of Congress, American parties have always been candidate-centered and this has affected campaigning strategies (Schudson, 1998). The presidential system may help to account for the prominence of candidate images over issues in modern U.S. campaigns. The first full-fledged campaign came in 1840 when candidates themselves were more active than ever before and the campaign was "full of theatrical innovations and extravagant rhetoric" (Schudson, 1998) and devoid of party issue platforms. The result was an impressive gain in turnout.

The noisy campaigning of the 19th Century, with parades and marching bands that drew thousands of supporters, gave way late in the century to a more restrained style of campaigning as a result of reform efforts to contain the spoils system and party excesses. Parties began to focus more on policies to attract uncommitted voters. The organizing of a host of national interest groups independent of parties had a similar sobering effect. Bias in reporting campaigns and other political news had already begun to decline as a result of the growing independence of newspapers from party support and from the relatively objective wire service news carried over the rapidly developing telegraph system. Perhaps as a result, voter turnout began to fall.

Campaign coverage began to change as a result of the innovations in journalistic techniques. The *news interview*, an American invention, was perhaps the most important of these, and it still dominates contemporary reporting. Before the 1860s, reporters did talk with sources, but their articles did not directly quote the conversations or even refer to them (Starr, 2004). Today journalists' habitual use of opposing interview quotes as a way of balancing news stories may be problematic when there are more than two points of view. The routine also may be questionable when both quotes are treated as equally valid when they are not. Another innovation was the *inverted pyramid* style of story structure starting off with a lead paragraph condensing facts instead of presenting events in a narrative or chronological order. It was developed to help the reader save time by scanning the headlines and the leads, a strategy that is likely to result in overall reduced learning from the story. This reporting style that emphasized factuality and objectivity endured into the 21st Century.

Media Structure

Average Americans spend about one hour daily consuming news (Pew Research Center, 2005). They can choose from the long menu of newspapers, network, public, cable and local television channels, magazines, radio, and online sites. With about 70% of Americans going online for news, use of the Internet for news has approached levels of other traditional media. However, the rise of Internet use has likely contributed to declining audiences for the traditional news platforms. In 2005, there were 1,452 daily newspapers in the United States, 20% fewer than in 1970, and only about 200 more than a century and a half ago. Since the late 1970s, circulation has fallen by 14% to 53.3 million copies sold. The audiences for three network news channels, ABC, CBS, and NBC, and their flagship evening news broadcast was 26 million in 2006, just about one half of the number in 1980. Their audiences are considerably older than ever before. Cable TV prime time news audiences, at 2.5 million in 2006, has shrunk by one million in three years.

On the other hand, the Public Broadcasting System's program "The NewsHour with Jim Lehrer" has a steady, although relatively tiny, nightly viewership of about 3 million. The number of listeners to AM/FM radio news, talk, and information stations also remains constant although the amount of weekly listening has declined by one hour since 2002 to 19.5 hours. The Media Audit, a media market survey group, estimated that the commercial news/talk format has about 19.4 million weekly listeners, whereas National Public Radio, which distributes programming to over 800 public radio stations nationwide, has a news audience of about 13 million. The circulation of traditional weekly newsmagazines such as *Time, Newsweek,* and *U.S. News* remains unchanged while magazines such as *The Week* and *The Economist* report a double digit growth (Project for Excellence in Journalism, 2007b). Overall, there is little good news in the traditional news media landscape.

The health of the news industry can be measured by market indicators. Stock prices of publicly traded newspaper companies fell in 2005 and 2006, and advertising revenues, the bloodline of the media business, were flat. However, the weighted average of profit margins for the newspaper divisions of major media companies were nearly 20%—more than double the average profit margin of the Fortune 500 ("Something to Discover," 2005). Newspapers are clearly struggling to develop a new economic model in response to challenges of online news consumption and advertising. Other traditional news media confront similar problems, although local TV news, network, and cable news have all seen increases in revenues and profits. The main casualties of the flux have been full-time newsroom staffers whose numbers continue to decline. From 1992 to 2002 newsrooms lost about 6,000 people or about 5% of the workforce (Weaver, Beam, Brownlee, Voakes, & Wilhoit, 2007). Diminished economic potential seems to be the main threat to American news media according to the analyses by the Project for Excellence in Journalism (2007a). As a result, reporters are losing power to pundits and personalities, cheaper and less accurate journalism is gaining a foothold, and the range of stories is narrowing despite the greater number of outlets delivering news.

Below the surface of thousands of news media choices loom only a dozen media conglomerates that together own more than 90% of the media market. The ownership concentration of media outlets has led to the disappearance of two-thirds of independently owned newspapers since 1975. In 2004, the 21 biggest companies owned about 40% of the newspapers in the country and accounted for about 70% of national circulation. Similar consolidation trends are evident in the television news industry. Since 1995 the largest companies have tripled the number of local TV stations they owned. As a result, centrally produced content is distributed locally and fewer voices have a chance to be heard. Limiting the points of view in the news media is detrimental to making informed choices in a democratic society. Can the Internet with seemingly limitless choices save democracy? Most popular Internet news sites are also owned by the largest media companies, but since 2004 the number of sites they own continues to decline (Project for Excellence in Journalism, 2007a).

Media Content

American news media entered the new millennium facing accusations of having abandoned traditional straight news accounts for feature- and people-oriented approaches, and of shifting away from covering government and foreign affairs toward lifestyle, celebrities, and scandal (Project for Excellence in Journalism, 1998). Although all the news media outlets and their coverage of all topics are similarly affected by this general trend, the traditional inverted pyramid style emphasizing facts is still used in about a quarter of stories in the largest papers and in almost half of the stories in smaller ones (Project for Excellence in Journalism, 2005). Topics of government and elections were covered in more than 40% of all stories in newspapers and 27% of all stories in the network evening news (Project for Excellence in Journalism, 2005). Though these percentages may represent some increase over the previous presidential elections, the amount of network television coverage may be still lower than in 1992 and 1988 (Farnsworth & Lichter, 2007).

In 2004, network television news organizations decided to reduce coverage of the two party conventions, when parties present their cases to the nation, to no more than three hours of prime time each night because their increasingly ritualistic and stage-managed character promised very few newsworthy "surprising" events. The sharp decline in coverage since 1976, when networks devoted almost 10 hours of daily prime time to conventions, is offset by feeding convention reports to their nightly news and morning shows, and utilizing websites, cable affiliates, and radio networks.

The coverage of the first presidential election debate in 2004 attracted more than 62.5 million viewers, about 16 million more than the first presidential debate in 2000 and just about 4 million less than the first televised debate between Nixon and Kennedy in 1960, which was seen by more than a third of the entire U.S. population at the time. The coverage of debates, the only formal face-to-face contact that candidates have during campaigns, is constrained by their format which is controlled by The Commission on Presidential Debates and the agreement between the campaign managers. The commission, created in 1987, has allowed the candidates to avoid direct questioning of one another, limited follow-up questioning, and lets the candidates nominate and veto panelists. It has also insisted that a third-party candidate must have a 15% support rating in pre-debate polls to be included, despite the fact that a party needs only 5% of the vote to qualify for federal campaign financing (Farah, 2004). Heavily scripted debates have directed and amplified media attention to who won, general judgments of candidates' performance, their blunders, body language, and demeanor rather than on merit and the accuracy of what they said. Impressions passed by media analysts on candidates' performances in "post-debate spins" and relentless replaying of gaffes may have greater influence on audience opinions of candidates than the debates themselves (Chaffee & Dennis, 1979). For an overview of political campaign debates, see McKinney and Carlin (2004).

Election stories were most distinguishable from other topics by their focus on winners and losers (Project for Excellence in Journalism, 2005). The dominance of the "winners and losers" frame, typically used in an attempt to create more exciting and compelling stories, supports the longstanding view of the horse race character of American elections coverage (Cappella & Jamieson, 1997). Horse race coverage is by far the most common target of critiques and complaints of journalistic campaign coverage performance. Stories that discuss the status, strategies, or tactics of the candidates and their campaigns presumably take air time and page space, and divert attention of audiences from "substance" or candidates' stands on issues. Farnsworth and Lichter (2007) found that about half of the stories on network news discussed horse race aspects of the 2004 campaign, a somewhat lower proportion than in the 1988, 1992, and 2000 elections and about the same as in the 1996 election. Horse race aspects, along with politics as a game and strategy frames were also identified in about 60% of articles published in *USA Today,* the *New York Times,* and the *Washington Post* in 2004 (Strömbäck & Dimitrova, 2006). Kovach and Rosenstiel (2001) suggested that horse race coverage dominates American election coverage because it is easier and safer for reporters to assess candidates' campaign strategies than to get involved in explanations of their complicated and nuanced stands on issues. Another reason might be the tradition of reporters' reliance on public opinion polls, the all-American twentieth century invention, which during election time is reduced to its most superficial aspect—winning margins.

The election coverage of 2004 also saw clear splintering of the traditional professional model of journalism, with its emphasis on objectivity, toward more opinionated stands led by the Fox news cable channel. About 82% of Fox election stories included journalistic opinions, compared to about 44% in other network news, 13% in large newspapers, 7% on CNN, and only 3% on

PBS. PBS seems to represent one of the last bastions of traditional news values in American media. However, the opinionated accounts did not simply translate into negativity and cynicism. The Project for Excellence in Journalism (2005) study found that about half of the stories were neutral in tone, and in the other half they were twice as likely to be positive as negative in both newspapers and network news. Other studies have found that about half of the stories on the network news in 2004 contained negative evaluations of the candidates (Farnsworth & Lichter, 2007). There is little evidence of partisan bias in news reporting. Structural biases, rooted in journalistic norms and commercialism are mainly responsible for the patterns in news constructions (Gulati, Just, & Crigler, 2004).

Another staple of journalistic objectivity, balance, was also under attack by cable news channels. Overall, cable news, with only 27% of stories that presented a mix of different points of view, was only half as balanced as were networks or newspapers. The Project for Excellence in Journalism (2005) study also found that cable TV news stories have fewer sources and are less transparent about them than network news, contributing to "thinner" reporting. Whereas the "24/7" coverage of TV cable news channels may give an illusion of exhaustive reporting, about 60% of all stories aired through the day were simple repetitions of the same information.

Media Effects

The analysis of structural characteristics of media systems and content of media election coverage constitute a necessary context toward understanding the impact election news has on citizens. What perceptions people develop and what information they learn from their use of media election coverage content is crucial for understanding their electoral behaviors. Contemporary research emphasizes various cognitive and affective processes through which news media indirectly influence citizens' political participation and preferences (McLeod, Kosicki, & McLeod, 2002). These processes are central in four types of media effects that have recently received considerable attention in the election context: agenda setting, priming, framing, and knowledge gain.

Agenda setting effects are produced by frequent media coverage of certain issues prioritized by candidates and the public's adoption of those issues as the most important in elections (Weaver, McCombs, & Shaw, 2004). Similarly, frequent presentations of certain attributes of a candidate, such as issue positions, biographical information, qualifications, personality, integrity, may lead the public to think about those attributes as more important (McCombs, Lopez-Escobar, & Llamas, 2000). Priming effects are considered to be a consequence of agenda-setting effects because the news media, by calling attention to some matters while ignoring others, set the standards and influence the criteria by which people evaluate and judge election candidates (Iyengar & Kinder, 1987). Framing effects result from the media's consistent use of various symbolic (e.g., catchphrases) and reasoning (e.g., causes and consequences) devices to focus public attention on particular aspects of the issues and problems and promote their corresponding definitions, interpretations, evaluations, and treatment recommendations (Gamson, 1992; Entman, 1993).

News media coverage of election campaigns provides an abundance of various types of information that public says it wants: candidates' stands on issues, their records, experience, public demeanor and character (Project for Excellence in Journalism, 2001; Lipsitz, Trost, Grossmann, & Sides, 2005). There is something to meet the desires of both those who are more politically involved and want substance and those who are not and are more concerned with candidates' images. Majorities, and in particular those who are most politically informed and involved, dislike campaigns, believe that negative campaigning is damaging to democracy, and think that unethical practices in campaigns occur often (Lipsitz et al., 2005). Whereas interactive campaigns and additional substantive information may prove beneficial to the most involved citizens, campaigns that provide simple cues and clear choices would please those less involved who also find ads helpful.

The news media's most basic function of providing accurate facts has been long recognized as central in promoting democratic competence and political participation (Delli Carpini, 2004). Citizens' knowledge of who public officials are, various rules of how government works, and substantive features of major public affairs issues, captures the most *general* skills necessary for participating in democracy. Knowledge gain from news media use has been documented since the 1960s, and research has shown positive effects of exposure to news independent of formal education, demographics, attitudinal factors, and cultural differences (Norris, 2000).

Communication research in particular has emphasized the importance of distinguishing between use of different media and various types of content when knowledge gain is measured. In general, newspaper reading has a stronger positive effect on knowledge than does viewing of television news, whereas exposure to entertainment-based and "soft" news has no effect or even negative relationships with political knowledge (for an overview, see Sotirovic & McLeod, 2004). Political debates and media analyses following these debates are sources of issue information (McKinney & Carlin, 2004). When the Internet is used for researching political information and accessing campaign news it has a positive effect on political knowledge (Shah, McLeod, & Yoon, 2001). Users of the Internet are more likely to be consumers of newspapers and television news, suggesting that as a new medium the Internet is not replacing traditional media but supplementing their information. In the studies conducted during the last five presidential elections, Drew and Weaver (2006) found that attention to television news, televised debates, and Internet news are important predictors of voter learning of candidate issue positions and voter interest in the election campaigns.

Media in the 2004 Campaign: Levels and Effects.   The following analyses of the American National Election Studies (ANES) 2004 U.S. presidential election data confirm that media effects on political knowledge and campaign participation are not uniform, but medium and content specific.[2] Table 2.1 shows two attributes of media impact: their *dosage* indicated by levels of use and the *potency* shown by the size of effects. Dosage, in terms of the number of days used, is overall highest for watching television news but considerably greater for national than for local news. The potency of general exposure to media news varies more widely. Local news viewing contributes to neither.

Attention to the campaign among users of each medium revealed little variation in levels, though they were somewhat higher for television than for the print media. Attention to newspaper articles had the strongest effects on knowledge (.24) followed by attention to the campaign on television news and in magazines. All four campaign attention measures had equally strong effects on campaign participation.

Exposure levels to campaign stories differed widely. Almost everyone (86%) watched programs about the campaign on television, about half read about it in newspapers, listened to speeches or discussions on the radio, and sought campaign information on the Internet, and less than one-third read about it in magazines. Each of the five campaign exposure measures was strongly related to both campaign knowledge and participation. Effects on knowledge were strongest for newspaper campaign exposure (.22) and weakest for television news (.10). Radio listening had the strongest effect on participation (.29).

Additional mediation analyses provide a better understanding of the power and importance of media use in the 2004 campaign.[3] In addition to contributing 11.2% of incremental variance to political knowledge and 15.9% to campaign participation, media use variables mediated 62.8%

TABLE 2.1
Levels of Media Use and Effects on Political Knowledge and Campaign Participation: 2004

Media Use Variables	Levels			Effects on	
				Knowledge	Participation
	Mean/ Percent	Range	SD	Beta	Beta
General Exposure					
Number of days read newspaper	3.08	0-7	2.88	.16**	.10**
Days watch national network news	3.58	0-7	2.76	.12**	.16**
Days watch local television news shows in the late evening	2.79	0-7	2.73	-.05	.20
Days read daily newspaper on Internet/Web	2.13	0-7	1.80	.13**	.06
Campaign Attention					
Attention to newspaper articles about the campaign	3.48	1-5	.94	.24**	.25**
Attention to network TV news about the campaign	3.62	1-5	.98	.16**	.21**
Attention to television news about the campaign (post)	3.86	1-5	.97	.18**	.24**
Attention to campaign in magazines (post)	3.34	1-5	.98	.17**	.00
Campaign Exposure					
Read about campaign in newspaper	53%			.22**	.19**
Watch programs about the campaign on television	86%			.30**	.17**
Seen campaign information on the Internet/Web (post)	47%			.14**	.17**
Read about campaign in magazines (post)	30%			.18**	.19**
Listened to campaign speeches or discussions on radio (post)	52%			.18**	.29**

Note. Data come from American National Election Studies (ANES) 2004 survey. N = 1212 (pre),1066 (post).
** p < .01, * p <,05. Means for attention measures are based only on respondents who read or watched the particular media content.
All measures are pre-election except those indicated as (post). The media effects shown are pre-entry before controlling for each other but after control for four demographics and two other variables.

of the influence of traditional variables (demographics, party ID, need for cognition) on political knowledge and 60% of their influence on campaign participation. Thus, attentive use of the news media and the Internet during the campaign was the major process by which older, more educated and affluent citizens, Democrats, and those with higher needs for cognition learned more about the campaign. Media use also the dominated the process by which older, more educated, and affluent citizens participate in the campaign.

Trends in Levels and Effects. Over the past several decades levels of use and attention to the American election campaigns have varied considerably (Table 2.2). Newspaper reading in 2004 continued the same downward trend begun in 1988. This is consistent with research showing that newspaper reading is lowest among the most recent cohorts of young adults. Reading about the campaign followed the same downward trend from 1976 to 2000, but in the 2004 campaign it increased by 7.2%. Television national network news viewing jumped markedly over the 2000 election. This contrasts to the downward trend of non-campaign network news viewing

TABLE 2.2
Levels of Media Use across Four Presidential Election Years

	1976	1984	1988	2000	2004
Number of days read newspaper	—	3.94	4.02	3.52	3.08
Read about campaign in newspaper	73.5%	—	50.0%	45.3%	52.5%
Attention to newspaper articles about the campaign	—	2.96	3.32	3.44	3.48
Days watch national network news	—	3.60	—	3.33	3.58
Attention to network TV news about the campaign	—	3.53	3.40	3.49	3.62

Note. Data come from National Election Studies (NES) 1976, 1984, 1988, 2000 and 2004 surveys. N = 1903, 1926, 1775, 1555, 1212 respectively. Means for attention measures are based only on respondents who watched and read the relevant campaign content.

of the past decades. Attention to network news during the 2004 campaign also showed a sharp increase.

Trends in the potency of five forms of media use and attention are shown in Figure 2.1.[4] Reading about the campaign in a newspaper, despite its recent increase in level of use, continued its sharp downward trend in effectiveness in conveying knowledge from .39 in 1976 to only .06 in 2004. Further, reading of newspapers more generally revealed a slight decline in effectiveness. The potency of effect among attentive readers of campaign stories, however, increased in 2004, reversing its downward trend since the 1984 election. This suggests that the content of newspaper election stories is becoming less relevant to political learning, but those who pay close attention are able to learn from them. Watching network television news became a slightly less effective source for political knowledge in 2004 despite its increasing level of use. Among those who watched network news, however, the effectiveness of paying attention to campaign stories increased markedly from .08 in 2000 to .15 in the 2004 election. Use of particular media and sources of information reflect secular trends driven largely by technology and changes in American life styles. Attention levels and potency of news media appear to coincide with the strategies and intensities of particular election campaigns.

Advertising and Election Coverage

Elections in the United States are the most costly in the world. Paid political advertising, the main budget item in Presidential campaigns, will reach a record $3 billion in the 2008 election—a staggering sum even for the lengthy two years of U.S. campaigning though it would cover only 11 days of Iraq war costs. Even more striking is the degree to which the 30-second television spots dominate the air time of the campaign. Heavy television viewers in the battleground state of Ohio in 2004 might have been exposed to more than an hour of political ads daily, but if they watched a network news broadcast they could have viewed only about nine minutes of news devoted to the campaign. Ohio and the other 15 battleground states constituting 32% of eligible voters received 87% of candidate advertising in 2004. Did the 7 to 1 ratio of advertising to news add up to greater effects of advertising? Were the viewers in half of the other states who were able to see very few political ads short-changed or should they have been grateful? Given the fact that over half of the 144 unique political spots shown in Ohio and other battleground states were negative, what impact might they have had on the campaign and its outcome?

Research has produced mixed results for television advertising effects. It is likely that frequent exposure to political spot ads does convey rudimentary awareness of candidates and issues

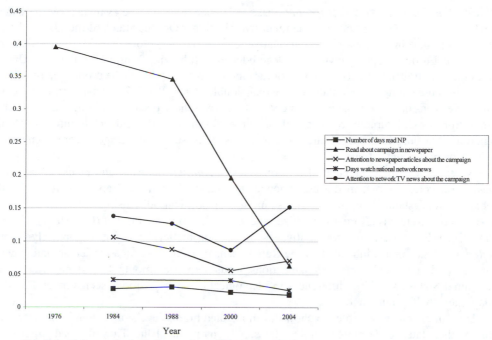

Note. Data points are unstandardized regression coefficients after controls.

Figure 2.1 Effect of five types of campaign media use on political knowledge.

though such effects may not be as strong as those of the traditional news media. Greater depth and a nuanced understanding of issues may not result *directly* from viewing 30-second spots. More subtle positive *indirect* effects have been identified in models where heavy dosages can increase campaign participation through stimulating campaign discussion and Internet messaging. However, at a high point of exposure the negative tone of ads may begin to have a negative impact that deters participation (Shah et al., 2007).

Beyond whatever effects the saturation levels of political advertising have on the audience, the domination of political advertising may to some extent exert undesirable control over the whole campaign. Candidates may be constrained by the strategic decisions of their advertising consultants and may not be able to explain their more complicated issue positions and policy proposals. Ads of the two campaigns most often emphasize different sets of issues and even those addressing the same issues use very different frames thus hindering citizens' ability to make direct substantive comparisons.

The news media coverage of campaigns includes stories about fund-raising and political ads. Early in the campaign and before adequate polling data are available, journalists tend to report on the money raised by each of the many candidates as a valid indicator of their viability. Those lagging in funding are subsequently treated as minor candidates and receive little coverage. Negative ads attract more media attention than positive ones. In the 2004 election, the "Swift Boat" group attack ads against Kerry were seen by more people as part of the news than when originally aired. It took the news media months to discover their inaccuracies. *Ad Watch* and other groups have used critical evaluation of specific ads to control the damage of false and misleading advertising. Most of these analyses have been quite well done, though some critics claim the increased attention to negative ads only increases their damaging effects by increasing public exposure to them. For a detailed review of political advertising, see Kaid (2004).

Election Turnout and Competitiveness.   Democracies can be evaluated by the extent to which their citizens participate in competitive elections. On this standard the U.S. political system falls short in having *low turnout* relative to other nations, more than 20% lower than the median for Europe. Rapid growth in college education following World War II in the United States failed to translate into rising levels of turnout. From 1960 to 1990 the proportion of college graduates in the voting age population more than doubled (from 9% to 20%), but turnout in presidential elections declined by approximately 10% between those decades. Among many possible reasons for low U.S. turnout, voters are often blamed for their apathy and lack of interest.[5] Media sometimes have used the lack of interest as an excuse to lessen the coverage of campaign events such as the party conventions and debates.

We examined the contextual effects of states' *campaign intensity* and *electoral competitiveness* on voter turnout, media use, knowledge, and participation. High campaign intensity in battleground states, indicated by the saturation of political advertising, frequent candidate appearances, strenuous efforts to mobilize voters, should stimulate turnout (Goldstein & Freedman, 2002). In contrast, low competitiveness in the non-battleground states (popularly known as *Red* and *Blue* states), indicated by the Republicans or Democrats in a particular state having consistently large-winning margins in elections, would depress turnout.[6] The characterization of the United States as lacking differences in ideological or issue positions seems much less true today than a half-century ago.

Turnout estimates in Table 2.3 show the anticipated higher levels of turnout in battleground than in other states, 8.9% more than Red states, 5.2% more than Blue. They also had larger 2004 increases in turnout over the 2000 election (6.6% vs. 6.0% Red, 4.1% Blue).[7] Our grouping of states also shows *consistency* in direction and margins in voting for candidates of the given party across seven elections. The last two elections were completely consistent in direction with margins of 16% and 17% above the national averages in Red states, 11% and 12% in Blue states. The strong Republican tides of the 1980s and the Clinton years of the 1990s resulted in many states falling to the opposition, but in over 90% of the cases the margins were less than the national trend. The increased consistency in recent elections has resulted in diminished campaign resources and less media coverage that reinforce the polarization of the Red and Blue states.[8]

TABLE 2.3
Vote Turnout and Outcomes by Red, Battleground and Blue States

		Presidential Years			
		1980–1988	*1992–1996*	*2000*	*2004*
Red states	Turnout	49.4	51.3	50.3	56.3
(n=22)	Margin	+17.9	+ 3.3	+16.3	+20.4
Battleground	Turnout	57.1	55.7	58.6	65.2
states (n=16)	Margin	+11.3	- 6.7	+ 0.9	+ 1.3
Blue states	Turnout	56.1	56.2	55.9	60.0
(n=13)	Margin	+ 9.0	-13.0	-11.7	- 8.6
U.S. (Total)	Turnout	54.1	54.8	54.2	60.3
	Margin	+11.8	- 7.1	- 0.5	+ 3.1

Note. Turnout is the proportion of citizens eligible to vote (VEP estimate) who cast votes for President. Outcome is the vote margin of the winning candidate over the main opposition candidate relative to the total votes cast for President. Margin is the vote margin of the winning candidate over the loser as a proportion of the total votes cast for president; a + indicating a Republican advantage, a – designating a Democratic winner in the given area.

The three elections 1980 to 1988 won by Republicans (Reagan and George H. Bush) have been combined as have 1992 and 1996 won by Clinton. States were classified in Battleground states by consensus judgments from the 2004 campaign.

In analyses of the ANES 2004 data, we found that residents of battleground states had the highest levels of attention to campaign stories in newspapers and on the Internet. They also were the most avid participants in the campaign.[9] The combined saturation of advertising and other campaign activities may have operated as important contextual stimuli for participation of those citizens living in battleground states.

The Off-Year Elections of 2006.   The congressional elections of 2006 included contests for 33 Senate and 299 House of Representative seats (36 incumbents were unopposed). The Democrats gained control of both houses of Congress for the first time in 12 years by unseating five Republicans in the Senate and 21 in the House, with pickups of six and 30 seats in total. The unusually large turnover in the House did little to change the picture of consistent party dominance within the Red and Blue states.[10] Within the non-battleground states, this dominance results in fewer stories that scrutinize claims of members of the dominant party or challenge their views. At the same time, the members of the weaker party are given much less access and exposure because of the tendency of reporters to rely on official and most powerful sources. On the federal level, control of both houses of Congress has not allowed Democrats to over-ride presidential vetoes but it has allowed them to hold committee hearings regarding various administration scandals. The power shift brought more previously oppositional views into the public forum and emboldened reporters to openly express their skepticism toward conduct and performance of the Bush administration. Particularly sore points are the Iraq war, alleged attacks on civil liberties in the name of combating terrorism, and intrusions of the executive into the judicial branch of government. The tight control that the administration exerted on the American public opinion by using various sophisticated propaganda strategies is showing cracks under pressures of dissent. The use of anonymous sources in traditional media and blogs in non-traditional media helped in voicing dissent. These developments will most likely carry over to coverage of the 2008 presidential campaign.

FUTURE DIRECTIONS

The 2008 presidential campaign involves some unusual circumstances that present challenges to news media coverage. First, an unusually large number, eight or more candidates in both major parties, entered the race because the incumbent president and vice-president are not running. To cover candidates' appearances and their within-party debates eight months before the primaries requires the news media to allocate many more resources than they possess. To reduce the load, the news media give more coverage to candidates perceived to be in the top-three tier than to the half-dozen "dark horses."

Second, at least 22 states, including the five largest, moved up the dates of their primaries to the beginning of February. The primary election season has traditionally been spread across five months starting in January with the Iowa caucuses and the New Hampshire primary election. Now, with a large number of states having primaries at about the same time, the campaign managers will have to rely more on advertising and the campaign will become even more expensive. For the news media it again poses a huge problem of distributing scarce resources, and will likely lead to more horse-race stories based on often-inadequate state polls. The front-loading of primaries made it almost certain that the presidential candidates will be selected by early February, resulting in a nine-month general election campaign run. Sustaining voter interest by organizing campaign events and producing compelling and meaningful stories over such a long period will be the challenge for both campaign managers and the news media.

Ten months before the primaries, and a year and a half before the 2008 presidential election, the amount of campaign news coverage was already unprecedented. The number of campaign stories was topped only by the Iraq policy debates (Project for Excellence in Journalism, News Coverage Index, 2007b). Whereas the amount of coverage is extraordinary for so early in the campaign, the content of the campaign news stories was much less exceptional. About 90% of the stories during the first quarter of 2007 were about campaign tactics and the horse race. The level of attention which has been given to backroom maneuvers, winning, and knockout punches means that citizens may be given little information about who the candidates are and what they would do for the country. Consequently, to find additional information, large numbers of campaign Internet users go to Web sources beyond those that are fed by traditional news media. In the 2006 Congressional campaign about a quarter of Internet campaign users got news and information from "issue-oriented" websites, one fifth from blogs and websites created by candidates, and about 10% visited websites of alternative news organizations (Pew Internet, 2007). In the heated presidential election environment these numbers are expected to increase.

Under business pressures for increasing revenues, the news media content decisions are made to attract the most profitable audiences: young people. Therefore, the best foresight into the future of news media coverage may be gained by looking at what the Internet generation, accustomed to interactivity and customization, likes to read and watch. First, they like to get both the national newspaper and TV channel content online but prefer the digested and consolidated news services such as Google, AOL, or Yahoo News to those traditional packages. Second, they like reality based fake news, indicated by the popularity of "The Daily Show" with Jon Stewart, and "personality" peppered news presented in *People* magazine. Third, they like to blog and form lifestyle and taste based, online social networks. The biggest losers of young audiences are formats such as PBS NewsHour with Jim Lehrer show, CNN's Larry King Live show, and Fox's O'Reilly Factor. The average person watching those shows is about 57 years old, about 17 years older than a regular user of the Google news, and about two years older than a typical regular user of national network news, Sunday morning interview shows such as Meet the Press, or news magazines such as 60 Minutes (Pew biannual media consumption survey, 2006).

Young people rely on the Internet to gather political information, and it may have served them well in the last presidential election. The young voter turnout increased from 2000 by 9% to 51%, compared to a 6% increase for all adults. However, the full contribution of the Internet to the electoral process should be evaluated by its ability to engage most of the citizens and make diverse groups more equivalent in their knowledge necessary for political participation. Online political news consumption among Internet users showed mixed results in terms of its adoption by segments of the population underrepresented in voting turnout. Compared to 2000, online news use grew more rapidly (23%) for those in the 21 to 29 age category and for Hispanics than for other citizens, potentially narrowing participation gaps. On the other hand, gaps may have been widened by the greater increase of online news use by college graduates (23%) and among those with high incomes (20%) compared to less educated and less affluent citizens.

Almost 90% of the public in the last presidential election indicated that they felt they learned enough about the candidates and the issues to make informed choices. Despite all the popular and academic criticism of media performance and the low public esteem of press conduct in campaigns, both subjective estimates and evidence we presented in this chapter indicate that the coverage of campaigns contributes to learning. The widely popularized trend of the public's increasing skepticism about news media professionalism, accuracy, caring, morality, and honesty (Project for Excellence in Journalism, 2007b) may be less alarming in the context of the confidence Americans have in other political institutions. About 70% of Americans have at least some confidence in television and newspaper news, about ten percentage points more than in Congress and the Presidency (Gallup Poll, 2006).

NOTES

1. See Chart 1 at https://netfiles.uiuc.edu/sotirovi/www/electioncoverageinus.pdf
2. Political knowledge was an index consisting of (1) knowing which party had the most members in the House of Representatives in Washington before the election; (2) knowing where to place the Democratic and Republican parties on a liberal/conservative scale; and (3) knowing what job or political office Dennis Hastert, (4) Dick Cheney, (5) Tony Blair, and (6) William Rehnquist held. Campaign participation was an index of five things people do to help a party or a candidate win an election: go to political meetings etc.; wear a campaign button etc.; do any other work; contributed money; and voted. Six control variables consisted of: gender, age, education, income, party identification, and need for cognition.
3. See Table 3 at https://netfiles.uiuc.edu/sotirovi/www/electioncoverageinus.pdf . We reduced the 13 media measures shown in Table 1 to six media-specific variables, combining campaign exposure and attention measures wherever possible. The six exogenous (control) variables (four demographic, party identification, and need for cognition), each having been shown to be influential in election campaigns, were used as antecedents to media use, knowledge and campaign participation. We then examined the extent to which the block of six media variables mediated the effects of the antecedent block by using reverse-order block regression analyses of the ANES data.
4. The knowledge effects indicated in Figure 2.1 are unstandardized regression coefficients for each media variable after the introduction of the six control variables. Unstandardized coefficients are necessary for comparisons across time because the variances of the media variables and knowledge are somewhat different across elections; however, readers should avoid making between-media comparisons based on unstandardized effect coefficients because their magnitude in part reflects differences in the underlying scales used in measuring the various media measures. The political knowledge measures are limited to two items common to all election years shown in the figure. This attenuates somewhat the coefficients shown here in comparison with the larger set of knowledge items used in Table 2.1.
5. Possible reasons given for low turnout include: the "laziness" of voters; the frequency of elections at all levels of government; the similarity between the two parties on issues; lengthy ballots with multiple contests and referenda items; media coverage that disdains politics and leads to voter cynicism; political candidates running against the "guvment;" and tactics used by parties officials discourage minority turnout by requiring poll challenging, moving polling places, etc. Efforts to stimulate turnout by mobile voter registration has had some limited success. Voting on weekends rather than on the present Tuesday voting day has been suggested but not tried.
6. The competitiveness of the states has been reduced by the Electoral College system of winner-take-all awarding of electoral votes in combination with recent redistricting by the state legislatures, which created more secure seats in the House of Representatives. Estimates are that no more than 37 of the 435 (8.5%) House seats are competitive. The homogeneity of parties within states also has led more recently to party politics more *polarized* in terms of campaign issues and positions and to acrimonious arguments rather than deliberation and compromise. Polarization also has been applied at the level of individuals referring to an alleged increase in extremity of opinions about public issues. Comparisons of public opinion on many issues over time seem to give little support to an increase in polarization so conceived.
7. To evaluate turnout, we divided the fifty states into Republican-dominant Red states (n =11), competitive Battleground states (n = 16), and Democratic-dominant Blue states (n= 13).
   Red states included: Utah, Wyoming, Idaho, Alaska, Nebraska, North Dakota, Montana, South Dakota, Oklahoma, Texas, Kansas, Mississippi, South Carolina, Indiana, Kentucky, Alabama, North Carolina, Georgia, Virginia, Louisiana, Arkansas, and Tennessee. These represent two solid blocks of states: the Great Plains-Mountain West and the South.
   Battleground states included: Florida, Ohio, Iowa, Missouri, New Mexico, Nevada, West Virginia, Arizona, Pennsylvania, Wisconsin, Minnesota, Michigan, Colorado, New Hampshire, Maine, and Oregon.
   Blue states included: Washington, Vermont, Illinois, California, Delaware, New Jersey, Maryland, Connecticut, Hawaii, New York, Massachusetts, Rhode Island, and the District of Columbia. These

represent two solid blocks of states: the Northeast-Mid Atlantic and the Far West, plus Illinois. Although the number of states in each category differs considerably, the proportion of eligible voters in each is almost equal. Turnout for each state for each of seven presidential elections from 1980 to 2004 was the total presidential vote cast (Federal Election Commission) divided by the estimated voting eligible voting population (VEP) for each state (McDonald & Popkin, 2001, McDonald, 2006). Voter election population (VEP) is a correction of previous estimates of the Voting-age population (VAP) minus the number of citizens legally ineligible to vote due to incarceration, probation or other reasons. Corrected for the growing U.S. prison population and some on parole and probation, the estimates show a less stark picture of turnout by increasing estimates from 2% in 1980 to 5% in 2004. Because eligibility varies by state and changes over time, correction is laborious and time-consuming. We thank Professor McDonald for making his data set estimating VEP 1980 through 2006 publicly available at http://elections.gmu/voter_htm. Some flawed analyses of turnout have used the gross estimates of voting age population that include the immigrant population in each state.

8. Another indication of consistency in the Red and Blue classification is party dominance in other offices. In 2004, in Red states Republicans held 80% of the Senate seats, 68% in the House of Representatives, 64% of the state Governors, and 56% and 55% in the upper and lower houses of the State Legislatures. The Blue states were solid at the federal level with 96% of the Senate and 65% of the House, but had only 33% of the state Governors, and 64% and 66% of the upper and lower houses of the State Legislatures, It appears that party domination in both the Red and Blue states carries down to both houses of Congress at the federal level and almost as well to the state level offices. On the other hand, the opposition holds one-third of these offices.

9. See Table 4 at https://netfiles.uiuc.edu/sotirovi/www/electioncoverageinus.pdf

10. Candidates for the dominant party won 64% of contested House seats, 91% of dominant party winners and only 52% of opposition party winners won with margisn of 20% or more. Relatively close races with less than 10% margin were most common in Battleground states, 20% compared to only 13% in both the Red and Blue states. The battleground states also had a disproportionate share of gains with 4 of 6 Senate seats and 17 of 30 seats gained in the House.

REFERENCES

American National Election Studies, The. (2007). Retrieved June 12, 2007, from http://www.electionstudies.org/nesguide/toptable/tab6d_6.htm

Cappella, J. N., & Jamieson, K. H. (1997). *Spiral of cynicism: The press and the public good.* Chicago: University of Chicago Press.

Chaffee, S. H., & Dennis, J (1979). Presidential debates: An empirical assessment. In A. Ranney (Ed.), *The past and future of presidential debates* (pp. 75–106). Washington, D.C.: American Enterprise Institute.

Delli Carpini, M. X. (2004). Mediating democratic engagement: The impact of communication on citizens' involvement in political and civic life. In L. L. Kaid (Ed.), *Handbook of political communication research* (pp. 395–434). Mahwah, NJ: Erlbaum.

Drew, D., & Weaver, D. (2006). Voter learning in the 2004 presidential election: Did the media matter? *Journalism & Mass Communication Quarterly, 83*(1), 25–43.

Entman, R. M. (1993). Framing: Toward clarification of a fractured paradigm. *Journal of Communication, 43*(4), 51–58.

Farah, G. (2004). *No debate: How the Republican and Democratic parties secretly control the presidential debates.* New York: Seven Stories Press.

Farnsworth, S. J., & Lichter, S. R. (2007). *The nightly news nightmare: Television's coverage of U.S. presidential elections, 1988-2004* (2nd ed.). Lanham, MD: Rowman & Littlefield.

FOIA at 40, *Sunshine Week.* Retrieved June 12, 2007, from http://www.sunshineweek.org/sunshineweek/foiaat40.

Gallup Poll (2004, December 5–8).

Gallup Poll (2006, June 1–4).

Gamson, W. (1992). *Talking politics*. Cambridge, UK: Cambridge University Press.

Goldstein, K., & Freedman, P. (2002). Campaign advertising and voter turnout: New evidence for the stimulation effect. *The Journal of Politics, 64*(3), 721–740.

Gulati, G. J., Just, M. R., & Crigler, A. N. (2004). News coverage of political campaigns. In L. L. Kaid (Ed.), *Handbook of political communication research* (pp. 237–256). Mahwah, NJ: Erlbaum.

Hallin, D. C, & Giles, R. (2005). Presses and democracies. In G. Overholser & K. H. Jamieson (Eds.), *The press* (pp. 4–16). New York: Oxford University Press.

Horwitz, R. B. (2005). Communications regulations in protecting the public interest. In G. Overholser & K. H. Jamieson (Eds.), *The press* (pp. 284–302). New York: Oxford University Press.

Iyengar, S., & Kinder, D. R. (1987). *News that matters: Television and American opinion*. Chicago: University of Chicago Press.

Kaid, L. L. (2004). Political advertising. In L. L. Kaid (Ed.), *Handbook of political communication research* (pp. 155–202). Mahwah, NJ: Erlbaum.

Kendall, K. E. (2000). *Communication in the presidential primaries: Candidates and the media, 1912–2000*. Westport, CT: Praeger.

Kovach, W., & Rosenstiel, T. (2001). Campaign lite. Why reporters won't tell us what we need to know. Retrieved July 15, 2001 from http://www.washingtonmonthly.com/features/2001/0101.kovach.rosenstiel.html

Lipsitz, K., Trost, C., Grossmann, M., & Sides, J. (2005). What voters want from political campaign communication. *Political Communication, 22*(3), 337–354.

McCombs, M., Lopez-Escobar, E., & Llamas, J. P. (2000). Setting the agenda of attributes in the 1996 Spanish general election. *Journal of Communication, 50*(2), 77–92.

McKinney, M. S., & Carlin, D. B. (2004). Political campaign debates. In L. L. Kaid (Ed.), *Handbook of political communication research* (pp. 203–234). Mahwah, NJ: Erlbaum.

McLeod, D. M., Kosicki, G. M., & McLeod, J. M. (2002). Resurveying the boundaries of political communication effects. In J. Bryant & D. Zillmann (Eds.), *Media effects: Advances in theory and research* (2nd ed., pp. 215–267). Mahwah, NJ: Erlbaum.

Norris, P. (2000). *A virtuous circle: Political communication in postindustrial society*. Cambridge, UK: Cambridge University Press.

Pew Internet & American Life Project, Election 2006 Online. (2007). Retrieved June 12, 2007, from http://www.pewinternet.org/report_display.asp?r=199

Pew Research Center for the People and the Press. (2005).Trends 2005.

Pew Research Center for the People and the Press. (2006). *Biannual media consumption survey*. Retrieved February 26, 2008, from http://www.people-press.org/reports/display.php3?ReportID=282.

Project for Excellence in Journalism. (1998). *Changing definitions of news*. Retrieved February 19, 2002, from http://www.journalism.org/ccj/resources/chdefonews.htlm

Project for Excellence in Journalism. (2001). Election coverage 2000: What people want ot know. Retrieved July 15, 2001, from http://www.journalism.org/publ–research/election5.html.

Project for Excellence in Journalism. (2005). *The state of the news media: An annual report on American journalism*. Retrieved April 11, 2007, from http://stateofthemedia.org/2005/topline

Project for Excellence in Journalism. (2007a). *The state of the news media: An annual report on American journalism*. Retrieved April 11, 2007, from http://stateofthemedia.com

Project for Excellence in Journalism. (2007b). *News coverage index*. Retrieved June 13, 2007, from http://www.journalism.org/node/5712

Schudson, M. (1998). *The good citizen: A history of American civic life*. Cambridge, MA: Harvard University Press.

Shah, D. V., McLeod, J. M., & Yoon, S. H. (2001). Communication, context, and community: An exploration of print, broadcast, and Internet influences. *Communication Research, 28*(4), 464–508.

Something to discover: The American newspaper at a crossroads. (2005, November/December). Editorial in *Columbia Journalism Review*, Issue 6. Retrieved June 12, 2007 from http://cjrarchives.org/issues/

Sotirovic, M., & McLeod, J. M. (2004). Knowledge as understanding: The information processing approach to political learning. In L. L. Kaid (Ed.), *Handbook of political communication research* (pp. 357–394). Mahwah, NJ: Erlbaum

Starr, P. (2004). *The creation of the media: Political origins of modern communications.* New York: Basic Books.

Stewart, P. (1975, January). Or of the press. *Hastings Law Journal, 26*, 633–634.

Strömbäck, J., & Dimitrova, D. V. (2006). Political and media system matter: A comparison of election news coverage in Sweden and the United States. *Harvard International Journal of Press/Politics, 11*(4), 131–147.

Top talk personalities. *Talkers* magazine. Retrieved June 12, 2007, from http://www.talkers.com/main/index.php?option=com_content&task=view&id=17&Itemid=34

University of Wisconsin Advertising Project. (2007). Advertising project based on Nielsen Monitor-Plus.

Weaver, D. H., Beam, R. A, Brownlee, B. J., Voakes, P. S., & Wilhoit, G. C. (2007). *The American journalist in the 21st century: U.S. news people at the dawn of a new millenium.* Mahwah, NJ: Erlbaum.

Weaver, D. H., McCombs, M., & Shaw, D. (2004). Agenda-setting research: Issues, attributes, and influences. In L. L. Kaid (Ed.), *Handbook of political communication research* (pp. 257–282). Mahwah, NJ: Erlbaum

Wood, G. (1993). *The radicalism of the American Revolution.* New York: Vintage Books.

3

Trends in Television Network News Coverage of U.S. Elections[1]

Stephen J. Farnsworth and S. Robert Lichter

Throughout recent decades, three national television networks, ABC, CBS and NBC, have dominated the U.S. media landscape. Although their audiences have fallen since the late 1970s as they have faced increasingly aggressive competitors, including CNN, Fox News, online newspapers, and a tidal wave of online commentators, the networks and their cable and online offshoots remain influential media players. Their flagship 30-minute evening newscasts still draw tens of millions of viewers, and the influence of network news is magnified further by the many cable and online outlets that follow their lead (Pew, 2000d; Seib, 2001).

This chapter examines the trends in U.S. television network news coverage over the past several presidential elections. Before doing so, we set the stage with a brief outline of campaign news coverage trends.

U.S. CAMPAIGN NEWS IN CONTEXT

Presidential elections, held every fourth November, have long been contentious spectacles. For nearly the nation's entire history, two hostile camps have dueled for power, using whatever means they could to win (Genovese, 2001). The raucous electoral tradition in the U.S. represents a sharp contrast from the more genteel electoral traditions of some other nations (Huntington, 1981). While the subjects of electoral disagreements have changed over time, conflict has been a constant electoral companion in the U.S. Just as recent presidential campaigns have done, early 19th century presidential campaigns featured allegations of sexual misconduct and attacks on the patriotism of rivals (Sabato, 2000; Smith, 1977).

The news media function as the ringmasters of the American political circus. The earliest 19th century newspapers were often financed by political parties, and they offered their readers one-sided fare that fueled a voter's passion more than a voter's reason. Circulation numbers for these newspapers were small—the best selling publications of the day printed a few thousand copies per issue—because the papers were expensive to produce and to buy.

By the mid-19th century, widespread literacy, the inventions of steam printing presses, the telegraph and rail engines dramatically expanded public interest in newspapers and also dramatically reduced the costs of printing papers. Commercial imperatives—that is, the desire to sell their products to as many citizens as possible—pushed news organizations to offer more even-handed coverage and cover controversies thoroughly throughout the 19th and 20th centuries. As the American economy expanded throughout this era, businesses demanded a wide audience for their advertisements, increasing the pressure for a paper (and later for radio and television news) to be both interesting and even-handed.

The media's future may not look like the past. In recent years, the American news environment has begun a process of rapid change. The traditional dominant news outlets—the three networks and a few elite national newspapers (the *New York Times*, the *Wall Street Journal,* and the *Washington Post*)—now face challenges from a wide range of new news sources. Both the traditional norms of more objective reporting and the huge market share enjoyed by the most popular media are under siege from aggressive online upstarts (Seib, 2001). Even the news agenda is no longer set by the traditional media gatekeepers, who increasingly are following the lead of stories first broken online (Hall, 2001).

One cannot generalize about the cacophony of the online media world. Some of the most prominent news voices are online versions of the news outlets that dominate offline. Other news outlets exist largely or entirely in cyberspace, and some of these voices are more committed to the advancement of an ideological agenda through one-sided commentary than conveying the news fairly (Seib, 2001). In addition, the online world is full of clips from late-night television and cable entertainment programs, like *The Tonight Show* and *The Daily Show,* where political satire is routine fare (Pew, 2004).

While U.S. news outlets are in transition, the traditional two-dominant party system in the U.S. seems as stable as ever. The Democratic and Republican parties have dominated politics in the U.S. since before the Civil War. Since the election of 1860, every single elected president has been either a Democratic or Republican nominee (Hetherington & Keefe, 2007). The two parties also control nearly all offices in Congress and at the state level. While voters tell pollsters they would like more parties, the rare third party movements that arise expire after an election or two. The Electoral College used in presidential elections, the first-past-the-post system used in nearly all other elections, and the near-universal failures of third party movements discourage voters from casting a ballot for someone other than a major party candidate (Hetherington & Keefe, 2007).

Given the dominance of national news messages in a nation of more than 300 million, presidential candidates have had to develop sophisticated media management strategies to present themselves to the public (Farnsworth & Lichter, 2007). Regardless of their substantive qualifications, candidates who fail to look and sound good on television become ex-candidates fairly quickly (Patterson, 1994; West, 2005). Character has become an important part of presenting oneself to the country, as the candidates become regular visitors (via the evening news) in America's living rooms (Barber, 1992; West, 2005). So far the Internet has been most useful for fundraising and for drawing attention to second-tier candidates, but overall the new media outlets remain less important than the old standby of television (Trippi, 2004).

The First Amendment and the largely private news sector are huge barriers to government control over news content on television, radio, and print. Media companies are highly profitable and generate sufficient revenues from advertisers that they have arisen without government subsidies provided to state broadcasters elsewhere. U.S. media policies do provide such things as special media access to policy-makers and government records, as well as discounted postage rates for printed media, but these modest benefits are provided regardless of a publication's editorial policies (Cook, 2005).

Probably the most powerful gift the government bestows on private media companies is a frequency allocation, determining who gets to be Channel 2 or Channel 3 in a given television market. Radio and television airwaves are public property in the U.S., and once given, a broadcast frequency is almost never revoked, no matter how negative the news coverage of the government (Graber, 2006). What the government obtains in exchange for this very valuable permit to use a particular frequency is a commitment by the broadcaster to provide news and public affairs programming, something that serves the financial interests of the stations by bringing in advertising revenue (Graber, 2006).

Self-policed goals—like that of journalistic objectivity—are not always met. Politicians of all ideologies have complained of media bias, but in the U.S. there is little they can do about it. A previous governmental attempt to mandate even-handed news coverage on radio and television news was abandoned two decades ago, and the so-called Fairness Doctrine has never been close to being reinstated after being eliminated (Graber, 2006).

In the analysis that follows regarding television's election news reports in the relatively unregulated U.S. media system, we pay particular attention to changes in the amount of news coverage; the subject of those election news reports; the ability of candidates to reach voters through these evening newscasts; and, of course, the tone of news coverage. The data used here were produced by the Center for Media and Public Affairs (CMPA), a nonprofit, nonpartisan media research firm that has examined network news coverage of every presidential election since 1988 (Farnsworth & Lichter, 2007).

This analysis is conducted through scientific content analysis, the careful dissection of each news story into fragments that can be coded along several different dimensions. With content analysis, media scholars and political scientists have demonstrated that the evening news programs on ABC, CBS, and NBC, for decades the dominant citizen sources for information on U.S. presidential elections, do a poor job of covering presidential elections. Over the past two decades, television news' portrayal of the past five presidential contests has been marked by a host of shortcomings: the damaging focus on horse-race coverage of who is winning and modest attention paid to matters of substance, the less-than-satisfactory performance with respect to the journalists' cardinal issues of accuracy and fairness, the declining amount of attention paid to candidates (as opposed to that lavished on the correspondents covering them), as well as the declining volume of coverage of the presidential election overall.

CHANGES IN THE AMOUNT OF COVERAGE

Even before the general election stage of the presidential selection process begins, the networks routinely face criticism for cutting back on their live coverage of the party conventions. Critics saw this reduction in coverage as the most recent instance in which the network news departments paid less attention to "hard" political news and more to "soft" news of lifestyle trends and human interest stories (Patterson, 2000). Broadcast executives themselves claimed that the conventions had grown too dull and too stage-managed to justify covering extensively and argued that interested viewers could find more coverage on cable television.

Even so, network television executives may be listening to their critics. During the 2004 presidential election—the second nail-biter in a row—the three evening newscasts aired 504 stories on the presidential election, the largest number since 1992 and a nearly 10 percent increase over the 2000 totals. When measured by number of minutes devoted to the election the results are even more striking: the 1,070 minutes (17 hours and 50 minutes) of campaign news in 2004 was 33 percent more airtime than in Election 2000 and 37 percent more than in the 1996 presidential election. Still the 2004 coverage remained well below the totals for 1992 and 1988.

As shown in Table 3.1, the three networks carried a combined average of 9 stories a night on

TABLE 3.1
Amount of General Election News, 1988–2004
Labor Day through the day before Election Day

	2004	2000	1996	1992	1988
Amount of Coverage					
Number of Stories	504	462	483	728	589
Stories per Day (average)	9.0	7.3	7.7	11.5	10.5
Total Time (minutes)	1,070	805	788	1,402	1,116

the 2004 election between Labor Day and Election Day, well above that of 2000 (7.3 a day for the three networks) and 1996 (7.7), although below both 1992 (11.5) and 1988 (10.5).

All three networks increased their campaign news coverage in 2004. The amounts of network coverage for the last three general elections, however, pale before the massive coverage CMPA recorded for Campaign '92—23 hours 22 minutes (Campaign '88 had 18 hours 36 minutes of news coverage). Presidential elections do not get much more interesting than they were in 2000 and in 2004, but the amount of coverage in those elections was far, far less than the general election phase of the 1992 presidential election. However, the trend, at least as of 2004, is improving.

HORSE RACE COVERAGE

Every four years in November, roughly 100 million Americans cast a vote for a presidential candidate. The campaigns for president, and before that the preliminary battles for the Democratic and Republican presidential nominations, are extended seminars on the state of the nation: primarily how well the incumbent has handled issues concerning the country's security and economic well-being. Candidates debate other issues that could affect presidential performance as well, which—depending on the year—could include energy, the environment, health care, taxes, and even the country's moral climate.

More than just a look back, presidential campaigns are also about looking forward. Candidates discuss where the country should go in the years ahead and how the nation can deal with some of its most vexing problems: crime, poverty, the massive federal debt, the tens of millions of Americans who lack health insurance, and the potential insolvency of Social Security and Medicare in the coming decades.

On network television's evening news programs, though, a different picture emerges. The debate is not primarily over whether Social Security needs fixing, and if so, how to fix it. The televised discussion is not over whether the American economy needs a boost, and if so, how to provide a little macroeconomic help. Instead, in most national elections over the past three decades, network television reporters have talked largely about who is ahead and who is behind in the presidential polls and the reasons for the disparity.

The discussion of public policy matters that does occur on network television is often framed in the context of this horse race. Proposals to fix Social Security or cut taxes or revamp welfare are seen as ways to woo farmers, senior citizens, or some other special interest group. Reporters often spend at least as much time talking about the "sport" of politics as presenting the policy proposal and evaluating its substantive merits, focusing on how effective the appeal, not the policy, seems to be.

A quarter century ago, political scientist Thomas Patterson (1980) observed that television focused greatly on the question of which candidate was ahead and who was behind, a far cry from the much more issue-oriented coverage of the 1940s. Although Patterson focused on the 1976 presidential election, the same trends were found in subsequent contests (Farnsworth & Lichter, 2007; Lichter & Noyes, 1995, 1998; Patterson, 1994; Robinson & Sheehan, 1983).

However, voters did more than learn regularly of each candidate's standing; they actually began to support in greater numbers the candidate who reporters said was winning. Patterson (1980) called this a "bandwagon" effect. Bandwagon effects make it harder for a candidate who is believed by reporters to be behind—or who really is lagging in the media-reported polls—to catch up with the front-runner. If news consumers are told over and over again that poll numbers are so important, it should come as no surprise that the voters think about polls when evaluating candidates.

The thoroughness of campaign news, along with its usefulness to voters, depends on the focus of the coverage as well as its sheer volume. This issue has long been raised by critics of the media's concentration on the horse race and, more broadly, the strategies and tactics adopted by the campaigns (Ranney, 1983; Sigelman & Bullock, 1991). It also involves the more specific topical agenda that the news features: the major foci of discussion. This has become more central to the debate over campaign news since the 1992 election.

Many journalists regarded the 1988 general election battle between Bush and Dukakis as a campaign marred by negativity, superficiality, and factual distortions. The network news divisions responded by vowing to pay greater attention to the topics that journalists considered most relevant to the public interest, regardless of the candidates' spin on issues and events.

In other words, after the 1988 election, broadcast journalism adopted a more active role in setting the campaign agenda, in order to serve better the voting public (Alter, 1988, 1992; Bode, 1992). This commitment towards a more heavily mediated approach has been a goal of network television since 1988, though the effects of this approach have been mixed at best (Farnsworth & Lichter, 2007; Kerbel, 1998; Lichter & Noyes, 1995, 1998; Owen, 2002).

With a more active role comes increased responsibility for the tone and substance of campaign news. How did the networks respond to this challenge in the past five presidential elections? As Table 3.2 illustrates, 48 percent of all stories during the 2004 general election contained a discussion of the candidates' standings and prospects (We defined "discussions" as lasting a minimum of 30 seconds of air time or one-third of very brief stories). This figure matched the 48 percent figure produced by Clinton's runaway victory eight years earlier, far less than the 71 percent of the discussions devoted to horse-race matters in the razor-thin 2000 election, or the 58 percent of stories that dealt with the horse race in both 1992 and 1988.

Of course the question of who is likely to win the election is a perfectly legitimate one for the voters to hear about. This question is particularly likely to be a focus of media coverage when

TABLE 3.2
General Election News: Horse Race Coverage, 1988–2004
Labor Day through the Day before Election Day

	2004	2000	1996	1992	1988
Focus of Coverage (percent of stories)*					
Horse Race	48	71	48	58	58
Policy Issues	49	40	37	32	39

*Stories can include a horse race and a policy focus (or neither focus); numbers therefore do not sum to 100 percent.

the answer is highly uncertain, as it was leading up to, and even for several weeks after, Election Day 2000. (The 2004 contest was also close, though an undisputed Bush victory in Florida that year prevented the weeks of uncertainty that followed Election Day four years earlier.) Even though the 2004 election turned out to be the second closest (behind 2000) of the five presidential contests considered here, it tied for the lowest focus on the sport of politics, and placed first in amount of coverage spent on policy matters (49 percent, up from 40 percent in 2000).

As television news has become more and more focused upon campaign standings and campaign strategy, evaluations of the news media remained consistently negative. Citizens surveyed by the Pew Research Center gave reporters a "C" average grade for their Election 2004 coverage, with the mean score of 1.9 (where a 4.0 is an "A" and a 2.0 is a "C"). The 2004 media GPA is higher than the 1.7 mean grade for 2000, the 1.8 mean grade for 1996, but below the 2.0 average for 1992 and tied with the 1.9 average for 1988 (Pew, 2004).

Polling data are not the only evidence that people are frustrated with the media's approach to campaign coverage. They also seem to be voting through their news consumption choices. Surveys of media use show that citizens clearly are not endorsing the heavy horse race coverage that network television provides. Pew Research Center surveys found that the percentage of people who listed network television as one of their two leading sources of news about presidential elections has fallen 26 percentage points between 1992 and 2004, down from 55 percent to 29 percent (Pew, 2000c, 2004).

The decline registered by network television, once the jewel in the crown of America's corporate media empires, was the sharpest of the seven media sources included in the survey. While network television and newspapers were virtually tied in the 1992 survey (55 percent versus 57 percent respectively), by 2004 more people listed newspapers (46 percent) and cable television (40 percent) than the networks as leading sources of campaign news. (Since people were allowed to give up to two responses, the percentages for media use exceed 100 percent). While newspapers also provide considerable horse-race coverage, CMPA content analyses demonstrate they provide less of it than network television (Farnsworth & Lichter, 2007). Further evidence that the networks are on the wrong track in paying so much attention to the horse race comes from the questions voters ask when they are given the chance to question candidates (Just et al., 1996; Patterson, 1994). The town meeting-style debate between Bush and Gore several weeks before the election—the third of three presidential debates in 2000—focused on middle-class needs and the merits of Bush's proposed tax cuts. In 2004, the candidates also devoted one their three debates to questions from the audience, and the questions in that debate also directed candidates towards health care, Social Security, and other policy matters, and away from the horse race.

MEDIATED COVERAGE AND THE SILENCING OF CANDIDATES' VOICES

To be sure, the horse race frame offered up by network television has the potential to degrade our democratic debates. A less visible, but perhaps equally dangerous frame is one that is the result of news media narcissism. Television correspondents increasingly seem to believe that elections are largely about themselves as reporters and as interpreters of political events.

U.S. election news increasingly has become a zero-sum game in which candidates lose out as journalists increasingly set the tone of reportage. In a study of front-page presidential election news stories from the *New York Times*, Patterson (1994, p. 114) found that candidates and other partisan sources set the tone of an article nearly two times out of three in 1960 and more than 70 percent of the time in 1964 and 1968. Since 1972, candidates and other partisan sources never again set the tone even 40 percent of the time, and by 1992 reporters were setting the tone of a story about 80 percent of the time. Patterson attributes the reversal to the weakening of norms that once worked against such advocacy by reporters.

This proved true for television as well. In his analysis of the differences between news programs on ABC and CNN during the 1992 presidential election, Matthew Kerbel found few differences worth noting between the broadcast and cable networks with respect to who tells the story. On both networks, Kerbel (1998, p. 22) found "better than three quarters of all statements were attributed to news personnel—correspondents, anchors or analysts solicited by the networks to make observations about the election."

In her analysis of the 2000 presidential election, political scientist Diana Owen (2002) observed that broadcast network reporters sometimes tried to focus attention on average voters and their views, one of the key differences from their cable news counterpart. Even they abandoned the practice as the campaign progressed, returning to the reporter-centered perspectives relatively quickly.

These media-centered trends in coverage are not trivial. Citing the Vanishing Voter Project at Harvard University, Kerbel (2001) reported that large numbers of citizens exposed to such self-referential media fodder predictably described the fall campaign as "boring." This was an astonishing assessment, given the photo finish nature of the November 2000 general election. However, when reporters talk a lot about their troubles on the campaign trail rather than the candidates' future plans for the country, it should not be surprising that many citizens do not find these campaigns interesting.

Of all the declines in the quality of network television election news in recent decades, perhaps none have been as dramatic as the reduction in a presidential candidate's ability to address the issues in his or her own voice. Candidate sound bites have been shrinking for several decades (Hallin, 1992). A study by Kiku Adatto (1990) found that the average length of time a candidate spoke in his own words on network television news during the 1968 campaign was 42 seconds. The average sound bite length in 1988 fell to 10 seconds, a decline of more than three-quarters over that twenty-year period (Adatto, 1990). The results triggered a good deal of soul-searching among reporters when they were first released, and the networks promised longer candidate sound bites in 1992 (Kurtz, 1992; Patterson, 1994). Despite that controversy, CMPA content analyses have since revealed a steady decline in the average length of on-air candidate statements from 9.8 seconds in 1988 to 8.4 in 1992, 8.2 in 1996, and 7.8 in 2000 and again in 2004. Lichter, Noyes, and Kaid (1999) reported that in 1996, for instance, journalists took up 73 percent of the campaign coverage time on the networks, and voters heard journalists speaking six times as often as they heard candidates. Thus, the average amount of time that a candidate speaks on-air without interruption seems to have stabilized. But the shrunken sound bite we now take for granted is about 20 percent below the figure that caused a furor when it was reported by Adatto five presidential elections ago. Details are found in Table 3.3.

TABLE 3.3
General Election News: Sound bites and Airtime, 1988–2004
Labor Day through the Day before Election Day

	2004*	2000	1996	1992	1988
Amount of Coverage					
Average Sound Bite (seconds)	7.8	7.8	8.2	8.4	9.8
Percentage of candidate airtime	12	12	13	12	n/a

*2004 data is based on a random 10 percent sample of election news stories.

Expressing an idea, even a relatively simple one, in eight seconds or less is a considerable challenge. The standard television commercial, which usually has a single, simple message to "buy this product," uses twenty to thirty seconds to make its case, about three to four times as much time as a presidential candidate has to say "Here is why you should vote for me" or "Here is why you should support this policy." (These sentences can be said in about three seconds each, so together they come close to an average sound bite.) Making the case as to why one should be president by speaking for eight seconds or less at a time is a daunting, perhaps an impossible challenge. After all, Coca-Cola would not try to sell a can of soda that fast.

When you add up all the sound bites on the three networks across the two month campaign, they still do not represent all that large a part of campaign discourse. Cumulative speaking time for the entire 2000 general election campaign was 53 minutes for Gore, 42 for Bush, and three for Ralph Nader. By contrast, cumulative speaking time for journalists was 9 hours 56 minutes during the roughly two-month general election campaign season. The total speaking time for presidential candidates dropped from 168 minutes in 1992 to 98 minutes in 2000, a 40 percent decline that represents a loss of more than an hour of direct communication with viewing audiences on the three networks.

The declining amount of news coverage and the shrinking sound bites encourage politicians to focus on raising money to pay for vast amounts of campaign advertising. Advertisements by the candidates, and by independent organizations that may or may not be linked to a specific candidates, is an important source of learning about the campaign, even though the often-nasty advertisements may be quite misleading in content (West, 2005).

Third party candidates without the vast personal fortune of Ross Perot face an impossible challenge when it comes to getting his or her message out on network television (Nader, 2002). Ralph Nader's three minutes of sound bites during the 2000 campaign averages out to just sixty seconds per network—the length of two commercials over the course of a two-month general election campaign. The nearly total absence of Nader on these news programs was particularly ironic, given his crucial influence on the final outcome of the 2000 presidential election.

These brief snippets from Gore, Bush, and Nader in the 2000 election and from other candidates in previous elections are hardly sufficient for a viewer to get a well-developed sense of a nominee and his or her policies. Of course, interested viewers can go beyond the nightly newscasts for other information, including the more extensive coverage found in most newspapers or on cable news networks. In fact, the declining overall coverage of the campaign, coupled with the tiny share of that coverage that allows the candidates to speak in their own words, practically invites voters to look elsewhere. More and more citizens are accepting the invitation, as the downsizing of network news campaign coverage has been accompanied by a decline in the viewing audience (Norris, 2001; Pew, 2000a, 2000b).

TONE OF COVERAGE: QUESTIONS OF NEGATIVITY AND BIAS

The news media's power to set the agenda is particularly troubling if reporters fail to meet standards of objectivity and fairness. Conservatives have long charged that reporters are biased. In the 1992 campaign, when allegations of media bias were particularly high, many Republicans put bumper stickers on their cars that said, "Annoy the Media: Re-Elect Bush." In the 2000 election, however, many liberals alleged the reporters were being too easy on Texas Gov. George W. Bush and were unfairly keeping Green Party candidate Ralph Nader off the air.

Scholars have a range of opinions on the question of whether reporters are biased. A recent meta-analysis of studies that examined possible partisan bias in news content have found barely measurable differences (D'Alessio & Allen, 2000) or no significant coverage differences at all (Niven, 2003). Some researchers have concluded that whatever bias that exists makes it way into the news because of deadline pressures and the need to make stories interesting for the public (Robinson, 1976). Others say that reporters try to be fair, but whatever bias that does find its way into stories—consciously or unconsciously—is predominantly biased towards the liberal perspective (Lichter et al., 1990).

Still other media researchers, generally found on the ideological left, focus on the corporate structures of the news business and argue that the generally conservative orientations of publishers, owners and other corporate executives are the true sources of bias (Ginsberg, 1986; Herman & Chomsky, 1988). As the diversity of opinion suggests, media researchers have not yet reached a consensus on the nature of an alleged media bias. In this project, we use the CMPA content analysis to search for evidence of bias on the network news across the past five presidential elections.

While scholars and politicians argue over the existence of ideological bias, there is much stronger evidence that television coverage has become increasingly negative in tone over the past several elections (Lichter & Noyes, 1995, 1998). This negativity, directed against nearly all viable candidates, can have a powerful impact on the public's orientation toward government. Above all, citizens exposed to the cynicism found in media portrayals of political candidates and public officials may become increasingly negatively disposed towards politics and government (Cappella & Jamieson, 1997; Hetherington, 2001).

More than a quarter century ago, Americans generally and journalists in particular were rocked by twin scandals of governmental deceit: Vietnam and Watergate (Gergen, 2000; Neustadt, 1990). In a televised moment eerily similar to President Bill Clinton's finger-wagging denial of any sexual relationship with Monica Lewinsky more than twenty years later, President Richard Nixon declared that he was "not a crook," while the Watergate scandal swirled around him (Gergen, 2000).

President Nixon, and President Lyndon Johnson before him, repeatedly misled the country about the ultimately failed U.S. military intervention in Vietnam. When the magnitude of their deceit became apparent, investigative reporters who exposed government malfeasance, such as Bob Woodward and Carl Bernstein of the *Washington Post*, became folk heroes and celebrities. The brightest of Hollywood's stars—Robert Redford and Dustin Hoffman—portrayed these enterprising reporters in a hit film on Watergate, *All the President's Men*. Reporters ever since have viewed government pronouncements with suspicion and governmental figures with contempt. For two generations now, reporters have resolved that they won't be fooled again (Kurtz, 1998; Sabato, 2000).

Campaign news coverage was not exempt from the growing media negativity of the post-Watergate years. A content analysis of news coverage of the 1980 presidential campaign found that all four major candidates that year—President Carter, Senator Edward Kennedy (D-MA), Ronald Reagan, and Republican turned Independent candidate John Anderson—received more negative than positive press on CBS (Robinson & Sheehan, 1983). Despite allegations of a liberal media bias, in 1980 there was no evidence to indicate that the most conservative candidate of the four—Ronald Reagan—received more negative press than the other leading candidates.

In a study of favorable and unfavorable references to major party nominees in *Time* and *Newsweek*, Patterson (1994) found a dramatic trend towards negativity in recent decades. The study, which excluded horse-race evaluations, found that in 1960, 75 percent of the references in America's two leading weekly news magazines were positive and that as late as 1976 over 60 percent of the coverage was positive. A majority of references were negative in 1980, and the figure rose to 60 percent negative in 1992 (Patterson, 1994).

If academic criticism has concentrated mainly on the superficiality and negativism of campaign news, the candidates and their supporters are most attuned to the fairness issue. Historically this complaint has been raised most often by Republicans, who see the national media as presenting the perspectives of liberals and Democrats (Bozell & Baker, 1990; Rusher, 1988). The Democratic voting patterns and relatively liberal personal perspectives of national media journalists are well documented, particularly on social and cultural rather than economic issues (Lichter, 1996; Lichter et al., 1990; Schneider & Lewis, 1985).

In recent years, however, Democrats have increasingly joined the chorus of media criticism. President Clinton's resentment of the media for its treatment of his personal life, beginning in the 1992 campaign, is well known. In the waning weeks of the 2000 campaign, several prominent liberal commentators charged that the media coverage was favoring George W. Bush, stemming either from journalists' personal antipathy toward Al Gore or their efforts to lean over backwards to avoid charges of partisanship.

In response to such criticism, journalists typically argue that their professionalism prevents their personal politics from influencing their coverage in any overt or systematic fashion (Deakin, 1983; Hunt, 1985). Some scholars have reached the same conclusion by pointing to economic and social constraints as counterweights to personal opinion in the news product (Epstein, 1975; Gans, 1979). However, this position should be treated as an empirical question rather than an article of faith.

CMPA's content analysis system was designed to examine this question with greater depth and precision than it usually receives. The system identified the tone as well as the source and topic of each statement about a candidate or issue; i.e., who said what about whom. This procedure allows for a more detailed and nuanced analysis than is possible when the entire story is treated as the unit of analysis. Our 2004 study was conducted in cooperation with Media Tenor, which coded election news according to CMPA's categories as well as their own. We are grateful for their generous assistance with this project.

Our coding procedure differentiated between the source and the object of each evaluative statement. We separated evaluations of candidate viability (horse race assessments) from those of candidate desirability (assessments of a candidate's qualifications, policies, personal character, or conduct). Only the latter were included in our definition of tone or valence, which is concerned with the merit of each candidacy rather than its likelihood of success. Second, we differentiated between evaluations made by (or attributed to) partisan and nonpartisan sources, respectively. In this case, "partisan" refers to sources identified as being affiliated with a particular candidacy; "nonpartisan" refers to all other sources. In practice, the vast majority of partisan evaluations in election stories come from the candidates and their campaign staffs. Nonpartisan sources of evaluative statements are most frequently journalists themselves, voters, experts (such as an economist who comments on a candidate's economic policies) and various pundits.

We followed the lead of Robinson and Sheehan's pioneering work (1983) in restricting our measure of tone to statements by nonpartisan sources. This was done for two reasons. First, they are more influential in the sense of predicting opinion change (Page, Shapiro, & Dempsey, 1987), presumably because voters give less credence to identifiably partisan opinion. Second, they represent the more discretionary portion of election news, the value-added element of a journalist's (and a media organization's) particular news judgment. So news accounts of partisan evaluations are more closely linked to the campaign trail give-and-take, whereas nonpartisan evaluations give more latitude to journalists' own judgments in selecting sources and topics.[2]

NETWORK NEWS TONE IN PRESIDENTIAL ELECTIONS

Throughout the final weeks of Campaign 2004 it was good to be John Kerry on network news. The Democratic nominee received highly positive coverage between Labor Day and Election Day—59 percent positive in tone. George W. Bush, in contrast, received coverage that was only 37 percent positive (i.e., 63 percent negative) in tone. In other words, Kerry easily won the battle for good press, which was calculated by tallying every positive or negative on-air evaluation of a candidate's record, policies, personal character, and behavior on the campaign trail by nonpartisan sources. This overall pattern differed little among the networks, as Kerry bested Bush by at least 19 percentage points for all three. Kerry received better press than Bush on policy matters (42 percent positive to 25 percent positive) and on personal evaluations (64 percent to 46 percent).

Kerry's advantages in media coverage were even more apparent when compared to major party candidates in previous presidential elections, as shown in Table 3.4. The tone of Bush's coverage was identical to that of 2000—and better than the coverage received by GOP nominee Bob Dole in 1996 or the elder George Bush in 1992. However, the tone of Kerry's coverage was the best of any major party nominee since CMPA began tracking election news in 1988.

Of course, the broadcast networks had competition this year from a cable channel that attracts a more conservative audience. Fox News Channel, an upstart cable news outlet that has seen a substantial rise in its audience in the past several years, was even more one-sided than the broadcast networks, but in the opposite direction. On Fox, Bush received coverage that was 53 percent positive versus only 21 percent positive coverage for Kerry. That 32 percentage point margin favoring Bush was greater than the overall 22 percentage point gap on the three broadcast networks.

Kerry's fortunes on all four networks improved considerably following a strong performance in the first presidential debate. On the broadcast networks, Bush received coverage that was 36 percent positive in tone during September—that is, before the first debate—compared to coverage that was 27 percent positive in tone for Kerry. Bush beat Kerry on Fox by a 58 percent to 9 percent margin during that month. (Kerry was also struggling to deal with questions raised by the Swift Boat Veterans for Truth during September). During October, the tone of Kerry's coverage rebounded to an unprecedented 73 percent positive on the Big Three networks, versus 38 percent positive for Bush. Even on the Fox News Channel, Kerry's coverage rose to 30 percent positive in tone during October, though still far below the 50 percent positive tone that Bush received.

Overall, in the last five presidential elections going back to 1988, CMPA studies three times found a significant imbalance in the tone of broadcast network news toward the major party candidates. In 1996 Democratic Bill Clinton enjoyed 50 percent positive evaluations versus only

TABLE 3.4
General Election News: Tone of Coverage, 1988–2004
Labor Day through the Day before Election Day

	2004	2000	1996	1992	1988
Tone of Coverage (% good press)					
Dem Nominee	59%	40%	50%	52%	31%
Rep Nominee	37%	37%	33%	29%	38%

Data based on campaign news stories from the ABC, CBS and NBC evening newscasts between Labor Day and Election Day for all years.

33 percent positive commentary for Republican Bob Dole. In 1992 Bill Clinton bested then-President George H.W. Bush by an even wider margin of 52 percent to 29 percent positive evaluations (Perot's coverage that year was 45 percent positive). Thus, during his two campaigns for the presidency, a slight majority of Clinton's on-air evaluations were positive, while over two out of three evaluations of his Republican opponents were negative. Clinton's advantage in election news coverage has also been independently replicated by other media scholars[3] (Just et al., 1996; Kerbel, 1998).

Network news was not alone in pumping up Clinton at the expense of the elder President Bush in 1992. That year, CMPA expanded its content analysis to include other media outlets, including the *Wall Street Journal*, the *New York Times*, the *Washington Post* and CNN and PBS. In all these media, Clinton received coverage that was better than Bush's by a margin of at least fifteen percentage points (Farnsworth & Lichter, 2007). These imbalances on network television and elsewhere cannot be dismissed as an accurate reflection of the loser's inferior political skills;, i.e., the reality of the campaign trail. Even after controlling for this subset of evaluations, Clinton enjoyed significantly better notices for his policy stands than his opponents did. (For all five elections we examined, the tonal directionality of policy judgments mirrored the overall pattern of candidate evaluations.)

The only time the Republican candidate fared better on network television than his Democratic opponent was in 1988, when coverage of then-Vice President George H.W. Bush was slightly more positive than that of Michael Dukakis, by the margin of 38 percent to 31 percent favorable assessments. Bush's slight advantage in 1988 and Gore's in 2000 can be treated as effectively balanced (or as canceling each other out). If we accept a 10 percentage point difference as the threshold for a clear advantage, then the Democrats' scorecard in this battle for better network news coverage reads three wins, no losses, and two ties in the five presidential elections between 1988 and 2004.

Of course, in two of the three instances of unbalanced coverage over the past four presidential campaigns, the advantage went to Bill Clinton. (Two of the three distinctly negative treatments were directed at an incumbent president who is a member of the Bush family.) Although it is difficult to imagine that this finding reflects a generalized pro-Clinton tilt (or anti-Bush family trend) in the news, we controlled for this factor by examining all evaluations of Democratic and Republican candidates during the two off-year elections of 1994 and 1998, from Labor Day through Election Day. The results were consistent with the pattern that we observed for general elections: In 1994 Democratic candidates fared better, collectively receiving 43 percent positive evaluations, compared to 31 percent for their GOP counterparts. In 1998 the tone was more balanced, with 43 percent positive judgments of Democrats and 40 percent positive for Republicans.

Our findings demonstrating tonal advantages that favor neither party in some years and favor the Democrats in others are consistent with the results of content analyses of the two presidential elections prior to those studied by CMPA. An examination of news coverage of the 1980 campaign concluded that Ronald Reagan and Jimmy Carter "both did about equally badly on television" (Robinson & Sheehan, 1983, p. 138). Studies of the 1984 campaign found that Walter Mondale received balanced news coverage, while Reagan's was predominantly negative (Clancey & Robinson, 1985; Graber, 1987).

Clancey and Robinson (1985) accounted for the good press gap between Mondale and Reagan by positing a general anti-frontrunner bias they termed "compensatory journalism." They argued that reporters are toughest on the candidates who are most likely to become president, in effect compensating those who are trailing with better press than the leaders. However, this hypothesis has since been contradicted by data from subsequent general elections. Clinton got far better press than both Bush in 1992 and Dole in 1996, despite his wire-to-wire leads in the polls.

And Bush led Dukakis in good press in 1988, albeit by a slight margin, despite his frontrunner status in preference polls throughout the fall.

In sum, a general pattern of negativism on network news has coincided with an intermittent tendency toward more favorable press for Democrats than Republicans. In four of the past nine elections for which exhaustive systematic content analysis data are available (1980, 1988, 1998, and 2000), both sides received mainly negative notices. In the other five (1984, 1992, 1994, 1996, and 2004), Democrats fared substantially better on the evening news programs than did Republicans.[4]

It appears that negativity and political ideology represent separate dimensions that contribute independently to the tone of election news. To paraphrase George Orwell, journalists may see all candidates as evil, but some as more evil than others. Democratic candidates did not always get better press than Republicans, but Republican candidates never got much better press than Democrats. To be sure, any difference in tone seems less pro-Democratic than anti-Republican. Nonetheless, these data suggest that allegations of ideological tilt in election coverage cannot be dismissed entirely as the special pleading of partisans. At the same time, neither negativity nor partisanship alone can fully account for the tilt in the tone of campaign news.

It is important to note that positive media coverage during the general election does not always help the candidate who received it. For the five elections in which the Democrats received significantly better coverage (the presidential election years of 1984, 1992, 1996, and 2004 and the mid-term congressional elections of 1994), the party was only two-for-five at the polls. Bill Clinton won his two presidential campaigns, but John Kerry lost narrowly in 2004 and Walter Mondale was trounced in 1984, winning only his home state of Minnesota and the overwhelmingly Democratic District of Columbia. In 1994, the off-year election in this group, the Republican candidates for the U.S. House and the U.S. Senate scored extraordinary victories on their way to taking majority party status away from the Democrats in both chambers (Jacobson, 2001a).

The four elections in which coverage was about equally negative for the two parties and their candidates (1980, 1988, 1998, and 2000) also offer mixed results. Reagan won easily in 1980, and the Republican Party took control of the U.S. Senate that year. George H.W. Bush won the presidency in an easy victory in 1988, securing nearly 54 percent of the popular vote and winning 40 states. In the mid-term election of 1998, when the air was thick with the presidential impeachment controversy, the Republicans broke even in the Senate and suffered a net loss of five seats in the House (Jacobson, 2001a). In 2000, of course, the presidential election ended in a virtual deadlock that was settled by the U.S. Supreme Court after a five-week struggle involving partisan activists, lawyers, and Florida ballot counters. Although the Republicans regained the White House that year, the party lost four Senate seats and two House seats (Jacobson, 2001b).

The mixed results demonstrate that the fears of an all-powerful or "imperial" media in the U.S. are overblown. In cases of both equally negative media and of more one-sided coverage, the results offer no evidence in support of the hypodermic effects model of media influence. The media don't tell us in a consistently decisive and effective way how to vote. But this doesn't mean television news coverage is unimportant. The mere fact that a "media candidate" did not win does not prove that the media did not influence voters. Further, the media have powerful agenda-setting effects, particularly relating to the framing of news stories, a process of telling viewers what issues to think about and in what ways.

Our content analysis of five presidential elections reveals that what we are told to think about by television—the horse race, candidates who seem to be scheming at every opportunity, and the human failings of those candidates—are not matters likely to make us informed citizens or congenial voters. Nor does the generally declining amount of coverage we have found on all networks remind citizens about the importance of political participation in presidential elections.

CONCLUSION

Media theorist Marshall McLuhan (1964) famously argued that "the medium is the message." But the evidence shows that in presidential campaigns the message matters a great deal to candidates and voters. So what messages do network television news programs offer us? The short sound bites and shrinking amount of news coverage of elections tell us that presidential candidates aren't worth listening to for long, and that presidential campaigns don't deserve much of our attention. The horse race-dominated coverage tells us that issues don't really matter much either. The embarrassing way the networks made mistake after mistake on Election Night 2000 raises questions about how seriously they take their central mission of being responsible, fair, and accurate transmitters of critically important information.

The heavily mediated and negative coverage that year told us that neither the Democratic liar nor the Republican lightweight deserved to be president. And the lack of coverage of third-party candidates like Ralph Nader and Pat Buchanan told us they hardly existed. (Ironically, the votes for both these candidates turned out to be decisive in Florida, and hence the entire election, in 2000. Gore would have won Florida with a fraction of either Nader's 97,000 votes in the state or less than one-quarter of the 3,400 apparently mistaken votes recorded for Buchanan in Palm Beach County.)

This multi-count indictment of network news is particularly troubling in light of the central role that the news media play in linking citizens to candidates. Since few of us ever meet presidential candidates in person, our views of Kerry, Bush, Gore, Clinton, and the rest develop largely from what we learn about them from the mass media. And if we rely on network television's evening newscasts, the flagship public representation of some of the world's largest companies—including General Electric (NBC) and Disney (ABC)—do not learn much beyond the basic fact that candidates are not nearly as important as reporters, that their positions and records don't matter much, and perhaps that neither major party candidate really deserves our vote, and other candidates barely exist. Of course, the networks' Election Night 2000 inaccuracies—together with the retracted CBS *60 Minutes II* September 2004 story on George W. Bush's alleged National Guard records—send an unintended message that the networks don't deserve our confidence any more than the candidates do.

Simply put, coverage that focuses on the horse race shortchanges candidates trying to talk about issues, and voters who are trying to think about issues. The questions voters ask of candidates are about a lot more than who is gaining or losing ground in the latest poll. The movement in recent years towards talk shows, cable television, and even the Internet suggests that increasing numbers of voters are hungry for the kinds of coverage that broadcast television news is increasingly unable and/or unwilling to provide. Of course, not all people have equal access to, or equal ability to use, these alternative sources of information.

News coverage of 2004 suggests that the considerable ferment and reform efforts by mainstream journalists in recent years, together with extensive criticisms of media content by scholars, may be pushing the news back towards levels of campaign coverage not seen since 1992. But one cannot be as optimistic about the shrinking sound-bites, which in 2004 remained at an abysmally low average of 7.8 seconds. Nor can one be sanguine about the strong differences in the tone of coverage of Kerry and Bush during the 2004 election. That year, Fox tilted towards Bush while the three broadcast networks' tilted toward Kerry.

In the early years of the 21st century, network news departments continue to struggle to redefine their role in a rapidly expanding media landscape that already includes such new venues for election news as talk radio, cable news networks, Internet sites, and entertainment formats that range from *Oprah* to late night comedy monologues (Farnsworth & Owen, 2004; Pew, 2000c,

2000d, 2004). Twenty years ago the broadcast network news departments had the field virtually to themselves among electronic media in setting the campaign news agenda. Today they struggle to remain *primus inter pares*.

Of course the broadcast networks are staking their own claims in the new media landscape. For example, NBC reaches voters through the cable networks CNBC and MSNBC, along with their associated web sites, not to mention other news programs like "Dateline" and Jay Leno's nightly thrusts at politicians during the *Tonight Show* monologues. The information at each network outlet is increasingly integrated with the others by cross-promotions that encourage viewers to learn more by watching another channel or visiting a website. But showing a web page address at the bottom of the screen is no substitute for doing a better job of covering the campaign, an area where there is considerable room for improvement on several dimensions we have examined here.

NOTES

1. Thanks to the staffs of the Center for Media and Public Affairs, especially Mary Carroll Willi, and of Media Tenor for their assistance with this project. Thanks also to the University of Mary Washington and McGill University for financial support and to Rowman & Littlefield for permission to use material drawn from the second edition of *The Nightly News Nightmare*. An earlier version of this chapter was presented at the Seventh Annual International Agenda Setting Conference, Bonn, Germany (2006). All errors remain the authors' responsibility.
2. Additional data analysis showed that the inclusion of partisan evaluations did not significantly alter the tonal balance between Bush and Gore. We could not make longitudinal comparisons, because only non-partisan source evaluations were coded for all five elections.
3. Just et al. (1996) found no clear tilt in terms of visual images in 1992. CMPA coded shot-by-shot visuals during the same contest and similarly found no clear pattern. We also concluded that few images could be reliably categorized for tone in a fashion that met the criteria of reliability and validity, i.e., replicable judgments that were substantively meaningful.
4. Hofstetter (1976) found negative but balanced network news coverage in the 1972 race between Nixon and McGovern. Unfortunately his coding system conflated what we have termed the viability and desirability dimensions of evaluative content. Robinson and Sheehan (1983, p. 311) cite this problem as a major drawback of this study. This convinced them to separate the two dimensions in their analysis of the 1980 campaign.

REFERENCES

Adatto, K. (1990, June). *Sound bite democracy*. Research paper, Kennedy School Press Politics Center, Harvard University, Cambridge, MA.

Alter, J. (1992, November 2). Go ahead, blame the media. *Newsweek,* p. 59.

Alter, J. (1988, November 28). How the media blew it. *Newsweek,* p. 81.

Barber, J. D. (1992). *Presidential character*. Englewood Cliffs, NJ: Prentice-Hall.

Bode, K. (1992, March). Pull the plug. *The Quill*, pp. 10–14.

Bozell, L. B., & Baker, B. H. (1990). *And that's the way it wasn't*. Alexandria, VA: Media Research Center.

Cappella, J. N., & Jamieson, K. H. (1997). *Spiral of cynicism: The press and the public good*. New York: Oxford University Press.

Clancey, M., & Robinson, M. J. (1985). General election coverage. In M. J. Robinson & A. Ranney (Eds.), *The mass media in campaign '84*. Washington, D.C.: American Enterprise Institute Press.

Cook, T. (2005). *Governing with the news: The news media as a political institution* (2nd ed.). Chicago: University of Chicago Press.

D'Alessio, D., & Allen, M. (2000). Media bias in presidential elections: A meta-analysis. *Journal of Communication, 50,* 133–156.

Deakin, J. (1983). *Straight stuff: The reporters, the White House, and the truth.* New York: William Morrow.

Epstein, E. J. (1975). *News from nowhere.* Chicago: University of Chicago Press.

Farnsworth, S. J., & Lichter, S. R. (2006). *The mediated presidency: Television news and presidential governance.* Lanham, MD: Rowman & Littlefield.

Farnsworth, S. J., & Lichter, S. R. (2007). *The nightly news nightmare: Television's coverage of U.S. presidential elections, 1988–2004* (2nd ed.). Lanham, MD: Rowman & Littlefield.

Farnsworth, S. J., & Owen, D. (2004). Internet use and the 2000 presidential election. *Electoral Studies, 23,* 415–429.

Gans, H. J. (1979). *Deciding what's news.* New York: Pantheon.

Genovese, M. (2001). *The power of the American presidency, 1789-2000.* New York: Oxford University Press.

Gergen, D. (2000). *Eyewitness to power: The essence of leadership.* New York: Simon & Schuster.

Ginsberg, B. (1986). *The captive public: How mass opinion promotes state power.* New York: Basic Books.

Graber, D. (2006). *Mass media and American politics* (7th ed.). Washington, D.C.: CQ Press.

Hall, J. (2001). *Online journalism: A critical primer.* London: Pluto.

Hallin, D. (1992). Sound bite news: Television coverage of elections, 1968-1988. *Journal of Communication, 42,* 5–24.

Herman, E. S., & Chomsky, N. (1988). *Manufacturing consent: The political economy of the mass media.* New York: Pantheon.

Hershey, M. R. (2001). The campaign and the media. In G. M. Pomper (Ed.), *The election of 2000.* (pp. 46–73). New York: Chatham House.

Hetherington, M. (2001). Declining trust and a shrinking policy agenda: Why media scholars should care. In R. P. Hart & D. R. Shaw (Eds.), *Communication in U.S. elections: New agendas* (pp. 105–121). Lanham, MD: Rowman & Littlefield.

Hetherington, M., & Keefe, W. J. (2007). *Parties, politics and public policy in* America (10th ed.). Washington: CQ Press.

Hofstetter, C. R. (1976). *Bias in the news.* Columbus: Ohio State University Press.

Hunt, A. (1985, July 23). Media bias is in the eye of the beholder. *Wall Street Journal.*

Huntington, S. P. (1981). *American politics and the promise of disharmony.* Cambridge, MA: Harvard University Press.

Jacobson, G. C. (2001a). *The politics of congressional elections* (5th ed.). New York: Addison Wesley Longman.

Jacobson, G. C. (2001b). Congress: Elections and stalemate. In M. Nelson (Ed.), *The elections of 2000* (pp. 185–209). Washington, D.C: CQ Press.

Just, M. R., Crigler, A. E., Alger, D. E., Cook, T. E., Kern, M., & West, D. M. (1996). *Crosstalk: Citizens, candidates, and the media in a presidential campaign.* Chicago: University of Chicago Press.

Kerbel, M. R. (1998). *Edited for television: CNN, ABC and American presidential election* (2nd ed.). Boulder, CO: Westview.

Kerbel, M. R. (2001). The media: Old frames in a time of transition. In M. Nelson (Ed.), *The elections of 2000* (pp. 109–132). Washington, D.C.: CQ Press.

Kurtz, H. (1992, June 21). Networks adapt to changed campaign role. *Washington Post,* A21

Kurtz, H. (1998). *Spin cycle: Inside the Clinton propaganda machine.* New York: Free Press.

Lichter, S. R. (1996, Fall). Consistently liberal: But does it matter? *Forbes Media Critic,* pp. 26–39.

Lichter, S. R., & Noyes, R. E. (1995). *Good intentions make bad news: Why Americans hate campaign journalism* (2nd ed.). Lanham, MD: Rowman & Littlefield.

Lichter, S. R., Noyes, R. E., & Kaid, L. L. (1999). No news or negative news: How the networks nixed the '96 campaign. In L. L. Kaid & D. G. Bystrom (Eds.), *The electronic election:Perspectives on the 1996 campaign communication* (pp. 3–13). Mahwah, NJ: Erlbaum.

Lichter, S. R. Robert, & Noyes, R. E. (1998). *Why elections are bad news.* New York: Markle Foundation.

Lichter, S. R., Rothman, S., & Lichter, L. S. (1990). *The media elite.* New York: Hastings House.

McLuhan, M. (1964). *Understanding media.* New York: New York American Library.

Nader, R. (2002). *Crashing the party: Taking on the corporate government in an age of surrender.* New York: St. Martin's Press.

Neustadt, R. E. (1990). *Presidential power and the modern presidents: The politics of leadership from Roosevelt to Reagan.* New York: Free Press.

Niven, D. (2003). Objective evidence on media bias: Newspaper coverage of congressional party switchers. *Journalism & Mass Communication Quarterly, 80,* 311–326.

Norris, P. (2001). A failing grade? The news media and campaign 2000. *Harvard International Journal of Press/Politics, 6,* 3–9.

Owen, D. (2002). Media mayhem: Performance of the press in election 2000. In L. Sabato (Ed.), *Overtime: The election 2000 thriller* (pp. 123–156). New York: Longman.

Page, B. I., Shapiro, R. T., & Dempsey, G. R. (1987). What moves public opinion. *American Political Science Review, 81,* 23–43.

Patterson, T. E. (1980). *The mass media election: How Americans choose their president.* New York: Praeger.

Patterson, T. E. (1994). *Out of order.* New York: Vintage.

Patterson, T. E. (2000, December). *Doing well and doing good.* Research paper, Kennedy School Press Politics Center, Harvard University, Cambridge, MA

Pew Research Center for the People and the Press. (2000a, July 27). *Voters unmoved by media characterizations of Bush and Gore.* Retrieved June 10, 2007 from http://people-press.org/reports/display.php3?ReportID=34

Pew Research Center for the People and the Press. (2000b, October 15). *Media seen as fair, but tilting to Gore.* Retrieved June 10, 2007 from http://people-press.org/reports/display.php3?ReportID=29

Pew Research Center for the People and the Press. (2000c, November 16). *Campaign 2000 highly rated.* Retrieved June 10, 2007 from http://people-press.org/reports/display.php3?ReportID=23

Pew Research Center for the People and the Press. (2000d, December 3). *Internet election news audience seeks convenience, familiar names.* Retrieved June 10, 2007 from http://people-press.org/reports/display.php3?ReportID=21

Pew Research Center for the People and the Press. (2004, November 11). Voters liked campaign 2004, but too much "mud-slinging." Retrieved June 10, 2007 from http://people-press.org/reports/display.php3?ReportID=233

Ranney, A. (1983). *Channels of power.* New York: Basic Books.

Robinson, M. J. (1976). Public affairs television and the growth of political malaise: The case of "The Selling of the Pentagon." *American Political Science Review, 70,* 409–432.

Robinson, M. J., & Sheehan, M. A. (1983). *Over the wire and on TV.* New York: Russell Sage Foundation.

Rusher, W. A. (1988). *The coming battle for the media.* New York: William Morrow.

Sabato, L. J. (2000). *Feeding frenzy: Attack journalism and American politics.* Lanham, MD: Rowman and Littlefield

Schneider, W., & Lewis, I. A. (1985). Views on the news. *Public Opinion, 8,* 6–11.

Seib, P. (2001). *Going live: Getting the news right in a real-time, on-line world.* Lanham, MD: Rowman & Littlefield.

Sigelman, L., & Bullock, D. (1991). Candidates, issues, horse races, and hoopla: Presidential campaign coverage 1888-1988. *American Politics Quarterly, 19,* 5–32.

Smith, C. (1977). *The press, politics, and patronage.* Athens: University of Georgia Press.

Trippi, J. (2004). *The revolution will not be televised: Democracy, the Internet and the overthrow of everything.* New York: HarperCollins.

West, D. (2005). *Air wars* (4th ed.). Washington, D.C.: CQ Press.

4

Media Matter:
Election Coverage in Canada[1]

Elisabeth Gidengil

Canada is a multicultural and increasingly multiracial country, with a large French-speaking minority which resides mainly in the province of Quebec. The country covers a vast geographical area, made up of regions that are economically and culturally distinct. As a result, voting in federal elections tends to be highly regionalized. National unity is a perennial concern. Quebeckers have twice voted in referenda on Quebec sovereignty, and in 1995 the "no" side won by a razor-thin majority. Meanwhile, residents of Canada's western provinces often feel alienated from the centers of power. The other perennial concern, at least in English-speaking Canada, relates to Canada's cultural sovereignty. As former Prime Minister Pierre Trudeau famously remarked to the National Press Club in Washington, D.C., in 1969, living next to the United States is like sleeping with an elephant: there is a risk of being crushed.

This helps to explain why Canadian broadcasting is highly regulated. Indeed, the Broadcasting Act, 1991 declares that "the Canadian broadcasting system...provides, through its programming, a public service essential to the maintenance and enhancement of national identity and cultural sovereignty" [Section 3(1)(b)]. It goes on to state that: "the Canadian broadcasting system should...serve to safeguard, enrich and strengthen the cultural, political, social and economic fabric of Canada" [Section 3(1)(d)]. This backdrop is essential for understanding election coverage in Canada.

THE CANADIAN POLITICAL SYSTEM

Canada has a highly decentralized federal system of government. It is made up of the federal government and the governments of the ten provinces and the three northern territories. Canada is a constitutional monarchy. The Queen's representative in Canada is the Governor-General, but the latter's role is largely ceremonial. By contrast, the Prime Minister, who is the leader of the party with the most seats in the House of Commons, enjoys considerable power. It is he or she who gets to choose the cabinet ministers who head the various federal government departments. The Canadian Parliament is bicameral. The upper house, or Senate, is appointed, with seats assigned on a regional basis. Appointments are made by the Governor-General on the recommendation of the Prime Minister. The provincial and territorial legislatures are all unicameral. The House of Commons, the provincial legislatures and the Yukon legislature operate under Westminster-style rules with strict party discipline; the Nunavut and Northwest Territories legislatures are nonpartisan and operate by consensus. As a result of changes to the Canada Elections Act in December 2007, there will be fixed four-year terms for the House of Commons beginning in 2009.However, an election can come at any time if the government loses the House's confidence. The provinces of British Columbia, Newfoundland and Labrador, and Ontario also have fixed terms. Members of Parliament and provincial and territorial legislators are elected in single-member districts according to the plurality rule.

Canada traditionally had a two-plus-one party system that was dominated by the two major parties, the Liberals and the Progressive Conservatives (PCs). That system broke apart in 1993 when the PCs suffered the most devastating defeat ever inflicted on a governing party in an established western democracy. It was left with only two parliamentary seats and temporarily lost official party status. Outside Quebec, the PCs were displaced by the Western Canadian-based Reform party. The fight to re-unite Canada's right continued until 2003 when Reform's successor, the Canadian Alliance, merged with the PCs to form the new Conservative Party of Canada. Meanwhile in Quebec the separatist Bloc Québécois established itself as the main rival to the Liberal party. At the federal level, Canada now has two party systems, one in Quebec and one outside. Outside Quebec, Canada seems to be returning to a two-plus-one party system, with the New Democratic Party (NDP) regaining its traditional position on the left as Canada's third party. Canada has witnessed a good deal of electoral volatility, with the two most recent elections, in 2004 and 2006, both resulting in minority governments. The provinces and territories have a variety of party systems, ranging from single-party dominance to multiparty systems.

CANADIAN MEDIA SYSTEM

The Canadian media system is dominated by a small number of multimedia conglomerates. Bell Globemedia owns both *The Globe and Mail*, generally considered Canada's newspaper of record, and CTV, Canada's largest private English-language broadcaster. Meanwhile, Canada's other national newspaper, the *National Post*, is owned by CanWest, which also owns Global, Canada's second private English-language national broadcast network. TVA, the largest private French-language broadcaster in North America, is owned by Quebecor, whose subsidiary, Sun Media Corporation, owns Canada's largest chain of community newspapers and tabloids. In addition to its radio stations and specialty TV channels, Rogers Media owns Canada's largest circulation news magazines, *Maclean's* and *L'Actualité*.

Canada also has a national public broadcasting network that operates in both English (the Canadian Broadcasting Corporation) and French (Société Radio-Canada) and four provincial public broadcasters. However, the distinction between public and private has become increasingly blurred. According to Marc Raboy, Canada has developed a "hybrid" broadcasting system which "can best be described as a semi-public, semi-private system" (Raboy, 1996, p. 117). Commercial and budgetary pressures have produced a growing "privatization of conventional public broadcasting," while increasing dependence on public funds and public policy measures have fostered a concomitant "publicization" of the private sector.

The Canadian broadcasting industry is regulated by the Canadian Radio-television and Telecommunications Commission (CRTC). Public and private broadcasters alike are bound by the CRTC's Canadian content guidelines that require them to produce and air a specified amount of domestic programming. However, many Canadian households have access to U.S. networks and specialty channels via cable or satellite (or direct signal if they live close to the border). While the CRTC limits the number of specialty channels that are licensed and requires broadcast distributors to maintain a specified ratio of Canadian to non-Canadian channels, any assessment of the impact of news coverage in Canada has to bear in mind that many Canadians may be watching American channels. Canadian content has also been an issue in the magazine industry. The federal government has imposed a special excise tax to discourage split run publishing where a U.S magazine like *Time* adds a few pages of Canadian content to attract Canadian advertisers. The dominance of U.S. media is much less of an issue in Quebec where the majority of the population is French-speaking.

The major issue with respect to newspapers has been the concentration of ownership. Osprey Media owns 21 of Canada's 100 daily newspapers while Quebecor/Sun Media owns another 17. In terms of circulation, CanWest leads with 28.4 per cent of all dailies, followed by Quebecor/Sun Media with 21 per cent (Canadian Newspaper Association, 2006). Gesca, a subsidiary of Power Corporation, owns seven of Quebec's 10 French-language dailies. However, newspaper ownership is actually more diversified today than it was in the 1990s.

THE REGULATORY FRAMEWORK

Throughout their history, Canadian broadcasters have been required to provide coverage of federal and provincial elections as part of their larger obligation under section 3 of the Broadcasting Act of 1968 to "provide a reasonable opportunity for the public to be exposed to the expression of differing views on matters of public concern." Broadcasters are obliged to provide equitable treatment. CRTC guidelines specify that,

> It is the broadcaster's duty to ensure that the public has adequate knowledge of the issues surrounding an election and the position of the parties and candidates…. From this right on the part of the public to have adequate knowledge to fulfill its obligations as an informed electorate, flows the obligation on the part of the broadcaster to provide equitable—fair and just—treatment of issues, candidates and parties. It should be noted that "equitable" does not necessarily mean "equal" (http://www.crtc.gc.ca/eng/INFO_SHT/b309.htm).

Under the Canada Elections Act, every broadcaster must make a certain amount of prime time air space available during federal election campaigns for purchase by registered and new political parties, even if this means pre-empting other advertisers. This applies to both radio and television broadcasters, including cable, satellite and multipoint distribution systems. The total amount of broadcasting time depends on the number of recognized political parties and is allocated among the parties by the Canadian Broadcasting Arbitrator. One-third of the available time is divided equally among the parties, while the remaining two-thirds are allocated according to seat and vote shares in the previous election. In the 2006 federal election, 408 minutes were made available, with the incumbent Liberals receiving 105 minutes and the Official Opposition Conservatives 85 minutes (The Broadcasting Arbitrator, 2006). Certain television (CBC-TV, SRC-TV, TVA and TQS) and radio (CBC Radio One, SRC Première Chaîne and Réseau Corus Québec) networks are also required to provide free time to political parties, again according to a formula determined by the Broadcasting Arbitrator. Since 1995 (when the Reform party successfully challenged the constitutionality of a cap in the courts), broadcasters have been free to sell extra time to a party, provided that they do not refuse to sell it to the others. However, the parties are bound by their overall election spending limits. They are also prohibited from purchasing time on stations outside the country. No political advertising is permitted on Election Day.

The publication of opinion polls is also banned on the day of the election under the provisions of the Canada Elections Act that relate to the premature transmission of election results (see section 5 below). The Act also specifies that certain information must be provided during the 24 hours when the results of an election survey are first transmitted to the public, including the names of the polling organization and the survey's sponsor, the timing of the field work, the population sampled, the number of people contacted, and the margin of error. The wording of the survey questions and information on how to obtain a report with additional methodological information must also be provided if the results are being published rather than broadcast. If the survey is not based on "recognizable statistical methods," this must be made clear when the results are first transmitted to the public.

THE EVOLUTION OF POLITICAL NEWS COVERAGE

Election coverage in Canada's early years was highly partisan, reflecting the close links between the press and political parties. Partisan organizations subsidized newspapers well into the twentieth century (Osler, 1993). However, the emergence of newspaper chains, the development of wire services, increasing literacy and the growth of mass readership, the lessening of competition within the industry, and the increasing dominance of the profit motive all worked to diminish partisan influence (Fletcher, 1981). Newspapers could no longer risk alienating their readers with partisan coverage. The growth of television also contributed to the waning of press partisanship (Fletcher, 1981). The regulatory framework governing broadcasting established norms of impartiality that came to influence newspaper reporting as well. By the 1960s all trace of a partisan press had effectively disappeared (Fletcher, 1987). Still, some newspapers have partisan leanings and editorial endorsements often appear at some point during the campaign in the larger dailies.

Television service first became available to Canadians in 1952, and the 1957 federal election qualifies as Canada's first "television election." Since then, election campaigns have routinely been extensively covered. The CTV network opened in 1961 and the Global network was launched in 1974. *CTV National News* is Canada's most watched national newscast, followed by *Global National*, with CBC's *The National* a distant third. The French-language TVA began broadcasting in 1971 and it was joined by a second private French-language network (TQS) in 1986. The CBC launched its English all-news channel in 1989; the French-language all-news channel followed in 1995. The three English-language networks focus their late-night election news coverage on the national campaign and especially the party leaders' tours, leaving local campaign coverage largely to their local affiliates. Beginning with the 2000 federal election, the television networks, as well as the major news magazines and the larger newspapers, routinely maintain election websites featuring a variety of tools and resources to help inform voters about the election.

RESEARCH ON ELECTION COVERAGE

Media Usage

Television is Canadians' main source of information about politics: when the 2000 Canadian Election Study (CES) asked people where they got most of their election information, television was named twice as often as newspapers and more than four times as often as radio (Gidengil, Blais, Nevitte, & Nadeau, 2004). It is difficult to pinpoint when television assumed its current dominance as a source of political information in Canada, but television was already coming out on top in the 1970s. Newspapers, though, were a more important source of information then than now.

Interpersonal communication is another important source of election information. Indeed, family or friends were the *main* source of information about the 2000 federal election for almost one Canadian in ten, and as many as one young Canadian in five (Gidengil et al., 2004). Almost as many people named family or friends as their main source of information as named radio, but the rise of "talk radio" and the growing number of people who have lengthy commutes to and from work make radio a more important source of political information today than it was 20 or 30 years ago (Gidengil et al., 2004).

In 2000, only one Canadian in eight reported that they had used the Internet to get information about the election (Gidengil et al., 2004), but the numbers are growing. By the time of the 2006 federal election, one in four reported paying at least some attention to election news on the Internet (2006 Canadian Election Studies). Still, fewer than one in twenty indicated that the Internet was their main source of information about the election. Predictably, younger Canadians are much more likely to use the Internet to track down political information. Interestingly, though, the young Canadians who are going on-line to get information about politics are also the most likely to be following politics in conventional media.

Media Bias

Coverage of the political parties tends to be more or less proportional to their seat share. This is true of both air time and newspaper space. A content analysis of coverage of the 2000 election on the principal English- and French-language nightly network newscasts found that the incumbent Liberals received the most attention, followed by their major rivals, the Alliance and, on the French networks, the Bloc Québécois (Blais, Gidengil, Nadeau, & Nevitte, 2002). The PCs and especially the NDP received much less attention. This was even more evident when the news headlines and story placement were analyzed. The NDP did not feature even once in the lead election story of the night. The party fared even worse during the 1997 election: it received *no* coverage in fully a third of the nightly newscasts, despite having more seats than the PCs going into the election. The PCs may have fared better because they had been one of Canada's two major parties until their devastating defeat in 1993, but the NDP's lack of coverage may also have reflected sex-differentiated treatment of their leader (see below).

Content analyses of newspaper coverage tell a similar story. Press coverage of the 2000 election focused heavily on the incumbent party and its major rival (see also Dornan and Pyman, 2001). Similarly, content analyses of press coverage of the 2006 election by McGill University's Observatory on Media and Public Policy (2006) found that the incumbent Liberal party enjoyed a visibility bonus. The Liberals received the most coverage, followed by their main rivals, the Conservatives, with the NDP receiving only about half as many mentions as the Liberals. The differences among the parties were even larger when first mentions were analyzed.

The 2006 analysis gave the press a clean bill of health: "It's not as sexy as saying there's huge bias in news but, the truth is, Canadian newspapers are relatively neutral in their news coverage."[2] This is not to say that the newspapers did not reveal their political leanings, but with the exception of the *Calgary Herald*, partisanship was limited to editorials and opinion pieces. Overall, the tone of the articles appeared to be driven by campaign events and party fortunes. Similarly, while Dornan and Pyman (2001) found that coverage of the 2000 election in the right-leaning *National Post* was much less favorable to the Liberal prime minister than that of *The Globe and Mail* or the *Toronto Star*, 40 per cent of its coverage of the Conservative leader was also unfavorable, and of the four newspapers analyzed, the paper actually had the highest percentage (50 per cent) of election coverage that was coded as straight news.

Evidence about possible bias in television coverage is scanty. A study of coverage of the

1997 federal election concluded that the there was an important element of evaluation to television news: only 36 per cent of stories on the French-language SRC news and 42 per cent of those on the English-language networks were judged to be neutral in tone (Nevitte et al., 2000). The negative tone of Reform coverage led the authors to conclude that any media biases were operating against parties of the right (but not in favor of the parties of the left). The CBC generated a good deal of controversy during the 2000 election for airing a program entitled "Fundamental Day" that highlighted the fundamentalist Christian views of Alliance (successor to Reform) party leader, Stockwell Day, including his belief in creationism. However, detailed analyses of network news coverage are needed before concluding that there is any anti-right-wing bias. Interestingly, "Fundamental Day" had surprisingly little lasting impact on voters' evaluations of Day or on Alliance vote intentions (Blais et al., 2003).

There has not been any systematic cross-time analysis of trends in descriptive versus interpretative reporting in Canada. However, Dornan and Pyman (2001) note a continuing trend toward more analytical and interpretive reporting, as opposed to straightforward descriptive coverage, in their analysis of election coverage in four Toronto newspapers.

News Frames

Leadership and the horse race dominate television coverage on Canada's networks. Matthew Mendelsohn's (1993, 1996a) analysis of CBC national nightly news coverage of the 1988 campaign and the opening week of the 1993 campaign found that the horserace frame predominated, with the leadership frame playing a secondary role.[3] The focus was on who was winning and why. Even the issues were interpreted through the leadership and horserace frames: "Policy positions are treated as mere campaign devices to attract votes" (Mendelsohn, 1993, p. 158). Such is the focus on party leaders that the party may not receive *any* coverage in the broadcast news if its leader takes a day off (Mendelsohn, 1993).

This type of framing is not confined to television news reporting. "Horse race journalism" is typical of newspaper, television, and magazine coverage alike (Wilson, 1980). Linda Trimble and Shannon Sampert's analysis of all the election-related headlines appearing in Canada's two English-language national newspapers during the 2000 federal election campaign revealed that both newspapers neglected the election issues and ideological differences among the parties in favor of a "game frame" that focused on the horse race, the party leaders' personalities and performance, and party strategy (Sampert & Trimble, 2003; Trimble & Sampert, 2004).

More recent work on framing has highlighted the stereotypically masculine narrative used in coverage of election campaigns. Metaphors of warfare, violence, and stereotypically masculine sports like professional ice hockey and boxing dominated television news coverage of the 1993, 1997, and 2000 televised party leaders' debates (Gidengil & Everitt, 1998, 2003a). Trimble and Sampert's analysis of election headlines in the national press revealed a similar reliance on images drawn from the battlefield and the boxing ring (Sampert & Trimble, 2003; Trimble & Sampert, 2004). When Anne-Marie Gingras (1997) asked journalists why war and sports metaphors dominate campaign coverage, they typically responded that they made it easier to communicate abstract and complex ideas while also making news reports more entertaining.

Gender and Election Coverage

This research on the use of imagery in campaign coverage was motivated by an interest in gendered patterns of media coverage. Research on gender and media coverage in Canada began with a focus on the lack of coverage of women politicians (Gingras, 1995) and the use of sex-specific narrative frames when covering prominent women politicians (Robinson & Saint-Jean, 1991, 1995, 1996). Robinson and Saint-Jean have traced how the narrative style evolved over a thirty-year period from a reliance on stereotypes associated with women's traditional social roles, such as "spinster," "woman of easy virtue," and "wife of," to stereotypes associated with power, such as "superwoman," "champion," and "one of the boys." When Manon Tremblay and Nathalie Bélanger (1997) analyzed editorial cartoons during the 1993 campaign, only three of their twelve indicators yielded statistically significant differences between the male and female leaders. To the extent that there were differences, the women tended to be portrayed as weak and not in control of the situation.

More recently, attention has focused on the implications for women politicians of the stereotypically masculine narrative used in election coverage. My colleague Joanna Everitt and I have argued that the use of metaphors of warfare and confrontation reinforces the perception that Canadian politics is still very much a man's world. Women in politics are faced with a classic "damned if you do, damned if you don't" dilemma. If they adapt to the dominant norms and behave confrontationally, the media are apt to focus undue attention on the conflictual behavior: conflict is newsworthy but conflictual behavior on the part of women is doubly newsworthy because it is unexpected. But if women in politics refuse to adapt to the dominant norms and try to do politics differently, their behavior fails both tests of newsworthiness and they risk being marginalized by the media.

The speech of the two female leaders in the 1993 federal election was typically reported in more negative and aggressive language than the men's: while the men were merely telling or saying, the women were blasting and hammering (Gidengil & Everitt, 2003b). A comparison of the coverage of the debates in the nightly network news with the party leaders' actual behaviour in the 1993, 1997, and 2000 televised leaders' debates showed that the coverage also played up the women's confrontational behavior through the disproportionate use of metaphors of warfare and violence (Gidengil & Everitt, 1998, 2003a) and the selection of video bites (Gidengil & Everitt, 2000). Meanwhile, the women leaders who opted for a more low-key style received much less coverage. Similarly, Trimble and Sampert have shown how the game frame worked to marginalize the lone female party leader in press coverage of the 2000 election (Sampert & Trimble, 2003; Trimble & Sampert, 2004). Finally, reflecting their novelty status, the two women in the 1993 election received much more interpretative reporting than the men and their performance was subject to harsher evaluation (Gidengil & Everitt, 2000; c.f. Robinson & Saint-Jean, 1991, 1995, 1996).

Publication of Opinion Polls

Before the Canada Elections Act came into force in 2000, there was no regulation of the publication of poll results (save for a publication ban during the final three days of the campaign that was enacted in 1993, but struck down by the Supreme Court as unconstitutional). Guy Lachapelle (1991) documented the sloppy reporting of opinion polls in the media, notably the failure to provide such basic information as the response rate, the size of regional samples, and question wording.

Debate continues about just how much the situation has improved since the enactment of the new legislation. Claire Durand (2002) concluded that newspapers complied rather well with the new reporting requirements during the 2000 election. Similarly, based on her analysis of poll reporting in six major English- and French-language newspapers and in the Canadian Press wire service during the 2004 election, she judged that "overall, the media respect the formal provisions of section 326 in their publications" (2005, p. 31).[4] The one notable exception to overall compliance related to informing readers of where to obtain a detailed report. However, Durand also highlighted some problems with the reporting of the margin of error, especially for regional sub-samples, a particular concern given the regionalization of the vote in federal elections.

Peter Ferguson and Christine De Clarcy (2005) render a much more critical judgment. They argue that Durand overstated the degree of compliance because she only analyzed first-hand reports as opposed to all reports published within the first 24 hours. She responds that it would be methodologically questionable to weight all reports equally since the second-hand reports are dependent on the first-hand reports (Durand, 2003). Looking at both first- and second-hand reports published in 18 newspapers during the 2004 election, Ferguson and De Clercy found that only the name of the polling firm was reported with any consistency. None of the other reporting requirements achieved more than a 60 per cent level of compliance. Barely half of the reports provided the margin of error, and a mere 20 per cent provided question wording. Only 4 per cent told readers where to obtain more information. Newspapers typically complied with more of the reporting requirements when they had sponsored the poll. Interestingly, smaller circulation newspapers tended to be more compliant than their large-circulation counterparts. Ferguson and De Clercy suggest that many journalists and editors may be unaware of the reporting requirements. They point to the need to disseminate the relevant information to the media and also to enforce the Act by prosecuting violators.

MEDIA EFFECTS

Since 1988, the CES have combined a rolling cross-section campaign survey with a post-election panel. In a rolling cross-section design, the total sample is broken down into replicates, one for each day of the campaign. Because each daily replicate is as similar to the others as random sampling variation allows, all that distinguishes the replicates (within the range of sampling error) is the date of interview (Johnston & Brady, 2002). When combined with a daily tracking of the media coverage, this methodology constitutes an extremely powerful design for capturing the dynamic interaction between media coverage and voters' reactions. It has been used to study both direct and indirect persuasive effects.

Indirect Persuasive Effects: Agenda-Setting and Priming

The most important indirect persuasive effects are agenda-setting and priming. Both assume that the power of the media lies not in telling people what to think, but in telling people what to think *about* (Cohen, 1963; Shaw & McCombs, 1977). Agenda-setting takes place when extensive media coverage of an issue increases people's perceptions of the issue's importance (Cohen, 1963; Shaw & McCombs, 1977). Priming occurs when extensive media coverage of an issue leads voters to attach more importance to that issue in their decision calculus (Ansolabehere et al., 1991).

During election campaigns, political parties compete to control the issue agenda, emphasizing issues on which they enjoy recognized expertise and downplaying issues that will hurt them. The media's role in communicating the parties' messages to the voters makes them critical players in this struggle to control the election agenda. The media do not simply serve as a neutral transmission belt between political parties and voters. As they distill the day's events into newsworthy stories, they highlight some messages and downplay others.

André Blais and his colleagues (Blais et al., 2002) have assessed the media's role in the agenda-setting process by comparing the issues that the nightly network news chose to highlight during the 2000 campaign with the issues that each party was attempting to play up. Their analysis showed that the media focused much more on some issues than on others, and this benefited some parties and disadvantaged others.

Several studies have demonstrated the media's power to prime. Mendelsohn (1994) showed that both television viewing and newspaper readership enhanced the impact of leadership on reported votes in the 1988 election and diminished the salience of partisanship. He went on to exploit the power of the rolling cross-section design to demonstrate that voters who were more highly exposed to the media became increasingly likely to base their vote on their evaluations of the leaders' trustworthiness as the campaign progressed, while party identification receded in importance (Mendelsohn, 1996b). He also showed that interpersonal communication served to prime the central issue of the campaign.

My colleagues and I (Gidengil et al., 2002) have shown how the priming effect varies with campaign context. Issue priming appears to be the exception rather than the norm, occurring only when a new and dramatic issue dominates the campaign (as it did in 1988). In the absence of such an issue, the priming of leadership is the more typical campaign effect, reflecting the leader-centered nature of campaign coverage. When the issue agenda is varied and reflects voters' ongoing priorities, interpersonal communication does not offset the media's power to prime leadership.

Indirect Persuasive Effects: Learning

Richard Jenkins (1999, 2002a) has sounded a warning note on the subject of priming: some of what appears to be priming may, in fact, be learning. Highlighting the role of media coverage in explaining Reform's stunning breakthrough, he argues that media coverage mattered because it enabled voters to learn about Reform's stands on the issues. He demonstrates that the increased impact of attitudes toward the welfare state on evaluations of Reform during the 1993 campaign mostly reflected increased awareness of the party's position on the federal budget deficit. As the PCs' campaign faltered, there was a dramatic increase in the amount of coverage devoted to Reform and Reform vote intentions surged in the wake of this enhanced media attention. Drawing on John Zaller's (1992) work, Jenkins develops a two-mediator model that links media effects to how much attention people pay to news about politics and their predisposition to accept the messages they receive. Over a two-week period, the percentage intending to vote Reform increased by 25 points among those who were *both* aware *and* predisposed (Jenkins, 2002b).

Direct Persuasive Effects

Studies combining content analyses of the nightly network news with rolling cross-section campaign survey data have also shown that the media can have a direct effect. Matthew Mendelsohn and Richard Nadeau (1999) have documented the rise-and-fall phenomenon in coverage of Kim Campbell, Canada's first female prime minister, in the 1993 election. First observed in U.S. presidential primaries (Zaller and Hunt, 1994, 1995), this occurs when the media initially give a new candidate very favorable coverage but become much more critical once the election gets under way. Chosen to lead the PCs only months before the election was called, Campbell initially received very favorable coverage, but once the election campaign began she was the target of intense and critical media scrutiny. Mendelsohn and Nadeau are able to show that both her ratings and PC vote intentions plummeted as a result. There was a significant relationship between the daily balance of positive and negative mentions of Campbell in the nightly news and PC vote intentions. Moreover, they find that "media shocks," defined as days when her coverage was more negative than average, affected perceptions of Campbell's leadership as well as PC vote intentions.

Drawing on theories about gender identity, Joanna Everitt and I (Gidengil & Everitt, 2006) have gone on to show that women and men reacted differently to the coverage. The more negative the coverage of Campbell's campaign, the less favorable men's ratings of Campbell became. Conversely, the more positive the coverage of Preston Manning's campaign, the more highly men rated the Reform leader. Women were much more resistant to both negative coverage of Campbell and positive coverage of her rival on the right.

Finally, Agnieszka Dobrzynska and her colleagues (2003) have combined two different approaches to examine the impact of television news coverage of the 1997 election. Using the "linkage" approach, they show that vote intentions for a party increased when the party received systematically positive coverage (and decreased when the coverage was negative), at least among people who followed the news *and* had not made up their minds before the campaign began. However, the "attentiveness" approach suggested that these effects were only temporary: those who paid more attention to election news on television did not vote any differently from those who did not (other things being equal).

The Televised Leaders' Debates

Few campaign events in Canada are covered as extensively as the televised leaders' debates, but research on their impact has produced mixed results. Based on post-election data from the 1979 election, Lawrence LeDuc and Richard Price (1985) concluded that the effect of watching the 1979 debate was mostly limited to reinforcement of pre-existing political preferences. Few viewers were converted. LeDuc and Price attributed this to the fact that the leaders were already well known to the electorate. This is borne out by David Lanoue's (1991) study of the 1984 debates, which featured two new party leaders. Watching the 1984 debates proved to have a significant effect on vote choice.

While these early studies had to rely on post-election data, Richard Johnston and his colleagues (1992) were able to draw on their rolling cross-section campaign data to study the impact of the 1988 debates. They showed that people who watched the debates were quick to form a judgment and, once formed, these judgments were relatively resistant to change. Although the debates were mostly watched by partisans, viewers did not necessarily react to the leaders' performances through the filter of partisanship. Non-viewers, meanwhile, seemed to be taking their cues from the subsequent media coverage.

A comprehensive assessment of the impact of the debates, which was conducted by André Blais and Martin Boyer (1996), underlined the importance of the indirect effect on non-watchers who get to hear about the debates from their friends or from the media. Using a panel analysis that included both watchers and non-watchers, they showed that people who thought a given leader had won the 1988 debate were more likely to vote for that leader's party than they were before the debate. Their time-series analysis confirmed that the 1988 debates had a substantial and lasting impact on vote choice, though the debates did not determine the election outcome.

Indeed, the debates have not proved to be critical events when it comes to deciding who wins an election (LeDuc, 1994), but this does not necessarily mean that they are inconsequential. André Blais and his colleagues' (2003) times-series analysis demonstrated that the 2000 debates saved the PCs from electoral annihilation by giving the party a four-point boost.

Their impact on party fortunes is not the only yardstick for evaluating the leaders' debates. Based on her study of the 1984 and 1988 debates, Cathy Barr (1991) concluded that the debates have an overwhelmingly positive influence, encouraging people who are not very interested to vote and providing information to help them decide *how* to vote. The debates also assist people in forming impressions of the leaders and their personal characteristics (c.f. Lanoue, 1991; Johnston et al., 1992), which may explain why their impact is often greatest when they feature leaders who are relatively new to viewers. The debates also seem to enhance people's evaluations of the party leaders in general. Thierry Giasson and his colleagues (2005) have shown in an experimental setting that the visual representation of the party leaders in the debates can provide information cues that help viewers to form judgments of the leaders.

The Impact of Polls

There is also evidence that opinion polls have an effect. Using a multi-method approach, André Blais and his colleagues (Blais, Gidengil, & Nevitte, 2006) showed that polls influenced voters' assessments of the parties' chances of winning the 1988 election. As a result, they had an effect on strategic voting: some voters became less likely to support their preferred party when they perceived that it had little or no chance of winning. Polls also had an impact on the vote, but there was little evidence of any bandwagon effect. Neither parties nor their leaders were evaluated more favourably simply because they were doing well in the polls.

CONTROVERSIAL ISSUES

One particularly contentious issue in regard to electoral communications in Canada relates to so-called third-party advertising: it pits claims to freedom of expression against concerns about the power of money. The 1974 Election Expenses Act prohibited any individual or group other than a candidate or a registered political party from spending money to promote or oppose the election of any party or candidate.[5] This restriction was successfully challenged in the courts in 1984 on the grounds that it violated the right to freedom of expression guaranteed by the Canadian Charter of Rights and Freedoms, adopted in 1982. Concerns about the role played by business interests in the so-called free trade election of 1988 led the 1992 Royal Commission on Electoral Reform and Party Financing to recommend limits on third-party spending. Accordingly, the government introduced legislation limiting third party spending on election advertising to a maximum of $1,000, but these provisions, too, were struck down as unconstitutional. The Canada Elections Act, which came into effect in 2000, limits third-party spending on election advertising to $150,000 in the country as a whole and to $3,000 in any one electoral district (subject to an inflation factor in subsequent elections). The constitutionality of these restrictions was also challenged in the courts, but the Supreme Court of Canada overturned the decision of the lower court on appeal.

A second source of controversy concerns the publication of election results. Canada has a vast territory spanning several time zones. As a result, the election outcome was often known on the basis of the results in eastern and central Canada before the polls even closed on the west coast. This reinforced westerners' sense of political alienation. Accordingly, the Canada Elections Act now prohibits the transmission of election results (or purported results) in any electoral district to the public in another electoral district until the latter's polls close. In 2000, a British Columbia resident was prosecuted for violating the Act when he posted real-time results from Atlantic Canada on his website. This initiated a series of court cases to decide whether the ban constitutes a reasonable limit on the freedom of expression. Finally, in 2007 the Supreme Court of Canada upheld the ban in a five to four split decision. Besides the constitutionality of the restriction, serious questions have been raised about enforceability: a number of websites maintained by Canadians living outside the country published results on election night in 2006.

The final issue is the televised leaders' debates, which have been a regular feature of federal election campaigns since 1980. There is typically one debate in English and one in French, held midway through the campaign. To date, only the leaders of parties which won seats in the previous election have been invited to take part. In 2006, the Green party challenged its exclusion, citing its current popularity in the polls, the number of votes that it won in previous elections, and the fact that it was planning to run candidates in every electoral district. Given the party's continued standing in the polls, the controversy is likely to continue.

TELEVISION ADVERTISING

Television advertising affords political parties an opportunity for unmediated communication with viewers. Not surprisingly, the ads themselves elicit coverage from the news networks, along with horse-race commentary focusing on the assumed strategic motivations and the anticipated effect on party fortunes. This is especially true of controversial ads. There have been a number of these in recent elections. In 1993, the PCs commissioned an ad that drew attention to the Liberal leader's facial palsy, cutting between a particularly unflattering head shot and actors voicing their embarrassment at the thought of his becoming prime minister. It was pulled almost immediately. In 1997, Reform was widely criticized for airing an ad that was perceived to be anti-Quebec. It featured unflattering close-ups of the three federal party leaders from Quebec and the Quebec premier, with a voice-over suggesting that it was time to have a voice for all Canadians, not just Quebec politicians. In 2006, a Liberal ad suggesting that the Conservative leader would deploy armed soldiers in Canadian cities attracted negative coverage, though the reaction was more one of derision than of condemnation.

There has not been any large-scale, systematic coding of campaign ads in Canada, and relatively little analysis of their impact. Denis Monière has analyzed the ads aired on the French-language networks during election and referendum campaigns. He observes (Monière & Guay, 1994, p. 122) that there appears to be little relationship between the amount spent on advertising and the parties' electoral performance: strikingly, in the 1993 campaign, the party that spent the least and that had the least visibility on television received the most votes in the province, while the party that spent the most received the fewest votes.

The evidence, such as it is, about the impact of campaign advertising on Canadian voters suggests that its effects may be limited. Johnston and his colleagues (1992) found that the PCs' 1988 ads only affected opinion about the free trade agreement and about the Liberal leader, but did not affect the vote. André Blais and his colleagues (1999) have examined the impact of the "no more leaders from Quebec" ad, using data from the 1997 campaign rolling cross-section survey. The ad did move vote intentions temporarily, but the effect had completely dissipated by election day.

THE FUTURE OF ELECTION NEWS COVERAGE

The 2000 federal election qualified as Canada's first Internet election. The verdict of Paul Attallah and Angela Burton (2001, p. 215) at the time was that "the Internet stands today where television stood in the 1950s and radio in the 1920s: a new medium, still overshadowed by its predecessors, and still seeking its own voice and form." That verdict still stands, at least as far as electoral communication goes. Rather than supplanting traditional news coverage, these websites appear to be providing an additional source of information for people who are following the election in the traditional print and broadcast media. As noted earlier, relatively few Canadians claim to rely on the Internet as their main source of election information. However, this may very well change as the Internet generation comes of age. Certainly, we can expect technological advances to make it much harder for regulatory bodies to ensure that electoral communications promote the twin goals of national unity and cultural sovereignty.

NOTES

1. I am grateful to Blake Andrew for his research assistance and to the Fonds Québécois de la recherche sur la société et la culture for financial support.
2. Stuart Soroka, quoted in MacLean's (2006, p. 2)
3. Following Todd Gitlin (1980), Mendelsohn defined frames as those "persistent patterns of cognition, interpretation, and presentation, of selection, emphasis and exclusion, by which symbol-handlers routinely organize discourse" (p. 7).
4. The polling firms consistently failed to comply with the reporting requirements. In 2004, two of the six firms did not even specify the sampling method used and two did not provide any information on weighting or other adjustments. The response rate was reported in only one of the 18 survey reports analyzed.
5. For a more detailed overview, see "Regulation of election activities by "third parties": Overview and statements by the Chief Electoral Officer" at www.elections.ca.

REFERENCES

Ansolabehere, S., Behr, R., & Iyengar, S. (1991). Mass media and elections: An overview. *American Politics Quarterly, 19,* 109–139.

Attallah, P., & Burton, A. (2001). Television, the Internet, and the Canadian federal election of 2000. In J. H. Pammett & C. Dornan (Eds.), *The Canadian general election of 2000* (pp. 215–241). Toronto: Dundurn.

Barr, C. W. (1991). The importance and potential of leaders debates. In F. J. Fletcher (Ed.), *Media and voters in Canadian election campaigns* (vol. 18, pp. 107–156), Royal Commission on Electoral Reform and Party Financing. Toronto: Dundurn Press.

Blais, A., & Boyer, M. M. (1996). Assessing the impact of televised debates: The case of the 1988 Canadian election. *British Journal of Political Science, 26,* 143–164.

Blais, A., Nadeau, R., Gidengil, E., & Nevitte, N. (1999). Campaign dynamics in the 1997 Canadian election. *Canadian Public Policy, 25,* 197–203.

Blais, A., Gidengil, E., Nadeau, N., & Nevitte, N. (2002). *Anatomy of liberal victory: Making sense of the vote in the 2000 Canadian election.* Peterborough, ON: Broadview Press.

Blais, A., Gidengil, E., Nadeau, R., & Nevitte, N. (2003). Campaign dynamics in the 2000 Canadian election: How the leader debates salvaged the Conservative Party. *Political Science & Politics, 36,* 45–50.

Blais, A., Gidengil, E., & Nevitte, N. (2006). Do polls influence the vote? In H. E. Brady & R. Johnston (Eds.), *Capturing campaign effects* (pp. 263–279). Ann Arbor: University of Michigan Press.

Broadcasting Act, 1991. (1991). Canada. Retrieved June 23, 2007 from http://www.crtc.gc.ca/eng/LEGAL/BROAD.htm

The Broadcasting Arbitrator. (2006). *Broadcasting guidelines: Federal general election.* Retrieved January 23, 2006 from http://www.elections.ca/med/bro/guidelines2006.pdf

Canadian Election Studies. (2006). Retrieved Marge 7, 2008, from: http://ces-eec.mcgill.ca/surveys.html#2006.

Canadian Newspaper Association. (2006) *Ownership of Canadian daily newspapers.* Retrieved December 31, 2006 from http://www.cna-acj.ca

Canadian Radio-Television and Telecommuniations Commission. (2005). *Election campaigns and political advertising.* Retrieved December 31, 2006 from http://www.crtc.gc.ca/eng/INFO_SHT/b309.htm

Cohen, B. (1963). *The press and foreign policy*. Princeton, NJ: Princeton University Press.

Dobrzynska, A., Blais, A., & Nadeau, R. (2003). Do the media have a direct impact on the vote? The case of the 1997 Canadian election. *International Journal of Public Opinion Research, 15,* 27–43.

Dornan, C., & Pyman, H. (2001). Facts and arguments: Newspaper coverage of the campaign. In J. H. Pammett & C. Dornan (Eds.), *The Canadian general election of 2000* (pp. 190–214). Toronto: Dundurn.

Durand, C. (2002). The 2000 Canadian election and poll reporting under the new elections act. *Canadian Public Policy, 28,* 539–545.

Durand, C. (2003). Reply, The new act has merit if enforced: Exactly what I said. *Canadian Public Policy, 29,* 373–375.

Durand, C. (2005). Opinion polls and the Canada Elections Act. *Electoral Insight, 7(1),* 28–31.

Ferguson, P. A., & De Clercy, C. (2005). Regulatory compliance in opinion poll reporting during the 2004 Canadian election. *Canadian Public Policy, 31,* 243–258.

Fletcher, F. J. (1981). *The newspaper and public affairs*. Vol. 7. Ottawa: Royal Commission on Newspapers.

Fletcher, F. J. (1987). Mass media and parliamentary elections in Canada. *Legislative Studies Quarterly, 12,* 341–372.

Giasson, T., Nadeau, R., & Bélanger, E. (2005). Televised debates and candidate evaluation: Does the visual representation of Canadian politicians affect the formation of preferences of the Quebec electorate? *Canadian Journal of Political Science, 38,* 867–895.

Gidengil, E., Blais, A., Nevitte, N., & Nadeau, R. (2002). Priming and campaign context: Evidence from recent Canadian elections. In D. M. Farrell & R. Schmitt-Beck (Eds.), *Do political campaigns matter? Campaign effects in elections and referendums* (pp. 76–91). London: Routledge.

Gidengil, E., Blais, A., Nevitte, N., & Nadeau, R. (2004). *Citizens*. Vancouver: University of British Columbia Press.

Gidengil, E., & Everitt, J. (1998). Metaphors and misrepresentation: Gendered mediation in news coverage of the 1993 Canadian leaders' debates. *Harvard International Journal of Press/Politics, 4,* 48–65

Gidengil, E., & Everitt, J. (2000). Filtering the female: Television news coverage of the 1993 Canadian leaders' debates. *Women & Politics, 21,* 105–131.

Gidengil, E., & Everitt, J. (2003a). Conventional coverage/unconventional politicians: Gender and media coverage of Canadian leaders' debates, 1993, 1997, 2000. *Canadian Journal of Political Science, 36,* 559–577.

Gidengil, E., & Everitt, J. (2003b). Talking tough: Gender and reported speech in campaign news coverage. *Political Communication, 20,* 209–232.

Gidengil, E., & Everitt, J. (2006). Gender, media coverage and the dynamics of leader evaluations: The case of the 1993 Canadian election. In H. E. Brady & R. Johnston (Eds.), *Capturing campaign effects* (pp. 336–355). Ann Arbor: University of Michigan Press.

Gingras, A-M. (1997). Metaphors in political language. *Politique et Société, 30,* 159–171.

Gingras, F-P. (1995). Daily male delivery: Women and politics in the daily newspapers. In F.-P. Gingras (Ed.), *Gender and politics in contemporary Canada* (pp. 191–207). Toronto: Oxford University Press.

Gitlin, T. (1980). *The whole world is watching: Mass media in the making and unmaking of the New Left*. Berkeley: University of California Press.

Jenkins, R. W. (1999). How much is too much? Media attention and popular support for an insurgent party. *Political Communication, 16,* 429–445.

Jenkins, R. W. (2002a). How campaigns matter in Canada: Priming and learning as explanations for the Reform Party's 1993 campaign success. *Canadian Journal of Political Science, 35,* 383–408.

Jenkins, R. W. (2002b). The media, voters, and election campaigns: The Reform Party and the 1993 election. In J. Everitt & B. O'Neill (Eds.), *Citizen politics: Research and theory in Canadian political behaviour* (pp. 215–230). Don Mills, ONT.: Oxford University Press.

Johnston, R. G., Blais, A., Brady, H. E., & Crête, J. (1992). *Letting the people decide*. Montreal and Kingston: McGill-Queen's University Press.

Johnston, R., & Brady, H. E. (2002). The rolling cross-section design. *Electoral Studies, 21,* 283–295.

Lachapelle, G. (1991). *The research studies for the Royal Commission on Electoral Reform and Party Financing: Vol. 16. Polls and the media in Canadian elections: Taking the pulse*. Toronto: Dundurn.

Lanoue, D. J. (1991). Debates that mattered: Voters' reaction to the 1984 Canadian leadership debates. *Canadian Journal of Political Science, 24,* 51–65.

LeDuc, L. (1994). The leaders' debates: Critical event or non-event? In A. Frizzell, J. H. Pammett, & A. Westell (Eds.), *The Canadian general election of 1993* (pp. 127–141). Ottawa: Carleton University Press.

LeDuc, L., & Price, R. (1985). Great debates: The televised leadership debates in Canada. *Canadian Journal of Political Science, 24,* 51–65.

The media message. (2006, January 30). *Maclean's.*

Mendelsohn, M. (1993). Television's frames in the 1988 Canadian election. *Canadian Journal of Communication, 18,* 149–171.

Mendelsohn, M. (1994). The media's persuasive effects: The priming of leadership in the 1988 Canadian election. *Canadian Journal of Political Science, 27,* 81–97.

Mendelsohn, M. (1996a). Television news frames in the 1993 Canadian election. In H. Holmes & D. Taras (Eds.), *Seeing ourselves: Media power and policy in Canada* (2nd ed.) (pp. 8–22). Toronto: Harcourt Brace.

Mendelsohn, M. (1996b). The media and interpersonal communications: The priming of issues, leaders, and party identification. *The Journal of Politics, 58,* 112–125.

Mendelsohn, M., & Nadeau, R. (1999). The rise and fall of candidates in Canadian election campaigns. *Harvard International Journal of Press/Politics, 4,* 63–76.

Monière, D., & Guay, J. H. (1994). *The Quebec battle: First episode, the 1993 federal election.* Saint-Laurent: Fides.

Nevitte, N., Blais, A., Gidengil, E., & Nadeau, R. (2000). *Unsteady state: The 1997 Canadian federal election.* Don Mills, ONT: Oxford University Press.

Observatory on Media and Public Policy (2006). *2006 federal election newspaper content Analysis.* McGill University. Retrieved December 31, 2006 from http://www.ompp.mcgill.ca

Osler, A. M. (1993). *News: The evolution of journalism in Canada.* Toronto: Copp Clark Pitman.

Raboy, M. (1996). Canada: The hybridization of public broadcasting. In M. Raboy (Ed.), *Public broadcasting for the 21st century* (pp. 103–119). Luton: University of Luton Press.

Robinson, G., & Saint-Jean, A. (1991). Women politicians and their media coverage: A generational analysis. In K. Megyery (Ed.), *Women in Canadian politics: Toward equity in representation* (pp. 127–169). Toronto: Dundurn.

Robinson, G., & Saint-Jean, A. (1995). The portrayal of women politicians in the media: Political implications. In F.-P. Gingras (Ed.), *Gender and politics in contemporary Canada* (pp. 176–189). Toronto: Oxford University Press.

Robinson, G., & Saint-Jean, A. (1996). From Flora to Kim: Thirty years of representation of Canadian women politicians. In H. Holmes & D. Taras (Eds.), *Seeing ourselves: Media power and policy in Canada* (2nd ed.) (pp. 22–36). Toronto: Harcourt Brace.

Sampert, S., & Trimble, L. (2003). Wham, bam, no thank you ma'am': Gender and the game frame in national newspaper coverage of election 2000. In M. Tremblay & L. Trimble (Eds.), *Women and electoral politics in Canada* (pp. 211–226). Toronto: Oxford University Press.

Shaw, D. L., & McCombs, M. (Eds.). (1977). *The emergence of American political issues: The agenda-setting function of the press.* St. Paul, MN: West.

Tremblay, M., & Bélanger, N. (1997). Female party leaders and editorial cartoons: The 1993 Canadian federal election. *Recherches féministes, 10,* 35–75.

Trimble, L., & Sampert, S. (2004). Who's in the game? Framing of the Canadian election 2000 by the Globe and Mail and the National Post. *Canadian Journal of Political Science, 37,* 51–71.

Wilson, R. J. (1980). Media coverage of Canadian election campaigns: Horserace journalism and the meta-campaign. *Journal of Canadian Studies, 15,* 56–68.

Zaller, J. R. (1992). *The nature and origins of mass opinion.* Cambridge, UK: Cambridge University Press.

Zaller, J. R., & Hunt, M. (1994). The rise and fall of candidate Perot: Unmediated versus mediated politics—part I. *Political Communication, 11,* 357–390.

Zaller, J. R., & Hunt, M. (1995). The rise and fall of candidate Perot: The outsider versus the political system—part II. *Political Communication, 12,* 97–123.

5

Election News Coverage in the U.K.

Margaret Scammell and Holli A. Semetko

THE POLITICAL SYSTEM

"England," declared 19th Century reformer John Bright, "is the mother of parliaments." In fact, England is the mother of a particular form of parliamentary democracy, known commonly as the Westminster Model, varieties of which have been adopted in Canada, Australia, New Zealand, and many former British colonies throughout Africa and Asia. The defining characteristics of the Westminster model are that it is a party system, it has majoritarian and disproportional (first-past-the-post) national elections, and it concentrates executive power in one-party cabinets headed by a prime minister, traditionally conceived as *primus inter pares* (Lijphart, 1999). These features distinguish the U.K. from presidential systems, such as the U.S., and from many countries in the European Union that exercise forms of proportional representation (PR).

A general strength of the model is its propensity to deliver unambiguous results. It almost always produces clear winners with no need for the protracted coalition bargaining common to many PR systems. Thus, in the U.K. general elections since 1945 in all but two races clear majorities have been delivered to either the Conservatives or Labour. However, this strength is also a weakness; its in-built disproportion favors winners but systematically disadvantages the smaller parties. Thus, in the 2005 general election Labour won 55% of all the 646 seats in parliament on just a 35% vote share, while the Liberal Democrats won just 10% of the seats on a 22% vote share. Unsurprisingly, the LibDems have been consistent advocates of electoral reform. However, their continuing strength in vote share, at or close to 20% since the 1980s, makes them the only "smaller" party to have made a significant impact at Westminster. Outside Northern Ireland, where Conservative and Labour do not compete, only the nationalist parties of Scotland and Wales (the Scottish National Party and Plaid Cymru) have consistently returned at least a few Members of Parliament (MPs) to parliament. The "others," including independents, greens, far right and left, single issue and anti-European Union parties, have registered only five successes between them in the seven general elections from October 1974. Of these the independents have won four, with Respect, the socialist, anti-Iraq War grouping, winning the other. The disproportion of the electoral system spills over into election news coverage (below); it is both reflected and partly redressed by broadcasting rules of fairness, balance, and the allocation of airtime for Party Election Broadcasts (PEBs).

However, while the Westminster Model still characterizes elections to the U.K. parliament, it has come under increasing challenge both formally and informally over the past decade. Formally, elements of proportional representation have been introduced for non-Westminster elections, most importantly for the European Union Parliament and for the devolved parliament and assemblies of Scotland, Wales, and Northern Ireland. Less formally the model has been pressured by a marked trend towards presidentialization of political affairs (Langer, 2007; Mughan, 2000). Presidentialization is indicated by three significant features: a concentration of executive authority in the person and office of the Prime Minister, increased significance of assessments of party leaders in voting decisions, and a heightened tendency for media to focus on leaders at the expense of other party spokespeople. The process appeared to reach new heights with Tony Blair, who strengthened the office of the Prime Minister at the expense of the Cabinet, "neglected parliament" (Riddell, 1999) and in 1997 and 2001 ran markedly personal election campaigns. There is also no question of the media's role in the presidentialization process, and, as indicated below, there has been a significant trend towards leader focus in electoral coverage.

THE MEDIA SYSTEM

Hallin and Mancini's (2003) typology of media systems places the U.K., along with the U.S., Canada, and Ireland, in the "North Atlantic" model; predominantly a free-market "liberal" media system in contrast to the more regulated "democratic corporatist" orders of northern Europe. However, as the authors admit, the U.K. has significant hybrid features. It shares with the U.S. a commitment to free markets, freedom of speech, and self-regulation as the guiding principles for newspapers. It shares with northern Europe a history of highly partisan newspapers and regulated television markets, dominated by well-funded public service broadcasters. There is in the U.K. a sharp marked regulatory split between the newspaper and broadcasting sectors (see Table 5.1) that has resulted in sharply contrasting rules, styles, and content of political reporting.

National newspapers, especially the popular tabloids, are highly opinioned, pick sides and push agendas; they are powerful and overt political players, willing and at times apparently able to shape the agenda and make or break political careers. The post-war history of politics is littered with the bodies of those whose heads were demanded by the press. The most infamous victim of recent times was former Labour leader Neil Kinnock, who led his party to two crushing defeats

TABLE 5.1
U.K. Media Market: News, Regulation and Trust

	Type of regulation	News content regulation	Paid political advertising	Public trust in news sources*
Newspapers	Self-regulation	Self-regulation No prior restraint on expression of opinion	Permitted	Low, especially for tabloid newspapers
Television	Statutory regulatory bodies: Ofcom BBC Trust	Broadcast code**: Demands due impartiality, accuracy and balance. Prevents expression of organizational opinion on political controversy. Requires news quotas in prime time on PSB providers (BBC, ITV, Ch. 4 & Five.)	Not permitted. Parties allocated free airtime for Party Election and Party Political Broadcasts (PEBs & PPBs) on specified TV & radio channels	High

*Source: Ofcom (2004) The Communications Market 2004. Television Appendix The Public's View: Survey Results.
**The Broadcasting Code is retrievable at: http://www.ofcom.org.uk/tv/ifi/codes/bcode/undue/

in 1987 and 1992. The *Sun,* in a now legendary character assassination, ran a multi-page spread under the banner "Nightmare on Kinnock Street," and on the day of the 1992 election it pictured Kinnock's head in a light bulb; if the ginger-haired Welshman should win, the paper told its readers, "would the last person in Britain please turn out the lights" (Harrop & Scammell, 1992). The power of the press is feared by politicians, and it is difficult to over-estimate the impact the Kinnock debacle had on his successors. It was a major task and ultimately historic achievement of Tony Blair's Labour to swing majority newspaper support away from the Conservatives to Labour (Gould, 1998; Scammell, 2001).

By contrast, television news is required by law to be impartial and balanced as between the parties; and television companies generally are prohibited from giving organizational (as opposed to individual) opinion on matters of political or industrial controversy. Additionally, all five analogue television networks are required to air news in prime viewing time. All the major national TV news organizations take seriously a partly formal, partly self-imposed duty to inform as well as entertain voters at election times. Television is easily the most accessed source of national and international political news (see Table 5.2). Moreover, it is also by some distance the most trusted source of news. This is the consistent result from a succession of Public View surveys for the broadcast regulator Ofcom (and its predecessor the Independent Television Commission). TV is cited by 65 to 70% of respondents as the most trusted source of national news, compared to a paltry 10% figure for newspapers.

New technology has transformed the communications market. Ofcom's (2006) annual review noted the extraordinarily quick uptake of digital TV services; 73% of U.K. households now have the multiple channel platforms of either satellite or terrestrial digital television. Thus, digital TV has achieved in just eight years something that took analogue 40 years. Broadband is also booming and installed in 41% of all homes, while Internet access had passed the 50% mark by the time of the 2005 general election. New technology massively expanded the number of available channels from four in 1990 to more than 270 in 2004, when for the first time the new competitors achieved a combined audience share greater than the old dominant duopoly of BBC and ITV1 (Scammell & Langer, 2006b). The audience share of these two has been in decline since 1981, falling from 39% and 49% on BBC1 and ITV respectively to 23% and 22% in 2005. By 2003 subscription had outstripped advertising as the major revenue source in the television industry, with Rupert Murdoch's BSkyB the major beneficiary.

The new media abundance is changing patterns of consumption, with an increase in entertainment viewing, a decline in news viewing, and an overall shift to niche TV channels, the overwhelming majority of which are politics-free zones. According to Ofcom's review (2006, p. 272), the "total television viewing share for news programmes has declined gradually since 2000." The U.K.'s premier commercial channel, the ITV, suffered most. Its flagship late evening news programme lost a 10% audience share, down from 25% in 2000 to about 15% in 2006, while in 2005 it decided to close its struggling 24-hour news channel. The irony, of course, is that

TABLE 5.2
Main Sources of U.K. and World News (%)

	UK news	World news
TV	68	72
Radio	15	9
Newspapers	11	10
Other	5	n/a

Source: Ofcom (2006) The Communications Market 2006

news audiences have declined while opportunities for news consumption have multiplied, via the Internet, two 24-hour news channels, and the BBC Parliament channel. Intense competition has pushed news to the margins of prime viewing time on both BBC1 and ITV, while the latter has all but abandoned political documentaries. Thus the inadvertent audiences for politics, those who catch the news purely by watching the two main omnibus channels, have fallen. Structurally, "British television has expanded exponentially with the digital age, but politically speaking only those awake, equipped (digitally) and interested (politically), stand a real chance of finding more political information on television at election time" (Semetko & Scammell, 2005).

Within the overall picture of decline, there is nonetheless surprising stability in the U.K. news market. It is consistent with the old adage that change comes quickly in the long-term and slowly in the short-term. Notwithstanding the new media explosion, the "old five"—the analogue TV channels of BBC1 and 2, ITV1, Channel 4, and Channel 5—continue to take the top five slots in the top 20 audience share ranking (Ofcom, 2006, p. 266). The dedicated 24-hour news channels, Murdoch's Sky News, and the BBC News 24, performed creditably: Sky News broke into the top 20 at 19th slot in 2005 (up from 25 in 2001), while the BBC News 24 moved up to 23rd place (from 41st in 2001). But compared with the big two their audiences were relatively meagre. Meanwhile, the newspaper market, despite a history of steady decline since 1945, has been remarkably stable over the last 15 years. The 10 titles that comprised the national daily press in the 2005 election were the same as in 1992; and despite some manoeuvring in the rankings, Murdoch's tabloid, *The Sun,* was still the country's most popular paper and the Conservative *Telegraph* the most-read broadsheet. The continued dominance of the old providers of election news is shown in Table 5.3. Grand predictions of an Internet election proved to be "another false dawn," as the Electoral Commission (2005) put it.

Aside from the paltry showing of the Internet, the importance of radio is the most notable, and often neglected, finding reported in Table 5.4. Radio listening has increased about 3% since 2000, fuelled by digital platforms, either online or through direct sales of digital radio sets. The BBC is dominant in the radio market, with 55% of the total audience share, thus outstripping all commercial radio combined. Overall, the digital revolution has been good for the BBC. Encouraged by the government to spearhead the national drive towards switchover from analogue to digital, it launched a suite of new digital channels and via Freeview, a consortium of the BBC and commercial providers, it is now the leading supplier of free-to-air terrestrial digital television. After the nervous years of the Thatcher era, the BBC has been accepted by both Conservative and Labour governments as the cornerstone of quality for the system as a whole. Its prime funding, a licence fee paid by all who own or rent a television set, has increased steadily. In 2005 licence fee

TABLE 5.3
Public Sources of News during the 2001 2005 General Elections

	2001 %	*2005** %
Watched election coverage on TV	89	89***
Read national newspaper	n/a	43
Heard election news on the radio	39	50
Used the internet for election information	2	7***

Source: The Electoral Commission (2005) Election 2005: Engaging the public in Great Britain (Retrievable at: http://www.electoralcommission.org.uk/files/dms/Engaging_19456-14157__E__S__W__.pdf)
* MORI survey June 2001
** ICM survey June 2005
*** MORI post-election poll 5-10 May, 2005

TABLE 5.4
Website Destinations: UK General Election 2005

Websites used for election news	% *
BBC news	22.2
Google/MSN/Yahoo	10
Guardian.co.uk	4.0
Any party site	3.5
Any blog	0.5
None	74

Source: BBC/MORI Citizenship Survey May 2005. Cited in Schifferes
et al. (2007)
* Percentages reflect multiple use of sites and hence add up to more
than 100%

income amounted to £2.4 billion, about 23% of the total revenue for the TV industry. The BBC has surpassed the ITV as the single largest television company by audience share and revenue, while BSkyB, the prime provider of subscription services, has emerged as the third national broadcast giant.

ELECTORAL NEWS ON TELEVISION:
HISTORY, DEVELOPMENT AND REGULATION

The history of electoral broadcasting is best understood in three stages. First, the era of politics ascendant and broadcasting deference; second, television's coming of age with increasing willingness to exercise discretionary power over the news agenda, subject leaders to in-depth interviews and audience questioning; and third, the current era, consumed by anxieties of crisis of citizen engagement and breakdown of trust between politicians, media, and public. Running through these stages is the common thread of a decline of deference towards politicians. In historical context, the transformation is all the more sharp because it is relative to extraordinarily supine beginnings (see Table 5.5 for timeline).

The television era opened with the BBC as the sole operator and it volunteered what now seem astonishing restrictions to ensure that it did not interfere with the processes of politics. It willingly adopted in peacetime the World War II 14 Day Rule which prohibited the reporting of any controversial topic in the two weeks preceding debate in Parliament. It was so concerned with impartiality that it avoided any campaign coverage at all, apart from the airing of Party Election Broadcasts (PEBs) and election-day results service. Non-coverage was deemed the safest way to avoid party bias. It took the advent of commercial television (ITV) in 1955 to sweep away these self-denying ordinances. The ITV pioneered campaign coverage, abandoned the 14 Day Rule, and rejected the BBC's custom of handing interviewees an advance list of questions. The BBC followed suit, but nervously. The 1959 general election brought its first opportunity to cover a national campaign, and the BBC "threw caution at the screen" (Cockerell, 1988, p. 68). It canceled a popular topical news show and instead broadcast a series of hustings programs in which the parties were invited to choose both the audiences and the spokesmen. Whatever enlightenment the BBC imagined backfired spectacularly; with audiences composed entirely of party activists the programs disintegrated into such raucousness that it was 15 years before party spokespeople returned to BBC studios for voter questioning.

TABLE 5.5
Landmark Dates in Electoral Nroadcasting History

1951 General Election	First PEBs broadcast on BBC
1955	Commercial TV (ITV) introduced
1959 General Election	First "TV election"
1964 General Election	PEBs increased to present ration of five each for Cons & Labour. First in-depth leader interviews
1979 & 1983 General Elections	Marked professionalization of campaigning. Leaders tours as photo-ops
1983 General Election	Simultaneous transmission of PEBs scraped.
1990	Broadcasting de-regulation encourages competition. Lightens PSB burden on commercial providers. PEBs given legal protection.
1992 General Election	ITV abandons stopwatch balance
1997 General Election	24-hour news (Sky) impacts election coverage
2005 General Election	Five 24-hour news channels. First quasi leader debate format – all three main party leaders appear in turn on 1½ hour audience question show.

Television gradually came of age over the 1960s and 1970s; virtually all homes had a TV set, the politicians adapted to the new medium, and the broadcasters became confident of their role. The 1964 contest introduced in-depth interviews with party leaders, an innovation that has remained ever since a staple of election coverage; while the parties have consistently resisted presidential-style debates it became unthinkable for a leader to refuse one-on-one interviews with celebrity presenters. The balance of power was shifting from politics to media, yet both channels continued to adopt a "sacerdotal" attitude to politics going into the 1970s (Blumler, Gurevitch, & Nossiter, 1989) and well beyond for election news. The ration of PEBs increased to five each for Labour and Conservatives, and their simultaneous transmission on both BBC and ITV ensured a huge near-captive audience. At the same time, the BBC and ITV typically extended their flagship news programs for the duration of the election from the launch of manifestoes until polling day (about three to four weeks). Their coverage was guided by an attitude of respectful distance: the campaign agenda was the domain of politicians, and the duty of broadcasting was to report fully and reflect upon their views and deeds.

The normal public service requirements to deliver impartial and balanced news were interpreted in particularly strict ways for elections. The allocation of PEBs provided the guidelines for appropriate balance as between the parties, with both Labour and the Conservatives receiving equal news time, while the Liberals were apportioned a share according to their ration of PEBs, normally one-third to four-fifths. This interpretation of balance ensured that election news coverage remained firmly within the ambit of the major parties. However, it also gave the Liberal Democrats a much larger share of coverage than their usual non-election helping. Thus, broadcasting effectively adopted proportional representation as a reporting guideline, in contrast to the electoral system itself. Both the parties and the broadcast organisations timed "balance" with a stopwatch to ensure fair dues.

Moreover, provisions in the Representation of the People Acts ensured that no parliamentary candidate feature in television news stories without roughly equal coverage for his or her competitors. While this rule was not applied to national leaders talking about national issues, it applied strictly to local constituency reports, or indeed any themes or issues that featured candidates in a non-leadership capacity. It meant that parties could have an effective veto over some stories by refusing to put forward a spokesperson. This combination of constraints and guidelines gave parties, if not a stranglehold, then certainly a strong grip on the TV news agenda.

The restrictions have gradually loosened over time, under pressure of increasing competition in the TV market. As the television market expanded from two to four channels (with the addition of BBC2 and Channel 4) so the practice of simultaneous transmission of PEBs became increasing unworkable, and it was scrapped in 1987. The commercial TV companies made clear their dislike of PEBs in the debates leading to the Broadcasting Act of 1990; they regarded them as schedule disrupters and audience losers. Ultimately, the Broadcasting Act compromised; it gave legal protection to PEBs but granted broadcasters greater scheduling power. The PEBs were duly shunted from their former peak viewing slots of just before the evening news to the margins of prime time. The effective downgrading of the PEBs was compounded in 1991 when Independent Television News, the commercial news provider unilaterally abandoned "stopwatch balance" for the 1992 general election. The allocation of PEBs was no longer to be arbiter of balance, and the stopwatch was rejected as a crude measure of fairness. From then on news values were to determine the stories and parties would have to compete with each other and with non-election news to lead the bulletins.

Electoral law reform further weakened the parties' power of veto, even at constituency level. By the 2001 campaign candidates of major parties still had to be invited to appear in a news item which featured their constituency rivals, but their refusal could no longer prevent the story being broadcast. The reform increased broadcasters' discretionary power, enabling items (for example, news analysis about women and ethnic minority candidates or specific regional issues) that had been rendered practically impossible by the former requirement to include all the candidates of all mentioned constituencies. A summary of the electoral broadcasting code is shown in Table 5.6.

These reforms effectively shifted the balance of agenda-setting power from politicians to journalists. However, more fundamental than the formal rule changes were the shifts in the cultural climate over the last 40 years. The decline of deference and a general weakening of the

TABLE 5.6
Summary of Broadcasting Regulations for Elections and Referendums*

Rule:	*Requires:*
Impartiality, accuracy & balance	Due weight to all major parties** & significant others. Balance assessed across campaign as a whole, but also expected within individual news programs.
Constituency reporting	Broadcasters must invite participation from all major candidates of any featured constituency. Must list names of all candidates at the end of the report.
Candidates	Banned from acting as news presenters & interviewers. Must not be invited to appear in non-political programs.
Election day	News analysis of election issues suspended until voting stations close. Opinion polls may not be reported on election day until after the voting stations close.

BBC imposes additional rules through its editorial guidelines. Its code prevents it leading news programs with opinion polls of voting intention, requires that polls be reported within context of trend, and does not give undue credibility to opinion poll findings.

* *Sources:* Ofcom Broadcasting Code, Section 6, Elections and Referendums (www.ofcom.org.uk) & BBC Editorial Guidelines, Politics and Public Policy (www.bbc.co.uk/guidelines/editorial guidelines).
**The Electoral Commission designates "major parties" currently Conservative, Labour, Liberal Democrats plus the Scottish National Party, Plaid Cymru and four parties in Northern Ireland.

social class system has been a much-noted trend in British society. It found its counterpart in political communication with the rise of no-holds-barred satire and a distinctly non-deferential style of journalism. The latter includes the forceful interviewing of politicians, a more interpretative rather than straight reporting approach, and the encouragement of blunt-to-belligerent audience-participation shows. The new style is embodied by the BBC's Jeremy Paxman, who famously draws inspiration from H. L. Mencken's advice that the correct relationship of a journalist to a politician is that of a dog to a lamppost. His robust one-on-one interrogations of politicians have become regular highlights of election coverage;[1] in 2005 he asked Liberal Democrat Charles Kennedy whether his doctor approved of how much he drank and smoked, and he pressed Blair 18 times on how many illegal immigrants were in the country.

Paxman and his ilk are celebrity journalists who confront politicians as equals and indeed are often more famous than the politicians they interview. They offer a colossal contrast to the early days of the BBC when journalists would meekly ask government ministers if they had anything to say to the public. It is a moot point the extent to which the Paxman-*esque* style of journalism is a cause or effect of the intensification of political news management and spin doctoring. Certainly, they have grown together in a mutually reinforcing way. As television came of age and wrested concessions from customary and regulatory shackles, so the politicians sensed, correctly, a loss of power. The latter responded with a new wave of professionalization, pioneered by Margaret Thatcher's Conservatives. They brought in professional advertisers, Saatchi & Saatchi, to coordinate campaign communication, transformed political advertising along commercial lines, and brilliantly exploited television's insatiable appetite for pictures by organizing Thatcher's tours as a series of photo opportunities (Scammell, 1995). Since Thatcher's trail-blazing, parties have become increasingly adept at news management through aggressive spinning, selective leaking, and the maximum extraction of news value from their PEBs and advertising billboard launches. Blair's New Labour ratcheted up the professionalization process, incorporating a fearsome media machine at the heart of government. It expanded all inherited sectors of the normal government apparatus of publicity, initiated several others, strengthened Downing Street control over the civil service, changed working relationships with the Westminster press lobby, and cultivated the Internet and non-political outlets to sidestep political journalists (Scammell, 2001).

A journalistic backlash was inevitable and duly came. There has been a colossal increase in both the volume and cynicism of spin coverage since Blair's first triumph in 1997. A mix of critics from politics, media, and the academy accused Labour of serial abuse of its communication powers; it had become government by "spin and focus group" (Ingham, 2003), "control freaks" (Jones, 2001), and had waged unparalleled efforts to "soft soap" the public (Franklin, 1999, pp. 17–18). The result according to Barnett and Gaber (2001), was a "crisis of political journalism"; informed critical reporting of policy was substituted by increasingly cynical coverage of spin as journalists attempted to demonstrate their independence.

Two major events compounded a mounting sense of crisis. The first was the slump in voter turn-out at the 2001 election; at just 59% it was the lowest turn-out since 1918. It created widespread fears of a crisis of democracy, sparked a rush of academic research into citizen engagement and public trust in politicians (Bromley, Curtice, & Seyd, 2004), and provoked journalistic and political soul-searching about campaign responsibilities (Gaber, 1998; Lloyd, 2004; Rusbridger, 2001; Scammell, 2004). The second event was the extraordinary public confrontation between Blair's spin doctor, Alastair Campbell, and the BBC in June 2003, concerning allegations that the government had lied about weapons of mass destruction to win support for the Iraq War. The episode culminated in the suicide of the BBC's informant, Dr. David Kelly, and the establishment of a public inquiry under Lord Hutton to investigate the circumstances surrounding his death. The Hutton Report in 2004 acquitted the government but condemned the BBC for fatal errors, not least a failure to check its facts and properly investigate the complaints made by Campbell. Hutton's conclusions led to casualties at the top of the BBC and generated considerable debate about journalistic standards and the role of public service news. However, whatever comfort Labour took from Hutton did not last long. With the failure to find weapons of mass destruction in Iraq, it was Blair, not the BBC, who lost public trust, according to the opinion polls (Scammell, 2004). It became settled popular opinion that Blair had "spun" Britain into a devastating war.

In the aftermath of these events, both politicians and media entered the 2005 general election nervously, each with a sense that their credibility was on trial and each concerned that their behaviour should not be blamed for another "apathy election." The ITV news organization was determined that it would not repeat its mistakes of 2001, when it had "failed creatively" by sending target teams to follow the party leaders and ended up with tedious coverage of "every cough of the politicians."[2] Its approach this time was to find "the real stories," to "de-code the politicians' language," get behind the spin, and to ensure that real people's concerns were reflected through audience questioning of politicians (*Ballot Box Jury*). Distrust of politicians was thus effectively built in to the ITV election coverage formats (Billig, cited in Electoral Commission, 2005, p. 40). The BBC, for its party, was determined to uphold "serious news values" (Michael Grade, BBC chairman, quoted in Harrison, 2005, p. 95) but would not repeat the 2001 election coverage overdose which broadcasters believed had bored voters. The BBC's main innovation, and a significant one, was to bring the three main party leaders together for a *Question Time Leaders Special*, the closest the U.K. has yet come to a presidential debate. Each leader was subjected in turn to often hostile questions from an invited and politically balanced audience. The program attracted a viewing audience of more than 4 million and is sure to be an experiment that the BBC would like to repeat.

MEDIA COVERAGE OF ELECTIONS

There is now a substantial body of research into the content of general election news. Martin Harrison (2005), for broadcasting, and Scammell and Harrop (2005), for newspapers, have provided commentaries and content analysis for every recent general election—in the Butler & Kavanagh series, *The British General election of… (1974, 1980, 1988, 1992)*. Blumler and colleagues (Blumler, Gurevitch, & Nossiter, 1986, 1989) provided analysis of BBC news over successive elections based on observation in the newsroom; and together with McQuail, Blumler (1968) presented the first detailed analysis of PEBs. Semetko et al. (1991) compared the formation of campaign agendas in the U.S. and U.K. in the 1980s; while Semetko and Scammell (2005) have tracked the changing content of election over for the period 1992 to 2001 (the results of this work are reported below). The Electoral Commission, established in 2000 with a remit *inter alia* to encourage participation, has provided reports of media coverage, using research by Loughborough University, and commissioned opinion surveys of voters' use and perception of media information. Norris et al. (1999) provided the single most comprehensive analysis of campaign communication, comparing the content of media and party agendas in 1997 and using survey and experimental data to examine the differential effects of positive and negative news. In addition to these major works, many other researchers have analyzed aspects of media coverage at specific elections (Bartle, 2005; Curtice & Semetko, 1994; Goddard, Scammell, & Semetko, 1998; Miller, 1991; Seymour-Ure, 1995). Hence, we now know a good deal about media treatment of elections and can track change over time with a reasonable degree of confidence. There is also a smaller but growing corpus on party advertising, which again allows comparison over time (Scammell & Semetko, 1995; Scammell & Langer, 2006a, 2006b); while Pattie and Johnston

(2002) have analyzed PEB effectiveness. However, we know much less about media in non-general elections, notwithstanding Semetko et al's internationally comparative work on media reporting of elections to the European parliament. Thus, the focus here is on general election campaigns, media content and effects.

Media Content: Key Features

The key features of electoral coverage are these: it is U.K. -focused, leader-focused, and is characterized by tendencies towards strategic framing and a widening gulf between party and media agendas.

One regular result of all the research is that elections are predominantly domestic affairs. U.K. issues, normally the bread-and-butter of the economy and social welfare dominate the substantive issue agendas. Occasionally foreign affairs can disrupt the pattern, and it is usually relations with the European Union that ignite the passions of the right-wing press and politicians. In the 2005 campaign, the Iraq War burst through as a leading news item, but the framing was distinctively British, concerned with the legality of U.K. involvement and whether Blair had misled Parliament and his own Cabinet. Intriguingly, but hardly surprisingly, the domestic focus appears to be as much a feature of European elections as U.K. ones.

A second consistent finding is the trend towards strategic framing. This is evident in the amount of news devoted to campaign trail activities, tactics, and strategies; "process" stories at the expense of coverage of substantive issues. Across all media in 2005 44% of media coverage was concerned with process (Electoral Commission, 2005), and about half of the process category was composed of stories discussing campaign strategies. A further 8% was concerned with political impropriety (the integrity of politicians, primarily Blair) and just 22% with core issues (economy, crime, social welfare). Despite the public service obligations of television, there was relatively little difference between the broadcast and print sectors (see Table 5.7).

It seems clear that the concentration on process is a relatively recent trend. When Semetko et al. (1991, p. 142) compared U.S./UK media during the 1980s they concluded:

> British election coverage on television is almost comprehensively different from campaign news on U.S. television…it is more ample, more varied, more substantive, more party oriented, less free with unidirectional comment, and more respectful. By contrast American election television is more terse, concentrated, horse-racist, guided by conventional news values, ready to pass judgment and ready to be occasionally disrespectful in passing such judgment.

Thus, U.K. news, as it becomes an intensively competitive model, is converging on traits noticed in the ultra-competitive U.S. market. The trend was picked up first in analysis that compared

TABLE 5.7
Top Themes in U.K. Media Coverage of the 2005 General Election

Ranking	All media	Coverage %	Broadcast	Coverage %
1	Electoral process	44	Electoral process	42
2	Impropriety	8	Iraq	10
3	Iraq	8	Asylum/immigration	8
4	Asylum/immigration	7	Impropriety	8

Source: Deacon et al (LCRC), in Electoral Commission (2005) "Engaging the public in Great Britain: media coverage of the campaigns" p.34

the main BBC and ITV news programs for the 1992 to 1997 elections (Norris et al., 1999). There was a marked increase in process coverage across the two elections, most notably on the BBC; while the proportion of substantive issue subjects fell, again most significantly for the BBC, although it continued to carry more substance than the ITV. The degree of convergence should not be over-stated; there is still a huge amount of election coverage on U.K. television by comparison with many other countries, and indeed in contrast to the U.K. tabloid newspapers, whose interest seems to dwindle by the race (Scammell & Harrop, 2005). According to Harrison (2005), the election led the main evening TV news programs for 21 of the 28 days before polling, a strong testament to television attention to the campaign. Nonetheless, there is an evident trend emerging, to present less political news overall and within that giving less attention to substantive issues.

A significant side-effect of strategic framing is a widening gulf between party and media agendas. Comparing the two in 1997 Norris et al. (1999, p. 80) found that "journalists and politicians were marching to different beats"; the agendas were miles apart. Moreover, the disparity seemed to have increased since 1983, although the authors noted that there was still a far closer correspondence in the U.K. than the U.S. It is not yet possible to extend the agenda comparison to include the 2005 election.[3] but it is reasonable speculation that overall there was a significant, and most likely, growing chasm.

Presidentialism was noted earlier (see "Political System") as an informal challenge to the Westminster Model. It is reflected both in the parties' campaigns and in media selection of sound bites. As Figure 5.1 shows, the leaders again dominated the sound bites on the evening news on the main two TV channels. Between them the three leaders took 75% of all politicians' speaking time. However, while there is little doubt that presidentialization is the trend over several elections now (Semetko & Scammell, 2005), it is not a purely linear one, either in the media or for the parties. The extent to which campaign strategies highlight leaders depends upon their perceived strength as a vote-winner. Hence, Blair had eclipsed all other Labour spokespeople in the party's 1997 and 2001 campaigns, but in the troubling aftermath of the Iraq War he was used more sparingly, and others, notably Gordon Brown, elevated to more prominent roles. As Figure 5.1 suggests, Labour were unable to protect Blair from the spotlight, but were reasonably successful at raising the profile of other spokespeople.

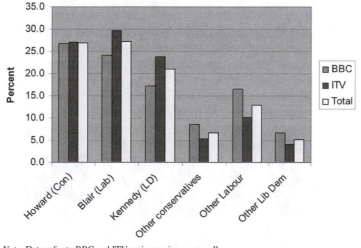

Note: Data refer to BBC and ITV main evening news onlly.

FIGURE 5.1 Time devoted to leaders' speaking (as a proportion of all main party spokespeople): UK general election 2005.

The leader focus is emphasized in all the main accounts of the 2005 race (Electoral Commission, 2005; Scammell & Harrop, 2005). For the newspapers especially it was a two-leader race, with the Liberal Democrats never making the front-page lead. In this respect, Figure 5.1 demonstrates the continued importance of television for balanced coverage. The stopwatch may have been thrown out the window, but the main two leaders get roughly equal coverage, while Kennedy was not too far behind.

Electoral News on the Main Channels: Diminishing Visibility

A comparative analysis of BBC and ITV news (ITN) over three elections (1992–2001)[4] offers grim reading for politicians: It reveals that on the flagship news programmes of the two most popular TV channels attention to the campaign decreased consistently (see Figure 5.2). The proportion of stories mentioning the campaign declined, while the proportion devoted to non-politics increased. Moreover, the time given to campaign stories decreased sharply; not only were there fewer stories, they were shorter. In total on both channels there was about 40% less time for the election in 2001 (about 8.5 hours) compared to 1997 (about 15 hours). Such a large fall is partly accounted for by broadcast decisions not to extend the news especially for the election.

Additionally, politicians became substantially *less* visible in the news, both absolutely and in relation to the increasing visibility of journalists and other non-political actors. The total time devoted to politicians' voices fell fairly dramatically on the BBC, less spectacularly on the ITV, but from a lower base (see Figure 5.3). However, Figure 5.3 demonstrates again the value of public service to the Liberal Democrats; there is no evidence of the two-party squeeze that is such a marked feature of newspaper reporting, while attention given to spokespeople of the minor parties increased fairly substantially on the BBC.

The one good piece of news for the politicians, and it runs contrary to expectations and trends in the U.S., is that the tone of news reporting did not become more negative overall. Story tone in 2001 was more favorable to each of the parties than it had been in the previous campaigns. A strict comparison with 2005 is not yet possible, and therefore one cannot speculate about trends. The bald figures for 2005 suggest that reporting has become more evaluative, but that the evaluation is by no means uniformly or even predominantly in a negative direction.

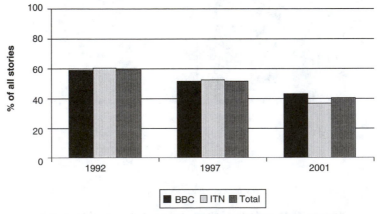

FIGURE 5.2 Attention to the campaign (BBC/ITV: 1997–2001).

Length of quotes political actors

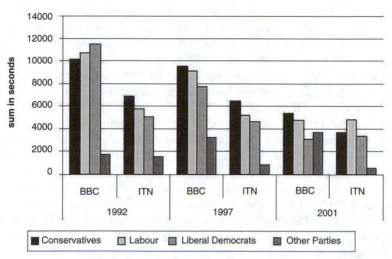

FIGURE 5.3 Politicians voices in U.K. elections.

Electoral Coverage and the Public: Perceptions and Effects

Public perceptions of news sources are monitored annually by the broadcasting regulator, and additionally, the Electoral Commission and the British Election Survey provide campaign-specific research into media use and voters' views of it. This research for the 2005 race is summarized in the Electoral Commission report (2005, pp. 37–39). It confirms overall that television was the most important source of election news, that a significant minority (about two fifths), thought there was too much news about the campaign, and that a large majority (69%) found TV reporting "fair, accurate, balanced, informative and impartial." Respondents' self-assessments rank media relatively highly compared to other sources as an influence on their voting decisions. About 18% said that television had influenced their vote; 14% said that newspaper coverage had done so; 12% said that they were influenced by their local candidate, and just 2% cited the Internet. PEBs, despite their reputation as audience-losers, were appreciated by at least 30% of respondents who said they had helped them understand what the parties stood for.

Political scientists continue to be skeptical about the value of self-reported assessments and it remains notoriously difficult to isolate media from other influences and provide hard proof of substantial effects. However, there is increasing recognition that the media matter in election campaigns. The old orthodoxy that campaigns serve merely to reinforce pre-existing voting dispositions is being extended to more nuanced concerns: the ways in which media may contribute to political knowledge, to voters' sense of efficacy, mobilization and issue priorities, and perceptions of party and leader images, competence and credibility. These concerns fall into three broad groups: agenda-setting effects, persuasion effects and impacts on citizen engagement.

Media power to set the agenda, and thus prioritize the issues that influence voters' decisions, has been a major strand of U.S. research. However, evidence for the U.K is mixed. Miller's study (1991) of the 1987 race concluded that television had relatively little impact on the public agenda. Norris et al.'s (1999, pp. 182–183) experimental research for the 1997 election concluded that TV raised the saliency of "unobtrusive" issues but had no agenda-setting impact on issues that were already high priority—the "bread-and-butter" issues, jobs, health, and social welfare.

Panel survey data for the 2005 contest offered mixed results: immigration, a key media and Conservative party issue, rose in public salience; but the Iraq War—the top substantive issue across all media—actually fell slightly (Norris, 2005). Thus, it appears that the media *do* have some agenda-setting power, but it is conditional and does not operate across the board.

A key benefit of campaigns *should* be that they promote citizen learning about politics. The U.K.'s relatively short official election period offers an information-dense three to four weeks. Notwithstanding the decline in prime time news, there are abundant opportunities to access political information. Voters' self-assessment is that they do learn from media reporting and also from the PEBs, despite the significant minority (29%), who complained that media coverage "made it difficult to learn what the parties stood for" (Electoral Commission, 2005, p. 37). Overall, it appears the U.K. media are good for citizen engagement. In contrast to the "spiral of cynicism" anxieties of the U.S. (Cappella & Jamieson, 1997), attention to the news is positively associated with higher levels of political knowledge and a greater propensity to vote. In place of the spiral of cynicism there is a "virtuous circle" of news consumption and political participation (Norris et al., 1999; 2000; Electoral Commission, 2005). While Norris has consistently argued that the source of news has little differential impact (Norris, 2005), voters themselves claim the source is highly significant. The 2005 highlight for voter learning was the BBC's *Question Time Leaders' Special*, which nearly three-quarters of the viewing audience claimed helped them understand better the parties' policies.

Against the limited effects orthodoxy, U.K. research also suggests that the media may be highly significant in influencing voting preferences. The key here is less the agenda priorities, or the amount of news devoted to each party, but the tone of the news. This was a prime conclusion from the Norris et al. (1999) study; it provided powerful experimental evidence that exposure to favorable (positive) news benefits the featured party or leader; conversely exposure to negative news had far less impact, a finding that once again contrasts with the conclusions of U.S. research. Norris et al. (p. 185) concluded: "what matters is *how* favorably parties are depicted in television news, in particular with positive coverage, rather than *how much* coverage they receive or on what topics." Typically for experimental research the results do not translate straightforwardly into the real world; the effects of positive news for one party can be quickly canceled by positive news for another. Nonetheless, it is an important finding and one that should direct research to crucial questions of story tone and the tone of reporters' remarks. It is also valuably corrects a tendency to dismiss television's persuasive influence (because it is required to be impartial) compared to the vociferously partisan tabloid press. The latter are more commonly ascribed modest but significant persuasive power to affect party images, economic evaluations and vote choice (Curtice & Semetko, 1994; Miller, 1991).

CONCLUSIONS

A snapshot of British election coverage shows information abundance and stability. The election seems everywhere but the down-market tabloids. The pre-digital providers from television and newspapers are still the media giants; and public service, for all its progressive regulatory lightening, still infuses broadcasting decisions with respect to balance, impartiality, and attention to substance. However, there is fundamental movement beneath the surface. Media abundance is multiplying news choice but squeezing its availability. Politics and politicians are becoming less visible, and their voices less frequently heard. Journalists are becoming less respectful, and "news with attitude" is deemed the new way to grab and keep declining audiences. Any visitor returning to Britain after a 30-year absence would be shocked at the decline in deference towards politicians. This seeps through not just into entertainment satire but the most respected news programs themselves; where once the BBC scrapped lampooning satire during the election period, it now employed a resident poet on its flagship Radio 4 morning news, whose verses ended with the line: "They're lying, they're lying, they're lying" (Harrison, 2005, p. 111).

The problem for television now is how to retain mass audiences for news. For politicians the task increasingly seems to be to find ways to bypass political journalists. Part of this effort involves up-rated Internet use, not just to develop party sites, but to reach the public through hi-tech fashion, for example posting video on Youtube, or, as for new Conservative leader David Cameron, hosting a video webblog (WebCameron). However, thus far the Internet has made little dent in the overall election news picture. Internet use has grown rapidly but has largely supplemented and replicated off-line news consumption, not recruited from the ranks of the politically uninterested. Patterns of use suggest that Internet significance will increase as broadband becomes more pervasive. One day there will be an Internet election in Britain.

NOTES

1. Examples of Paxman's most celebrated encounters with politicians can be found on the BBC website, including his 2005 election night interview with anti-Iraq War candidate George Galloway. See http://news.bbc.co.uk/1/hi/uk_politics/vote_2005/blog/4519553.stm).
2. Interview with Craig Oliver, executive producer, ITN. 7 April, 2005.
3. The data to allow comparison of media/party agendas for the 2005 election have been collected by Scammell and Semetko. However, analysis was not complete at the time of writing.
4. The study used similar codebooks for the three elections and the comparisons presented are based on identical measures. The programs analyzed were the BBC's Nine O'clock News (1992 and 1997), BBC Ten O'clock News in 2001, and the ITV's News at Ten for the three elections. These programs are the main news shows on each channel. The entire output of these programs, bar the weather reports, was analyzed over the official election period. The coding unit was the individual news story.

REFERENCES

Barnett, S., & Gaber, I. (2001). *The Westminster tales: The changing relationship between politicians and the media*. London: Continuum.

Bartle, J. (2005). The press, television and the Internet. *Parliamentary Affairs, 58*(4), 699–711.

Blumler, J. G., Gurevitch, M., & Nossiter, T. J. (1986). Setting the television news agenda: Campaign observation at the BBC. In I. Crewe & M. Harrop (Eds.), *Political communications: The general election campaign of 1983* (pp. 104–124). Cambridge, UK: Cambridge University Press.

Blumler, J. G., Gurevitch, M., & Nossiter, T. J. (1989). The earnest versus the determined: Election news-making at the BBC, 1987. In I. Crewe & M. Harrop (Eds.), *Political communications: The general election campaign of 1987* (pp. 157–174). Cambridge, UK: Cambridge University Press.

Blumler, J. G., & McQuail, D. (1968). *Television in politics*. London: Faber & Faber.

Bromley, C., Curtice, J., & Seyd, B. (2004, June). Is Britain facing a crisis of democracy? Working paper 106, Center for Research into Elections and Social Trends. Retrievable at: www.crest.ac.uk.

Butler, D., & Kavanaugh, D. (1974). *The British General Election of February, 1974*. New York: Macmillan.

Butler, D., & Kavanaugh, D. (1980). *The British General Election of 1979*. New York: Macmillan.

Butler, D., & Kavanaugh, D. (1988). *The British General Election of 1987*. New York: St. Martin's Press.

Butler, D., & Kavanaugh, D. (1992). *The British General Election of 1992*. New York: St. Martin's Press.

Cappella, J., & Jamieson, K. (1997). *Spiral of cynicism: The press and the public good*. Oxford, UK: Oxford University Press.

Cockerell, M. (1988). *Live from Number 10*. London: Faber & Faber.

Curtice, J., & Semetko, H. (1994). Does it matter what the papers say? In A. Heath, R. Jowell, & J. Curtice (Eds.), *Labour's last chance? The 1992 election and beyond* (pp. 43–64). Aldershot, UK: Dartmouth.

De Vreese, C., S., Banducci, H., Semetko, H., & Boomgaarden (2006), The news coverage of the 2004 European Parliamentary election campaign in 25 countries. *European Union Politics, 7*(4), 477–504.

Electoral Commission. (2005). *Election 2005: Engaging the public in Great Britain.* London: Electoral Commission. Retrievable at http://www.electoralcommission.org.UK/files/dms/Engaging_19456-14157ESW.pdf

Franklin, B. (1999). Soft-soaping the public? The government and media promotion of social policy. In B. Franklin (Ed.), *Social policy, the media and misrepresentation* (pp. 17–38). London: Routledge.

Goddard, P., Scammell, M., & Semetko, H. (1998). The campaign on TV: Too much of a good thing?' In I. Crewe (Ed), *Political communications: The General Election campaign of 1997* (pp. 149–175). London: Cass.

Gould, P. (1998). *The unfinished revolution: How the modernizers saved the Labour party.* London: Little Brown.

Hallin, D., & Mancini. P. (2003). *Comparing media systems.* Cambridge, UK: Cambridge University Press.

Harrison, M. (2005). On air. In D. Kavanagh & D. Butler (Eds.), *The British General Election of 2003* (pp. 94–118). Basingstoke, UK: Palgrave;

Harrop, M., & Scammell, M. (1992). A tabloid war. In D. Butler & D. Kavanagh (Eds.), *The British General Election of 1992* (pp. 180–210). Basingstoke, UK: Macmillan.

Ingham, B. (2003) *The wages of spin.* London: John Murray.

Jones, N. (2001). *The control freaks: How Labour gets its own way.* London: Politicos.

Langer, A. I. (2007). A historical exploration of the personalisation of politics in the print media: The British Prime Ministers (1945–1999). *Parliamentary Affairs, 60*(3), 371–387.

Lijphart, A. (1999). *Patterns of democracy: Government forms & performance in thirty-six countries.* New Haven, CT: Yale University Press

Lloyd, J. (2004). *What the media are doing to our politics.* London: Constable.

Miller, W. (1991). *Media and voters: The audience, content and influence of press and television at the 1987 General Election.* Oxford, UK: Clarendon Press.

Mughan, A (2000). *Media and the presidentialization of Parliamentary elections.* London: Macmillan.

Norris, P. (2000). *A virtuous circle: Political communications in post-industrial societies.* New York: Cambridge University Press.

Norris, P. (2005, September). *Did the media matter? Persuasion, priming and mobilization effects in the 2005 British General Election campaign.* Paper presented to EPOP, Political Studies Association.

Norris, P., Curtice, J., Sanders, D., Scammell, M., & Semetko, H. (1999). *On message: Communicating the campaign.* London: Sage.

Nossiter, T. J., Scammell, M., & Semetko, H. A. (1995). Old values versus news values. In I. Crewe & B. Gosschalk (Eds.), *Political communication: The General Election campaign of 1992* (pp. 85–103). Cambridge, UK: Cambridge University Press.

Ofcom. (2006). *The communications market 2006.* London: Office of Communication, Department of Culture, Media and Sport. Retrievable at http://www.ofcom.org.uk/research/cm/cm06/

Patterson, T. E. (2002). *The vanishing voter: Public involvement in an age of uncertainty.* New York: Alfred A. Knopf.

Pattie, C. J., & Johnston, R. J. (2002). Assessing the TV campaign: The impact of party election broadcasting on voters' opinions in the 1997 British General Election. *Political Communication, 19*(3), 333–358.

Riddell, P. (1999). *Parliament under Blair.* London: Politicos.

Rusbridger, A. (2001). *Politicians, the press and politcal language.* The Hetherington Memorial Lecture 2001. Retrieved November 2005 from: http://fms.stir.ac.uk/research/hetherington/2001/index.html.

Scammell, M. (1995). *Designer politics.* Basingstoke, UK: Macmillan.

Scammell, M. (2001). Media and media management. In A. Seldon (Ed.), *The Blair effect* (pp. 509–534). London: Little, Brown.

Scammell, M. (2004). Crisis? What crisis? Political communication in the Blair era. *Political Communication, 21*, 501–516

Scammell, M., & Harrop, M. (2005). The press: Still for Labour despite Blair. In D. Kavanagh & D. Butler (Eds.), *The British General Election of 2005* (pp. 119–145). Basingstoke, UK: Palgrave.

Scammell, M., & Langer, A. (2006a).Political advertising: Avoiding disbelief, Inviting boredom. *Media, Culture, & Society, 28*(5), 763–784.

Scammell, M., & Langer, A. (2006b), Political advertising in the United Kingdom. In L. L. Kaid & C. Holtz-Bacha (Eds.), *The Sage handbook of political advertising* (pp. 65–82). London: Sage.

Scammell, M., & Semetko. H. (1995). Political advertising on television: The British experience. In L. L. Kaid & C. Holtz-Bacha (Eds.), *Political advertising in Western democracies* (pp. 19–43). London: Sage.

Schifferes, S., Ward, S., & Lusoli, W. (2007). What's the story…? Online news consumption in the 2005 UK election. Unpublished manuscript. Retrievable at: http://www.esri.salford.ac.UK/ESRCResearch-project/output.php.

Semetko, H. A., Blumler. J. G., Gurevitch, M., & Weaver, D. H. (1991). *The formation of campaign agendas: A comparative analysis of party and media roles in recent American and British elections*. Hillsdale, NJ: Erlbaum.

Semetko, H., & Scammell, M. (2005, Sept. 1–4). *Television news and elections: Lessons from Britain and the U.S.* Paper presented at the annual conference of the American Political Science Association, Washington D.C.

Seymour-Ure, C. (1995). Characters and assassinations. In I. Crewe & B. Gosschalk (Eds.), *Political communication: The General Election campaign of 1992.* Cambridge, UK: Cambridge University Press.

6

Free Journalism under Control: Election Coverage in France

Eric Darras

In 2007, because of what was dubbed by the media as the "beauty and the beast struggle," the macho style coverage of Segolene Royal, the first woman candidate with a real chance to win the French presidency, is seen as having ruined her chance to win against her opponent, Nicolas Sarkozy. In 2002, almost 5 million French citizens voted for the far-right leader Jean-Marie Le Pen, thus placing him in the presidential election run-off. In 2002, the *election coverage* was and still is considered as the main cause not only of voter apathy (28.4% of the eligible voters did not bother to vote, a record in a presidential election) but also of the motivation for the vote for the extreme-right candidate. If other explanations are associated with the main one (the election coverage), they are considered to be secondary.[1]

The arguments encompass, in a more visible manner, every aspect of French election coverage since the seventies, including (1) the influence of political marketing with the communication faux-pas of the main left-wing contender Lionel Jospin;[2] (2) the generally boring campaign; (3) the role of the media with its cynical treatment of the political leaders' programs and institutions; (4) the media's responsibility for framing the issues with sensational coverage of crime and violence;[3] and (5) the role of the pollsters who were accused, among other biases, of having generated underdog effects by predicting the (wrong) result (they all predicted up until the last days the first round victories of Lionel Jospin and Jacques Chirac). But one cannot understand French election coverage without first recalling some important national characteristics of the political and media systems: the interrelationship between a country's political and media institutions will explain most of the national political communication issues (Hallin & Mancini, 2004).

OVERVIEW OF THE POLITICAL AND MEDIA SYSTEMS

The Political System: A Super-Presidential Regime

The presidential election is increasingly at the core of the French political system. For the presidential election, there is no real intra-party primary selection process (except within the Green Party and the Socialist Party for the 2002 and 2007 presidential elections), but "the designation of nominees by the multiple political parties is accomplished in informal and varying ways" (Swanson, 1991, p. 14). Thus, many candidates compete in a first ballot (there were no less than

12 candidates in 2007). The two top vote-getters in this first round can compete for a majority in the second ballot two weeks later. The direct election of the president of the Republic every five years since 2002 (every seven years before that date) takes place immediately before the direct election of the deputies. This new schedule reinforces the presidential nature of the French fifth Republic.[4] The personalization is prominent in the French political system not only because national elections are direct[5] and use a majority principle (and are thus uninominal), but notably because the schedule of the elections reinforces the control by a few national leaders of the candidates' investiture to the national assembly elections: the president of the republic, the prime minister, and the chiefs of the two dominant parties, the Socialist Party (PS) and the Union for a Popular Movement (UMP). Almost every political incumbent who wants to be reelected is thus required to declare allegiance to one hopeful "présidentiable," sometimes long before knowing who will be the winner in the first round of the next presidential election.

The political centralization in Paris is exacerbated by the centralization of the media: all the newsrooms of the national media are located in Paris. Such a concentration is aggravated by the common educational background of political journalists and national political leaders who notably attend the same institutions of higher education. Thus, the Parisian press and television channels and radio stations are the only ones to cover the entire nation. The domination of the two main terrestrial television channels (TF1 and France 2) accomplishes the personalization. The recent and weak French local radio (since the 1980s) and television (2000s) channels are notably difficult to compare with the U.S. syndicated media system. This structural fact explains much of the French geographic bias, in election coverage as elsewhere: the nationalization of every issue and even of local elections (Gerstlé & Piar, 2005) as well as European elections (Gerstlé, Semetko et al., 2001).

However important the media have become in French elections, grass-root communication strategies are still required mainly because of the persistence of a strong local democracy. Despite the concentration of media power in Paris, however, an influential local press is still powerful: *Ouest France* remains the most popular French newspaper far ahead of the second-place *Le Monde*. Presidential candidatures are thus regularly announced in a strategically selected regional newspaper. A national leader must build up and strengthen a local network: in the 1983 local elections, Jacques Chirac made 92 trips to support the right wing contenders, in 1986 one-third of the 577 legislative contenders of his party (the RPR, formerly UMP) welcomed him; and after Chirac's defeat in the 1988 presidential election, his advisors went further by systemizing his grass-roots political strategy (Bacqué & Courtois, 1998; Le Bart & Lefebvre, 2005; Gaxie & Lehingue, 1984).

The Broad Political Spectrum in France

The recent history, instability, and complexity of the party system has led to a growing dispersion of the votes: at the first ballot of the presidential election, the two major candidates shared only 36% of the votes in 2002, compared to 76% in 1974 (but 57% in 2007). Among other European countries, the growing influence of the extreme right since the eighties reached a very high level.[6] The significant electoral influence of the extreme left in France is less common in European countries. Extreme left and communist leaders support anti-systemic platforms that have no equivalents in most other countries. Despite the lack of proportional representation at the parliamentary level and gerrymandering-like successive operations in order to favor the dominant parties, France's exceptional political pluralism persists. Besides essential historical and socio-economical factors, this may be due to the state financial support of political parties, journals, and elections. In addition, the regulatory system requires television and radio to also provide air time to minority candidates, especially in state-owned and operated media. State financial support to the ideological press is also crucial: the communist newspaper *L'Humanité,* as well as the extreme-right magazine *Présent,* could not survive without indirect aids provided by the State. National newspapers, and newsmagazines are still left/right oriented (*Libération-Le Nouvel Observateur* vs. *Le Figaro-Le Point*) and even *Le Monde* is commonly associated with the center left. French TV viewers consider the private (since 1986) national broadcaster TF1 as oriented toward the right in comparison with the other dominant channel, France 2, that is supposed to diffuse its news within a leftist bias (*Télérama,* 2002a, 2002b; Vedel, 2007, p. 118). Another particularity of the French journalistic field is the survival of the historically influential humor and investigative weekly newspaper *Le canard enchaîné.* Satirical political TV programs *Le Bébête-show* and *Les guignols de l'info* have been broadcast since 1982 and play a significant role in election coverage in each presidential election. At the very least, they act as a two-step flow effect within the journalistic field: facts and candidates framed in satirical programs obtain a broader circulation via the national media, newspapers, and news magazines (Collovald, 1991).

Regulation of Political News Coverage during Elections

Increased Fine Tuning of the CSA for Dominant Media.   The law of September 30, 1986 (modified several times) created the Conseil Supérieur de l'Audiovisuel (CSA), a durable independent but state-funded authority which succeeded two former regulatory agencies of the audiovisual media. The 1986 law on the freedom of audiovisual communication delegated to the CSA the role of monitoring and controlling the balance of political expression in the electronic media. It included broadcasts by cable and satellite but excluded the diffusion online since the law of June 21, 2004. As an interesting consequence, minor but younger media seem less and less controlled. Like the print media, they can only be sanctioned *a posteriori* by the judges in accordance with the ordinary press legislation (for example, for deliberate errors of fact, for defamation, or, in theory, for an offense to the president of the Republic). But at the same time, dominant media journalists seem increasingly limited in their ability to carry out their real function during electoral periods. For the most part, this is due to the improvement of the computerized means available at lower costs for the CSA.

"There are eight or more different ways of equalizing candidates that I can legally offer to the CSA," affirmed the host of the major political program of the 1980s, François-Henri de Virieu.[7] He was pretty correct in terms of the situation in the 1980s, but the formal constraints have been more and more solidified for national broadcasters. According to the president of the CSA, Dominique Baudis, "strict submission to our democratic rules gives to our French political life a media coverage equilibrium without any equivalent in the world" (Baudis, 2006, p. 1). Before every campaign, the CSA sends a detailed recommendation to radio and television operators about the need to respect pluralism. During the electoral period, the CSA calculates more precisely than ever, twice a month and then week after week, the amount of coverage for every candidate in order to control the application of the rules related to the access of candidates and their supporters. It distinguishes more precisely the speaking time (the amount of interview time devoted to each candidate and members supporting his or her own team as well as anonymous people interviewed in the street who defend the candidate's platform); and the time of visibility (the amount of speaking time plus the amount of news coverage for every candidate and his or her supporters) for the five main television channels. The other radio and television broadcasters have to do their own calculations and communicate the results to the CSA.

On the one hand, the "equity rule" is as applicable for non-electoral (but political) news during a non-electoral period as it is during an election campaign. Since 2000, the CSA has nuanced the old-fashion Gaullist tradition of the particularly unfair "three-third rule" by the "reference principle." Before 2000, radio and television were supposed to provide one-third of the political coverage to the government, one-third to its majority, and one-third to the parliamentary opposition. The most victimized are the spokespersons of non-governmental or "little" parties, even if those parties are regularly supported by far more than 5% of the electorate (Chasse-Pêche-Tradition, Lutte Communiste Révolutionaire) and sometimes for more than two decades (Front National, Lutte Ouvrière, Parti Communiste). The CSA now requires a more fair coverage of these politicians but also of the members of the parliament that do not belong to the majority or to the opposition (notably the center-right party UDF).

On the other hand, for electoral news specifically and only for journalistic programs, three periods are now distinguished. The "equity rule" during the prior trimester to the election is required. This pre-campaign ("preliminary period") takes place from December 1st before the election year up to the day before the official proclamation of the candidates by the Constitutional Court (around a month before the second ballot). This preliminary period has been extended by the CSA (it started before 2007 with the calendar year, January 1) in order to facilitate respect for global equilibrium by radio and television professionals within a longer time period. The political information supported by government office holders (e.g., prime minister, president of the Republic) who are also candidates have to be distinguished ("reference principle") from their "electoral" messages ("electoral news"). Another major intricacy for the CSA remains that many candidatures are often not "declared" or have to be "presumed." Moreover, most of them cannot be known before the deposit of the 500 signatures at the Constitutional Court. Therefore, journalists and the CSA have to take into account the media fairness for every expected candidate by gauging their notoriety, their support, and their involvement in the campaign. This is a delicate mission since the credibility of the minor challengers is correlated to their amount of media coverage: to persuade 500 local politicians to sign their candidature act, a minimum of notoriety appears necessary; and media visibility is more required for the unknowns.

The second or intermediary period begins when the constitutional court makes public the names of the candidates and continues until the first day of the official campaign: in 2007 it was April 8. The "equity rule" is then applicable for the news coverage of every candidate, and the much more simple "equality rule" is applicable for the weekly amount of spoken time allotted to the candidates and their supporters. Equal time rules were initiated as early as 1956 for the very first televised national assembly election.

During the final or official campaign period, the equality rule is applicable for the weekly amount of spoken time and of news coverage for every candidate (two weeks prior to the first ballot, one month before the second ballot). Nowadays, during the election period non-journalistic programs (infotainment, talk shows) must also follow these rules, but only for the spoken time of the candidates and their supporters. Thus, they have to avoid every kind of political discourse if they cannot respect the CSA rules. Actually, the CSA has stricter control over non-journalistic programs. The CSA can more easily reprimand TV and radio talk-show hosts as long as it is encouraged to do so by influential political journalists. On the other hand, every warning given a journalist by the CSA provokes a strong reaction amongst journalists. The CSA also fixes the rules concerning the conditions of production, programming, and broadcasting of the programs that report on the official campaign; that is, the free air time that is provided to every candidate. Official programs of the electoral campaign are now mainly broadcast on state television channels, often at the worst hours and for only a few minutes. In addition, with few exceptions,[9] they clearly also fail to attract more viewers because of the old-fashion Soviet-television style that persists despite the CSA's repeated instructions since 1992. Indeed, the members and professionals of the CSA consistently deplore the candidates and their campaign teams' lack of interest in these official broadcasts. Excessively suspicious, candidates' strategists seem terrified by the idea of their candidate making a faux-pas in the media just a few days before the ballot.

These principles were strictly applied by the leading radio and TV stations for the very first time in 2007. CSA members have repeatedly warned at four levels (informally, officially with a recommendation, a direct warning, and a strict warning) the executives and journalists of national broadcasters to better conform to the rules. Indeed, the CSA is deprived of a real punishment capacity mainly because of the self-censorship of the nine council members themselves. Politically oriented and selected, their own credibility is fragile. They fear a political false move, and they do not want to compromise the economy of the audiovisual sector: it remains notably impossible for them to threaten the company that operates on an allocated frequency even if the renewal of each frequency is in theory decided by the CSA. In addition, the CSA's resources are weak and its budget depends on the prime minister.

However, the mere existence of the CSA's threat is at least somewhat efficient: it leads to regular recommendations by media executives and therefore leads to consistent self-censorship inside the newsroom. During the 2005 referendum on the European Treaty, which was rejected by the French, the CSA's fine tuning played a key role in re-balancing pluralism in favor of the partisans of the No vote. The repetitive warnings, even on the dominant broadcaster TF1, were based on increasingly precise calculations and thereby became less open to criticism.

From midnight on the last day before the ballot until 8 pm on election day, it is forbidden to broadcast any kind of electoral message from the candidates ("propaganda" in French) on any of the audiovisual media. In addition, evaluations by opinion polls cannot be communicated before the last location for voting has closed at 10 pm, and this applies also to the print media. This election coverage silence has been required since the 19th century in order to "calm the passions" and let "the citizen choose in the privacy of his consciousness" (Offerlé, 1992, p. 77).

The Prohibition of Political Advertising.   Under a law passed on January 15, 1990, the campaign funds of every candidate for every kind of electoral office must be disclosed, and a maximum amount is fixed by law. The election costs are strictly limited and controlled but actually the winner cannot be easily invalidated because he overspent the authorized amount. However, at the local level, the law certainly favors or protects the grass-roots candidates against their richer but locally unknown challengers who could otherwise invest in a costly media image campaign. Above all, political advertising is forbidden, and this remains the main protection against the "Americanization" of French election coverage (Gurevitch & Blumler, 1990; Kaid & Holtz-Bacha, 1995). French candidates are not allowed to pay for air time on radio and television even in the independent or non-state media. Thus, in comparison with the U.S., political marketing does not play such a key role in France where "political strategy, institutional communication and the part played by the candidates themselves have a greater influence on the final results of the election" (Habib). Omnipresent posters and stickers are plastered everywhere (although it is strictly forbidden except on the official political panels), even in the smallest villages. They surround and inform everyone that the political show is on. Negative ads seem inappropriate to communication experts, and the posters are still very classical: a picture of the candidate's face plus a catch-all though vague slogan (Haiman, 1991, p. 28). Besides the plastering of posters every night, the daily distribution of leaflets in mailboxes and at every city's weekend markets begins long before the official campaign and reveals the persistence of the belief in the crucial role of street-level party members.

Above all, electoral candidates are invited to appear on influential political interview shows on every leading national radio and television channel a few months before the first ballot. During election periods, political speeches are easier to sell to the average targeted viewer, just because of the mobilization of the opinions nourished by the general political climate that activates a civic sense of duty. But even in electoral periods, it remains hard work to sell politics on TV. In order to attract more viewers, television and radio journalists try to modernize their news programs by creating media events, with more movement, more external footage, and more aggressive questioning, or by orchestrating debates between the contenders. It is notably quite impossible to organize a real debate between the major candidates just because the candidates do not want to be involved in such a risky business. Debating on TV is not a legal obligation even at the local level. Nevertheless, the great "presidential election debate" between the two ballots is quite inescapable since 1974, even if Jacques Chirac refused to debate with Jean-Marie Le Pen in 2002. These "great debates" constitute the acme of election coverage, and sometimes the tone between the contenders is very harsh. The 2007 debate between Ségolène Royal and Nicolas Sarkozy was described as particularly abrasive. It was broadcast on the two major channels for more than 20 million viewers. After the debate, Ségolène Royal was described by political journalists as too "sensitive" (she accused her opponent of reaching the "summit of political immorality" when he was speaking of handicapped children) whereas Nicolas Sarkozy showed his "serenity" (*Le Monde,* May 4, 2007).

The overall gendered news coverage of the 2007 election must be highlighted. The gendered tone of Ms. Royal is due first of all to her communication strategy: she tried to personify the political renewal of the left after the 2002 electoral trauma *as a woman.* Actually, Ségolène Royal had to show both that she could fit the role of president, in its dominant male historical definition and simultaneously convince the electorate that the role of the president should be redefined in a more feminine way. She described herself more or less exclusively as a woman with the so-called feminine qualities and as a mother and a wife. For example, in the official campaign television spot she declared "I am a mother, a woman with a sense of reality and with both feet on the ground"; as an attractive woman she commented: "Why should one have to be sad, ugly and boring to go into politics" after paparazzi shots of her in a bikini. Trapped within the boundaries of such a gendered scheme she consequently had to face sexist discourses pro or con. The classical headline: "Sarko to face Sego" is a good illustration: it works as an implicit depreciation of the female candidate. Sarko refers to a family name (Sarkozy) and Ségo to the familiar first name. No French journalist suggested the similar attractive title but with a less gendered frame "Nico to face Ségo."

To prepare for the interviews, shows, and debates and to spin the overall news coverage of their campaign, amateurism is clearly ineffectual, and reliance on party members' advice is no longer sufficient, so candidates have had paid professional campaign specialists since the 1970s (Legavre, 1996).

French elections are not very costly, but the bill is paid by the taxpayer: according to an official survey, the 2002 presidential election cost €200 million (twice the cost of the 1988 presidential election). Sixty percent of that amount paid for propaganda material (ads, programs, bulletins). One can argue after Pippa Norris (2000) that the diffusion of television oriented, personality driven, and money driven campaigning, seen as characteristic features of the Americanization of campaigning, is more or less empirically validated with respect to France. More important, it seems that the horse-race coverage, the television programming, but also opinion polls could have a similar or even greater influence in France than in the U.S., despite the marginal role of money and the broader political field in France. A comparative perspective would show that the same apparent consequences (personalization, opinion polls) can be due to different causal factors (money or centralization).

DEVELOPMENT OF POLITICAL NEWS COVERAGE

Relationship between Political and Journalistic Fields: Rival Partners

Political emancipation of political television journalists in France is not a linear historical process (Bourdon, 1994; Neveu, 2001). Cayrol's (1977) ethnographic study of the 1st channel's newsroom during the 1973 legislative electoral period showed that governmental control of political content was continuous despite the lack of explicit censorship and the claims of TV journalists' unions. Top TV executives are designated by the government at different levels, and most of them belong to majority parties. Leading journalists make known inside the newsroom the rewards or warn powerful majority leaders about the latest newscasts and follow their suggestions for the next one. Direct telephone calls from government officials reach the reluctant journalists themselves. Top civil servants in each ministry are considered as prominent sources, official rules but also local and informal forms of internal regulations favor both the government and the majority candidates.

Three decades later, one could argue that governmental control is far less crude or visible because of growing professionalism amongst journalists. However, some of these instruments of political control are still at work: on the one hand, as for the members of the CSA themselves, top executives of the publicly owned radio and television channels are still agreed to, if not informally chosen by the president of the republic, "the spoils system is more effective in television than in any other elite spheres of [French] society" (Dagnaud & Mehl, 1992). Indeed the political interviewers of the 1970s and 1980s became the top television executives of the nineties both in the public and the private sectors, thanks to their top political connections. On the other hand, partisan contacts and involvements are no more required, but the closer a political journalist is to the political elite, the more he or she will benefit. At the local level the gentleman's agreement relationship between elected politicians and journalists also remains uneasy (Le Bohec, 1997; Restier-Melleray, 2002).

Journalist Objectivity.   On the one hand, French political journalists are usually objective if it means that they allocate fair time or space to the major candidates. There are rare exceptions. In 1995, the CSA itself officially denounced the independent leading channel TF1 for its too obvious over-coverage of right wing candidate and actual prime minister, Balladur. Journalists could be more democratic in applying a more proportional visibility to candidates, but they essentially work within the mainstream of the French political system.

On the other hand, political journalists are also commonly "objective" if it means that they refrain from framing the political information through their own ideological preferences. However, there are several exceptions: when they deal with the EU, Le Pen (Collovald, 1991; Le Bohec, 2005, Lehingue, 2003) or other anti-system candidates such as the far left tickets. According to academic standards, French political journalists are not objective if it means that they tell or at least try to "approach the truth" when asking or answering politicians or when they cover the main issues of the candidates' platforms: with rare exceptions, when journalists deal with immigration, foreign affairs, unemployment, and so on, their lack of knowledge doesn't allow them to challenge the figures and facts that are alleged by the candidates. Moreover, talk show hosts, who are not journalists, became in the 1990s the primary authorized interviewers of political leaders (Neveu, 1999). Insufficient professionalism by journalists facilitates control over the agenda by dominant candidates and institutions.

Changes in the Media Hierarchy?   Watching television is the most popular campaign "activity" in France for every type of election. According to the Eurobarometer, 51% of the

French people watched a TV program "during the two or three weeks before the European election," while 3% attended a public rally or meeting, 5% spoke to a party worker, 8% tried to persuade someone to vote, 18% read election material sent to his or her home, 19% listened to a program on the radio about the election, 25% read an election poster, 26% read a newspaper report about the election, and 39% talked to friends, family, or workmates about the election. Thus, television is the most "helpful" source of information for European elections according to 44% of the French, ahead of newspapers and magazines (23%), personal discussions (15%), radio (14%) and polls (4%) (Norris, 2000, pp. 156–159). These trends have been rather stable since the 1970s.

Content Analysis of News Coverage

There have been major concerns regarding the decline in election news coverage. In 2002, the CSA was so worried that it made an official statement in which it declared itself as "preoccupied by the rarity of political debate, especially for a major event of our democracy [the presidential election]" (CSA, 2002). Table 6.1 shows a sharp decline in television coverage of candidate remarks in 2002.

Actually, rather than declining regularly, the overall election coverage depends first of all on the intensity of the election at stake and of the polarization between the candidates (Gaxie, 1989). Secondly, the decline is more apparent on non-government channels and a new development in journalism is taking place: since the 1990s, state television stations have assumed an increasing amount of the overall political coverage. This change became obvious with the 2005 referendum (Table 6.2) when the three public broadcasters shared 79% of the total of the electoral news. Thirdly, there is a considerable intensification of the election coverage as we approach the ballot: for commercial reasons, the timetable of coverage is shrinking but not necessary the total amount of coverage. Gerstlé established for the 1999 European election that "nearly 90% of the articles dedicated to the elections are published in the last two weeks of the campaign" (Gerstlé et al., 2001, p. 6). Fourthly, the growing audience of M6 (the former French MTV) and of Canal Plus (the former French HBO) has allowed these two broadcasters to become more generalist or catch-all in their programming. It means that they have to put more money into information programs and especially into seasonal election coverage.

Last but not least, the hundred or so digital channels inevitably deal with politics. Nevertheless, increased political offerings on television have not necessarily led to increased consumption of political programs. Since the mid-1980s, political speeches on television have been broadcast late at night or on Sundays mornings and political programs have had to face competition from attractive entertainment programs, even in the less profitable segments of the television schedule.

TABLE 6.1
Speak Time for Candidates during the Three Last Presidential Elections

	Overall election coverage (minutes)	Theoretical average coverage per candidates (mn)	Theoretical average coverage per day and per channel (mn)
1995 (9 contenders)	6310'	701'	11,5'
2002 (16 contenders)	4669'	292'	8,5'
2007 (12 contenders)	8451'	704'	17'

Source: CSA (newscasts and public affairs shows of the five main national broadcasters: TF1, France 2, France 3, Canal +, M6 from January,1st till april, 19th – 109 days ; 2007 : from January the 1st till april 8th: 98 days)

TABLE 6.2
News Coverage of the 2005' Referendum on the European Treaty

	Global time	%	Average audience 2005
TF1 (private)	9h14'	8%	32,3%
M6 (private)	6h26'	6%	12,6%
Canal + (private)	8h54'	8%	3,6%
France 2 (state television)	31h06'	27%	19,8%
France 3 (state television)	47h09'	41%	14,7%
France 5 arte (state television)	12h14'	11%	4,9% (est)
TOTAL	115h04'	100%	(other TV:13% est)

Source : CSA and Mediamétrie

The Visibility of the Candidates

Mainly because of the equal time rule observed by TV channels since 1956 minor candidates are much more visible on TV during the actual campaign period than their counterparts in the U.S. (Gerstlé et al., 1992, p. 67). Following Olivier Duhamel (1996), French political scientists constantly take apart two types of campaign coverage of the presidential election depending on the uncertainty of the verdict of the first round on the right side: in 1974 (Chaban Delmas-Giscard d'Estaing), 1988 (Barre-Chirac), 1995 (Balladur-Chirac), and 2007 (Bayrou-Sarkozy) more than two contenders competed for the run-off. Actually, that's the way the pollsters and market-oriented journalists manage the election coverage toward its center. The description of the challenger of the center right as a possible winner looks like a pseudo-event that can be explained by the commercial journalistic need for more political suspense: everybody, including audiences, wants to believe that another candidate can win, not only those of the two main parties. Another explanation could be found in the center-right orientation shared by most political journalists in dominant newsrooms (a political position that also fits, in a way, their professional standards and "objectivity"). The dual configuration of the other presidential elections since 1965 (1969, 1981, 2002) comes out more simply: the first round is perceived as "already done." In this case, everybody knows that the two candidates of the main dominant parties will be chosen by the electorate (even if this belief was revealed as a false truth in 2002 when no one was seriously expecting the victory of Jean-Marie Le Pen against Lionel Jospin for the second place in total votes cast). As Gerstlé points out, in the duopoly configuration, the departure of the campaign is at first considerably delayed. Secondly, communication strategists guide the political discourse to the political center target, and thirdly, they favor frontal sound bites against their one real challenger. Finally, the duopoly configuration benefits outsiders and marginal contenders because they are more visible before the official campaign. Consequently, this overall election coverage acts as a self-fulfilling prophecy that produces its effects on the degree of openness and political involvement of the voters since it shrinks the useful (or realistic) vote, which profits minor contenders (Gerstlé, 2003a, pp. 32–35).

Despite the journalistic pledge to be objective, imbalances in the news coverage help to maintain the dominant candidates. Dominant party candidates benefit not only from more coverage but also receive more flattering treatment. French journalists argue that they are well-known by their voters, better trained, and more credible than their challengers. They can provide to television interviewers sound bites that are fit to print. Of course, this argument is not always empirically corroborated. Every election produces a different configuration of the forces: the unequal distribution of the political resources has to be objectified for each election to explain the media coverage. Journalists have to take into account the political "rapport de force en presence."

Candidate Visibility: Not So Simple Correlations

It remains very difficult, not to say impossible, to identify the causal role played by party loyalty, by the main political issues, and by the candidate's image (Garrigou 1989, p. 361). It is even true of the public images of the former victorious generals Eisenhower and De Gaulle that were mainly connected to voter partisanship (Converse & Dupeux, 1966). Moreover, it remains impossible to separate an individual's exposure to a mediated political discourse from other selective perceptions of other political or background news messages; from the normative pressure exerted by friends, parents, or colleagues; from the person's own real-life experiences and those of relatives; and from social dispositions incorporated in the individual's political habitus. Other media exposure, daily discourse, and personal experiences mediate each political message that is then thoroughly reinterpreted by the individual. Against essentialist explanation, one cannot make a distinction between an "easy" and a "hard" issue (even the so-called breaking news, such as of a terrorist attack) without taking into account not only the personal experience of the voter (Kiewet, 1981) but also the voter's interpretation of his or her personal situation. For example, unemployment can be experienced on a continuum from not so bad to life-threatening, it depends on the the individual's present circumstances and objective chances of finding another job. Then again, some or most unemployed poor people don't believe in the political leaders' responsibility for unemployment but rather in their own inadequacy. The experience of violence in one's neighborhood, say, differs sharply from members of the upper-class, who have a very low level of tolerance toward violence, to the poorest and immigrant neighborhoods where daily violence is ongoing and includes police harassment.

Spin Control

If the impact of the leader's image remains uncertain for political scientists, it has a real impact within the political field even in the Communist Party or the Green Party where the "media factor" is now considered as crucial long before the ballot: the "charisma factor" can play a key role in the selection of candidates (Neveu, 1998). The notoriety or the popularity of a candidate, as recorded by opinion polls, is a powerful argument inside the party for investing the "notable" as opposed to less well-known challengers (Restier-Melleray, 2002). As a political tool more than a scientific one, opinion polls are actually used to boost a challenger's media visibility inside a dominant party, sometimes for ludicrous reasons but with a real effect on the political agenda. An example of this is when polls "revealed" that Segolene Royal, at that point a candidate among others for the PS presidential investiture, was considered by French males as the sixth sexiest women in the world (FHM). In almost every presidential campaign, an inside challenger to the main leader of a dominant party has benefited from media coverage thanks to opinion polls that are paid to boost his or her support within the particular party: Michel Rocard in 1981, Raymond Barre in 1988, Jacques Delors and Edouard Balladur in 1995. Opinion polls can be seen as participating in political modernization because they increase transparency and efficiency (Cayrol & Mercier, 2002, p. 42) or as a new technology for the newsmakers, dominant parties and institutions, by which they can control both the media and the political agenda (Champagne, 1990; Lehingue, 2007). Pollsters exert a major influence on the campaign's marketing, on the selection of the issues highlighted in the candidates' speeches, but also for the selection of the candidates themselves and finally the voters' behavior.

Mobilization Effect

The 2007 election, with its historical turnout of 84%, confirmed that "a virtuous circle" was at work when increased election coverage boosted the public's interest in the election. According to Gerstlé, "the turn-out rate increases in proportion to campaign activity" (Gerstlé et al., 2001, p. 12). More precisely it looks like a classical egg and chicken dilemma: if the media contribute to the increase in voter attention, audience interest is also clearly responded to by commercial journalism. Moreover, the intense interest in the 2007 presidential election could be due to better "activation not only of the traditional political parties' set of connections but of other nearby networks" such as those of the poor suburban areas (Offerlé, 2007, p. 9).

Agenda Effect

For the 1988 presidential election, Gerstlé, Davis, and Duhamel (1991; Gerstlé 1997) note the lesser visibility of Raymond Barre and the growing presence of Jean-Marie Le Pen on television and the contribution of their levels of visibility to their respective final scores: it was obviously less than expected for the former prime minister but more than anticipated for the extreme right leader. Such a correlation does not imply the existence of a causal liaison. Gerstlé's studies are firm on the role of the media treatment rather than the too simple analysis in terms of the number of occurrences. There are too many counterexamples to conclude that the more visible you are, the more votes you will earn. The 1994 European election campaign confirmed "the lack of a direct link between the time spent on the air and the electoral results...ceteris paribus if 80% of the airtime generates 47% of the votes, 20% of the airtime produces 52%" (Gerstlé, 1995, p. 221). In 2007, the correlation between the visibility of the candidates on the three main television channels and their final scores seems almost perfect: 0.97 (Figure 6.1).

However, one should not conclude too quickly that the more visible you are on TV the more votes you get. As Figure 6.2 shows, in 2002 the correlation was 0.82 between the final votes and the TV coverage for every candidate, and the exceptional case of Jean-Marie Le Pen suggests that the election process is much more complex than we often assume. According to the CSA in 2002,

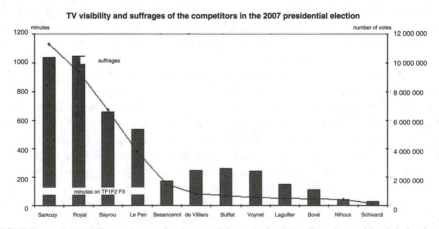

FIGURE 6.1 TV visibility and votes for the candidates in the 2007 French presidential election.

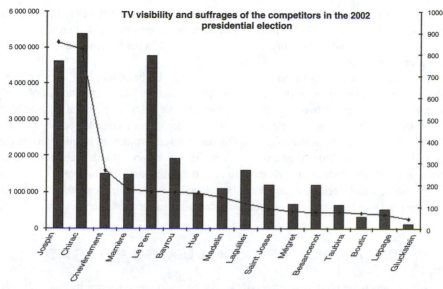

FIGURE 6.2 Visibility and votes for candidates in the 2002 French election.

the total airtime accorded to Lionel Jospin by the three leading television channels was almost five times higher (858 minutes) than that accorded to Jean-Marie Le Pen (182 minutes) from January 1st until election day, but the latter won 194,600 votes more than Lionel Jospin.

The Contrast Effect

In discussing the gap between Le Pen's surprising electoral score and his meager visibility during the 2002 presidential election, Gerstlé argues that one has to take into account the *contrast* between the lack of coverage before the electoral period (21 minutes for the FN on the three main televisions coverage for the whole year 2001) and his weak but ongoing visibility during the presidential election (169 minutes during the overall campaign before the first ballot) as for other marginal candidates. Gerstlé suggests an analogy with the presidential election of 1965 which surprised French viewers when for the first time they could see opposition leaders on television (Gerstlé, 2003a, p. 39). The visibility argument thus appears reversible: in certain circumstances the less visible you are, the more votes you will finally earn. This hypothesis by which a sudden visibility can exert a potentially positive effect seems admissible, but it is only obvious for the (almost) unknowns and for those who produce a political message that is in contrast to the often unanimous discourses of the major left and right candidates. But it does not work for every new contender (Darras, 2005a).

The Background News Effect

The overall volume of law and order topics had been prominent for years in the background news at the time of the 2002 presidential election. As this media obsession with crime is ongoing, one cannot conclude that it benefited Le Pen in 2002. In addition "the insecurity issue was a public opinion concern even before being put on the agenda" (Le Gall, 2003. p. 53). Gerstlé argued that the preoccupation with security could have been transformed in a more intense or solid evaluation: a political judgment. Gerstlé adds that if the security issue is clearly not a new one in 2002, it became more and more visible in the press as we moved closer to the presidential election (Gerstlé, 2003a, pp. 43–45). Moreover he sketches a correlation between the growing importance of the security issue in the press and its importance in public opinion when compared to the unemployment issue.

Academic publications on political communication can be heuristic, but they are also inevitably read by political advisors and thus become performative. The best example of this phenomena came in 2007 when Royal and Sarkozy applied the rules of political communication scholars by following the background news closely (in order to gain a greater echo performative effect …) that the electoral agenda changed day by day, and no prominent issue could be clearly distinguished. However, toward the end of the campaign, Sarkozy attracted attention from extreme-right voters by announcing his intention to create a "minister of immigration and national identity," a proposal which created controversy but placed the right-wing candidate as the owner of the immigration issue in spite of the extreme-right leader Le Pen (Mayer, 2007).

MEDIA TREATMENT OF POLITICAL LEADERS AND ISSUES

A comparison between the media coverage of the issues and voters' preoccupations reveals that an important gap has developed since the 1986 election. The media's main concern then was "coalition" whereas it was not at all a priority for the citizens themselves (Bregman & Missika, 1988). From 1981 to 1995 public opinion priorities remained remarkably stable. Institutional issues and foreign affairs are typically not considered as decisive by voters when they actually vote. Unemployment, social and medical care, social inequalities, and education can be considered as the main issues along with law and order since the mid-1990s (Bregman & Missika, 1988; Gerstlé, 1996, p. 746; Gerstlé, Semetko et al., 2001). As a consequence, the potential effect of election coverage needs to be nuanced because media political preoccupations are not those of the electorate. However, the election coverage contributes not only to mobilizing voters but also to orienting the electorate in several ways.

Balance between the Horse Race and Issues

In France since 1981 at least, the political game (political competition, the horse race aspects of the campaign attacks, evaluation, events, affairs, campaigning, images and polls) represents about the three-fourths of the political information disseminated by TV newscasts when this category is opposed to the TV coverage of political issues or problems (Gerstlé, Davis, & Duhamel, 1991. p. 59; Gerstlé & Pirat, 2005; Piar, 2007, p. 105). For the 2007 presidential election, Piar and Gerstlé (2008) found that the rate of political issues climbed by one-third. but the crime issue was reduced to half the coverage in 2002. They conclude this is a sign of improved quality in the coverage. A less optimistic explanation is plausible: because of the 2002 obsession with crime, TV journalists were accused of contributing to the success of Le Pen in reaching the second ballot. Thus, in 2007 TV journalists were subject to extreme scrutiny by the CSA, their colleagues, and academics, and of course they knew it. French journalists in the print media share with their U.S. equivalents an expertise in the critical analysis of campaign tactics and events. Such a repeated bubble style of election coverage could contribute to an overall discrediting of political leaders and a demobilization of many citizens. It remains certain that the superficial and sometimes unpleasant coverage of the immigration issue contributes to the political disengagement of younger residents whose parents are immigrants and who themselves live in the poorest urban areas. Moreover, the media coverage of immigration issues is described as rather poor. Causal explanations and public-policy issues seem more and more neglected. This is so true that questions formulated by ordinary people on television issue-oriented talk-shows seem more profound and less profane than those asked by political journalists themselves (Neveu, 1997).

It is, however, too easy to blame the media entirely because political leaders have always liked coverage of their personal lives (Darras, 2005b; Le Grignou & Neveu, 1993). Their communication strategists observe closely every faux pas of their competitors to feed to the media, such as Ségolène Royal's gaffes when she was abroad. Moreover, they insist on the "extrinsic characteristics of the political game" (Gaxie, 1978) in order to "reach a demobilized and inattentive audience" (Gerstlé & Piar, 2005).

Competition inside the media produces a classical snowball or bandwagon effect. This effect is not only generated because of the competition between TV channels but also because of the cross-dependence between journalists and newsmakers. One cannot understand the "crime obsession" of the 2002 presidential election without considering that the major candidates fed the media by formulating newsworthy comments on law and order. Political leaders and influential journalists joined forces in playing on people's anxieties for a variety of purposes that Bourdieu subsumed into one: maximizing short term profits by which the logic of the plebiscite in the political field joins the logic of the immediate audience in the media (Bourdieu, 1994).

Priming Effect

Gerstlé, Davis, and Duhamel (1991) first drew attention to the growing visibility of "insecurity" (fear inducing) issues (immigration, French hostages, civil insecurity) during the 1988 presidential election. They suggested that it could support extreme right discourse and an extreme right leader. Garrigou (1989) confirmed that voters are sensitive to this connection. However, according to Gerstlé "one should not assimilate [voters'] priorities and attention. Media agendas respond to public needs but not to the short-term ranking of the main problems [priorities]" (Gerstlé, 1996, p. 747). The electorate's behavior does not depend exclusively on short-term factors, and Gerstlé considers the various ways by which the information is received. He advocates for a typology that ranks the uses to which available political information can be put with the models of the neo-rational voter, the sensitive voter, and the volatile voter, the enlightened preference voter (Gerstlé, 1996, p. 752).

In 1995, Gerstlé explained the low electoral score of the prime minister and candidate for the presidency Edouard Balladur by analyzing the progressive and parallel decline in his public opinion ratings concerning his personal qualities, with a turning point in February. This decline has to be connected to an increase in negative news for the government. Thus the media transferred public attention from candidate human being Balladur to Balladur the prime minister who was in charge, and "this mechanism is an example of a priming effect" (Gerstlé, 1996, p. 750). Gerstlé adds that similar mechanisms were at work in previous elections also characterized by the greater than ever media coverage of political affairs or scandals.

On the other hand, many examples in both older and more recent French electoral history tend to invalidate the hypothesis of the media having a decisive effect on voters since the first analysis concluded that television does not play a key role in the election result (Blumler, Gurevitch, & Cayrol, 1978). Despite a hegemonic pro-EU media during the 1992 referendum campaign, the Treaty of Maastricht was ratified by a very small majority: According to Arnaud Mercier's content analysis of the press coverage of the 2002 presidential election, the daily newspaper *Le Parisien* did not pay much attention to Le Pen and certainly did not support him. However, 27% of the readers of *Le Parisien* voted for Le Pen, which was a much greater percentage than readers of the right oriented national newspaper *Le Figaro* (22% CSA-Télérama, 2729 April 30th, 2002 quoted in Mercier, 2003, p, 68). And this took place despite a unanimous negative angle.[10] Le Pen gained 720,000 votes between the two ballots. According to Mercier (2003, p. 71), one can see in these figures one more proof of the limits of media power.

New Media

In 1966 50% of French households had TV sets. In 2006 the Internet was present in 50% of French homes. Therefore the influence of the Internet was studied from every angle during the 2007 presidential election. However, the new free metropolitan journals (*Metro*, 20 *minutes*) certainly played a more significant role than the Internet notably among the strategic new voters (18–20 years old) despite a weaker academic interest in the French importation of a Scandinavian press model. Less than 5% of French voters used the Internet as a source of information to make up their mind (but 14% of 18–24 year-olds did so); a little more than 10% of the French people seemed "confident" in the political contents of the Internet. This was more than in previous elections, but remained marginal compared to the confidence in radio (39%), television (65%), or newspapers (38%) (Vedel, 2007, pp. 115–116). The Bayrou Web site attracts at best an audience of 45,000 people a day, less than 10% of a mediamat TV audience rating point. The Internet did not change the nature of the French election coverage for many reasons. In 2007, as in 2002, it was still considered as a minor medium by campaign strategists, despite their noisy discourse on the strategic importance of the new media. The technological possibilities of the media were once again considerably under-used by political leaders and their teams. The Internet is still used by political professionals as a political technology that celebrates their *majesté* or their role as representatives of the people: 10 years after the first political communication uses of the Internet, the new media can still be seen more like a "show room than a chat-room" (Serfaty, 2002, p. 149). Professionals and bloggers of every party were online, both to produce and to consume ideological messages, and the Internet was used for many disinformation strategies. Internet activists certainly share the same sociological profile as their predecessors, the former traditional militants who tried to convince the public by using traditional forms of political participation a few years ago. Finally, the interdiction of the publication of the election results before 8 pm was strictly applied in France (there was a €75,000 fine for violating this rule). If the first estimates were available in French-language Swiss or Belgium newspapers or on radio and Web sites at 6.30 pm the the SSR estimates were far from the final results (26.5% for Nicolas Sarkozy who attracted 31% of the voters). Anyway, these Swiss or Belgian borderline Web sites rapidly became too overwhelmed to be reachable.

The influence of the Internet was greater on political journalists themselves who took advantage of the new medium as a major source, and it remains to be seen whether the Internet will become a major influence on political campaigning or public opinion in France.

NOTES

1. Among other explanations for this electoral verdict there were the sixteen candidates that especially fragmented the overall leftist vote, the Socialist Party already having had two incumbents fighting for the top seats (Lionel Jospin was already the Prime Minister and Jacques Chirac the President of the Republic), the replacement of the French franc by the Euro (a radical shift in the daily life of the French people—and an object of political communication studies—although its effects were denied by the academic literature).

2. The communication gaffes are generally retrospectively considered as such, after the defeat. The socialist Cambadélis highlighted the point that Lionel Jospin's anti-Chirac obsession could have been

counter-productive; Bacqué and Courtois deplored his "sin of pride" that led him and his advisors to exclusively consider the second round (see below).

3. Writing for an international audience implies a few precautions. The worst French evening newscasts remain far ahead of their crime obsessed U.S. counterparts. There are many reasons for this: the local economy of U.S. television, the more competitive U.S. television markets (the leading channel TF1 shares more than 50% of the advertising market and its domination explains most of the durable "seriousness" of the French evening newscasts), the strength of state owned television channels in France, etc. (see Benson & Hallin, 2007).

4. The president's legitimacy is supported by universal suffrage and direct election since 1965 with a two rounds scrutiny on a majority basis. The presidentialism is, however, only effective during non-cohabitation periods when the president assumes the most important governmental decisions and not only when he presides over the ministers' council every Wednesday: De Gaulle's 1958 constitution provided him with key responsibilities from the spoils system nominations giving greater power to the presidency while the French parliament remained weak by comparison.

5. A significant difference from the U.S. presidential election is that the French presidency results from a direct election in France, and therefore the popular vote cannot be threatened as it was in the 2002 U.S. presidential election. It provides a more powerful legitimacy to the French chief of the state (who has only to face his prime minister especially but not only when there is a coalition government).

6. Nevertheless, international comparisons of political tendencies are a difficult issue, since the categories of left and right do not refer to the same content. To intentionally take a provocative example, one should keep in mind that many topics such as the death penalty or limitation to abortion rights are only supported in France by extreme right leaders whereas in the U.S. even dominant liberal candidates can defend them. On the other hand, affirmative action, for example, has long been a quasi-taboo in the dominant French political sense, notably on the left, because of "republican faith." The division between U.S. Republicans and Democrats still isn't paralleled by the French opposition between the right and the left.

7. Interview with François-Henri de Virieu.

8. Présentation de l'organisation de la campagne par M. Peyreffite: ina pour tous.

9. Campagne électorale officielle Chirac 1988 : Ina pour tous.

10. A huge militant and, sometimes "hysterical" anti-Le Pen coverage (Mercier, 2003, p. 85) ; so obvious that the CSA itself was constrained to highlight the "critical tone" of the journalists against Le Pen and his supporters (CSA Rapport, 2002, p.28).

REFERENCES

Bacqué, R., & Courtois, G. (2003). Le choc des personnalités [The impact of personalities]. In P. Pascal & C. Ysmal (Eds.), *Le vote de tous les refus: Les élections présidentielle et législatives de 2002* [The vote of the refusers: The presidential and legislative elections of 2002] (pp. 89–99). Paris: Presses de Science-Po.

Baudis, D. (2006). *La letter du CSA* [Letter to the CSA]. No. 200.

Benson, R., & Hallin, D. (2007). How states, markets and globalization shape the news: French and U.S. national press, 1965–1997. *European Journal of Communication, 22*(1), 27–48.

Blumler, J. G, Gurevitch, M., & Cayrol, R. (1978). *Le télévision fait-elle l'élection?* [Does television make the election?]. Paris: Presses de la fondation nationale des sciences politiques.

Bourdieu, P. (1994). L'emprise du journalisme [The influence of journalism]. *Actes de la recherche en sciences sociales, 101–102*, 3–9.

Bourdon, J. (1994). *Haute fidélité: Pouvoirs et télévision 1935-1994* [High fidelity: Capacities and television, 1935–1994]. Paris: Seuil.

Bregman, D., & Missika, J-L. (1988). La campagne: la sélection des controverses politiques [The campaign: The selection of political controversies]. In E. Dupoirier & G. Grunberg (Ed.), *Mars 1986: la drôle de défaite de la gauche* [March 1986: The comic defeat of the left] (pp. 97–116). Paris: PUF.

Brugidou, M., & Mandran, N. (2002). Des campagnes électorales verrouillées, mais des coups de théâtre [The locked-in election campaigns, but with a dramatic turn of events]. *Revue politique et parlementaire, 1020–1021*, 34–60.

Cayrol, R. (1977). L'ORTF face aux élections de 1973 [The ORTF face of the 1973 elections]. *Revue française de science politique, 27*(4–5), 668–690

Cayrol, R., & Mercier, A. (Eds.) (2002, March-April). Télévision et élection [Television and the election]. *Dossiers de l'audiovisuel, 102*.

Champagne, P. (1990). *Faire l'opinion: Le nouveau jeu politique* [Creating opinion: The new political game]. Paris: Minuit.

Collovald, A. (1991). The "Bebete Show": Satire in the 1988 French campaign. In L. L. Kaid, J. Gerstlé, & K. R. Sanders (Eds.), *Mediated politics in two cultures: Presidential campaigning in the United States and France* (pp. 211–220). New York: Praeger.

Collovald, A. (2004). *Le populisme: Un dangereux contresens* [Populism: A dangerous, misinterpretation]. Broissieux: Le croquant.

Collovald, A., & Neveu, E. (1996). Les guignols ou la caricature en abîme [Puppets or the caricature of the abyss]. *Mots, 48*, 87–113.

Conseil Supérieur de l'Audiovisuel (CSA). (2002). *Rapport annuel*. Paris: CSA.

Converse, P. E., & Dupeux, G. (1966). De Gaulle and Eisenhower: The public image of the victorious general. In A. Campbell, P. Converse, W. E. Miller, & D. Stokes (Eds.), *Elections and the political order* (pp. 292–345). New York: Wiley.

Dagnaud, M., & Mehl, D. (1992). Patrons de chaînes [Owners of chains]. *Pouvoirs, 63*.

Darras, E. (2004). Media consecration of the political order. In. R. Benson & E. Neveu (Eds.), *Bourdieu and the media field* (pp. 156–173). Cambridge, UK: Polity Press.

Darras, E. (2005a). Et pouvoir de la télévision? Sornettes, vieilles lunes et nouvelles approches [The capacity of television? Twaddles, old moons and new approaches]. In A. Cohen, B. Lacroix, & R. Bernard (Eds.), *Les formes de l'activité politique: Eléments d'analyse sociologique (18è–20è siècles)*[The forms of political activity: Elements of sociological analysis (18th–20th centuries)] (pp. 457–484). Paris: PUF.

Darras, E. (2005b). La politique télévisée entre ruptures et continuités [Televised politics between abrupt change and continuity] *Recherches en communication, 25*(4), Université Catholique de Louvain (Belgium), 109–128.

Darras, E. (2006). La force supposée des *hardnews*. [The supposed force of hard news]. *Nouveaux dossiers de l'audiovisuel*. Paris: INA-La documentation française.

Duhamel, O. (1996). *Election présidentielle: le moment décisif in SOFRES, L'Etat de l'opinion* [Presidential election: The decisive moment in SOFRES, the state of opinion]. Paris: Seuil.

Garrigou, A. (1989). Conjoncture politique et le vote [Political conjecture and the vote]. In D. Gaxie (Ed.), *L'explication du vote* [An explanation of the vote] (pp. 357–385). Paris: Presses de la fondation nationale des sciences politiques.

Gaxie, D. (1978). *Le cens caché* [The hidden census]. Paris: Seuil.

Gaxie, D. (Ed.) (1989). *L'explication du vote* [An explanation of the vote]. Paris: Presses de la fondation nationale des sciences politiques.

Gaxie, D. (2002). Appréhensions du politique et mobilisations des expériences sociales [Political apprehensions and mobilization of social experiences]. *Revue française de science politique, 52*(2–3), 145–178.

Gaxie, D. (2003). Une construction médiatique du spectacle politique? Réalité et limites de la contribution des médias au développement des perceptions négatives du politique [Media construction of the political spectacle? Reality and limits of the media contribution to the development of negative political perceptions]. In J. Lagroye (Ed.), *La politisation* [The politization]. Paris: Belin.

Gaxie, D., & Lehingue, P. (1984). *Enjeux municipaux: La constitution des enjeux politiques dans un eélection municipale* [Municipal stakes: The nature of the political stakes in a municipal election]. Paris: PUF, CURAPP.

Gerstlé, J. (1995). La dynamique nationale d'une campagne européenne [The national dynamic of the European campaign]. In P. Perrineau & C. Ysmal (Eds.), *Le vote des douze. Les élection européennes de juin* [The vote of twelve: The European elections of June 1994] (pp. 203–228). Paris: Presses de Science-Po.

Gerstlé, J. (1996). L'information et la sensibilité des électeurs à la conjoncture [Information about and sensitivity of the voters to the economic situation]. *Revue française de science politique, 46*(5), 731–752.

Gerstlé, J. (1997). La persuasion de l'actualité télévisée [The persuasiveness of television news]. *Politix/ Travaux de sciences politiques, 10,* 81–96.

Gerstlé, J. (2003). Une fenêtre d'opportunité électorale [A window of election opportunity]. In P. Perrineau & C. Ysmal (Eds,). *Le vote de tous les refus. Les élections présidentielle et législatives de 2002* [The denial vote: The presidential and legislative elections of 2002] (pp. 29–52). Paris: Presses de Science-Po.

Gerstlé, J., Davis. D. R., & Duhamel, O. (1991). Television coverage of the presidential campaigns in the United States and France. In L. L. Kaid, J. Gerstlé, & K. R. Sanders (Eds). *Mediated politics in two cultures: Presidential campaigning in the United States and France* (pp. 119–143). New York: Praeger. Also reprinted in French in La couverture télévisée des campagnes présidentielles. L'élection de 1988 aux Etats-Unis et en France [Television coverage of the presidential campaigns: The election of 1988 in the United States and France]. *Pouvoirs, 63*(1991), 53–69.

Gerstlé, J., & Piar, C. (2005). La campagne des régionales dans l'information télévisée. Le cadrage national d'un scrutin local [Television coverage of regional campaigns: The national framing of a local poll]. In B. Dolez, A. Laurent, & C. du Patriat (Eds.), *Le vote rebelle. Les élections régionales des 21 et 28 mars 2004* [The protest vote: The regional elections of 21 and 28 March 2004]. Dijon: Presses Universitaires de Dijon.

Gerstlé, J., Semetko, H. A., Schoenbach, K., & Vila, M. (2001). The faltering Europeanization of national campaigns. In G. Grunberg, P. Perrineau, & C. Ysmal (Eds.), *Europe at the polls, The European elections of 1999* (pp. 59–77). New York: Palgrave.

Grunberg, G., & Mayer, N. (2002). *La démocratie à l'épreuve: Une nouvelle approche de l'opinion* [The test of democracy: A new approach to opinion]. Paris: Presses de Science-Po.

Gurevitch, M., & Blumler, J. G. (1990). Political communication systems and democratic values. In J. Lichtenberg (Ed.), *Democracy and the mass media* (pp. 269–289). New York: Cambridge University Press.

Haiman, F. S. (1991). A tale of two countries: Media and messages of the 1988 Frecnh and American presidental campaings. In L. L. Kaid, J. Gerstle, & K. Sanders (Eds.), *Mediated politics in two cultures: Presidential campaigning in the US and France.* New York: Praeger.

Hallin, D. C., & Mancini, P. (2004). *Comparing media systems. Three models of media and politics.* Cambridge, UK: Cambridge University Press.

Kaid, L. L., Gerstlé, J., & Sanders, K. R. (Eds.). (1991). *Mediated politics in two cultures: Presidential campaigning in the United States and France.* New York: Praeger.

Kaid, L. L., & Holtz-Bacha, C. (Eds.) (1995). *Political advertising in western democracies: Parties and candidates on television.* Thousand Oaks, CA: Sage.

Kiewet, R. D. (1981). Policy oriented voting in response to economic issues. *American Political Science Review, 75*(2), 448–459.

Legavre, J-B. (1996). D'un groupe à l'autre: Le passage de l'expertise en communication à la pratique professionnelle [From one group to another: The passing of communication expertise to professional practitioners]. *Politix, 9*(35), 131–148.

Le Bart, C., & Lefebvre, R. (Eds.). (2005). *La proximité en politique* [Proximity in politics]. Rennes: PUR.

Le Bohec, J. (1997). *Les rapports presse-politique. Mise au point d'une typologie idéale* [The press-policy connection: The development of an ideal typology]. Paris: L'Harmattan.

Le Bohec, J. (2005). *Sociologie du phénomène Le Pen* [Sociology of the Le Pen phenomenon].Paris: La découverte.

Le Bohec, J. (2007). *Télévision et élections* [Television and elections]. Grenoble: Presses Universitaires de Grenoble.

Le Gall, G. (1994). Les Français et la sécurité [The French and security]. In *SOFRES, L'Etat de l'opinion* [The state of opinion] (pp. 117–139). Paris: Seuil.

Le Grignou, B., & Neveu, E. (1993). Intimités publiques: Les dynamiques de la politique à la télévision [Public intimacies: The dynamics of politics on television]. *Revue française de science politique, 43*(6), 940–969.

Lehingue, P. (2003). L'objectivation statistique des électorats: que savons-nous des électeurs du front national? [The statistical objectivation of the electorate: How does it affect the National Front electorate?]. In P. Lagroye (Ed.), *La politisation* [The politization] (pp. 247–278). Paris: Belin.

Lehingue, P. (2007). *Subunda. Coups de sonde dans l'océan des sondages* [Subunda: Opinion soundings in an ocean of polls]. Bellecombe-en-Bauges: Le croquant.

Mayer, N. (2007). Comment Nicolas Sarkozy a rétréci l'électorat Le Pen [How Nicolas Sarkozy shrank Le Pen's electorat]. *Revue française de science politique, 57*(3–4), 429–445.

Mercier, A. (2003). Les médias en campagne [The media in the campaign]. In P. Perrineau & C. Ysmal (Eds.), *Le vote de tous les refus: Les élections présidentielle et législatives de 2002* [The vote of the refusers: The presidential and legislative elections of 2002] (pp. 53–102). Paris: Presses de Science-Po.

Neveu, E, (1997). Des questions "jamais entendues." Crise et renouvellements du journalisme politique à la télévision? [Unasked questions: Crisis and renewal of political journalism on television?]. *Politix, 10*(37), 25–56.

Neveu, E. (1998). Media and politics in French political science. *European Journal of Political Research, 33*(4), 439–458.

Neveu, E. (1999). Politics on French television. Towards a renewal of political journalism and debate frames? *European Journal of Communication, 14:* 379–409.

Neveu, E. (2001). *Sociologie du journalisme* [Sociology of journalism]. Paris: La découverte.

Norris, P. (2000). *A virtuous circle: Political communications in postindustrial societies.* Cambridge, UK: Cambridge University Press.

Offerlé, M. (1993). *Un homme, une voix? Histoire du suffrage universe* [One man, one vote: History of universal suffrage]. Paris: Gallimard.

Offerlé, M. (2007, April 29-30). Interview in *Le Monde,* p. 9.

Piar, C., & Gerstlé, J. (2008). Les campagnes dans l'information télévisée : la structuration de l'agenda et ses consequences [The campaign in televised information: The agenda structure and its consequences[. In P. Perrineau (Ed.), *Le vote de la rupture. Les élections présidentielle et législatives de 2007* [The ruptured vote: The presidential and legislative elections of 2007]. Paris: Presses de Sciences Po.

Piar, C. (2007). Images des candidats et enjeux de la campagne [Images of the candidates and the campaign stakes]. In P. Perrineau (Ed.), *Atlas électoral* [Election atlas] (pp. 101–106). Paris: Presses de Sciences-Po.

Restier-Melleray, C. (2002). *Que sont devenues nos campagnes électorales?* [What happened to our election campaigns?]. Pessac: Presses Universitaires de Bordeaux,

Riutord, P. (2004). *Sociologie de la communication* politique [Sociology of political communication]. Paris: La découverte.

Serfaty, V. (Ed.). (2002). *L'Internet en politique. Des Etats-Unis à l'Europe* [The Internet in politics: The United States and Europe]. Strasbourg: Presses Universitaires de Strasbourg.

Swanson, D. (1991). Theoretical dimensions of the U.S.–French presidential campaign studies. In L. L. Kaid, J. Gerstlé, & K. R. Sanders (Eds.), *Mediated politics in two cultures: Presidential campaigning in the United States and France* (pp. 9–23). New York: Praeger.

Télérama, 2729, 30 April 2002.

Télérama, 2730, 7 May 2002.

Traïni, C. (Ed.) (2004). *Vote en PACA. Les élections 2002 en Provence-Alpes-Côte d'Azur,* [The vote in PACA: The 2002 elections in Provence-Alpes-Côte d'Azur]. Paris: Karthala.

Vedel, T. (2007). Les électeurs et les médias [The voters and the media]. In P. Perrineau (Ed.), *Atlas électoral* [Electoral atlas] (pp. 115–118). Paris: Presses de Sciences-Po.

7

Australia: Gladiatorial Parties and Volatile Media in a Stable Polity

Rodney Tiffen

Australia is one of only a handful of countries that have been democracies continuously since the beginning of the twentieth century. When the Federation of Australia was formed, it took most of its traditions from the British colonisers, and embraced central tenets of the Westminster tradition, such as a parliamentary system based upon single member electorates. As it represented the consolidation of six self-governing colonies, it also looked to the other major English-speaking democracy, the United States, and adopted a federal system and a strongly bi-cameral system with a Senate which had equal legislative powers with the House of Representatives. The resulting hybrid has sometimes been dubbed the Washminster mutation (Thompson, 1980).

Like Britain, the party enjoying a parliamentary majority forms the Government, the Cabinet is the centre of executive power, and ministers are accountable to Parliament on a continuing basis. Both countries have essentially two-sided party systems; in Australia's case the Labor versus anti-Labor party system being in key respects constant since 1910 (Butler, 1997; Jaensch, 1992). On the one side has been a more conservative party, gaining its major electoral support from the middle classes and the bulk of its financial support from business. On the other has been a more left wing, social democratic party, gaining its core electoral support from the working class and its most constant financial support from the trade unions. In contrast to the British Conservatives, the conservative side of politics in Australia is always a coalition. The National Party began life as the Country Party in the 1920s to represent rural interests. Since World War II, at the federal level, it has always operated in tandem with the Liberal Party, the major party on the conservative side. Their relationship is much closer than a coalition between two independent parties. Giovanni Sartori (1976) describes it as a coalescence.

The Australian political system is in Lijphart's terms (1999) a majoritarian democracy, although with some important qualifications. An Australian government enjoying majority support in the House of Representatives does not have the unfettered power of the idealised Westminster model. First, in the federal system it shares a division of powers with state governments. Second, the two houses of parliament—the House of Representatives and the Senate—have equal powers, and they are elected on different bases: the latter having an equal number of senators from each state based on a proportional representation, multi-member electoral system. The government therefore often lacks a majority in the upper house and must negotiate to get its legislation passed.

There is another important difference between Australia and other countries with single member electorates such as Britain, Canada, and the United States. In those plurality systems, the candidate with the largest vote wins, irrespective of whether it is a majority or not. The voter casts a single vote. If he or she supports a minority candidate, then two choices must be made: a preferential one about whom to support, and a strategic one about whether that would mean wasting their vote by casting it for someone with no realistic chance of winning. In the Australian preferential system, such a voter also gets the opportunity to express their second (and subsequent) preferences. So they can vote for a minority candidate either out of conviction or as a protest vote, and then their second preference will still help to decide who wins, because the counting of preferences continues until one candidate has reached 50% of the vote. This majority preferential voting (sometimes called the alternative vote) is friendlier to minor parties than the Anglo-American first past the post systems. Moreover, the proportional representation voting system in the Senate also gives minor parties the chance of winning seats, and perhaps holding the balance of power.

Table 7.1 illuminates several central characteristics of Australian electoral competition. Perhaps most basic is the sheer number of elections. Among established democracies, only Denmark had as many in the same period (Tiffen & Gittins, 2004), and Denmark comes from the other

TABLE 7.1
Australian House of Representatives Elections 1946-2004

Year	Winning party	Winning leader	LNP primary vote %	ALP primary vote %	Total other %	Winner: loser two party preferred %*	Winner's % seats	Swing to government (% 2PP)*
1946	ALP	Chifley	43.7	49.7	6.6	53.7: 46.3	58.1	- 5.4
1949	LNP	Menzies	50.3	46.0	3.7	51.0: 49.0	61.2	- 4.7
1951	LNP	Menzies	50.3	47.7	2.0	50.7: 49.3	57.0	- 0.3
1954	LNP	Menzies	47.1	50.0	2.9	49.3: 50.7	52.9	- 1.4
1955	LNP	Menzies	47.6	44.6	7.8	54.2: 45.8	61.5	+ 4.9
1958	LNP	Menzies	46.5	42.8	10.6	54.1: 45.9	65.8	- 0.1
1961	LNP	Menzies	42.1	47.9	10.0	49.5: 50.5	50.8	- 4.6
1963	LNP	Menzies	46.0	45.5	8.5	52.6: 47.4	59.0	+ 3.1
1966	LNP	Holt	50.0	40.0	10.0	56.9: 43.1	66.1	+ 4.3
1969	LNP	Gorton	43.4	47.0	10.6	49.8: 50.2	52.8	- 7.1
1972	ALP	Whitlam	41.5	49.8	8.9	52.7: 47.3	53.6	- 2.5
1974	ALP	Whitlam	45.7	49.3	5.0	51.7: 48.3	52.0	- 1.0
1975	LNP	Fraser	53.1	42.8	4.1	55.7: 44.3	71.7	- 7.4
1977	LNP	Fraser	48.1	39.6	12.3	54.6: 45.4	69.4	- 1.1
1980	LNP	Fraser	46.3	45.1	8.6	50.4: 49.6	59.2	- 4.2
1983	ALP	Hawke	43.6	49.5	6.9	53.2: 46.8	60.0	- 3.6
1984	ALP	Hawke	45.0	47.5	7.4	51.8: 48.2	55.4	- 1.4
1987	ALP	Hawke	46.1	45.8	8.1	50.8: 49.2	58.1	- 1.0
1990	ALP	Hawke	43.4	39.4	17.2	49.9: 50.1	52.7	- 0.9
1993	ALP	Keating	44.3	44.9	10.9	51.4: 48.6	54.4	+ 1.5
1996	LNP	Howard	46.9	38.8	14.3	53.6: 46.4	62.8	- 5.0
1998	LNP	Howard	39.2	40.1	20.7	48.9: 51.1	54.1	- 4.7
2001	LNP	Howard	42.7	37.8	19.5	51.0: 49.0	54.0	+ 2.1
2004	LNP	Howard	46.7	37.6	15.7	52.7: 47.3	58.0	+ 1.7

Note: ALP = Australian Labor Party, LNP = Liberal and National Parties.
* For explanation of the two-party preferred vote (2PP), see text. This data is drawn principally from the electoral websites of Peter Brent (2007), Campbell Sharman (2007), Antony Green (2007) and the AEC (2007).

end of Lijphart's spectrum being a multi-party system with many coalition and minority govern-ments resulting in frequent dissolutions of parliament. In Australia's case, the key reason for the frequency of elections is that the maximum election interval is only three years, whereas for most other democracies it is four years or more. Australian elections can be even more frequent for several reasons. One stems from the peculiar constitutional provisions laid down for the two houses, and the wish to have elections for both simultaneously. Moreover, if the government's legislative program is thwarted in the Senate, the Prime Minister has considerable latitude in how to respond, including seeking a fresh mandate. So elections are often called early to try to win a political advantage.

A second aspect that emerges from the table is the relative infrequency of changes of gov-ernment. As columns two and three show, only five of these 24 elections resulted in one party displacing the other. After the wartime Labor Governments of Curtin and Chifley, the Liberal coalition governments of Sir Robert Menzies (Prime Minister 1949–1966) and his successors lasted 23 years. Then came the short and dramatic interlude of the Whitlam Labor government (1972–1975). But since then there has been a return to long-lasting governments: the Fraser Gov-ernment (1975–1983) lasted just over seven years, the Hawke and Keating Labor governments lasted 13 years (1983–1996), while the Howard Government lasted from 1996 to 2007.

The stability of outcomes is qualified by two aspects, however. One is that in almost three quarters of the elections the swing was against the government. On only 7 of 24 occasions did the government improve its position, either in seats won or percentage of the votes. Four of these seven occurred during the long period of Liberal dominance from 1949 on, and they occurred in the five elections following the momentous Labor Party split in 1955. In the 40 or more years since 1966, it has occurred only three times. In 1993, Prime Minister Keating, facing what had been called an unwinnable election, mounted a very effective scare campaign against the Liber-als' economic package labeled "fightback." Then in 2001 and 2004, Prime Minister Howard increased his share of the vote. In 2001 the combination of the anti-asylum seeker campaign and the September 11 attacks allowed him to reverse his electoral fortunes, which had looked precarious. In 2004, again after the election first looked to be close, Howard increased his lead substantially as polling day neared, with fears about the Labor opposition increasing. Thus, in 24 elections, the government only changed five times, but the incumbent only improved its posi-tion seven times. So the "normal" Australian election (12 out of 24) involves a swing against the government but not sufficient to unseat it.

Another central feature revealed by Table 7.1 is the closeness of the competition. Column seven reports the result in terms of two-party preferred vote percentages. The "two-party pre-ferred" vote is a calculation, originally devised by Malcolm Mackerras, to take account of the two primary facts about Australian elections: (1) that it is a preferential voting system in which the distribution of second preference votes for minor parties may be crucial; and (2) that the basic question in deciding who forms a government is which side—Labor or LNP—has the majority. In 13 of the 24 elections, the two-party preferred vote was 52:48 or closer, and in 7 of the 10 elec-tions since 1980 it has been this close. A small shift of votes can thus change the outcome of an election. Table 7.1 also reveals that in five elections, the winning side actually received just under 50% of the two-party preferred vote, and so except for the distribution of votes seats would have been lost. All these elections (1954, 1961, 1969, 1990, and 1998) involved an incumbent govern-ment, actually being less preferred than its opponent, but managing to win because it retained its most vulnerable seats.

The two-sided nature of the system is evidenced not only by the two major parties always forming the government, but also by their share of the vote. In 13 of the 24 elections, the two major blocs received more than 90% of all votes. However, in the years between 1946 and 1987, the average vote for minor parties and independent candidates to the House was less than 10%, but since 1990 voting for other candidates (Greens, Australian Democrats, One Nation, and independents) has averaged 16%, showing an increasing disillusion with the major parties. Indeed the table only gives the House of Representatives results, and voting for minor parties is usually greater in the Senate.

This institutional and electoral context reveals two characteristics fundamental to understanding the media's role in Australian elections. One is the intensity of the two-sided contest, fanned by the frequency and closeness of elections. The two-sided battle between Labor and non-Labor to form a government is a zero-sum, winner-take-all game, resolved by public opinion (Tiffen, 1989). It is zero-sum in that elections involve preferential rather than absolute judgements. Either one party or the other will form the next government, and as one becomes more likely to succeed, the other necessarily becomes less so. No win-win outcome is possible. Moreover the prize is indivisible. Whatever the margin, the victor forms government and the loser is in opposition. It is not a situation conducive to a strong sense of fair play. Winning by whatever means is preferable to losing nobly. It is the party contest as such which generates the conflicting interests, irrespective of the parties' differing social bases or policy clashes. It is a conflict in which there are always incentives to find profitable points of opposition, to overstate differences, and where there are few pressures towards restraint.

The second characteristic is that the campaign period has become more crucial in determining electoral victory. Not only is the winning margin typically narrow, but during almost all electoral cycles over the last 30 years, there have been extended periods when the opposition is in front, and when election campaigns begin there is typically a large pool of undecided voters, whose decisions could easily change the result one way or the other. In the 1940s Prime Minister Ben Chifley said that the poll that counts is the one six months before the election. Chifley, diffident about campaigning even by the standards of his own age, practised what he preached. He was so unconcerned with selling his government's policies that in the 1949 election he recorded his policy speech in a studio rather than at a public meeting, and used only 36 minutes of the hour's broadcast time allotted to him (Tiffen, 1989). In the four election campaigns in the 1990s, the proportion claiming they decided how to vote during the election campaign itself ranged between 32 and 42% (McAllister, 2002). The head of the leading public opinion company, Newspoll, wrote that their 'poll taken after the (2004) federal election found that 49% of voters said they did not finally decide who to vote for until the month before the election, including 30% who said they decided in the final week' (Lebovic, 2006). These figures almost certainly exaggerate the actual degree of indecision, but they are indicative that the electoral contest is characterised by a greater proportion of very softly committed voters, allowing more pronounced and sudden swings than in earlier periods. Thus, the influence of the election campaign on the late deciders can be critical to electoral success.

AUSTRALIAN MEDIA INSTITUTIONS AND ELECTION CAMPAIGNING

Just as Australia's political institutions are a Washminster mutation, so its media institutions and policies reflect an Anglo-American hybrid. Whereas Britain's broadcasting heritage began as a public service monopoly, and America had a wholly commercial structure, Australia adopted a mixed system in radio, with the ABC (Australian Broadcasting Commission, now Corporation) modelled on the BBC (Inglis, 1982), but sharing the airwaves with several commercial stations in each city. When television was introduced in 1956, Britain had moved to a mixed system, although one still with public service dominance. Australia adopted a mixed system, but with commercial dominance. Television began with one public service channel, the ABC, and two commercial channels. A third commercial channel in the four biggest cities was begun in 1964. In 1980, a second public channel, the SBS (Special Broadcasting Service), was set up with a mandate as a multi-cultural broadcaster, to cater to the large proportion of immigrants in the Australian population, many of them from non-English speaking backgrounds. In very rough terms, the three commercial channels between them account for over 80% of the prime time audience, the ABC for perhaps 15%, and SBS for around 3%. Of course these figures are not constant, and, for example, over 80% of viewers tune to the ABC at some time each week.

Australian television channels were bound by the Broadcasting Act to be impartial. Just as importantly, TV news services have audiences that are broadly split 50-50 in terms of party support, which means that commercial incentives broadly align with what were the official regulations. So in the prime time news bulletins, there has rarely been overt editorialising or politically loaded commentaries. Neither, however, has there ever been any attempt at regulating the media's political performance. Moreover, since the introduction of the Broadcasting Services Act in 1992 (Davies & Spurgeon, 1992), with its greater emphasis on co-regulation and self-regulation, the capacity for any enforcement is greatly reduced.

Indeed, Australian election campaigning and election news coverage is most remarkable for the lack of regulations. The conduct of the elections themselves is of course subject to detailed rules, the most important being that, within some constraints, the Prime Minister has the right to call the election on the date he chooses. The statutory minimum campaign period for Australian elections is 33 days (Australian Electoral Commission, 2007). Occasionally there is a longer campaign, but the usual pattern is for the Prime Minister to call an election one weekend for a Saturday five weeks ahead.

There are no special restrictions on campaign reporting. Public opinion polls, for example, can be reported right up to polling day, and normally are. This is not as sensitive as in some other countries, because with Australia's compulsory voting, they will not have an influence on turnout, although there is always a concern among political leaders that a strong lead in the polls may induce a backlash. Australia used to have restrictions forbidding any election coverage on radio and television in the last three days of the election. This was abandoned as unrealistic in the 1980s, although it still applies to election advertising in broadcasting.

Australia is also one of the democracies most permissive about political advertising. It is possible for political parties to buy unlimited amounts of advertising space in the media. The net result is that election campaigning has become ever more expensive. The coalition parties and the Labor Party both now raise more than $100 million each in a three-year electoral cycle (Young & Tham, 2006). Associated entities used by the parties raise another 50% on top of this (Young & Tham, 2006). Importantly, the major parties are buttressed by larger degrees of state subventions, with public subsidies for campaigning. This has been accompanied by more regulations about public disclosure of private donations, although the loopholes are still considerable.

Professionalism of Campaigning

James Q Wilson (1980) argued that "organisations in conflict with each other come to resemble each other." Not surprisingly, both major parties have thus changed in similar directions in their internal organisation. This is not an argument about the disputed issue of policy convergence (Goot, 2004; Lavelle 2004; Marsh, 2006), but rather that both major parties are overwhelmingly guided by electoral pragmatism, and they have also developed their campaigning capacities in similar ways. The leaders' staffs, national secretariats, pollsters, and advertisers form centralised, leader-centred teams professionally guiding both overall marketing strategies and daily tactics, with speedy responses to the other side. Both sides are guided by marketing imperatives based upon substantial and sophisticated polling data. Parties' relations to their pollsters (Mills, 1986), and their use of those polls, in the presentation, timing, and even framing of policies has become steadily more sophisticated. Not only is campaign planning more thorough, but both parties have also developed an accelerating ability to respond to developments during the campaign, in advertising and leaders' rhetoric.

Australian political parties have followed a similar broad trajectory to other liberal democracies (Blyth & Katz 2005; Katz, 1996; Ward, 2006), from loose groupings of individuals to mass parties, then to 'catch-all parties', where parties reached out from their social bases to maximise their vote, and finally to 'cartel parties', where party membership has substantially eroded, campaigning has become more centralised and capital-intensive, and the electoral appeals of both parties is to managerial efficiency as much as their articulation of policy differences. The term *cartel party* is appropriate in that the capital intensive nature of contemporary party competition and the various means of state support for parties with a strong parliamentary presence create barriers for minor parties and newcomers. However, it is at the same time inappropriate because in a commercial market a company enjoying 45% of market share would be reaping large profits, but a political party is failing in its central purpose, to win government. Commercial cartels are often marked by cosy, constrained competition. In contrast, the two-sided contest between the major political parties has become ever more ruthless.

Not only do both major parties subordinate all other concerns to the pursuit of electoral victory; both have also accepted some common presumptions about the surest route to success. Both are chasing the same swinging voters. Unlike most other democracies, Australia has compulsory voting (Tiffen & Gittins, 2004). The path to victory in the 2004 American election, attributed to President Bush's strategist Karl Rove, of mobilising the base is not possible in Australia, as the base for both parties will vote anyway. The key to victory is appealing to the swinging and uncommitted voters, and although this group is more heterogeneous than sometimes claimed, both parties share a common view of their dominant characteristics. This was articulated most graphically in a leaked memo from Labor opinion pollster Rod Cameron (Kelly, 1984) written in the lead-up to the 1980 election.

> The people who determine elections in this country are the least interested and the least informed about politics. You're talking about people who vote on whims. The next election will be decided solely on the votes of the 15 per cent of "swingers" who show any willingness to change.... They are basically ignorant and indifferent about politics. They vote on superficial, ill-informed and generally selfish reasons.

In similar vein, the Liberals' planning for the 1996 campaign targeted "Phil and Jenny," an archetypal couple, married for eight years, worried about their mortgage, not much interested in politics, resentful of the taxes they had to pay, and that "they seemed to be carrying everyone else." The punch line was "they would vote against the party they despised most rather than for the party they liked most" (Williams, 1997, pp. 64–65).

This view of swinging voters has two central consequences for the style of parties' campaigning. One is that the projection of leader images is more important than detailed policy exposition. The brevity of media formats combines with the short attention span attributed to swinging voters to emphasise the need for sharpness rather than depth. The other is that it is easier to persuade swinging voters to vote against the other side than for themselves, to convince them of the defects of their opponents rather than of their own virtue. Because swinging voters are cynical about politics they are sceptical about what social improvements governments will achieve, but fearful about how much harm they might do. Moreover, because embarrassments and unfavourable accusations are more likely to develop into big, running stories in the media than any conceivable positive policy announcement, parties have decided that negative appeals are more potent than positive ones.

Campaigning in the Media Arena

The media are an intense, assertive, and volatile presence on the political stage, the central arena for election campaigning. Media skills are indispensable for a leader and party to succeed. However, over the last generation the increase in resources devoted by parties to election campaigning has increased far more than those committed by the media to covering the campaign. Moreover, their clarity of purpose—the wish to be elected and to do whatever is needed to achieve that—is much clearer than the media's.

Both parties have made central to their planning the requirements of the media-centred campaign. The greater proportion of the campaign consists of events designed solely for the media. The local public meeting has dwindled in importance, not only because it reaches only small numbers, with those attending more likely to be the already committed, but also because of the wish to minimise the possibilities for embarrassment, such as the appearance of dissent.

The prime-time evening TV news reaches the largest single audience, so it is where political leaders place most emphasis (Lloyd, 1997). During an election campaign, coverage of the leaders by the main media is all but obligatory. The parties' main aim then is to determine that that coverage will focus where they want it. Their itineraries have thus been radically transformed. While many aspects of electioneering have become ever more frantic, leaders' schedules have become somewhat less so. The pace of leaders' campaigning probably reached its peak in the 1970s, when media logistics and the national networking of TV news were less developed. In 1974, for example, both leaders Whitlam and Snedden maintained punishing schedules. By 1987 Prime Minister Hawke had "basically one major engagement per day" usually in a telegenic setting. In contrast Opposition Leader Howard still had a program packed with engagements, with constant last-minute cancellations and changes, "a nightmare for the TV crews" and with "little control over the pictures that appear on that night's television news bulletins" (Tiffen, 1989). By the time he became prime minister nine years later, it was a lesson Howard had learned thoroughly (Williams, 1997).

He also learned another lesson. In the middle of the 1987 campaign, Australian Pat Cash won Wimbledon, which was decided somewhat after midnight. Howard had gone to bed, but Hawke stayed up and watched, of course surrounded by TV crews in his motel room, so that the nation could share his joy at Cash's victory (Tiffen, 1989). As Prime Minister, like Hawke, Howard saw a major part of his job as being the country's most visible sports fan, especially in moments of Australian victory.

The parties have become far more skilful in calculating which avenues will give them access to the greatest audiences, but with the minimum amount of critical scrutiny. There is much effort devoted to finding "lighter" outlets, such as on pop music programs and chat shows, where the candidate can appear human, without awkward probing. Party leaders have realised that securing positive news coverage is not the same as making a favourable impression on journalists. As a result, there is as much effort in seeking to bypass the press gallery, or to neutralise them into being passive ciphers for the messages they want to convey, as to persuade them.

A central aspect of the parties' media planning concerns the rhythms needed for a five week campaign, aiming to maximise their vote on election day, and ensuring that there is a fresh supply during the whole period, while making sure that on any one day the focus is on the story the party wants and not some negative distraction. Rationing the news is as important as supplying it.

One consequence is that the policy speech has declined in importance, because it is does not fit the timing imperatives of the media campaign: to spread news generating announcements across the whole campaign, rather than concentrate them in one occasion. Thus the terminology has changed from policy speech to campaign launch, but even that is a misnomer, as they have edged ever closer to election day itself, hoping to maximise electoral impact. In the last five elections, the party launches have on average been just 10 days before the vote, as opposed to 21 days in earlier decades.

The biggest television audience for any single campaign event is the debate between the leaders. At least one of these has been held in each election since 1987. But there is always considerable shadow play about the arrangements, with the incumbent, particularly if he or she is likely to win, typically reluctant to have more than one and to want it as far out from the election as possible. Whatever its defects, the debate is the only occasion on which both leaders appear on an equal footing, and with at least some semblance of mutual engagement and dialogue.

AUSTRALIAN ELECTION NEWS COVERAGE

Although the biggest audience for any single campaign event is the televised debate between the party leaders, the day to day coverage is probably more important in the long run for how people perceive the competing parties, their policies, and their prospects. In Australia as elsewhere, modern politics is mediated politics. Thus, in the following sections different aspects of the election news coverage will be described and discussed.

Partisan Impacts on Election Campaigns

As in other democracies the most publicly debated media impacts concern allegations of partisan bias. Unlike television, the press has a long history of partisan support and faces few legal inhibitions in its expression. Concern with partisan bias in the press is heightened by the concentrated nature of Australian press ownership and structure. In newspaper structure, demography is to some extent destiny. In countries such as Britain, France, and Japan the largest city is also the political capital and the centre of commercial and cultural life, and so the capital city press tends to be the national press, and these national newspapers tend to have more intense competition, and are relatively large enterprises. In contrast, in Australia the political capital is not the largest city, or the commercial or cultural centre. Instead of a national press, with a segmented, competitive market, local monopolies or very circumscribed competition is the common pattern. Trends over the decades have greatly narrowed the range of competition in each city market. Indeed no afternoon newspapers remain, and only in the two largest cities, Sydney and Melbourne, are there locally produced competing morning newspapers. Elsewhere monopoly reigns, although there are two nationally circulating newspapers, politically important, but with very limited circulation in each major city.

Not only is the Australian newspaper market characterised by local monopolies or near-monopolies—the overall level of ownership concentration is the greatest among Western democracies (Tiffen & Gittins, 2004). Newspapers owned by Rupert Murdoch's News Limited account for around two thirds of metropolitan daily newspaper circulation. Of the 11 daily titles, Murdoch owns 6, and has the largest circulating newspaper in every major city except Perth and Canberra.

Murdoch, who became an American citizen in the 1980s to enable him to enter the television market there, is a controversial figure in all countries in which he operates (Chenoweth, 2001; Page, 2003).

For most of Australia's history that editorial support has gone to the Liberals (Lee, 1992). Before 1983, the major exceptions were the Fairfax press in 1961 (Souter, 1981) and the Murdoch press in 1972 (Page, 2003). After the election of the Hawke Government in 1983 the balance of partisan support shifted, and for the next several elections Labor enjoyed at least conditional support or neutrality from most of the major papers. Under Keating, when Labor's electoral fortunes had gone into decline, most papers swung back to the Liberals, and Howard has enjoyed strong majority editorial support in all the elections he has faced since 1996.

What is less amenable to easy measurement, but more important, is how the editorial partisanship manifests itself. British scholars have documented the changing trends best. Seymour-Ure (1974) saw a steady decline in the degree of partisanship leading into the 1970s, but after Murdoch's embrace of Thatcher there was both a very heavily right-skewed press and an increasing partisan vociferousness (Tunstall, 1996). This development reached its peak in 1992, after her departure, with the biggest selling tabloid claiming that "It was the Sun who won it." From the election of Blair on, however, some have seen the Tory press replaced by the Tony press (Deacon & Wring, 2002).

The Australian picture is less neat. The peak of partisanship in the last 40 years was reached with the Murdoch press's campaign against the Whitlam Government in 1975. The Murdoch press remained virulently anti-Labor for the next seven years, paralleling its embrace of conservative parties in Britain and the United States. In recent years, there have been some claims by Labor that the Murdoch press is still biased against it, although the nature of media politics now is that a company like Murdoch's also has an interest in being perceived as supportive of whoever wins the election.

Simms and Bolger (2000) examined the number of positive, negative, and balanced editorials about the parties in the 1998 election. While most papers supported the re-election of Howard's conservative coalition, in all papers' editorials, balanced and negative commentary outweighed positive comments. In the case of the *Sydney Morning Herald*, there was no correlation between its editorial stance and the content of its front-page election coverage. In 2004 Simms (2005) replicated the exercise, finding that as the election neared and the likely result became clearer the editorial support for the coalition became more clear-cut.

The most valuable set of polling data on Australian elections comes from the Australian Electoral Survey, conducted on fairly large samples for every federal election since 1987. However, none of the surveys has found a strong correlation between party vote and any patterns of media consumption.

Nevertheless, the media environment is not the same for the two major parties. Apart from editorial endorsements, and the extent to which they carry into news judgements, the Liberals carry the weight of opinion in two other media forums. Talk radio, which has become an increasingly important political forum in recent decades, is dominated on commercial radio by strongly conservative commentators, including some who openly parade their partisanship (Masters, 2006). Moreover, among regular columnists in daily newspapers there is a clear weighting to the right. Both of these resemble what David Brock (2002) in America has termed the Republican noise machine.

On the other side, conservatives charge that the ABC and the Canberra Press Gallery have a liberal left bias. The charges against the press were strongest during the period of the Hawke-Keating governments (Parker, 1990). Nevertheless, such charges are on a different level. They are generally about subtle influences on judgements of newsworthiness or interpretations of the political meaning of events, of broad political sympathies and world-views, rather than any ongoing commitment to a party or a wish to publicly embrace an ideology.

Interestingly the most debated cases, such as 1972 and 1975, are ones where the electoral tide was flowing so strongly that press partisanship would likely not have had any impact on the result. More interesting are the impacts on say the 1980 election, where the Murdoch press's news priorities, and its escalation of the Liberals' theme of Labor's secret wealth tax plans, may have inhibited the swing towards that party in what was a very close election (Goot, 1983). Nevertheless, although many 'biases' occur which might not balance each other out, and which may sometimes have some electoral impact, the most important impact of the media on elections is not in partisanship, but in their interaction with campaigning processes.

The Advantages of Incumbency

The deliberate exercise of power is not the most important impact of media on election campaigns. Two biases built into news values and journalistic practices have a more pervasive influence on political coverage and interact with electioneering outcomes and processes. The first is the importance of incumbency. The second is the tendency of the election news coverage to fan the growth of bandwagons and political momentums.

While there are many similarities in the way the two parties face the challenges of campaigning, there is a basic asymmetry between them. One is in government, while the other is not. Incumbents have won seven of the last eight elections in Australia federally, and have a similar success rate in recent state and territory elections. There is an old saying that oppositions don't win elections, governments lose them. It is an over-simplification, but it does point to where the political initiative and the media focus lie.

The political advantages of incumbency are considerable and increasing. Governments have always had the ability to fashion budgets, tax cuts and discretionary spending to maximise political benefit for their re-election, in other words to release good news before elections and bad news afterwards. They have always had the ability to direct largesse towards marginal electorates or strategic groups to enhance their electoral prospects (Jackman, 2005). They have always had the right to call the election on a date of their choosing. However, each of these advantages is now pursued more professionally and calculatingly. Moreover, in areas where there was a reliance on tradition to constrain the pursuit of partisan advantage, barriers have steadily eroded. For example, governments' capacity to conduct information campaigns for the common good, using taxpayer funds, has increasingly been used for partisan purposes. The Howard Government has shamelessly broken new ground here, with its tax changes advertised to a song about breaking the chains, and then in mounting advertisements for its industrial relations changes even before the legislation was introduced. So the traditional government advantage in fund raising—itself becoming more important as the expense of political advertising increases—is now compounded by the increasing use of tax funds to advance its own agendas. The increasing staff support for members of parliament (Jones, 2006) and their increasing allowances (Kelly, 2006) have also become increasingly important resources in the electoral battle.

Incumbency is also fundamental in understanding how the electoral contest is played out in the media. Governments have always had publicity advantages over oppositions in that they act where oppositions only criticise. They can use this leverage to seek to influence the political agenda in directions they wish.

The most common pattern is for governments, despite their publicity advantages, to gather various scars during their term of office, and for them often to be equal or somewhat behind in the polls for substantial periods, but when the election approaches there is much more scrutiny of the opposition as well, and then for the government to claw back support.

Central to the incumbent's recovery is the mounting of 'scare' campaigns about the consequences of what the opposition would do if elected. For example, under the Howard Government the scare campaign centred on claims that interest rates would rise under a Labor Government. Under the Fraser Government it centred on what secret, new, or increased taxes a Labor Government would bring. Under the Hawke Government it focused on cuts in government services, especially in health and education, a Liberal victory would bring. Putting to one side the validity of the various claims, what they have in common is that incumbents counter criticisms of their own performance by promoting fears about what their opponents would do. In other words, their path to victory is to be the less disliked alternative.

Furthermore, if the government can puncture the image of the Opposition Leader, depicting him as a risk, an unknown quantity, someone who can't be trusted, then re-election is closer. The viciousness and directness of attacks against opponents thus seems to be exponentially increasing. The Fraser Government labelled Opposition Leader Bill Hayden a sissy, while the Hawke Government made much fun of 'little Johnny Howard'. The Howard Government then accused Opposition Leader Kim Beazley of lacking 'ticker' (heart). In 2004, the age difference between the two leaders was the greatest ever, with Howard 20 years older than his opponent Latham. The Liberals exploited Latham's inexperience with their advertisements all spelling his name with the L character done in the same way as the L plates showing a learner driver. Equally, both parties have a strong interest in prosecuting scandals involving their opponents (Tiffen, 1999) in order to undermine their credibility at the core.

The Battle for Agenda Control

The use of scare campaigns means that defensive campaigning is important to success. While in 1980, the Hayden campaign was wrong-footed by Fraser Government claims that they had secret plans to introduce a wealth tax, in 1983 Hawke was judged to have run "an excellent defensive campaign systematically denying Fraser the peg on which to hang the big scare" (Kelly, 1984, p. 396). It poses strategic and tactical dilemmas for the opposition in the content of their campaigning, in Australian political jargon usually framed as one about small target campaigns. In 1987 under Howard, and then in 1993 in what was supposed to be the unlosable election under Hewson, the Liberals ran 'big target' campaigns, proposing radical policy changes. In each case this made them the focus of attention with both the Labor Government and a range of other groups zeroing in on likely costs. By 1996, Howard's path to victory was based upon reassurance rather than the prospect of radical change. In the post-mortems following the three elections Labor has lost since, the degree to which they should adopt a clear alternative versus small target strategy has been a central and contentious theme.

An incumbent government's capacity to seize the political agenda was shown most graphically in the election of 2001. Early that year, the Howard Government was at the nadir of its electoral fortunes, with all the indicators showing them well behind. In the next months the Liberals reversed some of their more unpopular policies, but were still trailing substantially. The turning point came on August 26, when the Norwegian merchant vessel the *Tampa* properly responded to the distress calls of a sinking boatload of asylum seekers, and set out to land at the Australian territory of Christmas Island to offload its extra cargo of 433 people, mainly Afghans and Iraqis.

The Australian government refused permission for it to land, saying it had to go back to Indonesia. Then there followed a tense stalemate, after which the asylum seekers eventually were transferred to the tiny Pacific Island nation of Nauru. This was the first of several government actions to dramatize the problem of what they called illegal immigrants. Two weeks later the terrible events of September 11 made security concerns far more urgent than they had been at least since the end of the Cold War.

When the election campaign began in October, with a continuing parade of both security related and "illegal immigrant" news stories, the changed political atmosphere had transformed the parties' prospects (Goot, 2002). The Howard Government vigorously pursued security and "illegal immigration" as a winning electoral agenda. Its advertising quoted the Prime Minister: "we will decide who comes to this country, and the circumstances under which they come" (Solomon, 2002). In contrast, Labor had done badly during the campaign in the daily battle to dominate page one. As Geoff Walsh, Labor's secretary, ruefully noted, of the 30 front page stories in Sydney's *Daily Telegraph* in those weeks, only 10 had headlined Labor's agenda, while over 20 were devoted to asylum seekers, the war against terrorism, anthrax, and jihads (Marr & Wilkinson 2003, p. 275). The changed agenda was crucial in winning victory for the government on November 10 (McAllister, 2003).

Momentum, Bandwagons and the Framing of Politics as a Horse Race

Agenda battles such as the ones described above are intertwined with another central aspect of the interaction of media practices and political campaigning, namely the building of political momentum. While the focus of many commentators and political practitioners is upon the extent of media power, in some ways, the election campaign puts the media in a difficult position. The parties are determined to cast them into a passive role. Reporting the campaign is the epitome of "herd journalism," with great caravans of media following the leaders. The media outlets are fiercely competing with each other, but the bulk of coverage is a study in conformity. The journalists have limited access, limited scope for initiatives, and few opportunities to score competitive scoops. Moreover, it is a time of acute sensitivity with politicians and partisans in their audiences ever ready to accuse them of bias.

On the other hand, they do not want to be purely parroting what the politicians want them to say. One response to their frustration at being manipulated by the parties is to react with alacrity to any unplanned embarrassments, to any chance to break out of the campaigners' control. They swarm to the spontaneous, to gaffes and foul-ups, and visual embarrassments. To take just one example: In 1996, when John Howard tumbled down the steps from a podium, and the same day had to correct a mis-statement on radio, all TV news programs linked the visual with the political slip, and it received saturation coverage, being repeated on TV several times in the next 48 hours (Lloyd, 1997, p. 92).

The most common frame journalists use to distance themselves from the politicians and parties is to cover the campaign as a strategic game or as a horse race (see further Patterson, 1994). While journalists would be loath to say they favoured one side or the other, or say one policy is superior to another in substance, they feel increasingly able to comment on the progress of the campaign, to say that one side or the other is on the defensive, that a policy move has been widely greeted or criticised, that a campaign is smoothly functioning or not, or whether each party camp is feeling confident.

Reporters also then try to distance themselves from the combatants in this fierce election game by searching for scoreboards and referees. Most problematically there is a search for independent arbiters—experts or professional or interest groups—who can comment on the politicians' claims, but reputations for impartiality dissolve quickly in the heat of the partisan conflict. Most commonly, each new opinion poll is seized upon, and its entrails dissected at length. Until the 1972 election, there was only one commercial poll, the Morgan Gallup poll, which often provided a markedly inadequate record of movements in public opinion (Goot & Tiffen, 1983). It failed to register, for example, the large swing against the government before the 1961 election (Butler, 1973). However, ever since, each election has seen several competing polls, and as in most democracies they have become a prominent part of the election coverage.

The Australian pollsters' task is somewhat easier because compulsory voting takes one unknown out of the equation, namely who will actually vote on the day. It also removes one of the major worries about polls in other countries, that they will depress the turnout if they indicate one candidate will win easily. More difficult for the pollsters is that in very close elections, it is the distribution of the vote into winning seats rather than the totals that will be crucial. In the close 1998 election, the major pollsters were properly cautious about the importance of the distribution of the vote (Goot, 2000). Despite some hiccups the leading pollsters have a good record of picking the winner in recent elections (Goot, 2005), although the very late swing in 1993 back to the Keating Labor government caught some unprepared. The reporting of the polls varies, especially of the smaller polls and of local polls, with too little attention paid to how confidence limits are affected by sample size as the most common defect.

The tendency to frame politics as a strategic game or as a horse race is probably inevitable in election reporting, but it does have its downsides. For example, after televised debates the press typically focus on whether there was a knock out blow and any indicators of 'who won' more than an examination of what was said. Such framing, signalling momentum and calling winners, means policy differences often come pre-interpreted. The audience hears something is controversial before they hear its substance. Debates come filtered through the lens of commentary focused on appearances and effects on the competition for votes. This adds to any bandwagon effects a winning side may be generating. In addition, a politically safe frame for reporters, which also resonates with parts of their audiences, is to project an anti-political, sceptical 'spin' on all developments. A plague on both your houses appears impartial and also appears to be showing independence from the politicians they are covering, but it is not necessarily healthy for the democratic process.

CONCLUSION

While the focus of most analysts is naturally on election outcomes and policy content, the more elusive processes of electioneering, and how they interact with media coverage, have changed fundamentally. It is always difficult to capture degrees of change, particularly when it comes to charting qualitative changes that do not lend themselves to simple quantification. Politics has always involved cynicism and hypocrisy. Leaders have always been important for electoral success. Each party has always been aggressive towards its opponents, and sought to portray them negatively. Nevertheless, with the ever-increasing professionalisation of campaigning, and with the news media as its central arena, it also seems that contemporary electioneering has increased in each of these aspects. Such changes can have very profound implications for democratic ideals of accountability and choice, as well as for the factors fostering political success. However, it is not clear whether any of them will be changing in ways that enhance the accountability of governments and the public's ability to make informed choices.

REFERENCES

Australian Electoral Commission (2007). http://www.aec.gov.au.

Blyth, M., & Katz, R. (2005). From catch-all politics to Cartelisation: The political economy of the Cartel Party. *West European Politics, 28*(1), 33–60.

Brock, D. (2002). *The Republican noise machine: Right-wing media and how it corrupts democracy.* New York: Random House.

Butler, D. (1973). *The Canberra model: Essays on Australian government.* London: Macmillan.

Butler, D. (1997). Six notes on Australian psephology. In C. Bean, M. Simms, S. Bennett, & J. Warhurst (Eds.), *The politics of retribution: The 1996 federal election* (pp. 228–240). Sydney: Allen & Unwin.

Chenoweth, N. (2001). *Virtual Murdoch: Reality wars on the information highway*. London: Secker & Warburg.

Davies, A., & Spurgeon, C. (1992). The Broadcasting Services Act: A reconciliation of public interest and market principles of regulation? *Media Information Australia, 66*, 85–92.

Deacon, D., & Wring, D. (2002). Partisan de-alignment and the British press. In J. Bartle, R. Mortimore, & S. Atkinson (Eds.), *Political communications: The general election of 2001* (pp. 197–211). London: Frank Cass.

Goot, M. (1983). The media and the campaign. In H. Penniman (Ed.), *Australia at the polls: The national elections of 1980 and 1983* (pp. 140–215). Sydney: Allen & Unwin.

Goot, M. (2000). The performance of the polls. In M. Simms & J. Warhurst (Eds.), *Howard's Agenda* (pp. 37–47). St Lucia: University of Queensland Press.

Goot, M. (2002). Turning points: For whom the polls told. In J. Warhurst & M. Simms (Eds.), *2001. The centenary election* (pp. 63–98). St Lucia: University of Queensland Press.

Goot, M. (2004). Party convergence reconsidered. *Australian Journal of Political Science, 39*(1), 49–74.

Goot, M. (2005). The polls: Liberal, labor or too close to call? In M. Simms & J. Warhurst (Eds.), *Mortgage nation: The 2004 Australian election* (pp. 55–70). Perth: Australian Studies Series.

Goot, M., & Tiffen, R. (1983). Public opinion and the politics of the polls. In P. King (Ed.), *Australia's Vietnam*. Sydney: George Allen & Unwin.

Green, A. (2007). *Elections: ABC coverage of elections*. Retrieved from http://www.abc.net.au/elections/

Inglis, K. (1982). *This is the ABC*. Melbourne: Melbourne University Press.

Jackman, S. (2005). Incumbency advantage. In M. Simms & J. Warhurst (Eds.), *Mortgage nation: The 2004 Australian election* (pp. 335–348). Perth: Australian Studies Series.

Jaensch, D. (1992). *The politics of Australia*. Melbourne: Macmillan.

Jones, K. (2006). One step at a time: Australian Parliamentarians, professionalism and the need for staff. *Parliamentary Affairs, 59*(4), 638–653.

Katz, R. S. (1996). Party organisations and finance. In L. LeDuc, R. G. Niemi, & P. Norris (Eds.), *Comparing democracies: Elections and voting in global perspective* (pp. 107–132). London: Sage.

Kelly, P. (1984). *The Hawke ascendancy: A definitive account of its origins and climax 1975–1983*. Sydney: Angus & Robertson.

Kelly, N. (2006). MPs incumbency benefits keep growing: Democratic audit of Australia Discussion Paper 27/06 . Retrieved from http://democratic.audit.anu.edu.au

Lavelle, A. (2004). A critique of Murray Goot on convergence. *Australian Journal of Political Science, 39*(3), 645–650.

Lebovic, S. (2006). Parkers: The key to ALP prospects. *The Australian*, October 7.

Lee, M. (1992). *News and fair facts: The Australian print media industry*. Report from the House of Representatives Committee on the Print Media. Canberra: [Parliament of the Commonwealth of Australia] Australian Government Publishing Service.

Lijphart, A. (1999). *Democracies. Patterns of Majoritarian and consensus government in twenty-one democracies*. New Haven, CT: Yale University Press.

Lloyd, C. (1997). Television and the election. In C. Bean, S. Bennett, M. Simms, & J. Warhurst (Eds.), *The politics of retribution: The 1996 Australian federal election* (pp. 88–98). Sydney: Allen & Unwin.

McAllister, I. (2002). Calculating or capricious? The new politics of late deciding voters. In D. M. Farrell & R. Schmitt-Beck (Eds.), *Do political campaigns matter? Campaign effects in elections and referendums* (pp. 22–40). London: Routledge.

McAllister, I. (2003). Border protection, the 2001 election and the coalition victory. *Australian Journal of Political Science, 38*(3), 445–463.

Marr, D., & Wilkinson, M. (2003). *Dark victory*. Sydney: Allen & Unwin.

Marsh, I. (2006). Policy convergence between major parties and the representation gap in Australian politics. In I. Marsh (Ed.), *Political parties in transition?* (pp. 116–142). Sydney: The Federation Press.

Masters, C. (2006). *Jonestown: The power and the myth of Alan Jones*. Sydney: Allen & Unwin.

Mills, S. (1986). *The new machine men: Polls and persuasion in Australian politics*. Ringwood Vic: Penguin.

Page, B. (2003). *The Murdoch archipelago*. London: Simon & Schuster.

Parker, D. (1990). *The courtesans: The press gallery in the Hawke Era*. Sydney: Allen & Unwin.

Patterson, T. E. (1994). *Out of order*. New York: Vintage.

Sartori, G. (1976). *Parties and party systems*. Cambridge, UK: Cambridge University Press.

Seymour-Ure, C. (1974). *The political impact of mass media*. London: Constable.

Sharman, C. (2007). *Australian government and politics database*. Retrieved from http://elections.uwa.edu.au

Simms, M. (2005). The print media: Lap dog or watch dog? In M. Simms & J. Warhurst (Eds.), *Mortgage nation: The 2004 Australian election* (pp. 71–82). Perth: Austrilaian Studies Series, Perth, API Network.

Simms, M., & Bolger, D. (2000). The Australian print media and partisan bias in the campaign. In M. Simms & J. Warhurst (Eds.), *Howard's agenda* (pp. 25–36). St. Lucia: University of Queensland Press. Perth: Australian Studies Series.

Solomon, D. (Ed.). (2002). *Howard's race: Winning the unwinnable election*. Sydney: HarperCollins.

Souter, G. (1981). *Company of Heralds*. Melbourne: Melbourne University Press.

Thompson, E. (1980). The "Washminster" mutation. In P. Weller & D. Jaensch (Eds.), *Responsible government in Australia* (pp. 32–40). Richmond: Drummond.

Tiffen, R. (1989). *News and power*. Sydney: Allen & Unwin.

Tiffen, R. (1999). *Scandals. Media, politics and corruption in contemporary Australia*. Sydney: University of New South Wales Press.

Tiffen, R., & Gittins, R. (2004). *How Australia compares*. Melbourne: Cambridge University Press.

Tunstall, J. (1996). *Newspaper power: The new national press in Britain*. Oxford: Clarendon Press.

Ward, I. (2006). Cartel parties and election campaigns in Australia. In I. Marsh (Ed.), *Political parties in transition?* (pp. 70–93). Sydney: The Federation Press.

Williams, P. (1997). *The victory: The inside story of the takeover of Australia*. Sydney: Allen & Unwin.

Wilson, J. Q. (Ed.). (1980). *The politics of regulation*. New York: Basic Books.

Young, S. (2004). *The persuaders: Inside the hidden machine of political advertising*. North Melbourne: Pluto Press.

Young, S. (2006a). The convergence of political and government advertising: Theory and practice. *Media International Australia, 119*, 99–111.

Young, S. (2006b). Australian election slogans, 1949–2004: Where political marketing meets political rhetoric. *Australian Journal of Communication, 33*(1), 1–19.

Young, S. & Tham, J-C. (2006). Political finance in Australia: A skewed and Ssecret system? Report for the Democratic Audit of Australia. Retrieved from http://democratic.audit.anu.edu.au

8

Elections in India: One Billion People and Democracy

Lars Willnat and Annette Aw

India's 2004 parliamentary election was one of the largest democratic exercises the world has seen ever. On 13 May, 2004, the ruling Hindu-nationalist Bharatiya Janata Party (BJP) conceded defeat after an unexpectedly strong showing by the Indian National Congress (INC), which was able to put together a majority under the direction of Sonia Gandhi, the Italian-born widow of former Indian Prime Minister Rajiv Gandhi. Most opinion polls suggested that Prime Minister Atal Bihari Vajpayee, campaigning on the slogan "India Shining" which celebrated the country's 8% growth rate, would win a third successive term. In the end, millions of impoverished Indians, angered over being left out of their country's economic boom, handed the opposition INC party a stunning victory. However, Gandhi surprised many political observers by declining to become the new prime minister, citing the division that her rule would bring. Members of Vajpayee's BJP had demonstrated against the possibility of a foreign-born prime minister, pledging to boycott Gandhi's swearing-in were she named prime minister. Instead, Gandhi asked former Finance Minister Manmohan Singh, a well-respected economist, to take control of the new government.

The sheer size of the Indian electorate creates enormous logistical challenges for the organizers of national elections. India's cultural and religious diversity—the many hundreds of languages and dialects, the widespread poverty, and a 39% illiteracy rate—make democratic elections a seemingly impossible task. In addition, the majority of the Indian population lives in rural, often remote, areas of the country, making it difficult to provide polling facilities to all eligible voters.

Overall, more than 671 million Indians were eligible to vote in the 2004 election—almost twice as many people as were eligible to vote in the European parliamentary elections. Because of the extremely large number of voters in India, polling was staggered in five phases over a three-week period in April and May 2004. Indian voters, assisted by nearly five million election officials, were faced with a total of 5,435 political candidates from which they needed to select 543 members of the *Lok Sabha*, the lower house of the Indian parliament (Ramkumar, 2004). Making a proper choice was not easy, given the diverse backgrounds of many political candidates, who included former royalty, movie stars, holy men, convicts, war heroes, farmers, and even a former Miss India.

The 2004 election was further complicated by the fact that Indians voted for the first time entirely on electronic voting machines, introduced to eliminate invalid votes and to increase the accuracy and speed of the counting process (Murthy & Paditar, 2005). Overall, more than one million voting machines were transported with elephants, boats, bullock carts, and off-road vehicles to 687,402 polling stations located in 25 states and seven federally-administered areas (Electoral Commission of India [ECI], 2007a). In addition to the logistical challenges such a massive democratic exercise created, ethnic and religious disturbances have been the norm during India's recent elections. More than 1.5 million police officers, army personnel, and paramilitary troops were on high alert throughout the 2004 election, but by the time the vote was completed, at least 43 people had been killed in election-related violence (Associated Press, 2004). As shocking as this high number of deaths might be, it was much lower than the 100 election-related deaths that occurred during the previous election in 1998.

As Tekwani and Shetty (2007, p.151) note, "the necessity of campaigning to a population divided along diverse social, cultural, religious, linguistic, and political lines, turns the entire exercise into a Babel-esque festival." Yet, every five years, hundreds of millions of Indians go to the polls and elect their government in what can only be described as an exercise in democratic determination. According to Dhirubhai L. Sheth, a political scientist at the Center for the Study of Developing Societies in New Delhi, "people [in India], and especially the poor, see their vote as an asset that must be used. There is a lot of enthusiasm at election time…. Maybe it's because so many other things in life are not so easy, and here you can get a sense of one's efficacy, what one vote can do" (cited in Baldauf, 2004).

Given the importance of such a large part of the world population voting regularly in fair and democratic elections, it is odd that so little is reported about Indian elections in the Western media. India's 2004 national election, for example, was completely ignored by the *Washington Post* and the *New York Times*, two newspapers that pride themselves on their international coverage. The few stories that reached Western audiences about India's landmark election originated mostly with European news services such as the British *BBC News* or the German *Deutsche Presse Agentur*. The fact that such an enormous democratic event has been mostly ignored by the Western media underscores the importance for a better understanding of the social and cultural factors that differentiate elections in India from those conducted in Western societies. Since many Indians are still illiterate, it seems especially intriguing to explore the potential impact of the mass media in political campaigns that need to be much more focused on verbal and visual cues than typical Western-style campaigns. While Indian media scholars are still catching up with the more established field of media studies in other countries, India provides ample opportunities to explore the role of the media in elections that are characterized by an intriguing mix of traditional and modern election campaign techniques.

The goal of this chapter is to provide the reader with an introduction to the fascinating democratic events that take place in India every five years. To explain the vast social and cultural diversity found in India, we will first provide a short overview of India's social and cultural background. Next, we will discuss India's media system and the electoral rules and procedures that govern Indian elections. Finally, we will provide an analysis of the existing research on political media effects and election coverage in India.

SOCIAL AND POLITICAL BACKGROUND

India is often described as the "largest democracy in the world," a well-deserved title it has earned in half a decade of independence from Great Britain. India became independent in 1947 with the partition of British India into the predominantly Hindu India and the mostly Muslim Pakistan. Today, India is a democratic republic modeled after the British parliamentary system with distinct executive, legislative, and judicial branches.

The Indian parliament is a bicameral legislature composed of a lower house, the *Lok Sabha* (House of the People), and an upper house, the *Rajya Sabha* (Council of States). Except for two appointed seats for Indians of European descent, the 552 members of the *Lok Sabha* are directly elected for five-year terms. The 250 members of the *Rajya Sabha*, on the other hand, are either elected by the state legislatures or nominated by the president, and serve staggered six-year terms. The prime minister is the leader of the majority party in parliament, but is formally appointed by the president. The president, who serves as head of state, is elected for a five-year term by state and national lawmakers.

Since independence, there have been 14 parliamentary elections in India with voter turnout ranging from 55 to 64% of eligible voters (about 671.5 million voters were eligible in the 2004 election). National and state elections are similar to the British House of Commons and United States House of Representatives, in which members gain office by winning a plurality of votes in their local constituency. During the first five decades of India's independence, the left-of-center, secular Indian National Congress (INC) and its factions have ruled almost continuously. While the Hindu nationalist Bharatiya Janata Party (BJP), in alliance with several other parties, won the 1998 national election, the INC returned to power with Manmohan Singh as prime minister in 2004.

Despite the resilience of the Indian political system, political infighting and widespread corruption have undermined some democratic advances. According to the Freedom House (2006a), for example, the electoral system largely depends on black money obtained though tax evasion. In addition, Indian politicians and civil servants are regularly caught accepting bribes or engaging in other corrupt behavior, but are rarely prosecuted. Not surprisingly, the "2006 Corruption Perceptions Index," which is published annually by the nonprofit organization Transparency International (www.transparency.org), ranked India 70 out of 163 countries surveyed.

Nevertheless, the fact that Indian elections have been free and fairly peaceful during the past 50 years is an astonishing accomplishment given the size and diversity of the country. India is the seventh largest country in the world, about one-third the size of the United States. In 2007, India's total population was estimated to be 1.13 billion with an annual population growth of about 1.4% (World Bank, 2007).

One of the biggest problems facing India today is widespread illiteracy among the fast-growing population. In 2004, the literacy rate among those 15 years or older was only 61%, with significantly lower rates among women (47.8% for females and 74.4% for males). Despite the fact that the literacy rate has nearly doubled since 1961 and is higher than in most other South Asian nations, it is still far lower than in most East Asian nations (Library of Congress, 2004).

Another challenge confronting India is economic change and widespread poverty. Agriculture employs nearly 60% of the population, but accounts for only 22.6% of the gross domestic product. In the past two decades, economic production has been transformed from primarily agriculture and textile manufacturing to various heavy industries, transportation, and telecommunications with economic growth rates of around 4 to 7% annually. However, a majority of Indians still live in poverty and often earn less than one U.S. dollar per day. According to the World Bank, the 2005 per capita income in India was about U.S.$730 (World Bank, World Development Indicators, 2007).

The development problems caused by illiteracy and poverty in India are compounded by the huge geographic dispersion of the Indian population. There are 28 states and seven union territories in India, including the national capital territory of New Delhi. India's population is characterized by a large divide between the urban and the rural population. Despite the fact that India has 35 cities and urban metropolitan areas with more than one million people, about 72% of the population resides in rural areas (UNESCO, 2007). The three most populous cities are Mumbai (Bombay, 16.4 million people), Kolkata (Calcutta, 13.2 million), and Delhi (12.8 million).

India's cultural diversity is reflected in the large number of religions and languages that can be found across the country. Approximately 80.5% of the population is Hindu, 13.4% Muslim, 2.3% Christian, and 1.9% Sikh (2001 Census of India). While the Indian constitution guarantees religious freedom and prohibits religious discrimination, significant tensions between Hindus and Muslims have persisted during the past decades (Library of Congress, 2004). Twenty-two languages are officially recognized by the Indian constitution, but the most commonly spoken languages are Hindi (40.2% of the population), Bengali (8.3%), Telugu (7.9%), Marathi (7.5%), and Tamil (6.3%). English also has official status and is widely used in business and politics. Overall, an estimated 850 languages are in daily use, and the Indian Government claims there are more than 1,600 dialects (Library of Congress, 2004).

One of India's biggest development challenges is to provide the people with better access to mass media and new communication technologies. While the number of telephones, radios, and television sets has increased substantially since the late 1990s, India's telecommunication and media environment is still extremely underdeveloped. In 2005, for example, there were only about 50 million land-based telephones and 69 million cell phones available in India (UNESCO 2005 estimate). Telephone density remains low at about 7.3 main telephone lines per 100 people nationwide and only one line per 100 people in rural areas (ITU, 2005). Access to new communication technologies is even more limited: while the number of Internet users reached 38 million in 2006, only about 1.5 personal computers are available per 100 people nationwide (ITU, 2005). The inadequate access to communication technologies is matched by the nominal availability of mass media across India: only about 12 radios and 6.5 television sets are available for each 100 people nationwide. Similarly, about six newspaper copies are shared by each 100 people in India (UNESCO 2007 estimate).

THE MEDIA LANDSCAPE IN INDIA

The Press

Despite its low literacy rate, India has more newspapers than any other nation. Driven by a growing middle class and the demands of a culturally diverse population, newspaper circulation has risen annually by millions and new titles appear every day. According to the official Registrar of Newspapers for India (2006), more than 62,000 newspapers were published in 2006 with a total circulation of almost 181 million copies. This astounding number includes more than 2,100 daily newspapers with a combined circulation of about 89 million copies. The highest numbers of newspapers is published in Hindi (4,131), followed by English (864), Gujarati (775), Urdu (463) Bengali (445), and Marathi (328).

According to Karan (in press), the free and mostly privately owned newspapers have played an important role in India's struggle for political independence by being generally supportive of the government's efforts towards nation building. Bhoopathy (2003a) notes, however, that by the 1960s, the relationship between the press and the government was transformed, and many newspapers took an adversarial role. Today, most print media in India, particularly the English-language press, provide diverse coverage and frequently criticize the government (Bhoopathy, 2003a; Vohra, 2000).

The Broadcast Media

Radio and television reach almost the entire Indian population, therefore representing the most efficient way of communicating with the Indian electorate. Until the mid-1990s, the Ministry of

Information and Broadcasting maintained firm control over the government-owned television network Doordarshan and the radio broadcaster All India Radio (AIR). Both national broadcasters were used extensively to promote the Indian government's educational and economic development programs. Through its broadcasting monopoly, the government was also able to control and ban any unwanted information, thus allowing the long-ruling INC party to heavily influence political news coverage to its own advantage (Karan, in press). As a result, Doordarshan's and AIR's news reporting customarily presented the government's point of view.

The government broadcasting monopoly ended in 1993 with the conversion of Doordarshan and AIR into public broadcasting services. Today, about 90% of the Indian population can receive Doordarshan's national, regional, and local television programs through a network of nearly 1,400 terrestrial transmitters. Presently, Doordarshan has 26 television channels (4 national channels, 11 regional satellite channels, 8 state networks, 1 international channel, and 2 channels for live broadcast of parliamentary proceedings) with programs produced in all 28 states (Ministry of Information and Broadcasting, Annual Report, 2005).

Over the past decades, Doordarshan's viewership has increased exponentially. According to the most recent estimate, 119 million homes in India have television sets (CII-KPMG, 2004), which means that about 654 million people can watch Doordarsham's programs in their homes (based on UN estimates of 5.5 people per household). In addition, Doordarshan can be received in 147 countries around the world, mostly serving the large Indian overseas populations. While Doordarshan has come under increasing pressure from competing private broadcasters to include more entertainment programs in its daily schedule, the public broadcaster continues to maintain a focus on cultural, educational, and development programs.

Doordarshan's televised broadcasts are complimented by AIR's national radio programs, which are transmitted in 24 languages and 146 dialects through a network of 223 radio stations and 358 transmitters that covers about 99 percent of the Indian population. Similar to Doordarshan's programming objective, AIR's radio broadcast "keep[s] Indians informed about government initiatives and policies with a variety of with a variety of programs on culture, education, science, health and hygiene, as well as social and economic aspects"(AIR, 2007). Apart from AIR, there are also 69 privately-owned FM stations in major cities across India. However, private radio stations in India are not allowed to broadcast news and public affairs programming.

The end of the government's broadcasting monopoly in 1993 also opened the Indian media market to private cable and satellite providers who have since attracted large audiences across India. India's cable television market, for example, is one of the world's largest, with more than 60 million subscribers (BBC, 2007). Major international news broadcasters such as STAR TV, CNN, BBC News, and CNBC have entered the Indian market and are now competing fiercely with the public broadcaster for audience share. The competition from cable and satellite stations brought radical change to Doordarshan, cutting its audience and threatening its advertising revenues at a time when the government was pressuring it to pay for expenditures from internal revenues (Library of Congress, 1995). Overall, the number of news and business channels grew from virtually none in 1995 to around 11 mainstream news channels and a slew of regional news channels in 2007. In addition, several 24-hour news channels were launched in 2004, providing Indian audiences with more and faster news from a variety of national and international sources (CII-KPMG, 2004).

The Internet

The political potential of the Internet in a democratic nation of more than one billion people is hampered by India's lack of a sufficient telecommunication infrastructure and the fact a majority of Indians cannot afford computers or Internet connections. According to recently released survey report of the Internet and Mobile Association of India (2006), the number of Internet users in India reached 38 million or about 3% of the total population by the end of 2006. This number includes only about one million users in rural areas. Most users in India are between the ages of 18 and 35 and spend about 8.2 hours per week on the Internet. The report notes, however, that the time Indian users spend on the Internet is primarily limited by the high cost of Internet access and the slow transmission speeds of the still dominant dial-up connections in India. As a consequence, cyber cafes continue to be the most popular access point for most Indian Internet users (39%), followed by access at home (31%), and the office (22%). Access from schools and colleges, on the other hand, is at a mere 6%, which, according to the study, "remains a cause of concern since internet access from schools and colleges help in reducing the digital and socio-economic divide." According to the U.S. State Department, Internet access in India is unrestricted, although some states have proposed legislation that would require the registration of customers at cyber cafes (Freedom House, 2006b).

POLITICAL RIGHTS AND CIVIL LIBERTIES

The "Fundamental Rights" contained in the Indian constitution guarantee all citizens equality before the law and freedom of speech, expression, religion, and association. Article 19 ensures freedom of speech and expression, but also allows the government to place "reasonable restrictions" on the exercise of those rights under various circumstances, such as maintenance of public order, state security, and public morality (Library of Congress, 2004). Potentially inflammatory books and films produced within or outside India, for example, are occasionally banned or censored by India's national or state governments (Freedom House, 2006b).

According to the Freedom House (2006b), India's private press "continues to be vigorous and is by far the freest in South Asia." In recent years, however, the government has occasionally used its power under the Official Secrets Act to censor security-related articles. The Press Council of India, an autonomous body set up under the Press Council Act 1978, serves as a self-regulatory mechanism for the print media through its investigations of complaints of misconduct or irresponsible reporting. It is headed by a chairman and has 28 other members from the press, the government, the private sector, and academia (Ministry of Information and Broadcasting, Annual Report, 2005).

While much of the Indian broadcast media is in private hands, the Public Broadcasting Act of 1997 established Doordarshan and All India Radio as public broadcasters. It also created the Prasar Bharati Corporation, which is a regulatory agency that distributes the airwaves between the public cooperation and the private channels.

The Election Commission of India

The Election Commission of India (ECI), established in 1950, is an independent constitutional body that supervises and conducts parliamentary and state elections in India, a task it calls the "management of the largest event in the world" (ECI, 2007a). The ECI performs routine functions, such as voter registration, deploying and training of election officials, registering the political parties, conducting the actual voting, and declaring the voting results. The Election Commission enjoys complete autonomy and is insulated from any kind of governmental interference (Murthy & Paditar, 2005). The ECI consists of three commissioners who are appointed for five years. The Chief Election Commissioner can only be removed by the president of India, a step that requires a formal parliamentary impeachment and proof of misconduct or incapacity. All political parties are registered with the Election Commission and are granted recognition at the state and national levels on the basis of their performance in previous elections. The ECI also functions as a quasi-judiciary body in electoral disputes and other matters involving the conduct of elections.

The ECI also controls a scheme that allows recognized political parties to use the state-owned television and radio network for free advertising broadcasts during election times. Time is allotted in five-minute blocks to the recognized parties according to their popularity, which is determined according to the votes polled to them during the last election (N.B.R. Roa, 2003). In the 2004 parliamentary election, free airtime on Doordarshan and All India Radio was allocated to six national and 45 state parties recognized by the ECI, totaling 125 hours on each of the two broadcasters. This included ten minutes given to each state party on the local satellite channels of Doordarshan and All Radio India. In addition, the Prasar Bharati Corporation was authorized to organize two national debates broadcast on the national channels of Doordarshan and All India Radio, in which each national party could nominate one representative (ECI, 2004a).

The Election Commission tries to ensure a level playing field for all political parties through a strict observance of a "Model Code of Conduct," which was created with the consensus of the political parties shortly before the 2004 parliamentary election (ECI, 2007b). The code states that parties and candidates should not "cause tension between different castes and communities, religious or linguistic" and should refrain from appealing to "caste or communal feelings for securing votes." Criticism of other political parties or candidates, when made, should focus on policies and programs rather than on private lives. In addition, all parties and candidates are asked to avoid all "corrupt practices and offences" under the election law, such as bribing and intimidation of voters, canvassing close to polling stations, or transporting voters to and from polling stations. The code also contains rules about the conduct of political meetings and processions during the election. This contains a set of detailed instructions about the organization of election day and various restrictions meant to limit any advantages the party in power might have during the election because of its control over government facilities (ECI, 2007b). In addition to the more self-regulative Model Code of Conduct, the Representation of the People Act 1951 requires all political candidates to file affidavits declaring their assets and liabilities, educational qualifications, and any criminal cases pending against them. These affidavits are then placed on the website of the Election Commission to enable voters to make a more informed choice (ECI, 2007b).

Another important function of the ECI is to assign pictorial symbols to each recognized political party. The symbols' main function is to allow illiterate voters to cast their votes in secrecy by recognizing parties and candidates by the symbols printed on the ballots. As a result, Indian elections depend heavily on the promotion of these pictorial symbols especially among the illiterate voters in India's rural areas. According to Bhoopathy (2003a, p. 414), "the main campaign technique of each and every candidate is to lay great emphasis on his election symbol rather than his political label. The most popular method of communicating the symbol to voters is through posters, handbills, and signs on the walls."

Regulation of Political Advertising

Until the year 2004, the Cable Television Network (Regulation) Rules 1994 did not allow any political advertising on India's private broadcast media. This advertising ban was part of an effort to provide a level playing field to political candidates with different financial means. In April

2004, however, the Supreme Court ruled that banning such political advertisement is against the fundamental right to free speech and expression and therefore violated the Indian Constitution. Unfortunately, while the Court's rule allowed political advertising on private cable networks and satellite television channels, these advertisements also had to comply with the rules of the Advertising Code of the Cable Television Networks (Regulation) Act, which prohibits any commercials that are "shocking, disgusting or revolting" or that "offend morality, decency and [the] religious susceptibility of viewers." To resolve this issue, the Supreme Court directed the ECI to monitor all political advertisements on India's television networks during the 2004 election and ensure that they conformed to existing laws—a task that quickly overwhelmed the ECI.

Since 2004, large amounts of party funds have begun to flow toward political advertising in electronic media, but no firm estimates on the actual amounts are available yet. Murthy and Paditar (2005), however, estimate that the parties spent between 100 and 150 million rupees (about US$2.6 million to US$3.9 million) on political advertising during the 2004 campaign. These costs are in addition to what the parties incurred in traditional print advertising, for which the authors estimate an expenditure of approximately 100 million rupees.

The Representation of the People Act of 1951 laid down ceilings on election spending by candidates. These expenditure limits were recently revised upwards to 2.5 million rupees (about US$62,000) per candidate for *Lok Sabha* constituencies and one million rupees (about US$26,000) per candidate for state constituencies (Government of Tamil Nadu, 2007). Campaign funds are mostly supplied through private contributions, although some contributions from public companies are permitted (up to 5% of the company's net profits). Unfortunately, there is little transparency for the contributions received by political parties and candidates (Murthy & Paditar, 2005), and many politicians are suspected of accepting bribes from dubious contributors. Frustrated by this lawless but persistent tradition, the Indian Supreme Court (1996) noted in a 1996 judgment that "...there is no accountability anywhere. Nobody discloses the source of the money. There are no proper accounts and no audit. From where this money comes, nobody knows. In a democracy where rule of law prevails this type of naked display of black money, by violating the mandatory provisions of law, cannot be permitted."

The Exit Poll Controversy

The persistent belief that exit polls can significantly influence voting decisions in elections that allow polling stations to close at different times caused an interesting controversy during India's 2004 parliamentary election. In April 2004, the ECI asked the government to ban all exit polls conducted by the mass media during the official election time. The Commission, which also conducts polls throughout the election, complained that the publication of opinion polls by television channels and newspapers during the election "are likely to influence the minds of the voters" (ECI, 2004b). The Commission's lawyers pointed out that the 2004 national election would be held in five stages that lasted eight weeks. Therefore, the publication of exit polls after one round's conclusion would negatively influence the voters in the next round. Fortunately, India's Attorney General refused to support a ban on exit polls, pointing out that any such ban would undermine the fundamental right to freedom of speech and expression. He also noted that "information from divergent and antagonistic sources would help voters to make an informed choice after reading articles and editorials in different newspapers." On April 26, 2004, the India's Supreme Court agreed with this opinion and subsequently refused to issue a decree banning the publication of opinion polls and exit polls during election time (International Press Institute, 2004).

MEDIA AND ELECTION STUDIES IN INDIA

The field of political communication studies in India is much less developed than comparable studies in East Asia, the United States, or Europe. The earliest studies, which can be traced as far back as the late 1960s, concentrated mostly on descriptive analyses of political parties, candidates, policies, campaigns, and voting behavior (Brass, 1986; Eldersveld & Ahmed, 1978; Meyer, 1989; Pattabhiraman, 1967; Prasad, 1967; Prasad & Kinni, 1968; Sheth, 1975; Siriskar, 1965, 1973; Varma & Narain, 1973; Weiner & Field, 1974-77). Similar to election studies conducted in Western nations, these analyses tried to explain voting behavior with a number of socio-economic variables, such as age, sex, education, and income.

Accounting for the unique social and cultural environment found in India, some election studies also considered the influence of religion, caste, community, and interpersonal communication on voting behavior in rural and urban India (Ahmed, 1970; Brass, 1984; Kaur, 1989). Varma and Bhambri's (1967) analysis of the campaign techniques used in the 1962 parliamentary election, for example, showed that rural voters had a more developed political consciousness than urban voters—a finding confirmed in two later studies on voters in Rajasthan (Bhambri & Varma, 1973; Varma & Narain, 1973).

The political engagement of rural citizens in India can be explained at least partly by the often inadequate public services found outside large metropolitan areas. Thus, the combined effects of widespread poverty, illiteracy, and insufficient government services have increased rather than suppressed the political involvement of rural Indians. The political impact of the mass media, however, has been limited because of the low levels of literacy found among the rural population in India. As expected, Varma and Bhambri (1967) found that newspapers were more popular sources for political information in urban areas, while rural people mostly depended on grassroots workers, rallies, and public meetings with candidates and leaders for information about politics. Similarly, Kaur's (1989) study of voters in the city of Hyderabad found that newspapers were the main source of information for more than three-quarters (77%) of the respondents.

Overall, political communication studies conducted in the 1960s, 1970s, and 1980s primarily described Indian elections and voting behavior during that period. While many of these studies analyzed the potential impact of demographic background factors on voting behavior, most studies did not move much beyond reporting on "who voted for whom." Moreover, given India's size, variability, and plurality, the generalizations that emerged from such studies had only limited application at the macro level (Suri, 2006).

More recent studies of political media effects have stressed the growing importance of news media in Indian elections and their impact on voter behavior (Kumar, 1991; Ahuja & Paul, 1992; Pathak, 1992; Prasad, 2003). Karan (in press) argues that with the growth of Indian mass media during the 1980s and 1990s, political awareness increased rapidly among Indian voters, now able to access more extensive and diverse election media coverage. Vakil's (1994) analysis of the 1991 parliamentary election, for example, found higher levels of political awareness among urban voters in India who used mass media and interpersonal communication to gather political information. Similarly, Karan's (1994) analysis of the 1991 election documented high levels of interest among the voters who followed the campaign in the media, particularly through newspapers and television. Interpersonal communication was an important factor in voting decisions when candidates and political workers approached people though door-to-door campaigns or public rallies and meetings.

It is important to note, however, that Indian voters traditionally have been concerned with very different political issues than voters in more developed nations. Election polls conducted in 1996, for example, show that Indian voters attach a high importance to problems such as poverty, drinking water, electricity, housing, food, and clothing. According to Suri (2006, p. 5), "most people in India seem to give priority to the fulfillment of their basic needs, unlike people in the postmodern societies of the industrialized west."

A number of recent studies also noted that political parties in India have started to use public relations and research companies to run and supervise their election campaigns more successfully through the mass media (Dua, 1999; Karan, 1994, 2000; Sarwate, 1990). The style of political campaigning in India first changed in the 1984 national election, when Rajiv Gandhi took over the leadership of the INC party after the assassination of his mother, Indira Gandhi. The young, Western-educated leader believed that he could win the election with a professional advertising campaign focusing on his family's political heritage and taking advantage of the emotional impact his mother's assassination had throughout India. Consequently, Gandhi asked the Indian advertising agency Rediffusion to create a national multi-media campaign, which stressed Rajiv Gandhi's connections to his famous mother and played up the emotional trauma of her assassination. To nobody's surprise, Gandhi's INC party won the 1984 election with a landslide victory, gaining 415 of the 543 directly elected seats in the *Lok Sabah* (Karan, in press). While it is reasonable to assume that the sympathy factor helped Gandhi to become prime minister in 1984, his professional media campaign was recognized by many academic observers as a central factor in his political victory (Butler, Lahiri, & Roy, 1991; Karan, 1994; Sarwate, 1990).

While Western-style media campaigns have had some success in India, social and cultural factors have prevented them from becoming ubiquitous. Plasser (2000), for example, notes that while India has embraced media- and television-driven politics, the cultural barriers and a general lack of campaign money make India a special case. His comparative study of the adoption of U.S. campaign techniques in forty countries found that most Indian party and campaign managers distance themselves from the U.S. campaign style and instead choose campaigns in Britain, Spain, and Sweden as possible role models for more professional Indian election campaigns. Plasser's interviews with political consultants and leading party managers found that only 25% of the party officials in India believed that U.S. campaign strategies could be implemented in their country. This compares with 52% in East Central Europe, 58% in Russia and Ukraine, 68% in South Africa, and 83% in South America. The author concludes that a "profound skepticism about foreign campaign know-how currently still dominates among Indian party managers" (Plasser, 2000, pp. 49–50).

India's Alternative Media Campaigns

The fact that four out of ten Indian voters cannot read or write and live primarily in remote areas of the country greatly undermines the effectiveness of modern, media-based election campaigns. In order to reach the largely illiterate voters in rural India, political audio- and videocassettes were introduced by the main political parties in the 1991 elections (Karan, in press). Since political parties were not allowed to promote these videos on national television until 2004, the campaigns developed trucks equipped with large projection screens that could show political videos to large groups of voters at a time. These "videos-on-wheels" moved from village to village to promote the party's messages even among the most remote regions of India. To make the political videos more attractive to Indian voters, they were usually interspersed with popular songs or tales based on Indian mythology, all presented in the languages or dialects of the regional populations (Dickey, 1993; Karan, in press).

In addition to the political videos that have been shown throughout the country, the parties also used music to reach younger and less engaged voters. During the 1998 election, for example, the BJP employed a team of lyricists whose entire job it was to remix popular film or pop music with political messages that attacked the opposition parties (Bhoopathy, 2003b). The BJP's version of Altaf Raja's popular hit song *Tum to Thehre Pardesi* was used to comment on Sonia Gandhi's foreign looks by altering the original lyrics to: "After all you are a foreigner, how long will you stay by our side. You'll catch the first flight and go away to Italy" (Kazmi, 1999). Both the BJP and the INC distributed a number of such political "hits" on audiocassettes, which reached even the least politically involved citizens.

Indian politics has been also influenced by the prominent role of cinema in Indian public life (David, 1983; Dickey, 1993; Forrester, 1976; Hardgrave, 1975; Pentane, 1992; Pandian, 1992; A. M. Rao, 2003; Sivathamby, 1981). India is the world's largest producer of feature films, and cinema is extremely popular among the urban and rural poor, who comprise the great majority of the electorate. Not surprisingly, several present and past politicians in India have benefited politically from their popularity as film actors. Maruthur Gopala Ramachandran, one of India's best known movie stars, became Chief Minister of Tamil Nadu in 1967 by reminding voters of his carefully cultivated movie image as a protector of the poor and the weak. Similarly, the late Nandamuri Taraka Rama Rao, former chief minister of Andhra Pradesh, was closely associated in the voters' minds with the role of the Hindu god Krishna, whom he played throughout his successful movie career (Tekwani, 2005). As a consequence, Indian politics has been very personality-oriented where every major political party is largely dependent on the 'charisma' and 'public image' of its individual leaders rather than on any ideology, economic or political philosophy. Boopathy (2003b, p. 511) argues that "the hero-villain mesh of Indian cinema fits in ideally with the cult-dominated Indian politics to promote such personalities."

India's First Television Election

The growing importance of television as a campaign medium in India became especially evident during the 1998 parliamentary election. India's first "television election" allowed voters to follow the campaign live around the clock on Doordarshan and almost a dozen satellite channels, including BBC and CNN (Chopra, 1998). The large number of competing news organizations covering the 1998 election and the much faster news cycle of the new 24-hour news channels dramatically changed the way Indian politicians used the mass media. According to Chopra (1998, p. 67), "normally taciturn politicians, realizing the immediacy and the impact of television, became instantly available. They began to understand that live, two-minute sound bites were easier to control than pesky press conferences." This new perspective on Indian politics, of course, contrasted sharply with the exclusive but somewhat staunch news coverage of the 1996 election by the public broadcaster Doordarshan.

A survey conducted by the Delhi-based Centre for Media Studies (1998) supports the notion that television became the dominant political medium even in remote areas of India during the 1998 election. The survey found that while about a third (32%) of the interviewed respondents in a rural pocket of Andrah Pradesh had heard of the INC's leading political candidate, Sonia Gandhi, through the medium of newspapers, almost half of the respondents (49%) had heard of her through television. A similar survey conducted in Delhi found that a staggering 93% of all respondents had seen political advertisements on India's public television station Doordarshan. Moreover, about 49% said that the advertisements had changed their attitude towards the 1998 election and its candidates. The study concludes that the weight given by television to the role of personalities in the 1998 election has become the single most important and influential factor in public perception of political candidates and their parties in Indea (Media Advocacy Group, 1998).

Vijaypur and Balasubramanya (2003) argued that mass media exposure during the 1998 election encouraged political discussion among a sample of 340 Indians. However, according to the authors, the media did not have a consistent impact on the various types of political activities tested. For example, while regular television viewers and magazine readers were more likely to participate in public demonstrations, higher media exposure did not play any role in persuading respondents to deliver speeches at political meetings. In addition, the study found that education and income correlated positively with exposure to political content in the mass media. The use of television ranked first in providing access to political information, followed by newspapers, radio, and magazines.

In a similar study, Madhavi (2003) analyzed the potential impact of the mass media on voting behavior among a sample of 450 female respondents who voted in the 1999 state election that took place in Andrah Pradesh. Madhavi compared voters in the less developed district of Anantapur with voters in the economically more advanced district of Chittoor. Surprisingly, the study found that exposure to newspapers and election campaign advertising in the less developed district actually decreased the likelihood of voting. In the more developed district, on the other hand, exposure to radio, television, and election advertising had a positive effect on voting behavior, but exposure to newspapers was associated with lower levels of voting. The author explains these findings primarily with the different development levels of each district—women in the more developed district simply were able to access more media sources than women in the less developed district. Therefore, they were more likely to show positive correlations between media use and voting behavior. The negative associations found between media use and voting behavior, on the other hand, might be explained by the fact that women in the less developed district, who generally had lower levels of literacy than the women in the more developed district, were more likely to prefer entertainment programs rather than election news. Overall, this study shows that political media effects in India are influenced by the deep economic and educational divides that still separate India's rural and urban population.

The 2004 Election Campaign

With the rapid expansion of cable and satellite television throughout India in the late 1990s, India's election campaigns quickly became more media-centered. The most recent 2004 parliamentary election, for example, was covered extensively by multiple 24-hour television news channels, making it India's first true "live television" election. In addition, the number of dedicated political news shows increased significantly compared to the previous election in 1998. In March 2004, for example, India's television stations announced more than ten new programs that were exclusively dedicated to the coverage of the 2004 election (R. Gupta, 2004).

Anticipating the central role television would play in the 2004 election, the ruling BJP created the "India Shining" advertising campaign, which emphasized the BJP's successes on the economic front and highlighted the country's booming high-tech industry. To reach even more voters with their political message, the BJP also dispatched Deputy Prime Minister Lal Krishna Advani on a 5,000-mile bus tour through 16 states—an Indian tradition called the *Uday Yatra*. The tour bus was equipped with all modern communication technologies as well as a conference and press room. The bus also featured a built-in elevator allowing Advani to address public gatherings from the roof of his bus. The *Yatra*, of course, was also an ideal vehicle to attract media coverage since journalists were courted by the BJP to join it on its progress through the country (Deutsche Presse Agentur, 2004). The INC, on the other hand, announced that Mrs. Gandhi would conduct her own "road show" and would travel to different parts of the country by private car.

While the 2004 parliamentary election was covered extensively by both the private and the public broadcasting media, political news coverage of the 2004 election was heavily biased in favor of the ruling BJP party. According to a study by the Viewers Forum and Center for Advocacy and Research (2004), for example, the BJP party received 13% more news coverage than the INC from the private and public broadcasters (BJP 44.5%, Congress 31.5%). Moreover, while the top six BJP candidates accounted for about 23% of all sound bites found in the political news coverage of the public and private broadcasters, the top six INC candidates accounted for only 12% of all sound bites. In addition, the BJP's bus campaign received almost six times the amount of news coverage from the private and public broadcasters than Sonia Gandhi's "road show." The study monitored a total of 871 news bulletins broadcasted on the public broadcasting station Doordarshan News and the top five private 24-hour news channels in India between March 8 and May 7, 2004.

The 2004 election also featured the most high-tech political campaign ever conducted in India. Non-traditional media were particularly important in reaching urban and literate voters during the election. Especially the BJP excelled in using prerecorded voicemails and SMS messages to reach voters with cell phones. According to claims by the BJP, Prime Minister Vajpayee's campaign messages reached 46 million people by landline telephones and an additional 25 million people via cell phones. In addition, the BJP targeted between 100 and 120 million voters through e-mail (Ramaswany, 2004).

The 2004 election campaign also introduced the Internet as a serious campaigning tool in India. While the first political party sites were launched by the BJP and the INC during the 1998 election, most of these websites were geared toward the more educated and wealthier voters living in India and abroad. In 2004, most of the larger political parties in India maintained Web sites that allowed voters to directly access election-related information. Tekwani and Shetty's (2007) analysis of a sample of 100 political websites used during the 2004 election, however, shows that the political reach of these websites was rather limited in a country where many voters are illiterate and often live in rural areas with minimal access to the Internet.

Moreover, the study found that a majority of the political websites provided very little information about the election, the parties, or the candidates. Instead, most candidate and party sites simply listed the candidates' biographies and issue positions without providing voters with the opportunity to take an active role in some aspect of the election. Most of the opposition websites, for example, did not allow voters to send e-mails to candidates, distribute campaign material offline, express support for a party or candidate, or volunteer their help in the campaign. The government websites, on the other hand, provided users with the opportunity to register to vote, to donate money, to contribute to forums and online discussions, and to distribute relevant election material offline. The authors conclude that the Internet did not influence the outcome of the election but rather reinforced a perception of India "in which the middle and upper classes are given greater political efficacy through the use of information technology and the lower classes are reliant almost entirely upon traditional, low-cost media for election information" (Tekwani & Shetty, 2007, p. 150).

CONCLUSIONS

As this chapter has shown, India's election campaigns are difficult to compare with Western-style election campaigns. The country's enormous size and cultural diversity, the large number of eligible voters in each national election, and the high levels of poverty and illiteracy have limited the usefulness of media-based campaigns. Because a large part of the population is illiterate and lives in rural areas with limited media access, the print media, especially, has had limited effects as a political campaign tool.

Indian campaign managers have come up with unique solutions to these challenges, creating campaigns that rely on alternative forms of communication to transmit their political messages to the electorate. Traditional campaign methods such as public rallies or door-to-door campaigns still work best. In addition, alternative forms of communication with the voters, such as political films, video-on-wheels, or political songs have been very successful in Indian elections because they reach a large number of voters who either do not have access to the traditional news media or are simply not interested in politics. It is therefore no surprise that most Indian campaign managers have rejected U.S. campaign methods as a possible model for modernizing Indian election campaigns.

Nevertheless, it is clear that India's news coverage of election campaigns has changed dramatically since the late 1990s, when private broadcasters were first allowed to compete with the news coverage of the public broadcaster Doordarshan. As a result, the two most recent Indian elections in 1998 and 2004 have received more diverse and more in-depth news coverage by the private and the public broadcasters in India. The most important change came from the introduction of national and international 24-hour news channels allowing both literate *and* illiterate voters to follow the campaigns live on television.

Today, India's election coverage is as vibrant and diverse as those found in other nations, even though the impact of this dramatic change has not yet been analyzed sufficiently by Indian media scholars. Recent studies have found some evidence that Indians pay close attention to what is offered and that they might be influenced by political media messages. Unfortunately, most of these analyses are rather rudimentary and do not present reliable conclusions. It should be clear, however, that the increased diversity in election coverage (especially the more "entertainment" oriented political news coverage of the private broadcasters) should draw more Indian voters into the elections in the long run. Moreover, the increased focus on televised election coverage should allow even illiterate voters to better participate in the campaign and the political process overall.

Indian media scholars agree that the public broadcaster Doordarshan still dominates political news in India; however, the private news channels are increasingly successful in their competition for audiences across the country. It is also obvious that the quality of political news coverage in India is still far from perfect. While Doordarshan has been accused of routinely favoring the government in their political news, private broadcasters have exhibited the same pro-government bias during the 2004 parliamentary election. However, it remains unclear why private broadcasters have favored the candidates of the ruling party during the 2004 election. One possible explanation might be that most political observers expected the ruling BJP to win the election. As a result, the private media focused more attention on the projected winners than the likely losers. But no matter the real reason for this bias, both private and public broadcasters in India must balance their political news coverage of future elections.

Another reason for India's unique election campaign environment has been the strict limits on political advertising in the Indian broadcast media. Until 2004, political parties were not allowed to run full-fledged ad campaigns on Indian television or radio stations. Instead, the parties were restricted to free but pre-set advertising segments on the television and radio stations of Doordarshan and Air India Radio. While political advertisements in newspapers and magazines were permissible, the widespread illiteracy among Indian voters limited the impact of print advertising campaigns severely. As a consequence, the art of political advertising is a relatively young and unexplored field in India and has only recently shifted from traditional street and billboard advertising (Tekwani, 2005) to the more sophisticated televised campaigns many of us are familiar with.

The 2004 election showed, however, that Indian campaign managers have recognized the political potential of new communication technologies. A large number of political parties used the Internet as well as text- and voicemail messages to reach urban and literate voters throughout India. However, because of the high illiteracy rate and the limited access to these technologies by the average citizen, the impact of such new campaign techniques has been limited. Moreover, such high-tech election campaigns are still a novelty in a country where most voters have to be drawn to public rallies by dancing Bollywood stars or the promise of better heath services and clean drinking water.

While elections in India are characterized by an astonishing mix of traditional and modern campaign methods, very little is known about the impact of these campaigns on voters. Despite a 50-year tradition of democratic elections, only a small number of studies on media and elections have been conducted in India. Moreover, most of the existing studies from India are descriptive and far behind the standard of similar analyses from the United States, Europe, and East Asia. It is rather curious that most of the studies here discussed lack any kind of theoretical foundation and often get lost in descriptions of very specific events or processes that do not really advance our understanding of the interactions between media and elections in India. Overall, Indian media scholars have made very little progress beyond the early studies that tried to analyze the potential effects of people's social and cultural background on voting behavior.

It should be noted, though, that India's social and cultural environment provides a fascinating backdrop for studying media effects in elections within a non-Western context. Indian media scholars have identified a number of interesting venues for more research on political communication within an Indian context (for example, the impact of political films or music among rural and/or illiterate voters), however, no systematic effort has been made to explore these research topics with a coherent set of *empirical* analyses that are grounded in existing media *theories*. While it is true that very little is known about Indian elections (at least outside India), what is needed at this point are more theory-guided analyses that are based on empirical survey data or experiments—studies that show how the Indian media might affect voters who are likely to be swayed by very different campaign strategies and political processes than voters in more economically advanced but culturally less diverse nations.

We acknowledge that this could be a difficult undertaking. Western media theories cannot be easily adapted to India's social, cultural, and political environment, and many of the assumptions behind established media theories do not necessarily hold in India. The media agenda-setting hypothesis, for example, assumes that people are exposed to a fairly similar set of mass media messages. Obviously, such an assumption is problematic in India, where many different people consume many different types of media in many different languages. It seems to us, however, that such a lack of common assumptions is exactly what makes the study of political media effects in India interesting and challenging. We therefore believe that Indian media scholars should try to develop a unique Indian perspective on how the media might influence elections in "the world's largest democracy." Such a new perspective would help us all to better understand how the media influence elections in democracies around the world.

REFERENCES

Ahmed, B. (1970). Caste and electoral politics. *Asian Survey, 10*(11), 979–992.

Ahuja, M. L., & Paul, S. (1992). *The 1989-91 general elections in India.* New Delhi: Associated Publishing.

All India Radio (2007). Retrieved June 20, 2007, from http://www.allindiaradio.org/about1.html

Aram, I. A. (2003). Mass media and image-traps in contemporary politics. In K. Prasad (Ed.), *Political communication: An Indian experience* (Vol. 2, pp. 625–642). New Delhi: B. R. Publishing.

Associated Press (2004, May 19). Indian voters in final phase: Police on alert after 43 killed in election-related violence, *Edmonton Journal*, p. B14.

Baldauf, S. (2004, April 20). Dance of democracy; India heads to the polls: "There's a lot of enthusiasm at election time. It's turned into a carnival," *Hamilton Spectator*, p. A10.

Bhambri, C. P., & Varma, P. S. (1973). *The urban voter: Municipal elections in Rajasthan*. New Delhi: National Publication House.

Bhoopathy, D. (2003a). Mass media politics and political campaigning in India. In K. Prasad (Ed.), *Political communication: An Indian experience* (Vol. 2, pp. 413–465). New Delhi: B. R. Publishing.

Bhoopathy, D. (2003b). Cinema and politics in India. In K. Prasad (Ed.), *Political communication: An Indian experience*. (Vol. 2, pp. 505–532). New Delhi: B. R. Publishing.

Brass, P. R. (1984). Caste, faction and party politics in Indian politics. *Election Studies, I.* New Delhi: Chanakya Publications.

Brass, P. R. (1986). The 1984 parliamentary elections in Uttar Pradesh. *Asian Survey, 26*(6), 653–669

British Broadcasting Corporation (BBC). (2007). *Country Profile: India.* Retrieved June 20, 2007, from news.bbc.co.uk/2/hi/south_asia/country_profiles/1154019.stm.

Butler, D., Lahiri, A., & Roy, P. (1991), *India decides: Election 1952–1991*. New Dehli: Sage.

Chandra, B., Mukherjee, M., & Mukherjee, A. (2000). *India after independence 1947–2000*. New Delhi: Penguin.

Chopra, M. (1998, May/June). TV wins the elections. *Columbia Journalism Review*, pp. 67–69.

David, C . R . W . (1983). *Cinema as medium of communication in Tamil Nadu.* Madras: Christian Literature Society.

Deutsche Presse Agentur. (2004, March 10). Vajpayee's BJP starts "India shining" election campaign.

Dickey, S. (1993). The politics of adulation: Cinema and the production of politicians in South India. *The Journal of Asian Studies, 52*(2), 340–372.

Dua, M. R. (1999, July/September). Campaigning on television. *Communicator,* pp. 17–18. New Delhi.

Elder, J. W., & Schmitthenner, P. L. (1985). Film fantasy and populist politics of South India: N. T. Rama Rao & the Telugu Desam Party. In R. E. Fryenberg & P. Kolenda (Eds.), *Studies of South India: An anthology of recent research and scholarship* (pp. 373–387). Madras: New Era Publications.

Eldersveld, S. J., & Ahmed, B. (1978). *Citizens and politics: Mass political behaviour in India.* Chicago: Chicago University Press.

Election Commission of India, Press Notes. (2004a, August 1). *General election to Lok Sabha and certain state legislative assemblies, 2004—Telecast/Broadcast facility to Political Parties during elections.* Retrieved June 20, 2007, from http://www.eci.gov.in/press/current/PN_010404.pdf

Election Commission of India, Press Notes. (2004b, August 2). *Electoral reforms.* Retrieved June 20, 2007, from http:// http://www.eci.gov.in/press/current/PN_030804.pdf

Election Commission of India. (2007a). *About ECI.* Retrieved June 20, 2007, from http://eci.gov.in/about-eci/the_setup.asp

Election Commission of India. (2007b). Model Code of Conduct for the Guidance of Political Parties and Candidates. Retrieved June 20, 2007, from http://eci.gov.in/Model_Code_Conduct.pdf

Forrester, D. (1976). Factions and filmstars: Tamil Nadu politics since 1971. *Asian Survey, 16,* 283–296.

Freedom House. (2006a). Report on freedom in the world, India 2006. Retrieved June 20, 2007, from http://www.freedomhouse.org/inc/content/pubs/fiw/inc_country_detail.cfm?country=6980&pf

Freedom House. (2006b). *Press freedom report on India 2006.* Retrieved June 20, 2007, from http://www.freedomhouse.org

Gupta, D. (2004, March 12). Ban drives political parties online. *Media Asia.*

Gupta, R. (2004, March). Poll boosters: India's TV stations are as excited as the country's politicians in the run up to the general elections. Television Asia.

Hardgrave, R. L. (1975). *When stars displace the gods: The folk culture of cinema in Tamil Nadu.* Occasional Paper Series, No 3, Centre for Asian Studies, University of Texas at Arlington.

Hindu Online, The. (2004, April 5). *Smear advertising.* Retrieved June 20, 2007, from http://www.hindu.com/2004/04/05/stories/2004040500981000.htm

International Press Institute. (2004). World press freedom review. Retrieved June 20, 2007, from http://www.freemedia.at/cms/ipi/freedom_detail.html?country=/KW0001/KW0005/KW0116/&year=2004

International Telecommunications Unition (ITU). http://www.itu.int/net/home/index.aspx.

Internet and Mobile Association of India. (IAMAI) and IMRB International (2006). *Internet in India 2006.* I-Cube 2006 Report. Retrieved June 20, 2007, from http://www.iamai.in/book.pdf

Jefferey, R. (2000). *India's newspaper revolution: Capitalism, politics and Indian language press, 1977–99.* New Delhi: Oxford University Press.

Karan, K. (1994). Political communication and the 1991 general elections in India. Unpublished Ph.D. thesis, London School of Economics & Political Science, University of London.

Karan, K. (2000). *Media networking and the political communication strategies in the 1999 midterm elections in India.* Report for the Minor Research Project. University Grants Commission. Osmania University Hyderabad. India.

Karan, K. (in press). Political communication in India. In L. Willnat, & A. Aw (Eds.), *Political communication in Asia.* New York: Routledge.

Kaur, T. (1989). Effects of mass media and interpersonal communication on voting behaviour of new voters: A study of undergraduates in Hyderabad. MCJ Project Report, Department of Communication and Journalism, Osmania University, Hyderabad.

Kazmi, F. (1999). *The politics of India's conventional cinema: Imaging a universe, subverting a multiverse.* New Delhi: Sage.

Kumar, A. (1991). *The tenth round: Story of Indian elections.* Calcutta: Press Trust of India. Rupa & Co.

Library of Congress. (1995). *Country study India.* Retrieved June 20, 2007, from http://lcweb2.loc.gov/cgi-bin/query/r?frd/cstdy:@field(DOCID+in0165)

Library of Congress. (2004). *Federal Research Division Country Profile: India.* Retrieved June 20, 2007, from http://lcweb2.loc.gov/frd/cs/profiles/India.pdf

Madhvi, R. K. (2003). Mass media, election campaign and voting behaviour of women. In K. Prasad (Ed.), *Political communication: An Indian experience* (Vol. 2, pp. 563–595). New Delhi: B. R. Publishing.

Malhotra, S., & Crabtree, R. D. (2002). Gender, internationalization, and culture: Implications of the privatization of television in India. In M. J. Collier (Ed.), *Transforming communication about culture* (pp. 60–84). Thousand Oak, CA: Sage.

Media Advocacy Group. (1998). Assessing the role of television in the general election 1998. Retrieved June 20, 2007, from http://www.thehoot.org/story.asp?storyid=webhoothootL1K098024&pn=1

Meyer, R. C. (1989). How do Indians vote? *Asian Survey, 29*(12), 1111–1122.

Ministry of Information and Broadcasting, India. (2006). *Annual report 2005–2006.* Retrieved June 20, 2007, from http://mib.nic.in/informationb/POLICY/frames.htm

Mitra, S. K., & Singh, V. B. (1996). *Democracy and social change in India: A cross-sectional analysis of the national electorate.* New Delhi, Thousand Oaks, CA: Sage.

Murthy, T. S. K., & Paditar, V. (2005). Case Study 2. In R. Lopéz-Pintor & J. Fisher (Ed.), *Cost of registration and elections (CORE) project* (pp. 67–84). Washington, D.C.: Center for Transitional and Post-Conflict Governance. Retrieved June 20, 2007, from http://www.gsdrc.org/docs/open/PO50.pdf

Pandian, M. S. S. (1992). *The image trap: M.G. Ramachandran in film and politics.* New Delhi: Sage.

Pathak, D. N. (1992). *Political behaviour in Gujarat with reference to the fourth general elections.* ICSSR Studies. New Delhi: Allied Publishers.

Pattabhiraman, M. (1967). *The fourth general elections in India.* Bombay: Allied Publishers.

Pentane, M. S. (1992). *The image trap: M.G. Ramachandran in film and politics.* New Delhi: Sage.

Plasser, F. (2000). American campaign techniques worldwide. *Harvard International Journal of Press/Politics, 5*(4), 33–54.

Prasad, K. (2003). *Political communication: The Indian experience,* Vol 2. New Delhi: B. R. Publishing Corporation.

Prasad, N. (1967). *Ideology and organization in Indian political parties: A study of political parties at the grassroots.* New Delhi: Allied Publishers.

Prasad, N., & Kinni, N. G. S. (1968). *The city voter in India: A study of the 1967 general election in Nagpur.* New Delhi: Abhinav Publications.

Prateek, J. (1999). The Indian parliamentary election of 1998. *Electoral Studies, 18*(1), 124–27.

Ramaswamy, A. (2004, April 18). India's e-campaign is electioneering via e-mail, cellphone, Deutsche Presse Agentur.

Ramkumar, V. (2004, May 14). India: The largest democratic election in human history. Retrieved June 20, 2007, from http://www.freedominfo.org/news/20040514.htm

Rajgopal, A. (2001). *Politics after television: Hindu nationalism and the reshaping of public in India.* Cambridge, MA: Cambridge University Press.

Rao, A. M. (2003). Radio and political awareness in India. In K. Prasad (Ed.), *Political communication: An Indian experience* Vol. 2 (pp. 495–504). New Delhi: B. R. Publishing.

Rao, N. B. (2003a). *Miles to go. The Indian media scene.* New Delhi: Centre for Media Studies

Registrar of Newspapers for India. (RNI). (2007). Press in India. Retrieved June 20, 2007, from http://rni.nic.in/pii.htm

Sarwate, D. M. (1990). *Political marketing: The Indian experience.* New Delhi: McGraw Hill.

Sheth, D. L. (Ed.) (1975). *Citizens and parties: Aspects of competitive politics in India.* Bombay: Allied Publishers.

Singh, B., & Vajpeyi, D. K. (1981). *Government and politics in India.* New York: Apt Books.

Siriskar, V. M. (1965). *Political behaviour in India: A case study of the 1962 general elections.* Bombay: Manaktalas.

Siriskar, V. M. (1973). *Sovereigns without crowns: A behavioural analysis of the Indian electoral process.* Bombay: Popular Prakasam.

Sivathamby, K. (1981). *The Tamil film as a medium of political communication.* Madras: New Century Book House.

Standard, The. (2004, May 17). Stunning election upset revives storied Gandhi dynasty in India, p. D8.

Supreme Court of India. (1996). *A registered society v/s Union of India,* Writ Petition (Civil) No. 24 of 1995, dated 4 April 1996. Substituted by section 4 of the Amendment Act 46 of 2003 for the explanation I to section 77 (1) in the Representation of People Act (1951).

Suri, K. C. (2006, November). *Patterns of electoral support and party leadership in India: Some observations based on empirical research.* Paper presented at the International Conference on Election Systems and Electoral Politics in Bangalore. Retrieved June 20, 2007, from http://www.cses.org/plancom/2006Bangalore/Suri2006.pdf

Tekwani, S. R. (2005). *Visual culture in Indian politics: The gaudy billboard as political communication.* Paper presented at the annual meeting of the International Communication Association, New York City, 2005. Retrieved June 20, 2007, from http://www.allacademic.com/meta/p14010_index.html

Tekwani, T., & Shetty, K. (2007). Two Indias: The role of the internet in the 2004 elections. In R. Kluver, N. W. Jankowski, K. A. Foot, & S. M. Schneider, *The Internet and national elections: A comparative study of web campaigning* (pp. 150–162). New York: Routledge.

United Nations Educational, Scientific and Cultural Organizations (UNESCO). www.unesco.org.

Vakil, F. D. (1994). The urban voter. Hyderabad: Booklinks.

Varma, S. P, & Bhambri, C. P. (1967). *Elections and political consciousness in India.* New Delhi: Meenakshi Prakasam.

Varma, S. P., Narain, I., & Associates (1973). *Voting behaviour in a changing society: A case study of Rajasthan.* New Delhi: National Publications.

Vijaypur, B. S., & Balasubramanya, A. S. (2003). Mass media and influence of political news on young adults. In K. Prasad (Ed.), *Political communication: An Indian experience* (Vol. 2, pp. 533–559). New Delhi: B. R. Publishing.

Vohra, R. (2000). *The making of India.* New Delhi: Vision Books Pvt. Ltd.

Weiner, M., & Field, J. O. (1974–1977). On electoral politics in Indian states, 4 vols. Delhi: Manohar.

World Bank (2007). World Bank country profile for India. Retrieved June 20, 2007, from http://devdata.worldbank.org/external/CPProfile.asp?PTYPE=CP&CCODE=IND

II

ELECTION NEWS COVERAGE IN COUNTRIES WITH PROPORTIONAL ELECTIONS

9

The Netherlands: Media Logic and Floating Voters?

Claes H. de Vreese

The Netherlands is a key example of a Northern European "democratic corporatist" media system (Hallin & Mancini, 2004). It is characterized by a consensual political system, a welfare state model, a tradition of political–press parallelism, a professionalized news and journalism culture, a strong public broadcasting ethos, and a strong state intervention to protect press freedom. In this chapter the specifics of the country are discussed and the implications for election coverage are outlined.

THE DUTCH MEDIA SYSTEM

The Dutch media system is characterized by high newspaper circulation and a tradition of strong links between political parties and social and religious organizations on the one hand, and the press on the other. This political parallelism has co-existed and developed along with a high level of journalistic professionalization, including a consensus on professional standards of conduct, a notion of a commitment to the public interest, and a high degree of autonomy from social power, all organized within a primarily self-regulatory regime. The public broadcasting tradition is strong, and pluralism in the media market is obtained by the sum of the presence of different media organizations, newspapers, and channels. The Dutch system of public broadcasting is "a particularly strong and unusual case of a system based on the representation of organized social groups" (Hallin & Mancini, 2004, p. 165).

"Pillarization and Depillarization"

Indeed the "organized representation of social groups" is a prominent feature of the Dutch media system and society. For the better part of the twentieth century the Dutch media system was organized along political and religious cleavages that shaped the rest of Dutch society. The segmented structure of the Dutch media system has its origins in protracted political conflict in the later nineteenth and early twentieth centuries (Van der Eijk, 2000). These conflicts gave rise to a strongly organized cleavage structure organized in so-called "zuilen" (pillars) (Lijphart, 1968).

The pillarization of Dutch society has important implications for the media landscape. The circulation of newspapers increased simultaneously with the emergence and consolidation of the

pillars. The press became an integral part of the different pillars and a way for the different constituencies to communicate. This dynamic was driven by the Constitutional guarantee of press
freedom which allowed the newspapers to develop their own profiles. The newspaper industry
was therefore somewhat of a reflection of societal cleavages, and the system at the beginning of
the twentieth century remained until the 1960s. Key newspapers were the voices of Protestant,
Catholic, socialist, and liberal pillars of society while a number of papers maintained less explicit
ties with these and other movements in society (Hemels, 1979). Newspapers not only provided
news, but also "signature" features and editorials in which specific views and ideas about society
prevailed.

The organization of radio became an institutionalized part of the pillar system. A regulatory
regime imposed the regulation that broadcasters should "manifest cultural or religious needs in
the population," effectively suggested that they should be associated with one of the pillars, and
they should provide comprehensive programming (Van der Eijk, 2000, p. 306). Four organizations were originally granted a license (NCRV, Protestant; KRO, Catholic; VARA, social democratic; and AVRO, general). Each organization was granted 20 percent of the broadcasting time
with the remaining 20 percent available for national programming including newscasts and official events. In this system, news was produced outside of the pillarized system. When television
was introduced in 1948 its organization became embedded in the already existing broadcasting
system, also including the ratio-allocated broadcasting time.

The pillarization of Dutch society and media lasted until the 1960s when changes, often
referred to as depillarization, took place. Several mutually reinforcing phenomena could be observed (see also Van der Eijk, 2000). First, the loyalty to the respective pillars decreased, and
citizens started using media from other pillars, visiting other sports clubs, choosing other schools
for their children, and voting (less frequently) for "their" party. Second, the pillars themselves
changed, and the unique profile of each pillar became less identifiable, making it harder for the
pillars to claim loyalty. The internal cohesion of the pillars decreased, and ties with societal organizations dissolved. By the 1970s the process of depillarization of Dutch society was almost
complete.

Brants and McQuail (1997, p. 154) summarize the "segmented pluralism" like this:

> Dutch society between the beginning of the twentieth century and the mid-1960s (and notably the
> first twenty years after the Second World War) was a principal example of "segmented pluralism"
> with social movements, educational and communications systems, voluntary associations and
> political parties organized vertically (and often cross cutting through social strata) along the lines
> of religious and ideological cleavages.

The antecedents of the depillarization process have been observed from different perspectives, but all center on a declining raison d'etre for this form of organization (Lijphart, 1989; Van
der Eijk 2000). The success of integrating religious and ideological perspectives into the national
debate made the pillars superfluous (Ellemers 1984). The pillars had satisfied different groups'
demand for representation; and, once established, the pillars themselves were without function.

The media were both affected by and affected the process of depillarization. Ellemers (1984,
p. 142) suggested that media and "in particular television made people aware of the ideas and
values of other groups and subsequently eroded existing cleavages." With the depillarization, the
ties between newspapers and religious, political, and social movements were significantly loosened. By the end of the twentieth century newspapers were no longer specifically tied to societal
institutions, and most consider themselves without an explicit bias. This is not to say that the
influences have vanished completely. Most newspapers maintain Editorial Statutes that define

the paper's identity and profile and during elections, most newspapers make explicit partisan endorsements in editorials, mostly along the lines of the former pillar structure.

As the importance of these religious and ideological cleavages declined throughout the 1970s, the structure of (public) broadcasting was challenged. With the introduction of commercial broadcasting, de facto introduced in the Netherlands in 1989 with RTL broadcasting in Dutch from Luxembourg, public broadcasting faced new challenges and a continuous battle for funding and legitimacy. The broadcasts by RTL, along with foreign cable channels, led to gradual policy shifts (Brants & McQuail, 1997). By 2007, the Netherlands had reached a competitive and mature dual system of broadcasting with the major domestic commercial channels—RTL (3 channels), *SBS*, and *Net5*—and several international cable channels competing directly with the three public service networks.

The provision of television news is primarily undertaken by the public broadcasting organization NOS and the news department of RTL. NOS's *Acht Uur Journaal* (8 o'clock news) is comparable to the BBC's main evening news bulletin, both in terms of "national authority" and audience share. Comparative analyses of the public NOS and the private RTL news have revealed some differences between the two programs, both in their election coverage (van Praag & Brants, 2000; van Praag & van der Eijk, 1998) and during routine periods (Semetko & Valkenburg, 2000), but also many similarities. The fundamental differences between public and commercial news programs, as found in a comparative study of British and American election coverage (Semetko et al., 1991), have not been found to apply to NOS and RTL in the Dutch case. The 1995 introduction of the commercial entertainment channel SBS brought along a new mode of news reporting in the Netherlands. Human interest journalism programs have contributed to the popularity of new channels, and posed new competitive challenges for RTL and public broadcaster NOS.

The political leanings in favor of a specific religious or ideological standpoint are less pronounced in broadcasting compared to the press. Van der Eijk (2000, p. 320) writes: "One important reason is that, via their federated organization, NOS, the different broadcast organizations produce the newscasts on the public channels jointly; consequently these newscasts are unlikely to reflect the central values of any one of the [broadcast] organizations."

During past decades and particularly in recent years, Dutch politics has gone through a period of change. The changes are notable when looking at electoral behavior in the country. While elections for a long period produced similar outcomes and were thus relatively boring and predictable, instability and rapid change have become a reality of Dutch politics. Prior to 1990 an election meant that 10% of the seats in Parliament changed to other parties. Since 1990 this has increased to between 25 and 30%. At the same time, more than 40% of the electorate reports making their voting decision in the final week before the election, which compares to 20% prior to 1990 (Aarts, 2005). Of course significant electoral change had been witnessed before, but the instability in recent elections is unique in Dutch parliamentary history. While this development is inconvenient and annoying to established political parties, it can be seen as a healthy antidote of choice and competition in an otherwise stable democracy.

REGULATORY REGIME AND CONVENTIONS

The Dutch regulatory regime for media and political communications contains few restrictions and is designed to enable access and to safeguard fairness. There are no restrictions on the collection or publication of polls, there are no restrictions on direct funding or subsidies, there is no limit on financial contributions, and there are no restrictions on the use of ads. All political parties are provided free air time on television, larger parties participate in election debates, and news programs are trusted to bring a fair, balanced, and unbiased coverage of politics and elections.

In terms of providing (public) funding to the media, many of the same principles are followed. Press policies include measures to support the press and enhance the diversity of titles (Brants, 2004). Public broadcasting used to be financed via a license fee and membership contributions. This was abandoned in 2000 and replaced by a levy on the income tax which, together with membership fees and revenues from commercials, funded public broadcasting organizations.

For public broadcasting, the policy is designed to secure content diversity through a "systemic openness" which implies that new organizations (provided they have 60,000 members and that their programming is seen to contribute to the representation of different movements and currents in Dutch society) are given air time. The Media Act further explicated that the three public channels must provide a full range and variety of programs, defined as a minimum of 35% information and educational programming (which should be fair and balanced) and at least 25% cultural programming. Since 2001, a classification system has been in place that places all programs in specific categories, a system which is used to monitor whether public broadcasters are "delivering" the agreed content.

In general, the Dutch system relies on a notion of "external diversity," meaning that diversity is achieved by having a variety of organizations offering programming (which as a total is believed to be diverse). This is different from the "classic" BBC model of public broadcasting where diversity is to be insured internally, within the branches of the BBC. In terms of the news coverage of elections, the public broadcaster NOS is supposed to report in a balanced and fair fashion and to give access to different parties. This obligation is not monitored strictly, and some dissatisfaction is always part of the campaign period since the sheer number of political parties in the Netherlands (which can amount to 20 in one election) makes it hard to provide access to all parties and actors.

THE DEVELOPMENT OF ELECTION COVERAGE

The contents and forms of election coverage are a function of (changes in the) political system and culture and in the media landscape itself. This section concentrates on (1) *journalistic styles*; (2) the *contents*; and (3) the *effects* of election coverage. First of all, research suggests that journalists may fulfill different roles (Patterson, 1998). This also applies to the election period where Blumler and Gurevitch (1995) distinguish between a "sacerdotal" and a "pragmatic" journalistic approach to elections. In a sacerdotal approach, elections are perceived as the fundamental element of democracy, and campaigns are considered newsworthy per se. The attitude towards politicians is respectful, cautious, and reactive. In a pragmatic approach campaign news is evaluated against conventional news selection criteria and is not automatically given special attention. The pragmatic orientation implies that the "amount of time or space allocated to [political events] will be determined by strict considerations of news values, in competition with the newsworthiness of other stories" (Semetko et al., 1991, p. 6).

Previous research has suggested that European public broadcasters have been cautious, respectful towards politicians, and reactive towards the political party agendas (Asp, 1983; Gurevitch & Blumler, 1993). Earlier studies of election coverage at the Dutch public broadcaster NOS Journaal have reached similar conclusions. NOS Journaal was seen to treat politics "respectfully" (van Praag & van der Eijk, 1998), and it adhered to the political party agenda rather than setting its own agenda (Meurs, van Praag & Brants, 1995). This situation appears to have changed somewhat over time (de Vreese, 2001). The change in the basic principle for election coverage was formulated by one of the news executives. NOS was reporting "about *the campaign, rather than reporting the campaign*" (de Vreese, 2001, p. xx).

Indeed, contrary to its campaign coverage of the national elections in 1986, 1989, and 1994, NOS, from 1998 and onwards, refrained from a daily campaign segment. Election news was to be evaluated according to conventional news values and not be artificially inflated by the fact that it was election time. According to an internal memorandum from 1998 (de Vreese, 2001):

> We shall no longer adhere to the slogan "campaign time is news time." We will depart from our policy of a daily campaign segment with a visit to all the rallies including sphere visuals and staged media events, as has been the case in earlier elections. We must challenge the old notion of campaign coverage (seen at least from 1986 and onwards): that the campaign in itself is so news-worthy that it justifies a daily display of activities. The consequence hereof is that it is no longer self-explanatory that we have a daily campaign segment.

During earlier campaigns, NOS was found to follow the political agenda (de Vries & van Praag, 1995; van Praag & van der Eijk, 1998) and be relatively reactive towards politicians (van Praag & Brants, 1999). In relation to the 1998 elections, de Vreese (2001) found that rather than being only "agenda-sending," NOS in its election coverage also assumed a role of "agenda-setting." An agenda-sending approach with a daily visit to party activities, the policy applied at the 1994 and earlier national elections, was abandoned.

The discretion displayed by NOS in defining the news agenda and providing an interpretative context to the issues covered was inherent to the role of an analytical political commentator, which was a central feature of the news show during the 1998 national elections. His role was to bring together the news of the day, put it in perspective, and offer analyses and interpretations of the events for the campaign. An analysis of the air-time devoted to politicians in the news on the Dutch public networks during the 1994 and 1998 national elections suggested that the proportion of time reserved for politicians decreased by 40% from 1994 to 1998 (van Praag & Brants, 1999). This observation dovetails with studies of election news in the U.S. (Hallin, 1992) and similar trends have been found in the BBC's coverage of the 1992 and 1997 British general elections (Blumler & Gurevitch, 1998).

An additional element suggesting the discretion of *NOS* in its election coverage was found in a concern with balance and impartiality. While balance in political reporting is inherent in the public service ethos (McQuail, 1992), NOS appeared to have departed from the concise "stop watch interpretation" of balance. Demands for balanced reporting at NOS were neither to be fulfilled within a single nor in a couple of news stories, but rather within and between the different bulletins over the course of the campaign. A similar observation was made for the British general election in 1992 where newsroom executives formally announced that their organizations would not be fulfilling balance requirements by monitoring all election news with a stop watch (Semetko, 1996).

Election Coverage in the Netherlands: More Horse Race, But Still Substantive

Elections enjoy strong media attention in the Netherlands. The national newspapers devote much space in both the news sections and in the editorial/opinion sections to elections. The amount of campaign news in the newspapers does not appear to be decreasing. Heijting and De Haan (2005, p. 47) show that the five national newspapers devoted, on average, 6.3 articles per day during the campaign to the elections in 1998. In 2002 this number was 5.5 and in 2003, on average, 8.6. There is some expected variation between different newspapers with quality broadsheet papers such as *de Volkskrant*, *NRC Handelsblad*, and *Trouw* devoting more articles to the elections than the more populist *Algemeen Dagblad* and *De Telegraaf*.

Given the importance of television, not only in general terms for election coverage, but also specifically for Dutch voters as well as better availability of comparable data (over time) most attention will be paid to the content of television election coverage. In terms of the visibility of national elections in the news, the public broadcaster news show *NOS Journaal* devoted 37% of its main evening news bulletins to the elections in 1998 compared to 30% at the commercial broadcaster. In 2002 this was 27% and 25% respectively, and in 2003 the elections took up 42% and 31% of the main evening news (Van Praag & Brants, 2005, p. 83). Indeed, the 2003 elections were highly visible, and the elections were mentioned in the headlines of the main news bulletins daily (with the exception of one day) during the campaign.

Turning to the *content* of the election news, the literature suggests that election coverage can be focused on issues or more on the polls and the horse race (Patterson, 1993), politicians' motives and strategies (Cappella & Jamieson, 1997), or on the role of the media in the campaign (for which the phrase "meta-coverage" has been coined) (Esser & d'Angelo, 2006). In general terms issue coverage is said to decrease at the expense of these other foci. Altheide and Snow (1979) and Mazzoleni (1987) two to three decades ago discussed the emergence of "media logic" in which the content of the news is decided by the media and where political actors adapt their performance to the needs of the media. Entman (1989, pp. 49–50), worrying about this development, concluded that "the need to manufacture news that attracts and retains mass audiences and thus to address and see the public as consumers is holding journalists in a tightening grip."

In the Netherlands, some evidence may be found of such developments. Brants and van Praag (2006) suggest that given the increased competition and commercialization, one would expect the Netherlands to also adhere more to the media logic, but the picture is less clear. When distinguishing between substantive (issue-driven) news, horse race news (taking the form of either opinion polls or reflections, interpretations, and coalition speculations), or hoopla news (focusing on campaign events and stunts), we can note an increase in horse race coverage during the past 20 years (both in terms of poll-based reporting and news stemming from polls) (see Table 9.1). However, this increase does not seem to come (clearly) at the expense of substantive news which is still high and relatively stable. The increase seems to come more from a decrease in the focus on events on the campaign trail.

In a longitudinal analysis looking at sample elections between 1956 and 2003, Brants and van Praag (2006) conclude about the 2003 general elections that the "campaign showed clear signs of media logic: performance driven campaign communication, media orientation on the

TABLE 9.1
Election News on Dutch Television 1986-2003 (Percentages)

	1986	*1989*	*1994*		*1998*		*2002*		*2003*	
	NOS	*NOS*	*NOS*	*RTL*	*NOS*	*RTL*	*NOS*	*RTL*	*NOS*	*RTL*
Substantive news	51	41	35	28	52	53	50	34	45	26
Horse race news	18	31	29	30	33	24	21	38	43	44
- opinion polls			10	3	13	18	3	22	11	25
- reflections			19	27	20	6	18	16	32	19
'Hoopla' news	32	27	37	42	15	23	29	29	11	28

Note: NOS is the public broadcaster, RTL started in 1989
Source: Brants and van Praag, 2006.

TABLE 9.2
News Types in Dutch Election News, Television and Newspapers, 1994–2006

	1994	1998	2002	2003	2006
Issue news	34	35	28	32	38
Conflict news	47	49	51	49	45
Horse race news	19	15	21	19	17

Note: percentages are based on election news in the major national newspapers and most important television news outlets.
Source: Kleinnijenhuis et al., 2007.

public, on the whole less substantive and more horse race and poll driven reporting." They also note, however, that the share of issue news is still substantial.

In another series of studies, a distinction was made between issue news, conflict news, and horse race news (Kleinnijenhuis et al., 2007). Corroborating the evidence provided by Brants and van Praag (2005)—and contrary to what the general literature suggests—they too find that issue news is high and has remained high (see Table 9.2). The differences in the absolute level of issue news between the two series of studies can be explained by the different methods and operationalization used. These differences notwithstanding it is safe to say that Dutch election coverage is still relatively substantive in focus, and there are no clear signs of a change in this.

Another feature of election coverage that is allegedly on the increase is the degree of *personalization*, which may refer to news that focuses on politicians' personalities and the presence of politicians in talk show and entertainment programming—see Brants, Cabri & Neijens (2000) and van Zoonen (2000) for Dutch examples and Baum and Jamison (2006) for a recent U.S. study. Other research has addressed the tendency to place more emphasis on the candidates and party leaders (and de facto less on the party and ideology). Kleinnijenhuis et al. (2003, p. 80) report findings suggesting that while parties and candidates were covered evenly in the elections in 1994 and 1998, by 2002 65% of all news focused on candidates while only 35% of all news focused on a political party. They take this as evidence of personalization in the news. That said, a comparative study of Dutch and German election news concluded that Dutch television news applies a principle of "equal access" in which not only top candidates are given access to the news (Schoenbach, de Ridder, & Lauf, 2005).

A third feature of election news that is often considered is the degree of *conflict* reporting. Conflict news is often said to distance voters from politics (Lichter & Noyes, 1996), but news focusing on disagreement, conflict, and differences of opinion between political actors may provide mobilizing information by showing what is at stake and that there is a genuine choice (de Vreese, 2006). Semetko and Valkenburg (2000) and de Vreese et al. (2001), outside an electoral context, show that the conflict frame is present in Dutch news, together with the economic consequences and responsibility frames. Specifically in relation to elections, Kleinnijenhuis et al. (2003, p. 63) demonstrate that conflict news, news focusing on support and criticisms of opponents and allies, and news about successes and failures, has increased and was very high during the 2002 elections. There is little systematic and comparable knowledge, however, about the presence and visibility of the conflict frame across elections over time.

Election Coverage in a System of Multi-Level Governance

Dutch national politics, as is the case in most European countries today, has become part of an intricate system of local, regional, national, and supra-national levels of governance. One of the defining features is the push towards European integration. Research on the EU and European elections in the news is burgeoning. By and large, European affairs in the news tend to be *marginal*, *cyclical*, *domestic,* and slightly *negative*. Coverage of European affairs is cyclical in nature with coverage of the EU virtually absent from the news agenda and then peaking around important EU events to vanish off the agenda again (de Vreese et al., 2001; Norris, 2000). EU actors (such as candidates for the EP and members of EU institutions) tend to be only marginally represented in the news. In fact, most European issues are discussed by national political actors (de Vreese, 2002; de Vreese et al., 2006). Finally, news about European issues is largely neutral, but when it contains evaluations, these tend to be negative (de Vreese et al., 2006).

However, there is huge variation to this pattern. While television news in, for example, Denmark devoted more than 20% of the news leading up to the 1999 and 2004 European elections to these elections, news in the Netherlands devoted between 2 and 8% of the time to the elections, almost making the Netherlands "European Champions" in neglecting Brussels. Table 9.3 shows that the European elections were essentially off the screen in 1999 and increased (in time more than quadrupled) at the European elections in 2004. This increase notwithstanding, the Netherlands is still in the category of countries that only devotes limited time to European elections (de Vreese et al., 2006). It should be noted however, that the national referendum in the Netherlands on the EU Constitutional Treaty in 2005 generated a lot of news coverage and dominated the news agenda in the weeks leading up to the referendum (Neijens et al., 2005; Schuck & de Vreese, 2006).

The Effects of Campaign and Election News: Small But Increasing

We finally turn to uses and effects of election coverage in the Netherlands. First, news availability (and newspaper readership, as highlighted above) is high and a significant part of prime time television on the public broadcasting channels is devoted to news and current affairs programs. A considerable share of the electorate is, therefore, frequently exposed to election news. As a second introductory remark, it should be noted that despite the plethora of political parties in the Netherlands, up until the early 2000s Dutch electoral politics had been characterized by stability. This explains why a significant portion of the literature has found only marginal effects of campaigns and election news on vote *choice*. In the words of Van der Eijk (2000, p. 331):

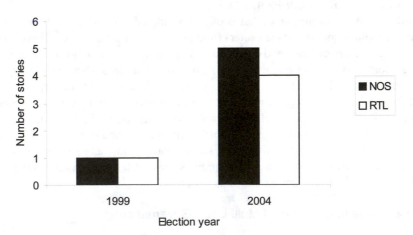

Note: Number of stories about the European elections in the main evening television news in the two weeks leading up to the elections. Source: De Vreese, 2005, p. 213.

FIGURE 9.1 Visibility of European elections on national television news 1999 and 2004.

It must be said that survey-based research in the Netherlands has come to largely negative conclusions on the issue of media effects during election campaigns. Changes in the voters' party preference, in the party for which they actually vote, or in their evaluation of party leaders are far more often than not unrelated to the use of specific media or to exposure to a specific message.

This general reservation notwithstanding, research focusing on effects of campaigns and election coverage is accumulating. When studying effects of news and campaigns, we may distinguish between effects on cognitions, attitudes, and behavior such as turnout and vote choice (see McLeod et al., 2002; de Vreese & Semetko, 2004). The relationship between media use and political knowledge, efficacy, trust, and political participation in the Netherlands found support for a "dual effects hypothesis" with regular watching of public service channels being positively related with cognition, efficacy, and turnout while opting for commercial channels had negative effects (Aarts & Semetko, 2003). These findings were interpreted in the light of the changing media landscape in Europe where audiences for public channels are decreasing but increasing for commercial channels. This might lead to a "virtuous circle" happening only for a small and decreasing part of the citizenry while other media choices contribute to diminishing political engagement and participation. Using panel survey data and a media content analysis from the Netherlands (but outside an election context), de Vreese and Boomgaarden (2006) extended the notion of differential effects to show that it is not so much the choice of channels or news outlets per se that matters, but rather the content and political information in these outlets.

While research has not produced clear-cut findings of campaign effects and election coverage exposure effects on vote choice, it has been shown that campaigns might well produce effects, but that these can be across-the-board, and thus not vary by news media use. This was the case in the 1998 elections (van der Brug and van der Eijk, 1998). Other research showed that exposure to television news in the 1994 elections reduced the loss of the social democratic party (Couvret et al., 1995), but van der Eijk (2000) notes that even studies relying on both survey data and media content analyses found only sporadic and no systematic effects (Kleinnijenhuis et al., 1995).

Recent research, based on the 2002 and 2003 elections, concluded that the campaigns both generated modest across-the-board effects and some effects on voting preference as a function of news exposure (Van der Brug & Van der Eijk, 2005). A more dynamic model of the campaign and news showed, on the basis of a biweekly seven-wave panel study and a daily content analysis of television news and newspapers, that negative news had a significant negative effect on trust in party leaders. The distrust in party leaders produced a delayed sleeper effect on turnout and on the actual vote. These findings were used to explain why the Christian Democrats could win the 2002 elections in defiance of the polls (Kleijnnijenhuis et al., 2006). In a study of the 2006 elections, it was demonstrated that not only news about the elections affected vote choice, but that online self-help voting advices also affected vote choice, in particular for those with lower levels of political knowledge (Kleinnijenhuis et al., 2007).

In relation to *European Parliamentary elections*, Peter (2004) found that exposure to news about the 1999 elections decreased citizens' perceptions of European integration being an important issue. This might be explained by the consensus among Dutch political parties about most issues of European integration in 1999 and the, related, virtual absence of news about the elections which might have conveyed the impression that Europe was neither a particularly important nor problematic issue. For the 2004 European elections, however, Banducci and de Vreese (2006) found that the visibility of anti-European actors in the news, which was considerable in the Netherlands in 2004, had a mobilizing function and increased turnout. Finally, in relation to the national referendum on the EU Constitutional Treaty in 2005, Schuck and de Vreese (2006) investigated the dynamics of the campaign and the effects of the election coverage on turnout. They found that the framing of the referendum and the Treaty as a potential benefit in the news mobilized Euroskeptic voters to turn out to vote due to the perceived risks that a yes outcome would bring.

POLITICAL COMMERCIALS AND TELEVISION DEBATES

Turning to paid and organized publicity (political commercials and television debates), a number of things are important. First, it should be stressed that political campaigns in the Netherlands up until the turn of the millennium could be described as relatively dull given the high degree of stability in the political system and the electorate's voting behavior. Second, the campaigns themselves, partially as a function of the above, were amateurish and low cost (Koole, 1992; van Praag, 2005). There seems to be some change in this situation though, with campaigns becoming slightly more aggressive, expensive, and professionalized.

To start with the political campaigns, they have tended to be on the dull side and most politicians, especially in the ideological center, have refrained from using attack strategies. This is largely due to the multiple party, coalition government tradition of the country in which it would become difficult to form a coalition with opponents after the election if the opponents had been attacked heavily. This would also make the attacking party lose credibility if voters would immediately see two or more "sworn enemies" link up in a new coalition. However, the most recent campaigns in 2002, 2003, and 2006 did contain elements of politicians using the attack mode. Especially in 2002, the later murdered leader of the LPF party, Pim Fortuyn, received and gave harsh criticism. And in 2006, the incumbent government managed to make the leader of the Social Democratic party look like an inconsistent flip-flopper, much in the way that the Republications in the United States managed to create doubts about the consistency of the policies of the Democratic presidential candidate in 2004, John Kerry.

The first changes in campaign style and the incorporation of elements of late-modern campaign techniques (Farrell, 1996) were already noticed during the 1994 elections when the largest parties (the Christian Democrats and the Social Democrats) employed part-time election and opinion researchers. This, however, is by no means a widespread phenomenon and the campaign is largely an "internal party affair" with campaign managers, media strategists, and researchers being recruited from the party membership (Brants, 2006). Indeed, in relation to the 2004 European Parliamentary elections, de Vreese (2008) found that the campaign in the Netherlands was indeed short and not very labor or capital intensive.

In reaching the electorate with their messages, Dutch politicians have to a large extent relied on the ample space provided by the news media. Use has been made of newspaper ads (both national and local), but one of the more important communication tools has been the "party spot" and later political ads on television. Party spots have been aired on the radio since 1925 and in 1959 the first party spots were broadcast on television (Brants, 1995). Party spots are allocated to political parties in equal amounts, are free of any legal restrictions on form or content, and they are broadcast throughout the year with a slightly higher frequency during the campaign period. The length of the spots has been reduced from the original ten minutes to three minutes today. Brants (2006) noted that the reduction in time and changes in the formal features of the spots have made them somewhat comparable to "regular" political ads.

Regular political advertising was experimented with on the radio and local television in the late 1980s and early 1990s. However political ads on national television were only introduced in 2002. One interpretation suggests that there was great reluctance on the side of the commercial broadcasters because they feared that advertisers might not want to be placed next to a political party ad (Brants, 2006). In 2002, two parties, the Socialist party (SP) and the Lib-Dems (D66) both bought air time and during the elections in 2003, the Social Democrats ran commercials on local television while SP, the Liberals (VVD), the Christian Union (CU), and the LPF (remains of the List Fortuyn) advertised on national television. The introduction of ads in Dutch politics was comparatively late. And the use of and amount of money going into political ads in the Netherlands is still very limited but it is increasing.

While advertising is (still) of limited impact, television debates have gained in importance and have also become the focus of news coverage of the elections. Since the mid-1970s a party leader debate on the evening before the elections has been customary. The specific form of the debates changes from election to election, but it typically consists of one or more prominent political journalists asking the participants initial questions and then giving them the opportunity to comment on each other. Negotiations take place about which party leaders to include. The debates are popular and in the 1980s and 1990s enjoyed very large audiences, sometimes almost half of the electorate (Brants & van Praag, 1995; van der Eijk & van Praag, 1987).

In recent years, the number of debates has gone up, primarily because the commercial broadcaster RTL also hosts a debate. In the 2006 elections, there were several debates between both the leaders of the smaller parties and of the larger parties and between the party leaders of the largest parties (the Social Democratic PvdA party and the Christian Democratic CDA party). In 2002, 2003, and 2006 the debates were important events in the campaign and generated much subsequent news coverage.

DUTCH ELECTION NEWS IN THE FUTURE

Politics and political communication in the Netherlands appear to be in some state of flux. Voters are increasingly disloyal to political parties and change parties between elections; political parties emerge and disappear; the pillarization and stability of Dutch political culture and society are things of the past; media channels and outlets proliferate; and audiences fragment. Journalists are starting to adhere somewhat to principles of media logic and politicians are slowly discovering (the need for) attack campaign strategies and the use of targeted strategic communication.

However, these larger changes have not (at least not yet) fundamentally changed the nature and contents of election coverage. National elections are still covered widely in both newspapers and on television and the visibility of European elections is even rising. Substantive issue news has *not* been replaced in large amounts by other news, though there seems to be a significant increase over time in the attraction for poll driven, horse race coverage. This development is, however, not to be taken at face value as simply bad or damaging for Dutch democracy and electoral processes. Polls can serve the function of showing an electorate what is on offer and who is likely to win (and thus be part of a coalition government). The latter can be potentially important information in a multi-party system where any election produces a coalition government.

Moreover, conflict news, which is strongly present in the election news coverage, should also not necessarily be discarded as undesired. In some literature, there seems to be an aversion towards and fear of disagreement and conflict. The media's endless focus on conflict and political strategy fuels a spiral of cynicism, Cappella and Jamieson (1997) conclude. And an emphasis on conflict and battles portrays politics as a game and may undermine democracy (Fallows, 1996). However, from the viewpoint of democratic processes and informed citizenship, conflict in news about politics has more advantages than disadvantages. Conflict is inherent to political reasoning and in democratic theory conflict is an essential part of decision-making (Sartori, 1987). News focusing on disagreement, conflict, and differences of opinion between political actors therefore provides mobilizing information by showing what is at stake and that there is a genuine choice. If citizens, through the media, realize that there is something to choose from, conflict has positive effects on citizens' political attitudes and participation (de Vreese 2006).

One other development, traces of which can also be detected, is the development towards a stronger focus on individuals. This may play out in regular news coverage but is even more strongly seen by the increase in appearance of politicians in other genres and outlets. Except for observing this trend, very little is known about the extent and consequences of this. The 2006 elections produced memorable situations of politicians in game shows, gossip television "news shows," and a prime minister trying to ride a skateboard. In the Dutch case, Van Zoonen (2004) argues for the potential of popular culture to expand the scope and appeal of politics, but Aalberts (2006) demonstrated that other forms of addressing (potential) young voters in the Netherlands had no positive effects on engagement and mobilization. Research from the United States suggests that political information in non-traditional news formats can spark political engagement and consistent voting behavior (Baum & Jamison, 2006). Suffice to say that these developments challenge political communication scholars to conceptualize the scope of a campaign differently and maybe not only include "traditional" news outlets.

On a related note it seems evident that politicians feel a greater need for a strategic and controlled form of political communication in which they can by-pass the selection and framing filters of political journalism. This would lead to the expectations that ads would play an increasingly important role in the future of Dutch campaigns. However, other developments are both observable and plausible. In an attempt to communicate directly with voters, most parties have turned to the Internet for not only creating informative websites, but also to offer opportunities for chatting, blogging, etc. Again the uses and effects of these developments are largely unknown at this point, though with the high penetration and use of the Internet in the Netherlands this is likely not to emerge merely as a marginal complementary form of campaign communication. Indeed recent research, contrary to conventional wisdom, has shown that Internet usage among young people can be diverse and include peer communication, entertainment, and consumption of politics online, which seems to be positively related to most forms of political engagement and participation (de Vreese, 2007).

From a systemic perspective it seems that one of the key features of the democratic corporatist model (Hallin & Mancini, 2004), namely the strong public service broadcasting tradition, in particular when it come to news provision, might also be under pressure. In a competitive media landscape public broadcasters can be put in a position where it becomes questionable whether they can provide the same share of news and in particular political news during the prime time hours.

Finally, it is worth pointing out that in the aftermath of the tumultuous elections of 2002 and 2003, the topics of "media, journalism, and politics" have been much contested. The Council for Social Development, the Council for Public Administration, and the Scientific Council for Government Policy have all issued reports that dealt specifically with the relationship between journalism and politics. Gloomy pictures of a not too healthy relationship dominate these reports and result in the academic literature also suggesting that mistrust is increasing not only between politicians and citizens, but also between politicians and media and between media and citizens. In the future, political journalism will have to come to terms with this discussion and show whether these are fundamental changes or "merely" self-reflection on the side of both politics and the media in a society still coming to terms with a political assassination in 2002 and the murder of film maker Theo van Gogh in 2004. With (parts of) the Dutch electorate drifting and the media in flux, there should be ample room for political communication research in the future to identify the changes, explicate the antecedents, and investigate the consequences.

REFERENCES

Aalberts, C. (2006). *Aantrekkelijke politiek? Een onderzoek naar jongeren en popularisering van politiek* [Attractive politics? A study of youth and popularization of politics]. Amsterdam: Sphinhuis.

Aarts, C. (2005). Dwarse kiezers. [Inaugural lecture], University of Twente.

Aarts, C., & Semetko, H.A. (2003). The divided electorate: Effects of media use on political involvement. *Journal of Politics, 65*(3), 759–784.

Altheide, D. L., & Snow, R. P. (1979). *Media logic*. Beverly Hills, CA: Sage.

Asp, K. (1983). The struggle for the agenda: Party agenda, media agenda, and voter agendt in the 1979 Swedish election campaign. *Communication Research, 10,* 333–355.

Banducci, S., & de Vreese, C. H. (2006, June). *Media, Euroskepticism and turnout in European elections.* Paper presented at the International Communication Association Convention, Dresden, Germany.

Baum, M., & Jamison, A. S. (2006). The Oprah effect: How soft news helps inattentive citizens vote consistently. *Journal of Politics, 68*(4), 946–959.

Blumler, J. G., & Gurevitch, M. (1995). *The crisis of public communication*. London: Routledge.

Boomgaarden, H. G., de Vries, H., & van Praag, Ph. (1995) De inhoud van het campagnenieuws [The contents of the campaign news]. In K. Brants & Ph. van Praag (Eds.), *Verkkop van de politiek* (Selling politics]. Amsterdam: Het Spinhuis.

Brants, K. L. K. (1995). The blank spot: Political advertising in the Netherlands. In L. L Kaid & C. Holtz-Bacha (Eds.), *Political advertising in western democracies* (pp. 143–161). Thousand Oaks, CA: Sage.

Brants, K. L. K. (2004). The Netherlands. In M. Kelly, G. Mazzoleni, & D. McQuail (Eds.), *The media in Europe* (pp. 145–156). London: Sage.

Brants, K. L. K (2006). Sure to come, but temporarily delayed: The Netherlands in search of the political ad. In L. L. Kaid & C. Holz-Bacha (Eds.), *Handbook of political advertising* (pp. 227–240). London: Sage.

Brants, K. L. K, Cabri, E., & Neijens, P.C. (2000). Hoe informatief en hoe leuk? Infotainment in de campagne [How informative and how nice? Infotainment in the campaign]. In P. van Praag & K.L.K. Brants (Eds.), *Tussen beeld en inhoud. Politiek en media in de verkiezingen van 1998* [Between image and content. Politics and media in the elections of 1998] (pp. 134–153). Amsterdam: Het Spinhuis.

Brants, K. L. K., & McQuail, D. (1997). The Netherlands. In B. S. Oestergaard (Ed), *The media in Western Europe* (pp. 153–167). London: Sage.

Brants, K. L. K., & van Praag, Ph. Jr. (1995). *Verkoop van de politiek* [Selling politics]. Amsterdam: Het Spinhuis.

Brants, K. L. K., & van Praag, Ph. Jr. (2006). Signs of media logic. Half a century of political communication in the Netherlands. *Javnost—the Public, 13,* 25–40.

Brug, W. van der, & Eijk, C. van der (2005). Welke effecten hadden de campagnes nu eigenlijk? [What effects did the campaigns in fact have]. In K. Brants & P. van Praag (Eds.), *Politiek en media in verwarring* [Politics and media in flux] (pp. 244–267). Amsterdam: Spinhuis.

Cappella, J. N., & Jamieson, K. H. (1997). *The spiral of cynicism: The press and the public good*. New York: Oxford University Press.

Couvret, E., van der Eijk, C., & van Praag, Ph. Jr. (1995). Effecten van de campagne [Effects of the campaign]. In K. Brants & Ph. van Praag (Eds.), *Verkoop van de politiek* [Selling politics] (pp. 211–227). Amsterdam: Het Spinhuis.

Eijk, C. van der (2000). The Netherlands: Media and politics between segmented pluralism and market forces. In R. Gunther & A. Mughan (Eds.), *Democracy and the media: A comparative perspective* (pp. 303–342). Cambridge, UK: Cambridge University Press.

Eijk, C. van der, & van Praag, Ph. Jr. (1987). *De strijd om de meerderheid: De verkiezingen van 1986* [The battle over the majority. The 1986 elections]. Amsterdam: CT Press.

Ellermers, J (1984). Pillarization as a process of modernization. *Acta Politica: International Journal of Political Science, 19,* 129–144.

Entman, R. (1989). *Democracy without citizens: Media and the decay of American politics*. New York: Oxford University Press.

Esser, F., & D'Angelo, P. (2006). Framing the press and publicity process in German, British and U.S. General Election campaigns: A comparative study of metacoverage. *Harvard International Journal of Press/Politics, 11*(3), 44–66.

Fallows, J. (1996). *Breaking the news. How the media undermine American democracy.* New York: Pantheon Books.

Farrell, D. (1996). Campaign strategies and tactics. In L. LeDuc, R. G. Niemi, & P. Norris (Eds.), *Comparing democracies and voting in a global perspective* (pp. 160–183). London: Sage.

Gurevitch, M., & Blumler, J. G. (1993). Comparative research: The extending frontier. In D. L. Swanson & D. Nimmo (Eds.), *New directions in political communication: A resource book* (pp. 305–325). Newbury Park, CA: Sage.

Hallin, D. (1992). Sound bite news: Television coverage of elections, 1968–1988. *Journal of Communication, 42,* 5–24.

Hallin, D., & Mancini, P. (2004). *Comparing media systems: Three models of media and politics.* Cambridge, UK: Cambridge University Press.

Heijting, K., & de Haan, R. (2005). De gestage teloorgang van politike inhoud [The slow decrease of political substance]. In K. Brants & P. van Praag (Eds.), *Politiek en media in verwarring* [Politics and media in flux] (pp. 44–64). Amsterdam: Spinhuis.

Hemels, J. (1979). *De Nederlandse krant 1618–1978* [The Dutch newspaper 1681–1978]. Baarn: Ambo.

Kleinnijenhuis, J., Hoof, A., & Oegema, D. (2006). Negative news and the sleeper effect of distrust. *Harvard Journal of Press/Politics, 11,* 86–104.

Kleinnijenhuis, J., Oegema, D., & de Ridder, J. (1995). De democratie op drift (Democracy afloat]. Amsterdam: Free University Press.

Kleinnijenhuis, J., Oegema, D., de Ridder, J., van Hoof, A., & Vliegenhart, R. (2003). *De puinhopen in het nieuw.* Alphen a/d Rijn: Kluwer.

Kleinnijenhuis, J., Scholten, O., de Ridder, J., van Hoof, A., van Atteveldt, W., Ruigrok, N. & Takens, J. (2007). *Nederland vijfstromenland: de rol van media en stemwijzers bij de verkiezingen van 2006.* [The Netherlands, five-stream country: The role of the media and the vote helps in the 2006 elections]. Amsterdam: Bert Bakker Prometheus.

Koole, R. (1992). *De opkomst van de moderne kaderpartij* [The arrival of the modern party]. Utrecht: Het Spectrum.

Lichter, S. R., & Noyes, R. E. (1996). *Good intentions make bad news: Why Americans hate campaign journalism.* Lanham, MD: Rowman & Littlefield.

Lijphart, A. (1968). *The politics of accommodation: Pluralism and democracy in the Netherlands.* Berkeley: University of California Press.

Lijphart, A. (1989). From the politics of accommodation to adversarial politics in the Netherlands. In H. Daalder & G. Irwin (Eds.), *Politics in the Netherlands—How much change.* London: Frank Cass.

Mazzoleni, G. (1987). Media logic and party logic in campaign coverage: The Italian general election of 1983. *European Journal of Communication, 2,* 81–103.

McLeod, D. M., Kosicki, G. M., & McLeod, J. M. (2002). Resurveying the boundaries of political communications effects. In J. Bryant & D. Zillmann (Eds.), *Media effects: Advances in theory and research* (pp. 215–267). Mahwah, NJ: Erlbaum.

McQuail, D. (1992). *Media performance.* London: Sage.

Meurs, E., van Praag, Ph., & Brants, K. L. K. (1995). De produktie van het campagnenieuws: NOS-journaal en RTL-nieuws' [The production of campaign news: The NOS Journaal and RTL News]. In K. L. K. Brants & P. van Praag (Eds.), *Verkoop van de politiek: De verkiezings-campagne van 1994* [Selling politics: The 1994 election campaign] (pp. 141–149). Amsterdam: Het Spinhuis.

Norris, P. (2000). *A virtuous circle.* Cambridge, UK: Cambridge University Press.

Patterson, T. (1993). *Out of order.* New York: Alfred Knopf.

Patterson, T. (1998). Political roles of the journalist. In D. Graber, D. McQuail, & P. Norris (Eds.), *The politics of news: The news of politics* (pp. 17–32). Washington, D.C.: CQ Press.

Peter, J. (2004). Our long 'Return to the concept of powerful mass media'—a cross-national comparative investigation of the effects of consonant media coverage. *International Journal of Public Opinion Research, 16*(2), 144–168.

Praag, Ph. van (2005). De veranderende Nederlandse campagnecultuur [The changing Dutch campaign culture]. In K. Brants & P. van Praag (Eds.), *Politiek en media in verwarring* [Politics and media in flux] (pp. 21–42). Amsterdam: Spinhuis.

Praag, Ph. van, & Brants, K. L. K. (Eds.). (1999). *Tussen beeld en inhoud: Politiek en media in de verkiezingen van 1998* [Between image and content. Politics and media in the elections of 1998]. Amsterdam: Het Spinhuis.

Praag, Ph van, & Brants, K. (2005). Gefascineerd door de horse race [Fascinated by the horse race]. In K. Brants & P. van Praag (Eds.), *Politiek en media in verwarring* [Politics and media in flux] (pp. 66–91). Amsterdam: Spinhuis.

Sartori, G. (1987). *The theory of democracy revisited*. New Jersey: Chatham.

Schoenbach, K., de Ridder, J., & Lauf, E. (2005). Politicians on TV news: Getting attention in Dutch and German election campaign. *European Journal of Political Research, 39*(4), 519–536.

Schuck, A. ,& de Vreese, C. H. (2008). The Dutch no to the EU Constitution: Assessing the role of EU. *Journal of Elections, Public Opinion & Parties, 18*(1), 101–128.

Semetko, H. A. (1996). Journalistic culture in comparative perspective: The concept of "balance" in U.S., British and German TV News. *Harvard International Journal of Press/Politics, 1*(1), 51–71.

Semetko, H. A., Blumler, J., Gurevitch, M., & Weaver, D. (1991). *The formation of campaign agendas: A comparative analysis of party and media roles in recent American and British Elections*. Hillsdale, NJ: Erlbaum.

Semetko, H. A. & Valkenburg, P. M. (2000). Framing European politics: A content analysis of press and television news. *Journal of Communication, 50*(2), 93–109.

Van Praag, P., & Eijk, C. van der (1998). News contents and effects in a historic campaign. *Political Communication, 15,* 165–183,

de Vreese, C. H. (2001). Election coverage—New directions for public broadcasting: The Netherlands and beyond. *European Journal of Communication, 16*(2), 155–179.

de Vreese, C. H. (2002). *Framing Europe: Television news and European integration*. Amsterdam: Aksant.

de Vreese, C. H. (2006). *10 observations about the past, present and future of political communication*. Inaugural lecture delivered at the University of Amsterdam, Chair in Political Communication. Amsterdam: Amsterdam University Press.

de Vreese, C. H. (2007). Digital renaissance: Young consumer and citizen? *The Annals of the American Academy of Political and Social Science*.

de Vreese, C. H. (2008). Second-rate election campaigning? An analysis of campaign styles in European parliamentary elections. *Journal of Political Marketing*.

de Vreese, C. H., Banducci, S., Semetko, H. A., & Boomgaarden, H. A. (2006). The news coverage of the 2004 European Parliamentary election campaign in 25 countries. *European Union Politics, 7*(4), 477–504.

de Vreese, C. H., Peter, J., & Semetko, H. A. (2001). Framing politics at the launch of the euro: A crossnational comparative study of frames in the news. *Political Communication, 18*(2), 107–122.

de Vreese, C. H., & Semetko, H. A. (2004). *Political campaigning in referendums: Framing the referendum issue*. London: Routledge.

Zoonen, L. van (2000). De talkshow: Personalisering als politieke strategie [The talk show: Personalization as political strategy]. In K. L. K. Brants & Ph. Van Praag (Eds.), *Tussen beeld en inhoud: Politiek en media in de verkiezingen van 1998* [Between image and content. Politics and media in the elections of 1998] (pp. 154–174). Amsterdam: Het Spinhuis.

Zoonen, L. van (2004). *Entertaining the citizen: Politics in the fan democracy*. Boulder, CO: Westview.

10

Swedish Election News Coverage: Towards Increasing Mediatization

Jesper Strömbäck

The 2006 Swedish election campaign might prove to be historical. This was the first time that the four center and right-wing parties had entered into an "Alliance for Sweden," whose purpose was to oust the Social Democrats from power. This was partly the result of the Moderates—traditionally a conservative party—transforming itself into "The New Moderates," thus following in the footsteps of the British Labour Party. The Alliance parties duly won the election. This was the first time since 1991, and only the fourth time since the 1930s, that the Social Democats did not form the government. Finally, this was the first election when political advertising on TV was allowed in Sweden, although only on some niche channels.

Taken together, these examples suggest that Sweden might be at an important junction between old and new with regards to media and politics. This chapter will describe and discuss both the old characteristics and the new trends with regards to Swedish election news coverage.

THE SWEDISH POLITICAL SYSTEM

Sweden is the largest of the Scandinavian countries with a population of approximately 9.1 million people. Stockholm is the capital city and also the country's political, economic, and cultural center. It is also the city where most major media companies are located.

Sweden is a parliamentary monarchy. The parliament (Riksdagen) has one chamber with 349 seats. Since 1994 the elections have been held on the third Sunday in September every fourth year. On the same day people also vote for the regional parliaments and city councils. Thus, with the exception of referenda and elections to the European Parliament, Swedish citizens cast their ballots only once every four years. Voter turnout is high, although it has decreased somewhat over the last decades. In the 1970s turnout was above 90%, whereas it was 82% during the 2006 election. Voting is not compulsory, so this is a high turnout, although the perception in Sweden is that the drop in turnout is a democratic problem (SOU 2000:1).

The electoral system is strictly proportional, although there is a 4% threshold in order to gain parliamentary representation. People vote for party lists set up by the parties. It is possible to express a preference for a particular candidate, but less than a quarter of the voters did so in the latest election. Until the 1988 election only five parties were represented in parliament: the

Moderates, the Center Party, the Liberal Party, the Social Democrats, and the Left Party. During this period it was considered almost impossible for new parties to win representation.

In 1988 things started to change, however, when the Green Party won representation. This was, however, lost in 1991 but regained in 1994. In 1991 the Christian Democrats and New Democracy, a right-wing populist party, won representation. Since then, the Christian Democrats have remained in parliament, whereas New Democracy suffered from internal conflicts and has ceased to exist. Since 1994 the Swedish party system has thus consisted of seven significant parties.

Ever since the 1930s the Social Democrats have been, and continue to be, the largest party. Between the 1930s and the 1976 election, the Social Democrats were the ruling party with over 40% of the votes. When the center and right-wing parties won power in 1976, this was considered to be almost revolutionary, as it was the first time since the 1930s. Different coalitions of center-right-wing parties formed minority governments between 1976 and 1982 and 1991 and 1994 and a majority government after the 2006 election.

The Social Democrats' "subscription of governmental power," together with the electoral system and the fact that minority governments have been the rule, form part of the explanation as to why Sweden has a tradition of consensus-seeking and corporatism. The strong welfare state and high taxes have also had support from all major parties, although the right-wing parties started to challenge "the Swedish Model" in the 1980s. However, it is significant that the change from the "old" to the "New" Moderates involved taking a more positive stance towards the welfare state and less emphasis on the need to reduce taxes.

From this perspective one can agree with Hallin and Mancini's (2004) classification of Sweden as a typical example of the *Democratic Corporatist Model* of media and politics. Sweden has moderate political pluralism, a political culture of consensus-seeking, organized pluralism, a strong welfare state, and a strong development of rational-legal authority. In addition, Sweden has often been considered a "most different case" in comparison to the U.S., the prototypical example of *the Liberal Model* (Åsard & Bennett, 1997; Granberg & Holmberg, 1988; Hallin & Mancini, 2004; Strömbäck & Dimitrova, 2005).

However, it is also important to note some important trends which have implications for Swedish political communication. One such trend is that the former political stability has been replaced by increased volatility. The share of voters switching parties between elections has increased from approximately 10% in the 1960s to more than 30% in the 2002 election. The share of voters switching parties during the election campaign—which lasts three to four weeks—had increased to 19.1% in 2002. In 2002, fully 57% percent stated that they had made their final voting decision during the election campaign. Moreover, split-ticket voting has quadrupled since 1970. Thus, all measures indicate increasing electoral volatility (Holmberg & Oscarsson, 2004). This, in turn, can partly be explained by decreasing party identification. In 1968, 65% stated that they identified with a particular party, whereas in 2002, the corresponding share was 40%. Only 18% identified themselves as strong identifiers in 2002. During the same period, political trust also decreased sharply (Holmberg & Oscarsson, 2004).

These trends indicate that the parties have lost much of their anchorage among the voters and that the level of uncertainty has increased. This has not, however, changed the importance of the left–right ideological dimension with regards to how people vote. Furthermore, there is little evidence that Swedes base their voting on the party leaders' personalities. Rather, people tend to vote for the party they perceive as being closest to them in terms of the issues being discussed and the left–right ideological dimension (Holmberg & Oscarsson, 2004).

It should also be noted that there are no signs of decreasing political interest. During the last few decades, 50 to 60% have stated that they are interested in politics. This indicates that politics is considered to be relevant by most people, particularly at election time when Swedes are mobilized politically (Strömbäck & Johansson, 2007).

As high relevance and a high degree of uncertainty equals a strong need for orientation (McCombs, 2004; Weaver, 1980), which shapes the degree to which people are susceptible to agenda-setting effects, the Swedish election news coverage has become more important as a source of political information and in terms of affecting people's opinions. Two other indications of this should be mentioned. The first is that close to 50% say that they read at least a good part of the political information offered by the newspapers. Approximately 60% also report watching or listening to the party leaders' debate which is traditionally held on TV on the last Friday before the Election Day (Petersson et al., 2006). The second is that Sweden is one of the democratic countries in which citizens are most passive during election campaigns. For example, only 3% of Swedish voters in 2002 reported showing active support for a particular party, and only 7% reported having been contacted by anyone from a political party during the election campaign (Petersson et al., 2006, p. 136). This suggests that Swedish politics is clearly mediated with the election news coverage playing a major role in the opinion formation processes.

THE SWEDISH MEDIA SYSTEM

In terms of media consumption, Sweden is a newspaper-centric country. More than 70% read a newspaper on a daily basis (Andersson, 2006), although newspaper sales are falling. The Swedish press is further highly local, in that most people subscribe to local newspapers, and only four newspapers count as "national newspapers." All of these are now tabloid in format, but two of them—*Dagens Nyheter* and *Svenska Dagbladet*—are quality papers in style, whereas the two other—*Expressen* och *Aftonbladet*—are tabloids both in format and style.

Traditionally, Swedish newspapers used to be closely affiliated with political parties. The "party press" was strong, and the political affiliations were visible not only in editorials but also within the news pages. People tended to read newspapers which reflected their own political views, which employed journalists sharing the political view of the newspaper, and which in terms of ownership were directly or indirectly linked to the parties (Hadenius & Weibull, 2003; Nord, 2001). Political parallelism was thus strong.

However, this situation started to change in the 1960s. One reason was the advent of TV, which was organized as a public service monopoly with an obligation to follow rules regarding impartiality. Similar rules had been in place for radio, which was also organized as a public service monopoly, for decades, but the growing importance of TV still had an effect upon the perceptions of journalistic professionalism. Even within public service broadcasting there was a strong movement towards increasing professionalism and independence from the political system, a movement which gained momentum in the 1960s (Djerf-Pierre & Weibull, 2001; Esaiasson & Håkansson, 2002). The journalistic credo successively changed from "mirroring society" in the 1950s to "scrutinizing society" in the late 1960s and then, in the mid-1980s, to "interpreting society" (Djerf-Pierre & Weibull, 2001). Within broadcasting these normative shifts took place within the framework of journalistic objectivity and impartiality, ideals which came to dominate newspaper journalism.

In 1987, the public service monopoly started to break down as a Swedish cable channel, TV3, started to broadcast to a Swedish audience, but from London, thus circumventing the Swedish legislation in this area. In 1991, the first terrestrial and commercial TV channel, TV4, was allowed to broadcast in Sweden. The monopoly was broken, and in 1993, private radio was allowed to broadcast at a local level.

Whereas Sweden had two TV channels and four radio channels in the mid-1980s, all of which were public service channels, Sweden now has more than forty terrestial, cable, and digital TV channels, the majority of which are private or commercially owned. Regarding TV4, however, it is important to note that even though it is a commercially driven media company, it is obliged to follow the conditions of its charter, which is similar to that which the public service channels are obliged to follow (see below).

The Swedish media landscape has thus become more competitive and fragmented. However, it should be pointed out that the focus of most of the new TV channels is almost exclusively on entertainment. Of the major commercial channels only TV4 offer a significant amount of news and current affairs programmes. The three major TV news programs are *Aktuellt* and *Rapport* in the public service channels, and *Nyheterna* in TV4. In 2004, the proportion of viewers stating that they watched each of these news shows at least five days a week was 43, 43, and 32% (Jönsson & Strömbäck, 2007).

To sum up, at the national level, four newspapers and three TV channels are considered to be the most important with regards to news and current affairs: *Dagens Nyheter* and *Svenska Dagbladet* (quality papers), *Aftonbladet* and *Expressen* (newsstand tabloids), *Aktuellt* (public service), *Rapport* (public service), and *TV4 Nyheterna* (commercial channel). In addition to these, the public service radio channels constitute an important part of news and current affairs programming and, apart from local newspapers, devote most news space to election coverage. Furthermore, whereas external diversity—diversity between different media—used to dominate the media landscape, today internal diversity within different media is the rule.

Regulations that Apply to Political News Coverage during Elections

Considering the Swedish tradition of strong state intervention within various sectors of society, it might be considered an anomaly that there are, in fact, no regulations which apply exclusively to the political news coverage during elections, including the publication of opinion polls. There are, however, some general regulations which are relevant in this context. Firstly, all newspapers must follow the requirements stipulated in the Freedom of the Press Act, which covers general issues such as libel. Secondly, in broadcasting, the public service channels and TV4 are required by their charters to produce news and public affairs programming. They are also regulated under the Radio and Television Act. The TV channels are, for example, obliged to maintain an impartial stance and are banned from carrying political advertising. However, they are not required to provide equal airtime for the parties.

Thirdly, the obligation to carry news and public affairs imposed on public service radio and TV as well as TV4 is rather similar but not very detailed. The charters for the public service media state that they "shall present news, stimulate debate, comment on events and processes and provide citizens with the all-round information they need to be well-oriented and to be able to form opinions on social and cultural issues." How they go about doing this is left up to the media to decide. Thus, journalism in Sweden is largely regulated on the principle of "freedom under responsibility" (Petersson et al., 2005).

Fourthly, all this suggests that Sweden does indeed belong to the *Democratic Corporatist Model* with regards to its media system (Hallin & Mancini, 2004). Mass-circulation press developed early and is still strong, but there has been a shift towards commercial journalism. Journalism is strongly professionalized and institutionalized but mainly self-regulated. Although state intervention exists within parts of the media system, there remains strong protection for press freedom and for journalistic autonomy. Political ads are still banned in the main TV channels, although since 2006 they are allowed in newer niche channels that broadcast from countries in which paid political ads are allowed, such as Finland. This new opportunity was seized by some parties, although only to a limited extent.

THE MEDIATIZATION OF SWEDISH POLITICS: A BRIEF HISTORY

Viewed from the perspective of the four phases of mediatization (see chapter 1), the development of the Swedish election news suggest that major changes have taken place during the last few decades. Until the 1960s, the party press was still strong whereas broadcast news journalism was rather passive vis-à-vis the political system. Journalism had not yet become professionalized, and the degree of journalistic independence from politics was rather low.

However, Swedish politics was clearly mediated. To a significant extent people obtained information about elections from the election news coverage or the special election programs which have been broadcast since the 1930s. These election programs can be divided into two main genres: Debates between the party leaders and interviews with each of the party leaders (Esaiasson & Håkansson, 2002).

Until the mid-1960s, the parties had a decisive say with regards to both these genres. A major change took place in 1966, however, when journalists gained control of the interview programs, and now the broadcast media have taken full control of both genres (Esaiasson & Håkansson, 2002). Although negotiations between the media and the parties occasionally take place with re-gards to, for example, which issues to discuss, it is ultimately the media that make the decisions (Nord & Strömbäck, 2003; Petersson et al., 2006).

It is thus clear that Swedish politics has reached the second phase of mediatization. Evidence also shows that the format and content of the debates and the interview programs has changed considerably since journalists took control. The tone of the interviews has become more critical and the attitudes of the journalists have become more querulous. The tempo has hastened, and it has become commonplace for journalists to interrupt the politicians who are being interviewed. Nowadays the party leaders are interrupted almost every second time they attempt to answer the questions posed (Esiasson & Håkansson, 2002, p. 121). The change in tone is also evident in how politicians are addressed, in how journalists and politicians are dressed, and in the introduction of a lighter atmosphere with elements of satire and entertainment. These changes have all been introduced by the media.

These interview programs and debates belong to the most watched political programs dur-ing election campaigns. They certainly make a significant contribution to the voters' knowledge of the parties and their positions. They also make a significant contribution to how politics is covered in the news media, as they have become important events in themselves. The tabloids in particular devote a great deal of news space in their coverage of these events, and polls regarding "who won" the debates or how the party leaders performed have become regular features of the election news coverage in these newspapers.

This brings us to the development of the Swedish election news coverage during the last couple of decades. During this period it can be argued that the election news coverage has freed itself from its former ties to political parties. Newspaper and broadcast journalism both pride themselves with their professionalism. From a scholarly point of view, present day news journal-ism is, by and large, professionalized, independent from political actors as well as with regards to news values and news selection, and it takes a neutral-active stance towards political and social actors. Non-partisan and impartial news reporting is the norm, and the understanding of journal-istic objectivity most dominant among Swedish journalists is "going beyond the statements of the contending sides to the hard facts of a political dispute" (Patterson, 1998).

In the following sections I will summarize the academic research on the content of the Swedish election news coverage. The focus will be on the three most recent elections, held in 1998, 2002, and 2006. Five themes will be addressed: the amount of coverage of national elections, the degree of partisan bias, the framing of politics, the use of opinion polls, and, finally, journalistic style.

ELECTION NEWS IS STILL GOOD NEWS: THE AMOUNT OF ELECTION COVERAGE

Although the Swedish media landscape has become more commercialized, the news media still pay considerable attention to political news (Table 10.1). However, there are substantial differences between the different media. In 2006, the TV channels, and in particular public service TV, contained more extensive coverage than ever before. The newspapers, on the other hand, had less extensive coverage in 2006 than in 2002. This was particularly true for *Dagens Nyheter*, which changed to a tabloid format between these two elections. The number of articles for the 2006 election declined by 42%, as compared to 2002. Taking the four major newspapers together, the decline in the number of articles was 26% (Asp, 2006, pp. 11–16).

Thus, while there are indications that Swedish newspapers have cut down on their election news coverage, the trend with regards to TV news is in the opposite direction. It is also obvious that there are clear differences between public service TV and commercial TV. Despite *Dagens Nyheter* cutting down on its election news coverage, it is still the newspaper which contains the greatest amount of coverage. The tabloids lag far behind.

This suggests that the Swedish news media have a pragmatic rather than a sacerdotal approach to politics (Semetko et al., 1991). This is further underlined by evidence that the news media published approximately four times as many news stories concerning the 2002 national election than for the 2004 European Parliamentary election (Strömbäck & Nord, 2008). The latter election was considered a second-order election without much drama and excitement and about which the electorate showed only minimal interest. Hence, the media coverage was limited, further contributing to low interest in this election.

This indicates that it has become more important than previously for the news media to consider the attention-grabbing potential of politically relevant news when deciding *what to cover* and *how to cover it*. It is not only the intrinsic importance of potential news that matters, but whether the potential news is important, relatively cheap to cover, and at the same time can be

TABLE 10.1
The Amount of the Swedish Election News Coverage in 2006

	Total number of news stories	News stories per day
Dagens Nyheter	551	29
Svenska Dagbladet	504	18
Expressen	316	11
Aftonbladet	370	13
Rapport	134	4,8
Aktuellt	138	4,9
TV4 Nyheterna	122	3,5

Source: Asp, 2006, p. 10.

told in a way that is competitive in the struggle to capture a wide audience. Thus, if a potential news story can be told using storytelling techniques such as simplification, polarization, stereotypization, and personalization, it adds to its news value and increases the likelihood that it will be reported.

This suggests that the media logic (Altheide & Snow, 1979) is more important to the news media that any kind of party-political or democratic logic. If this is indeed the case then partisan bias should be rather uncommon in the Swedish election news coverage.

BIAS IN THE SWEDISH ELECTION NEWS COVERAGE

The degree to which the election news coverage expresses partisan bias has been studied extensively by Asp (2003, 2006) for every election since 1979. His analyses start from the notion that parties can be part of news stories as objects (of others' comments) or as active subjects. He summarizes the data in an "actor treatment index," constructed on the basis of the extent to which the parties receive media attention and the extent to which their mention is either positive or negative. Parties that are much criticized are thus considered to receive unfavorable treatment, irrespective of the source of criticism, whereas parties that are frequently mentioned and in positive terms are considered to receive favorable treatment.

The results show that some party or parties always receive favorable coverage, whereas other parties receive unfavorable coverage. What is more important, however, is that different parties receive favorable and unfavorable coverage in different elections (Asp, 2003, 2006; Petersson et al., 2006). Moreover, a party that receives positive treatment in one election campaign, tends to receive more negative treatment in the next campaign, further illustrating that there does not seem to be any systematic partisan bias in the Swedish election news coverage. This is the main conclusion.

The tendency with regards to the treatment of the two main governing alternatives is rather similar (Asp, 2006). Although the left-wing parties have tended to receive more negative coverage on the whole than the center or right-wing parties, this tendency is not particularly strong. Furthermore, the treatment of the two blocs has varied between elections, and it is also related to which bloc is in government. The main conclusion, therefore, is that parties in government receive more scrutiny and criticism than parties in opposition, regardless of whether they belong to the left or the right. Research also shows that the media tend to join together with regards to changes in their treatment of the blocs (Asp, 2003).

Taken together, this research thus shows that the Swedish news media does not display any systematic partisan bias. In each election, some party or parties are favored and some party or parties are disfavored, but which party receives which treatment differs between elections. What this suggests is that partisan bias is not the problem. Rather, the problem appears to be structural bias.

The concept of structural bias can be traced back to Hofstetter (1976) who suggested that structural bias "occurs when some things are selected to be reported rather than other things because of the character of the medium or because of the incentives that apply to commmercial news programming" (p. 34). Similarly, Graber (2005, p. 236) writes that, "Political bias reflects ideological judgments, whereas structural bias reflects the circumstances of news production" (see also Gulati et al., 2004; Strömbäck & Shehata, 2007). When different news media treat a particular party favorably or unfavorably in a similar manner, no matter what their linkages are to political predispositions among owners or journalists, then this suggests that structural rather than partisan bias is at work.

Similarly, Schudson (2003, p. 55) has noted that news reporting tends to be event-centered, detached, focused on bad news as well as on strategy and tactics rather than policies, and highly dependent on official viewpoints, and that this is due to prevailing notions of journalistic professionalism. Commercial media are also highly dependent on finding a formula which offers low costs in terms of news production, and high returns in terms of an ability to be competetive in the ongoing race for ratings and newspaper circulation (Hamilton, 2004; McManus, 1994). This might favor certain issues or parties at a particular point in time, regardless of political viewpoints.

Thus, the end result of both structural and partisan bias might be that particular candidates or parties are favored in the news. The end result might also be that particular ways of framing the news are favored, whereas others are not. Hence, the Swedish election news coverage certainly is not neutral, but neither is it politically biased. Rather, it is structurally biased. One of the manifestations of this structural bias is the framing of politics as a strategic game, rather than as issues (Gulati et al., 2004).

FRAMING OF POLITICS IN THE SWEDISH ELECTION NEWS COVERAGE[1]

The notion that the media have a tendency to frame politics as a strategic game, rather than as issues, is certainly not new. It has been documented in many countries, particularly the U.S. (Patterson, 1980, 1993). There has been heavy criticism of this as it turns people's attention away from the issues which they, supposedly, should have knowledge about in order to cast informed votes. There is also evidence showing that the framing of politics as a strategic game might lead to increasing levels of political cynicism, as it, implicitly or explicitly, tells people that all that matters for politicians is the winning or losing—not how to reform and improve society in the interest of the citizenry (Cappella & Jamieson, 1997).

In Sweden, the first study of the framing of politics was performed on the news coverage of the 1998 election (Strömbäck, 2001). In that study a distinction was made between issue framing, game framing, and scandal framing, and which of these frames dominated each article or news item during the final three weeks before Election Day.[2] Using the same methodology and definitions of the frames, this study was followed up after the 2002 and 2006 elections (Strömbäck, 2004). The results are displayed in Table 10.2.

The results show that the Swedish news media as a whole does have a tendency to frame politics as a game or as scandals, but also that issue framing is more prominent. In fact, issue framing has been more dominant than game framing in all three elections in the quality papers and the public service TV news, but not in the tabloids or the commercial TV news. This suggests that there is indeed a linkage between the degree of commercialism and how politics is framed (Patterson, 2000). This is also suggested by a study by Johansson (2008), covering the

TABLE 10.2
The Framing of Politics in the Swedish Election News Coverage 1998-2006 (%)

	Issue frame			Game frame			Scandal frame		
	1998	2002	2006	1998	2002	2006	1998	2002	2006
Quality papers	56	65	55	37	32	30	7	3	15
Tabloids	39	48	37	50	46	40	11	6	23
Public service TV	57	69	60	33	26	28	10	5	12
Commercial TV	36	45	39	44	49	23	20	6	39

Total N: 1998=963, 2002=1102, 2006=1099.

TABLE 10.3
The Framing of Politics in Four Major Swedish Newspapers in 2006 (%)

	Issue frame	Game frame	Scandal frame	N
Dagens Nyheter	56	27	17	279
Svenska Dagbladet	53	34	13	203
Expressen	41	40	19	173
Aftonbladet	32	40	28	160

election news in every election between 1979 and 2006. Although not investigating the framing of politics, his results also suggest that news coverage is increasingly focusing on campaign news, scandals, or opinion polls. According to his data, 54% of the articles in the quality papers in 2006 were dramatized in that they focused on campaign news, polls, or scandals, whereas the corresponding share for the tabloids, public service TV news and commercial TV news were 70%, 50% and 65%, respectively.

However, more detailed analyses show that there are differences across the media and within categories. As an example, Table 10.3 shows how politics was framed in the four main newspapers in 2006.[3]

In this election, the quality papers were clearly more prone to frame politics as issues and less likely to frame it as a game, than the tabloids. At the same time, the scandal frame was much more prominent in *Aftonbladet* than in *Expressen*, in which the issue frame was more prominent. There are, however, variations across time, which are particularly evident with regards to the usage of a scandal frame. This frame has never been as prominent as it was in 2006, and it has been discussed whether this was an exception or whether this signals a more fundamental change of Swedish political journalism. This discussion has been fuelled by the opinion that the underlying events, triggering this focus on scandals, were rather minor and not particularly relevant with regards to the election.

Most of this scandal-framed coverage focused on two events. The first was related to how the Swedish government, and one high-ranking governmental official in particular, handled the 2004 Tsunami in Asia in which more than 500 Swedes were killed. The second was related to the Liberal Party. In early September the breaking news was that this party had obtained access to a password for the Social Democrats' intranet, which they had repeatedly used from November 2005 to March 2006. This behavior was widely condemned as unethical and perhaps even illegal. A few high-ranking officials in the Liberal Party had to resign, as their involvement became known. There was also much speculation concerning whether the party leader was involved, but, as yet, there is no evidence that this was the case.

Nevertheless, this event became major news. Research (Asp, 2006) also shows that it was the Liberal Party which received the most negative coverage of all the parties in the 2006 election, which was in contrast to the 2002 election when it had the most positive coverage of all (Asp, 2003). What can be questioned is whether this event was so important that it deserved to be the main topic in 9% of all news stories during the final four weeks before the election (Asp, 2006).

To many this coverage appeared excessive, and also as an indication of the increasing commercialization, dramatization, and fictionalization of the election news (Johansson, 2008). It can also be perceived as an indication of journalists' increasing power vis-à-vis politicians with regards to the agenda- and frame-setting processes. Although the Social Democrats were part of sponsoring the issue when the news first broke, it was mainly journalists who pushed it.

Stated differently, the focus on political scandals can be perceived as an indication that journalists favor news that they, rather than the politicians, control. It gives them an increased sense of autonomy and independence, and it can be perceived as evidence that they are fulfilling their role as watchdogs.

THE PUBLICATION OF OPINION POLLS
IN THE SWEDISH ELECTION NEWS COVERAGE

One common type of Swedish election news story concerns the results from a variety of opinion polls. The first polling firm was established in Sweden as early as 1941. Among the first subscribers of the polls was *Dagens Nyheter*, and it did not take long until other newspapers followed suit and also started to publish the results of opinion polls (Holmberg & Petersson, 1980).

Although the Swedish media's interest in opinion polls has fluctuated over the years, there is no doubt that polls are considered highly newsworthy by journalists. It also appears as if the perceived news value of polls might have increased during the more recent election campaigns as compared to those of the 1980s (Johansson, 2008; Strömbäck, 2004). The majority of the polls are published in the newspapers. In the last three elections—1998, 2002, 2006—the four major newspapers taken together published 86, 76, and 93 polls, respectively, during the final three weeks of the election campaign. The majority of these polls, 72% in 2006, were commissioned by the media.

The object of most polls, especially those commissioned by the media, is vote intention or how the party leaders performed in TV performances, such as debates or major TV interviews. 25% of all polls published in 2006 focused on issues. Of those commissioned by the media, only 16% focused on issues. The tabloids particularly focus on polls regarding how the party leaders performed in their various TV performances. In 2006, 92% of the polls in *Aftonbladet* and 77% of the polls in *Expressen* were based on this concept.

Thus, it is evident that the publication of polls contributes to the framing of politics as a strategic game and as a horse race. Research also shows that the media often fail when it comes to following the "Esomar International Code of Practice for the Publication of Public Opinion Poll Results." Important information, such as the margin of error, is often omitted (Petersson & Holmberg, 1998; Strömbäck, 2004) with the consequence that it is often difficult to assess the reliability of the results.

From the perspective of the news media, however, this is not particularly significant. What appears to matter more to the news media is that they are in control of the news, that polling data is easy to report on and lends itself to dramatic news narratives with regards to winners and losers, and that polling data offers the journalists a "quasi-objective" and proactive role as interpreters of the campaigns (Lavrakas & Traugott, 2000). Whereas journalists hesitate to criticize the policy proposals of the different parties, they have no problem criticizing how the parties or party leaders perform in debates or in the campaign, as long as they can refer to polls. The availability of polls thus enables them to be active as interpreters, while also seemingly being objective. In this sense, the media play a triple role in connection with polls: they commission them, then report on them, and also interpret the results (Petersson et al., 2006). Thus, polls not only sponsor the framing of politics as a game and a horse race. Polls also sponsor an interpretive journalistic style.

DESCRIPTIVE OR INTERPRETIVE JOURNALISTIC STYLE

As noted previously, the understanding of journalistic objectivity favored by journalists in Sweden is "going beyond the statements of the contending sides to the hard facts of a political dispute"

(Patterson, 1998). This understanding arguably fosters an interpretive journalistic style, as it allows journalists to decide what constitute the "hard facts." Thus, it is perhaps not surprising that an interpretive journalistic style appears to have become more common in Swedish political news journalism (Djerf-Pierre & Weibull, 2001; Strömbäck, 2004).

This tendency can manifest itself both directly and indirectly. Regarding indirect measures, there is evidence that the political news coverage in general, including the election news coverage, has become more personalized than it used to be (Asp, 2006; Johansson, 2006, 2008; Petersson et al., 2006; Strömbäck, 2004). First and foremost this is obvious in the media's focus on the party leaders. In the media, they have become and are often treated as symbols for the parties, despite the fact that, other than in this regard, Swedish politics is very party-centered. On a 4-point scale, with 1 being the lowest level of personalization and 4 the highest, one study furthermore categorized approximately 70% of all election news stories in 2002 as somewhat or highly personalized (cf. Strömbäck, 2004), in the sense that they focused on individuals or on actions or opinions of individual as opposed to collective actors.

There are also more direct measures of an interpretive journalistic style. For one thing, so called "news analyses" have become rather common in the Swedish press. These are articles with some kind of vignette, such as "Analysis," which signals a more subjective approach. In 1998 and 2002, approximately 8% of all election news stories had such vignettes, whereas in 2006, it was approximately 5%. However, some newspapers are more consistent in their use of such vignettes, and it might be misleading to take only this kind of articles into account when judging the prevalence of interpretive journalism. A more direct measure is to code the dominant journalistic style in single news articles (Table 10.4).

Briefly, this measure builds on Patterson's (2000, p. 250) distinction between descriptive and interpretive journalism: "Whereas descriptive reporing is driven by the facts, the interpretative form is driven by the theme around which the story is built. Facts become the materials with which the chosen theme is illustrated…. The descriptive style places the journalist in the role of an observer. The interpretative style requires the journalist to act also as an analyst."

As shown in Table 10.4, an interpretive journalistic style is rather common in all major newspapers (as well as on TV), regardless of whether they have the appearance of straight news articles or are labeled as some kind of "news analysis," and regardless of the type of newspaper. However, it is not unrelated to the framing of politics. On the contrary, there is a positive correlation between game framing and an interpretive journalistic style.

On the other hand, there is also a genre in which the journalistic style is almost exclusively descriptive. This is the so called "issue guide," where the parties are allowed the opportunity to spell out their policies for different topics. The media choose the questions that the parties are to answer, but the parties are allowed to answer them in a largely unedited fashion within the space limitations set by the media. During the last three elections this genre accounted for 3 to 6% of all election news stories—more in 2006 than in previous elections.

TABLE 10.4
The Frequency of an Interpretive Journalistic Style in Swedish Election Coverage (%)

	1998	*2002*	*2006*
Dagens Nyheter	38	34	34
Svenska Dagbladet	34	44	34
Expressen	30	52	39
Aftonbladet	33	35	35
Mean	34	41	36

This does not, however, mean that it is mainly the politicians who set the agenda and decide how the different issues are to be framed. On the contrary, research indicates that both politicians and journalists agree that journalists have more power than politicians in terms of how different issues are framed. With regards to the power over the agenda, evidence is more mixed. The most recent study (Nord & Strömbäck, 2003), based on interviews with leading politicians and journalists from the major media, showed that politicians from the larger parties claimed that they, rather than the media, set the agenda, and that most of the journalists agreed with this statement. Politicians from the smaller parties, however, disagreed. However, as noted, the consensus regarding the media's power over how politics or different issues are framed, is striking. Survey evidence furthermore suggests that both journalists and politicians think that journalists are as powerful, or even more powerful, than politicians in terms of influencing politics and society (Strömbäck & Nord, 2006). Thus, if the relationship between journalists and their political sources is like a tango (Gans, 1980), then evidence suggests that in the Swedish case, and in the context of election campaigns, it is the journalists who take the lead for the majority of the time.

EFFECTS OF THE SWEDISH ELECTION NEWS COVERAGE

Unfortunately, Sweden does not have a strong tradition with regards to research into media effects. However, there are some studies documenting rather strong media effects in terms of agenda-setting and information-aquisition (Asp, 1986; Johansson, 1998). There is also recent evidence from the 1998 and 2002 elections that people who either daily or frequently read about politics in the newspapers are more knowledgeable with regards to politics, than people who only read occasionally or never about politics. The same pattern is evident with regards to watching or listening to public service TV or radio, but not with regards to commercial TV. Those who often listen to or watch the news on commercial TV are in fact less knowledgeable than those who rarely or never watch the news, even after controlling for factors such as education, age, and political interest. High media consumption is also positively correlated with political trust, but not with regards to consumption of commercial TV news or *Expressen* (Petersson et al., 2006). Interestingly, these differences bear a correspondence to how the respective media framed politics in 2002. The media most prone to framing politics as a strategic game were also those with a negative correlation between media consumption, political knowledge, and political trust (Petersson et al., 2006).

There also appears to be a strong correlation between election news coverage and election outcomes. As noted by Asp (2006, p. 82), when referring to the elections between 1979 and 2006: "During all nine investigated election campaigns there are clear correlations between how the media covered the parties and their salient issues, and how the parties did at the polls."[4] For example, an analysis of his data, measuring the percentage of all news stories in which the parties were covered as main acting party in the 2006 election, and the election outcome, shows that the rank order-correlation (Spearmans Rho) is 0.94. However, more research, using panel studies in addition to content analyses and experiments, is required in order to assess the importance of the election news in the Swedish context.

THE FUTURE OF SWEDISH ELECTION NEWS COVERAGE

In the introduction it was noted that Sweden might be at an important junction between old and new with regards to media and politics. To briefly summarize, it is evident that both the parties and the news media are under increasing pressure to reach out to their potential audiences and voters. As a consequence of this and due to the commercialization of the media system, some media give less priority to politics and elections than previously. The media logic has become more important, to some extent weaking the public service ethos which used to be strong among Swedish news media. The election news coverage appears to have become more popularized and personalized, especially in the tabloids and in commercial TV. It is also obvious that an interpretive journalistic style is common, although a descriptive journalistic style dominates. Finally, political advertising has been allowed on some channels, and it is likely to become more important in future elections.

What role does the Internet play in all this? Before the 2006 election, some thought that this would be the first "Internet election," and many hoped that the Internet would lead to a more politically active citizenry. However, so far the evidence suggests that no fundamental changes have taken place. For example, a survey done during the 2006 campaign showed that Swedes, when ranking the importance of potential sources of political information, rank TV as being the most important source, followed by newspapers and radio. The Internet was only ranked to fourth as the most important source of information.[5] Furthermore, only 9% in 2002 visited a party´s website before the election. With regards to blogs, during the latter part of 2005 only 4% said that they had read a blog written by a politician at least once during the past 12 months (Bergström, 2006).

Thus, the main conclusion so far must be that the Internet has not revolutionized Swedish political communication. Changes might, however, be underway, as young people rely more on the Internet than older people and as people who have grown up with the Internet will successively replace older voters. On the other hand, research indicates that the driving force with regards to all kinds of political behaviour is the level of interest and engagement. Thus, the crucial question is not what the Internet will do to the electorate and Swedish political communication, but whether people will be more or less interested in political information, transmitted through old as well as new media.

Another crucial question is what kind of election news coverage people will be looking for. A more volatile electorate, and a media landscape increasingly diversified, fragmented, and commercialized, will force both political parties and the news media to become more attuned and responsive to the wants and needs of the people in their roles as voters and media consumers. It remains to be seen whether this will weaken or strengthen Swedish democracy as we know it.

NOTES

1. When references are made to research on the 1998, 2002, and 2006 elections, and no sources are mentioned, the research was done by this author but hitherto unpublished.
2. News items which did not fit any of these categories were classified as "other" and here treated as missing. With regards to the news articles, the percentages reported refer to the main body of the articles. Headlines, lead paragraphs, and end paragraphs were also coded, but this coding is not included here.
3. See note 2.
4. Translated by this author.
5. This survey was done by the Center for Political Communication Research at Mid Sweden University.

REFERENCES

Altheide, D. L., & Snow, R. P. (1979). *Media logic*. Beverly Hills, CA: Sage.

Andersson, U. (2006). Nya vanor påverkar dagspressens spridning [New habits affect newspaper readership]. In S. Holmberg & L. Weibull (Eds.), *Du stora nya värld* [Brave new world] (pp. 299–314). Göteborg: SOM-institutet.

Åsard, E., & Bennett, W. L. (1997). *Democracy and the marketplace of ideas. Communication and government in Sweden and the United States.* New York: Cambridge University Press.

Asp, K. (1986). *Mäktiga massmedier: Studier i politisk opinionsbildning* [Powerful mass media: Studies in political opinion formation]. Stockholm: Akademilitteratur.

Asp, K. (2003). *Medieval 2002. Partiskheten och valutgången: En studie av valrörelsens medialisering* [The media election 2002: Bias and election outcome. A study of the mediatization of the election campaign]. Göteborg: JMG/Göteborgs universitet.

Asp, K. (2006). *Rättvisa nyhetsmedier: Partiskheten under 2006 års medievalrörelse* [The fair news media: Bias in the 2006 election campaign]. Göteborg: JMG/Göteborgs universitet.

Bergström, A. (2006). Nyheter, bloggar och offentliga sajter [News, blogs, and official websites]. In S. Holmberg & L. Weibull (Eds.), *Du stora nya värld* [Brave new world] (pp. 391–402). Göteborg: SOM-institutet.

Cappella, J. N., & Jamieson, K. H. (1997). *Spiral of cynicism: The press and the public good.* Chicago: University of Chicago Press.

Djerf-Pierre, M., & Weibull, L. (2001). *Spegla, granska, tolka: Aktualitetsjournalistik i svensk radio och TV under 1900-talet* [To mirror, scrutinize and interpret: News and current affairs in Swedish radio and TV during the 20th century]. Stockholm: Prisma.

Esaiasson, P., & Håkansson, N. (2002). *Besked ikväll! Valprogrammen i svensk radio och TV* [Election programming in Swedish radio and TV]. Stockholm: Stiftelsen Etermedierna i Sverige.

Gans, H. J. (1980). *Deciding what´s news: A Study of CBS Evening News, NBC Nightly News, Newsweek and Time.* New York: Vintage.

Graber, D. A. (2005). *Mass media and American politics* (7th ed.). Washington, D.C.: CQ Press.

Granberg, D., & Holmberg, S. (1988). *The political system matters: Social psychology and voting behavior in Sweden and the United States.* New York: Cambridge University Press.

Gulati, G. J., Just, M. R., & Crigler, A. N. (2004). News coverage of political campaigns. In L. L. Kaid (Ed.), *Handbook of political communication research* (pp. 237–256). Mahwah, NJ: Erlbaum.

Hadenius, S., & Weibull, L. (2003). *Massmedier* [Mass media] (8th ed.). Stockholm: Albert Bonniers Förlag.

Hallin, D. C., & Mancini, P. (2004). *Comparing media systems: Three models of media and Politics.* New York: Cambridge University Press.

Hamilton, J. T. (2004). *All the news that's fit to sell: How the market transforms information into news.* Princeton, NJ: Princeton University Press.

Hofstetter, C. R. (1976). *Bias in the news: Network television coverage of the 1972 election campaign.* Columbus: Ohio State University Press.

Holmberg, S., & Petersson. O. (1980). *Inom felmarginalen* [Within the margin of error]. Stockholm: Publica.

Holmberg, S. M., & Oscarsson, H. (2004). *Väljare: Svenskt väljarbeteende under 50 år* [Voters. Swedish voter behavior over 50 years]. Stockholm: Norstedts juridik.

Johansson, B. (1998). *Nyheter mitt ibland oss: Kommunala nyheter, personlig erfarenhet och lokal opinionsbildning* [News among us: Local news, personal experiences, and local opinion formation]. Göteborg: JMG/Göteborgs universitet.

Johansson, B. (2006). Blir nyhetsbevakningen bättre ju närmare valdagen vi kommer? [Does the election news coverage improve as election day comes closer?] In H. Bäck & M. Gilljam (Eds.), *Valets mekanismer* [The mechanisms of elections] (pp. 286–302). Malmö: Liber.

Johansson, B. (2008). Popularized election coverage? News coverage of Swedish parliamentary election campaigns 1979–2006. In J. Strömbäck, T. Aalberg, & M. Ørsten (Eds.), *Political communication in the Nordic countries.* Göteborg: Nordicom.

Jönsson, A-M., & Strömbäck, J. (2007). *TV-journalistik i konkurrensens tid: Nyhets- och samhällsprogram i svensk TV 1990-2004* [TV-journalism in an era of competition: News and current affairs in Swedish television 1990–2004]. Stockholm: Ekerlids.

Lavrakas, P. J., & Traugott, M. W. (2000). Why election polls are important to a democracy: An American perspective. In P. J. Lavrakas & M. W. Traugott (Eds.), *Election polls, the news media, and democracy* (pp. 3–19). New York: Chatham House.

McCombs, M. (2004). *Setting the agenda: The mass media and public opinion*. Cambridge, UK: Polity Press.

McManus, J. H. (1994). *Market-driven journalism: Let the citizen beware?* Thousand Oaks, CA: Sage.

Nord, L. W. (2001). *Vår tids ledare: En studie av den svenska dagspressens politiska opinionsbildning* [The contemporary editorial: A study of political opinion making in the Swedish press]. Stockholm: Carlssons.

Nord, L., & Strömbäck, J. (2003). *Valfeber och nyhetsfrossa: Politisk kommunikation i valrörelsen 2002* [Political communication in the 2002 election]. Stockholm: Sellin & Partner.

Patterson, T. E. (1980). *The mass media election: How Americans choose their president*. New York: Praeger.

Patterson, T. E. (1993). *Out of order*. New York: Vintage.

Patterson, T. E. (1998). Political roles of the journalist. In D. A. Graber, D. McQuail, & P. Norris (Eds.), *The politics of news, The news of politics* (pp. 17–32). Washington, D.C.: CQ Press.

Patterson, T. E. (2000). The United States: News in a free-market society. In R. Gunther & A. Mughan (Eds.), *Democracy and the media: A comparative perspective* (pp. 241–265). New York: Cambridge University Press.

Petersson, O., Djerf-Pierre, M., Strömbäck, J., & Weibull, L. (2005). *Mediernas integritet* [The integrity of the media]. Stockholm: SNS Förlag.

Petersson, O., Djerf-Pierre, M., Holmberg, S., Strömbäck, J., & Weibull, L. (2006). *Media and elections in Sweden*. Stockholm: SNS Förlag.

Petersson, O., & Holmberg, S. (1998). *Opinionsmätningarna och demokratin* [Opinion polls and democracy]. Stockholm: SNS Förlag.

Schudson, M. (2003). *The sociology of news*. New York: W. W. Norton.

Semetko, H. A., Blumler, J. G., Gurevitch, M., & Weaver, D. H. (1991). *The formation of campaign agendas: A comparative analysis of party and media roles in recent American and British elections*. Hillsdale, NJ: Erlbaum.

SOU (2000). *En uthållig demokrati: Politik för folkstyrelse på 2000-talet* [A sustainable democracy: Democratic policies for the 21st century]. Stockholm: Fritzes.

Strömbäck, J. (2001). *Gäster hos verkligheten: En studie av journalistik, demokrati och politisk misstro* [Guests in reality: A study of journalism, democracy and political distrust]. Stockholm/Stehag: Brutus Östlings bokförlag Symposion.

Strömbäck, J. (2004). *Den medialiserade demokratin: Om journalistikens ideal, verklighet och makt* [The mediatized democracy: On the ideals, reality and power of journalism]. Stockholm: SNS Förlag.

Strömbäck, J., & Dimitrova, D. V. (2006). Political and media systems matter: A comparison of election news coverage in Sweden and the United States. *Harvard International Journal of Press/Politics, 11*(4), 131–147.

Strömbäck, J., & Johansson, B. (2008). Still a second-order election. Comparing Swedish media coverage of the 2004 European parliamentary election and the 2002 national election. In L. L. Kaid (Ed.), *The EU expansion. Communicated shared sovereignty in the parliamentary elections* (pp. 137–152). New York: Peter Lang.

Strömbäck, J., & Nord, L. W. (2006). Do politicians lead the tango? A study of the relationship between Swedish journalists and their political sources in the context of election campaigns. *European Journal of Communication, 21*(2), 147–164.

Strömbäck, J., & Nord, L. W. (2007). Still a second-order election. A comparison of the Swedish media coverage of the 2004 EP election and the 2002 national erlection. In L. L. Kaid (Ed.), *The expansion election*. New York: Peter Lang.

Strömbäck, J., & Shehata, A. (2007). Structural bias in British and Swedish election news coverage. *Journalism Studies, 8*(5), 798–812.

Weaver, D. H. (1980). Audience need for orientation and media effects. *Communication Research, 7*(3), 361–376.

11

Election Coverage in Spain: From Franco's Death to the Atocha Massacre

Esteban López-Escobar, Teresa Sádaba,
and Ricardo Zugasti

The death of Franco in 1975 marked the beginning of a period of political uncertainty in Spain. It was obvious that Spain could not continue as an authoritarian regime, and the debate centered on the means by which political changes should be introduced to bring Spain into line with the democracies of Western Europe. However, if the Spanish political situation constituted an anomaly in the Western European panorama, the same was true of its media system. Therefore, some important changes had to take place in the media system, not only due to the appearance of new media, but above all as a necessity to overcome a very *sui generis* situation.

A consideration of the election coverage in the Spanish media, limited for obvious reasons to a period of thirty years, should take into account all those changes. This analysis begins with those first changes and ends with the last general election held on March 14, 2004, three days after the terrorist massacre at Madrid's Atocha train station, which included attacks on some other trains arriving in Madrid, with a tragic outcome of almost two hundred casualties.

TRANSITION TO DEMOCRACY

The political and institutional transition to democracy, which began in Spain after the death of General Franco in November 1975, ended in December 1978 when the new democratic Constitution was approved by a referendum. King Juan Carlos I, designated by Franco as his successor in 1969 and crowned two days after the death of the dictator, became the new head of state. He was not merely a parliamentary monarch with symbolic functions, but actually enjoyed considerable political power (Ferrando, 1975). From this moment and thanks to his powers, the acts of the King were important steps toward democracy and reconciliation among Spaniards (Powell, 1991).

The democratic aim of the King was shared by many of the francoist politicians, especially the younger ones who had not lived through the Second Republic (1931–1936) and the Civil War (1936–1939). They thought, as the King did, that a francoism without Franco was impossible in a Western European country in the last years of the twentieth century. In addition to this, Spanish society had experienced deep changes since the sixties. When Franco died, Spain was a developed and industrialized country with a reasonable level of welfare and a broad-based middle class. These social characteristics, to a great extent very different from those which conditioned political life during the Republic, worked as an antidote against extremism (Sastre, 1997). Democratization was definitely seen as the only way to put an end to the uncertain period that Franco's death had opened.

At the center of the reformist way was the Law for Political Reform in December 1976, which dissolved the non-democratic francoist parliament and called for the free election of a new parliament whose job would be to draft a Constitution. In June 1977, the first democratic elections were won by The Center Democratic Union (UCD), a coalition of parties mainly formed by francoist reformists whose leader was the Prime Minister, Suárez. The Partido Socialista Obrero Español (PSOE) has remained on the left of Spanish parties since then. The third party in importance was the Spanish Communist Party (PCE). Only a few months later, the parliament decreed a total amnesty, even for prisoners convicted of terrorist attacks, which followed several pardons decreed by the King and the government since Franco's death.

The New Constitutional System

The main result of the consensus between all the political forces was the new Constitution, currently in force, which was drawn up and approved by both the right and the left and finally by the Spanish people through a referendum in December 1978. This Constitution turned the francoist monarchy into a parliamentary monarchy, lacking any political power and therefore compatible with a democracy.

The Constitution made provision for a parliamentary system in which the Spanish people are represented in a bicameral parliament. In this system the main house is the Congreso de los Diputados (Chamber of Deputies), whose members have the power to name the Prime Minister. The second chamber, with a considerably less important role, is the Senate. The members of both houses are elected at the same time in legislative elections which take place every four years, although the Prime Minister has the power to dissolve the parliament and call early elections. Legislative elections actually are seen as presidential elections because the new Chamber of Deputies appoints the candidate of the party which has the majority in the chamber as Prime Minister. In a system where the Head of State has a mere symbolic role representing the unity and continuity of the State, the Prime Minister is the key figure in Spanish politics.

The members of the Chamber of Deputies are elected following the D'Hondt system, a proportional election system modified to reduce the proportionality in order to benefit the two parties with the most votes—especially the frontrunner—in every electoral district. The result of that is a two-party system which also allows the representation of other parties (Román, 2001; Santaolalla, 2004).

Once the Constitution had come into force, the first legislative election was in 1979 and the winners were again UCD and Adolfo Suárez. After a difficult term which included divisions within UCD, the resignation of Suárez as Prime Minister, and an attempted coup, the PSOE won the 1982 elections with a hegemonic majority in parliament. As a consequence, Felipe González was appointed as the new Prime Minister.

In 1986, Spain became a full member of the European Community, an event that introduced a new election for Spaniards: the election for the European parliament. The PSOE and Felipe González also won the next two general elections (1986 and 1989) with an absolute majority. However, several serious political scandals and the effects of an important economic crisis led to a loss of political support, thus causing the loss of an absolute majority in 1993 and defeat at the hands of the Popular Party (PP) in 1996. PP is a center-right party founded in the transition years which became the first opposition force after the dissolution of the UCD in 1983. José María Aznar, who was the "popular" candidate since 1989, was elected Prime Minister, and after a successful period in terms of economic policy, the PP and Aznar repeated their victory in 2000, in this case with an absolute majority. Everything pointed to a new victory of PP in the 2004 general elections, even if Aznar was not running again, in accordance with his promise at the beginning of his first mandate. However, the Madrid bombings, three days before the elections, and the political turmoil after the terrorist attack, changed the situation drastically giving the victory to the PSOE, whose candidate was José Luis Rodríguez-Zapatero. Many voters considered the bombings to be a consequence of the support of Aznar's government for the invasion of Iraq, and a great number of voters went to the ballot as a way of punishing the Aznar government.

The Constitution established a quasi-federal state as regards regional decentralization. Spain is now divided into seventeen regions, called Autonomous Communities, which enjoy a considerable degree of self-government. The institutional model of each Autonomous Community reproduces almost exactly the central model: one regional parliament, in this case with only one chamber, and a president of the Community. The members of the parliament are elected by regional elections every four years following the D'Hondt system and they possess the power to elect the president of the Autonomous Community (Aja, 1999).

Fragmentation is one of the main characteristics in the Spanish political arena because of the parliamentary system. This is due to the fact that the electoral system promotes two main national political parties (now PSOE and PP) on one side, but also a number of other small political parties (including among them the regionalist or nationalist parties). However, those small parties have had a relevant role in political history because in some important situations they have been the key to reaching an absolute majority.

The New Media System

The political changes were paralleled by changes in the media system. As far as the printed media are concerned, the transition to democracy had begun in 1966 with the approval of a new Press Act. This law ended censorship—established during the Civil War by the 1938 Press Act—and made possible a certain ideological pluralism among Spanish newspapers and magazines. The print media began to enjoy some degree of freedom and were referred to as "The parliament of paper" in contrast with the real and non-democratic parliament. The print media and radio after 1977, have played an important role in supporting the democratic transition (Giner, 1983a).

After Franco's death, a royal decree in 1977 established complete freedom of the press. The definitive legal recognition of freedom of information came with the Constitution of 1978, whose article 20 states: "Every Spaniard has the right to freely communicate or receive true information by any means."

A challenge for the new rulers was the dismantling of the press chain owned by the state. The Franco regime had created the so called Press of the Movement (the name given to the only party that was permitted), which was the main publisher in Spain with about forty daily newspapers. Most of them yielded no profits after Franco's death, and those which did not fold up were auctioned off to private owners in 1984 (Zalbidea, 1996).

By 1984, approximately 115 newspapers were published, but only half of these existed in 1975, which gives an idea of the transformation that the market of dailies experienced during the transition period (Iglesias, 1989). In 1976, for instance, two new dailies were founded in Madrid, the principal market of the country: *El País* and *Diario 16*. Another important daily, *El Periódico de Catalunya*, was founded in Barcelona in 1978. The three had a center-left bias and played an important role during the transition process because their direct and successful democratic discourse spurred the other more conservative dailies to be less shy in talking about democratic values. In two regions with important nationalist and separatist movements, Catalonia and the Basque Country, nationalist newspapers were founded: *Avui* (entirely published in the Catalan language) in 1976 and the Basque titles *Deia*, in 1977, and *Egin* in 1978. Meanwhile, many of the more established newspapers, such as *ABC* and *Ya* in Madrid and *La Vanguardia* in Barcelona, had to face new obstacles. Some were able to survive but others folded up in the 1980s or 1990s.

Very few newspapers created after the democratic transition, were able to survive in a very competitive and saturated market. *El Mundo*, a national newspaper set up in 1989, was destined to play an important role in Spanish politics, especially because of its intense opposition to socialist governments. Nowadays, it has the second highest circulation figures.

The majority of newspapers supported the main guidelines of political reform and the strategy of consensus led initially by the francoist reformists and later by the opposition political parties. The press forgot its role as fourth state or watchdog of its own free will, in order to give almost complete support to the politicians who were making the transition. The reason was a shared goal: the achievement of a stable democratic regime. Owners, editors, and journalists saw clearly that the transition period was exceptional and joined the general consensus which worked until the Constitution came into force (Barrera & Zugasti, 2006; Zugasti, 2007).

Broadcasting

Post-Franco Spain inherited a broadcasting structure at that time unique in Europe: a mixed commercial and public radio system and state-run national television financed by both public funds and advertising. News content in all sectors was tightly controlled by the government (López-Escobar, 1992b).

In the radio sector, besides the oldest commercial network (SER), there were basically three main radio stations: the state run Radio Nacional de España (RNE), the network linked to the Falange (REM-CAR), and the COPE, linked to the Catholic church hierarchy. A November 22, 1977 decree, concerning the "freedom of information on radio" ended the state news radio monopoly, and encouraged competition and initiative among the non-state networks leading to higher credibility and bigger audiences (López-Escobar & Faus, 1985).

By the time of Franco's death in 1975 there were 210 stations in operation. During the transition period towards democracy, the public radio stations included in Radio Nacional de España and other official networks were incorporated by a royal decree within the state body Radiotelevisión Española, which drew together the public television station and all the public radio stations. As a result, the old broadcasting machinery created for the Franco regime was placed at the disposal of the new democratic state and its successive governments.

In contrast to the press and radio, television in Spain was instituted as a state monopoly, financed both by advertising and state subsidies. The only national television station which broadcast in Spain from the mid-1950s until the early 1980s was *Televisión Española* (TVE), the public channel whose contents have been completely controlled by successive governments either in dictatorship or in democracy (Palacio, 2001). But on December 26, 1983, a law was passed to regulate the so-called third channel, meaning channels directly managed by the Autonomous Communities, when Catalonia and the Basque Country had already created regional broadcasting corporations, and had launched television channels taking for granted that they had a right to do so, even before the passing of the 1983 law. The parliaments of a number of other Autonomous Communities also passed laws to establish their own broadcasting bodies, even if some of them never took the decision to set up a television station (López-Escobar, 1992a).

After several attempts and high pressure on the government, the Spanish Parliament passed a law authorizing the government to license three commercial television channels, nationwide in scope but with an obligation to provide some regional programming. The licenses were awarded in 1990 to Tele 5, Antena 3, and Canal+, the last being a pay TV service in spite of the fact there were no specific provisions for pay television (Barrera, 1995; López-Escobar, 1992b). More recently the government has licensed two new national channels: the Sexta (Channel Six) and the Cuatro (Channel Four), the last one using the connections of Canal+'s local television operations.

A characteristic of the current Spanish media scene is the proliferation, especially since the nineties, of powerful multimedia groups. As a result, it is not easy to find important means of communication outside these groups. PRISA, the most powerful group, is the owner of the most important daily in terms of circulation figures (*El País*), the most listened to radio station (SER), one of the national private televisions (Cuatro), and many other media. This group can be taken as a paradigmatic example of this trend toward ownership concentration.

LEGAL FRAMEWORK FOR ELECTIONS AND FOR MEDIA COVERAGE

Elections have been held in Spain since 1977 (see Table 11.1) and, as in many other countries, at several levels: state (9 years), regional (23 years), local (7 years), and European (5 years). Only in 2002 were Spaniards not called to the ballots. Some of these elections have received careful scholarly attention (Gifreu & Pallarés, 2001; Crespo, 2004). Due to space limitations, we will focus specifically on the state or national elections.

The most important norm ruling elections is the so called 5/1985 LOREG (Ley Orgánica del Régimen General Electoral). This law, partially modified in 1994, governs the duration of the campaign, the finance model, including a limit on expenses, and the use of political advertising in the mass media. It also establishes some basic principles regarding the election news coverage.

Whereas the 1985 law established that electoral campaigns would last at least fifteen days and no more than twenty-one, the new 1994 law (Ley Orgánica 13/1994, March 30) limited electoral campaigns in Spain to fifteen days. The day before voting is a reflection day and electoral activities are forbidden, which means that it is only during the prior fifteen days that parties can organize electoral activities to ask citizens for their vote.

Campaigns are mostly financed with public money. The Spanish model is mainly based on public subsidies granted to the political parties by the state in order to cover all the electoral expenses. Two laws, LOREG and the 3/1987 law on political parties' finances rule this area. The main principle is that the state subsidizes the national (and local) campaigns. Political parties receive an amount of money from the national budget according to the number of parliamentary seats and the votes they got in the previous election. Subsidies coming from other public entities or from foreign entities or individuals are forbidden. Private funding is allowed, but very limited. The permitted donations to the campaign by corporations or individuals are limited to an amount of €6,000. The 1994 law established a limit for electoral expenses, fixing the maximum at an amount which results from multiplying a small quantity of money by the number of citizens in the constituencies where the political parties present their candidates (the same rule applies also to local and European elections).

The legal framework regarding political advertising and propaganda is complex (see Table 11.2). We will focus here specifically on advertising in the press, on radio, and television.. Advertising in the streets is allowed, and public spaces are distributed by local governments to political parties also according to their number of votes and seats in the previous election.

TABLE 11.1
General, Regional, Local and European Elections in Spain since 1977

	General	Regional	Local	European
1977	*			
1978				
1979	*		*	
1980		* (Catalonia and Basque Country)		
1981		* (Galicia)		
1982	*	* (Andalusia)		
1983		* (13)1	*	
1984		* (Basque Country)		
1985		* (Galicia)		
1986	*	* (Andalusia and Basque Country)		
1987		* (13)	*	*
1988		* (Catalonia)		
1989	*	* (Galicia)		*
1990		* (Andalusia and Basque Country)		
1991		* (13)	*	
1992		* (Catalonia)		
1993	*	* (Galicia)		
1994		* (Andalusia and Basque Country)		*
1995		* (13 + Catalonia)2	*	
1996	*	* (Andalusia)		
1997		* (Galicia)		
1998		* (Basque Country)		
1999		* (13 + Catalonia)	*	*
2000	*	* (Andalusia)		
2001		* (Galicia and Basque Country)		
2002				
2003		* (13 + Catalonia)	*	
2004	*			*

Based on the Spanish Home Office data

(1) Meaning the thirteen Autonomous Communities whose elections take place at the same time than the local elections.

(2) In some cases Catalonia also held its regional elections at the same time than the local elections.

(3) In 1978 the Constitutional referendum was held.

There are different rules for each one of the mass media. There are no limits concerning the print media—every political party can contract for as many ads as they want, without paying more than is usually paid by commercial advertisers, provided they comply with the provision establishing a limit of 20% of campaign expenses invested in advertising in the press and on commercial radio. This last statement indicates that advertising on commercial radio stations or radio networks is virtually free with the indicated percentage limit. But public radio has a different regime, as we will explain.

Television, considered as a powerful medium, constitutes a special case in Spain. For many years public television has been a clear target for all the political forces. Tightly controlled since

TABLE 11.2
Main Principles Regarding Political Advertising, Electoral Propaganda and Electoral Campaign Coverage in Spain

	Printed press	*Commercial Radio*	*Public radio*	*Public television*	*Commercial television*
Political advertising is…	Freely purchased Only limited with reference to the total campaign expenses	Freely purchased Only limited with reference to the total campaign expenses			Banned
Electoral propaganda is…			Free According to the proportion of the vote Not specifically restricted regarding content	Free According to the proportion of the vote Not specifically restricted regarding content	
Coverage principles	Freedom	Freedom	Principles of pluralism and balance	Principles of pluralism and balance	Principles of pluralism and balance

the beginning of the fifties under Franco, it is well known that it is controlled by the government and, although it should be objective and neutral as the laws require, every political party in power has tried, in one way or another, to use it for their convenience. Now private channels compete with public television not only for audiences but also for the commercials and money, but Spanish politicians have remained extremely cautious in this area and have approved more restrictive rules regarding television, both public and commercial, than those for radio and the print media. A proof of that has been the ban under the 1988 law on broadcasting political ads on commercial television channels (Ley Orgánica 2/1988, May 3) whereas there is freedom to broadcast political ads on commercial radio and publish them in the press.

Notwithstanding, even if the political parties are not allowed to contract advertising time with the public radio and television stations and networks, they have, in accordance with the 1988 law, a right to broadcast unpaid slots of electoral propaganda in these media. The distribution of time for those free slots follows some complex rules, but the main principle is that it should correspond with the number of votes each party got in the previous similar election. The Central Electoral Authority has the power to distribute the slots for the free electoral propaganda in the public media, examining the specific proposals made by a radio and television committee, representing the political parties in Parliament, being the value of each vote related with the number of seats each party has in Parliament. This pattern is also followed at the local and regional level.

An interesting point is that the free slots for political propaganda are not considered as commercial advertising, and therefore legal restrictions for commercials (such as subliminal, comparative, etc.) do not apply to electoral advertising. One can understand the explicit interest among legislators to restrict *television* advertising with a clear restriction of *channels*, but what is not understandable is their apparent indifference as regards content. Consequently there are no restrictions regarding negative propaganda, and as a matter of fact there is an interesting episode linked with this which we shall turn to later.

The Central Electoral Authority (article 65) decides the length of time and moment of emission of electoral propaganda spots, based on the proposal of the specific *ad hoc* organizing committee, and taking into account the number of votes obtained in the previous elections (article 67). As an example, in the 2004 general election, the PP and the PSOE got 45 minutes each, to broadcast twenty-two ads, two minutes long, and an additional one with a length of three minutes. Izquierda Unida got 30 minutes distributed in a similar fashion, and three regional parties—Convergencia I Unió (CiU), Partido Nacionalista Vasco (PNV), and Coalición Canaria (CC)—had 15 minutes each in the geographic area where the party presented candidates. The same amount of time was given to those parties emission time of the public radio.

One can take for granted that the big political parties, having more time, can be more explicit and that this inequality established by law prevents the small parties from presenting their proposals in a better way (Sádaba, 2003). Also, having more money, the big parties produce better spots in terms of quality. Nevertheless, the advantage of the present regulation is clear, because it guarantees free electoral propaganda time, both on radio and television, to all the parties which can then compete even if their budget is low.

Concerning the content of news campaign coverage (see Table 11.2), the LOREG stated a principle for the public media—at that time Spain only had public television—saying that respect for political and social pluralism and also neutral coverage and reporting would be guaranteed by the managing staff of those media and controlled in accordance with the law. Legitimate claimants can appeal to the Electoral Authority at the corresponding level.

But the Spanish legislators went farther in the 1988 law when, after banning political ads on commercial television channels, they made it an obligation also for the commercial television channels to respect pluralism and the balance principle in those programs broadcast during the period of campaign. Regarding this point, the electoral authorities are also empowered to take decisions at each level: local, regional, and national.

As a matter of fact, public television is required to give proportional coverage time to political parties, what is called "mathematical balance": Each party has a right to a space in the news broadcasts that is proportional to the vote obtained in the previous elections. The Council of Administration of RTVE (Radio Televisión Española) decides on the specific distribution of coverage time for each campaign.

The electoral coverage system in the public media is not an ideal solution for media practitioners. It seems that in some cases parties' activities are not newsworthy and a purely balanced coverage would mean a bureaucratic instead of a professional coverage. Canel (2006) has recently illustrated this situation regarding several elections in Catalonia.

Polling is another point that should be mentioned. Both the Centro de Investigaciones Sociológicas (CIS), a state agency whose history goes back to the Franco period (Giner, 1983b), and independent firms conduct polls before and during the electoral period. The CIS, whose declared aim is "the scientific study of Spanish society," and which is required to work in accordance with "the principles of objectivity, neutrality, equal access to its data and respect for citizens and the statistical secret," has been the object of intense controversy. Dependent on the government, it was accused of a partisan use of its resources, of manipulation, of presenting biased results in favor of the government, of delaying the public presentation of data which was not favorable to the government, and so on. Some months before the election in which Felipe González was defeated, the Parliament passed an act linking CIS more to Parliament than to the government (Law 39/1995, December 19). Nevertheless, the criticism has remained both under Aznar's PP government and now with Rodriguez Zapatero's socialist government.

Polls conducted by CIS, which are open to all the media, and other polls published by specific media, have now become a relevant part of the electoral campaign coverage, thus fostering the horse-race style of the political contest. The LOREG includes some provisions dealing with polls. On the one hand, the provisions are related to the obligation of reporting about who carried out the poll and who was the sponsor, about the technical aspects (sampling method, sample size, sample error, level of confidence, etc.), and also the wording of the questions and number of people not answering specific questions. On the other hand, the LOREG, without limiting the freedom of political parties to conduct polls for their own purposes, prohibits the publication of polls in any medium in the five days prior to election day. In spite of this provision and also as a sign of the controversial nature of the CIS, there was an interesting case in which a CIS poll was published just before the election. That happened in the Basque 2001 elections when the CIS was accused of delaying the publication of the last poll to favor the government. Nevertheless, because of the increasing use of new technologies, the concept of publishing is somehow ambiguous and it is easily avoided.

Perhaps paradoxically, the media that hire the pollsters are very critical of them when failures happen. That happened for instance in the 1993 and 1996 elections (see Table 11.3). In 1993 some Spanish pollsters predicted a possible PP victory, but as it turned out the socialists maintained a reduced but effective majority. And in 1996 the pollsters overestimated the eventual PP victory. Perhaps due to this experience the pollsters were much more cautious in 2000 and reduced Aznar's expectations when his party got the absolute majority.

In conclusion, the legal framework for campaigns in Spain is more concerned with the use of television than other techniques of political communication. Also, it is relevant that it details how often political parties' ads may appear but does not say anything about the content. Finally, the law, as it was settled in 1985, reflects the broadcasting situation at that moment when there was no commercial television, and new technologies were not included.

COVERAGE PATTERNS

Academic research has outlined that coverage during electoral campaigns has followed several patterns. In the Spanish case, we can state that there is not much research on this specific topic although here we collect some of the most outstanding literature in the field. In accordance with the international literature, we can establish at least six coverage models: horse-race coverage, issues coverage, personalization coverage, quoting coverage, civic journalism coverage, and campaign strategies coverage. We suggest an additional model that could be named "entrenched" journalism. The models converge and overlap, but one of them can become especially relevant in a specific campaign, as we can see when considering the Spanish elections (see Table 11.4).

Patterson has carefully explained the horse-race pattern coverage, as a model that highlights the competitive character of the campaign, as opposed to the issue coverage (Patterson, 1980). The horse-race coverage pays attention to who is going to win and what are the possibilities of the candidates. Therefore, they follow the polls and what pollsters explain narrowly. Valentino,

TABLE 11.3
Predictions for the Number of Seats (only PSOE and PP) in the Spanish Chamber of Deputies made by Some Leading Pollsters and de facto Results

		Demoscopia El País	Opina La Vanguardia	Sigma Dos El Mundo	Final results
1993	PSOE	135 to 145	138 to 142	135 to 145	159
	PP	143 to 153	138 to 146	139 to 148	141
1996	PSOE	118 to 128	135 to 145	113 to 123	141
	PP	170 to 178	160 to 170	170 to 179	156

Beckman, and Buhr (2001) say that this kind of coverage has negative effects on people who have no interest in politics, whereas it does not affect those who with a greater interest in politics.

Issues coverage is characterized by the explanation of the proposals each political party defends during the campaign. This model has two possible focuses. On the one hand, the coverage can inform about the political parties' programs, and on the other hand, the media themselves can establish which are the most important issues for the elections and cover them. In other words, the media can follow the political agenda or set it themselves (McCombs, 2004).

Besides, the media approach to the issues could be different depending on the subject. For instance, Weaver and Elliot (1985), in their study in a local newspaper on the coverage of a municipal meeting, conclude that with social and recreational issues the media establish a greater filter than with economic subjects. According to the researchers, this happens because of the professional routines applied to economic information, such as: confidence in the official sources, the absence of other sources, the time pressure, the norm of objectivity, or the journalistic values that give priority to conflict and to controversy.

Opposed to issues coverage, there is a third model, namely personalization coverage (Dader, 1990; Berrocal, 2003), which stresses the role of the candidates during the campaign, putting emphasis on their personal characteristics. In a comparative study of the Spanish television channels during the 2000 elections, Martín (2002) concluded that the coverage was focused on the candidates.

Another model of media coverage basically consists in quoting the statements of each candidate and the answers to other candidates, following the scheme: A says something, B answers A, A responds to B, etc. This is the "quoting coverage," declaratory journalism. In this sense, the media follows "the track of the power"; that is to say, they speak for the candidates (Bennett, 1996). Bennett also suggests that this type of coverage is included within the professional routines for political topics; journalists go to official sources, and they look for the controversy that exists between different sources (for example, government-opposition). Being focused on the cross-fire, this coverage model introduces problems for the audience, since it is easy to get lost in the course of the events. Getting lost means that people would not see the sense of the controversy, so this situation could provoke a logical saturation effect.

Civic journalism with its proposals for coverage tries to avoid this possible saturation by involving citizens in the electoral coverage: citizens and their concerns would be the authentic protagonists (Rosen, 1992), so the public agenda gets more attention than the political or the media agendas. In Spain, like in the United States (Martín & Alvarez, 2003) this type of coverage has been experimented with in some local newspapers, without obtaining significant changes in the citizens' perspective of the campaign.

TABLE 11.4
Election Coverage Models: Attempted Typology

Types or styles of election news coverage	Main focus
Horse-race coverage	Which candidate is ahead
Issues coverage	Parties' proposals
Personalization coverage	Candidates' image
Quoting coverage	Statements and counter-statements
Civic journalism coverage	Audience's participation
Campaign strategies' coverage	Campaign's tricks and devices
Entrenched coverage	Taking sides, "militancy"

Finally, we can talk about campaign strategies coverage when the media emphasize the communication strategies developed during campaigns (Arterton, 1984). Under this model, the media try to carry out electoral pedagogy, showing the audiences the communication tools which political parties use during campaigns. This was the case during the 1993 general elections in Spain when the first and only television debate between the two main candidates running for the post of prime minister took place. There are no legal norms regarding electoral debates, but in the case of there being one or more, the Central Electoral Authority has some supervising competences.

In the 1993 election Felipe González (PSOE) had been the incumbent prime minister for eleven years, and José Mª Aznar (PP) was trying to defeat him (Gunther, Montero, & Wert, 2000). Polls were saying they were almost equal. Both candidates agreed to two television debates, which the Central Electoral Authority approved. Interestingly, the Aznar electoral team rejected the possibility of having a debate on public Spanish television, arguing that Television Española's reporting had been systematically biased against Aznar (Díez Nicolás & Semetko, 1995). The debates were held on two national commercial channels (Antena 3, May 24 and Tele 5, May 31).

Expectations were very high and both debates were very successful in terms of audience reach, with the first getting an audience of 9.6 million and the second 10.5 million. They were the second and third most watched programs during that year (the first one was a soccer game). The atmosphere of the debate resembled a boxing match, with a challenger trying to defeat the incumbent champion. In one of the debates, the background music was even taken from the feature film *Rocky*. Probably because expectations were more with Gonzalez than Aznar, the media said he had won the first debate.

Another example of this type of coverage took place in 1996, when the PSOE decided to create a negative campaign based on a spot called the "Doberman spot." In 1996 the Socialists had a lot of problems because of corruption issues and the economic situation in Spain was not good. Results during local elections in 1995 and European elections in 1994 had not been good for the party in power. The PP, for the first time, was seen as the likely winner. Therefore, the PSOE tried to avoid this or at least, made an attempt to avoid an absolute majority for PP. They contracted a famous ad agency (José Luis Zamorano Associates) and followed a strategy based on fear-appeals (like the U.S. "Daisy Spot"). More specifically, there was a scene with a Doberman which threatened the audience in a very brief image. The media began to say that this was subliminal or at least, not legal, taking into account that it was a very negative spot (Sádaba, 2003). The result was that the audience for the spots increased because everyone wanted to check for themselves if they could see the Doberman or not. The strategy was more than the spot: all the media were talking about it. The election went to the PP, but with no absolute majority. Was it because of the Doberman effect?

Entrenched Journalism

The peculiarities of the Spanish media lead us to include a new model of election coverage that we call "entrenched" journalism, meaning a journalism that clearly takes sides, with the media playing a militant role. We do not argue that this is an exclusively Spanish feature, but this approach is clear in Spain. The polarization is more evident in the print media and commercial radio where there is in principle freedom in terms of election coverage, but it also appears in public and commercial television. National and regional public television have close links with the respective governments and usually there is a leaning towards the ruling political party, unless inner tensions hamper the government influence.

This entrenched model coverage explains that since the media are very effective in promoting knowledge about the political candidates, they promote at the same time more or less

TABLE 11.5
**Percentage of Positive, Neutral and Positive Statements in the 2000 Election
Campaign, Regarding the PP (Aznar) and PSOE (Almunia) Candidates in
Some National Newspapers (El País and El Mundo) and National Television
Channels (Public TV1, and Commercial Antena 3 and Tele 5)**

		% Negative statements	% Neutral statements	% Positive statements
El País	**Almunia**	13,3	29,7	57
	Aznar	**53,1**	21,2	25,7
El Mundo	**Almunia**	**44,7**	28,2	27
	Aznar	34,3	22,1	**43,7**
TV1	**Almunia**	8,9	43,3	**47,8**
	Aznar	**23,4**	30	46,7
Antena 3	**Almunia**	8,1	37,8	54
	Aznar	**24**	12,7	**63,4**
Tele5	**Almunia**	23,2	48,1	28,7
	Aznar	**27,2**	39,7	**33,1**

Source: our content analysis data of the 2000 election coverage

favorable images of those candidates. A 2000 study (López-Escobar, Tolsá, McCombs, & Martin, 2000), based on content analysis of the media during the electoral period and a regional survey made in Navarra, made a comparison among (1) the media coverage index, related to the number of news items about the national and regional candidates and the photographs, appearances in cartoons, and other references to the candidates; and (2) the number of marks on a barometer and number of mentions of the candidates by the public. The correlation among the media coverage index and the knowledge index was .81 in the case of the national candidates and .99 in the case of the regional ones.

But each candidate is framed by the media in a different light. Let us take, for example, the 2000 election coverage of the main candidates, Aznar (PP) and Almunia (PSOE). A content analysis of the main news items mentioning both candidates in two national dailies (*El País* and *El Mundo*) and three national television channels (the public TV1 and the commercial Antena 3 and Tele 5) shows clear differences in the tone of the coverage. *El País* put the emphasis on the positive attributes of the PSOE candidate (57% of the statements were positive) and on the negative characteristics of the PP candidate (53.1% of the statements were negative). Conversely, *El Mundo* emphasized the negative aspects of the PSOE candidate (44.7%) and the positives of the PP candidate (43.7%), notwithstanding its being more balanced than *El País*. The television coverage was also more balanced, complying with the legal principles. The two commercial channels included more positive statements about Aznar (TV1, even being public under a PP government, favored Almunia), but also emphasized Aznar's negative attributes. This difference in framing could be a result of the editorial policy of each medium as such and also a consequence of the stance the media take for competitive reasons.

The 2004 Election

This study ends with a reflection on the 2004 election and its media coverage, another good example of the entrenched journalism model, which we are referring to here. Virtually all the polls

TABLE 11.6
Vote Distribution among the PP and PSOE in the 1996, 2000 and 2004 Spanish National Election

	Valid votes	Turnout	Abstention	Party	Votes	Percentage
1996	25.046.276	77,38	22,62	**PP**	9.716.006	38,79
				PSOE	9.425.678	37,63
2000	23.181.272	68,71	31,29	**PP**	10.321.178	44,52
				PSOE	7.918.752	34,16
2004	25.891.299	75,66	24,34	**PP**	9.763.144	37,71
				PSOE	11.026.163	42,59

Based on Spanish Home Office's data

published during the campaign predicted a victory for the PP, with a new leader (Mariano Rajoy), but the possibility of getting the absolute majority was very unclear. The terrorist attack on trains at the Atocha train station in Madrid, the management of the reporting policy by the government, the media behaving as political actors, and the final turmoil activated by new communication media, increased turnout, with more than two million people, leading to an unexpected victory of PSOE with its new leader Zapatero.

The 2004 elections received very passionate treatment in the media, and a balanced and detached analysis of the situation is still required, in spite of the several books and papers published. This is so, above all, because the explanation about that terrorist event is still very blurred and incomplete. Based on a number of observations, it is clear that there was a polarization following a well-established pattern. TVE (Television Española) controlled by the Partido Popular government, two public regional channels (TeleMadrid and TV Valencia) of Autonomous Communities governed by the PP took a more favorable stance toward the government during the Atocha crisis, whereas Canal+, Tele5, and some public regional channels in Autonomus Communities ruled by the socialists backed the PSOE. The same adversarial situation occurred in the print media, with *El Mundo* and *La Razón* in favor of PP, and *El País* in favor of the socialists, while ABC took a rather more neutral position. Something similar happened with radio: SER favored very much the socialists whereas COPE and Onda 0 leaned towards the "populares," and RNE was more balanced. This polarization also happened in the new media that contribute very actively to the debate, feeding the controversy as many scholars have outlined (Vara, Virgili, Giménez, & Díaz, 2006).

A study conducted in 2004, immediately after the election, among Navarra's citizens (López-Escobar, Sádaba, Tolsá, & Lozano, 2005), explored how the public perceived two important issues, depending on the media they had used. The authors wanted to know public perceptions of how the government had reported the terrorist attack and if the media had been in favor, neutral, or unfavorable towards the government in those tense days. The hypothesis was that people that had consumed media reports that were more inclined to support the government would be more prone to say the government had reported "very well" or "well" in a larger proportion than those that had consumed the reports of the media less favorable towards the government. And that was what happened. Most of those interviewed said that the government had reported badly or very badly, but the proportion is much higher when we pay attention to those television channels (the national Tele5 and the Basque regional channel ETB2), newspapers (the national *El País* and the local *Diario de Noticias*, close to the leftist and Basque nationalist proposals), and radio networks (above all SER, but also that theoretically controlled by the government RNE).

Another interesting point was to know how people had perceived the media coverage

TABLE 11.7
"How Did the Government Report about the Terrorist Attack?"

		Very well/well	In between	Bad/very bad	DA/DK	N=
Television	TV1	36	19	38	7	284
	Antena3	30	18	45	7	423
	Tele5	19	15	**60**	6	284
	ETB2	10	5	**79**	5	204
Dailies	D. Navarra	30	19	45	5	573
	El Mundo	30	30	37	3	57
	El País	18	16	**65**	2	96
	D. Noticias	12	14	**71**	3	219
Radio	COPE	**47**	21	28	4	128
	Onda 0	**38**	21	**38**	3	133
	RNE	39	13	**43**	5	121
	SER	9	12	**73**	5	130

Based on our own sources

regarding the government—favorable, neutral, or unfavorable—in those crucial March 2004 days. The authors' assumption was that consumers of media less favorable towards the PP government, as a result of their own selective exposure and the influence of the media used by them, would think the media in general had been too benevolent to the government in a higher proportion than those consuming media with more leanings towards the PP government. In spite of the high proportion of those who did not answer or say they did not know, the pattern was clear: consumers of media less favorable towards the government (Tele5, ETB2, *El País*, *Diario de Noticias* and SER) thought the media had carried out a coverage more favorable towards the government than consumers of media more in favor of the government, who were less satisfied with the coverage.

TABLE 11.8
Spain: "How Was the Media Coverage Regarding Government?"

		Favourable	In between	Unfavourable	DA/DK	N=
Television	TV1	19	21	**34**	27	454
	Antena 3	17	18	**34**	31	284
	Tele5	**28**	17	27	28	424
	ETB2	**40**	10	16	34	206
Dailies	D. Navarra	21	20	**32**	27	572
	El Mundo	21	25	**30**	24	57
	El País	**30**	18	24	28	96
	D.Noticias	**35**	16	24	25	218
Radio	COPE	16	21	**37**	26	128
	Onda0	18	26	**35**	22	133
	RNE	25	19	**28**	29	120
	SER	**33**	16	24	27	130

Based on our own sources

EXPLORING THE FUTURE WITH A CRYSTAL BALL

Fortune telling is not one of those activities in which academic researchers tend to excel. Nevertheless, some signs could help to anticipate some aspects of the next national electoral campaign and its coverage by the media. The exceptional circumstances of the 2004 election, that accidentally gave power to the PSOE led by its new leader, Rodríguez Zapatero, are still coloring political events. Also the particulars of the terrorist attack, whose multisided manipulation before public opinion characterized the last general election, remain unclear. It is not easy to imagine the development of Rodríguez Zapatero's policy, which is focused on reaching an agreement with ETA, the Basque terrorist association. The consequence of this in terms of public opinion is to cause problems with defining him: the interpretations go from his having a genuine determination to negotiate peace with ETA, to his being an ETA hostage, with ETA as the electoral agenda-setter.[1]

Whatever happens in the country, it is clear than the media, having played their role, as we have said, guided partly by editorial policy and partly by tactical decisions related to their intense competition, will maintain and probably stress their positions, in accordance with the proposed entrenched model.

NOTE

1. Unfortunately, a day before the print proofs of this chapter were returned to the publisher, and two days before the 2008 national election day, ETA terrorists killed a former socialist member of the Arrasate-Mondragon (Basque country) community council. The coverage pattern of this election had also followed the entrenched model.

REFERENCES

Aja, E. (1999). *El Estado autonómico: Federalismo y hechos diferenciales* [State and autonomous communities: Federalism and differential features]. Madrid: Alianza.

Arterton, C. (1984). *Media politics*. Lexington, MA: Lexington Books.

Barrera, C. (1995). *Sin mordaza: Veinte años de prensa en democracia* [Gags out: Twenty years of the press in a democratic regime]. Madrid: Temas de Hoy.

Barrera, C., & Zugasti, R. (2006). The role of the press in times of transition: The building of the Spanish democracy (1975–1978). In K. Voltmer (Ed.), *Mass media and political communication in new democracies* (pp. 23–41). London: Routledge/ECPR.

Bennett, L. W. (1996). An introduction to journalism norms and representations of politics? *Political Communication, 13*, 373–384.

Berrocal, S. (2003). La personalización en la política [Personalization in politics]. In S. Berrocal (Ed.), *Comunicación política en televisión y nuevos medios* [Political communication in televisión and new media] (pp. 55–79). Barcelona: Ariel.

Canel, M. J. (2006). *Comunicación política: una guía para su estudio y práctica* [Political communication: A guide for its study and practice]. Madrid: Tecnos.

Crespo, I. (2004). *Las campañas electorales y sus efectos en la decisión del voto: Vol. 1. La campaña electoral de 2000: partidos, medios de comunicación y electores* [Electoral campaigns and their effects on voting: Vol. 2. The 2000 electoral campaign: Political parties, media and voters]. Valencia: Tirant lo blanch.

Dader, J. L. (1990). La personalización de la política [Personalization in politics]. In A. Muñoz-Alonso, C. Monzón, J. I. Rospir, & J. L. Dador (Eds.), *Opinión pública y comunicación política* [Public opinion and political communication] (pp. 351–367). Madrid: Eudema.

Díez Nicolás, J., & Semetko, H. (1995). La televisión y las elecciones de 1993 [Television and the 1993 election]. In A. Muñoz-Alonso & J. I. Rospir (Eds.), *Comunicación política* [Political communication] (pp. 243–304). Madrid: Universitas.

Ferrando, J. (1975). *Teoría de la instauración monárquica en España* [A theory of the monarchic establishment in Spain]. Madrid: Instituto de Estudios Políticos.

Gifreu, J., & Pallarés, F. (2001). *La campanya més disputada: mitjans, partits i ciutadans a les eleccions catalanes del 1999* [The most competitive campaign: Media, political parties and citizens in the 1999 Catalonian election]. Barcelona: Pòrtic.

Giner, J. A. (1983a). Journalists, mass media, and public opinion in Spain. In K. Maxwell (Ed.), *The press and the rebirth of Iberian democracy* (pp. 33–54). Westport, CT: Greenwood.

Giner, J. A. (1983b). Political opinion polling in Spain. In R. Worcester (Ed.), *Political opinion polling: An international review* (pp. 178–197). London: Macmillan.

Gunther, R., Montero, J. R., & Wert, J. I. (2000). The media and politics in Spain: From dictatorship to democracy. In R. Gunther & A. Mughan (Eds.), *Democracy and the media: A comparative perspective* (pp. 28–84). Cambridge, UK: Cambridge University Press.

Iglesias, F. (1989). Las transformaciones de la prensa diaria [Changes in the daily press]. In J. T. Álvarez (Ed.) *Historia de los medios de comunicación en España: Periodismo, imagen y publicidad (1900–1990)* [History of the Spanish media: Journalism, audiovisual media and advertising] (pp. 436–444). Barcelona: Ariel.

López-Escobar, E., (1992a). Vulnerable values in Spanish multichannel television. In J. G. Blumler (Ed.), *Television and the public interest* (pp. 161–172). London: Sage.

López-Escobar, E. (1992b). Spanish media law: Changes in the landscape. *European Journal of Communication, 7*(2), 241–259.

López-Escobar, E., & Faus, A. (1985). Broadcasting in Spain: A history of heavy-handed state control. *West European Politics, 8*(2), 122–136.

López-Escobar, E., Tolsá, A., McCombs, M., & Martín, M. (2000). *Widening the scope of the agenda-setting paradigm: The case of radio.* Paper presented at the WAPOR annual conference, Portland, Oregon.

López-Escobar, E., Tolsá, A., Sádaba, T., & Lozano, P. (2005). Aznar's public image and media framing. In *Elections, news media and public opinion.* Navarra: Servicio de Publicaciones, Universidad de Navarra.

Martín Llaguno, M., & Alvarez de Arcaya, H. (2003). Comunicación electoral e interés ciudadano [Electoral communication and citizens' interest]. *ZER, 14,* 75–96.

Martín Salgado, L. (2002). *Marketing político: Arte y ciencia de la persuasión en democracia* [Political marketing: Art and science of persuasion in democracy]. Barcelona: Paidós.

McCombs, M. (2004). *Setting the agenda: The mass media and public opinion.* Malden, MA: Polity.

Palacio, M. (2001). *Historia de la televisión en España* [History of televisión in Spain]. Barcelona: Gedisa.

Patterson, T. E. (1980). *The mass media election: How Americans choose their president.* New York: Praeger.

Powell, C. (1991). *El piloto del cambio: El rey, la Monarquía y la transición a la democracia Planeta.*

Román, P. (Ed.). (2001). *Sistema Político español* [The Spanish political system]. Madrid: McGraw-Hill.

Rosen, J. (1992). Politics, vision and the press: Towards a public agenda for journalism. In J. Rosen & P. Taylor (Ed.), (pp. 3–33). New York: Twentieth Century Foundation

Sádaba, T. (2003). Los anuncios de los partidos en Televisión: El caso de España (1993–2000) [Political parties advertsing in television: The Spanish case]. In S. Berrocal (Ed.*)*, *Comunicación política en televisión y nuevos medios* [Political communication in televisión and new media] (pp.163–205). Barcelona: Ariel.

Sádaba, T., Lopez-Escobar, E., Tolsá, A., & Martín A. M. (2005). Elections in a time of deep uncertainty. In *Elections, news media and public opinion.* Navarra, Spain: Servicio de Publicaciones, Universidad de Navarra. ISBN 84-8081-018-1.

Santaolalla, F. (2004). *Derecho constitucional* [Constitutional law]. Madrid: Dykinson.

Sastre García, C. (1997). *Transición y desmovilización política en España (1975–1978)* [Transition and political dismobilization in Spain]. Valladolid: Servicio de Publicaciones de la Universidad de Valladolid.

Valentino, N. A., Buhr, T.A., & Beckmann, M. N. (2001). When the frame is the game: Revisiting the impact of "strategic" campaign coverage on citizen's information retention. *Journalism and Mass Communication Quarterly, 78*(1), 93–112.

Vara, A., R. Virgili, J., Giménez, E., & Díaz, M. (Eds.). (2006). *La comunicación en situaciones de crisis: del 11-M al 14-M* [Communication crisis: From May 11 to May 14]. Pamplona: Eunsa.

Weaver, D., & Elliot, S. N. (1985). Who sets the agenda for the media? A study of local agenda-setting. *Journalism Quarterly, 62*, 87–94.

Zalbidea, B. (1996). *Prensa del Movimiento en España: 1936–1983* [The movement's press in Spain]. Bilbao: Servicio Editorial de la Universidad del País Vasco.

Zugasti, R. (2007). *La forja de una complicidad: Monarquía y prensa en la transición española (1975–1978)* [The forging of an understanding between the monarchy and the press in the Spanish transition]. Madrid: Fragua.

12

Election News Coverage in Greece: Between Two Logics

Nicolas Demertzis and George Pleios

AN OVERVIEW OF THE MEDIA AND POLITICAL SYSTEM

The type, volume, and density of election news coverage is not only contingent upon the available communications technology, but on the structure of political opportunities as well. What the media cover and how they cover it during an election campaign depends on the dynamic of the political system, the dynamic of the media system, and their interconnections. It is through an examination of these interconnections that it might become easier to understand the particularities of election news coverage in Greece.

Historical Roots

As in most western countries, in Greece the political and the media systems have developed in tandem within the coordinates of the nation's road to modernity. In Greece, as in other countries, the state has played a decisive role in the media sector. In the nineteenth century, the making of the Greek state and polity, including the parliamentary sub-system, took place principally in a quasi-capitalist socio-economic environment (Charalambis & Demertzis, 1993; Mouzelis, 1986). As a consequence, Greek economic capital in general has been commercial rather than productive and industrial. Socio-economic development has been carried out for the most part by the state and not by a robust capitalist market. This socio-economic model produced a prominently middle-class life style at that time, and it also led to loose party structures, which has been conducive to clientelistic electoral politics, and it has contributed to an atrophic civil society; that is, to the absence of strong intermediary political/civic "bodies" between the central state and the private sector.

From the outset, the development of the Greek press has been marked by enormous numbers of stillborn newspapers addressing a very limited readership; open partisanship or even sectarianism among party lines; and sizeable financial state aid to the press on which individual enterprises became dependent because they could not cover their production costs. As early as in the 1850s, with the population size of the country being almost three times smaller than it is today, there were 26 newspapers and a variety of magazines on the market. In 1890, 131 newspapers were circulating, of which 87 were strictly political and partisan (Bickford-Smith, 1893; Dakin, 1972).

During the major part of the twentieth century the relations between the media, the state, and the parties remained the same. In spite of the fact that in the interwar period the first press moguls arrived on the scene, the press has never managed to disentangle itself from clientelistic intermediations, and journalists have been at pains to defend themselves as the watchdogs of power. Due to this style of newspaper governance, political power has often become the watchdog of newspapers. Legally, however, newspapers were free. Since 1844 Greek constitutions have clearly declared the freedom of the press and denounced any form of censorship. Yet, form and substance do not always coincide. In practice, clientelistic arrangements, as well as the repeated interruptions of democratic rule, especially during the interwar period, have kept the press and journalism in a semi-independent position vis-à-vis the state and political personnel. This plight of print journalism remained unchanged and has dominated the landscape of print and public communication ever since. Radio began airing on a regular basis in 1938 under the direction of Metaxas's dictatorial regime, and television broadcasting began in 1966 and expanded further during the Colonels' junta which in 1970 installed its own nationwide network (Armed Forces' Information Service-YENED). This did not end until 1982. Given the constitutional provision that they operate under "direct state control," which does not necessarily mean state monopoly, this autocratic and statist legacy marked the culture of both media (Dimitras, 1997). Until the early 1990s one could thus discern two tendencies in Greek state television's programs; on the one hand, a somewhat modern and "Europe oriented" tendency, which was presented by the "civic" ERT1, and YENED's more popular and "tradition oriented" presentation.

Undoubtedly, many fundamental changes occurred in Greece after World War II and especially after the fall of the military junta in 1974. Contemporary Greece is an intensively urbanized, thoroughly consumer-oriented country, which since 1981 has been a full member of the European Union. Yet the unequal situation of a non-articulated and potent civil society and an overriding paternalistic central state remains one of its most important structural features. This affects both the media and the political system.

1. Despite the harsh deregulation that took place in the late 1980s, which led to a sudden proliferation of private radio stations, newspapers addressing a small market, as well as TV, both commercial and state/public, none of these elements managed to become an integral part of a flourishing civil society. Instead, the media succumbed to commercialization and to government legislation. Since the mid-1980s, entrepreneurs, bankers, and ship owners have gradually become the new press barons, and the commercial electronic media have been controlled by fewer and fewer hands through cross-ownership. With almost a decade time lag, since the mid-1990s there have been efforts by the state to (re)regulate the broadcasting sector according to EU directions on advertising time, program quotas, awarding of television and radio licenses, and media ownership concentration (Papathanassopoulos, 2001, 2004).

2. The contemporary Greek political system is a parliamentary democracy with political parties holding a strong position in it. This system has deep historical roots stemming from the 1915 to 1922 period (characterized by antagonism between democrats and monarchists) and the 1944 to 1949 period (characterized by the civil war between communists and nationalists). Due to the process of modernization, the most fundamental changes in Greek political life appeared after 1974. Some examples of such changes are: the abolition of the monarchy; the end of the state of emergency that followed the civil war; the diminishing of the power of "veto groups" such as the military; and the lessening of para-constitutional crises; the improved reputation of political personnel; the establishment of an openly competitive political system; the reorganization of the party system; and the expansion of political communication. Yet, as manifest as changes such as these might be, political modernization did not transcend traditional statism, (party) clientelism,

or the weak civil society, three of the fundamentals of the country's political culture (Demertzis, 1997; Papadopoulos, 1989).

The Current Situation

Since the early 1990s, the Greek political system has gone through a number of transformations. The most salient of these are: First, the gradual change in the party system from polarized pluralism into two-partyism, to the extent that the two main catch-all parties, PASOK (Panhellenic Socialist Movement, a center-left party) and ND (New Democracy, center-right party), managed to minimize or even eliminate other significant political forces (Pappas, 2003). Second, in spite of mass voting turnout, fostered by compulsory voting, rising levels of political apathy, cynicism, and disenchantment with public affairs have been systematically documented. Third, the style of electoral politics and policy formation is mostly conducted according to what has been called "Americanization" (Kavanagh, 1995, pp. 218–227), including extensive spin doctoring, mass reliance on opinion polls, telepolitics, and permanent campaigning. Fourth, the political and economic systems in Greece have been brought into compliance with the European environment.

It is striking that these changes in the political system and political culture are coterminous with changes in the Greek media system, such as deregulation, commercialization, and globalization. Yet, one should think in terms of elective affinity, since there is little evidence of any causal relationship between them (Demertzis & Kafetzis, 1996). Changes in both systems have taken place within a wider international environment, which in turn has led to a convergence among media systems, giving rise to a global media culture. This has shaken national polities and economics, and contributed to legitimation crises worldwide. Due to these processes, in particular the commercialization of the media, political communication in Greece as well as in other countries increasingly appears to be shaped by "media logic" rather than "political logic" (Mazzoleni, 1987). Yet, at the end of the day, one can argue that an antagonistic symbiosis frames the political–media nexus in Greece. For the most part, the two systems depend on, compete, and complement each other in a way similar to how Swanson (1992, p. 399) described the political–media complex several years ago: "within this complex, particular institutional interests often conflict with each other in the battle to control the public's perceptions, but mutual cooperation is required for each institution to achieve its aim."

This antagonistic symbiosis has been described as an oedipal symptom (Paraschos, 1995), and it is made possible in and through sophisticated forms of political clientelism; but this is not by definition incompatible with commercialization (Hallin & Papathanassopoulos, 2002). It is furthermore not incompatible with corruption and fraud, so far as the real or assumed bonds between the entrepreneurial sector and the mass media sector are concerned, especially during election campaigns. The media coverage can thus function as an efficient means for the media moguls to use for putting pressure on the policy agenda; for example, by focusing on "social problems" like unemployment, crime, public health, inflation, etc., so as to affect public opinion for or against the incumbents or the opposition. The efficiency of such means is enhanced all the more due to the absence of a robust civic society which otherwise, presumably, could filter and cope with these problems through non-governmental organizations (NGOs) and voluntarism.

THE DEVELOPMENT OF THE ELECTION NEWS COVERAGE

During the last 30 years or so, electoral campaigning in Greece has been going through Norris's three-facet developmental model of campaigning (Norris, 2000). According to this model, it is possible to make a distinction between three phases of political campaigning: the pre-modern, modern, and post-modern. Yet it should be noted that there is no clear-cut transition from the pre-modern to the modernand thereafter to the post-modern type of campaign. They may coexist and complement each other either in the very same electoral contest or in different campaigns. As an example, present day (2006) local elections in Greece are largely carried out through the pre-modern style of campaign, in contrast to campaigns in national or even European parliamentary elections.

Nevertheless, and although Norris's typology refers to electoral campaigning, it is possible to analyze the evolution of election news coverage using the distinction between three different phases, at least in the Greek case. Therefore, we suggest the following typology concerning the development of election news coverage in Greece within the historical context of the Third Republic (1974 to the present day).

Pre-Modern Phase (1974–1990)

The prominent characteristics of this phase, which derived from the pre-dictatorial electoral routines, were enormous and passionate rallies in the big cities and especially in Athens; very high partisanship and polarization; the central, if not exclusive, role of the party organization and leadership in the design and implementation of the campaign master plan; heavy reliance on the press; extensive use of political posters and slogans; and restricted use of television. As for the latter, the first time state TV channels awarded free time to political forces was during the campaign for the 1974 national elections and the referendum over the question of monarchy. This was a period when ideology saturated political discourse and political discourse dominated the mass media (Pleios, 2001).

Throughout the 1970s, television lagged behind other means of political communication because of limited know-how and technical infrastructure, and the reluctance of the political leaders to make use of the then-new medium because they were accustomed to the traditional means of press, radio, and interpersonal political communication. In the same period a way of covering pre-election campaigns was established which was characterized by: (1) An analogy between the number of parliamentary seats of the parties and the television news time which was spent covering the parties, and (2) a polemic, mainly symbolic and ritual, confrontation between representatives of the parties on political talk shows. From then on, however, the state channels have covered all central rallies of the period under discussion (1981, 1984, 1985, 1989, 1990) in national and European parliamentary elections, thus rendering most of them newsworthy media events. Since the mid-1980s, television's role in covering the election campaigns has continued to increase.

Modern Phase (1990–2000)

The basic contours of this phase are the abatement of populist and clientelistic politics, rising levels of political disaffection despite massive voter turnout, decrease of partisanship, proliferation of opinion polls and exit polls, rapid increase of television coverage, and the professionalization of electoral strategy with foreign and Greek communication experts being involved. It was a period when politicians were becoming increasingly comfortable with television routines and politics saturated television coverage before and during the campaigns (Papathanassopoulos, 2000). The 1993 and 1996 national elections signaled irrevocably "telepolitics" and "teledemocracy" in the Greek political landscape since political talk shows, television debates, and television political advertising, positive as well as negative, came to the fore, whereas at the same time public rallies in major cities and personal contacts with party workers were seriously curtailed. In contrast to the first period, in this phase the political discourse was much less shaped by ideology as it was widely guided by the power of the (moving) image and consumer-oriented mass media (Pleios, 2001).

It can be argued that in this phase, citizenship was gradually supplemented, if not replaced, by spectatorship (Swanson & Mancini, 1996); it is not accidental, at any rate, that the 1996 national elections were dubbed the "elections on the couch." To be sure, however, newspapers remained an arena for confrontation between contrasting politics and party ideology. The press still offers information, commentary, and analysis along traditional partisan lines, though to a much lesser degree than was once the case. With respect to television, the election news coverage has followed a market-oriented infotainment pattern leading to more personalization of politics evidenced in the promotion and the vote of celebrities from show business, sports, and TV journalism.

Post-Modern Phase (2000–Onward)

The main components of this phase are the amplified fluidity of the electorate mostly in the second order elections, with bipartisanship being dominant in general elections; the rise of the permanent campaign; the fixed consolidation of political marketing as a major component of election campaigning; and the use of the Internet as well as television as a means of political communication (Demertzis et al., 2005a). As is well known, through its "grammar" (interactivity, individual use, speed in information processing etc.) the Internet allows a shift from the mass-broadcasting model to a narrowcasting model. With the bypassing of journalists and the gradual abandonment of mass political communication, the three-way relation between politicians–mass media–audience takes new and unpredictable forms, whose future in Greece is open because the whole procedure is in its infancy, and the political use of the Internet in Greece is still limited. For the time being, however, the post-modern election news coverage in Greece is marked by an infotainment-like style, the inability of big political parties to engage their members in the implementation of their election campaign master plans, and the continuous professionalization of image making.

REGULATING ELECTORAL COVERAGE

Naturally, in such a state-centered communication landscape as the Greek one, any regulation of the election news coverage is a controversial endeavor for the stakeholders involved. Attempts to regulate it started early on, with the restoration of democracy and can be classified into two periods: before and after the deregulation of the entire television sector that took place in 1989. In the first period (1974–1989) there was a top-down regulation of the election news coverage, since the authorities of the state television and the government itself was ahead of the field. This, however, did not prevent them from asking the political parties to submit their suggestions or even form ad hoc consultative electoral committees with regard to the way campaigns should be covered. Yet, it was up to the governmental agencies to take the initiative and decide. In the 1974, 1977, and 1981 general elections, when partisanship in Greece was very high, state television offered free time for party political broadcasting in the prime time zone proportional to the parties' parliamentary strength. Besides, the rallies of all parties represented in the parliament in the major cities of Athens and Salonica were covered live whereas the rallies of the two stronger parties in two or three big cities were transmitted on video. Highlights of the smaller parties' rallies in these cities were given. Parties without seats in parliament were given free time for political broadcasting.

In the second period (1989 onwards) a number of different formal regulations were implemented, before each major electoral contest (Karakostas & Tsevas, 2000). As a consequence, the coverage itself has been part of the political contestation and a highly ambivalent issue. First, the newly formed National Radio and Television Council (NRTC) was responsible for the allocation of television time to the political parties. A year later (1990) the Council of State withdrew this responsibility from the NRTC and assigned it to the head of the state, which in Greece is the President of the Republic. Later, in 1993, a special law made provision for a presidential decree after the consolatory response of the NRTC and the advice of the parties and the ministers of interior and communications. For the 1996 general elections, regulation of television coverage was organized according to a ministerial decree based on the consolatory response of the NRTC and an inter-party electoral committee composed according to the party balance in parliament. According to that decree, state/public as well as private channels had to give some time (5 minutes) to each party for its electoral campaign (Samaras, 1999, pp. 189–190). As to electoral budgets, all parties' total electoral expenditure should not exceed 4.3 billion drachmas (about US$16.8 million). Also, each party's expenditure should not exceed 40% of the public finance it received. Of this amount, only 50% could be used for radio and television advertising of parties whereas radio and television advertising of the candidates were forbidden. Additionally, candidates were forbidden to use huge posters and banners (Heretakis, 2002; Papathanassopoulos, 2002).

In the 2000 elections a new law (3023/2000, article 28) foresaw that regulation should be made according to a ministerial decree based only on the advice of an inter-party electoral committee appointed three days after the announcement of elections. The premises of the coverage remained almost the same as in 1996.

According to the law mentioned above, just a few appearances for the candidates on the commercial as well as the public television channels were allowed in the 2004 national election campaign. The same regulation was held for the European parliamentary election as well. All party leaders were given 60 minutes free time for an interview by the public channel ERT, and 60 more minutes of free time for a televised press conference which the commercial TV and radio stations transmitted either live or on video. They should also cover four round tables and one pre-electoral rally for each party. Besides that, the parties were given free television and radio time for their political spots in both public and private channels according to their electoral rate. The advertising time should not exceed four minutes per hour, and the total cost (of US$6.9 million) was paid for by the state. Accordingly, 33% of news bulletins on public and private channels were reserved for the parties' activities (Demertzis, 2006).

All in all, it could be said that, although it has been part and parcel of the political contest itself, gradually the regulation of the electoral television coverage in Greece is becoming an integral aspect of campaigning which has contributed to its normalization.

GREEK ACADEMIC RESEARCH ON ELECTION COVERAGE

While developments in professional political communication in Greece move at a fast pace, academic research has been relatively restricted due to the rather late appearance of university and other academic communication research units. It was only in the early 1990s, as a response, as it were, to the deregulation of the communication landscape, that such units were established and began doing research, mostly quantitative. In order of priority the hitherto political communication research focuses on: (1) political attitudes, political culture, and mass media; (2) analysis of political news coverage; (3) institutions, the political system, and mass media; (4) electoral behavior and mass media (Demertzis, 2002). Detailed and specific academic research on election coverage has only recently been initiated; nevertheless, it is scattered, under-funded, and pursued principally on an individual basis. As a consequence, there has been no research on the descriptive vs. interpretive style of journalism in covering the elections, nor is there any research on the question of political bias. Nevertheless, there has been some research on the news framing and the publication of opinion polls. In the remainder of this section we shall refer to some representative pieces of this research, much of which was conducted at the Laboratory for Social Research in the Media at the Faculty of Communication and Media Studies of the University of Athens.

The 2004 General Elections

The parliamentary elections of 2004 were conducted on March 7 and resulted in a landslide victory for the major opposition party ND over PASOK, the party in office. Voting turnout was 76.5%, and four parties entered the parliament: ND, PASOK, along with KKE and SYN (the two dominant parties of the left). The campaigns were closely covered by the media, especially by television. However, this did not have a major impact on the outcome of the election, in the sense that the vast majority of the electorate had made their voting decisions long before March 7. At the end of the day, it was the long-term political strategies of the parties rather than the short-term media coverage that determined the outcome (Samaras, 2005). George Pleios (2004) conducted a content and discourse analysis of the 2004 election news coverage in the TV news. The research material was selected between February 15, 2004 and March 6, 2004 (the official period of the electoral campaign) and was drawn from 146 news bulletins of seven nationwide TV channels (two public/state and five private). By monitoring those 146 news bulletins, a total of 2,674 news stories were selected, out of which 1,355 focused on electoral issues and 1,319 focused on non-electoral issues. A sample of 356 (out of 1,355 cases or 26.3%) was analyzed in terms of visibility, categorization, focus on parties and society, party identity of talking heads, and dramatization. The units of analysis were grouped in two main categories: everyday issues and "high politics" issues (Olympics, E.U., terrorism, etc).[1] Among the conclusions, were these:

1. Half of the television news stories were *about elections*, which sounds paradoxical, even in the absence of detailed research, when compared to earlier electoral periods where newscasts were almost saturated by news about elections. The transitional character of the Greek political system and the ambivalence of the media coverage of the campaign are reflected in the duration of news stories focused on electoral and non-electoral issues, respectively, and the priority given to them. Two findings support this conclusion. First, the average duration of electoral issues in television news bulletins was much higher (5.5 minutes) than of the non-electoral issues (2.6 minutes). Second, in priority scale, electoral issues were ranked among the first three pieces in the news bulletins, especially in the state/public service TV channels.[2]

2. Different *types of television channels* covered the election differently. The two state/public TV channels aired 300 out of the 1,355 election news stories (or 22%), which means 150 news stories per state/public channel. The five commercial channels broadcast 1,055 election news stories (78%), or 211 news stories per channel. Beyond that, however, state/public channels were oriented to the "logic of politics"[3] (Meyer & Hinchman, 2002) more than the private ones. This is supported by the fact that the visibility of election news was greater on state/public television channels. According to an Index of Visibility,[4] the private channels scored 7.34 whereas the state/public TV channels scored 8.75. The average score across all TV channels was 7.95. Thus, although the private TV channels aired a greater number of election news stories, the stories broadcast in the state/public channels had greater depth and longer duration.

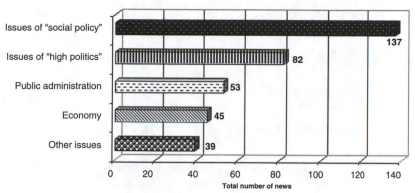

Source: Laboratory for Social Research on Mass Media.

FIGURE 12.1 Categories of issues in election news stories in the 2004 Greek election.

3. During the election campaign, the "political agenda" of the then center-right opposition party of Nea Democratia (ND), which is now in office, dominated the television news. ND planned its electoral campaign around "everyday life" and "social policy" issues. As some analysts pinpoint, heavy viewers are more likely to place themselves in the center of the left–right political scale, and they are attracted by issues of this sort (Shanahan & Morgan, 1999). Our research shows that this type of issue was presented more than any other category (Figure 12.1).

4. An important finding from the tele-democracy or "mediapolitik" point of view (Edwards, 2001) is that television news in private as well as in state/public channels presented politics mainly as an issue of parties and party leaders (Edelman, 1988), rather than as part of wider societal processes (Figure 12.2). More than two-thirds of the political news items in all TV channels adopted an elite-oriented angle, as if all politics centers round party leaders and party cadres. Other agents of the political process, like pressure groups, citizens' movements, and the like, were underrepresented.

This style of coverage is concomitant not only to the partycratic system of governance in Greece but also to the bipartyism that dominates the Greek party system. In Figure 12.3 one can see that the great majority (73%) of the talking heads on TV belonged to the two major political parties, that is ND and PASOK. Here there was no difference between private and state/public

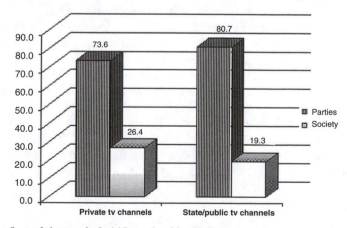

Source: Laboratory for Social Research on Mass Media.

FIGURE 12.2 Focus on parties vs society in the 2004 Greek election news stories (persent).

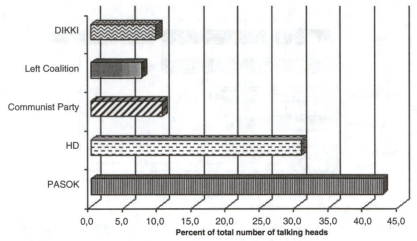

Source: Laboratory for Social Research on Mass Media.

FIGURE 12.3   Party identity of talking heads in the Greek 2004 election news stories (percent).

television channels, which means that the logic of politics in TV news appears to prevail regardless of ownership.

As important as duration and visibility might be, at the end of the day the discursive features of the election news coverage may be of more significance. Overall, on this point our research documented the "media logic," rather than the "political logic," as this is expressed through infotainment and, especially, through dramatization (Bennett, 1996).[5] To be sure, though it is an ingredient of the standardized journalistic beats and routines everywhere, dramatization varies in different countries and in different kinds of media. In our particular case it was found that an evident but not considerably high degree of dramatization was instigated in the election news coverage; using an index of dramatization[6] where the lower score is 0 and the highest 4, it was found that, on average, dramatization of the TV election news coverage was 0.5. Also, it was found that dramatization on the private channels was greater (0.84) compared to the public stations (0.18).

In their content analysis, Samaras and Papathanassopoulos (2005) explored the representation of politics in the talk shows that are integrated into the newscasts of three television channels (ANTENNA, ALPHA, ALTER) of the first and third campaign week. Their units of analysis were the statements (sound bites that contained political information) rather than simple references. The codebook incorporated, among other things, the issue vs. image dichotomy, issue topic, issue specificity, elements of issue reference, attributes of the image making process, focus of the image making process (MP image, party leader image, party image, government image, image of politics), the positive vs. negative dichotomy, fear appeal, and the focus of attacks. Among other things, they found that regarding the image vs. issue dichotomy there was a dominance of image over issue. They also found that candidate issues overwhelm policy issues, which means that the media logic promoted persons at the expense of parties. On top of this it was found that a high level of statements incorporated negativity, and the thesis of Trent and Friedenberg (1995) that challengers produce more negativity than incumbents was verified with the smaller parties producing higher negativity that the two larger ones.

The 2004 European Elections

In tandem with research on European news, Demertzis (2006) conducted a content analysis of the media coverage of the 2004 European Parliamentary election campaign. The time period covered the last two weeks of the campaign. The unit of analysis was every single principal publication or video (news item, opinion article, etc.) referring to the European Parliamentary elections (either the previous or the imminent one), to the EU, the European integration, or EU governance with regards both to the European and national political institutions.

The research material was selected from twelve news media: six national circulation newspapers, two regional papers, three commercial and one public television channels We selected 1,357 cases from 102 copies of the eight newspapers and 245 cases (units of analysis) from 52 prime time television news bulletins. Among other things, the results show that:

1. Most of the news about the European parliamentary elections referred to the Greek political parties and domestic public issues rather than to European issues; this is something that the Greek media appears to have in common with other European media in almost every single contest for the European Parliament.
2. There was a significant difference between television and the press. With the broadsheets leading the way, newspapers gave much more attention to the procedures, the workings, the structure, and the function of the EU than television channels (Table 12.1). It should be noted, however, that in comparison to the other three channels the public channel NET reported more extensively on the EU.
3. For the most part, the tone of the news stories was highly ethnocentric. Thus, the Greek media approached European news events from a "Greek" angle. Yet, there was a great difference between press and television: The latter's tone was almost totally ethnocentric whereas the former left sizeable space for Eurocentric as well mixed approaches.
4. Bipartyism was promoted once again, and the politicians were the chief communicators on television news. In the newspapers, journalists and experts were the most prominent sources for a variety of European news.
5. For several reasons, the electoral milieu was peaceful. Only during the last week of the campaign did it get somewhat harsher, due to PASOK's efforts to increase turnout. The media thus covered party strategies in a non-conflictual way. A non-conflictual framing dominated the coverage (Table 12.2).[7]

In a somewhat different way they covered the issues of the campaign (either European or national). Only stories about the activities of European and Greek political parties were framed to some extent in a conflictual style, which is only natural enough.

TABLE 12.1
Election News Stories per Medium in the 2004 Greek European Parliamentary Election

Medium	Press		Television	
Issues	Number of articles	Percent	Number of articles	Percent
Activities of the Greek political parties	729	53.7	176	71.8
EU modus operandi	395	29.1	32	13.1
Social and economic issues	251	18.5	32	13.1
Activities of the European political parties	69	5.1	14	5.7
Miscellaneous	92	6.8	33	13.5
Total	1536	113.2	287	117.2

Note: Overlapping in the coverage of different issues within a single news story explain why the percentage exceed 100.

TABLE 12.2
Media Framing in the 2004 Greek European Parliamentary Election

Medium	Press		Television	
Frame	Number of articles	Percent	Number of articles	Percent
Non-conflictive – strategic	364	26.8	91	37.1
Non-conflictive – thematic	623	45.9	76	31.0
Conflictive – strategic	168	12.4	41	16.7
Conflictive – thematic	202	14.9	37	15.1
Total	1357	100.0	245	100

The 2006 Local Elections

The 2006 elections for *local authorities* (municipal and prefecture) were conducted in two rounds, October 15 and October 22.[8] For the nation-wide TV networks, the campaigns that took place in Athens and in other big cities like Piraeus, Thessalonica, and Patras were of special interest. However, they also paid some attention to other cities and regions like Attica and Thrace due to their special nature (for instance, in Thrace there is a Muslim and Turkish ethnic minority which always attracts the media's attention during elections). Compared to the 2004 national election described earlier, the TV coverage of the local elections was characterized by fewer and shorter news stories, ranked in the middle or at the end of the news bulletins. It is indicative that the average priority was 15, which means that these election news stories were placed almost at the end of the news bulletins. In some detail the following conclusions can be drawn:

1. Elections for local authorities in Greece are regarded as second order elections with a lesser degree of partisanship and quite intense personalization of candidates; not infrequently they serve either as a pre-test or a post-test of national elections. If, as we saw above, during the 2004 campaign half of news stories focused on national elections, only 4% (or 149 out of 3,266 news stories) of TV news stories were about local elections.
2. Again, different TV channels covered the electoral campaign differently. In this case, however, the state/public channels covered the elections much more extensively than the commercial channels. The three TV state/public channels broadcasted 72% of the total number of TV electoral news (107 news stories out of 149), while the five commercial channels aired only 28% of them (42 news stories). Perhaps this finding documents the persistence of the "logic of politics" in a political system which is still modern rather than post-modern.
3. In contrast to the coverage of the 2004 general elections (see above), there was a great disparity of the relevant issues reported. More than 50% of all issues connected with local elections in the TV news could not be categorized in some specific and unified category. Instead, they were classified as "other," which means that in second order elections in Greece, there is ample room for personified news stories, not necessarily subdued to specific policy issues. The other two main categories were social policy issues (12%) and employment and administration (7.7%).
4. Once more, bipartyism was promoted in the election news coverage, though not in such steadfast way as in the 2004 general elections. According to the results, the focus (in terms of frequency of talking heads) was greater on candidates of the ND ruling party,

and less on candidates of PASOK and the other parties. Talking heads belonging to the ND appeared 102 times, whereas talking heads belonging to PASOK appeared 87 times. The corresponding number of appearances for the Communist Party, the Left Coalition, and LAOS were 65, 57, and 21, respectively.

5. Findings about dramatization support previous research on the dramatization of TV news in general elections and the coverage of political issues by television (Pleios, 2005). With an average rate of 4.87 (highest rate 40 and minimum 0), one can conclude that dramatization of local elections is too low. But it must be added that oral dramatization is much higher (12.2) than iconographic (1.64), a characteristic of the modern rather than postmodern communication systems. Accordingly, it can be claimed that the lower priority local elections news stories are assigned, the less dramatization is employed. Naturally, those news stories that were ranked first in the bulletin's agenda were more dramatized.

POLITICAL ADVERTISEMENT, POLL, AND THE INTERNET

The first political spots in Greece appeared in the 1990 election campaign. A set of factors contributed to that. First, the commercialization of the Greek media system limited governmental control of media organizations, and made advertising revenue crucial for independent channels' budgets. Second, the gradual predominance of television in the electoral campaigns introduced media logic into the campaigns. Third, the leading position of private TV channels (decreasing the audience share of the state/public channels) pushed political parties to opt for paid campaigns (Samaras, 2003). Fourth, the spread of political apathy led more and more citizens to tele-mediated participation and to emotionally laden political judgements. Nowadays, political advertising is absolutely crucial to the overall understanding of the election news coverage in Greece because of a number of interrelated reasons:

First of all, paid political spots on television take the lion's share of the parties' and candidates' electoral budgets. This is not without consequences. As has been documented elsewhere (Heretakis, 2002), not only did the cost for political ads in the 2000 national elections exceed the legally mandated ceiling, but the total amount paid was also much higher than the entire state allowance to the parties. Therefore, political ads are closely connected to political money and corruption.

Secondly, political ads produce an inter-textuality effect. They redefine the media agendas during election campaigns by simply being included by journalists and the candidates themselves in the short list of political talk shows. Since 1993 fervent discussions has been initiated on the occasion of negative political ads both in the media and in personal talks. The same holds true with the debates. Thus, it seems as if political discourse has become more or less a self-referential construction that buttresses the political spectacle. In the 2004 national election, news about the single debate that took place between the leaders of five political parties (ND, PASOK, Left Coalition, Communist Party, and DIKKI) represented 19% of the first three news stories on all TV stations. The number of news stories about the debate in all commercial stations taken together was 182 (mean value: 36.4), and 39 in the two public channels (mean value: 19.5).

Thirdly, the gradual erosion of partisanship among the electorate has reduced the overt political content of the spots. For example, it was found that the emphasis on the party declined radically, from 92% in 1996 to 65% in 1999 and to 46% in 2000 (Samaras, 2003). The emphasis is now on the candidate, and the aesthetic implemented in the ads follows a consumerist media logic (Vamvakas, 2006, pp. 178–260). Consequently, after 1996 the use of music dominates over text in 90% of the spots, and more emphasis is put on image rather than on issues (Samaras, 2003, pp. 81–82).

At the same time, political ads, especially the negative ones, do not transform political discourse overnight, nor do they undermine partisanship altogether. Negative spots connote an "anti-politics frame" and evoke, as it were, an anti-party sentiment (Poguntke, 1976), but the Greek electorate is still highly selective in terms of party preferences and media use. Therefore, it is not accidental that negative spots decreased from 73% in 1993 to 31% in 1996 (Samaras, 2003, p. 99). Nor is it accidental that research shows that 94.5% of the electorate was not affected by political ads (including both positive and negative ads) in their voting decision during the 2000 election campaign (Kakepaki, 2002, pp. 165–166). The reason is that 75% of the electorate had decided how to vote before the beginning of the campaign.

The bulk of the electorate seems to be highly sensitive to the election polls as well. Election polls entered the Greek political scene on a massive scale in 1993. As in other countries (Medvic, 2003, p. 34), the central role pollsters eventually would come to occupy as campaign strategists was not foreseen. Nowadays, they are an indispensable part of the political system. Together with the media and political consultants they contribute to the Americanization of political communication in Greece. Naturally, a long debate has been taking place regarding the role of public opinion polls in today's democracy, their possibly detrimental impact on public deliberation, and the bandwagon effect they might contribute to during a campaign. These and other relevant issues are still open in the Greek public sphere; the only formal regulation that has ever been put into effect is the banning of the publication of any poll results one week before Election Day. In the 2004 national election, news about various polls conducted in that period represented 4% of the first three news stories on all TV stations' bulletins. The number of news items about polls on all commercial stations was 35 (mean value: 36.4), and 11 in the two public channels (mean value: 19.5).

In addition to the traditional print and electronic media, the Internet is emerging as a new interactive medium employed both as a political marketing tool and as a source of information. Yet, use of the Internet is still limited, as the overall penetration of the Internet in Greece lags behind other Western countries. At large, the audience does not systematically use the Internet for getting information about the election campaign, nor do the political parties and politicians in Greece use it for enhancing bottom up flow of information or online interaction with their constituencies. In two recent studies on the 2000 and 2004 general election, it was documented that although the Internet in Greece is being acknowledged as the most recent political marketing tool and used instrumentally (normally as a digital poster or something like that), it failed to impact on the existing configurations of the Greek political arena (Demertzis et al., 2005a, 2005b). Perhaps in a few years, tele-democracy will be succeeded by "digital democracy," as the Internet may carve out new politician–citizenry nexuses and civil society networks (Katz & Rice, 2002). Another new medium that has been employed in recent electoral contests is the mobile phone. A host of SMS circulated in the last days of the campaigns in favor of specific candidates, something novel and unusual to the electorate, especially to the younger cohorts.

CONCLUSIONS

Due to an insufficient development of a market economy in the past, for a long time the state has played a decisive role in the formation of the media sector in Greece. Since the late 1980s, structural changes in the local and international environment (political apathy, European integration, deregulation, commercialization, and globalization) have shaped and reshaped the relationships between the political and the media systems, affecting the way the media cover electoral contests.

Electoral coverage in Greece is undergoing a transitional process. The logic of politics is gradually being replaced by media logic. This is evidenced by academic research: In the 2004 general elections, election news stories were more visible, with a longer duration than non-electoral ones, placed prominently in news programs (the logic of politics). At the same time however, TV channels presented politics dramatically as if it was exclusively about parties and party leaders' contestations (media logic). In the 2004 European election the tone of the news stories was highly ethnocentric, bipartyism was promoted once again, and the electoral milieu was peaceful (intermingling of the two logics). In the 2006 local elections, just a tiny amount of the TV news was about elections (a mixture of media logic and the logic of politics), with a great disparity of the issues presented (media logic). Bipartyism was considerably promoted, and dramatization was low.

Although political ads appeared relatively late, they now take the lion's share of the parties' and candidates' electoral budgets, and they constitute the most central means for electoral communication. The shift of emphasis from the party to the candidate or the leader is a clear indication of the strong presence of media logic in the election news coverage in contemporary Greece. Finally, the Internet has emerged as a new interactive medium, and is currently, although only to a limited degree, employed in political communication as a political marketing tool and as a source of information. In the future, this might contribute to a gradual post-modernization of electoral campaigning in Greece.

NOTES

1. A similar method was used in researching local elections.
2. Although the nominal values in the figure are higher between private channels, we have to take into account that the research included five private versus two state/public channels.
3. According to Meyer and Hinchman (2002, pp. 1–26), the "logic of politics" means to communicate about politics in an "appropriate" way. In other words, the "logic of politics" refers to discussion of political issues without the media transforming them into something else such as "drama" or "entertainment." "Media logic" promotes a theatrical style in depicting politics based on "personalizing" the participants and image creation through marketing techniques. Their distinction is similar but not identical to Mazzoleni's (1987) differentiation between "party logic" and "media logic," meaning chiefly the balance of power between party and media organizations in setting the public agenda, rather than promoting a style of representing politics.
4. The Index of Visibility is constructed by a combination of the following items: the duration of a news story, the position of a news story in priming, the presence of a news story in headlines, and its embedding in the news release.
5. Dramatization is the construction and presentation of news where events and information are described in the form of a story and newscasters employ various aesthetic means, such as drama, sensation, tragedy, suffering, or comedy (Bennett, 1996). We distinguish two principal means of dramatization relevant to television newscasts: (a) oral means (tone and type of discourse etc) and (b) iconographic (use of captions, graphics, and other techniques of moving image). Thereafter we bring together all separate elements in an "index of dramatization." Of course, such an index cannot imprint the exact dramatization of news coverage, and its value is therefore only indicative.
6. The index of dramatization used here includes: type and tone of discourse, use of music, metaphors, evaluative adjectives, use of caption, or graphics.
7. There have been a variety of categorizations in the media-framing literature (Entman, 1993). In this chapter, "strategic" framing during an electoral period means that the news media's coverage of the political and electoral process refers to the parties' and candidates' plans and tactics as if they are participating in a horse race; others might call it "game frame." The "thematic" framing refers to a style

of coverage that emphasizes the issues and the stakes of the electoral contest, and places them into an analytical perspective.

8. If no candidate succeeds in gaining a minimum of 42% of the ballots, elections are carried out again one week later between the two candidates with the most votes.

REFERENCES

Bickford-Smith, R. A. H. (1893). *Greece under King George*. London: R. Bentley.

Bennett, L. (1996). *News: The politics of illusions*. New York: Longman Publishers.

Charalambis, D., & Demertzis, N. (1993). Politics and citizenship in Greece: Cultural and structural facets. *Journal of Modern Greek Studies, 11*(2), 219–240.

Dakin, D. (1972) *The unification of Greece*. London: Benn.

Demertzis, N. (1997). Greece. In R. Eatwell (Ed.), *European political culture* (pp. 107–121). London: Routledge.

Demertzis, N. (2002). Εισαγωγή σε ένα νέο ερευνητικό πεδίο [Introduction to a new research field: Political communication in Greece]. In N. Demertzis (Ed.), *ΗΠολιτική Επικοινωνία στην Ελλάδα* [Political communication in Greece] (pp. 15–36). Athens: Papazissis Publishers.

Demertzis, N. (2006). Europe on the agenda? The Greek case. In M. Maier & J. Tenscher (Eds.), *Campaigning in Europe–Campaigning for Europe* (pp. 277–293). Berlin: Lit Verlag.

Demertzis, N., & Kafetzis, P. (1996). *Πολιτικός Κυνισμός, πολιτική αλλοτρίωση αμδ μαζικά μέσα επικοινωνίας: Ηπερίπτωση της Τρίτης Ελληνικής Δημοκρατίας* [Political cynicism, political alienation and mass media: The case of the Third Hellenic Republic]. In C. Lyrintzis, E. Nikolakopoulos, & D. Sotiropoulos (Eds.), *Κοινωνία και Πολιτκή: Όψεις της τρίτης Ελληνικής Δημοκρατίας 1974–1994* [Society and politics: Facets of the Third Hellenic Republic 1974–1994] (pp.174–218). Athens: Themelio.

Demertzis, N., Diamantaki, K., Gazi, A., & Sarzetakis, N. (2005a). Greek political marketing online: An analysis of parliament members' websites. *Journal of Political Marketing, 4*(1), 51–74.

Demertzis, N., Diamantaki, K., Gazi, A. & Sarzetakis, N. (2005b). Ιστοσελίδες Ελλήνων Βουλευτών κατά την Προεκλογική Περίοδο 2004. *Ζητήματα Επικοινωνίας, 2,* 103–112 [Webpages of members of the Hellenic Parliament during the election campaign of 2004. *Communication Issues, 2,* 103–112].

Dimitras, P. E. (1997). Greece. In B. S. Oestergaard (Ed.), *The media in Western Europe: The Euromedia handbook* (pp. 98–109). London: Sage

Edelman M. (1988). *Constructing the political spectacle*. Chicago: University of Chicago Press.

Edwards, L. (2001). *Mediapolitik: How the mass media have transformed world politics*. Washington, D.C.: Catholic University of America Press.

Entman, R. M. (1993). Framing: Towards clarification of a fractured paradigm. *Journal of Communication, 43*(4), 51–58.

Hallin, D., & Papathanassopoulos, S. (2002). Political clientelism and the media: Southern Europe and Latin America in comparative perspective. *Media, Culture & Society, 24*(2), 175–195.

Heretakis, M. (1997). *Τηλεόραση και Διαφήμιση: Η Ελληνική Περίπτωση* [Television and advertisement: The Greek case]. Athens: Sakkoulas.

Heretakis, M. (2002). Πολιτική Διαφήμιση: Μια εφαρμογή στις βουλευτικές εκλογές του 2000 [Political advertising: An application in the 2000 parliamentary elections]. In N. Demertzis (Ed.), *Η Πολιτική Επικοινωνία στην Ελλάδα* [Political communication in Greece] (pp. 95–140). Athens: Papazissis Publishers.

Kakepaki, M. (2002). *Τηλεόραση και Εκλογική Συμπεριφορά: Οι εκλογές της 9ης Απριλίου 2000* [Television and electoral behavior: The April 9, 2000 elections]. In N. Demertzis (Ed.), *Η Πολιτική Επικοινωνία στην Ελλάδα* [Political communication in Greece] (pp. 141–171). Athens: Papazissis Publishers.

Karakostas, I., & Tsevas, A. (2000). *Το Δίκαιο των ΜΜΕ* [Media regulation]. Athens: Sakkoulas.

Katz, J. E., & Rice, R. E. (2002). *Social consequences of Internet use: Access, involvement, and interaction*. Cambridge, MA: MIT Press.

Kavanagh, D. (1995). *Election campaigning: The new marketing of politics*. Oxford: Blackwell.

Mazzoleni, G. (1987). Media logic and party logic in campaign coverage: The Italian General Election of 1983. *European Journal of Communication, 2*, 81–103.

Medvic, S. K. (2003). Campaign pollsters and polling: Manipulating the voter or taking the electorate's pulse? In R. P. Watson & C. C. Campbell (Eds.), *Campaigns and elections: Issues, concepts, cases* (pp. 31–46). London: Lynne Rienner.

Meyer, T., & Hinchman, L. (2002). *Media democracy*. Cambridge, UK: Polity.

Mouzelis, N. (1986). *Politics in the semi-periphery: Early parliamentarism and late industrialism in the Balkans and Latin America.* London: Macmillan.

Norris, P. (2000). *A virtuous circle: Political communications in post-industrial societies*. New York: Cambridge University Press.

Papadopoulos, Y. (1989). Parties, the state and society in Greece: Continuity within change. *West European Politics, 12*, 55–71.

Papathanassopoulos, S. (2000). Election Campaigning in the Television Age: The Case of Contemporary Greece. *Political Communication, 17*, 47–60.

Papathanassopoulos, S. (2001). Media commercialization and journalism in Greece. *European Journal of Communication, 16*(4), 505–521.

Papathanassopoulos, S. (2002). *Τηλεόραση και Εκλογές στην Ελλάδα* 1990-2000 [Television and elections in Greece 1990–2000]. In N. Demertzis (Ed.) Η Πολιτική Επικοινωνία στην Ελλάδα [Political communication in Greece] (pp. 39–94). Athens: Papazissis Publishers.

Papathanassopoulos, S. (2004). Greece. In M. Kelly, G. Mazzoleni, & D. McQuail (Eds.), *The media in Europe: The Euromedia Research Group* (pp. 91–102). London: Sage.

Pappas, T. (2003). The transformation of the Greek party system since 1951. *West European Politics, 26*(2), 90–114.

Paraschos, M. (1995). The Greek media face the Twenty-first Century: Will the dam Smith complex replace the Oedipus complex? In D. Constas & T. Stavrou (Eds.), *Greece prepares for the twenty-first century* (pp. 253–266). Baltimore: John Hopkins University Press.

Pleios, G. (2001). *Ο Λόγος της Εικόνας: Ιδεολογία και Πολιτική* [The discourse of the image: Ideology and politics]. Athens: Papazissis Publishers.

Pleios, G. (2004). *Η προεκλογική εκστρατία του 2004 στις τηλεοπτικές ειδήσεις.* [Electoral campaign 2004 in television news]. Unpublished research summary. Athens: Laboratory for Social Research on Mass Media at the Faculty of Communication and Mass Media, University of Athens.

Pleios, G. (2005). Περιεχόμενο και ποιότητα της τηλεοπτικής ενημέρωσης: η πολιτική θεματολογία. *Ζητήματα Επικοινωνίας, 3*, 105–113 [Content and quality in television newscasts: The political agenda. *Communication Issues, 3*, 105–113].

Poguntke, T. (1996). Anti-party sentiment—Conceptual thoughts and empirical evidence: Explorations into a minefield. *European Journal of Political Research, 29*, 319–344.

Samaras, A. (1999). Party-centered campaigns and the rise of the political advertising spot in Greece. In L. L. Kaid (Ed.), *Television and politics in evolving European democracies* (pp 187–205). New York: Nova Science Publishers.

Samaras, A. (2003). *Τηλεοπτική Πολιτική Διαφήμιση. Μια ποσοτική έρευνα στην Ελλάδα* [Television political advertising: A quantitative research on Greece]. Athens: IOM.

Samaras, A. (2005). The 2004 Parliamentary elections in Greece: Chronicle of a defeat foretold. In A. Bolberitz (Ed.), *The European yearbook of political campaigning 2004* (pp. 106–129). Austria: Hartinger Consulting.

Samaras, A., & Papathanassopoulos, S. (2005). Η πολιτική στα 'παράθυρα' των τηλεοπτικών δελτίων ειδήσεων. *Ζητήματα Επικοινωνίας 3*, 58–80 [Politics on the talk shows of newscasts. *Communication Issues, 3*, 58–80].

Shanahan, J., & Morgan M. (1999). *Television and its viewers: Cultivation theory and research*. Cambridge, UK: Cambridge University Press.

Swanson, D. L. (1992). The political-media complex. *Communication Monographs, 59*, 397–400.

Swanson, D. L., & Mancini, P. (Eds.). (1996). *Politics, media and modern democracy: An international study of campaign innovations in election campaigning and their consequences*. Westport, CT: Praeger.

Trent, J. S., & Friedenberg, K. L. (1995). *Political campaign communication*. New York: Praeger.

Vamvakas, V. (2006). *Εκλογές και Επικοινωνία στη Μεταπολίτευση: Πολιτικότητα και Θέαμα* [Elections and communication after 1974: Civicness and spectacle]. Athens: Savvalas.

13

Campaigns in the Holy Land: The Content and Effects of Election News Coverage in Israel

Tamir Shaefer, Gabriel Weimann and Yariv Tsfati

THE POLITICAL AND MEDIA SYSTEMS IN ISRAEL

Established in 1948 as a parliamentary democracy, Israel has a 120-member parliament, the Knesset, which is elected by a closed-list system of proportional representation with the entire country serving as one constituency (Rahat & Hazan, 2005). The closed-list system does not allow the voters in the national elections an opportunity to influence the composition of the candidate lists. It is a multiparty system in a multicleavaged society (Lijphart, 1993), with an average number of parties in each Knesset that is usually never fewer than a dozen (Rahat & Hazan, 2005). Parties were the dominant actors in the Israeli polity in the first decades after independence (Galnoor, 1982; Horowitz & Lissak, 1989).

Seventeen national elections for the Knesset have been held between 1949 and 2006. Although each Knesset is elected for four years, some Knesset terms did not last for the whole period, when the prime ministers have asked the president to call for new elections. In the elections between 1949 and 1992, and since 2003, voters could cast only one ballot for a political party. The electoral system was temporarily changed in the 1996 and 1999 elections, where voters could cast two ballots, one for a party and one for the direct election of the prime minister. In 2001 special elections for the position of prime minister only were held. Following these elections, the direct election of the prime minister was abolished, after it was heavily criticized for failing to cure the ills of the Israeli electoral system (see Rahat & Hazan, 2005 for extended discussions of this issue).

The Israeli Media System

Television was introduced to Israel only in 1968. The dominant medium at that time was the printed press, and Israelis were exposed to many newspapers, in addition to a national, government-owned radio station. Many of the newspapers were owned by political parties, but they have gradually disappeared, most of them by the mid-1960s, and two other central newspapers of the Israeli Left by the early 1990s. Today there are only a few newspapers that are associated with political parties, mostly with religious parties (Caspi & Limor, 1999). The newspapers that have the highest circulation are all privately owned.

For more than two decades following the introduction of television, Israelis "were exposed to one monopolistic channel, which was controlled completely and later influenced by the government" (Peri, 2004, p. 23). The revolution in the Israeli media market occurred in the 1990s. Cable television was introduced at the end of the 1980s, and at the end of 1993 the privately-owned Channel 2 television station began broadcasting. Finally, in 2000 a third terrestrial channel and the second commercial channel, Channel 10, began broadcasting. According to Peri (2004, p. 25), "Despite the fact that television broadcasting had begun as far back as the 1970s, and although the overall circulation of the print media had grown, it was in the 1990s that television replaced the press as the dominant medium." Although exposure to television news declined compared with the time when there was a single television channel (Katz, Haas, & Gurevitch, 1997), it still remained rather high, with nightly ratings of 30 to 40 percent for all three major news programs (Channels 1, 2, and 10) combined.

Election Coverage Regulations

One unusual regulation of the television coverage of elections was the prohibition against presenting the candidates, either their faces or their voices, during the last 30 days before Election Day. This regulation aimed to prevent incumbents from using the medium unfairly for their electoral goals. It sometimes resulted in humorous situations, such as showing only the legs of Prime Minister Begin, when he met the Egyptian President Sa'adat. This regulation was removed before the 1999 elections (Wolfsfeld & Weimann, 2001).

However, the Electoral Propaganda Law still prohibits any political propaganda on radio and television news coverage during the last 60 days before the elections. The only exception is a daily designated hour reserved for the parties to present their political spots. This broadcast time is allocated to the various parties free of charge according to their current representation in the Knesset. Campaign funding is guaranteed by the state (and, again, is allocated according to the size of the parties). Personal and institutional campaign contributions are heavily regulated.

The chair of the Central Election Committee is responsible for upholding these laws. For instance, on January 9, 2003, during the elections for the 16th Knesset, Prime Minister Sharon, at that time the Likud party leader, planned a press conference to confront allegations about financial corruption. Believing that such a press conference was important for the public, High Court Judge Heshin, the chair of the Central Election Committee, used his authority and ordered the three main television channels to broadcast the press conference live for about ten minutes (something they would have done anyway). However, as Judge Heshin testified later, soon after Sharon began to talk, "it was clear to me that this was not a press conference at all, but rather, blatant electoral propaganda." The chair used his authority a second time that day, ordering the three television channels to immediately end the live coverage of Sharon's press conference, arguing that such blatant political propaganda was against the law.

NEWS COVERAGE OF ELECTIONS IN ISRAEL

Political communication scholars point to a process of "mediatization" of politics, which is characterized by an "increasing intrusion of the media in the political process" (Mazzoleni & Schulz, 1999, p. 248). This process underlines the centrality of media coverage of campaigns as the main source of political information during campaigns (Just et al., 1996), and hence calls for evaluations of its role, its strengths, and especially its weaknesses. We will focus here on a few major aspects of campaign coverage: issue frames vs. game frames and the horse race coverage; personalization of campaign coverage; increased negativity; and political bias.

Issue Frames vs. Game Frames

Scholars often distinguish between issue frames and game (or strategic) frames of campaign coverage when analyzing the function of the media during electoral campaigns (Cappella & Jameison, 1997; Patterson, 1994). An issue frame is a media focus on substantive issues like the economy, on ideology, and on candidates' positions on the issues. Media coverage of such substantive issues and candidates' positions on the issues may assist voters in making an educated and enlighten political decision. A game (or strategic) frame, on the other hand, "is structured around the notion that politics is a strategic game." It is a schematic framework "according to which candidates compete for advantage" (Patterson, 1994, p. 57). Such a strategic frame therefore leads to a media portrayal of the campaign as a race between two or several contenders who are fighting for an advantage; it leads to a focus on candidates' strategies and tactics, rather than an examination of issue positions and larger political forces. It therefore leads to a portrayal of the campaign as a horse race between a few leaders. According to Robinson and Sheehan (1983), journalists are defining the news as events, an approach which leads to horse race-style coverage. "'Horse races' happen; 'horse races' are themselves filled with specific actions. Policy issues, on the other hand, do not happen; they merely exist. Substance has no events; issues generally remain static. So policy issues...have been traditionally defined as outside the orbit of real news" (p. 148).

We first tested whether the TV coverage of Israeli campaigns is characterized more by issue frames or by game frames (Shamir et al., 2008; Weimann et al., in press; Weimann & Wolfsfeld, 2002; Wolfsfeld & Weimann, 2001). We relied on systematic content analyses of TV election coverage to provide the issue dimensions around which the campaigns were run and the relative focus upon substance vs. campaign strategy and game frame. These were based on the major news programs and the special election magazines on television throughout each election campaign since the 1992 campaign. An issue frame in a news item was defined as coverage of any substantive issue, such as the state of security or the economy, and candidates' issue positions. A game frame in a news item was defined as coverage of party strategies and tactics, as well as the candidates' traits.[1] The findings are presented in Figure 13.1.

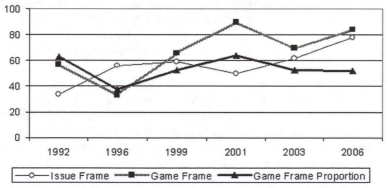

Notes: Each item was coded separately for the existence of issue frames and game frames. Therefore, the total percentages of issue and game frames sometimes exceed 100% because most media items included more than a single frame. The game frame proportion is its proportion out of the total of issue and game frames.

FIGURE 13.1   Issue vs. game frames in TV elections coverage 1992–2006.

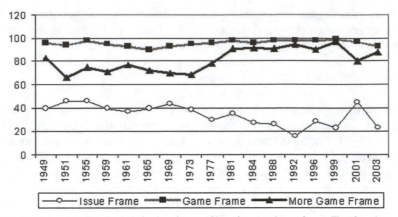

Notes: Each item was coded separately for the existence of issue frames and game frames. Therefore, the total percentages of issue and game frames sometimes exceed 100% because most media items included more than a single frame. In a different category, coders were asked to code the dominant frame in the item. This category is represented in the graph as "more game frame."

FIGURE 13.2   Issue vs. game frames in newspaper elections coverage 1949–2003.

The graphs are quite balanced, revealing almost an equal focus on issue frames and game frames. This finding is quite surprising in light of the substantial literature about the domination of game frames in TV election coverage. Nevertheless, in most elections the game frame still dominates over issues and ideology. This coding, however, did not account for the relative dominance of each frame in each item. Such an examination was conducted in another analysis of newspapers election coverage, as presented in Figure 13.2.

This figure is based on a content analysis of newspaper coverage of all 16 election campaigns for the Knesset that took place in Israel between 1949 (the first elections) and 2003, and of the 2001 special elections for prime minister only.[2] Looking at the figure, one may be surprised to see that the game frame has always been present. Since the first elections, almost all news items have included this frame. Yet, as can be expected from findings in other countries, especially the U.S., the findings do point to a trend of a declining number of issue frames in the news items and an increase in the domination of the game frame. Most election stories, most of the time, are dominated by a game frame, and are presented as a horse race between candidates.

There are some similarities and one major difference between the findings in Figures 13.1 and 13.2. In both figures, the 1992 elections are particularly low on the issue frame. The reason for this is unclear. It is also unclear why in the 2001 special elections for PM there is an increase in the proportion of the game frame on TV, but a decline in the prevalence of this frame in the newspapers. One explanation for this difference is the different coding definitions in the two studies. In the TV coding, the three (or fewer) main substantive issues and the three (or fewer) campaign-strategic topics were coded for each item. We specifically provided a list of substantive and strategic issues. The substantive issues included general issues, such as "the economy" or "security," even if these topics were not directly related to the candidates. In the newspaper coding, we were more restrictive in the issue frame area, including an item only when it dealt with the specific *policy positions of the candidates*. We also did not provide lists of substantive and strategic categories in this study.

Overall, however, our findings are quite similar to those from other democracies: The media "portray the candidates as strategists more than as leaders of electoral coalitions..." and therefore "make[s] it difficult for them to get their message across to the voters" (Patterson, 1994, p. 84).

The game frame can be broken down into several characteristics. Given that the game frame portrays the campaign as a horse race between candidates, it tends to focus primarily on the candidates. Personalization of the campaign is therefore a common characteristic of media coverage of campaigns. A portrayal of the campaign as a horse race is also said to increase the media's use of polls, which provide up-to-the-minute information about who is ahead and who is behind. And finally, the focus on the campaign as a race and a game and the obsession with strategies and tactics is also said to sharply increase the negativity of campaign coverage and attacks against the candidates who are presented in the news. Below we analyze these issues in Israeli election coverage.

Personalization

Political personalization in the media refers to a change in media coverage of politics in general, and of political campaigns in particular, manifested in an increase in journalists' focus on the activities of individual politicians at the expense of abstract collective entities such as parties, organizations and institutions (Rahat & Sheafer, 2007). Some Israeli scholars have argued in the past that political personalization has indeed occurred in Israel. The decline of political parties (Galnoor, 1996; Korn, 1998) and their role in politics (Medding, 1999), the central role of television (which was introduced in 1969), the growth of commercial media (Caspi & Limor, 1999), the game frame in election coverage (Caspi, 1996; Wolfsfeld & Weimann, 2001) and the accounts suggested by Caspi (1996), Galnoor (1998), and Peri (2004) supply a rather firm foundation for the hypothesis that a process of personalization has taken place in Israel. Until recently, however, there has been no systematic empirical analysis of the phenomenon itself.

Such an empirical analysis was recently done by Rahat and Sheafer (2007). They analyzed the occurrence of political personalization in the media coverage of Israeli elections from independence (1948) to the 2003 elections.[3] Figure 13.3 presents the percentage of news items that focused mainly on the parties, on the candidates, or equally on both, for the period of six months before each election.

Two phases in the development of the process of personalization in the media coverage can be identified. The first (1949–1977) witnessed a continued process of decline in the exclusive focus on covering the parties, and at the same time an increase in the combined focus on both parties and candidates. During this period, coverage of candidates incrementally gained equal status with that of the political parties. The second phase started in 1981 with an upsurge in the share of media coverage that focused mainly on candidates. Since then, the percentage of news items

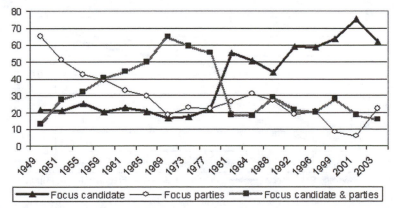

Notes: Based on Rahat and Sheafer (2007). The percentage of news items that focused mainly on the parties, mainly on the candidates and equally on both.

FIGURE 13.3   Personalization in media coverage of elections.

that focused on candidates has generally remained at the same high level while the percentage of news items focusing on parties or both parties and candidates has remained low.

Due to the changes in the election law, it is interesting to focus on the period from the 1990s onward. Until the 1996 elections, Israeli voters cast a single ballot for a party only. In the 1996 and 1999 elections, voters cast two ballots, one for a party and another for the prime minister. The 2001 elections were special elections for prime minister only. That electoral law was subsequently revoked, and in the 2003 elections voters returned to voting with a single ballot for a party. As Rahat and Sheafer (2007) hypothesize, changes in the conduct of elections are likely to have an effect on media personalization. Specifically, it is logical to expect that the introduction of direct elections for prime minister in the 1996 and 1999 elections resulted in an increase in media personalization. This trend is likely to have peaked in the 2001 special elections for PM only, and then to have decreased back to its level before the 1996 elections. We would expect similar results in the 2003 elections. Figure 13.3 provides support for most of these expectations. The focus on candidates did indeed peak in the 2001 elections. This trend began as early as the 1992 elections, which makes sense because the decision to change the electoral law in the 1996 elections was made about four months before the 1992 elections. Note, though, that in the 2003 elections the focus on the candidates did not decline to its level prior to the introduction of direct elections for prime minister (while the focus on the parties increased). The media obsession with individual candidates is therefore at least partially independent of the electoral law. The norms of campaign coverage that have developed in the era of direct, personal, elections have persisted despite the fact that direct elections were cancelled. This finding offers evidence for the strong focus on the game frame.

Media Coverage of Election Polls

The coverage of election polls as part of the horse race coverage of election campaigns is demonstrated in many studies (Paletz et al., 1980; Rokeach, 1968). This issue was studied in Israel by Weimann (1990, 1998), who analyzed the changes in the coverage of election polls in the years 1969 to 1996.[4] No newspaper reports about polls appeared prior to the 1969 election. Only three newspapers provided reports about polls in the 1969 campaign, and none of these polls was conducted by the newspaper. The number of newspapers reporting polls has steadily increased, to 11 in 1981 and finally to 16 in 1996 (Weimann, 1998).

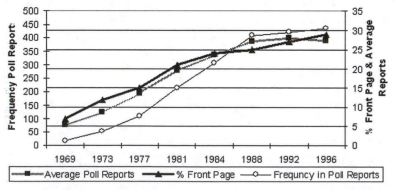

Notes: Based on Weimann (1996). "Frequency of poll reports" is the total number of poll reports in newspapers during the election campaign. "Average poll reports" is the average number of poll reports in each newspaper. And "% front page" is the percentage of polls appearing on newspaper front pages.

FIGURE 13.4. Media coverage of Israeli election polls.

Figure 13.4 demonstrates the sharp increase in the prominence of media coverage of polls. As can be seen, there was a steady increase in the total number of poll reports as well as in the average number of reports by each newspaper. Moreover, there was a similar increase in the number of polls appearing on the front page of the newspapers, demonstrating the increase in the news value of polls.

The media's taste for different kinds of polls has changed as well. Weimann (1998) found that while there was a decrease in the proportion of polls that focused on the positions of the public on various issues (from 46% in 1969 to 5% only in 1996), there was a sharp increase in the proportion of forecasting polls detailing who was ahead in the electoral race (from 52% in 1969 to 95% in 1996). In other words, the media gradually lost interest in reporting about the positions and issue preferences of the public in favor of monitoring the horse race; the forecasting polls function like a stopwatch in a sporting competition, showing the standing of each candidate or party in the race in different phases of the campaign. This is a clear strategic usage of polls that fits the game frame.

Negativity

Scholars argue that one of the most noticeable characteristics of horse race coverage and the game frame is a focus on the issue of "sleaze" (Blumler & Gurevitch, 2001), resulting in attacks against candidates and in general, an increase in negative coverage of the campaign (Cappella & Jamieson, 1997; Patterson, 1994; Swanson & Mancini, 1996). We first tested this issue in a previous study that revealed a sharp increase in negativity in TV coverage of the parties and candidates in the last decade (Sheafer & Weimann, 2005). Figure 13.5 presents the findings from that previous study, in addition to the 2006 data.[5] Our analysis is based on the question, "Did the television news item include an attack on or some criticism of the candidate or the party?" Figure 13.5 about here

The most salient finding in Figure 13.5 is the dramatic increase of the negativity expressed on television towards candidates and political parties. In the 1996 election campaign, only 5% of the television news items that referred to candidates or parties contained attacks or criticism. During the next election campaign, this percentage rose, and in the 2001 election campaign it passed the 20% mark. A giant jump occurred in the 2003 campaign, where nearly 60% of the

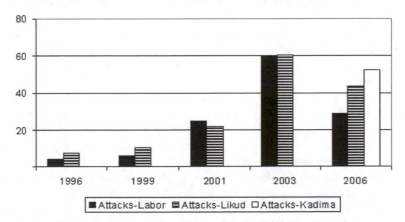

Notes: The values represent the percentage of TV news items in which there was an attack on or a criticism of a party and its candidate out of a total of news items that referred to a party or a candidate.

FIGURE 13.5   Negative coverage of the parties and their leaders (TV).

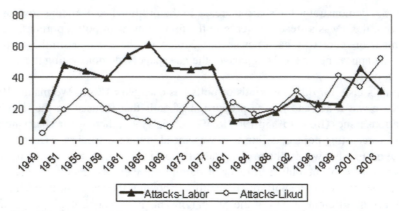

FIGURE 13.6 Negative coverage of the parties and their leaders (newspapers).

television news items referring to the parties and their candidates included attacks or criticism. Then a small decrease in the amount of criticism occurred in the 2006 elections (the analysis of the 2006 election includes three rather than two parties, due to the establishment of the Kadima party by the then PM Sharon). In general, our analysis of TV coverage supports findings from other countries about the increased negativity in the coverage of election campaigns in the last decade. Moreover, comparing this figure to Figure 13.1 shows quite a similar trend in the levels of negativity (Figure 13.5) and the proportion of the game frame (Figure 13.1).

Yet, is negative coverage of candidates and parties really a new phenomenon? We tested this question through a content analysis of newspaper coverage of the Israeli elections since 1949 and up to the 2003 elections (Figure 13.6).[6] The results are shown in Figure 13.6.

It can be clearly seen that negative coverage is not a new phenomenon in Israeli election coverage. Actually, the levels of attacks against the ruling Labor party were even higher during the 1960s than they were in the last decade. The level of attacks against Labor declined after it lost for the first time to the Likud party in the 1977 elections, and it has steadily increased since, in accordance with the level of attacks against the Likud (the ruling party is always the target of more attacks).

The nature of the attacks has also changed during that period. Until the beginning of the 1980s, the parties were the main target of attacks. Since that time, most attacks have been directed against the leading candidates. This trend is in complete accordance with the increased media personalization trend presented above.

How can the earlier high levels of negativity be explained? We conducted a qualitative content analysis of all elections[7] and found that until the late 1960s, election coverage was based mainly on quotations from campaign speeches. The high levels of negativity against the ruling Labor party (at that time, it was called *Mapai*) reveal the attack strategy of the other political parties against Labor, not journalistic practices. The attacks against Labor reached their peak in 1961 and 1965 due to a major political crisis in that party, which eventually led its historical leader, David Ben-Gurion, and his followers (among them Shimon Peres) to desert *Mapai* and form a new party. It was not until the 1970s that reporters took the lead in election coverage when election news began to look like it does today, with independent reporting of campaign events being the main focus of election stories. The gradual increase in negativity since the late 1970s is therefore comparable to a similar pattern found in other countries as well.

Political Bias

The more the media distanced themselves from affiliation with political parties, the more the issue of political bias of the media became a central issue in political campaigns. In Israel, the demise of party-owned media started in the 1960s, and by the mid-1980s most of it had disappeared (Caspi & Limor, 1999). Since then, most allegations of political-ideological media bias have come from right wing politicians, who argued that because most journalists hold a left-liberal world view, their coverage is clearly tilted to the left (Sheafer & Weimann, 2005). For example, in the final stages of the 1999 campaign Prime Minister Netanyahu attacked the media for having a clear bias in favor of the One Israel Party (the new Labor) and the left. In a notable speech that received prime media coverage, Netanyahu claimed that the media and journalists were "afraid" that Likud and the right would win the elections.

Research examining the issue of bias (or balance) in media coverage of parties and candidates during an election campaign usually focuses on two main areas of possible imbalance: media access and media valence. Access to the media is indicated by the time and space given to each one of the political parties and candidates competing in the campaign (Arian et al., 1999; D'Alessio & Allen, 2000). Media valence refers to the degree of positive or negative coverage of parties and candidates (D'Alessio & Allen, 2000).

In a previous study we have conducted on this matter (Sheafer & Weimann, 2005a), we argued that there are two significant, additional reasons for balance or imbalance in media coverage of parties and candidates during an election campaign: political bias or journalists' partisanship and newsworthiness bias. Political bias is usually the first bias that comes to mind when discussing balance in media coverage. It refers to a deliberate twisting of the media coverage in one direction based on the journalist's personal political views. Newsworthiness bias refers to a preference for candidates and parties that are simply more newsworthy, either because of their political standing or their performance. As Arian et al. (1999) argue, "It is not unreasonable to give wider coverage to a candidate who happens to be the incumbent prime minister or president, especially if his actions affect the welfare or security of the country" (p. 360). The newsworthiness bias is supposed to manifest itself through a lack of balance in media coverage but not in a systematic lack of balance in the direction of one party or political faction.

Figure 13.7 illustrates the amount of television coverage of the parties in the last five elections.[8] As can be seen, there is a nearly perfect balance in the accessibility of the two big parties,

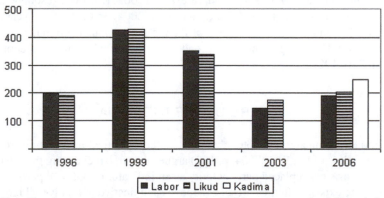

Notes: The values represent the number of news items in which the party was mentioned. The analysis disregarded additional news items in which other parties were mentioned but in which there was no mention or reference to Likud, Labor or Kadima.

FIGURE 13.7   Media accessibility of Likud, Labor and Kadima in five election campaigns (TV).

Likud and Labor (and of Kadima in 2006), in each of the election campaigns. Minor differences are always in favor of the party holding power during the campaign period. Based on these findings, it may be claimed that maximal balance is maintained in the parties' accessibility to the media. The minor differences that exist can be explained by newsworthiness, or more specifically, by the ruling party's higher status, which renders it more newsworthy. Further analyses that support this conclusion may be found in Sheafer and Weimann (2005a). Our newspaper analysis (1949–2003) provides similar results (not shown).

Analyses of media valence do not support the claim of political bias either. The analysis of balance on TV is presented in Figure 13.5 above. It shows that in general, the incumbent party suffers from more attacks compared to the other party (or parties, in 2006). The exceptions to this rule are 1996, in which the incumbent party Labor was attacked to a lesser degree compared with the Likud, and 2003, in which the incumbent Likud party was not attacked more than Labor. But even these exceptions work against the argument of political bias (Sheafer & Weimann, 2005a). Similar findings are evident in Figure 13.6. In newspaper articles in all elections since 1948 and up to the 2003 elections, the incumbent party always received a greater amount of criticism than the other large party. In sum, no support was found in our analysis for the political bias hypothesis in Israeli election coverage.

Exposure to Campaign News

A question regarding the reading of newspapers by Israelis has been included in election polls regularly since the 1988 elections. These surveys[9] show that the levels of newspaper reading during elections are quite high, with 50% of respondents in 1988 reporting that they read a newspaper almost every day, 51% in 1992, 54% in 1996, 44% in 1999, 50% in 2001, 44% in 2003, and 41% in 2006.

Voters' exposure to TV news during the elections was not regularly included in these surveys, but when asked, the answers also reveal high levels of exposure. For example, 71% of the respondents in the 2001 poll claimed to watch television news almost every day during the previous week. The 2006 rates were lower, with 51% claiming to watch television news almost every day during the previous week. These rather high percentages may be somewhat misleading, though. According to the data of the Israel Audience Research Board, the average rating of the leading news program (Channel 2's evening news) in the last week of the elections was 24.3% in 1999, 20.3% in 2001, 28.6% in 2003, and 18.8% in 2006.[10] However, respondents may have been exposed to other news programs. According to Peri (2004), in the first five years of the commercial Channel 2 (established in 1992), two of the ten most popular programs belonged to the political genre, "and this on top of the news broadcasts, each of which reached about 25 percent of the exposure" (p. 122).

VOTERS' USE OF THE MEDIA

In the era of modern campaigning, voters get most of their political information from the media (Swanson & Mancini, 1996). Peri (2004, p. 122) argues that in Israel during the 1990s, exposure to political broadcasts has replaced party activity as an indicator of political participation. While some may view the exposure figures presented above as indicative of relatively high levels of political engagement in Israel, an important question to ask relates to the motivations for exposure and to whether or not those exposed indeed use the political spots and news information they gather to guide their voting decision.

The most comprehensive study examining motivations for exposure to political spots in Israel was conducted during the 1992 campaign (Wolfsfeld, 1995). Results demonstrated that most respondents watching election spots (64%) did so for entertainment purposes. Only 17% reported using the ads to guide their electoral choice. While this rate was significantly higher among floating voters, Wolfsfeld (1995) concluded that election broadcasts were not meeting the needs of the voters.

More recent data concerning the usefulness of election news coverage point to the same conclusion. A majority of respondents in polls conducted in 2003 and 2006 by the Chaim Herzog Institute at Tel Aviv University reported that the coverage of elections would not have any influence on their vote choice (61.3% in 2006, and 63% in 2003). Only 27% reported in 2003 that election news coverage contributed to their political knowledge to a "great extent" or "to some extent," while 37% reported that the coverage had not contributed to their political knowledge at all. Answers to these questions were not significantly associated with political ideology or vote choice, but young and Arab respondents were more likely to report that news coverage had benefited their political knowledge, while those with higher degrees of formal education were significantly less likely to report knowledge gains from news coverage.

Trust in Media and Satisfaction with the Election Coverage

Israeli voters not only report that their exposure to campaign advertising and news contributes little to their knowledge about the position of the parties and the candidates. They also express low levels of trust in and high levels of dissatisfaction with campaign news. Nearly half of Israeli adults state that they mistrust the mainstream news media. In the 2006 survey, 61.9% of respondents said they were "dissatisfied or "very dissatisfied" with the news coverage of the elections. Only 38.1% of respondents were on the satisfied end of the continuum. While 31.7% of respondents said that they would like to have more information regarding parties' platforms and programs, only 9.6% said they felt the news media provided them with such information. On the other hand, 38.4% felt that the news media's emphasis was on polls and assessments regarding the likely winners, but only 15.9% of respondents said they actually needed such information. All in all, when combining the questions relating to the kind of information people needed and what they felt they were actually getting from news, 80% of respondents felt they were not getting the kind of information they needed the most from media.

POLITICAL EFFECTS OF ELECTION COVERAGE

Few Israeli elections studies have examined the possibility of actual media effects on the public. Here we focus on two studies that have recently analyzed agenda setting and priming effects, and present some additional data.

Agenda Setting

According to the agenda-setting hypothesis (first-level agenda setting), the media influence public opinion by emphasizing certain issues over others. The amount of media attention, or the media salience, devoted to certain issues increases their accessibility and consequently influences the degree of public concern for these issues (Dearing & Rogers, 1996; McCombs, 2004; McCombs & Shaw, 1972). Figure 13.8 represents a simple graphic examination of agenda setting in the years 1969 to 2003 (the 2001 special election for PM only is excluded from this analysis).[11] It

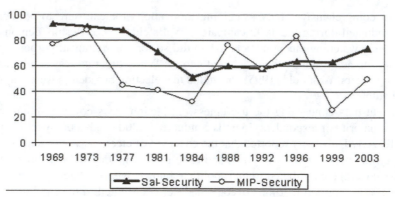

Notes: Sal-Security is the proportion of articles related to the security issue out of the total number of articles in the newspapers. MIP-Security is the proportion of respondents naming security as the most important national problem.

FIGURE 13.8. Agenda setting 1969–2003.

appears that there is a strong association between media and public agendas, as is demonstrated by both lines "moving" together.

Two other analyses of agenda setting that we have conducted provide more systematic evidence for this agenda-setting effect of the media in Israeli elections (Sheafer, 2007; Sheafer & Weimann, 2005b). This effect was found to be significant in both studies even after controlling for the effects of real world security and economic variables. Some scholars argue that the effect of agenda setting might be weaker when people have direct experience with a given issue (Watt et al., 1993). This makes the evidence of the influence of agenda setting in these studies, where Israelis have direct and strong experience with the security and economy domains, even more impressive. Moreover, Sheafer (in press) demonstrates that the public's naming of an issue as the most important issue (the dependent variable in agenda-setting studies) is strongly and negatively influenced by the valence of this issue's news coverage: the more negative the presentation, the stronger the agenda-setting effect.

Priming

The priming hypothesis states that the media agenda affects the criteria people use to evaluate the performance of political actors. Individuals use those issues that are most salient and accessible in their memory to evaluate the performance of political actors (Iyengar & Kinder, 1987). If, for example, the issue of the economy were primed, it would become the basis for evaluating the president's performance (Iyenger & Simon, 1993; Krosnick & Kinder, 1990; Pan & Kosicki, 1997). Sheafer (2007) demonstrates the impact of media priming on the evaluations of the incumbent parties in Israeli elections. As in his analysis of agenda setting, he demonstrates that media tone has an important role in voters' evaluations of the incumbent party, in addition to the "regular" salience dimension of the priming hypothesis.

Sheafer and Weimann (2005b) contribute to the priming hypothesis in a different way. Their analysis is focused on priming effects on electoral *behavior*, rather than on evaluations of the incumbent's performance. They demonstrate that the priming effect might have an influence on an individual's voting decision. By emphasizing certain issues and not others, the media may thus influence electoral results, because it appears that people tend to vote for parties that "own" the issues primed by the media.

Effects of Election News Coverage on Political Engagement

However, in recent decades more and more research has been dedicated to examining the possibility that election campaigns and their news coverage affect not only voting preferences, but also whether or not people vote at all. The argument is that exposure to negative and personalized campaigns and to their sensationalized and trivialized "strategic" news coverage negatively affects voter turnout and other forms of participation (Ansolabehere & Iyengar, 1995). Furthermore, it is often argued that media depictions of politicians as motivated by self-interest cultivate cynicism and mistrust towards politics (Cappella & Jamieson, 1997). Other studies present opposite findings, indicating that exposure to negative campaigns actually increases voter turnout (Finkel & Geer, 1998; Freedman & Goldstein, 1999).

To date, only a few studies have explored the possibility of negative media effects on political engagement and trust in Israel. The general trends demonstrate a substantial decrease over time in voter turnout, and on the other hand, an increase in negative campaigning and personalization (reported above), raising the possibility of the latter affecting the former. However, the association between collective level indicators of participation and campaign negativity and personalization requires systematic examination, with adequate controls, and to date, such an examination has not been conducted in the context of Israeli elections.

However, survey data collected by the Herzog Institute for Media, Politics and Society (Weimann et al., 2006) allows us to examine the associations between exposure to news media, and political participation and trust, on the individual level. These data offer little evidence for video malaise in Israel. On the contrary, controlling for demographics, news exposure[12] was significantly and *positively* associated with trust in Israeli democracy[13] (partial $r = .14$, $p <.01$), frequency of engagement in political conversation[14] (partial $r = .32$, $p <.001$), and borderline significantly also with political efficacy[15] (partial $r = .08$, $p = .08$). While news exposure in general was not associated with political participation and voter intentions, respondents who reported they were "closely following" campaign[16] coverage were significantly more likely to report they intended to vote in the coming elections (partial $r = .09$, $p < .05$).

These data indicate that if news media exert any influence on Israeli political engagement, it is probably a mobilizing influence. Of course, given that this analysis utilizes cross-sectional survey data, we cannot negate the very plausible reverse causality hypothesis—that is, that those trusting and involved in politics to begin with selectively expose themselves to news coverage, and not the other way around. In any case, the positive associations between news exposure and political engagement and trust is consistent with U.S. data reported by Norris (2000), and her "virtuous circle" argument, namely that the news media make those involved in politics even more involved in politics. On the other hand, Norris's claims that entertainment media make those disinterested in politics even more disinterested and uninvolved (an argument that is in line with Putnam's thesis about the role of television in the decline of social capital in the U.S.) has not been put to rigorous test in Israel to date.

CONCLUSION

All in all, the data presented above demonstrate that Israeli campaigns and their coverage have grown more negative and personalized over the years, and more focused on election polling and on political strategies. Citizens' exposure to political advertising and to campaign news coverage has decreased over the years. Israelis tend to hold negative opinions regarding news media coverage of campaigns, and to be relatively distrustful of mainstream news media. Despite these negative attitudes, several studies on the effectiveness of news media coverage on the vote have yielded support for agenda setting and priming effects. Also, somewhat surprisingly, news media exposure was associated with more trusting attitudes towards Israeli democracy, efficacy, and political conversation, and an indicator of exposure to campaign coverage was positively associated with intentions to vote in the coming elections.

What does Israeli research on media and elections have to offer to the worldwide community of campaign scholars? First, the research reported above extends some important political communication research theories to a radically different political system and political culture. The electoral system in Israel is fundamentally different from that in the U.S. and much more extreme (in terms of proportional representation) than most European electoral contexts. Given the continued state of conflict with the Arabs, the replication of theories such as agenda setting and priming, as well as the documentation of mediatization and personalization trends in Israel contribute substantially to these theories by increasing their generalizability. Second, as discussed above, Israeli campaign research not only offers replication, but also theoretical advancement and extension of both priming and second level agenda-setting theories. Third, Israeli campaign research offers several methodological tools for scholars interested in media and elections, especially in the context of analyzing emotional appeals in campaign advertising (Marmor Lavie & Weimann, 2006).

Thus, while campaign research in Israel is relatively young, it is quite fruitful. Nonetheless, many important questions remain for the future. The video malaise hypothesis has not been rigorously tested in Israel, nor have many other theories of communication and elections (e.g., the spiral of silence theory). Second, Israeli campaign research tends to focus on national elections and to ignore municipal campaigns, labor union elections, and primary elections, that may serve as a fruitful and interesting arena for theorizing and research. We obviously still lack a clear understanding of the answers to lingering questions such as what issues will dominate an election campaign. Do campaigns matter? Why do journalists cover elections the way they do? Does this coverage help voters make up their minds? Much work is left for research on media and elections in the future, in Israel and elsewhere.

NOTES

1. These data originate from the Israel Democracy Institute (IDI) Election Study Project initiated in 1996 and were expanded for the purpose of another study to include the 1992 elections as well (Shamir et al., in press). The leading TV news programs and the special election magazines throughout each election campaign were analyzed. In 1992 there was only one channel (Channel 1). For the 1996 to 2003 elections, we analyzed Channels 1 and 2, while for the 2006 elections we also included Channel 10. All items that mentioned the campaign, parties, or candidates were coded. The content analyses included: 96 items over a period of about 60 days in 1992; 627 items over a period of about 60 days in 1996; 1, 285 items over 60 days in 1999; 570 items over 50 days in 2001; 286 items over 27 days in 2003; 438 items over 29 days in 2006. The different time periods analyzed represent different campaign lengths. There is no theoretical or practical reason to believe that these differences have any impact on our conclusions. The coding team for each election included between two and seven students, interns in the IDI, and workers at Ifat, a company that conducts commercial content analyses. All coders were given instructions and intensive training by the same research team. For each news item, the three (or fewer) main substantive issues and the three (or fewer) campaign-strategic topics were coded. Inter-coder agreements were no less than 82% (for the lowest category).

2. For a period of six months prior to each election, we sampled every third day. Then we selected for analysis all election-related articles that covered the two largest parties (Alignment/Labor and Gahal/Likud or their components prior to the establishment of electoral alliances and later unified parties) in two of the leading Israeli daily newspapers, *Yediot Aharonot* and *Ha'aretz*. Overall, 4,711 items were analyzed. Two trained master's students conducted the content analysis. The inter-coder reliability (Scott's pi), tested in a session in which the two coders participated for 100 coding items was no lower than .81 (for the coding category with the lowest reliability).

3. A coding system was devised to measure media personalization. The most important of these is the focus of the news item on candidates compared with its focus on parties, measured as the percentage of news items that focus mainly on the party, the candidates or both. See note 2 for further information on the content analysis.

4. The study is based on analyses of daily newspapers printed in Israel during a period of three months before each election. Since 1992 the data include television coverage of Channel 1 (1992 and 1996) and Channel 2 (1996). See Weimann (1990; 1996) for further information.

5. See note 1 for methodological details about this study.

6. See note 2 for methodological details about this study.

7. The qualitative content analysis was conducted together with the quantitative content analysis. We would like to thank our research assistant, Rami Shalheveth, for this observation.

8. See note 1 for methodological details about this study.

9. The 1988–2003 surveys are part of the Israeli National Elections Survey project, supervised by Asher Arian and Michal Shamir. Sample sizes were 416 in 1988; 1,192 in 1992; 1,168 in 1996; 1,225 in 1999; and 1,234 in 2003. The surveys are available through the Israel Social Science Data Archive at The Hebrew University (http://ssda.huji.ac.il). The 2006 survey was supervised by Gadi Wolfsfeld and Tamir Sheafer. Sample size was 601.

10. Data were provided by the Israel Audience Research Board (http://www.midrug-tv.org.il/).

11. The media's coverage of the security issue was measured through a content analysis of the media coverage of all election years in Israel in the period 1949 to 2003. For the main analysis in the current study, only the data regarding the elections since 1969 was used (2001 was excluded). The reason for starting the analysis with the 1969 elections is that no public opinion surveys were conducted before that date. For a period of a year prior to each election (but only up to approximately three weeks before Election Day, just before the election surveys were held), we sampled every third day, and then selected for analysis all security-related and economy/interior-related front-page articles in two of the leading Israeli daily newspapers, *Yediot Aharonot* and *Ha'aretz*. The percentages of the security issue in Figure 13.8 represent the proportion of this issue out of the total of the security and economy/interior issues. See Sheafer and Weimann (2005a) for further discussion. Two trained master's students conducted the content analysis. The inter-coder reliability (Scott's pi), tested on 100 coding items, was .90.

12. News media exposure was composed of survey items tapping exposure to TV, radio, print and online news media (alpha = .55).

13. Trust in democracy was measured using a single survey item, worded "To what extent do you trust Israeli democracy?" (1–4 response categories).

14. Political conversation was measured using a single survey item, worded "To what extent do you talk about political matters?" (1–4 response categories).

15. A scale composed of four 1–4 items was used to measure efficacy: "There are almost no differences in the positions of the large parties on the different issues, " "It does not matter who you vote for, it doesn't change anything," "I really don't care about who wins the coming elections," and "Politicians care only about their personal future; they are not interested in the future of the state"(alpha = .69).

16. The question was worded "To what extent do you follow the coverage of the current campaign?" Answer categories varied between "not at all" (1) to "to a great extent" (4).

REFERENCES

Ansolabehere, S., & Iyengar, S. (1995). *Going negative: How political advertisements shrink and polarize the electorate*. New York: Free Press.

Arian, A., Weimann, G., & Wolfsfeld, G. (1999). Media balance in election coverage [in Hebrew]. In A. Arian & M. Shamir (Eds.), *The elections in Israel 1996* (pp. 7–28). Jerusalem: The Israel Democracy Institute.

Blumler, J. G., & Gurevitch, M. (2001). "Americanization" reconsidered: U.K.–U.S. campaign communication comparisons across time. In L. W. Bennett & R. M. Entman (Eds.), *Mediated politics: Communication in the future of democracy* (pp. 380–403). New York: Cambridge University Press.

Cappella, J. A., & Jamieson, K. H. (1997). *Spiral of cynicism. The press and the public good*. New York: Oxford University Press.

Caspi, D. (1996). American-style electioneering in Israel: Americanization versus modernization. In D. L. Swanson & P. Mancini (Eds.), *Politics, media & modern democracy* (pp. 173–192). Westport, CT.: Praeger.

Caspi, D., & Limor, Y. (1999). *The in/outsiders: Mass media in Israel*. Cresskill, NJ: Hampton Press.

D'Alessio, D., & Allen, M. (2000). Media bias in presidential elections: A meta-analysis. *Journal of Communication, 50*(4), 133–156.

Dearing, J. W., & Rogers, E. M. (1996). *Agenda-setting*. Thousand Oaks, CA: Sage.

Finkel, S., & Geer, J. (1998). A spot check: casting doubt on the demobilizing effect of attack advertising. *American Journal of Political Science, 42,* 573–595.

Freedman, P., & Goldstein, K. (1999). Measuring media exposure and the effects of negative campaign ads. *American Journal of Political Science, 43*, 1189–1208.

Galnoor, Y. (1982). *Steering the polity: Communication and politics in Israel*. Beverly Hills, CA: Sage.

Galnoor, I. (1996). Hamashber Bama'arechet Hapolitit Hayisraelit: Hamiflagot Cagorem Mercazi [The crisis in the Israeli political system: The parties as a central factor]. In M. Lissak & B. Knei-Paz (Eds.), *Yisrael Likrat Shnat 2000*. [Israel towards the year 2000] (pp. 144–175). Jerusalem: Magnes.

Galnoor, I. (1998). Miflagot, Tikshoret VeHademocratia HaIsraelit [Parties, media and Israeli democracy]. In D. Koren (Ed.), *The demise of parties in Israel* (pp. 195–214). Tel Aviv: Hakibbutz Hameuchad.

Horowitz, D., & Lissak, M. (1989). *Trouble in utopia: The overburdened polity of Israel*. Albany: State University of New York Press.

Iyengar, S., & Kinder, D. R. (1987). *News that matters: Television and American opinion*. Chicago: University of Chicago Press.

Iyengar, S., & Simon, A. (1993). News coverage of the Gulf crisis and public opinion: A study of agenda-setting, priming, and framing. *Communication Research, 20*(3), 365–383.

Just, M. R., Crigler, A., Alger, D., Montague, K., West, D., & Cook, T. (1996). *Crosstalk: Citizens, candidates, and the media in a presidential campaign*. Chicago: University of Chicago Press.

Katz, E., Haas, H., & Gurevitch, M. (1997). 20 years of television in Israel: Are there long-run effects on values, social connectedness, and cultural practices? *Journal of Communication, 47*(2), 3–20.

Korn, D. (Ed.). (1998). *The demise of parties in Israel*. Tel Aviv: Hakibbutz Hameuchad.

Krosnick, J. A., & Kinder, D. R. (1990). Altering the foundations of support for the president through priming. *American Political Science Review, 84*(2), 497–512.

Lijphart, A. (1993). Israeli democracy and democratic reform in comparative perspectives. In E. Sprinzak & L. Diamond (Eds.), *Israeli democracy under stress* (pp. 107–123). Boulder, CO: Lynne Rienner.

Marmor-Lavie, G., & Weimann, G. (2006). Measuring emotional appeals in Israeli election campaigns. *International Journal of Public Opinion Research, 18*(3), 1–26.

Mazzoleni, G., & Schulz, W. (1999). "Mediatization" of politics: A challenge for democracy? *Political Communication, 16*(3), 247–62.

McCombs, M. E. (2004). *Setting the agenda: the mass media and public opinion*. Cambridge, UK: Polity Press.

McCombs, M. E., & Shaw, D. L. (1972). The agenda-setting function of the mass media. *Public Opinion Quarterly, 36,* 176–187.

Medding, P. Y. (1999). From government by party to government despite party. *Israel Affairs 6*(2), 172–208.

Norris, P. (2000). *A virtuous circle: Political communications in postindustrial societies*. Cambridge, UK: Cambridge University Press.

Paletz, D. M., Short, J. Y., Baker, H., Campbell, B. C., Cooper, R. J., & Oeslander, R. M. (1980). Polls in the media: Content, credibility, and consequences. *Public Opinion Quarterly, 44*(4), 495–513.

Pan, Z., & Kosicki, G. M. (1997). Priming and media impact on the evaluations of the President's performance. *Communication Research, 24*(1), 3–30.

Patterson, T. E. (1994). *Out of order*. New York: Vintage Books.

Peri, Y. (2004). *Telepopulism: Media and politics in Israel*. Stanford, CA: Stanford University Press.

Rahat, G., & Hazan, R. Y. (2005). Israel: The politics of an extreme electoral system. In M. Gallagher & P. Mitchell (Eds.), *The politics of electoral systems* (pp. 333–351). New York: Oxford University Press.

Rahat, G., & Sheafer, T. (2007). The personalization(s) of politics: Israel 1949–2003. *Political Communication, 24*(1), 65–80.

Robinson, M., & Sheehan, M. (1983). *Over the wire and on TV*. New York: Russell Sage Foundation.

Rokeach, M. (1968). The role of values in public opinion research. *Public Opinion Quarterly, 32,* 547–559.

Shamir, M., Shamir, J., & Sheafer, T. (2008). The political communication of mandate elections. *Political Communication, 25*(1), 47–66.

Sheafer, T. (2007). How to evaluate it: The role of story evaluative tone in agenda setting and priming. *Journal of Communication, 57*(1), 21–39.

Sheafer, T., & Weimann, G. (2005a). An empirical analysis of the issue of media bias in Israeli elections, 1996-2003. In A. Arian & M. Shamir (Eds.), *The Israeli elections 2003* (pp. 123–142). New Brunswick, NJ: Transaction.

Sheafer, T., & Weimann, G. (2005b). Agenda-building, agenda-setting, priming, individual voting intentions and the aggregate results: An analysis of four Israeli elections. *Journal of Communication, 55*(2), 347–365.

Swanson, D. L., & Mancini, P. (Eds.) (1996), *Politics, media and modern democracy*. Westport, CT.: Praeger.

Watt, J. H., Mazza, M., & Snyder, L. (1993). Agenda-setting effects of television news coverage and the effect decay curve. *Communication Research, 20*(3), 408–435.

Weimann, G. (1990). The obsession to forecast: Pre-election polls in the Israeli press. *Public Opinion Quarterly, 54*(3), 396–408.

Weimann, G. (1998). Be aware of polls? The coverage of election polls in the Israeli media [in Hebrew]. In E. Fuchs & S. Bar-Lev (Eds.), *Surveys: Some good, some less* (pp. 123–146). Tel-Aviv: Hakubbutz Hameuchad/Haifa University Press.

Weimann, G., Tsfati, Y., & Sheafer, T. (in press). The media and the 2006 elections: The needs and opinions of the public vs. the function of the media. In A. Arian & M. Shamir (Eds.), *The Israeli elections 2006*.

Weimann, G., Tsfati, Y., & Tuchachinski, R. (2006). *News coverage of the elections to the 17th Knesset: Media trust index (5)*. Tel Aviv: Chaim Hertzog Institute for Media, Society and Politics.

Weimann G., & Wolfsfeld, G. (2002). Elections 2001: The propaganda that changed nothing [in Hebrew]. In A. Arian & M. Shamir (Eds.), *The elections in Israel-2001* (pp. 101–126). Jerusalem: The Israel Democracy Institute.

Wolfsfeld, G. (1995). Voters as consumers: Audience perspectives on the election broadcast. In A. Arian & M. Shamir (Eds.), *The elections in Israel 1992*. Albany: State University of New York Press.

Wolfsfeld, G. & Weimann, G. (2001). The competition over the media agenda, 1996 & 1999 [in Hebrew]. In A. Arian & M. Shamir (Eds.), *The elections in Israel-1999*. Jerusalem: The Israel Democracy Institute.

14

Election News Coverage in Poland

Bogusława Dobek-Ostrowska and Bartłomiej Łódzki

The collapse of communism in 1989 in Poland and other Central European countries resulted in changes in many areas of social, political, and economic life. One important area of change was the mass media in general and political communication in particular (Dobek-Ostrowska, 2001). Curry (2006) rightly observes that the transformation of the mass media in this region of Europe was part and parcel of these societies' transitions out of communism and toward democracy, and notes that one could not have happened without the other.

The transition towards and the consolidation of democracy was a very difficult process for all of the nations of the region (Cichosz, 2006). Those countries that joined the European Union in 2004, Poland, the Czech Republic, Slovakia, Hungary, Slovenia, Estonia, Latvia, and Lithuania, are arguably more advanced in the democratization process than others. However, Agh (2001) shows the many difficulties and obstacles that must be managed to continue to develop democratic processes and civil society in this region of Europe (see also Solarz, 2006). Agh discusses the early consolidation efforts and posits that the region still operates with what might be described as a low quality of democracy. In this context, the media coverage of politics and elections is crucial because the media constitute the most important channel for political communication and information.

AN OVERVIEW OF THE POLITICAL AND MEDIA SYSTEMS

Political System

The present political system in Poland was created in 1992 by what is known as the "small constitution" and was instantiated by the Constitution adopted in 1997. Legislative power is held by the parliament, which has two chambers, the Seym and the Senat, elected every four years. Executive power resides with the president, elected in general elections every five years, along with the government, which is appointed by the president (Lisicka, 2002; see also Godlewski, 2005). Table 14.1 shows the elections and outcomes since 1989.

Founded on a parliamentary model of political system, the following political structures were adopted: (1) the parliament is derived from general elections; (2) the government is accountable to the parliament; (3) the parliament has the right to express a vote of no confidence to the government; and (4) ministers can take a seat in the parliament. Other structures were adopted from the presidential model of political systems: (1) the president is elected in general elections

TABLE 14.1
Alternation of Power in Poland between 1989–2006

	Year of election	Presidential election	Legislative election	Local election
1.	1989		**Semi democratic election** the first non-communist government of Tadeusz Mazowiecki, and J. Bielecki	
2.	1990	Lech Wałęsa		The first free local election
3.	1991		**Post solidarity governments** Prime ministers: J. Olszewski, H. Suchocka	
4.	1993		**Post communist government SLD** Prime ministers: W. Pawlak, J. Oleksy, W. Cimoszewicz	
5.	1994			Local
6.	1995	Aleksander Kwaśniewski		
7.	1997		**Post solidarity coalition AWS** Prime minister: J. Buzek	
8.	1998			Local
9.	2000	Aleksander Kwaśniewski		
10.	2001		**Left coalition SLD** Prime ministers: L. Miller, M. Belka	
11.	2002			The first direct election of majors
12.	2005, IX		**Coalition** of the conservative party PiS, with the populist parties Samoobrona and LPR Prime minister: K. Marcinkiewicz, J. Kaczyński	
13.	2006, X	Lech Kaczyński		
14.	2006			Local

and (2) the president appoints the government. The political system in Poland is called a semi-presidential, mixed, or a dual executive model (Godlewski, 2005; Lisicka, 2002).

A multiparty system, characterized by fragmentation, polarization, and a lack of stability took shape in Poland in the early 1990s. The political parties developed during this time are rather weak, plus there are many conflicts between them (Sobolewska-Myslik, 1999; see also Antoszewski, 2002a; Markowski & Cześnik, 2002). Until 2005, the Polish party system was characterized by a competition of two blocs based on a strong axiological division: post-communist left parties (SLD and SdPl) vs. post-solidarity centre-right parties (PiS and PO). However, during the parliamentary and presidential elections in 2005, a growing level of competition emerged between the two post-solidarity parties—liberal PO vs. conservative PiS.

As a result of the legislative elections in 2005, the balance of political power in Poland was altered (Jednaka, 2004). After four years of left parties' governance (2001–2005), political power shifted to the right wing parties. The conservative party Prawo i Sprawiedliwość (Law and Justice)[1] brought into the parliament the highest number of deputies, yet they did not have parliamentary majority. Thus, an unstable coalition was created with minority and populist parties like Samoobrona (leader Andrzej Lepper) and nationalist Liga Polskich Rodzin (LPR; leader

Roman Giertych) (Ociepka, 2005). Kazmierz Marcinkiewicz, appointed as prime minister after the legislative election in 2005, was replaced by the leader of PiS, Jarosław Kaczyński, in July 2006. The leaders of Samoobrona and LPR became the vice prime ministers.

The political situation in Poland is unique. In 2005, after 10 years of popular Aleksander Kwaśniewski's presidency, a former Solidarity Movement member, Lech Kaczyński, was elected as the president of the country. He is the twin brother of Prime Minister Jarosław. This situation generates strong connections between two institutions of executive power both on the political and family levels. The second largest party in Poland, the liberal PO (leader Donald Tusk), was in political opposition along with the post-communist SLD and the peasant party PSL.[2]

Media System

In the early 1990s, the Polish media began to undergo a profound structural transformation, from one that was primarily based on a state media controlled by the communist party, to one dominated by an independent and free media market (Dobek-Ostrowska, 1999). Print media were transformed into private and self-managing commercial enterprises, operating within an open market. The dual model of broadcasting was transplanted by the broadcast act in December 1992 and implemented in 1994. The National Broadcasting Council (KRRiT) was created in 1993 and the first licenses for private broadcasters were distributed. The state Polish Television TVP changed its status and began to broadcast as a public television, beginning on the January 1st, 1994 (Goban-Klas, 1997).

After 18 years of transformation, the Polish media system has many features of the "polarized pluralist" or "Mediterranean" model presented by Hallin and Mancini (2004). Jakubowicz (2006) argues that the post-communist countries share some of the features of the countries with the Mediterranean media system such as late democratization, insufficient economic development, and weak rational-legal authority combined with a dirigist state. He adds that the modernization of media systems in this region of Europe is also incomplete, or at least minimally advanced.

The Polish media system is primarily comprised of small circulation daily newspapers, with electronic media occupying a central position (Jakubowicz, 1996). The media, above all the press, is marked by a strong focus on political life, an external pluralism, and a tradition of commentary-oriented journalism. The instrumentalization of public broadcasting media by the government and political parties is visible. Professionalism of journalism is lower than in countries that form part of the "democratic corporatist" or the "liberal" model (Hallin & Mancini, 2004). The relationship between the media and the political elites is one of constant conflicts over the autonomy of journalism. The state plays a key role in these relationships as the owner of both public radio and television. In addition, the state controls private broadcast media by regulation along with the limitation of licenses. The Polish patterns are typical of the Mediterranean model, and they are rooted to a large extent in the high degree of ideological diversity and conflicts (Goban-Klas, 1997; Jakubowicz, 1996; Ociepka, 2003).

Print Media.   Although more than a thousand newspaper and magazine publishing companies operate in Poland, the majority of them are small and locally oriented. At the beginning of 2007, the Press Circulation Audit Union (ZKDP) audited 47 dailies and 391 magazines.[3] Only 203 companies are members of the ZKDP, but their titles constitute 93% of the overall circulation of the Polish press. These are the major groups (in terms of circulation and revenue) of publishers in Poland:

- The "Big Four" media groups consist of three Germany-based publishers: (1) Bauer (magazines); (2) Polskapresse/Passauer (regional dailies); (3) Springer (quality national daily, tabloid, magazines); and (4) the Polish-based company AGORA (national daily, free daily, magazines, radio-stations, Internet).
- The next group consists of five relatively large publishers: (1) Mecom (regional dailies); (2) Media Express (tabloid); (3) Presspublica (national dailies); (4) G+J Poland (magazines); and (5) Edipresse Poland (magazines). In 2005 those companies included capital from Norway,[4] Germany, Switzerland, and Sweden.
- The third group is made up of (1) Swiss Marquard Media Poland (sports daily, magazines); (2) Polish Infor Publishing Group (financial daily, financial and law magazines); (3) *Polityka* Publishing Cooperative (opinion magazines); (4) Advertising Agency *Wprost* (opinion magazine), and (5) Murator Publishing Company (magazines).

The biggest share of the Polish press market, with regard to total sales, belongs to Bauer (53.2%), Axel Springer (7.7%), and Edipresse (5.4%).[5] Polish publishers perform better in more narrow submarkets and compete with foreign companies fairly successfully, especially with regards to news magazines (*Polityka, Wprost, Ozon, Przegląd, Angora*) as well as the financial, business, and law markets.

The Polish national daily newspapers market is highly dynamic and changeable. The growth of Polish daily press is caused by an increase in the number of free dailies and the introduction of Springer Polska's new tabloid, *Fakt,* in 2003, plus the new national quality daily, *Dziennik,* in 2006. The year 2005 saw distribution of 971 million dailies (paid and free), an increase of 124 million compared to 2001. In general, there has been an increase in the sales of national dailies, whereas regional dailies sales have declined.

In 2006, the three general quality newspapers (*Gazeta Wyborcza, Rzeczpospolita, Dziennik*) together had about 33% of the national newspaper circulation. The two paid tabloids (*Fakt* and *Super Express*) have about 27% and the two free tabloids (*Metro* and *Metropol*) have about 12% of total circulation (see Table 14.2).

The Polish opinion magazine market is relatively vast in reach and characterized by external pluralism. There are a lot of titles representing different political opinions and ideologies. The majority of them belong to either Polish media companies or small entrepreneurs. There are several categories of magazines (see Table 14.3).

The first group is "the big three" with *Polityka, Wprost,* and Springer's *Newsweek.* Their economic position is relatively stable. They have a loyal readership and the strongest advertising revenues in the opinion magazine segment. The second collection is made up of *Przekrój, Angora, Nie, Przegląd,* and *Ozon.* The catholic magazines *Gość Niedzielny, Tygodnik Powszechny,* and *Przewodnik Katolicki* constitute the next category. *Forbes, BusinessWeek, Businessman Magazine,* and *Manager Magazine* belong to the economic and business category of magazines.

Broadcast Media. In Poland there are both public service radio (PR S.A. Public media) and public service TV (TVP S.A) broadcasting. Compared to privately-owned media, they have an obligation to air political messages, free of charge, during electoral campaigns. The public media are financed by broadcasting fees and revenues derived from their own productions and advertising. Private media do not have the same burden; their revenues are primarily from advertising.

The Polish radio market operates like an oligopoly, with three main stations shaping the market. In 2005, the largest market share was held by the commercial stations, RMF FM (22%) and Radio ZET (18.6%). PR1 (14.6%) and PR3 (5.8%) had the best position among the public

TABLE 14.2
Structure of Poland's National Daily Newspaper Market in 2006[1]

p.	Title	Type	Average circulation in 2006 (number of copies) [2]	Readers of newspapers VI-XII 2006 (percent of respondents)[3]	Ownership
1.	GAZETA WYBORCZA	Quality newsp (left-center)	472 078	19.5	AGORA (Polish)
2.	FAKT	Tabloid	504 755	18.6	SPRINGER (German)
3.	SUPER EXPRESS	Tabloid	210 729	8.7	ZPR -BONNIER (Polish-Swedish)
4.	METRO	Free tabloid	No data	7.5	AGORA (Polish)
5.	DZIENNIK	Quality newspaper (conservative)	211 610	8.1	SPRINGER (German)
6.	RZECZPOSPOLITA	Quality newspaper (independent)	136 423	5.2	PPW- MECOM (Polish-British)[4]
7.	PRZEGLĄD SPORTOWY	Sport daily	64 295	5.2	MARQUARD (Swiss)
8.	METROPOL	Free tabloid	No data	4.2	METRO INTERNATIONAL GROUP (Swedish)
9.	GAZETA PRAWNA	Quality business/law newspaper	65 561	2.2	Grupa Wydawnicza INFOR (Polish)
10.	PULS BIZNESU	Quality business newspaper	20 399	0.5	BONNIER (Swedish)
11.	GAZETA GIEŁDY PARKIET	Quality business newspaper	11 225	0.2	PARKIET MEDIA S.A
12.	TRYBUNA	Quality newspaper (left)	No data	No data	AD NOVUM sp. z o.o.

[1]Data from "Press. Bezpłatny Dodatek: Dzienniki 2006", no. 8/2006, [2]http://wirtualnemedia.pl/document,,2082281,Gazeta_Wyborcza_dogania_Fakt.html, retrieved February 5, 2007.
[3]www.wirtualnemedia.pl/document,,2092836,PBC, retrieved February 19, 2007.
* The British MECOM Group bought "Rzeczpospolita" and other Polish local newspapers from the Norwegian ORKLA Media Group in 2006.

stations, but in general public radio loses listeners every year. There are more than 230 commercial stations in Poland, which broadcast in both national and regional markets (*The Broadcasting Landscape in Poland*, 2006).

The biggest terrestrial commercial broadcasters operating in Poland are TV POLSAT and TVN and two smaller stations, TV4 and TV PULS. There are 36 satellite stations licensed by the National Broadcasting Council (KRRiT) (*The Broadcasting Landscape in Poland, 2006*). Two public television channels, TVP1 and TVP2, are still leaders in market share, with over 46% of the audience. TVP1 dropped in audience share during 2005, whereas TVP2 and commercial TVN and TVPOLSAT gained ground. At the beginning of the twenty-first century, the expansion of new thematic channels created by the media holding ITI began. Its channels, TVN24, TVN, Meteo, TVN Style, and TVN Turbo, became more popular (Figures 14.1 and 14.2).

TABLE 14.3
Structure of the Poland National Opinion Magazine Market in 2006

Data from ZKDP (number of copies)	October			
	2006		2005	
	Average circulation	Average sales	Average circulation	Average sales
NEWSWEEK (center)	256117	161170	269659	154271
POLITYKA (left-center)	263821	158146	256693	162148
GOŚĆ NIEDZIELNY (catholic)	181089	127175	167932	121032
WPROST (right)	251423	127028	277031	151832
PRZEKRÓJ (center)	146262	70345	143930	65577
PRZEGLĄD (left)	78407	28647	86000	33110
TYGODNIK POWSZECHNY (catholic)	40990	19469	50580	22303

Source: http://wirtualnemedia.pl/document,,2062173,Newsweek_obronil_pozycje_lidera.html, retrieved January 8, 2007.

Layout of Media Regulation

Election law in Poland is regulated by the act governing election to the Seym and the Senat, the act governing the presidential election, the regulations concerned with elections to local councils and mayors, and the act governing election to the European Parliament (Antoszewski, 2002b). These kinds of elections have a direct, general, equal, proportional, and secret character. They are different in both manner and timing. Elections in Poland are organized on four different levels: (1) legislative elections (to Seym and Senat) every four years; (2) presidential elections every five years; (3) local elections every four years; and (4) elections to the European Parliament every five years (Antoszewski, 2002b).

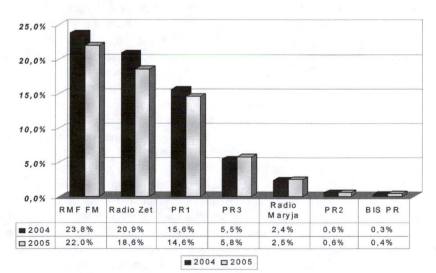

	RMF FM	Radio Zet	PR1	PR3	Radio Maryja	PR2	BIS PR
2004	23,8%	20,9%	15,6%	5,5%	2,4%	0,6%	0,3%
2005	22,0%	18,6%	14,6%	5,8%	2,5%	0,6%	0,4%

Source: AGB Nielsen Media Research.

FIGURE 14.1   The ratings of radio stations in Poland, 2004 and 2005.

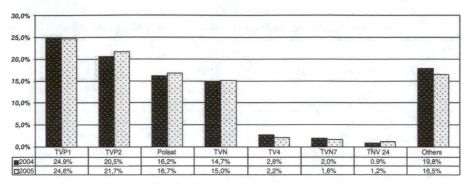

Source: AGB Nielsen Media Research.

FIGURE 14.2   The ratings of TV stations in Poland, 2004 and 2005.

Two constitutional institutions, the State Electoral Commission (PKW; Państwowa Komisja Wyborcza)[6] and the National Broadcasting Council (KRRiT), are responsible for the regulation of election information in the mass media. Election campaigns are mainly monitored by KRRiT, independent research institutes, and academic centers.

The State Electoral Commission (PKW) is the most important election organizing body. PKW controls and enforces action based on prevailing election law. It also tabulates and announces the results of the voting process. After announcing the election time, PKW has a right to present information, explanations, and announcements in national TV and radio stations, free of charge as long as they are related to campaign and election law.

The National Broadcasting Council (KRRiT) is the regulatory body that usually controls the broadcast media market, and thus it allocates time on the public media during the election campaign. The time is free of charge and is reserved for the electoral committees.[7] KRRiT oversees the process of registration, the way of preparing election messages, and the manner of their diffusion in media.

Public media are obligated to provide free election spots, at their own expense, from the 15 days before election day to the end of the election campaign. The amount of free advertising time depends on the level of the campaign, as noted in Table 14.4. There are 34 hours in television and 61 hours in radio allocated for legislative election messages. The presidential election is covered by 31 hours in television and 43 hours in radio.

Free advertising time is allocated in proportion to the number of registered electoral committees, and cannot be conferred to other committees. In addition to the free advertising time, each committee also has the opportunity to buy paid advertising time between the 15th day before election day and the end of the political campaign, and this is allowed in both public and commercial media. These kinds of messages cannot constitute more than 15% of total time which is reserved to each committee. Broadcasters cannot refuse to air these messages. The price is created according to the advertising price-list on the day when elections are announced and is the same for every committee. Time for paid advertising is not included to the free advertising time.

The period known as "election silence" starts a day before election day. Political agitation, both free and paid advertising, are not permitted during this period. During election campaigns, accelerated judicial proceedings can be launched when committees believe information broadcast about rivals is untruthful. The candidate or political party that suffers from inaccurate information as represented by their electoral committee has a right to lodge a complaint with the Court.

TABLE 14.4
Free Political Advertising Time in Public Broadcasting Media in Poland (hours)

	Legislative election to SEYM	Legislative election to SENAT	Presidential election I vote	Presidential election II vote	Local election	European election
TV national (TVP1,2)	10	5	20	6	-	15
TV regional (TVP3)	10	3	-	-	15	10
TV sat TVP Polonia	3	1	5	-	-	-
Radio national	25	10	30	8	-	20
Radio regional	15	6	-	-	20	10
Radio sat	5	-	5	-	-	-

Note: Data from The State Electoral Commission (Państwowa Komisja Wyborcza) www.pkw.gov.pl

The complaint can refer to the prohibition against publishing these kinds of materials, and can include rectification or apologies to the person whose rights were infringed. Proceedings cannot last longer than 24 hours and the decision made by the judge is final.

THE DEVELOPMENT OF POLITICAL NEWS COVERAGE

Print Media

After 1989 print media first became an important channel of political communication. A thriving and prosperous press offered the voters brand new quality newspapers, tabloids, and new opinion magazines. Paid advertising, articles, interviews, analysis, reports, commentaries, and other journalistic forms began to be published as never before. Once the long period of communism came to an end, the press started to cover political campaigns and helped the voters to make decisions.

In the early 1990s, the number of national dailies was limited. In the beginning of the transition to democracy, an important role was played by left-center *Gazeta Wyborcza*. The title was created by intellectuals within the left wing of the Solidarity Movement (e.g., Adam Michnik) a few weeks before the first semi-democratic legislative elections in 1989. *Gazeta Wyborcza* is still very active in public debate. The independent *Rzeczpospolita* was the second important channel of information and opinion in the election communication process. These quality newspapers belonged to the Polish state enterprises until 2006, then to the Norwegian media group, Orkla Media; each strives to be neutral and independent.

In the mid-1990s, the tabloid *Super Express* was created. However, its participation in the public debate has always been limited. In 2003 another tabloid was created when Springer launched *Fakt*.

There are many opinion weeklies that present different kinds of political options, from left oriented titles like *Przegląd* and *Nie*, to center-left *Polityka,* and the right-oriented *Wprost*. Some catholic weeklies like *Gość Niedzielny* and *Tygodnik Powszechny* have a small part of the market.

All of them have covered every presidential and legislative election and have taken part in public debate. Besides these titles there are about 20 different weeklies, which are addressed to particular market niches and have a stable but very small group of readers.

Free Political Advertising (Free Media) in the Public Broadcasting Media

The idea of free time in public media for parties and candidates during electoral campaigns was introduced in the early 1990s as a TV program titled *Studio Wyborcze* (Electoral Studio). Poles watched these kinds of programs very often at that time. The average audience size of *Studio Wyborcze* in prime time was about 37 to 51% (Mazur, 2002). Parties and candidates presented themselves in special election blocks in what may be described as a very amateurish way. Thus, *Studio Wyborcze* was not rated very highly by citizens, despite the high audience share in the beginning of the 1990s (Mazur, 2002). Consequently, the program lost viewers towards the end of the 1990s, as the competition for audiences became tougher. Free advertising time lost its justification in 2005. A large number of hours (Table 14.4), which were reserved to established parties and candidates for campaign communication, were in practice wasted.

The Main Political Television News Programs

In the early 1990s, Polish television continued its policy of giving very limited coverage to campaigns and campaign issues (Jakubowicz, 1999). During that period the public broadcaster had a monopoly on political news. At the end of the 1990s, some new competitors appeared, thanks to a dynamically developing television market. The commercial media group ITI started with the evening political news program *Fakty*, aired by its main channel, TVN, and launched the first information channel TVN24. In the early 2000s the biggest commercial channel TVPOLSAT renewed its political news program *Wydarzenia* and joined the "battle for viewers."

All of these channels with their main evening news shows engaged in fierce competition during the 2005 election campaign. They covered all aspects of the political campaigns (Kolczynski & Mazur, 2007). The main evening news shows and the information channel TNV24 created a hierarchy of information and a media agenda. They were one of the main sources of knowledge about campaigns, political parties, and candidates.

Other TV Political Emissions

The main channels have had their own political shows hosted by famous Polish journalists. Despite a late time slot, they influence the media agenda in very different ways. These shows are often discussed by other media. Thus, to some extent they set the media agenda.

The Polish TV channels have created a lot of political shows, especially during the campaign period. On the day of elections, when the voting process ended, TVP1 and TVN offered special coverage: they presented preliminary results, comments of politicians, and the latest information about the campaigns. Sociologists, economists, political science experts, and other specialists participated in many different debates.

These kinds of shows became one of the main areas of competition between public and commercial channels, especially TVP1 and TVN. Such competition had both positive and negative consequences. On the one hand Polish voters have received a rich source of news and commentary on which they could base a choice. On the other hand a majority of this programming could be characterized as infotainment, where the information value sometimes was questionable.

Political Debates

Political debates appeared on Polish television for the first time in 1995, before the second round of the race between Lech Wałęsa and Aleksander Kwaśniewski. Two debates were held on public television during prime time. Kwaśniewski was better prepared (Mazur, 2002) and worked with his political consultants and image specialists. About 70% of respondents thus agreed that Kwaśniewski presented himself in a better way than Wałęsa did. Polls of OBOP suggested that the political debates on television in 1995 played a big role in influencing the voting results (CBOS, 1995).

There were no televised debates during the presidential elections in 2000, and the next debates took place in 2005. The political debates were broadcast by the public TVP1 and the commercial TVN. The presidential debate on TVN was a disappointment, however, as it resembled infotainment rather than a serious debate. The debate on public television was better organized and exhibited a higher level of journalistic professionalism. Viewers could learn the arguments of both rivals and their economic and political programs.

Media Events

Campaigns of the year 2005 accelerated the process of an Americanization of Polish election campaigns. The big parties, especially PiS and PO, began their campaigns from professionally organized electoral conventions. Candidates were traveling through the whole country, had many meetings with citizens, members of trade unions, and organizations (catholic, business social, non-governmental). They participated in official celebrations of national and catholic holidays. They took part in ceremonies, opened exhibitions and conferences, gave lectures and press conferences. They did everything possible to generate news coverage. The hard work of public and media relations specialists and press agents was clearly visible.

THE CONTENT OF POLISH ELECTION NEWS COVERAGE

Content analyses of election news coverage do not have a long tradition in Poland, although the last election in 2005 provided very interesting materials for empirical research. Kolczyński and Mazur (2007) did a content analysis of free advertising media time in the public television and political news on TVP1 (*Teleekspress* and *Wiadomości*), TVP2 (*Panorama*), and TVN (*Fakty*). A group of researchers and students from the University of Wroclaw conducted an empirical content analysis of six national newspapers, seven quality opinion magazines, and the three political news programs of TVP1, TVN and TVPOLSAT.[8] They investigated how the news media covered both the presidential and legislative campaigns. These studies focused on questions pertaining to media bias in coverage, concluding that the media exhibited favoritism in their selection and presentation of political candidates, issues, and events. This is one of the first empirical studies of political communication in Poland, and we will thus base our continuing discussion mainly on the research from the team at the University of Wroclaw.

Content Analysis of the National Newspapers

The content analysis covered six newspapers during the time period between June 1 and October 31, 2005: *Gazeta Wyborcza, Rzeczpospolita, Fakt, Super Express, Nasz Dziennik,* and *Trybuna*. The sample consisted of 130 issues from each title. The number of articles in each

TABLE 14.5
Content Analysis of Polish Newspapers, June 1 – October 31, 2005

Title of newspaper	Number of articles	Parties' coverage	Candidates' coverage	Parties and candidates' coverage	Other
GAZETA WYBORCZA	1294	606 (46.8%)	406 (31.4%)	189 (14.6%)	93 (7.2%)
RZECZPOSPOLITA	884	No data	No data	No data	No data
FAKT	421	183 (43.5%)	238 (56.5%)	0	0
SUPER EXPRESS	429	213 (49.7%)	146 (34.0%)	31 (7.2%)	39 (9.1%)
TRYBUNA	303	114 (37.6%)	149 (49.2%)	30 (9.9%)	10 (3.3%)
NASZ DZIENNIK	383	112 (29.2%)	186 (48.6%)	38 (9.9%)	47 (12.3%)

newspaper is displayed in Table 14.5, which also shows the focus of the coverage in each newspaper.

The newspapers favored three main political parties. Most articles in *Gazeta Wyborcza* referred to PiS (410 articles) and PO (329 articles). Parties which were not as strong in the polls, such as SLD (165 articles), Samoobrona (138 articles), and LPR (146 articles), were in the second group. In the third group there were parties with polling numbers that were marginal. Only one of them, PSL (58 articles), managed to get some seats in the parliament. The other five parties were mentioned in only 38 articles.

Rzeczposopolita presented a more balanced and equal coverage, with a similar number of articles related to the three biggest parties. PiS was mentioned in 241 articles, PO in 255 articles, and SLD in 281 articles. Parties like Samoobrona (138 articles), LPR (146 articles), and SDPl (129 articles) were present in more articles than PD (88 articles) and PSL (81 articles).

The two tabloids focused primarily on scandals, sensations, and candidate attractiveness. These articles were not in any way objective. *Trybuna* and *Nasz Dziennik*, with a small but loyal group of readers, presented articles which reminded the researchers of the kind of political propaganda that was common during communism. Left oriented *Trybuna* wrote a lot about the left parties SLD (62 articles) and SDPl (17 articles). Catholic *Nasz Dziennik* published articles that favored the two biggest parties, PiS and PO. The journalistic professionalism of these four newspapers was very low (Figure 14.3).

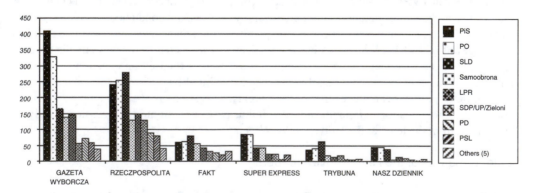

Source: Authors. The sample consists of 150 issues of each title.

Figure 14.3   Coverage of political parties in Poland in national newspapers, June 1–October 31, 2005.

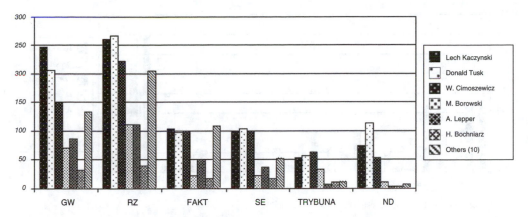

Source: Authors. The sample consists of 150 issues of each title.

FIGURE 14.4   Coverage of Polish candidates in national newspapers, June 1–October 31, 2005.

All six of the newspapers concentrated on the three main candidates in the presidential election: Tusk, Kaczyński, and Cimoszewicz (Figure 14.4). *Gazeta Wyborcza* published 246 articles about Kaczyński. It was 40 articles more than about Tusk. Cimoszewicz was mentioned in 150 articles. The most relevant and balanced articles were presented in *Rzeczpospolita*. This newspaper published 261 articles about Kaczyński, 266 about Tusk, and 222 about Cimoszewicz. The tabloids concentrated on the three main candidates too. *Fakt* wrote 104 times about Kaczyński, 98 about Tusk, and 100 about Cimoszewicz. *Super Express* covered the main candidates in similar numbers of articles. *Trybuna* preferred the left candidates and published 63 articles about Cimoszewicz and 34 about Borowski. Paradoxically the most number of articles in *Nowy Dziennik* concentrated on Tusk (113) but substantially speaking they were strongly critical of this candidate.

Content Analysis of the Opinion Magazines

The content analysis included the seven opinion magazines with the highest circulation. Table 14.6 displays the news magazines included, the number of articles published, and the focus of

TABLE 14.6
Content Analysis of Polish Opinion Magazines, June 1–October 31, 2005

Title of newspaper	Number of articles	Parties' news	Candidates' news	Parties and candidates' news	Other news
WPROST	270	70 (26%)	137 (50.7%)	54 (20%)	9 (3.3%)
POLITYKA	140	76 (54.3%)	44 (31.4%)	4 (2.9%)	16 (11.4%)
NEWSWEEK	229	No data	No data	No data	No data
PRZEKRÓJ	173	57 (32.9%)	72 (41.6%)	15 (8.7%)	29 (16.8%)
ANGORA	148	9 (6.1%)	76 (51.4%)	4 (2.7%)	56 (37.8%)
OZON	135	23 (17%)	43 (31.9%)	10 (7.4%)	59 (43.7%)
PRZEGLĄD	551	126	138	157	130

Source: Authors. The sample consists of 22 issues of each title.

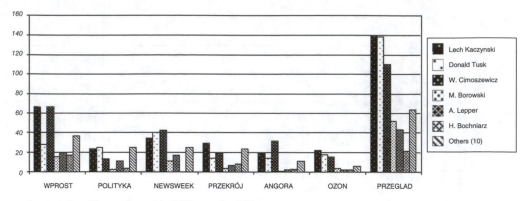

Source: Authors. The sample consists of 22 issues of each title.

FIGURE 14.5   Coverage of the Polish political parties in the opinion magazines, June 1–October 31, 2005.

the articles. All magazines, except for *Polityka*, concentrated on the presidential campaign. The election coverage of *Wprost* and *Angora* was characterized by a lack of balanced and even-handed coverage. *Wprost* published 137 articles focused on the presidential campaign and only 70 articles concerned with the legislative election. *Angora* published 76 articles which covered the presidential election and only nine which covered the legislative election.

Polityka published a similar numbers of articles about the main parties: 12 about PiS, 14 about PO, and 15 about SLD. *Wprost* wrote 67 times about PIS, 44 times about PO, and 34 times about SLD. The other parties were rather marginalized (Figure 14.5).

Quantitative data show that the three main candidates were presented in more articles than the others. A qualitative analysis shows that some magazines, such as *Wprost* and *Przegląd*, were partisan and non-objective. *Wprost* created a positive image of Kaczyński in 66 articles and an extremely negative image of Cimoszewicz in 67. There were only 28 publications about Tusk. This limited coverage of Tusk in *Wprost* could be interpreted as a clear declaration of political support for Kaczynski. *Polityka*, *Newsweek,* and *Przekrój* published more balanced and equal news. They attempted to be objective and neutral, although they did not always succeed (Figure 14.6).

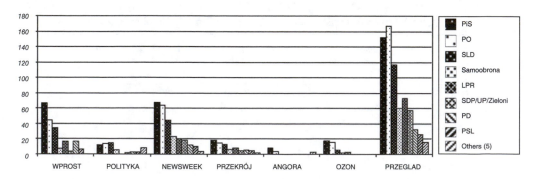

Source: Authors. The sample consists of 22 issues of each title.

FIGURE 14.6   Coverage of the Polish candidates in the opinion magazines, June 1–October 31, 2005.

TABLE 14.7
News Coverage of Polish Legislative and Presidential Elections, July 1–September 30, 2005, in *Wiadomości* TVP1

News coverage	Legislative & presidential election (mixed news)	Legislative election	Presidential election
July	11 (22%)	21 (42%)	18 (36%)
August	8 (19.5%)	13 (31.7%)	20 (48.8%)
September	32 (46.4%)	25 (36.2%)	12 (17.4%)

Source: Authors. The sample consists of 87 editions of *Wiadomości* TVP1.

Content Analysis of the Main Political News, Wiadomości (TVP1)

This study covers the evening news on the public television channel TVP1 between July 1 and September 25, 2005. We used a sample of 87 shows. *Wiadomości* broadcast 855 news programs during this time, but only 160 of them contained coverage of elections. There were 50 news spots of elections (124 seconds) in July, 41 (130 seconds) in August, and 69 (151 seconds) in September. The news coverage of elections took 16.5% of all program time in July, 14.1% in August, and about 27 % in September.

It is impossible to analyze both political campaigns, legislative and presidential, separately, because they occurred at the same time and were linked. A lot of news was classified as mixed news (22% in July, about 20% in August and about 46% in September). About 42% of all news coverage was related to legislative and 36% to the presidential campaign in July, but it changed in August. More than 48% of all news covered the presidential election and about 31% the legislative election. The legislative election was present in 36% and the presidential election in 17% of the news in September (Table 14.7).

The main television channels competed hard during the campaign period. Commercial channels presented many different polls and some special analyses before the final election. *Wiadomości* presented new polls almost every day. This kind of presentation could have misled less oriented viewers who could not watch TV systematically. The news based on polls dominated the content related to parties and candidates. The qualitative analysis suggests that television stories did not try to explain the differences among the candidates and their propositions of political, economic, and social reforms (Table 14.8).

PiS was shown as a party with a well-prepared and concrete political program. PO was seen as a party which wanted to fight fair. News related to SLD was rather negative and partisan. SDPl (second left-oriented party) started to appear only when SLD presidential candidate Cimoszewicz resigned. *Wiadomości* did not believe in the potential for success for SDPL, LPR,

TABLE 14.8
Focus on Parties' Program vs. Public Opinion Polls, July 1– September 30, 2005, in *Wiadomości* TVP1

	Number of news referred to parties' program	Number of news referred to public opinion polls
July 2005	7 (14%)	14 (28%)
August 2005	8 (19.5%)	8 (19.5%)
September 2005	19 (27.5%)	24 (34.8%)

Source: Authors. The sample consists of 87 editions of *Wiadomości* TVP1.

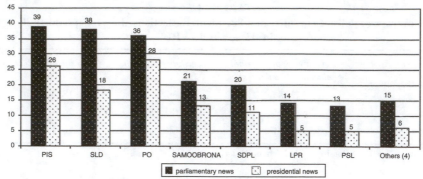

Source: Authors. The sample consists of 87 editions of *Wadomości* TVP1

FIGURE 14.7 The quantity of the news coverage of Polish Legislative and Presidential elections, July 1–September 30, in *Wadomości* TVP1.

Samoobrona, and PSL. They marginalized them and referred to them as second line parties. The conflict between the two main parties (PO and PIS) was characterized as one of confrontation, disunion, and many political differences (Figure 14.7).

In their comparative analysis of evening news programs in public and commercial TV channels, Kolczyński and Mazur (2007) pointed to a process of convergence. Similarities were seen in that they tended to select the same news and concentrate their attention on the same politicians, parties, and issues. There was an increase of legislative election news during the last week before election day. *Wiadomości* provided about 8 minutes and commercial *Fakty* 6 minutes of election news each day.

The next period of news intensification in both channels took place before the presidential election. TVN was more active that TVP1 in the last three days prior to voting. The commercial broadcaster treated the election news as an attractive media product (Kolczyński & Mazur, 2007). *Fakty* showed 88 minutes and *Wiadomości* 69 minutes of election news in the last week of the presidential campaign.

Descriptive versus Interpretative Journalism and Questions of Political Bias

Quantitative and qualitative content analysis of six newspapers, seven opinion magazines, and the main news television programs provides support for the claim that the mass media are in the main free and independent. On the one hand, they expressed different and plural opinions and Polish voters had free access to many sources of information about the various campaigns. But on the other hand, we noted a tendency in the news to deviate from an accurate, neutral, balanced, and impartial presentation. This tendency characterized some kinds of print and broadcast media, above all the tabloid and ideological newspapers and magazines but also sometimes the public and commercial televisions. The media concentrated on a control function (McNair, 1995). They informed about the parties and candidates who were leading in pre-election polls and ignored the others. Medium and smaller political actors did not have equal and proportional access to the media. Some media outlets had a problem with factuality of news. They were often characterized by a lack of relevance and were uninformative.

The content analysis of print media shows that the Polish press represented varied levels of journalistic professionalism. Generally speaking, the media standards were respected by quality newspapers, such as *Rzeczpospolita* and *Gazeta Wyborcza,* and opinion magazines, such as *Polityka*, *Przekrój*, and *Newsweek*. Interpretative journalism and commentary-oriented political reporting were typical for the tabloids, politicized newspapers such as *Trybuna* and *Nasz Dziennik,* some magazines such as *Przegląd, Wprost,* and sometimes for television political news.

The content analysis of *Wiadomości* TVP1 provides us with a lot of information about the journalistic professionalism of Polish public television. We observe an evolution of the main evening political news towards commercialization with short and attractive news illustrated by videos and still photos. The strong competition among the TV channels had some negative consequences for journalistic professionalism and started to mitigate against the mission of the public media. Rather interpretative and commentary-oriented journalism was typically for news presented by *Wiadomości.* The public broadcasters often did not accept the principles of objectivity, factual accuracy, and impartiality. The presentations of parties and candidates were in many cases not neutral and balanced.

Publication of Opinion Polls

Pre-election polling in Poland is very dynamic. An explosion in the number of polls started in 2000. An increased focus on polls took place during the 2005 election campaigns, when, for example, *Gazeta Wyborcza* published 70 news items about polls. The polling was produced by five different firms. The pre-election polling in 2005 was not without controversies, however, including extensive news coverage of different methodological issues, especially the omission of cell phones in standard samples and the differences in methods for estimating "likely voters" (Kamyk, 2005, p. 83). The pre-election polling in the 2005 campaign surveys we should treat as a defeat for research firms and mass media too. The firms produced a lot of polls under pressure from mass media which treated it as attractive news. The mass media often presented the results without professionalism. They did not explain methods and confused a probe and poll. A month before the parliamentary election more than 71% of respondents treated the choice between political parties as difficult (CBOS, 2005). A high percentage of undecided voters made a decision at the last moment. In the case of the second round of the 2005 presidential election, the lines of candidate support intersected exactly two days before election day, when publication of poll results was prohibited.

ROLE OF TELEVISION ADVERTISING IN ELECTIONS

Television political advertising is one of the most important elements of Polish political campaigns. However, at present there are only a few empirical studies on political advertising on television, conducted by psychologists (Francuz, 1999; Falkowski & Cwalina, 1999; Cwalina, 2000), and in more descriptive studies by political scientists (Mazur, 2005).

Nevertheless, political advertising on television evolved from 1989 to 2006. The first campaigns were very amateurish. The use of political advertising was limited to free election messages on public channels. The first political advertisements were not so attractive to viewers and did not become an efficient political communication channel. Its advantages were not seen until the 1995 presidential campaign, when advertisements were prepared by some special communication agencies. The professional advertising and an increase in cost then began. During the 2000 presidential election, candidates began buying airtime in addition to using their free airtime (Mazur, 2002).

In 2005 the Polish viewers consumed about 3788 advertising spots and 1314 election announcements on all television channels, and political television advertisement was one of the most popular sources of information. The use of political advertising depended on the size of the political party, and the position of its leaders. The big parties like PO, PiS, and coalition SLD paid attention to this form of political communication. Their advertising was rather professional (Mazur, 2005). They used free media and bought airtime during prime time on public and commercial television. Smaller parties had smaller budgets, which limited their activities to free time offered by public broadcast. They usually created their own spots, which weren't very attractive.

Negative political advertising has become more popular in Poland, although the first negative advertising was used as early as 1990. In both campaigns in 2005, negative advertising was rather common. PiS attacked the political program of PO and their tax propositions; PO did the same. Negative advertisements coming from these parties appeared again during local campaigns in 2006. The media accused these parties of imitating American political campaigns, as their spots were similar to American spots used by President Bush in 2004.

NEW DIRECTIONS OF NEWS COVERAGE OF ELECTIONS

Political parties and candidates promote their images and programs not only in print and on television, but also on the Internet. Polish politicians started to use the Internet for political communication in the late 1990s. However, they did not use all the possibilities offered them by this new technology. Their activities were limited to creating websites which were active only during the election campaign. In 2005 a significant development of new technologies occurred, and their impact on campaigns was visible.

Along with an increase in the number of Internet users in Poland (30% in 2005), an interest in this channel of political communication appeared. In 2005 all presidential candidates and all parties had their own websites. They published their political programs, multimedia news, and fragments of TV reports, political advertising, and public relations materials. The Internet stimulated a process of political personalization. The politicians published photos from their childhood as well as family photos. The blogs of politicians and candidates created a new way of political communication.

Internet chat with candidates and leaders was the other novelty at that time. This form of mediated but interpersonal relationships between political actors and voters dominated the major Internet portals, such as onet.pl, wp.pl, or interia.pl. The creators of Internet websites formed special links to election information sources. They organized meetings with politicians who could speak to voters. As the quantity of chat users on the Internet increases, so does the number of politicians writing blogs.

Paradoxically, during the local campaign one year later only the biggest political parties and the most significant candidates used the Internet. The quality of these websites was worse than in the national elections. In 2006, only one party, the liberal PO, had the highest professionalism of Internet communication; it had a better educated and a more affluent constituency. PIS and the others parties undervalued the Internet and plainly neglected their websites during the local campaign in 2006.

In addition to the Internet, political advertising was distributed by mobile phones and land lines. The leader of SLD used it for the first time in 2005 and Marcinkiewicz, the PIS candidate in a local election in Warsaw, repeated it in 2006.

CONCLUSION

The 2005 election was exceptional in the history of free elections in Poland. For the first time two campaigns—both the legislative and presidential—took place at the same time. This meant that Poles had to endure more that nine months under the pressure of election communications. Both campaigns were covered by print, broadcast media, and the Internet. Outdoor political advertisements were pervasive and intrusive. The candidates were presented in all accessible public places on thousands of billboards and millions of posters, on streets and in buses. Mail boxes were stuffed with leaflets and and full-color brochures. The accumulation of so many political messages at the same time and in the same space was unique.

These campaigns were really difficult for the electorate. No great personalities and charismatic leaders were identified by public opinion. Voters did not know who would decide to be a candidate until a few months before the presidential election (CBOS, 2005). The pre-election polls presented different outcomes every week and demonstrated unstable support for parties and candidates. It did not facilitate a decision by voters. Many respondents could not define their preferences even a few days before the election. We can interpret this phenomenon as being the consequence of the changeable outcome of polls, many similarities in the political offerings of the main political actors, and very intensive media campaigns that influenced voters up to the last moment. Poles were tired of politics and politicians. A lot of them were not interested in campaigns and did not vote. PiS and the Kaczynski brothers won the elections.

Both the 2005 national campaigns and the 2006 local campaign were conducted in a professional manner, with the help of political consultants and media experts. They took an active role in constructing campaign communication. We should stress that television occupied a central position in the media and was the main source of political information.

More that 10 years ago, Jakubowicz (1996, p. 151) said: "When television begins to play a crucial role in elections and the more telegenic candidates stand a better chance of getting elected, we will know that the process of transformation has been successfully completed." Nowadays, after 18 years of the Polish experience with democracy, we know that television plays a crucial role in elections and that a strong presence and positive coverage in the media is a prerequisite for electoral success (Dobek-Ostrowska, 2005).

NOTES

1. It is difficult to define a character of PiS. It is a conservative party on the level of values but rather socialist on the level of its political and economic programs.
2. PO won the earlier parliamentary election in 2007 and is the ruling party.
3. Data from February 2007. Retrieved February 15, 2007 from http://www.zkdp.pl/download/kontrolowane1.pdf
4. The British Group Mecom bought the media from Orkla Press Poland in 2006.
5. According to ZKDP see: "Press, Dodatek Specjalny," September 2006, p. 10.
6. The State Electoral Commission (Państwowa Komisja Wyborcza, PKW) is a constitutional and independent organization which is responsible for monitoring campaign proceedings. It is obligated to make sure that all political actors act according to election law and norms accepted in Poland.
7. An electoral committee according to Polish electoral law is an official structure created by political parties, candidates, or other political or social organizations in order to take part in an election. Only an electoral committee can submit official candidatures in election for registration by the State Electoral Commission. An electoral committee act during election campaign and after that they are closed.
8. The analysis of a huge empirical data set has not yet been completed.

REFERENCES

Agh, A. (2001). Early consolidation and performance crisis: The majoritarian-consensus democracy debate in Hungary. *West European Politics, 24*(3), 89–112.

Antoszewski, A. (2002a). Ewolucja Polskiego systemu partyjnego [Evolution of the Polish party system]. In A. Antoszewski (Ed.), *Demokratyzacja w III Rzeczpospolitej* [Democratization of III Republic] (pp. 137–156). Wrocław: Wydawnictwo Uniwersytetu Wrocławskiego.

Antoszewski, A. (2002b). Ewolucja systemu wyborczego do sejmu [Evolution of electoral system to the parliament]. In A. Antoszewski (Ed.), *Demokratyzacja w III Rzeczpospolitej* [Democratization of III Republic] (pp. 51–72). Wrocław: Wydawnictwo Uniwersytetu Wrocławskiego.

Broadcasting landscape in Poland. Retrieved June 20, 2007 from http://www.krrit.gov.pl/angielska/index.htm

CBOS Komunikat. (1995). *December, 1995: Debaty prezydenckie jako reklama polityczna* [Political debates as political advertising].

CBOS Komunikat. (2005). September 2005: *Trudny wybór Polaków* [Difficult choice of Poles].

Cichosz, M. (2006). Transformacja demokratyczna—Przyczyny, przebieg i efekty procesu [Democratic transformation—Causes, proceedings and consequences of process]. In A. Antoszewski (Ed.), *Systemy polityczne Europy Środkowo-Wschodniej:Perspektywa porównawcza* [Political systems in Central and Eastern Europe: A comparative perspective] (pp. 35–66). Wrocław: Wydawnictwo Uniwersytetu Wrocławskiego.

Curry, J. L. (2006). Transformacja mediów w Europie Środkowo-Wschodniej: Komplikacje wolności dla każdego [East European media's transition: The complications of freedom for everybody]. In B. Dobek-Ostrowska (Ed.), *Media masowe w demokratyzujących się systemach politycznych* [Mass media in democratizing political systems] (pp. 99–114). Wrocław: Wydawnictwo Uniwersytetu Wrocławskiego.

Cwalina, W. (2000). *Telewizyjna reklama polityczna* [Political television advertising]. Lublin: Wydawnictwo KUL.

Dobek-Ostrowska, B. (1999). Mass communication in Poland after the collapse of communism. *The Global Network, 11*, 85–104.

Dobek-Ostrowska, B. (2001). Process of transition to democracy and mass media in Central and Eastern Europe. In J. Adamowski & M. Jabłonowski (Eds.), *The role of local and regional media in the democratization of the Eastern and Central European society* (pp. 55–64). Warsaw: Oficyna Wydawnicza ASPRA-JR.

Dobek-Ostrowska, B. (2005). Profesjonalizacja kampanii wyborczych we współczesnym świecie i jej konsekwencje [Professionalization of political campaigns in the world and its consequences]. In B. Dobek-Ostrowska (Ed.), *Kampania wyborcza: Marketingowe aspekty komunikowania politycznego* [Political campaign: Marketing`s aspects of political communication] (pp. 11–33). Wrocław: Wydawnictwo Uniwersytetu Wrocławskiego.

Falkowski, A., & Cwalina, W. (1999). Methodology of construction effective political advertising: An empirical study of the Polish presidential election in 1995. In B. Newman (Ed.), *Handbook of political marketing* (pp. 283–304). Thousand Oaks, CA: Sage.

Francuz, P. (Ed.). (1999). *Psychologiczne aspekty odbioru telewizji* [Psychological aspects of television's reception]. Lublin: Wydawnictwo KUL.

Goban-Klas, T. (1997). Politics versus media in Poland: A game without the rules. In P. O`Neil (Ed.), *Postcommunism and the media in Eastern Europe* (pp. 24–41). London: Frank Cass.

Godlewski, T. (2005). Od systemu prezydencko-parlamentarnego do zracjonalizowanego systemu parlamentarno-gabinetowego [From a presidential-parliamentary system towards a rational parliamentary-cabinet system]. In R. Bäcker & J. Marszałek-Kawa (Eds.), *Drogi i bezdroża ku demokracji* [Ways and pathways towards a democracy] (pp. 28–35). Toruń: Wydawnictwo MADO.

Hallin, D. C., & Mancini, P. (2004). *Comparing media systems: Three models of media and politics*. Cambridge, UK: Cambridge University Press.

Herbut, R. (2006). Systemy partyjne w państwach Europy Środkowej i Wschodniej [Party systems in the countries of Central and Eastern Europe]. In A. Antoszewski (Ed.), *Systemy polityczne Europy*

Środkowo-Wschodniej: Perspektywa porównawcza [Political systems in Central and Eastern Europe: A comparative perspective] (pp. 145–166). Wrocław: Wydawnictwo Uniwersytetu Wrocławskiego.

Jednaka, W. (2004). *Gabinety koalicyjne w III RP* [Coalition's governments in the 3rd Polish Republic]. Wrocław: Wydawnictwo Uniwersytetu Wrocławskiego.

Jakubowicz, K. (1999). Television and elections in post-1989 Poland: How powerful is the medium? In D. L. Swanson & P. Mancini (Eds.), *Politics, media, and modern democracy: An international study of innovations in electoral campaigning and their consequences* (pp. 129–154). Westport, CT: Praeger.

Jakubowicz, K. (2006). Finding the right place on the map: Prospects for public service broadcasting in post-communist countries.

Jakubowicz, K. (2008). Finding the right place on the map: Prospects for public service broadcasting in Post-Communist countries. In K. Jakubowicz & M. Sükösd (Eds.), *Finding the right place on the map: Central and Eastern European media change in global perspective*. Britol: Intellect Books.

Kamyk, T. (2005). Sondaże polityczne. Prawda czy fałsz? [Election polls: Truth or false?]. *Brief, 12*, 83–87.

Kolczyński, M., & Mazur, M. (2007). *Wojna na wrażenia. Strategie wyborcze i telewizja w kampanii wyborczej 2005 w Polsce* [Impression's war. Election strategies and television in the election campaigns 2005]. Warsaw: Wydawnictwo Sejmowe.

Lisicka, H. (2002). Ewolucja reżimu politycznego w Polsce po 1989 roku [Evolution of political regime in Poland after 1989]. In A. Antoszewski (Ed.), *Demokratyzacja w III Rzeczpospolitej* [Democratization of the 3rd Polish Republic] (pp. 27–50). Wrocław: Wydawnictwo Uniwersytetu Wrocławskiego.

Markowski, R., & Cześnik, M. (2002). Polski system partyjny: Dekada zmian instytucjonalnych i ich konsekwencje [Polish party system: The decade of institutional changes and their consequences]. In R. Markowski (Ed.), *Polski system partyjny i zachowania wyborcze* [Polish party system and electoral behaviors] (pp. 17–48). Warsaw: Instytut Studiów Politycznych PAN & Fundacja im. Friedricha Eberta.

Mazur, M. (2002). *Marketing polityczny* [Political marketing]. Warsaw: Wyd. Naukowe PWN.

Mazur, M. (2005). Negatywna reklama polityczna: Doświadczenia amerykańskie i polskie [Negative political advertising]. In B. Dobek-Ostrowska (Ed.), *Kampania wyborcza: Marketingowe aspekty komunikowania politycznego* [Political campaign: Marketing's aspects of political communication] (pp. 77–95).Wrocław: Wydawnictwo Uniwersytetu Wrocławskiego.

McNair, B. (1995). *An introduction to political communication*. London: Routledge.

Newman, B. (Ed.) (1999). *Handbook of political marketing*. Thousand Oaks, CA: Sage.

Ociepka, B. (2003). *Dla kogo telewizja? Model publiczny w postkomunistycznej Europie Środkowej* [For who television? Public broadcasting service model in the post-communist Central Europe]. Wrocław: Wydawnictwo Uniwersytetu Wrocławskiego.

Ociepka, B. (2005). Populism as good communication with people: The Polish case during the referendum campaign. In B. Ociepka (Ed.), *Populism and media democracy* (pp. 207–226). Wrocław: Wydawnictwo Uniwersytetu Wrocławskiego.

Sobolewska–Myślik, K. (1999). *Partie i systemy partyjne Europy Środkowo-Wschodniej po 1989 roku* [Parties and party systems in Central and Eastern Europe after 1989]. Cracow: Wydawnictwo Naukowe Księgarnia Akademicka.

Sobolewska–Myślik, K. (2004). *Partie i systemy partyjne na świecie* [Parties and party systems in the world]. Warsow:Wydawnictwo Naukowe PWN.

Solarz, R. (2006). Kształtowanie się społeczeństwa obywatelskiego w krajach Europy Środkowej i Wschodniej [Formation of civil society in the countries of Central and Eastern Europe]. In A. Antoszewski (Ed.), *Systemy polityczne Europy Środkowo-Wschodniej: Perspektywa porównawcza* [Political systems in Central and Eastern Europe: A comparative perspective] (pp. 35–66). Wrocław: Wydawnictwo Uniwersytetu Wrocławskiego.

15

Media Coverage of Election News in the Republic of Serbia

Misha Nedeljkovich

Serbia and Montenegro dissolved their union recently and for the first time since 1917 became two independent countries. Both countries established themselves as independent parliamentary republics.

A SHORT HISTORY OF DEMOCRATIC ELECTIONS IN THE REGION

Between the end of World War II and the 1990s there was only one democratic election in this region. After World War II, the former Kingdom of Yugoslavia was transformed into the Socialist Republic of Yugoslavia, first under the rule of President Josip Broz Tito (until his death in 1980). Later (1980–1990), the collective presidency leadership of the Socialist Republic took over and led the country until the dissolution of the federal union in the 1990s. The last "democratic" elections in this region where held immediately after the Second World War. In May 1944, a new government of Yugoslavia was established under Ivan Subasic. Tito was made War Minister in this government. Tito and his partisans continued their fight against the German army and in October 1944 helped to liberate Belgrade. In August 1944, Churchill met with Tito in Naples and urged unity, suggesting that Yugoslavia should be a democracy. Tito assured him that he had no intention of introducing Communism into Yugoslavia. Tito, after his meeting with Churchill in August, engaged in discussions with Dr. Ivan Subasic, the Prime Minister of the Yugoslav Monarchy government-in-exile. In November, they reached an agreement on the formation of an interim united Yugoslav government. Under the terms of the agreement, a Regency Council would be established in which Tito would be Premier, Subasic would be Foreign Minister, and free elections would be held. Immediately after the war Tito started to mobilize every single power to win these "free elections." He was against monarchy and instructed all state services under his control to suppress the endeavors of pre-war politicians to return to power. Because of the non-democratic conditions for election campaigning non-communist members of the provisional government left their posts. Tito and his associates were the only powers. The People's Front changed its name to National Liberation Movement, which was the Communist party in reality. Every citizen older than 18, who did not give support to the monarchist forces during the war, could vote. Since voters could select delegates from a single list of members of the National Liberation Movement, November's elections secured Tito's victory over his political opponents.

After those elections, the first true democratic elections in this region (under the multi-party system instituted in 1990) and the first presidential/parliamentary elections were held in 1990. Unfortunately, at that time, Slobodan Milosevic had a firm grip on power in the State of Serbia. He controlled the media and the government apparatus and with a cadre of people changed the membership from the Communist Party of Yugoslavia into the Socialist Party of Serbia. Milosevic was a winner, and new political parties in their infancy were no match for his tightly controlled state apparatus. Two years later, the pressure from a newly developed democratic block was such that he had to allow another election. There was a second Parliamentary and Presidential election, December 20, 1992. This was actually the first democratic election where a serious pre-election campaign developed. This election was preceded by a six week long pre-election campaign (4 November to 17 December 1992). The situation was very complex, civil war had started, and it was difficult to create an atmosphere of impartiality and stability during the election campaign. However, these were the first steps towards a parliamentary democracy in this region.

This paper will discuss media regulation in the Republic of Serbia after the dissolution of its union with the state of Montenegro. Under existing Serbian broadcasting laws, there are two major regulatory bodies: Republic Telecommunications Agency (RTA) is responsible for technical area of broadcasting activities (oversees frequencies, mobile telephony, fixed telephony, radio-connections on ships and planes, Internet, cable distribution), and the Republic Broadcasting Agency (RBA) monitors the operation of broadcasters and decides on requests for physical and legal entities and broadcasters. As in the majority of European countries, the Serbian RBA Council adopts its decisions independently from other bodies and must implement them. However, the RBA has not been able to control the large number of broadcasting outlets operating without licenses—estimated to be as high as 650 active radio and TV stations, making the Republic of Serbia an undisputed leader in TV and radio piracy. The Republic Telecommunications Agency (RTA), despite the evident chaos in the air, has not exercised its right (and obligation) to regulate this situation (Nedeljkovich, 1998).

POLITICAL NEWS COVERAGE—REGULATIONS

Regulatory norms are prescribed by the Republic Broadcasting Agency (RBA), and the Council of the RBA establishes rules and regulations as general binding instruction to radio and television stations for conduct in the course of the pre-election campaign for local, parliamentary, and presidential elections. Radio and television stations of local and regional communities are obligated to ensure free-of-charge and equal broadcasting of presentations of the valid lists of candidates throughout the entire campaign for local elections. Candidates for municipality presidents and mayors may present their programs in person. The law specifies that public service stations are obliged "to ensure free-of-charge and equal broadcasting of the promotion of political parties, coalitions and candidates having accepted election lists for federal, province or local elections during the pre-election campaign; whereas they cannot broadcast paid pre-election…." (Broadcasting Law, Article 78, par 1.6).

In the event they shall decide to report on the course of the pre-election campaign for local elections in their programs, commercial radio and television stations ought to report both based on their editorial policy and the program interests of their audience, and based on the interest of the broader public. It is the right of commercial radio and television stations to determine the manner and portion of programs to be dedicated to the pre-election campaign. In the event commercial radio and television stations shall decide to dedicate a part of their program to presentation of candidate lists free of charge, then such program slots must be equally distributed among all candidates; that is, all lists. In the course of the pre-election campaign, commercial radio and television stations may broadcast paid pre-election advertisements, coverage, and clips of candidate lists under equal program, technical, and financial conditions, without discrimination against any candidate for municipality president or candidate list for aldermen.

The Law on Local Elections requires all radio and television stations "to ensure equality, timeliness, impartiality and completeness of information on all submitters of election lists and the candidates appearing in those lists, as well as on other events significant for the elections, throughout the election campaign" (Art. 4, Para. 2).

Reports on pre-election activities of all candidates from valid lists in daily news and special programs ought to be based on the principles of objectivity, equal representation, and public interest protection, as well as be equally available to all ethnic communities. Only respective election commissions are authorized to announce official information on the election course and results. Any other information must be designated as unofficial. Bearing in mind the conduct of broadcasters in previous pre-election campaigns, the Council emphasizes the following:

- All pre-elections shows, reports, advertising blocks, polls and so on, must be specially designated with a visible designation "pre-election program." Paid times must be designated in TV programs with a designation "paid time" continuously; whereas in radio programs paid times must be distinctly designated as such at the beginning and the end, as well as every 5 minutes during the show;
- All reports on pre-election activities in regular information programs ought to be based also on protecting the general interests of the region's citizens. Reports of agencies researching public opinion may be published provided that they indicate who ordered the poll, the sample polled, manner and duration of the research;
- Street, phone and similar polls with citizens may not be considered representative. In such cases, a broadcaster ought to warn the listeners or viewers of this fact, because their publishing violates the principle of objectivity of reporting;
- Reports on activities of government bodies and officers at all levels shall be published in accordance with the degree of significance of the event and cannot be used for advertising purposes;
- In the course of pre-election campaign, broadcasters ought to exclude from their programs any documentary, feature, and similar shows and films in which candidates from election lists appear, as well as to avoid other forms of indirect political propaganda in their regular shows. Advance announcements of party rallies, panels, and so on, may be broadcast only in paid times;
- Journalists and show hosts who are on election lists cannot appear in radio and television programs for the duration of the pre-election campaign;
- It is the obligation of radio and television stations to record their election related programs and to keep the recordings for a minimum period of 30 days from the date of the initial broadcast;
- Pre-election programs may not be re-broadcast, either directly or indirectly, by other broadcasters, unless they pay a fee;
- In harmony with Art. 38 of the Law on Public Information and Art. 21 of the Broadcasting Law, a broadcaster may refuse to broadcast advertising messages or shows if the broadcaster assesses that they instigate discrimination, hatred, and violence or offend the honor, reputation, or privacy of citizens or other participants in the campaign;
- A broadcaster is obliged to broadcast a reply, that is, correction of information related to pre-election campaign, the next day or before the end of pre-election campaign at the latest, in compliance with Arts. 47 through to 49 of the Law on Public Information.

Taking into consideration the large number of municipalities, elections lists, and candidates, the Republic Public Broadcasting Service (RTS–TV Beograd) is not required to present all candidates from all election lists individually, but is required to abide by the principle of objective reporting and equal representation of election participants. The Province Vojvodina Public Broadcasting Service (RTS–RTV Novi Sad) has special obligations related to adequate representation of the candidates of national and ethnic minorities. Commercial radio and television stations with national or regional coverage are required to cover the pre-election campaign without favoring any individual candidate or election list. This especially refers to broadcasters whose owners, directors, or editors-in-chief are members of a party or coalition.

Reports of scientific polls and surveys must include reports of their methodology. As mentioned above, street, phone, and similar polls with citizens may not be considered representative. Their publishing violates the principle of objectivity of reporting. As in other elections, broadcasters should exclude candidates from any other kind of programming, documentary, or film shown during the pre-election period, based on the Broadcasting Law, the Council of the Republic Broadcasting Agency (RBA) establishes the rules and regulations for presidential elections, and these are similar to those for parliamentary elections.

Media Use and Trust for Political News

It has been difficult for Serbia to move away from the strict centralized control of the media that characterized the system under communist and totalitarian regimes. Journalists were accustomed to being used as political and propaganda tools, and attempts to develop independent and alternative media voices were publicly met with "theats and intimidation and attack" (Matic, 2004). Even since the ouster of Milosevic, the party in power has continued to exert considerable authority over the content and operation of the major public television station, RTS (Bacevic, 1996; Erlangen, 2000).

As in most developed and developing nations, television is the major medium for political information in Serbia. During war periods, national radio broadcasts play an important role (Malešić, 2000). However, in 1998 a U.S. Information Agency (USIA) poll determined that 85% of the population gave television as the source of most of their information on upcoming elections (Malešić, 2000), although less than one-third were willing to acknolwedge that the media influenced their voting choices. One reason for this is the low level of trust in the media. Despite the necessity of relying on the media for news, other opinion research has found low credibility—when asked to judge the best source of conflicting information, 50% said television, 15% chose radio, only 5% trusted newspapers, and almost one-third (30%) felt they could not believe any of the media. The same respondents said that the news media is controlled (72%), performs as propaganda (74%), and can't be trusted (94%) (Malešić, 2000).

TRENDS AND CONTROVERSIAL ISSUES

However, despite the new codification of laws, the control of the media remained similar to the one-party communist controlled system.

> Even after the first multi-party elections, the monopoly of the ruling party over public information persisted. The new party in power strengthened government control over the major media in each country. In Serbia, in fact, the major media function now as a kind of bulletin news release apparatus for the ruling SPS party. (Nedeljkovich, 1998, p. 41)

However, When the SPS lost the local elections of 1996, local media began to tell a different story. This was an important turning point against Milosevic's grip on the country. Despite internal disorganization at the local level, the local newspapers and independent television media continued to provide an alternative, more critical story than that available from the national media, which were under the control of the governing regime (Branković, 1998).

Representatives of the RBA have solicited input from parties and electoral participants about the election broadcasting practices. Several concerns surfaced in these discussions including (1) the belief that TV broadcasters discriminate against some of the political parties and coalitions by their choice of participants in debates and contact shows, along with occasional favoritism toward state officials; (2) some broadcasters almost ignore certain parties and coalitions, not only in election programs but also during their daily news programs; (3) there are no objective criteria for the broadcasting of reports of pre-election party activities; and (4) polls are sometimes published without methodological details

For these reasons, it has been concluded that there is so-called "non-uniform permitted broadcaster practice" (Broadcasting Law, Art. 12, paragraph 2), which led the Council to publish its "Recommendations to Broadcasters" based on the same Article. The behavior of broadcasters will be registered and filed, and, based on Art. 53, paragraph 5, will be taken into account as one of the criteria for granting broadcasting licenses. Based on these discussions RBA had issued additional recommendations to the broadcasters, especially regarding reporting of poll methodologies and the inclusion of all parties in the coverage. In November of 2006, the RBA and RTA also announced new initiatives to shut down unlicensed broadcasters.

Research and Analyses of Media Election Coverage

Considering the fact that the country went through a very painful transition from a Socialist regime (1991–1995) during Milosevic's reign and the violent civil wars (Bosnia, Croatia, and most recently Kosovo), not much academic work could be devoted to electronic media, political communication, and electoral coverage. Some research, however, has documented the favoritism of the RTS system toward the ruling party. In the 1993 elections, RTS aired 184 news stories about parties during the pre-election period. However, smaller parties received very little of this coverage. Overall, eight parties were featured most frequently, receiving an average of 9.4 stories each, whereas 33 smaller parties received an average of just over one story each during the entire period. Overall, RTS gave the ruling party more than 7 times as much coverage as it gave other parties (Nedeljkovich, 1998).

The 1996 election news was just as imbalanced. The RTS goverment television system gave 11 news stories favoring the government party for every one news story on the opposition. For instance, in the first week of the 1996 campaign, the ruling party received 43.33 minutes of coverage; the combined total for opposition parties was a mere 3.1 minutes. In the last week of the campaign, the ruling party received 99.18 minutes of news coverage compared to only 3.40 minutes for opposition parties (Branković, 1998).

Even more recent changes have left uncertainty and instability in the major media establishment. Some monitoring projects have concluded that the national media now appear to be simply negative in their coverage of politics. Without visible political bias, the stories on national television were characterized by an independent institute as portraying the paraties as negative, "without much difference among them" (Radosavljevic, 2002).

The Internet may offer some hope for the future, but now its penetration is not sufficiently high to provide immediate help for the dissemination of political information in Serbia. Only 24% of population in Serbia has Internet access. However, some media outlets have been able to take advantage of Internet distribution capabilities. For instance, Radio B92 has the most frequently visited website in Serbia (Rankovic, 2007), and other media outlets will surely emulate its success in providing more outlets for diverse viewpoints.

The future for Serbia's media and their role in the continuing democratization are still evolving. The media still live in the shadow of the one-party communist domination followed by the same iron-fist control of the Milosevic era. Even now, the mainstream state media often find it difficult to sever the ties to a more subtle but still present authoritarian presence (Radosavljevic, 2002).

REFERENCES

Bacevic, L. J. (1996). Access to the media and the multiparty system in Serbia. *International Communication Gazette, 57*(3), 161–179.

Branković, S. (1998). The media in Serbia. *South East Europe Review, 3,* 135–142.

Erlangen, S. (2000, December 17). Milosevic's servile network now bows to its new masters, *New York Times*, p, 1.

Law on Broadcasting. (2002; amended 2005).

Law on Electing the President of the Republic of Serbia (1990, as amended 2004). Retrieved June 23, 2007, from: http://www.legislationline.org/legislation.php?tid=57&lid=411&less=false.

Law on Free Access to Information of Public Importance. (2004).Retrieved June 23, 2007, from: http://www.poverenik.org.yu/Dokumentacija/eng_23_ldok.pdf

Law on Local Elections. (2002). Retrieved June 23, 2007, from: http://www.legislationline.org/upload/old/0d8d99ead530542ed63af7e60f5fa07d.pdf.

Maleśić, M. (2000*). Peace support operations, mass media, and the public in former Yugoslavia*. Stockholm: Styrelsen för Psykologiskt Försvar.

Matic, J. (2004). Problems facing quality press development in Serbia. In O. Spassov (Ed.), *Quality press in Southeast Europe* (pp. 254–276). Sofia: SOEMZ.

Nedeljkovich, M. (1998). The making of post-socialist media: A case of F.R. Yugoslavia. *World Communication, 27*(1), 41–54.

Radosavljevic, V. (2002, February 18). Pressures on media in Serbia: Between black and white. *Southeast European Media Journal, Mediaonline*. Retrieved June 23, 2007 from: http://mediaonline.ba/en/?ID=194

Rankovic, L. (2007, April 19). Serbian media between alternative past and future. *EUMap.org*. Retrieved June 23, 2007, from http://www.eumap.org/journal/submitted.

16

Democratzation and Election News Coverage in Brazil

Mauro P. Porto

Brazilian elections have some distinctive features that lead to unique patterns of political communication. The sheer magnitude of the country's electoral and media systems is one of them. On the one hand, Brazil has the second largest electorate among the world's liberal democracies.[1] On the other, most electoral communication in this complex democracy is mediated by a television system dominated by one of the biggest global media empires. According to *Variety* magazine, Globo Organizations, TV Globo's parent company, is the planet's 16th largest media conglomerate.[2]

This general context suggests that analyses of electoral processes in Brazil that neglect the role of the news media are flawed. This is particularly true in relation to campaigns that followed the return of democracy in 1985, since they took place after the consolidation of a powerful cultural industry. Dominated by TV Globo, this complex and diversified media system became the main arena in which the drama of political power has been played out in Brazil.

This chapter analyzes trends in Brazilian electoral news in the last two decades. The objective is to identify the main features of campaign coverage by the media in general and by TV Globo in particular.

BRAZILIAN POLITICS

Electoral campaigns are always shaped by the broader political context, especially in terms of electoral and party systems, legal frameworks, and political history.

Brazil's current political system was deeply impacted by the military dictatorship that ruled the country between 1964 and 1985. During most of the authoritarian period, the regime imposed a two-party system.[3] To maintain a democratic façade, the military created an "Electoral College," made up of Congress members and representatives of state assemblies, which was put in charge of electing presidents for a six-year term. By the mid-1970s and early 1980s, economic stagnation, the electoral growth of the opposition, and a more organized civil society forced the regime to initiate a process of political openness that was designed to be "slow, gradual, and safe." Nevertheless, public support for the regime declined even further during General João Batista de Figueiredo's Presidency (1979–1985). The final blow came in 1984 when a massive pro-democracy movement led by opposition parties, including PMDB, as well as by civic groups, demanded direct elections for president. The campaign *Diretas Já* (Elections Now) gathered the largest demonstrating crowds in Brazil's history, with approximately 10 million people participating in rallies all over the country (Alves, 1988). Although the movement failed to get a constitutional amendment approved in Congress that would have restored direct elections for president, it had a devastating impact on the regime. PDS leaders, including its former president José Sarney, left the party and in 1985 formed the *Partido da Frente Liberal* (PFL; Liberal Front Party). The dissidents decided to join forces with the main opposition party (PMDB) and to take part in the indirect elections scheduled to January 1985. The "Democratic Alliance" between PMDB and PFL launched a ticket with the names of Tancredo Neves for President and José Sarney for Vice-President. Neves was a moderate PMDB member and was able to defeat the PDS candidate, Paulo Maluf, in the Electoral College.

Although the 1985 presidential election was indirect, the Neves-Sarney ticket was supported by a massive movement that gathered huge and enthusiastic crowds in rallies conducted around the country. The media in general, and TV Globo in particular, played a key role in mobilizing popular support for the transfer of power via the Electoral College by appropriating the symbols of the *Diretas Já* campaign and linking them to Tancredo's candidacy (Alves, 1988; Guimarães & Amaral, 1990). Popular enthusiasm was nevertheless soon replaced by bewilderment when Neves was hospitalized the night before he was supposed to take office. In an unexpected turn of events, José Sarney was sworn in as President on March 15, 1985. After several surgeries and weeks of a televised national drama, Neves died on April 21.

During José Sarney's term in the presidency (1985–1989), civil and political liberties were reestablished, and the bicameral Congress that was elected in 1986 was given the task of writing a new Constitution. Despite important advances in political democratization, Sarney's presidency was plagued by hyperinflation, failed economic stabilization packages, and corruption charges. The first presidential election of the democratic period took place in 1989 in this context of low presidential popularity and disillusionment with the new democracy.

The 1988 Constitution maintained presidentialism as the system of government, as well as a bicameral Congress, which includes a lower house (*Câmara dos Deputados*) and a Senate. The electoral system for selecting the members of the lower house is based on proportional representation, resulting in a multiparty system. Twenty political parties were represented in the 513-member *Câmara dos Deputados* that was inaugurated on February 1, 2007.[4] Nevertheless, four of these parties are dominant, accounting for 58% of the seats:

- *Partido do Movimento Democrático Brasileiro* (PMDB; Brazilian Democratic Movement Party): 90 seats. Centrist ideological orientation;
- *Partido dos Trabalhadores* (PT; Workers Party): 83 seats. Leftist ideological orientation;
- *Partido da Social-Democracia Brasileira* (PSDB; Brazilian Social Democracy Party): 63 seats. Center-left of the ideological spectrum;
- *Partido da Frente Liberal* (PFL; Liberal Front Party): 61 seats. Conservative ideological orientation.

These parties have been dominant forces in the electoral contests that took place in Brazil after the return of democracy in 1985. With the exception of the first election in 1989, presidential contests have been polarized between PT and PSDB candidates. PSDB was founded in 1988 by PMDB dissidents who became unsatisfied with the party's trajectory during the Constitutional Assembly (1986–1988) and with president Sarney's administration. One of its leaders, sociologist Fernando Henrique Cardoso, was elected president in 1994 and reelected in 1998. PT was founded in 1980 by a coalition of trade union leaders, intellectuals, small leftist groups, and sectors of the progressive branch of the Catholic Church. Particularly important in the foundation of the party was the new trade union movement that emerged in the industrial metropolitan areas surrounding the city of São Paulo. Led by metalworker Luís Inácio Lula da Silva (or simply "Lula"), the movement shook the foundations of the military dictatorship in the late 1970s through massive strikes. Lula became PT's leader and the party's presidential candidate in the five presidential elections that followed, becoming president in 2002 and being reelected in 2006.

A TELEVISION-CENTERED MEDIA SYSTEM

Electoral campaigns are shaped not only by features of the political system, but also by the structures that mediate the communication between elites, candidates, and voters. It is important to stress two key features of Brazil's media system: terrestrial television is the dominant medium, and TV Globo is the dominant force.

The centrality of television becomes clear when we compare it to other media. Brazil has a diversified print media market, with more then five hundred dailies, but only four of them sell more than 200,000 copies per day: *Folha de S. Paulo*, *O Estado de S. Paulo*, *O Globo*, and *Extra*.[5] These are small numbers for a country with more than 188 million inhabitants. Only 45 newspapers are sold per 1,000 inhabitants every day, putting Brazil in 50th place in the international ranking of newspaper circulation.[6] Although newspapers have limited penetration, they play an important agenda-setting function among opinion leaders, since the national elite monitors them very closely (Azevedo, 2006; Kucinski, 1998; Lima, 2006). There are three main weekly newsmagazines in Brazil (*Veja*, *Época*, and *Isto É*), but they also have a limited penetration.[7]

Radio reaches a broader audience and has a diversified market structure, but it has not developed a national character in Brazil and its fragmented audiences tend to use it mostly for musical entertainment, instead of as a news source (Straubhaar, 1996, pp. 223–224). Despite these limitations, radio talk shows are a significant source of political information, especially among the low-income population, as demonstrated by the significant number of show hosts who become politicians and achieve success in electoral processes (Esch, 1999; Moreira, 1998; Nunes, 2000). News programs on radio play an important role in state and municipal elections, although there are very few studies of campaign news coverage in this medium (see Chaia, Val, & Nepomuceno, 2003).

New technologies did not bring radical changes to Brazil's communications landscape. Only 12% of the population has access to subscription television, which includes cable and satellite services (GrupodeMídia, 2006, p. 221). In the case of the Internet, only 12% of households have access to the Web (Azevedo, 2006, p. 96). Brazil's high levels of social inequality help explain the limited impact of new technologies (Porto, 1999).

Television has a central position in Brazilian society and TV Globo is the dominant force. The network emerged when Roberto Marinho, the owner of the newspaper *O Globo*, launched his first TV station in the city of Rio de Janeiro in 1965, one year after the military coup. Marinho's entrance into the television market was facilitated by a financial and technical agreement signed in 1962 with the American Time-Life group, which included a $6 million interest-free loan.[8] In the late 1960s, the television market was integrated by a telecommunications infrastructure built by the state, which allowed the interconnection of broadcasting stations through the microwave and satellite systems. TV Globo's prime time newscast *Jornal Nacional* was launched on September 1, 1969, as the first program broadcast simultaneously to all affiliated stations of the same group. By the early 1970s, TV Globo had become a virtual monopoly, concentrating more than 70% of the national audience. As several authors have shown, TV Globo's consolidation was connected to the military's project of "national integration," which aimed at the creation of a national consumer market, as well as at establishing a platform to legitimate the regime and build ideological consensus (Caparelli, 1982; Fox, 1997; Jambeiro, 2001; Kehl, 1986; Lima, 1988; Mattos, 2000; Ortiz, 1989; Sinclair, 1999).

TV Globo faced a relative decline in its audience ratings in the late 1980s and early 1990s (Borelli & Priolli, 2000), but it maintains a dominant position in Brazil's communication system. In 2005, TV Globo had a 52% share of the national audience between 7:00 a.m. and midnight. Moreover, its share increases to 56% during primetime (6:00 p.m. to midnight), when more people watch television (GrupodeMídia, 2006, pp. 163–170). Thus, TV Globo's prime time programs (newscasts and *telenovelas*) are the main sources of information and entertainment for Brazilians. The prime time newscast *Jornal Nacional*, in particular, has a ubiquitous presence in Brazilian households, with very high audience ratings. In São Paulo and Rio de Janeiro, the biggest Brazilian cities, 34% of the households watch the newscast everyday, with an audience share (percentage of households with TV sets on) of 50% and 56%, respectively.[9] *Jornal Nacional* is also a major source of political information during elections. According to a survey that took place right after the 2002 general elections, 29% of voters watched *Jornal Nacional* everyday, 45% watched it at least once a week, while only 26% said they rarely or never watched the newscast (Porto, 2007a).

TV Globo's parent company, *Organizações Globo* (Globo Organizations), has a strong position not only in the terrestrial television market, but in the entire media and telecommunications sector.[10] Since television is the dominant medium and Globo Organizations are the dominant force, the analysis that follows focuses on TV Globo and its main newscast, *Jornal Nacional*.

MEDIA AND ELECTIONS IN DEMOCRATIC BRAZIL

In the last two decades, political communication has become a significant area of studies in Brazil. Previous literature reviews have demonstrated that the role of the news media in elections has been a major concern of the new field (Nunes, 2004; Rubim & Azevedo, 1998; Rubim & Colling, 2004). Nevertheless, most studies about journalism and elections in Brazil are impressionistic, failing to provide consistent evidence about general news coverage patterns. More recently, however, scholars have developed more systematic content analyses of electoral news coverage (Albuquerque, 1994; Alde, 2004; Azevedo, 2000; Cervi, 2003; Lattman-Weltman, Carneiro, & Ramos, 1994; Lima, 2001, pp. 269–322; Miguel, 2000a, 2004; Porto, Vasconcelos, & Bastos, 2004). Research about journalism and elections in Brazil also rarely investigates the effects of campaign news coverage on voters' behaviors and attitudes, with few studies using survey data to identify the effects of media exposure on voters' behaviors and preferences (e.g. Boas, 2005; Porto, 2007a; Straubhaar, Olsen, & Nunes, 1993).

This section summarizes academic research about news coverage patterns of the first five general presidential elections of the democratic period.[11] Whenever possible, the discussion will consider the effects of this coverage on voters' preferences and attitudes. Each of the five elections is considered separately.

1989: The Rise of Collor de Mello

The first presidential election of the democratic period sparked a wave of studies about the role of the media. The context of this election was characterized by corruption scandals, the rejection of President Sarney's administration, and popular disillusionment with the new democracy. The main candidates were all strong opponents of Sarney and his PMDB-led government. Early on, in late 1988 and early 1989, two leftist members of the opposition held the leading positions in the polls: Lula, from the Workers Party (PT), and Leonel Brizola, from the Labor Democratic Party (PDT). Candidates of stronger and more traditional political parties, which were part of Sarney's coalition, had a mediocre performance in the polls, including Ulysses Guimarães (PMDB) and Aureliano Chaves (PFL).

In the first months of 1989, a political phenomenon emerged. In April, the relatively unknown candidate Fernando Collor de Mello became the front-runner in the polls, leaving Lula and Brizola in the struggle for second place. Collor was the candidate of *Partido da Reconstrução Nacional* (PRN, Party of National Reconstruction), a label that was created by him the previous year to launch his candidacy. Collor was then governor of the small and backward state of Alagoas and began to attract national attention because of his strong opposition to President Sarney and because of his moralistic campaigns to clean his state and the country of corruption. Collor's dramatic rise in the polls took place right after his appearances in the television programs of PRN and of two other small parties that were broadcast between March 30 and May 18 (Lima, 2001). He would end up winning the election, with 30.5% of the valid votes in the first round (against Lula's 17.2%) and 53% in the second (against Lula's 47%).

The rise to power of outsider Collor de Mello has been explained in terms of several factors, including his sophisticated political marketing strategy and neopopulist rhetoric. One of the most frequent interpretations posits that biased news coverage, especially from TV Globo, was a key factor explaining his election (Boas, 2005; Lattman-Weltman et al., 1994; Lima, 1993, 2001; Rubim, 1999). These studies suggest that media mogul Roberto Marinho manipulated his communications empire to favor Collor and to prevent the election of either Lula or Brizola.

Although it is commonly argued that news coverage of the 1989 presidential election was consistently biased, few studies have applied content analysis to demonstrate this claim. The authors that cite more specific numbers about inequalities in terms of airtime distribution rely on data gathered by public opinion institutes, newspaper clipping services, or by an office of the Ministry of Communication, which were publicized at the time by the press (Lima, 2001; Rubim, 1999). Venicio Lima (2001) briefly mentions the results of a content analysis of TV Globo's *Jornal Nacional*, which found that Collor received more airtime in the first round (17.1%, compared to 12.2% of Brizola and 10.7% of Lula), as well as in the second round (54.4%, compared to 45.6% of Lula). Nevertheless, the author provides no details on the sample or on the methodological procedures of the content analysis.

Although evidence of a pro-Collor bias in TV Globo's news coverage of the 1989 presidential election is not always consistent, one famous episode demonstrated the partisan attitude of the network. In the eve of the second round of the election, on December 14, Collor and Lula participated in the last of two televised debates. The next day, the newscast *Jornal Nacional* presented a summary of the debate that clearly favored Collor. First, there were quantitative differences. The PRN candidate took 69.2% of the airtime (3 minutes, 28 seconds), while Lula got only 30.8% (2 minutes, 17 seconds).[12] Collor also appeared more frequently then Lula (8 and 7 times, respectively). Second, there were qualitative inequalities. While Collor appeared assertive and attacked his opponents several times, Lula was shown in a defensive position.

More evidence of the manipulation of news coverage by TV Globo in this election, which has not been considered by previous studies, are the two news stories broadcast by *Jornal Nacional* right after the controversial debate summary. The reports described and evaluated the performance of the two presidential candidates in the debate. First, there were quantitative inequalities. Collor's news story took more airtime (1 minute, 46 seconds, compared to Lula's 1 minute, 10 seconds). Collor also appeared more frequently (2 sound bites, compared to Lula's single sound bite) and spoke longer (34 seconds, compared to Lula's 18 seconds). Second, there were qualitative differences. While Lula was shown in a small room with PT leaders, Collor's report showed the enthusiasm of his supporters and suggested that the election was decided, since the candidate was already planning the formation of his cabinet.

It would be of course inappropriate to suggest that a single news broadcast can decide an election, but some evidence suggests that the editing of the debate by *Jornal Nacional* and these two news stories had an important impact in a close race. Daily tracking polls by the IBOPE Institute showed that support for Lula, which had been growing, began to fall slightly after the second debate and TV Globo's controversial edited version (Straubhaar, Olsen, & Nunes, 1993, p. 133). Carlos Matheus, then director of the Gallup Institute, argued that the media in general, and *Jornal Nacional* in particular, amplified the positive evaluation of Collor's performance in the debate (Conti, 1999).

Whatever effects the editing of the debate had on voting behavior, it became a major symbol of TV Globo's political manipulation of news coverage. Due to the controversies that followed, the network decided that it would never again broadcast summaries of debates between candidates.

1994: Cardoso and the New Consensus

Collor de Mello took office in March 1990, but he soon ran into trouble. His short-lived Presidency was characterized by failed attempts to stabilize the economy and by political scandals. In an interview to the newsmagazine, *Veja,* in May 1992, the president's brother, Pedro Collor, denounced a corruption scheme in the federal government led by Paulo Cesar Farias, the former campaign treasurer of Collor de Mello. After months of investigations, the Chamber of Deputies began an impeachment process in August, forcing Collor out of the Presidency. In December, the Senate concluded the process by voting to impeach the first elected president of the new democracy.

After Collor's downfall, Vice-President Itamar Franco took office and established a new government based on a broad coalition. Nevertheless, hyperinflation continued to plague the country and Franco searched for a plan to stabilize the economy. In May 1993, he invited then Minister of Foreign Affairs, Fernando Henrique Cardoso, to become the new Finances Minister. Cardoso was an internationally known sociologist and one of the founders of the Brazilian Social Democracy Party (PSDB). He launched a new economic plan, named *Plano Real*, which was able to contain inflation and bring the long-desired economic stability. Because of his achievements as head of the Ministry of Finances, Cardoso was launched as the official presidential candidate. His main opponent was PT's Lula, in his second presidential bid.

Scholarly analyses of news coverage of the 1994 presidential election have focused on how the media provided strong support for the new economic plan and his mentor, candidate Fernando Henrique Cardoso. Albuquerque (1994) developed a content analysis of *Jornal Nacional*'s coverage of the early campaign period, between March and May, identifying important inequalities. According to the author, Cardoso received 37% of the total airtime, while Lula came in second with 23%. Cardoso also was shown speaking more frequently, with 29 sound bites, compared to Lula's 16 sound bites. The two candidates were also framed in very different ways by TV Globo's main newscast. While Cardoso was presented in terms of his ability to unify political forces and build consensus, Lula was associated to interest groups (particularly to trade unions) and to conflict and discord. Several other studies stressed how the media contributed to build a consensus around the new economic plan, building a scenario that favored the candidacy of Cardoso (Kucinski, 1998; Miguel, 2000b; Rubim, 1999).

The role of the media in the 1994 election was revealed by a curious episode. When Cardoso left the Ministry of Finances to become a presidential candidate in March, he was replaced by diplomat and former U.S. ambassador Rubens Ricúpero. On September 1, one month before the election, Ricúpero was talking informally with TV Globo's journalist Carlos Monforte while waiting to give a live interview. Not aware that the conversation was being sent to the satellite, Ricúpero started to speak with the journalist about how he was allowing the media to support Cardoso in an indirect way. Ricúpero said that he was very useful to TV Globo because the network could give space and special treatment to him as the Finance Minister and to *Plano Real*, instead of supporting Fernando Henrique openly, and nobody could complain. Some viewers who owned parabolic antennas recorded the "informal" conversation and the candidates opposing Cardoso made it public. As a result of the exposé, President Itamar Franco fired Ricúpero.

Despite the scandal, the episode did not affect Cardoso's standing in the polls. He continued to lead and won in the first round, with 54% of valid votes, with Lula in second place with 27%. Although the scandal did not affect the outcome of the election, it revealed how *Plano Real* was making it possible for the media, particularly for TV Globo, to favor Cardoso in more subtle ways, by supporting his economic plan.

1998: The Invisible Election

Fernando Henrique Cardoso took office on January 1, 1995, enjoying a national consensus around his new economic plan that was partially built by the media. In the years that followed, he implemented a series of economic and political reforms, which included the privatization of major state-owned companies. With the continuous success of *Plano Real* in terms of inflation control and the resulting levels of popular support, Cardoso decided to initiate a movement to change the Brazilian Constitution, so as to allow presidents to run for a second term. The political coalition that supported Cardoso was successful in these efforts and he launched his bid for reelection in 1998. His main opponent was, again, PT's Lula.

Although the media was generally supportive of Cardoso and his policies, the news agenda in the first half of 1998 did not favor the incumbent. There were several reports about Cardoso's inability to confront urgent problems, including a drought in the Northeast, a fire in the Amazon rain forest, and growing unemployment (Azevedo, 2000; Lima, 2001; Miguel, 2000a, 2002). The reelection of *Plano Real*'s creator seemed threatened by this difficult scenario. In fact, Lula improved his standing in the polls and by the end of May he had achieved a technical tie with Cardoso.

In the case of TV Globo's *Jornal Nacional*, one study showed that there was no relevant bias in terms of airtime distribution or in the number of appearances of presidential candidates (Miguel, 2000a). But the more balanced coverage did not mean that *Jornal Nacional* did not affect the outcome of the election. One of the most consistent and striking findings of studies about the 1998 election is the decline of *Jornal Nacional*'s campaign coverage, which eliminated from the agenda the social problems that embarrassed the government in previous months. Greater emphasis was given instead to soft news, including reports on trivial events involving media personalities and bizarre cases with animals (Azevedo, 2000; Colling, 2000; Kucinski, 1998; Lima, 2001; Miguel, 2000a, 2002). Thus, *Jornal Nacional* helped Cardoso in more indirect terms, by de-politicizing and shrinking the campaign coverage. In this way, the negative social problems that had dominated the agenda in the previous months tended to disappear.

The media built a scenario favorable to the reelection of Cardoso not only by presenting a reduced and de-politicized news coverage, but also by framing the economy in particular ways. When the Brazilian economy begun facing severe difficulties in August, few months before the election, a major issue became how the media would frame the causes of the instability. Cardoso's campaign interpreted Brazil's difficulties as a result of problems at the international level, especially after the Russian crisis. The media in general, and *Jornal Nacional* in particular, strongly supported this frame, marginalizing alternative viewpoints, including those from opposition candidates (Azevedo, 2000; Colling, 2000; Lima, 2001; Miguel, 2000a, 2002; Soares, 2000).

Fernando Henrique Cardoso was reelected in the first round with 53% of the valid ballots, with Lula again coming in second place, with 32% of the vote. The 1998 election was the "coldest" in Brazil's recent history. The limited news coverage, the absence of television debates between the candidates, and the shrinking of the political advertising time period from 60 to 45 days, led to an electoral campaign with little debate of substantive issues. On the other hand, the issue that attracted most media attention, the economy, was framed in a way that supported the position of the incumbent candidate.

2002: Lula's Victory and the Shifts in News Coverage

Fernando Henrique Cardoso faced great difficulties in his second term. The consensus around him and his economic policies began to erode after he devaluated the real in January 1999, causing the Brazilian currency to lose about 40% of its value in relation to the dollar (Miguel, 2000a, p. 79). His popularity levels declined steadily after that. The period preceding the 2002 general elections was marked by popular disillusionment with Cardoso's administration and by a clear desire for change. It was in this context that Cardoso's PSDB launched his Minister of Health, José Serra, as a presidential candidate. The main opponent of the social democrats was, again, PT's Lula, in his fourth bid for the presidency.

The 2002 presidential election was marked by very significant shifts in electoral news coverage. In a clear contrast with the cold and depoliticized coverage in 1998, the media gave unprecedented levels of attention to the campaign. In the case of TV Globo's *Jornal Nacional*, the changes were dramatic. While in 1998 *Jornal Nacional* devoted only 5% of its total airtime to election coverage, in 2002 the topic took 31% of the newscast airtime (Miguel, 2004). There were several other significant changes in *Jornal Nacional*'s campaign coverage. For the first time in TV Globo's history, the newscast held live interviews with presidential candidates. There were two rounds of 10 minute-long interviews with the four main candidates (Lula, José Serra, Ciro Gomes, and Anthony Garotinho) before the first round of the election and two rounds of interviews with Lula and Serra before the second round. *Jornal Nacional* also created a thematic series with longer and in-depth analysis of national problems, including the economy, education, and social inequality. Thus, through live interviews and special thematic reports, there was a remarkable growth of issue news coverage on the part of the nation's main newscast.

Another significant change was the general "impartiality" of the media, in terms of the space and airtime dedicated to each of the four main candidates. A content analysis of four of the most important daily newspapers showed that the campaign news coverage was generally neutral in terms of candidates' visibility, with the official candidate, José Serra, benefiting from a slightly more positive coverage (Alde, 2004).[13] In the case of TV Globo, *Jornal Nacional*'s coverage was generally neutral in terms or airtime distribution and number of appearances of the four main presidential candidates. A content analysis of all broadcasts by *Jornal Nacional* between June and October showed that the four main candidates got almost the same number of news stories, the same amount of airtime, and the same number of sound bites (Porto et al., 2004). Interviews with *Jornal Nacional*'s anchor and with TV Globo's main news editors suggest that this equality in terms of airtime was a result of a deliberate policy aimed at avoiding accusations of bias and at recovering the credibility of the network (Porto, 2007b).

Although news coverage was generally balanced, the media played a significant role by framing the main campaign issue, the economy, in particular ways. In 2002 Brazil faced high levels of distrust by foreign investors, especially Wall Streets banks, which led to a rapid increase in Brazil's risk premium and a significant devaluation of the national currency (Martínez & Santiso, 2003; Porto, 2007a; Spanakos & Rennó, 2006). Content analysis data show that *Jornal Nacional* helped to frame the economy in a restricted way, supporting the interpretation that was promoted by Cardoso's administration and by financial markets, while marginalizing the perspectives of opposition candidates (Miguel, 2004; Porto et al., 2004). Moreover, this restricted news coverage had important effects on the campaign. Survey data show that exposure to *Jornal Nacional* had a positive and significant effect on voters' attitudes, increasing support for the interpretation that economic instability was the country's most important problem. In this way, news coverage contributed to marginalizing the interpretation promoted by the opposition, which emphasized Brazil's dramatic social problems, including poverty and social inequality, as the most important issues (Porto, 2007a).

The 2002 election represents a major shift in campaign news coverage in Brazil. The media in general, and TV Globo in particular, not only provided extensive news coverage of the elections, but increased the discussion of issues through live interviews with the candidates and thematic reports. In the case of *Jornal Nacional*, there were unprecedented levels of impartiality in terms of airtime distribution between the main candidates. The creation of a more balanced political field by the media is one of the factors that explains why challenger Luis Inácio Lula da Silva was able to succeed in his fourth presidential bid.[14]

2006: The Return of News Bias? Lula and Media Scandals

Lula took office in January 2003 enjoying high levels of popular support, but his first term was shaken by several political scandals involving some of the President's closest advisors and friends. In June 2005, the *mensalão* scandal broke when house representative Roberto Jefferson (PTB) denounced high ranking members of the president's party (PT) for paying a monthly allowance of 30,000 reais (about $12,500) to Congress members for their continuing support in passing legislation. The scandal of the *sanguessugas* (bloodsuckers) emerged in 2006, when it was discovered that dozens of Congress representatives, including members of the government coalition, received paybacks for approving budget amendments allocating funds for the purchase ambulances. One of the companies that manufactured ambulances and bribed representatives was Planam, owned by the Vedoim family. These and other scandals led to the firing or resignation of several members of the President's cabinet.

When Lula decided to run for reelection in 2006, another major scandal broke in the eve of the presidential election. It was discovered that two members of the family Vedoim, already involved in the *sanguessugas* scandal, had established contacts with high-ranking members of the Workers Party (PT). The Vedoims offered to sell a "dossier" containing a video and photographs involving two key PSDB leaders (presidential candidate Geraldo Alckmin and José Serra, candidate for governor in the state of São Paulo) in the illegal scheme used for the purchase of ambulances. On September 16, two weeks before the first round of the 2006 election, the Federal Police detained two PT members in a hotel with 1.7 million reais (approximately $790,000). The money was to be used to purchase the dossier against Alckmin and Serra. This was the beginning of the "dossier scandal," which involved at least seven leading figures of the Workers Party.

Until the time of this writing (February 2007), few studies have been concluded about the news coverage of the 2006 election. In an analysis that took place before the first round of the election, Venicio Lima (2006) argued that coverage of the main scandals in 2005 and 2006 by the print media and by TV Globo was severely biased against Lula and his party. According to the author, news coverage of scandals was dominated by the "guilty presumption frame," which was based on the assumption that the president knew about the irregularities and that he was responsible for them.

A systematic content analysis of election news coverage by the three newspapers with the highest circulation revealed that there was a significant increase of news coverage when compared to the previous election in 2002, with Lula attracting most coverage (Alde, Mendes, & Figueiredo, 2007). His strong presence in the press was a result of his dual status as president and as candidate, as well as of the extensive news coverage of scandals. Thus, despite his high visibility, the great majority of reports about the President had a negative tone, while news coverage of Lula's main opponent, Geraldo Alckmin, had a predominantly positive tone.

In the case of TV Globo, new accusations of bias emerged during the 2006 presidential campaign. On September 29, a few days before the first round of the election, the newscast *Jornal Nacional* presented several photographs taken by the Federal Police of the 1.7 million reais that had been apprehended with PT militants during the dossier scandal. The pile of notes on a table became a visual symbol of the scandal and the emphasis on the photographs given by *Jornal Nacional* contributed to amplify its impact. In a front page news story of its October 18 issue, the newsmagazine *Carta Capital* denounced the fact that the photographs had been leaked to the media by a Federal Police officer who wanted to damage Lula's candidature and prevent him from winning in the first round of the election. The newsmagazine alleged that TV Globo and several newspapers actively participated in the plot against Lula, failing to report the involvement of PSDB politicians in the *sanguessugas* scandal.[15]

In sum, the 2006 campaign news coverage was extensive and highly concentrated on scandals involving the party of the incumbent candidate. This focus on exposés and negative news for the PT raised new accusations of media bias. One remarkable aspect of the 2006 election is the fact that despite the negative tone of news coverage, Lula was reelected with relative ease, with 48.6% of the valid votes in the first round and 60.8% in the second round (against 39.2% of Alckmin). What explains Lula's successful electoral performance in the context of a highly negative news agenda? As several authors show, Lula's social policy was a major factor in the election (Hunter & Power, 2007; Oliveira, 2006). The centerpiece of the President's social policy was the *Bolsa Famiília* (Family Grant), a program that involves a monthly transfer of cash to low income families. Lula expanded the program in the second half of his first term in office. By the end of 2006, some 11 million families were receiving the benefit. Studies show that there was a strong correlation between Lula's vote share and the share of families covered by the Grant (Hunter & Power, 2007; Oliveira, 2006).

PATTERNS OF NEWS COVERAGE: A STUDY OF JORNAL NACIONAL

In the previous sections, I presented a brief review of academic research on electoral news in Brazil. As we have seen, most studies on campaign coverage focus on a single election and therefore fail to analyze patterns of news content across time.[16] This section presents the first systematic analysis of news coverage of the five presidential elections that took place after the re-democratization of the country in 1985. More specifically, it discusses the results of a content analysis of Brazil's main newscast, TV Globo's *Jornal Nacional*, during the presidential elections of 1989, 1994, 1998, 2002, and 2006. The sample includes 60 full broadcasts of the newscast, 12 from each year, which were aired in the three weeks preceding the first round of each election.[17]

The analysis is based on the assumption that the deepening of democracy in Brazil in the period under consideration (1985–2006) will lead to a process of "media opening," in which the media become more independent of official control and more representative of societal viewpoints

(Lawson, 2002). In particular, I argue that democratization will lead to significant improvements in election news in terms of balance and in terms of the growth of issue-oriented coverage.

As we have seen, most studies about media and elections in Brazil identify a tradition of political bias in TV Globo's journalism. Nevertheless, it is important to stress that the network has gone through an important process of openness since the mid-1990s. As I demonstrate in more detail elsewhere (Porto, 2007b), TV Globo reformed its News Division through changes in managerial roles and in news presentation styles, leading to a journalism model with less reliance on official sources and more balanced political coverage. One of the central aims of this process of reform was to recover the network's credibility in a period of increasing social and political democratization.

Based on these assumptions, I present the following hypothesis: the deepening of democracy in Brazil will lead to important changes in TV Globo's electoral news coverage, including: (1) an increase of issue news coverage; (2) a decline of horse race coverage; and (3) a decline of bias in terms of division of airtime between the main presidential candidates. Next, I test this hypothesis with content analysis.

Amount of Electoral News Coverage

I start by identifying the amount of electoral news coverage presented by Brazil's main newscast. Figure 16.1 below presents the airtime devoted by *Jornal Nacional* to electoral coverage in general and to presidential campaigns in particular. The results show very significant differences in the levels of attention devoted to elections, especially in 1998 and 2006. As far as 1998 is concerned, the data confirm the findings of other studies that showed the "invisibility" of the campaign in TV Globo's main newscast: only 7.8% of *Jornal Nacional*'s total airtime was devoted to elections. On the other hand, 2006 registered a significant increase of airtime devoted to electoral news, with more than two thirds of *Jornal Nacional*'s total airtime devoted to the topic. How to explain these differences?

In the case of the 1998 election, some accounts suggest that President Cardoso met with

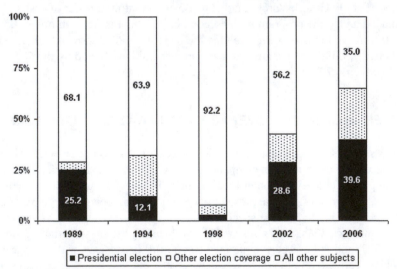

Note: the category "Other election coverage" includes all news stories about elections for Congress, Governorships, and State Assemblies. It also includes general reports about he electoral process that do not specify a specific level (presidential, congressional, etc.).

FIGURE 16.1   Airtime devoted to Brazilian elections by Jornal Nacional (percentages).

media owners in May to complain about the negative tone of the news agenda and to alert them to the fact that the continuation of such coverage could lead to Lula's victory. According to some authors, the media responded by cutting political coverage (Kucinski, 1998; Venturi, 2000). Another reason for the huge decline of election news coverage during Cardoso's reelection was the rise of a market-driven journalism at TV Globo, with a corresponding decline of political news coverage in general and electoral news coverage in particular (Lima, 2001; Miguel, 2000a, 2002; Porto, 2007b). This trend toward tabloidization took place during Mário Marona's term as editor-in-chief of *Jornal Nacional* (1996–1999), but it declined after anchor William Bonner replaced Marona in September 1999 (Porto, 2007b).

In 2006, the increase of campaign coverage was due to the focus on denunciations and exposés, especially those involving incumbent candidate Luís Inácio Lula da Silva. *Jornal Nacional* devoted an impressive 46% of its total campaign news coverage airtime to scandals or corruption. The great majority of reports in this category dealt with the "dossier scandal" that broke out in the period of analysis, in the two weeks preceding the first round of the elections.

Issues and Horse Race in *Jornal Nacional*'s Electoral Coverage

The main hypothesis of this case study about *Jornal Nacional* predicts an increase of issue news coverage. To test this hypothesis, I identify four main types of segments in the newscast's electoral coverage: agendas, polls, interviews, and general campaign reports. "Agendas" is a traditional format of electoral news coverage in Brazilian television. It includes news stories that describe candidates' campaign activities that day. Although in some cases, especially after 1998, candidates' positions on issues are discussed in these reports, their tone is mostly episodic. "Polls" includes segments that were entirely devoted to the results of public opinion surveys. "Interviews" includes live interviews with presidential candidates in the studios of *Jornal Nacional* by anchors William Bonner and Fátima Bernardes. This type of segment appeared only in the news coverage of the 2002 and 2006 presidential elections. Finally, "general campaign reports" includes all other news coverage about elections that does not fit the other three types of segments.

To identify the issue composition of *Jornal Nacional*'s campaign coverage, I ignore airtime devoted to polls, agendas, and interviews, focusing instead on the category "general campaign reports."[18] I also identify three main types of themes: issues, ethics, and campaign. The category "issues" includes reports devoted to substantive topics and candidates' platforms, including news stories on the economy, education, health, and infrastructure. The category "ethics" includes reports about scandals and corruption. Finally, the category "campaign" includes episodic news stories about the election itself, in terms of party conventions, preparations for the election, explanations about procedures and rules, or controversies about the nomination of candidates.

Table 16.1 below presents the thematic composition of *Jornal Nacional*'s campaign news coverage, excluding polls, agendas, and interviews. The main hypothesis of the study is generally confirmed. While there were no reports in 1989 and 1994 devoted to the discussion of issues, this type of coverage increased significantly in the following elections, especially in 2002. On the other hand, the airtime devoted to the campaign events went through a steady and linear decline, from 96% in 1989 to 9% in 2006.

Table 16.1 also shows that in each year *Jornal Nacional* emphasized a different aspect. In 1989, 75% of the airtime devoted to general campaign reports focused on "candidate nomination." This was a result of the entry of media mogul Silvio Santos in the presidential race. Santos is the owner of the second biggest television network, the Brazilian System of Television (SBT by its Portuguese acronym). He caused a political earthquake when he launched his candidacy to the Presidency 15 days before the first round of the election. According to several accounts, this

TABLE 16.1
Thematic Composition of *Jornal Nacional*'s Campaign News Coverage in Brazil (percentage of the total airtime)*

	1989	1994	1998	2002	2006
Issues					
Economy	–	–	–	13.1	–
Social inequality	–	–	–	4.5	–
Infrastructure	–	–	–	29.3	–
Candidates' platforms	–	–	19.0	6.0	1.0
Voters' aspirations	–	–	–	–	27.3
Total issues:	**0**	**0**	**19.0**	**52.9**	**28.3**
Ethics					
Scandals, irregularities	0	11.6	0	20.8	60.8
Campaign					
Explanation of rules, political system	–	29.6	41.3	15.9	–
Candidate nomination, party meetings	75.3	–	7.2	–	-
Preparation of elections	15.0	44.7	13.8	2.8	2.7
Television debates between candidates	6.0	–	–	–	6.7
Total campaign:	**96.3**	**74.3**	**62.3**	**18.7**	**9.4**
Other topics	3.7	14.1	18.7	4.2	1.5

* The table refers to airtime devoted to general campaign reports, and therefore does not include the segments agendas, polls, and live interviews with presidential candidates.

maneuver was planned and supported by President Sarney, as a way to create a strong alternative to the leading opposition candidates.[19] Thus, news coverage of the three weeks preceding the first round of the 1989 election was not only highly descriptive, with little discussion of substantive issues, but it was also heavily centered on the Santos affair.

In 1994, campaign topics also took most of their airtime, with a focus on preparations for the election and on descriptions of Brazil's political and electoral systems. Campaign news coverage centered on explaining the importance of the vote and the main features of the political system (the division of powers, functions of each branch of government, etc.), with little discussion of substantive issues (the economy, education, social security, etc.).

In 1998, campaign news coverage was not only drastically reduced, but it also lacked substance. Most of *Jornal Nacional*'s attention focused on campaign-related topics. This situation changed dramatically in 2002. As we have seen, TV Globo's electoral coverage in this year was characterized by a clear shift toward a more issue-oriented coverage, with the introduction of special thematic reports and live interviews with the four main candidates. Table 16.1 confirms this trend, showing a dramatic growth of issues coverage.

In the case of the 2006 election, there was a strong focus on ethics. Political scandals, especially those involving President Lula's party (PT), were the main topic of *Jornal Nacional*'s agenda. On the other hand, most of the issue-oriented coverage by the newscast focused on "voters' aspirations." This topic refers to a major innovation launched by TV Globo in its coverage of the 2006 election: the "*Jornal Nacional*'s Caravan." The Caravan was made up of a bus that traveled around the country to report on voters' desires, showing the different realities of the country. Nevertheless, most of the reports produced by the Caravan and by journalist Pedro Bial focused on curiosities and trivial aspects of the trip, with little attention to more substantive policy issues.

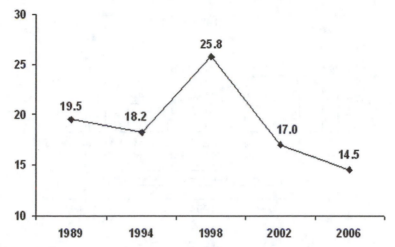

FIGURE 16.2   Percentage of *Jornal Nacional*'s campaign news coverage airtime taken by polls (horse race) in Brazil.

The main hypothesis also stated that horse race news coverage, operationalized in terms of airtime devoted to public opinion polls, would decline. To test this part of the hypothesis, I measured the amount of airtime devoted exclusively to publicizing the results of polls. Figure 16.2 below presents the proportion of the total campaign news airtime taken by polls. The results show a clear decline of horse race coverage, with the exception of 1998, when polls took one fourth of election news airtime. This is another piece of evidence demonstrating that in 1998 news coverage was not only extremely small, but also superficial. It focused on the performance of candidates in the polls with little coverage of substantive issues. With the exception of 1998, the general trend is clear: there is a decline of horse race news in *Jornal Nacional*'s coverage of elections.

The Question of Political Bias

The main hypothesis also stated that there would be less bias in *Jornal Nacional*'s news coverage in terms of airtime devoted to the main presidential candidates. To test this hypothesis, I measured the proportion of airtime taken by the main candidates, with the exception of the 1998 election.[20] Figure 16.3 below presents the results according to the number of valid votes candidates received in the first round of the presidential election. In the case of the 1989 dispute, the data confirm previous studies that argued that Collor de Mello attracted more airtime then his main opponents, Lula and Brizola. But the most interesting result, which conflicts with most analyses about the role of TV Globo in this election, is the clear bias in favor of candidates Mário Covas and Ulyses Guimarães. In the case of Guimarães, the data show a clear pro-government bias in *Jornal Nacional*. Guimarães was a historical leader of PMDB, the main party in President Sarney's coalition, but he had a disappointing performance in the election, receiving less the 5% of the valid votes. Despite his lack of electoral support during all the electoral period, *Jornal Nacional* devoted much more airtime to Guimarães than to other more competitive candidates.

Another significant finding about the 1989 election is the fact that Mário Covas was the candidate who received most airtime in *Jornal Nacional*'s coverage of the last three weeks of the campaign. Covas was a Senator and one of the founders of the Brazilian Social Democracy Party (PSDB). The fact that he got most airtime is surprising, since most studies about journalism and elections in Brazil argue that TV Globo manipulated news coverage to favor Collor de Mello. Although Collor did receive a substantial share of the airtime, he came in third place, after

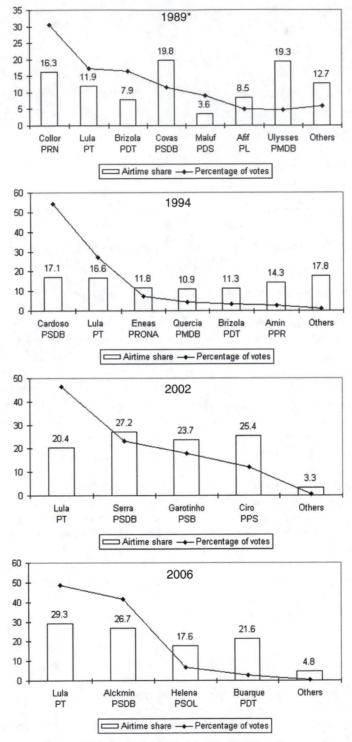

FIGURE 16.3   Presidential candidates' share of airtime in *Jornal Nacional*'s campaign coverage in the last three weeks preceding the first round, according to the percentage of valid votes received in the first round.

*The data does not include airtime devoted to Silvio Santos, who launched his candidacy 15 days before the first round of the election. The candidacy of Santos was later cancelled by the Superior Electoral Court (TSE).

Covas and Guimarães. These results provide support to the view that Collor de Mello was not the preferred candidate of TV Globo's owner, Roberto Marinho. Conti (1999, pp. 165–168) reports that TV Globo decided to give more visibility to Covas and boost his candidacy, since Marinho had reservations about Collor and his family. Although Conti reports that Marinho would later realize that Collor was the only candidate capable of defeating the leftists Lula and Brizola, the content analysis data reveal that TV Globo's support to Covas continued through the last three weeks of the first round.

Figure 16.3 also shows that after 1989 there was a general balance in terms of airtime distribution among the main candidates. These results confirm the main hypothesis of this study, which states that advances in democratization will lead to significant improvements in TV Globo's electoral news coverage. It should be noted, though, that balance in terms of airtime distribution does not necessarily mean lack of bias. As we have seen, *Jornal Nacional* played an active, although more subtle political role in 1994, 1998, and 2002 by framing the economy in particular ways. In the case of 2006 election, the strong focus on political scandals contributed to creating a hostile scenario for incumbent candidate Lula. Despite these caveats, Figure 16.3 shows a trend away from more explicit forms of political manipulation of electoral news coverage on the part of *Jornal Nacional*. Although some of the competitive candidates received less airtime then others in some cases, the tendency has been the elimination of the type of inequalities that characterized the coverage of the 1989 presidential election.

CONCLUSIONS

Based on the review of the literature about journalism and elections in Brazil, as well as on *Jornal Nacional*'s content analysis, this chapter identifies key trends in TV Globo's election news coverage. Looking across the five elections that took place after the country's return to democracy in 1985, I identify three key improvements in campaign coverage by the nation's main newscast. The first was a transition to a style of journalism with more focus on issues, especially after the 2002 election. The introduction of live interviews with presidential candidates in *Jornal Nacional*'s studios and the emergence of special thematic series is an indication of the trend. The content analysis has also shown a clear growth of issue-oriented news stories and the steady decline of descriptive reporting about campaign activities and features of the electoral process.

A second trend in TV Globo's News Division has been the reduction of horse race coverage. As we have seen, there is a linear decline in the total airtime devoted to polls, with the exception of the 1998 election. Finally, a third trend is the decline of political bias in terms of the airtime division among the main candidates.

It should be noted, though, that the process has been irregular and that in some regards regressions took place. In terms of the growth of issue-oriented reporting, the implementation of the "*Jornal Nacional's* Caravan" in 2006 contributed more to trivializing news coverage than to focusing on relevant issues. In the field of political bias, the strong emphasis on exposés and scandals in 2006 can be interpreted as an indicator of the hostility of the national media toward President Lula.

Despite these caveats, the analysis of campaign news coverage in Brazil shows positive trends. To explain these changes in journalistic practices and norms, it is important to consider the political context in which the media operate. The Brazilian case suggests that the deepening of democracy places important constraints on the news media. The negative repercussions of TV Globo's impartiality in 1989 and the rise of a more organized and active citizenry forced the network to change the way it had traditionally reported electoral processes. In the case of *Jornal*

Nacional, campaign news coverage became less biased and more focused on issues. As I show in more detail elsewhere (2007b), TV Globo's opening was aimed at changing its public image and recovering the credibility that was lost with more explicit political interventions. Thus, the general democratization of the country forced the powerful network to innovate and adapt. On the other hand, this process of media openness contributed to establish more fair and free elections. In interesting ways, media and political democratization contributed to reinforce each other.

NOTES

1. The size of the electorates of the world's largest democracies is as follows, according to the number of citizens who voted in the latest elections: India 671.5 million (2004); Brazil 125.9 million (2006); and United States 122.3 million (2004). I do not consider the electorates of China and Russia because their political systems are not democratic. In the 2006 edition of its "Freedom in the World Report," the Freedom House classifies both countries as "not free" (http://www.freedomhouse.org).
2. The ranking was based on TV Globo's revenues in the years 1999–2000 (see "Variety's Global 50," *Variety,* Auguest 28–September 3, 2000, p. 88).
3. The military abolished all parties in 1965 and allowed only two parties to function: the official *Aliança Renovadora Nacional* (ARENA; National Renewal Alliance), renamed *Partido Democrata Social* (PDS; Social Democratic Party) in 1980; and the opposition *Movimento Democrático Brasileiro* (MDB; Brazilian Democratic Movement), renamed *Partido do Movimento Democrático Brasileiro* (PMDB; Brazilian Democratic Movement Party) in 1980. As part of the process of political opening, but also as an attempt to divide the opposition, the regime allowed the legalization of three more parties in 1980, besides PDS and PMDB: *Partido dos Trabalhadores* (PT; Workers Party, discussed below); *Partido Democrático Trabalhista* (PDT; Labor Democratic Party), and *Partido Trabalhista Brasileiro* (PTB; Brazilian Labor Party).
4. Data retrieved from the *Câmara dos Deputados*' website: accessed February 2, 2007. http://www2.camara.gov.br/deputados/bancadas
5. Data from the website of the *Associação Nacional de Jornais* (ANJ; National Association of Newspapers), accessed Feb 2, 2007http://www.anj.org.br/; see also Azevedo (2006).
6. Data from the website of the *Associação Nacional de Jornais* (ANJ; National Association of Newspapers), accessed February 2, 2007 http://www.anj.org.br/ The data is from 2005.
7. *Veja* is the leading publication, with an average of 1.1 million copies sold per week in 2005, while *Época* comes in second place with 440,000 copies, and *Isto É* in third, with 366 thousand copies (GrupodeMídia, 2006, p. 284).
8. TV Globo's first channel appeared in a wake of scandal which was the object of an investigation by Congress, since the agreement with Time-Life was a flagrant violation of the Brazilian legislation (Caparelli, 1982; Herz, 1987).
9. Relatório Audência Domiciliar por Programa (ADP), IBOPE, Semana 12, 2006.
10. As a result of weak regulatory frameworks and processes of vertical and horizontal integration, the Globo corporation is present in all areas of the cultural industry, including newspapers (*O Globo, Extra*), a weekly newsmagazine (*Época*), radio stations (*Rádio Globo*), a publishing house (*Editora Globo*), a recording company (*Som Livre*), cable television (NET), Internet (www.globo.com.br), among many other sectors (Amaral & Guimarães, 1994; Brittos, 2000; Lima, 2001).
11. I will therefore not consider news coverage of elections to Congress, governorships, state assemblies, and local offices. For interesting analyses of news coverage of municipal-level elections, see Rubim (2002) and Carvalho (2003).
12. These numbers are slightly different from those presented by Conti (1999, p. 269) and Miguel (2002, p. 42). According to the authors, Collor got 3 minutes, 34 seconds, compared to Lula's 2 minutes, 22 seconds.
13. There are disagreements, though, on how "impartial" newspaper coverage of the election really was. By reanalyzing the same data of Alessandra Alde (2004), Emerson Cervi (2004) concluded that if

better measurements of favoritism are included, newspapers' bias in favor of the official candidate José Serra becomes clearer.

14. Lula won the Presidency in 2002 with 46% of the valid votes in the first round and 60.8% in the second, against Serra's 39.2%.

15. Raimundo Pereira (2006, October 18). Os fatos ocultos: a mídia, em especial a Globo, omitiu informações cruciais na divulgação do dossiê e contribuiu para levar a disputa ao 2°. turno. *Carta Capital*, n. 415.

16. In one of the few exceptions, Miguel (2004) compares *Jornal Nacional*'s news coverage of the 1998 and 2002 presidential elections.

17. The content analysis included 60 full broadcasts of *Jornal Nacional*, with 12 broadcasts from each year. The broadcasts were aired during the three weeks that preceded the first round of the elections. The complete composition of the sample follows:

    1989: October 25, 26, 27, 28, 30, 31, and November 1, 3, 4, 6, 7, and 8.
    1994: September 13, 15, 16, 17, 20, 21, 23, 24, 26, 28, 29, and 30.
    1998: September 12, 14, 16, 17, 18, 19, 21, 22, 25, 28, 29, and 30.
    2002: September 13, 14, 16, 17, 18, 20, 25, 26, 27, 28, 30, and October 1.
    2006: September 15, 16, 18, 19, 20, 21, 22, 25, 26, 27, 29, and 30.

    To calculate reliability, 15% of the materials (eight full broadcasts) were double-coded. The editions randomly chosen for the test were the following: November 3, 1989; September 17 and 26, 1994; September 19 and 21, 1998; September 25 and 27, 2002; September 15 and 18, 2006. The inter-coder reliability scores (Cohen's Kappa) were all .740 or higher. The main Kappa scores were (1) Subject of news stories (Figure 16.1) = .743 and (2) Candidates airtime measurement (Figure 16.3) = .876. No reliability tests were conducted on the airtime devoted to issues (Table16.1) and to polls (Figure 16.2) because they were added later on.

18. I exclude segments about candidates' agendas because of their episodic nature. Airtime devoted to polls is not considered because they almost always refer to candidates' standing in voters' preferences and rarely deal with issues. Finally, although airtime devoted to live interviews with presidential candidates is obviously important in terms of issue-oriented coverage, I do not include them here because they were introduced only in 2002. It should be noted, though, that the introduction of live interviews with candidates is another important indicator of the rise of issue coverage in *Jornal Nacional*.

19. Santos candidacy was later cancelled by the Superior Electoral Tribunal (TSE).

20. By "the main candidates" I mean individuals who received at least 2% of the valid votes in the first round of the presidential election. I do not include the year of 1998 in the analysis because of the reduced airtime devoted the campaign. In the 12 broadcasts aired in the last two weeks of the 1998 election, *Jornal Nacional* devoted only 3 minutes, 47 seconds to the three main candidates (Cardoso, Lula, and Ciro Gomes).

REFERENCES

Albuquerque, A. D. (1994). A campanha presidencial no 'Jornal Nacional': Observações preliminares [The presidential campaign on 'Jornal Nacional': Preliminary observations]. *Comunicação & Política, 1*(1), 23–40.

Alde, A. (2004). As eleições presidenciais de 2002 nos jornais [The 2002 presidential elections on newspapers]. In A. A. Rubim (Ed.), *Eleições presidenciais em 2002 no Brasil* [The 2002 presidential election in Brazil] (pp. 106–128). São Paulo, Brazil: Hacker.

Alde, A., Mendes, G., & Figueiredo, M. (2007). *Tomando partido: Imprensa e eleições presidenciais em 2006* [Taking sides: The press and the presidential elections in 2006]. Paper presented at the 16th Encontro da COMPOS, Curitiba, Brazil.

Alves, M. H. (1988). Dilemmas of the consolidation of democracy from the top in Brazil: A political analysis. *Latin American Perspectives, 15*(3), 47–63.

Amaral, R., & Guimarães, C. (1994). Media monopoly in Brazil. *Journal of Communication, 44*(4), 26–38.

Azevedo, F. (2000). Imprensa, campanha presidencial, e a agenda da mídia [The press, presidential campaign, and the media agenda]. In A. A. Rubim (Ed.), *Mídia e eleições de 1998* [Media and elections in 1998] (pp. 31-56). Salvador, Brazil: EdUFBa.

Boas, T. (2005). Television and neopopulism in Latin America: Media effects in Brazil and Peru. *Latin American Research Review, 40*(2), 27–49.

Azevedo, F. (2006). Mídia e democracia no Brasil: Relações entre o sistema de mídia e o sistema político [Media and democracy in Brazil: Relationships between the media system and the political system]. *Opinião Pública, 12*(1), 88–113.

Borelli, S., & Priolli, G. (2000). *A deusa ferida* [The wounded goddess]. São Paulo, Brazil: Summus.

Brittos, V. (2000). As Organizações Globo e a reordenação das comunicações [The Globo Enterprises and the reorganization of communications]. *Revista Brasileira de Ciências da Comunicação, 23*(1), 57–76.

Caparelli, S. (1982). *Televisão e capitalismo no Brasil* [Television and capitalism in Brazil]. Porto Alegre, Brazil: L&PM.

Carvalho, R. (Ed.). (2003). *A produção da política em campanhas eleitorais: eleições municipais de 2000* [The political production in electoral campaigns: The 2000 municipal elections]. Campinas, Brazil: Pontes.

Cervi, E. (2003). Imprensa brasileira e cobertura dos candidatos a presidente em 2002: Da objetividade anunciada à esquizofrenia de um sistema comercial de mídia [The Brazilian press and the 2002 coverage of presidential candidates: From the announced objectivity to the schizophrenia of a commercial media system] . *Revista da FDJ, 1*(1), 66–80.

Chaia, V., Val, H., & Nepomuceno, J. (2003). *Rádio e eleições 2002 no estado de São Paulo* [The radio and the 2002 elections in the state of São Paulo]. Paper presented at the 27th Encontro Anual da ANPOCS, Caxambu, Brazil.

Colling, L. (2000). *Agendamento, enquadramento e silêncio no Jornal Nacional nas eleições presidenciais de 1998* [Agenda-setting, framing, and silence in Jornal Nacional during the 1998 presidential elections]. Unpublished Master's Thesis, Universidade Federal da Bahia, Salvador.

Conti, M. S. (1999). *Notícias do planalto* [News from the congress]. São Paulo, Brazil: Companhia das Letras.

Esch, C. E. (1999). Do microfone ao plenário: O comunicador radiofônico e seu sucesso eleitoral [From the microphone to the plenary: The radio person and his electoral success]. In N. Del Bianco & S. V. Moreira (Eds.), *Rádio no Brasil* [Radio in Brazil] (pp. 69–94). Rio de Janeiro, Brazil: EdUERJ.

Fox, E. (1997). *Latin American broadcasting*. Luton, UK: University of Luton Press.

Grupo de Mídia. (2006). *Mídia dados 2006* [Media data 2006]. São Paulo, Brazil: Porto Palavra Editores.

Guimarães, C., & Amaral, R. (1990). Brazilian television: A rapid conversion to the new order. In E. Fox (Ed.), *Media and politics in Latin America* (pp. 125–137). Newbury Park, CA: Sage.

Herz, D. (1987). *A História secreta da rede Globo* [The secret story of Globo Network]. Porto Alegre, Brazil: Tche.

Hunter, W., & Power, T. (2007). Rewarding Lula: Executive power, social policy, and the Brazilian elections of 2006. *Latin American Politics and Society, 49*(1), 1–30.

Jambeiro, O. (2001). *A TV no Brasil do século XX* [The Television in Brazil in the twentieth century]. Salvador, Brazil: EdUFBa.

Kehl, M. R. (1986). Eu vi um Brasil na TV [I saw a Brazil on TV]. In I. Simões, A. Henrique & M. R. Kehl (Eds.), *Um país no ar* [A country in air]. São Paulo, Brazil: Brasiliense.

Kucinski, B. (1998). *A síndrome da antena parabólica* [The satellite dish syndrome]. São Paulo, Brazil: Editora da Fundação Perseu Abramo.

Lattman-Weltman, F., Carneiro, J. A., & Ramos, P. (1994). *A imprensa faz e desfaz um presidente* [The press makes and destroys a president]. Rio de Janeiro, Brazil: Nova Fronteira.

Lawson, C. (2002). *Building the fourth state: Democratization and the rise of a free press in Mexico*. Berkeley, CA: University of California Press.

Lima, V. A. d. (1993). Brazilian television in the 1989 presidential election: Constructing a president. In T. Skidmore (Ed.), *Television, politics and the transition to democracy in Latin America* (pp. 97–117). Baltimore: The Johns Hopkins University Press.

Lima, V. A. D. (1988). The state, television and political power in Brazil. *Critical Studies in Mass Communication, 5*(2), 108–128.

Lima, V. A. D. (2001). *Mídia: Teoria e política* [Media: Theory and politics]. São Paulo, Brazil: Editora da Fundação Perseu Abramo.

Lima, V. A. D. (2006). *Mídia: Crise política e poder no Brasil* [Media: Political crisis and power in Brazil]. São Paulo, Brazil: Editora Fundação Perseu Abramo.

Martínez, J., & Santiso, J. (2003). Financial markets and politics: The confidence game in Latin American emerging economies. *International Political Science Review, 24*(3), 363–395.

Mattos, S. (2000). *A televisão no Brasil* [The television in Brazil]. Salvador, Brazil: Edições Inamã.

Miguel, L. F. (2000a). The Globo television network and the election of 1998. *Latin American Perspectives, 27*(6), 65–84.

Miguel, L. F. (2000b). *Mito e discurso político* [Myth and political discourse]. Campinas, Brazil: Editora da Unicamp.

Miguel, L. F. (2002). *Política e mídia no Brasil* [Politics and media in Brazil]. Brasília, Brazil: Editora Plano.

Miguel, L. F. (2004). A descoberta da política: A campanha de 2002 na Rede Globo [The discovery of politics: The 2002 caimpaign on Globo Network]. In A. A. Rubim (Ed.), *Eleições presidenciais em 2002 no Brasil* [The 2002 presidential election in Brazil] (pp. 91–105). São Paulo, Brazil: Hacker.

Moreira, S. V. (1998). *Rádio palanque* [Radio stand]. Rio de Janeiro, Brazil: Mil Palavras.

Nunes, M. V. (2000). *Rádio e política* [Radio and politics]. São Paulo, Brazil: AnnaBlume.

Nunes, M. V. (2004). Mídia e eleição [Media and elections]. In A. A. Rubim (Ed.), *Comunicação e política* (pp. 347–378). Salvador, Brazil: EdUFBa.

Oliveira, F. D. (2006). Lula in the labyrinth. *New Left Review, 42*, 5–22.

Ortiz, R. (1989). *A moderna tradição Brasileira* [The Brazilian modern tradition]. São Paulo, Brazil: Brasiliense.

Porto, M. (1999). *Novas tecnologias e política no Brasil: A globalização em uma sociedade periférica e desigual* [New technologies and politics in Brazil: The globalization in a peripheral and unequal society]. Paper presented at the 21st International Congress of the Latin American Studies Association, Chicago.

Porto, M. (2007a). Framing controversies: Television and the 2002 presidential election in Brazil. *Political Communication, 24*(1), 19–36.

Porto, M. (2007b). TV news and political change in Brazil: The impact of democratization on TV Globo's journalism. *Journalism, 8*(4), 381–402.

Porto, M., Vasconcelos, R., & Bastos, B. (2004). A televisão e o primeiro turno das eleições presidenciais de 2002: Análise do Jornal Nacional e do horário eleitoral [Television and the first round of the 2002 presidential elections: An analysis of Jornal Nacional and the Free Electoral Political Advertising Time]. In A. A. Rubim (Ed.), *Eleições presidenciais em 2002 no Brasil* [The 2002 presidential election in Brazil] (pp. 68–90). São Paulo, Brazil: Hacker.

Rubim, A. (1999). *Mídia e política no Brasil* [Media and politics in Brazil]. João Pessoa, Brazil: Editora UFPB.

Rubim, A. (Ed.). (2002). *Mídia e eleições 2000 em Salvador* [Media and the 2000 elections in Salvador]. Salvador, Brazil: EdUFBa.

Rubim, A., & Azevedo, F. (1998). Mídia e política no Brasil: Textos e agenda de pesquisa [Media and politics in Brazil: Texts and research agenda]. *Lua Nova, 43*, 189–216.

Rubim, A., & Colling, L. (2004). Mídia e eleições presidenciais no Brasil pós-ditadura [Media and presidential elections in Brazil after the dictatorial system]. *Comunicação & Política, 22*(3), 169–189.

Sinclair, J. (1999). *Latin American television*. New York: Oxford University Press.

Soares, M. (2000). Veja e a contrução do CR-P nas eleições presidenciais de 1998 [Veja and the construction of the SR-P in the 1998 presidential elections]. In A. A. Rubim (Ed.), *Mídia e Eleições de 1998* [The media and the 1998 elections] (pp. 89–102). Salvador: Edições FACOM.

Spanakos, A., & Rennó, L. (2006). Elections and economic turbulence in Brazil: Candidates, voters, and investors. *Latin American Politics and Society, 48*(4), 1–26.

Straubhaar, J. (1996). The electronic media in Brazil. In R. Cole (Ed.), *Communication in Latin America* (pp. 217–243). Wilmington, PA: Scholarly Books.

Straubhaar, J., Olsen, O., & Nunes, M. (1993). The Brazilian case: Influencing the voter. In T. Skidmore (Ed.), *Television, politics, and the transition to democracy in Latin America* (pp. 118–136). Baltimore, MD: Johns Hopkins University Press.

Venturi, G. (2000). Imagem pública, propaganda eleitoral e reeleição na disputa presidencial de 1998 [Public image, political advertising and reelection in the 1998 presidential race] . In A. A. Rubim (Ed.), *Mídia e eleições de 1998* [Media and election sin 1998] (pp. 103–124). Salvador, Brazil: EdUFBa.

17

Media and Elections in South Africa: Finding a Foothold on the Democratic Path

Amanda Gouws and Arnold S. de Beer

MEDIA AND GOVERNMENT: TOWARDS THE FOURTH DEMOCRATIC ELECTIONS

It will be quite a different South Africa that moves towards the fourth democratic elections in 2009 than the body politic and media system that became part of the first democratic elections in 1994. Hope and uncertainty characterized the first elections. Democratic political and media discourse was in its infancy, still struggling with the legacy of apartheid. The second and third democracy showed a country finding its feet on the arduous road to democratic elections and a media system that supports the process. With the fourth general election looming in 2009, the mood has changed to find the country embroiled in boisterous and vociferous political discourse. However, as is the case in other democracies, the mood has changed. No longer was it a case of Archbishop Desmond Tutu's "rainbow nation," but a nation finding itself on a razor-sharp edge of political in-fighting, scandals, and mistrust between government and the media.

The years leading up to the 2009 elections have seen a bitter struggle within government and political structures. First and foremost was the succession battle for the African National Congress (ANC) presidency in 2007 and the burning issue of who would succeed Thabo Mbeki after his second term as president of the country.

It also became clear that there was little love lost between government and the media. Broadly, the relationship between the government and especially the print media could at best be described as acrimonious. Since the mid-1990s it has been clear that government and the print media were at loggerheads regarding the role the media should play in a democratic South Africa. Driving this relationship was a stark difference in the government's view that the media should serve the "national interest." While the government's characterization of the concept was at first rather vague (as being in the people's interest), it became increasingly clear that the government wanted the media to operate in a developmental mode, rather than in a typical Western mode of a liberal, but also market driven system. This approach resulted in the national broadcaster, the SABC, becoming more closely identified with the government and its policies. More and more, the SABC was seen to be "his master's voice" operating under the directorship of a former ANC political commissar.

Most of the main print media publications developed strong independent voices, often seen by the ANC to be pitted against the government and more specifically the ANC leadership. This rather discordant relationship saw government and media involved in two "indabas" (serious deliberations) on "finding a way forward" in the 2000s. Though these meetings were described as "amicable," the issue of basic mistrust was not yet solved in the period leading up to the 2007 election of a new ANC president, with the media maintaining that its primary duty was to serve the "public interest" which could mean criticizing, even vehemently, government, especially during election time (for a discussion of issues raised above, see De Beer & Wasserman, 2005).

THE POLITICAL SYSTEM IN SOUTH AFRICA

Since 1994 South Africa has been a liberal democratic system with a bi-cameral parliamentary system and an executive president. The *trias politica* has been institutionalized through an independent legislative (the National Assembly), executive, and an independent judiciary. The political system is a three-tiered system with a national government, provincial governments, and local governments. It is, however, not a federal system since the powers of the provinces are limited through the constitution.

Each sphere of government is autonomous but interlocked with other spheres and must operate in unison around the delivery of public services. Interlocking spheres of government imply equality between the spheres that contrasts with a more hierarchical concept of levels of government (Venter, 2001, p. 171).

The National Assembly consists of 400 popularly elected representatives—200 members are elected from national party lists and 200 from lists provided by the provinces (to be discussed later). It is the duty of the National Assembly to initiate, prepare, and discuss/debate legislation; and it has an oversight function over the national executive to monitor the implementation of legislation (Taljaard & Venter, 2001, p. 30).

The second house of parliament is called the National Council of Provinces (NCOP). This house provides direct representation of the provinces at the national level to make sure that provincial interests are taken into consideration in the legislative process. It also has to ratify all legislation made by the National Assembly. The NCOP has 90 members: 10 from each of the 9 provinces.

The cabinet is responsible for the implementation of legislation through a highly complex state administration. The cabinet is the link between the public interests of the country at large, the public service, and parliament (Venter, 2001, p. 57). Each minister heads a civil service department (like Domestic Affairs or Justice) and is responsible for the budget of their departments.

The President is an executive president who is the head of state and of government. He participates in the debates in parliament and also heads the cabinet. He has a presidency where power is increasingly concentrated. Political analysts fear that the way in which President Mbeki concentrated power in the presidency may weaken the executive. He has, for example, taken away the power of the provinces to appoint their own premiers. These are now appointed by the president. The president has, however, no power to veto legislation.

The cabinet consists of the president, the deputy president, and 28 ministers (the number may vary from time to time). The president appoints the ministers. All members of the cabinet are collectively and individually responsible to parliament for the performance of the functions of the national government and its policies (Venter, 2001, p. 63). The president can discharge a minister, and he or she cannot refuse to be dismissed. Each state department has a standing committee, the

Portfolio Committee which makes inputs into the legislative process. Portfolio committees do research and often write the first drafts of bills.

The Bill of Rights in the Constitution guarantees freedom of expression which includes: freedom of the press and other media, freedom to receive or impart information or ideas, freedom of artistic creativity, academic freedom, and freedom of scientific research. It does however prohibit hate speech.

The Chapter 9 bodies refer to the statutory bodies that are written into Chapter 9 of the Constitution. These bodies include the Human Rights Commission, the Commission on Gender Equality, the Public Protector, the Commission for the Promotion and Protection of the Rights of Cultural, Religious and Linguistic Communities, and the Auditor General with the aim of limiting the powers of cabinet. For the purposes of this study the Independent Broadcasting Authority is important because it is responsible for regulating broadcasting in the public interest and ensuring fairness and a diversity of views broadly representing the South African society. Another important body is the Independent Electoral Commission (IEC), which manages the elections of national, provincial, and municipal legislative bodies in accordance with national legislation and that ensures that elections are free and fair (The Constitution of the Republic of South Africa, Chapter 9).

Local government has been in a state of transformation since 1994 to rid local service delivery of its apartheid heritage. A demarcation process has resulted in metropolitan councils that govern big uni-cities or megacities, such as Johannesburg and Cape Town. There are 47 district councils, some of them with cross-provincial boundaries. Local councils are "stand alone" councils. In 2001 there were 231 local councils. The local council is the tier closest to the voter and delivers the most basic of services such as water, electricity, and garbage removal. They are also the most hamstrung by a lack of capacity and corruption.

Civil society plays an important role as a watchdog of government. South Africa has a strong and vibrant civil society. With regards to the media a very important non-governmental organization that monitors press freedom is the Freedom of Expression Institute.

The Electoral System

The electoral system is covered in more detail because of the way in which it influences election campaigns. The electoral system of any country is the mechanism used to translate support for parties and individuals into seats in government. It determines who will be in government and who will not. The electoral system is the constitutional and institutional process by which government by consent and fair representation is put into practice in a democratic system (Wessels, 1994, p. 143).

From the start of the transition process to the first election, a consensus grew around the desirability of proportional representation (PR) as the choice of the new electoral system. This broad consensus became apparent in the 1991 *Declaration of Intent of the First Convention for a Democratic South Africa* (CODESA). This declaration was signed by all the major participants in the negotiation process. While consensus existed around PR it did not bind the negotiating parties to any specific system of PR (Sisk, 1993, p. 84). In the 1992 *Policy Guidelines for a Democratic South Africa,* the African National Congress (ANC) committed itself to "an inclusive, accountable, and participatory multi-party democracy, with periodic elections, and an electoral system based on proportional representation" (Albertyn et al., 2002, p. 27). One of the main arguments was that it would benefit all parties, especially the smaller ones such as the National Party (NP) (now the New National Party, NNP) and the Democratic Party (DP). A PR List system would also prevent ethnic mobilization.

One of the most important inputs was the *Report of the Committee for Constitutional Affairs* of the President's Council of the previous government on "A Proportional Polling System for South African in a New Constitutional Dispensation." This report was released in 1992. This report recommended PR based on the following reasons:

- An almost complete consensus that a majoritarian electoral system is unsuited for deeply divided societies (in a majoritarian system the candidate who gets 50% plus one of the vote gets the seat).
- The fragmented nature of the South African society as shown by its party system indicated that PR would be a solution, due to the necessity to include fringe parties.
- PR includes smaller parties and thus protects minority rights.
- PR would establish participatory democracy in South Africa (Report of the Committee for Constitutional Affairs, 1992, pp. 60–64).

In the period between 1992 and 1994, major academic research showed that PR would be the most fitting electoral system for South Africa. In the period up to the 1994 election major political actors came to an agreement about the electoral system and confirmed the consensus around PR. Agreement about two ballots for each voter was also established—one vote for the national legislature and one for the provincial legislature (Faure, 1996, p. 92). Parties that formed part of the apartheid system all chose PR. This would have ensured them some representation in the future political system. The NP clearly expected to be a minority party in the new political system. The Inkatha Freedom Party (IFP) also expected to be a minority party and was concerned with devolution of power to the regions.

The African National Congress on the other hand would have benefited from a majoritarian system to push through its economic reforms, but it never argued that this support for PR was a major concession to minority concerns. The ANC understood the importance of addressing minority concerns and believed that PR was the fairest system. PR also serves the ANC's interests. The simplicity of the PR system is beneficial to illiterate voters and it helps to establish the legitimacy of the system (Sisk, 1993, p. 87).

For all political parties aiming to participate in the first democratic election PR provided certain benefits that enabled them to be included in the first parliament. The first electoral system of 1994 was based on a closed list PR system.

Explanation of the Electoral System as It Stands Today

The National Assembly consists of 400 members. Two hundred members are elected on the basis of regional party lists—each region or province gets a fraction of the 200 members in accordance with its relative population size. Ninety members are indirectly elected to the National Council of Provinces. The nine provinces are represented by a delegation of 10 members each. The delegation represents the different parties in accordance with their relative strength in the provincial legislatures (Faure & Venter, 2003, p. 3). Nine provincial legislatures reflect the population size of the province, and each legislature has a minimum of 30 and a maximum of 80 members.

Each voter receives two ballots. One is used to elect the members of the National Assembly and one is used to elect the members of the provincial legislatures. Voters cannot choose between various candidates of the different parties but only between competing party lists (Faure & Venter, 2003, p. 4). Voters have to accept the order of the candidates as decided by the parties.

The threshold for the election of one seat is very low. The threshold varies for the regional and national lists respectively, and those of the provincial legislature are about half the size of those for the regional allocation for the National Assembly. Approximately 1/400 of the votes cast for the national party lists of the National Assembly constitutes the threshold, but the number of seats already allocated regionally is subtracted from the seats won in this way—effectively making this threshold about 0.50%. The threshold for the National Assembly as a whole is 0.249% (Faure & Venter, 2003, p. 5).

Since this is a closed list PR system the names of candidates on the list are determined by party leaders, ensuring accountability to party leaders rather than to the voters. The order in which the names appear on the list is also determined by party leaders. The ANC is the only party that has accepted a one third quota for women, and since 2004 it attempts to make every third name on the list that of a woman—ensuring the election of 132 women to parliament in 2004.[1] Because South Africa uses a close list PR system, media campaigns very often tend to focus on parties and party leaders at the expense of policy issues.

Political Parties

South Africa is a multi-party system, but after three elections the country has developed into a one party dominant system. This is because of the overwhelming majority of the ANC, which got 62% of the vote in 1994, 67% in 1999, and 72% in 2004. Only three parties managed to get more than 2% of the vote in the 2004 election, with the official opposition, the DA, getting 12% of the vote and the Inkatha Freedom Party (IFP) 8%. All other parties, including the newly founded Independent Democrats (ID), got less than 2% of the vote which makes for a weak and fragmented opposition.

MEDIA SYSTEM IN SOUTH AFRICA[2]

South Africa has without doubt the most technically advanced media system on the continent of Africa (Teer-Tomaselli, Wasserman, & De Beer, 2007). It also has a strong history of a vibrant print media press which dates back to the early 1800s (for an historical overview, see Diederichs & De Beer, 1998).

At the time of the advent of democracy in the early 1990s, print media in the country were largely owned and edited by whites and split along ideological lines corresponding with language and, respectively, the interests of mining capital and the apartheid state. This led Nelson Mandela, president-in-waiting at the time, to remark on the skewed picture of social reality resulting from the state of media ownership. The alternative media responsible for much of the critical journalism during the apartheid period saw their funding dwindling. In the early 1990s, the papers largely disappeared or were taken up into the mainstream (e.g., the *Mail & Guardian*). To keep up with the political changes and new democratic atmosphere in the country, mainstream commercial print media subjected themselves to major ownership changes.

Two big transactions involving so-called black-empowerment consortiums (Johnnic and Nail) brought some of the biggest newspaper titles under black ownership in the 1990s. The Irish Independent group gained control of a series of newspaper titles, thereby opening up South African media for global competition and contributing to the increasing tensions between the local and the global economies. Restructuring was not as far-reaching in the Afrikaans media. Whereas the English-language print media have been on the receiving end of globalization, the largest Afrikaans media conglomerate, Naspers, only "unbundled" slightly by forming new companies and selling some of its "family silver" to black business groups.

The commercial pressure created by this opening up of the local media industry to global competition, had "devastating" results on the local media scene according to Anton Harber, Witwatersrand University Professor of Journalism (for reference, see note 2). It led to staff cutbacks, a "juniorisation" of newsrooms, a preference for commercial imperatives in making editorial judgments, and an erosion of specialized reporting. It also led to what has come to be referred to as the "tabloidization" of the mainstream print media, with more attention to entertainment, celebrity news, etc., often from wire copy produced abroad.

The shift to popular media formats had therefore already begun to take place well before the formal entry of tabloid newspapers to the market. Although broadsheet newspapers might have contributed to creating the environment for the entry of tabloid media, it eventually was intensified when tabloids began to exert pressure on the sales figures of the traditional broadsheets.

The editorial makeup of newsrooms also underwent significant changes with the shift to democracy. Most mainstream print publications now have black editors, and newsrooms have started to reflect the demographic diversity of the country. However, in spite of these changes to media ownership and editorial staff, mainstream commercial print media have not seen a fundamental change in perspective. Several critics have indicated that the print media's class-base remains the same and therefore would not result in a radical departure from their perspective on lucrative audiences. The print media still operate according to the same logic of circulation, distribution networks, price structure, and advertising that has in its sights the lucrative, and still largely white market.

The result was an industry largely operating on free-market principles—although attempts have been made by government to intervene in the market, for example through the establishment of a Media Diversity and Development Agency, and in the area of broadcasting, the awarding of community broadcasting licenses—and according to a neo-liberal functionalist logic, whilst market segmentation displayed continuities with the societal polarizations of the past.

Consequently, the development of the post-apartheid print media sphere left a gap for publications that would address the interests of the poor and working class black majority. This need was intensified through the growing frustration at a grassroots level with the lack of social delivery that had been promised by the new ANC government, the continuation of squalid living conditions in townships, and growing inequality (South Africa is the second most unequal society in the world, after Brazil). The disillusionment with the persistence of poor living conditions in post-apartheid society has led to the emergence of a range of social movements protesting what they see as the government's anti-poor macroeconomic policies and incompetence in service delivery. The mainstream media either ignored these social movements or covered them only when a conflict arose that registered on the radar of conventional news values. The groundswell of dissatisfaction had to find an outlet in the media, and the new tabloids rose to the occasion—which will have, according to most informed accounts, a considerable impact on the coming elections.

The emergence and unprecedented popularity of the South African tabloids, is evidence of a process of social mobility that part of the black working class is starting to enjoy. The tabloids are providing their readers with information to pave their way into the black middle class, where they will be a captive market for their advertisers. The tabloids tap into the aspirational culture of their readers, who fall in the lower LSM (Living Standards Measurement), but who are starting to earn a regular income. Of the *Daily Sun*'s regular readership, 95% of their readers are Black, and the majority of them (56%) are in the "young and starting-out life stages," with an average personal income of R2,739 per month (about U.S.$390). About half of its readership has completed school, while most of their readers are between 16 and 34 years of age. With readership running into the millions for a newspaper such as the *Daily Sun*, a new force in public discourse on elections was born.

ELECTION NEWS COVERAGE IN SOUTH AFRICA

After the transition to democracy it became increasingly clear that the news media would also have to transform away from its historical language divide. Under the apartheid regime the Afrikaans print media as well as the SABC favored the ruling NP while the English language press was the mouthpiece of left-leaning or liberal parties such as the Progressive Federal Party, that later became the Democratic Party and is now called the Democratic Alliance. The media would have to steer a more neutral path and attempt to be more even handed to give effect to press freedom (Teer-Tomaselli, 2005, p. 76).

A 1997 study found that 52% of South Africans listened to radio on a daily basis, 44% watched television, and only 16% read newspapers. In 2004 over 23 million watched television at least once a week and over 27 million listened to the radio. Television sets grew from 5.9 million in 1994 to 8.2 million in 2004 and radio sets tripled from 10.4 million to 33.7 million. The impact of broadcast media cannot be underestimated (Davis, 2005, p. 232). New and independent voices emerged through the sale of six SABC stations to private shareholders in 1996.

Elections were also enhanced by the SABC that gave discounted and free airtime to parties. During the 1999 election community radio stations actively participated in the dissemination of information since radio was used as the prime media for rural areas.

The Independent Electoral Commission augmented the election through regular press briefings by Commissioners and officials. As a result of their input a number of newspapers carried election maps and voting details free of charge (Report of Electoral Commission, 1999).

Content of Election Coverage

During the first election of 1994, the media coverage focused on the two strongest parties—the ANC and the NP and specifically on their leaders, Mandela and De Klerk. This made it difficult for other parties to compete. Zach de Beer, leader of the DP, was not really inspirational media material (Silke & Schrire, 1994, p. 121). The media also focused on practical issues of voter education, in an attempt to make citizens familiar with the voting procedure. The SABC gave parties free airtime to voice their campaign messages.

Jacobs (1999, p. 147) argues that mainstream media had a limited influence on black voter preference in the 1999 election. According to him the elections showed that campaigning through the media is more important for parties targeting minorities. A significant portion of the coverage was spent on the leaders of political parties in a more personalized type of coverage. In this, election opinion polls had an impact on how the campaigns were covered by speculation of which party would win and how parties were gaining on each other (to be discussed later).

In the 2004 election, *Media Tenor* (2004) showed in an extensive analysis, which included 10,409 reports in all the Gauteng daily newspapers, 7 national weeklies and the SABC news channels, as well as e-Tv from January 1 to 25, 2004, that the ANC received an overwhelming 58.7% of the news coverage and the DA 13%. The IFP received 10.3% and the NNP 6.3%. The Independent Democrats (ID) as a new party got the most coverage of the smaller parties. *This-Day* (now defunct) produced the most news on political parties of all newspapers. With regards to policy coverage the DP received 46% and the ANC 42%. There was also a focus of prominent party leaders with a consequence that men dominated the campaign to the exclusion of women (O'Donovan, 2004, p. 12).

Davis (2005, p. 237) underscores the important point that although newspapers do not have the reach of broadcast media, they are important for three reasons: they are the medium of choice for opinion makers and provide a deeper analysis than radio, and they have an investigative capacity that is unrivaled.

By 2004 over 5 million newspapers were read by black South Africans. Whites account for 1.7 million, coloreds 879,000, and Indians 339,000. All newspapers have, to a certain degree, mixed readership. For instance, the traditionally white Cape Town daily, *Die Burger,* now has more colored readers than white. Newspapers such as the Afrikaans *Beeld* and *Volksblad* are mostly read by whites, while the reading public of *Sowetan, City Press* and *Daily Sun* is almost exclusively black.

The Media Monitoring Project's analysis as well as that of *Media Tenor* showed that the ANC received most coverage in all newspapers during the 2004 election except in *Ilanga,* a Zulu paper that devoted space to the IFP. The IFP and NNP received higher coverage in the Afrikaans dailies. Davis (2005, p. 241) makes the argument that newspaper coverage was generally neutral. *The Sowetan* was the one newspaper that gave the ANC more positive than negative coverage and the *Sunday Independent* were more positive than negative toward the DP. The ANC and DA got the lion's share of print media but the argument is made that it is because they generated the most news.

Despite accusations of the SABC's favoritism towards ANC in its television news coverage, analyses show that the public broadcaster did not give undue coverage to the ANC or any other party, given the seventy odd percent of their electoral vote. Data of the Media Monitoring Project indicates that the ANC got a very big portion of TV news coverage, but that coverage came from independent e-TV, while the DA got a higher share of coverage on SABC (Davis, 2005, p. 234). *Media Tenor*[3] showed that ANC got slightly more coverage on SABC Nguni news than on the Afrikaans and English news of the public broadcaster. It also found that coverage of all parties was mainly neutral if not slightly positive, rather than negative. Coverage of the ANC on SABC was less sympathetic than on e-TV, and coverage of the DA was more negative on SABC and more positive on e-TV.

The ANC received most coverage on all radio stations, and the ANC and DA had the highest exposure to radio advertising. The Public Election Broadcasts (2 minute free advertising prime time slots allocated according to the seats parties hold in parliament) benefited the ANC as the party with the most seats (Davis, 2005, p. 236). This formula was used based on the argument that voters have to hear more from parties that will influence policy. The ANC's coverage on radio and television was further enlarged by other parties naming it. Its own voice consisted of only 23% of the coverage.

As the *Media Tenor* (2004) report points out, it does not take much in-depth research to determine that the ANC dominates political media coverage in South Africa. This is very much in line with the situation elsewhere in Africa, but to a degree also in established multi-party democracies where the ruling political party would under normal circumstances garner the most media coverage. For instance, in South Africa's most populated province with the highest concentration of media, a *Media Tenor* analysis of 5 073 reports show that in the seven Gauteng daily newspapers, seven national weekly newspapers, the various main evening SABC television news channels, and e-News in the first two weeks of January of 2004, the ANC received an overwhelming 69% of the political coverage. Following the ANC was the DA (13.4%), the IFP (5%) and the NNP (2%). Incidentally, this division correlates broadly with the division of Parliamentary seats held after the 2004 elections.

However, the positive and negative images of the ANC, the DA, and the IFP did not differ that much according to *Media Tenor.* The ANC received slightly more positive than negative coverage.

As a result of the focus on news about the horse race aspects of the campaign and on party leaders (personality-driven coverage), issues have received less coverage in South African election coverage. There was, nevertheless, a slight difference with regard to the news issues that could be linked to the news reports on the various political parties. In reports on the ANC, the issue of the economy was addressed the most, followed by social services and democratic values. Crime and AIDS were noticeably lower down the list. In reporting on the DA, the economy and social services played the biggest role. In the fewer reports on the NNP, crime was the most reported topic, while on the IFP most reports focused on the role of media. The latter showed an emphasis on an issue outside pressing political aspects related to election, but highlighted the IFP's ongoing battle with the media, due almost exclusively to what was conceived to be the media's negative treatment of IFP leader Mangosuthu Buthelezi.

Because the ANC has a massive advantage over other political parties in terms of media coverage (*Media Tenor*, 2004), it is clearly the political party that also has the highest level of awareness among the electorate. In the print media much of this coverage seems to be of a negative nature as far as the ANC is concerned, and it would be difficult to predict how the awareness factor and the image of the ANC as being victimized by the media will have an impact on voters in 2009 and following elections. As Papayya (2004) shows in a study based on interviews:

- Politicians in hotly contested areas always object to stories that "portrayed" them in a negative light.
- They also objected when their rivals were given publicity.
- They also felt personally "attacked" when journalists probed their actions.
- They felt "betrayed" when journalists who were once their "comrades" prior to 1994 began reporting about their organization in a critical manner.
- Certain high profile leaders would also pick up the phone and verbally insult editors and journalists.
- Politicians objected to the way certain stories were handled, the type of language used, or the treatment of a piece.

Another important factor that has influenced the flow of election information, and one that has been lingering since the beginning of the new century, is the issue of press freedom. From the outcome of a special high level discussion between cabinet members and the South African National Editors' Forum (Sanef) in June 2007, it was not quite clear what the future would hold. On the one hand, the media stressed the importance of the constitutional guarantee of a free press, but this was curtailed by ANC criticism that the print media was not supportive enough of the broader ideals that would serve the "national interest." Whichever way, in a Communiqué released by the Government Communication and Information Service and Sanef (2007, 06.17), it was noted by government and the media that:

- Both sides agreed on the importance of self-regulation…and it was noted that the media are strengthening their codes of ethics and conduct.
- Instances of inaccurate reporting and limited depth were raised by government and discussed. It was agreed that the credibility of the media as a source of reliable information is of vital importance to (the South African) society. The media would continue to take steps, including training and the application of their codes of ethics, to minimize publication of inaccurate information. For its part government would continue strengthening its communication capacity to assist the media in ensuring accuracy and promoting depth of coverage.
- Better mutual understanding of how the two institutions deal with information and communication should be promoted, including through internships and exchange of personnel.
- It was agreed that there was a need for greater working interaction between government and media to facilitate increased coverage of government, particularly in Pretoria, and to deal with problems before they become critical.

• In this regard it was agreed that changes in the media landscape and in (the South African) society are bringing major challenges for both media and government with regard to the quality of journalism. These include the pressure of the bottom-line on resources, and research and newsgathering infrastructure, increasing homogenization of content, lack of the flow of information from government and the need to increase the speed of the information flow, the challenge of broadening the reach of print media to those who prefer to receive information in African languages, the quality of (journalism) training institutions and the capacity of media and government to support the development of journalists and communicators. It was agreed that government and the media should discuss how such constraints can be addressed in order to strengthen (the South African) democracy.

What was absent from the above, was an unambiguous statement regarding the reality of the press in exposing government insufficiencies, ineptness, and corruption.[4]

Since major newspapers are no longer affiliated with any particular political party (though some gave explicit support to certain parties during the 1995 elections in terms of telling voters in leading articles who they should vote for), the impact of the print media on future elections, given the amount of negative reporting the government gets, has yet to be established. The SABC as national broadcaster was markedly changed in the 2007 elections compared with the past. Critics seem to agree that the organisation has already turned into a state, rather than a national, broadcaster (Green, 2007), not necessarily driven by its mandate as posited in an act by parliament to be a credible and reliable "public" broadcaster. To a certain extent, e-TV and its news channel with a much smaller footprint than the SABC will play a counter role.

Editorial Endorsements

Before 1994 the Afrikaans press endorsed the NP in national elections through the most prominent newspapers of Naspers (National Press), *Beeld, Burger,* and *Volksblad,* while the English press supported the liberal opposition. During the 1994 election the historical fault lines were still present.

Even though the 1994 election was a race between the National Party and the ANC, media endorsements did not go to the two main parties. The English press (in the form of the *Sunday Times, Sunday Tribune, Business Day, the Financial Mail, Cape Times and Argus*) in its loyalty to liberalism and therefore liberal parties continued to support the Democratic Party (Silke & Schrire, 1994, p. 122). Silke and Schrire make the argument that the English press (excluding *The Citizen*—a conservative paper founded through apartheid government funding that caused a big scandal) was out of touch with its readership at that time because many English readers supported the National Party (as indicated by the 1987 election when the Progressive Federal Party (the precursor to the DP) lost 10 seats to the NP). But the media campaign for the DP was rather lackluster.

The alternative press that developed out of resistance to the apartheid government, such as the *Weekly Mail* (now the *Mail and Guardian)*, the *Sunday Nation*, and *South* endorsed the ANC, while the latter two were scathing in their criticism of the NP and DP.

During this election, the ANC still used "traditional" ways of campaigning—that of big rallies and "walkabouts" in areas where it had support. The print media were only one source of information and had less impact than, for example, radio. In the two next elections the print media would become more important.

The SABC has in the past very blatantly supported the NP but changes in management since 1994 has made the pendulum swing in the other direction. Silke and Schrire (1994, p. 128) argue that the television coverage for the 1994 election was remarkable fair, however. Most of the airtime went to the ANC and the NP. One of the highlights of this coverage was the presidential style debate between Mandela and de Klerk on channels TV1 and CCV.

In the 1999 elections the print media were not so explicit in the endorsements of parties. This was a consequence of changing notions of the appropriateness of endorsing political parties through the mass media, as well as changing diversification and ownership in the print media due to the entry of foreign ownership as well as black ownership. The Afrikaans Nasionale Pers actually acquired newspapers aimed at the black market such as *City Press*. When the *Financial Mail* endorsed the United Democratic Front (UDM) it started an acrimonious debate about party endorsement causing other newspapers to be more cautious in that respect (Jacobs, 1999, p. 156).

When it became clear that there was a possibility that the ANC might get a two thirds majority in the 1999 election, the mainstream media started to indicate that the ANC might be a danger to democracy. The SABC, on the other hand, was accused of siding with the ANC, a situation caused by the change in management that seemed to have direct ties with the ANC as well as its editorial position.

In 2004 newspapers were even less willing to endorse a particular party than in previous elections, but it was clear that the *Sowetan, Sunday Times,* and *Mail and Guardian* endorsed the ANC. All newspapers of the Independent Group were reluctant to endorse the ANC. Newspapers of Media 24 (previously Nasionale Pers) also abstained from endorsement (Davis, 2005, p. 239).

Advertising

Teer-Tomaselli's (2005, 2006) research looks at party political advertising as a form of election coverage. As she argues, paid advertisements provide a particularly intense opportunity for parties to communicate to potential voters. Advertisements also provide a certain freedom to parties that are different from news coverage or editorial campaigns. Party messages can be disseminated in an unmediated way.

In the 2004 election, parties devoted the smallest portion of their advertising budgets to the print media. The ANC, which spent R3.8 million on advertisements in newspapers, spent a large portion of the money on the Afrikaans press such as *Die Burger, Beeld* and *Rapport*. The DA spent R790,000 on newspaper advertisements. The IFP and ACDP only advertised in community newspapers due to a lack of funds (Davis, 2005, p. 247).

The Role of Public Opinion Surveys

Opinion polling is an important feature of elections in the new South Africa. During the 1994 election there were at least 23 different polling organizations. Political parties used their own internal polls in 1994 to inform their campaigns. The ANC used an American pollster, Stanley Greenberg, to run its campaign and do its polling. The results were checked against more independent polling (Jacobs, 1999, p. 151).

In 1999 the media developed more sophisticated use of polls. A significant surge was *Opinion '99 SABC Radio and TV* as well as the omnibus of Markinor and the Institute for a Democratic South Africa (Idasa). Markinor also conducted polls for Naspers media, and the Human Sciences Research Council also did independent polling (Jacobs, 1999, pp. 151–152).

Public opinion polling became a more often used tool of analysis in elections after the 1994 election. The polls played an important role in the 1999 election to such an extent that it influenced election coverage because it informed media coverage as well as the priorities of political parties (Jacobs, 1999, p. 148).

Jacobs (1999) argues that a consequence of the opinion polls was the covering of the election in horse race terms. The focus of the polls was to try and determine which party was going to win and which one would come second—a focus on the margins of the victory between the parties. It also put an emphasis on whether the ANC would get a two thirds majority and speculated on which party would win the Western Cape and KwaZulu Natal. This diverted attention from the issues so that very little information on issues came out of these polls.

The IDASA-Markinor survey on what they called the "Public Agenda" for the 1999 election showed that there was a discrepancy between what the media reported as important issues singled out by voters and what the opinion polls found. Media indicated the following issues: immigration, land, rates and taxes, wages, the environment, the death penalty, and affirmative action. But as Jacobs (1999, p. 149) shows, these issues were not cited by more than 2% of the respondents. The majority of respondents cited job creation and unemployment as first priorities and housing and education as second most important. This survey also found that there was a very strong endorsement among the voters of the job performance of then deputy-president Thabo Mbeki—70% of the respondents were satisfied while 60% endorsed the performance of the national government. These findings were in sharp contrast with the media's coverage of the first 5-year term of the democratic government.

Jacobs (1999, p. 150) is of the opinion that the media do not reflect the opinions of the majority of the population but merely cater to the opinions of white voters. The issues singled out by the media were the issues that were important to white voters; for example, whites focused on crime as a problem and blacks on jobs, but the media only referred to crime as a problem.

Opinion '99, through their Public Participation poll and their Voter Registration poll, produced important information for the electoral process. These polls confirmed that a large portion of citizens lacked the correct identity documents to register and that they were also poorly informed about the registration process. The political debate that resulted from these findings led to an extension of the registration process. The surveys also revealed that voter apathy was not universal because there was a public willingness to register. Another important finding was that the political agenda of the respondents in the surveys differed significantly from the media and politicians. This finding helped the SABC to reorient the way it was covering the campaign (Jacobs, 1999).

CONTROVERSIES AROUND ELECTION MEDIA COVERAGE

During the 1994 election the SABC experienced controversy around its coverage of voter education. During the run up to the election the Democracy Education Broadcasting Initiative (DEBI) often referred to anti-apartheid activists who had relations with the ANC. Despite complaints by other parties this practice was continued. The National Party then laid a complaint at the Independent Electoral Commission (Silke & Schrire, 1994, p. 131). The outcome of the complaint is unclear but, given that DEBI continued its broadcasts, it is probably because the IEC did not act against it.

The SABC came increasingly under fire for what is perceived as bias in favor of the ANC. This issue came to a head during the 2004 election when it aired live coverage of the ANC's election manifesto and did not give other parties the same opportunity. During this coverage President Thabo Mbeki kicked off the meeting with the party-rallying cry of "Viva ANC Viva!" The opposition parties did not take kindly to this perceived favoritism of the SABC. The DA accused the SABC of creating a platform for the ANC and the UDM accused it of consistently favoring the ANC. The IFP was of the opinion that the new chairman of the Board, Eddie Funde who was in charge of the ANC's party list selection process, contributed to SABC bias. Independent media analysts were also of the opinion that the SABC favored the ANC (Davis, 2005, p. 233).

The matter was eventually taken to the Independent Communications Authority (ICASA) that ruled in the favor of the SABC on the grounds that the election period had not yet started and therefore it could not have been unfair coverage (Davis, 2005, p. 234). But this result did little to change perceptions of bias on the part of the SABC.

CONCLUSION

In the first years of its democracy since 2004, South Africa has constructed strong constitutional, legal, and media structures to facilitate the democratic process to run its course from one general election to the other: The national election commission keeps a lively website and oversees elections to a degree that garners the endorsement of critical observers. Also, a number of self-regulating mechanisms are in place in order to sustain and develop responsible media coverage of elections, such as those for the print press (http://www.sanef.org.za); the broadcast media (http://www.bccsa.co.za); and advertising (http://www.asasa.org.za).

South Africa has also broken the African spell of "one election once." The first three elections were different in nature (e.g., the first was characterized by great euphoria and the image and role of Nelson Mandela), but all were carried through in terms of what generally could be expected of a modern, developing democracy. There are no compelling reasons why the next election in 2009 and those following should turn out differently, except in worst case scenarios.

NOTES

1. For a more detailed discussion of the electoral system see Gouws and Mitchell (2005).
2. The authors are indebted to Herman Wasserman (2007), University of Newcastle, for permission to reprint the following abstract from his book (Indiana University Press) on South African tabloids for this section. For references, see Wasserman (2007).
3. Media Tenor South Africa is an institute for media content analysis.
4. See for instance the continuous coverage of these and related aspects in, amongst others, the quality weekly paper *Mail&Guardian* (2007-07-27, 2007-08-31, 2007-09-06) or on the online version *M&Gonline* at www.mg.co.za, "Dept of Home Affairs plagued by corruption." For an international comparison, see *Media Tenor*: "The media's role: Covering or covering up corruption," at http://www.mediatenor.co.za/download.php?download_cs=Corruption.pdf).

REFERENCES

Albertyn, C., Hassim, S., & Meintjes, S. (2002). Making a difference? Women's struggles for participation and representation. In G. Fick, S. Meintjes, & M. Simons (Eds.), *One woman, one vote—The gender politics of South African elections* (pp. 24–52). Johannesburg: Electoral Institute of Southern Africa.

Committee for Constitutional Affairs. (1992). Report on a proportional polling system for South Africa in a new constitutional dispensation, October.

Davis, G. (2005). Media coverage in election 2004: Were some parties more equal than others? In J. Piombo & L. Nijzink (Eds.), *Electoral politics in South Africa–Assessing the first democratic decade* (pp. 231–249). Basingstoke, UK: Palgrave.

De Beer, A. S. (2004). South Africa. In B. Lange & D. Ward (Eds.), *The media and elections*. Mahwah, NJ: Erlbaum.

De Beer, A. S., & Diederichs, P. (1998). Newspapers. The fourth estate: A cornerstone of democracy. In A. S. De Beer (Ed.), *Mass media: Towards the millennium.* South Africa: J.L. van Schaik.

Faure, M. (1996). The electoral system. In M. Faure & J. Lane (Eds.), *South Africa: Designing new political institutions* (pp. 89–104). London: Sage.

Faure, M., & Venter, A. (2003). *Electoral systems and accountability—A proposal for electoral reform in South Africa.* Unpublished paper.

Gouws, A., & Mitchell, P. (2005). South Africa: One party dominance despite perfect proportionality. In M. Gallagher & P. Mitchell (Eds.), *The politics of electoral systems.* New York: Oxford University Press.

Green, P. (2007). The rise and fall of the SABC. South Africa needs a credible, reliable public broadcaster. Will it get one? *Mail&Guardian,* July 27–August 2, 2007, p. 23.

Independent Electoral Commission. (1999, June 2). Report of the Electoral Commission of the Republic of South Africa—National and provincial elections.

Jacobs, S. (1999). The media and the elections. In A. Reynolds (Ed.), *Elections '99 South Africa* (pp. 147–158). Oxford: James Currey.

Media Tenor. accessed July 24, 2007 http://www.mediatenor.co.za/special_projects_sa2004.php

O'Donovan, M. (2004). Winning the attention of the media. *Election update South Africa,* 6. Southern African Institute of Electoral Studies.

Papayya, M. (2004). The role of the media in elections. In K. Adenauer-Stiftung (Ed.), Seminar report: *Media & election reporting In South Africa.* Johannesburg.

Silke, D., & Schrire, R. (1994). The mass media and the South African election. In A. Reynolds (Ed.), *Election '94 South Africa* (pp. 121–143). London: James Currey.

Sisk, T. D. (1993). Choosing an electoral system: South Africa seeks new ground rules. *Journal of Democracy,* 4(1), 79–91.

Taljaard, R., & Venter, A. (2001). Parliament. In A.Venter (Ed.), *Governmental politics in the new South Africa* (pp. 21–51) Pretoria: Van Schaik.

Teer-Tomaselli, R. (2005). Images of negotiation: The story of an election told through print advertisements. *Critical Arts, 19(1&2).*

Teer-Tomaselli, R. (2006). Political advertising in South Africa. In L. L. Kaid & C. Holtz-Bacha (Eds.), *The Sage handbook of political advertising* (pp. 429–442). Thousand Oaks, CA: Sage.

Teer-Tomaselli, R., Wasserman, H., & De Beer, A. S. (2007). South Africa as a regional media power. In D. Thussu, (Ed.), *Media on the move: Global flow and contra-flow* (pp. 153–164). London: Routledge.

Venter, A. (2001). The executive. In A. Venter (Ed.), *Governmental politics in the New South Africa* (pp. 3–19). Pretoria: Van Schaik.

Wasserman, H. (2005). Debating the media, shaping identity: postcolonial discourse and public criticism. *Communicatio, 31*(1), 49–60

Wasserman, H. (2006a). Globalised values and postcolonial responses: South African perspectives on normative media ethics. *The International Communication Gazette, 68*(1), 71–91.

Wasserman, H. (2006b). New media in a new democracy: An exploration of the potential of the Internet for civil society groups in South Africa. In K. Sarikakis & D. Thussu, *Ideologies of the Internet* (pp. 299–316). Creskill, NJ: Hampton Press.

Wasserman, H. (2006c). Les médias afrikaans après l'apartheid : un héritage encombrant? *Politique Africaine, 103,* 61–80.

Wasserman, H., & De Beer, A. S. (2005). Which public? Whose interest? The South African media and its role during the first ten years of democracy. *Critical Arts, 19*(1&2), 36–51.

Wasserman, H., & De Beer, A. S. (2006). Conflicts of interest? Debating the media's role in post-apartheid South Africa. In K. Voltmer, (Ed.), *Mass media and political communication in new democracies* (pp. 59–75). London: Routledge.

Wasserman, H., & Du Bois, M. L. (2006). New kids on the block: Tabloids as new entrants to the print media market in post-apartheid South Africa. In A. Olorunnisola, (Ed.), *Media in South Africa after apartheid: A cross-media assessment* (pp. 171–186). Lewiston, NY: Edwin Mellen.

Wessels, D.P. (1994). Electoral system and system of representation—Election of 27 April 1994. *Journal for Contemporary History, 19*(2), 141–179.

III

ELECTION NEWS COVERAGE IN COUNTRIES WITH COMBINED SYSTEMS

18

Characteristics and Dynamics of Election News Coverage in Germany

Frank Esser and Katharina Hemmer

The form and content of election news coverage in Western democracies is influenced by four structural macro-level factors: the strength of political parties, the government regulation of the media sector, the ownership structure of media companies, and the political and journalistic culture. With regard to the first impact factor, Germany's political structure is characterized by a stable multi-party system, covering a broad range of the political spectrum. Compared to the United States, party organizations are still strong and play a powerful role in the formation of governments, policy making, and the administration of campaigns. During election periods, they control which candidates are eventually selected and usually have the final word on political programs and the messages that should be conveyed to the public. Since German campaigns are fairly party-centered, election news is by implication more likely to be issue-focused and oriented to ideological goals.

With regard to the second factor, the regulatory framework of the German media sector is stricter than, for example, that of the United States, despite a considerable drive toward deregulation in the preceding decades. It applies stricter ownership rules to the print and broadcasting sectors in order to secure diversity and competition. In addition, press laws and broadcasting acts contain more detailed public interest obligations in their texts than can be found, for example, in the United States. On the German press market, which can be said to be relatively healthy in terms of economic revenue and political diversity, newspapers are required to follow principles of political balance. This is, however, notwithstanding that the prestigious opinion-leading national papers tend to follow distinct politically motivated editorial lines.

The third impact factor refers to the German broadcast sector which is divided into public service and private channels. Germany is the largest country in the European Union, and its television market is the most varied but also the most competitive. Surrounded by commercial rivals, the public service channels remain surprisingly popular. Public broadcasting is expected to provide more and better-quality public affairs coverage and to offer higher standards of informational, educational, and recreational programs. The means to achieve these goals are provided through license-fee funding, also designed to protect public channels from competitive market forces and direct government influences—at least in theory. In reality, the funding system forces public channels to remain widely popular, or at least respected, because otherwise the obligatory license-fee would lose its legitimate basis, in essence serving the general public and not just a niche market. Election coverage on public channels is subject to stricter regulatory rules than on private channels which have more leeway with regard to political advertising and journalistic content on their airwaves.

Journalistic culture, the fourth and last factor, is less adversarial than in the United States. German people in general and news people in particular seem a little less skeptical towards politicians and political institutions. This fits in with a political culture in which voting is considered a civic duty and where turnout levels consistently approach 80%.

HISTORICAL BACKGROUND

The tradition of democratic government in Germany can be seen as relatively short, but a tradition in which the media have played a prominent role. The first parliamentary system, introduced in 1919, rapidly deteriorated due to deficiencies in its first constitution and the success of Adolf Hitler. Exploiting the possibilities of a constitutional and political system that offered (too) many liberties, Hitler legally came to power in 1933. Soon after, a totalitarian order was established in which the media were used as a means to perpetuate the regime's grip on power; the freedom of the press was abolished, and all media underwent a process of political alignment. It was not until the postwar years that democracy was reinstituted, and it was with the experience of the preceding decades in mind that the new constitution, the "Grundgesetz" or Basic Law, was conceived. It is in the context of a country with a tradition of federalism and partisanship combined with the failure of the Weimar Republic and the events of the Third Reich that the contemporary situation of media and elections has to be understood. The chapter therefore continues with a detailed overview of the development and functional aspects of current structures in politics and the media that shape the election coverage in Germany. It then describes the developments that have taken place with regard to the content and effects of election coverage in recent years, and tries to illustrate the interrelations and implications that continue to influence German election coverage today.

THE GERMAN POLITICAL SYSTEM

In Germany, parties have a long tradition as important political organizations. While the first organizations resembling parties were founded in 1848, today's party system is based on the democratic, competitive party system the allies created after World War II. In the constitution, parties are described as a "necessary part of the free democratic constitutional structure," fulfilling a public duty in contributing to the political decision-making process of the people (German party law, §1).

After 1945, a number of parties without ties to the former Nazi government were licensed in democratic Western Germany.[1] Among them were the *Social Democratic Party* (SPD), which was close in philosophy to the SPD of the Weimar Republic, and the *Christian Democratic Union* (CDU), a newly founded party appealing to a less narrow ideological group. Parties in Germany are not, as in some other countries, oriented towards certain issues, but rather occupy a specific political stance, still more or less in tradition with their origin: the Christian Democrats (CDU) lean towards conservative, middle-class values, the Social Democrats (SPD) are oriented towards labor party values of the working and lower middle-class. Of the smaller parties in parliament, the FDP (*Free Democratic Party*) promotes civic liberties and free market values, the PDS (*Party of Democratic Socialism*) caters to a leftist, socialist audience, and the *Green* party focuses mostly on environmental and peace issues. However, the two biggest parties, SPD and CDU, today constitute catch-all parties (so-called *Volksparteien* or people's parties). They do not pursue any special interest politics for any certain class or group of people but are oriented towards common welfare and political compromise. Although party alignment has abated in the last few years (Gluchowski & Wilamowitz-Moellendorf, 1998; Jung & Roth, 1998), the long tradition of party membership and loyalty usually makes party identification a still relevant influence in elections.

Elections in Germany

Due to the importance of parties in its political landscape, Germany is often labeled a "party-driven democracy." It is organized as a parliamentary federal republic with proportional representation; the two institutions elected directly by the people are the federal parliament and the local state parliaments. Local state parliaments and municipal councils are elected by the voters every four to five years according to the local state constitution. Federal elections take place every four years and the chancellor, the head of the government, is in turn elected every four years by the federal parliament.

In federal elections, every citizen over 18 has two votes: the first vote is a direct vote for a candidate in the local constituency, who is elected by a majority of votes (even if he or she is not affiliated with any party); the second vote is given to a party. The parties are allocated seats in parliament by proportional representation. However, a party needs to receive at least 5% of the second votes (or three direct mandates from directly won constituencies through first votes) to form a "group" in parliament. This 5% barrier has been implemented following the experiences of the Weimar Republic, where the numerous small groups represented in its parliament led to constant disagreements and in turn to unstable governments, often incapable of any action due to lack of a majority in parliament. Despite this regulation, parties that receive at 0.5% of all votes are still eligible for government funding.

Parties usually have to form coalitions, since an absolute majority in parliament is needed to constitute a government. In the expectation of leading such a coalition, parties often nominate their candidate for the chancellorship in advance of the election campaign. This practice adds a personal aspect to an otherwise rather party-dominated election process.

THE GERMAN MEDIA SYSTEM

Newspapers as collections of news first emerged in Germany roughly around 1500. In the 19th century, a party press as well as an opinion and interest related press developed, and in 1916 Alfred Hugenberg founded the first newspaper conglomerate. In the Weimar Republic, however, freedom of the press was not guaranteed and with Hitler's seizure of power, the press was politically aligned. Newspapers were defined as "agencies of public duties" and used for propaganda purposes. It was not until 1945 that the American, British, and French allies "blacked out" all existing media in West Germany and founded new newspapers and publishing houses. Starting from 1949, anyone who was not affiliated with the Nazi regime could obtain a license to start a newspaper business.[2] When the new constitution was agreed upon the same year, it was with this history in mind that the freedom of the press was written into the constitution: "Everyone has the right to freely express and spread his opinion in word, writing and pictures and to unobstructedly inform himself through publicly available sources. The freedom of the press and the freedom of coverage through broadcasting and movies are guaranteed. No censorship is taking place" (Art. 5, Par. 1, German Basic Law).[3]

Today, Germany's press landscape is rather diverse: In 2006, there were 353 daily newspapers,

28 weekly papers, and six Sunday papers. Their combined circulation reached 27 million copies.[4] The press is regulated by acts of parliament of the 16 states, which do not specify any rules regarding election coverage. However, the press, like other media, is seen as a decisive factor in the formation of public opinion and therefore obliged to pay special attention to accuracy concerning content and sources of its coverage. A right of reply is guaranteed in all press laws in case of false reports; the press law of North-Rhine-Westphalia, for example, states that "the editor-in-chief and the publisher of a periodical are obligated to print a counterstatement of persons or institutions which are affected by an allegation made in the periodical" (Art. 11, Par. 1, Press Law of the State of North-Rhine-Westphalia).[5]

There is also a press code established by the German Press Council, which is jointly operated by several large publishing groups and journalist unions. Everyone can file complaints with the Press Council regarding media coverage. However, its sanctions are rather innocuous: the council can express its disapproval or, in harsh cases, give a reprimand to the publication in question, which is then obliged to publish the offence. The one publication with a reputation for not paying much attention to Press Council reprimands is Germany's one genuine tabloid: the *Bild*. Known for its lurid coverage and often rather conservative-leaning editorial drift, *Bild* is the best-selling newspaper in Europe, although its circulation dropped from 5 million in 1997 to 3.5 million in 2007. It is owned by the Axel Springer publishing house, which with a 23% market share[6] is the largest publishing group in Germany.

Together, the five largest publishing groups control more than 40% of the circulation of daily newspapers, of which most, like the *Bild*, have an implicit political leaning. Several opinion-leading papers can be identified across the political spectrum: The *Sueddeutsche Zeitung* (SZ) and the weekly *Spiegel* magazine are the most prominent and most influential representatives of the left range on the political scale. In this camp, we also find the smaller dailies *Frankfurter Rundschau* (FR) and *tageszeitung* (taz), as well as the news weeklies *Zeit* and *Stern*. The *Frankfurter Allgemeine Zeitung* (FAZ) and the *Welt* occupy more conservative positions, as does the weekly *Focus* magazine. For these nationally distributed papers, significant journalistic and social influence can be assumed (Wilke, 1999; Kleinsteuber, 2004). While the political leaning of the press is rooted in the country's tradition and history of party press and interest-driven publications, open editorial endorsements of political candidates are rare.

Broadcasting in Germany

Germany has a dual system of public and private broadcasting. Public broadcasting has existed since 1945, on a basis the allies helped establish. Public broadcast channels are designated to inform and educate citizens and to "function as a medium and element of the process of free individual and public formation of opinion" (Art. 11, State Treaty on Broadcasting in Germany, 2004). They are financed mainly through license fees and to a very limited degree through advertising revenue, and are self-regulated by independent public broadcasting boards. Their mixed revenue sources allow them independence from the state as well as the market. Commercial broadcasting was introduced in the 1980s, and today more than 50 different channels exist. In fact, the crowded German television market is the most competitive in Europe. Public television channels are still among the top five most watched channels in Germany as of 2006.[7] They are regulated by the State Media Treaty, which dictates that public broadcasting stations have to "respect and protect human dignity. They should contribute to strengthen respect for life, freedom, and physical inviolability, the respect for beliefs and opinions of others, [as well as] ethical and religious beliefs" (Art. 3, State Media Treaty 2004). Furthermore, public broadcasting is committed to "principles of objectivity and impartiality of coverage" as well as diversity of opinion, and coverage has to be "independent and factual" (Art 3, State Media Treaty, 2004).

On public channels, political newscasts cannot be sponsored, and commentary has to be separated from news coverage and labeled accordingly (Art. 10, State Media Treaty, 2004). If polls are used, their representativeness must be specified. Total advertising time is restricted to 20 minutes per day, and prohibited on Sundays, holidays, and after 8 pm on work days. Public channels are not constitutionally obliged to give airtime to political parties, but are often committed to do so by state broadcasting laws. They traditionally provide an appropriate amount of airtime to each party in any case as part of their public obligation of impartial information. Additionally, since public broadcasters are expected to cover the whole election with professional distance and impartiality, the boards have implemented certain rules regarding the time of the election campaign: no appearances of politicians in entertainment shows, and no active news work by journalists who are in any way affiliated with a party's campaign (Drück, 2004).

Private channels are partly regulated by the State Media Treaty as well, however they have no duty to inform or educate nor do they have the same strict obligations concerning advertising. While airtime is provided free of charge by public channels, parties have to pay (a reduced priced of 50% of the usually spot rate) on private channels (Holtz-Bacha, 2005, 2006).

Journalism Culture

Next to the political and media system, the role perceptions and normative orientations of journalists and the relationship between journalists and politicians is another important systemic factor to be considered. It is important to recognize that media in Germany do not merely constitute private enterprises, but rather fulfill a function as public institutions. Journalist unions and professional organizations register high membership, and the relationship between the media, the political system and the public can be seen as a strong system of organized social groups. Of special importance is the powerful role of political parties in many parts of society. Party politics also have an influence on media organizations because their executive boards are often either controlled by party representatives (in the case of the public broadcasting channels) or because media organizations pursue politically motivated editorial lines (in the case of national newspapers). As a result, Pfetsch (2001) argues that the political communication style in Germany has evolved around a press-party parallelism. In that setting, there is more consensual symbiosis between the news media and politicians. As a consequence, German news journalists lag behind their U.S. counterparts as far as their watchdog-mentality is concerned.

In line with this context, the German media landscape is characterized by external rather than internal pluralism, the editorial lines are often politically motivated, and the self-concept of journalists relies not only on conveying neutral information, but also on analysis and interpretation of complex issues (Weischenberg et al., 2006). This role perception can be traced back to the tradition of journalists as political commentators during periods when the press acted as party organs. With a history as political commentators as well as news workers, German journalists do not refer as strongly to professional norms of neutrality as their American colleagues do (Donsbach & Patterson, 2004).[8] Political communication is generally characterized by a more politically motivated style because journalists' news practices of and political positions of parties are more closely linked than, for example, in the United States (Pfetsch, 2001).

THE NEWS COVERAGE OF ELECTION CAMPAIGNS:
DEVELOPMENTS AND CHARACTERISTICS

The main concerns associated with recent changes in Germany's news culture (Esser & D'Angelo, 2006; Schulz & Zeh, 2005) are related to the democratic quality of the election coverage (whether or not it discourages political participation and perceived legitimacy of the system) and to Americanization tendencies (which are associated with decreasing amounts of election coverage, decreasing length of candidate sound bites, more personalized news, more interpretive news, more strategic news, and more negative news). The use of American campaign practices by German parties was first noticed in 1953, when the Christian Democrats began using opinion research and advertising agencies. 1961 is considered the year of the first entirely professionally organized election campaign, with the youthful candidate of the SPD, Willy Brandt, as a perfect fit for a personalized campaign with John F. Kennedy as a role model. Brandt even challenged his competitor Adenauer to a televised debate; Adenauer, however, declined, and TV debates between the two front runners were not introduced until 2002. Today, the diffusion of U.S. practices and structures is still a recurring topic in election campaign and media research; especially processes of personalization, the use of sound bites and game frames, and an increasing negativity are prominent issues in numerous studies. A driving force behind the research on these issues is concern over a decline of democratic values among the citizenry—political apathy and disinterest as well as dwindling political participation is dreaded. Voter turnout, which has traditionally been high in Germany, has fallen from constantly over 85% throughout the 1950s, 1960s, 1970s, and 1980s to 79% in 2002 and 78% in 2005.

Intensity of Election Coverage

Between the first democratic election in 1949 and 2005, 16 general elections have been held, four of them under "irregular" circumstances due to the retirement of a chancellor, a government coalition change, a motion of constructive non-confidence, and a failed vote of confidence. Over this period, election coverage rose in a continuous wave-like process from a mere 6% of overall political coverage in 1949 to almost triple this amount in the 1970s, and has since been more or less stable at this higher level (Schulz & Zeh, 2006, 2007; Wilke & Reinemann, 2001). Explanatory factors for these fluctuations over time include changes in the editorial space available for political news, competing and compelling news events (like German reunification in 1990), the closeness of individual races as well as the intensity of campaigning efforts (which has been increasing lately), and the introduction of media centered campaign events (like the TV debates in 2002). Figure 18.1 depicts the development in the German press.

Personalization of Election Coverage

Indicating a more personalized news style, the share of election stories with visual images and speeches from the main candidates has mounted steadily on the main evening news broadcasts. This increased degree of personalization, as documented in Figure 18.2, can be largely attributed to the introduction of televised debates. In 2002, the first on-stage duel between the two main candidates (Gerhard Schröder of SPD and Edmund Stoiber of CDU) was aired. The event received a vast amount of candidate-centered media coverage and more than 15 million people watched the debate. In 2005, the debate became the ultimate media event, broadcast simultaneously by Germany's four biggest television channels (the public ARD and ZDF as well as the commercial RTL and SAT1). The setup of the event was very similar to that of the U.S. debates, as were the analyses by experts and journalists that followed. The debates were publicly greeted as a chance to provide voters with a more direct source of information about the candidates, and the argument has been made that they were a major influence on the portrayal of the candidates for chancellor in the press (Reinemann & Wilke, 2007b; Weiss, 2005).[9] Although Genz et al. (2001) note that the amount of personalization was rather stable during the 1990s, the attention

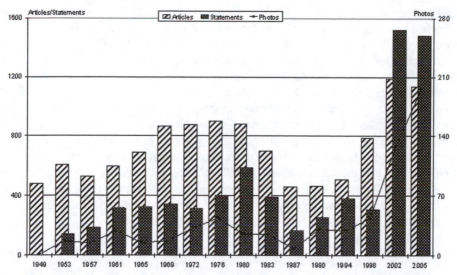

Basis: 11670 election-related articles, 7130 evaluative statements and 650 photographs in the national newspapers
Frankfurter Rundschau, Sueddeutsche Zeitung, Frankfurter Allgemeine Zeitung, and *Die Welt* in the last four weeks
before polling day (of which a 50% sample was coded).
Source: Reinemann & Wilke (2007a)..

FIGURE 18.1   Amount of election coverage in the German press.

paid towards the candidates has been clearly on the rise recently (Esser & D'Angelo, 2006)—at
least in part the result of debate-related follow-up coverage.

Despite the important role of the parties, single candidates attract the attention of the voters
more and more. The televised advertisements published by the parties during the 2002 and 2005
campaigns affirm this impression: All spots by the Green party and the FDP revolved around
their candidates, and at least half of the spots of SPD and CDU/CSU did the same. However,

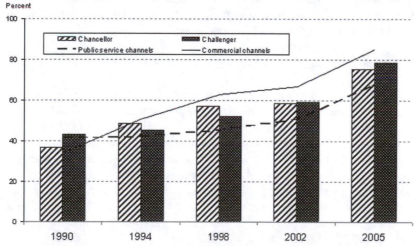

Note: Chart depicts the proportion of election stories with visual images (and original voice) of main candidates
on the evening newscasts of the major public service channels (ARD Tagesschau and ZDF heute) and the major
commercial channels (RTL Aktuell and SAT1 News) in the last four weeks before polling day.
Source: Schulz & Zeh (2007).

FIGURE 18.2   Personalization of election coverage on German television.

counterarguments against this macrotrend of personalization exist: First, regarding the televised ads, candidate appearance is often restricted to visual presence. As Holtz-Bacha (2003, p. 21) argues, "personalization in terms of an active role of the candidate is less frequent." Second, while personalization of campaign coverage has generally been higher after 1976 than before, the level of concentration on single candidates is still dependent on personality and political situation. Wilke and Reinemann (2001, p. 301) note "vast differences…among the individual elections" regarding personalized coverage, agreeing with Holtz-Bacha (2003) who states that "every election has its own face and is …dependent on the respective…context." This observation receives even more weight when considering a third counterargument: The amount of stories with a personal focus has been rising mainly because campaign coverage in general has been rising. Yet, these counterarguments cannot refute the general trend toward increased personalization of the campaign coverage. In sum, German television news conveys an increasingly lively, colorful, and exciting picture of the election campaign in which the chancellor candidates play an increasingly prominent role.

Incumbency Bonus

Despite the professional selection of news, there used to be a stable incumbency advantage in Germany. The "chancellor bonus" means that the incumbent generally receives more media coverage than his opponents, independently of the individual persons concerned (Semetko & Schoenbach, 1994). But this bonus is usually limited to attention, not evaluation —more coverage does not automatically mean better coverage (Holtz-Bacha, 2003). On the contrary: incumbents are generally criticized more frequently than their opponents (Genz et al., 2001; Krüger et al., 2005). Also, whenever the respective challengers appear in media reports they play a relatively important role (Schulz & Zeh, 2006)—it seems that the threshold for media attention is higher when it comes to the less well known challengers as opposed to the established and familiar figure of the chancellor. Recent studies have suggested that the chancellor bonus is on the decline (Krüger et al., 2005), partly as a result of the introduction of the televised debates in which the challenger per se is as important as the incumbent (Reinemann & Wilke, 2007b). With hindsight, the chancellor bonus was probably a historical phenomenon of the 1990s. In the 2005 campaign reporting the incumbent and the challenger were similarly portrayed.

Issue vs. Strategy Frames

Another topic that has caught the attention of election research concerning the level of direct confrontation between the two main candidates in the media is framing. Would German coverage follow the U.S. example and use game or strategy frames in the majority of election stories? With a reduction of persons of interest to two main characters and a focus on individual candidates rather than party organizations, election events could easily be boiled down to suspenseful duels: Who would prevail? And indeed, several studies have found that game frames (often used synonymously with strategy or horse-race frames) have become increasingly salient in German election coverage over the years (Klingemann & Kaase, 2001; Pfetsch, 1986; Schulz & Zeh, 2006; Wilke & Reinemann, 2001; Schulz, 1998). Genz et al. (2001) report a rising amount of horse race coverage, with "82% of the articles which concerned the election as central issue of their coverage focusing on the election as a contest" (Genz et al., 2001, p. 404). The most recent study by Schulz and Zeh (2007) found that strategy framing has been dominating television's portrayal of the candidates on German television news for the last decade. As Figure 18.3 illustrates, the only exception to this pattern was the 1990 election that closely followed German reunification.

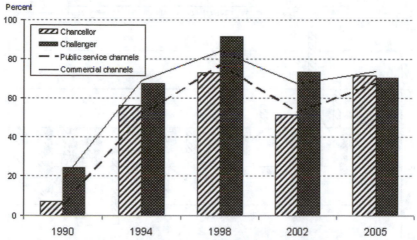

Note: Chart depicts the proportion of election stories that mention the two main candidates and are framed in strategic scenarios – aired on the evening newscasts of the major public service channels (ARD *Tagesschau* and ZDF *heute*) and the major commercial channels (RTL *Aktuell* and SAT1 *News*) in the last four weeks before polling day.
Source: Schulz & Zeh (2007).

FIGURE 18.3   Strategic framing of election coverage on German television.

The strategy prevalence was most clearly displayed during the 1998 election where it reached its present peak and, due to a ceiling effect, slightly fell from there. Schulz and Zeh's (2007) data in Figure 18.3 also show that commercial channels and public service channels do not substantially differ in their framing patterns.

Holtz-Bacha (2003) and Weiss (2005) both found that horse-race coverage increased especially after the broadcasting of the TV debates, which indicates an impact of the debate format on the perception and depiction of the two main candidates and the content-character of the election campaign itself. Especially candidates' publicity efforts and news management techniques are framed in strategic scenarios by the news media (Esser & D'Angelo, 2006). There has traditionally been much concern about a dominance of the game frame and the consequences for democracy in the spirit of Patterson (1993, p. 93), who suspected the press of "strengthening the voters' mistrust of the candidates and reducing their sense of involvement…because the game schema drives its analysis." Still, some German scholars view the trend towards a dominance of strategy frames in less negative terms. They attest to a dynamic impetus which the game frame can lend to election coverage (Brosius, 1995), and acknowledge that the "game schema" allows for more dramatic and vivid presentation (Schulz & Zeh, 2006, 2007).

Negativism

There has been a clear trend towards negativism in election coverage in the German press – both in quality papers (Reinemann & Wilke, 2007b) and the largest tabloid *Bild* (Semetko & Schönbach, 2003). The predominance of negative articles about the main candidates is especially pronounced since 1980, as can be seen from Figure 18.4. Only the 1990 election right after Germany's reunification brought positive evaluations for Chancellor Helmut Kohl. In all newspapers, notwithstanding their editorial polices or political preferences, there is a clear predominance of negative articles about both the incumbents and challengers. Thus, political leanings only rarely determined the evaluation of a specific candidate.

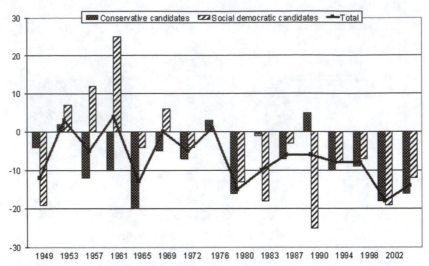

Basis: Chart depicts the balance of the proportion of positive and negative newspaper articles that mention the two main candidates and where published in the national newspapers *Frankfurter Rundschau, Sueddeutsche Zeitung, Frankfurter Allgemeine Zeitung,* and *Die Welt* during the last four weeks before polling day.
Source: Reinemann & Wilke (2007a).

FIGURE 18.4   Tone of candidate portrayals in the German press.

There is broad agreement that negative coverage has risen (Holtz-Bacha, 1999, 2000), if only parallel to the general increase in election-related media coverage (Schulz & Zeh, 2006). Genz et al. (2001), however, observe that while negativity is proliferating, it is not so much the journalists who voice criticism, but rather other politicians, experts, or citizens quoted in the media. This analysis is supported by Donsbach and Jandura (2003), who investigated the link between parties' press releases and media coverage and found that many media outlets did not adapt the rather destructive and negative rhetoric of most press releases: While the majority of press releases attacked the opponent, media reports often had a neutralizing tendency. This tendency is most pronounced on television, where Schulz and Zeh (2007) registered a surplus of references with a positive tendency for both candidates. They found that the tendency towards negative journalistic evaluations has abated, and that in 2005 the television presence of both main candidates was generally more favorable than unfavorable.[10] In sum, we see more negativity in the press than on television. This seems the result of strong principles of professionalism which demand a balanced and objective selection of broadcast news during election campaign time and restrict the integration of evaluative commentary into the news coverage. But across the board, we see more reporting of negative quotes or attacks by candidates, their parties or other campaign sources. Where we see an incline in negative evaluations by journalists themselves this may be related to adverse reactions by the press towards attempts of media manipulation by candidates.

Interpretive Coverage and Political Bias

Semetko and Schönbach's (2003) study of *Bild*'s coverage of the election showed that the tabloid included "more analytical pieces or commentaries alongside [its] tabloid style of routine political reporting" (p. 64). While *Bild* certainly does not set the standard for German journalism, there is some evidence for a tendency towards more interpretive coverage in the quality press also. Reinemann and Wilke's (2007b) analysis of broadsheet newspapers shows that since the 1950s, objec-

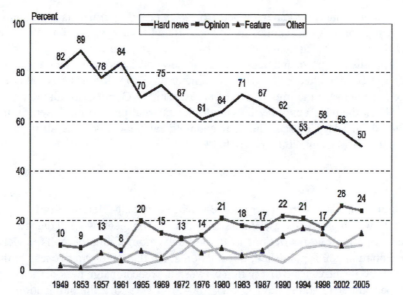

Basis: Chart depicts the share of subjective and objective story formats of election news articles published in the national newspapers *Frankfurter Rundschau, Sueddeutsche Zeitung, Frankfurter Allgemeine Zeitung,* and *Die Welt* during the last four weeks before polling day.
Source: Reinemann & Wilke (2007b).

FIGURE 18.5   "Objective" and "interpretative" story formats in the German press.

tive news coverage has been decreasing while the share of more subjective journalistic formats (features, opinion) has increased. Figure 18.5 reveals that the 2005 campaign saw the smallest proportion of hard news formats ever: Every fourth article was an opinion piece, every sixth a feature, and the rest were composed of other formats (portraits, interviews, and so on).

The tabloid *Bild* is an exception insofar as it publishes more explicit value judgments concerning politics than does any other German paper (Semetko & Schönbach, 1994, 2003). Still, many German media outlets do show clear and distinct tendencies towards certain political parties or candidates (Kindelman, 1994; Schulz 1991). They tend to synchronize news reporting with the editorial line of their political commentary and also prefer to publish poll results and expert assessments that are congruent with the editorial line (Donsbach 1997; Hagen, 1993). This partisan reporting is stronger in the daily than in the weekly press, and stronger in press media than in broadcast media. Donsbach and Weisbach (2005, p. 125) put forward the notion of a "double public opinion climate"—while opinion research in 2002 saw CDU/CSU as the frontrunner, the media suggested a rather tight race between CDU/CSU and SPD via editorial comments and subjective reporting. This practice of partisan coverage in German election reporting, however, has to be seen in the light of "the coexistence of political parallelism and professionalization that is one of the distinctive features of the Democratic Corporatist model" (Hallin & Mancini, 2004) to which one can assign the German media system. Working in a media system which has its roots in party press as well as commercialized media organizations,

the [German] journalist is a professional who respects rules and routines agreed upon by the profession as a whole and who insists on the autonomy of journalistic practice from political interference. At the same time he or she maintains a political/ideological identity, both as an individual and as part of a news organization and in many cases aspires actively to intervene in the political world. (Hallin & Mancini 2004, pp. 177–178)

In a comparative study by Patterson and Donsbach (1996), journalists were surveyed about their partisanship and news decisions, and it showed that both were significantly related in the U.S., the U.K., Italy, Sweden, and Germany. However, "the German news system is the most partisan [and] partisanship can and does intrude on news decisions, even among journalists who are conscientiously committed to a code of strict neutrality" (pp. 465–466). Another explanation for the difference between the importance of partisanship in Germany on the one hand and the U.S. and U.K. on the other could be that due to the external pluralism inherent in the German media system, the need for internal pluralism and political balance is not as strong as it might be otherwise (Hallin & Mancini, 2004, pp. 181–182).

Opinion Polls

Another example of this possible internal one-sidedness or self-referentiality is pointed out by Rössler (2003), who found that television news tend to rely on their own poll data for publication. Indeed, there are almost no restrictions as to the publication of opinion polls in Germany. But whenever an opinion poll is published, information about the representativeness of the data has to be included. While there is "no distinction between the precampaign period, the campaign, and a reflection period before voting day" (Drück 2004, p. 72) legally, the publication of exit polls before the closure of all polling stations is prohibited to prevent undue influence on voters (Art. 32, Par. 5, *Federal Election Law*). Also, only 6% of all political news during election time 2002 included statements about the status of politicians or parties in public opinion, and only every second of these statements reported opinion poll data. This amount has been stable since 1998 (Donsbach & Weisbach, 2005) and shows that opinion polls are only one source among several, and not one of the most important, either: Previous studies found that opinion polls only cause a very slight bandwagon-effect for the undecided and politically less interested. Only in few cases can they influence strategic voting in favor of a voter's second preference due to the electoral quota system (Rössler, 2003).

COVERAGE OF ELECTION CAMPAIGNS: USE AND EFFECTS

As mentioned before, voter turnout in Germany is relatively high compared to other Western democracies: Close to 80% of voters went to the polls in 2005, which is partly explained by the fact that voting is not only defined as a basic right, but also perceived as a civic duty (Esser & De Vreese, 2007). Observers of recent elections however have expressed concern about an increasingly volatile electorate: Between 23% and 68% of votes for each party in the 2002 and 2005 general elections were swing votes, and only the two biggest parties, CDU/CSU and SPD, received the majority of votes from their base (Infratest Dimap Wahlreport, 2005). The most significant cause for this development is the decline of party identification (Jung & Roth, 1998) and the dwindling importance of most socioeconomic status variables for voting decisions: "Traditional social cleavages or group identification, and social class in particular, once established as the determinants of the voting decision…have become less relevant" (Schönbach, 1996, p. 91). Instead, sources of communication have become more influential (Schulz et al., 2005); and although this includes mass media as well as interpersonal communication, television plays the most significant role as source of campaign information for the majority of voters (Schulz et al., 2005). While 56% of Germans over 18 used television as their main source of campaign information in the 2005 election, only 6% preferred the Internet, 8% radio, and 24% newspapers (Geese et al., 2005). Reliance on TV increases with age, and especially people with little interest in politics rank television highest as information source, which is attributed to the fact that the politically less interested care more for entertainment than information (Noelle-Neumann & Haumann, 2005). They turn to television as a main provider of entertainment also during election campaigns, and this behavior has fuelled the debate about the use and benefit of action- and entertainment-centered campaign coverage in the media (Klingemann & Kaase, 2001; Pfetsch, 1986; Schulz, 1998). Some recent studies argue that entertainment-centered television coverage has the advantage of reaching even the uninterested, whose importance in elections is growing as they tend to change their voting intention more often than do the more interested (Noelle-Neumann & Haumann, 1999). As Noelle-Neumann and Haumann (1999 2005, p. 21) put it: "if the politically remote citizens become providers of political majorities, all political impulses and information that reach their apolitical world acquire special relevance."

One televised event that has certainly reached this significance of late have been the TV debates. With 21 million viewers (Geese et al., 2005), that is every third person in the electorate, it seems that the debates have unified a public sphere that has been increasingly fragmented since the introduction of the dual media system in the 1980s. It might seem that it has become noticeably harder for candidates and parties to reach a large audience, although data on the 2005 election paints a rather positive picture: Close to 80% of the populace over 18 watched at least one of the special programs broadcast before the election (Geese et al., 2005). More than half of the electorate watched only public broadcasting programming during the 2005 election, and contrary to data about sinking public trust in the media (Kaase, 2000), the coverage in 2005 was well received: Especially the coverage of the two public broadcasting channels was evaluated very positively by the audience, independently of age, party ID, or residence. The quality of the reporting was perceived as high, with the most important factors being reliability, credibility, fairness, and comprehensibility, as well as objectivity (Geese et al., 2005). In general, only about 20% of the audience thought that the coverage in 2005 concentrated too much on the competition between the two main candidates, and only a small minority complained that the focus on the candidates instead of the party programs was too strong (Geese et al., 2005, p. 621). The majority of the electorate perceived the overall election coverage on ARD, ZDF, RTL and SAT1 as balanced and consequently also used one of these TV channels for information on the election outcome on Election Day (Geese et al., 2005).

Despite the obviously important role of television for voter information during election campaigns, the question about its influence on voting intention, turnout and decision and, in the larger scheme, democracy, remains: Studies find that voters who are not affiliated with any party and who frequently watch television news tend to base their voting intention on candidate preference instead of issue competence (Schulz et al., 2005). Data collected after the TV debates though shows that a majority of the audience was not influenced by the program in their opinion about the candidates (Geese et al., 2005). Furthermore, while newspapers have been found to be the least trusted among all media[11] they are still among the most important in influencing undecided voters in their voting decision (Schulz et al., 2005).

CONTROVERSIES

There have been some controversies which have been brought up frequently in public discussion concerning election coverage in Germany. They are usually centered on two areas: the question of media bias and the right of parties to access programs and receive airtime. Whereas the debate over bias (Donsbach, 1997; Hofmann, 2007; Hohlfeld, 2006; Noelle-Neumann et al., 2005) does not differ from other countries, the question of parties' access to the airwaves deserves more attention: Should, for example, parties with extremist right-wing views have the same right to airtime as every other, non-extremist party? In 1989 and 1993, the public channel ARD raised initiatives against the statutes that force broadcasters to provide airtime to all relevant parties, which was rejected both times. Similarly, demands for a weighted allocation of airtime to provide smaller fringe parties with as much presentation time on air as the larger mainstream parties, have not been fulfilled. Important in this regard is that the Federal Law of Political Parties states that "[w]here a public authority provides facilities or other public services for use by a party, it must accord equal treatment to all other parties. The scale of such facilities and services may be graduated to conform with the importance of the parties to the minimum extent needed for the achievement of their aims" (Art. 5). This equal treatment is based on their relevance for the public good. And in this, it is argued, the already established parties differ significantly from the smaller ones and therefore merit a different treatment—even if this might mean a preferential treatment in terms of media presence and gaining popularity.

A related controversy concerns the access of parties to editorial programming: the law does not explicitly include editorial content in its wording; however, especially the public broadcasting stations usually remind their editors to pay special attention to balanced reporting. How far a station has the duty to invite representatives from every party to a program instead of presenting only the parties represented in parliament already has been a debated issue. In every case which has been brought before court in this matter, it has been ruled that the stations are free to decide in what way they inform their audience about the elections. If they want to provide information via a debate between members of the current parliament, they are not obligated to invite representatives of all campaigning parties. However, if a program contains a debate between candidates of the campaigning parties, a representative of every campaigning party has to be invited, because in this case "a station is considered to violate the principle of equality and objectivity if only those parties that represent the power structures and the established opposition are invited" (Drück 2004, p. 72). While the discussions surrounding these issues of party access are of a more legal nature, the matter of media bias and media campaigning is frequently the topic of public debates. In 2002, for example, the *Financial Times Germany* published an explicit endorsement of a presidential candidate/party—a practice until then widely frowned upon among Germany's media. Gerhard Schröder, German chancellor from 1998 until 2005, more than once criticized broadcasters and newspapers for providing unbalanced reporting on his government and, later on, his election campaign in 2005.

CONCLUSION AND OUTLOOK

To sum up, there are at least four macro-trends that can be observed in German election news coverage: Increased personalization, a dominance of strategy frames, growing negativity, and a tendency towards analysis and interpretation. However, these trends are less strong and more ambiguous compared with election coverage trends in the United States. There is no doubt that political campaigning has become more professional during the last decades, and the role of the media has become more important over time—parties and politicians pay attention to media logic, and the media is wary of the parties' use of spin doctors or pseudo events. Still, interaction between the media and politicians is much more politically and less media oriented in Germany than it is in the United States. And Germany's multi-party system as well as unique media history shape election campaign reporting until today. Journalists' professional standards differ from their American counterparts in that they refer more strongly to social norms like ethical behavior, honesty and exchange relationships with politicians than to professional norms like objectivity or diversity (Pfetsch, 2001). Journalists seem to be slightly more partisan in their commentaries and news decisions than most of their American and European colleagues (Patterson & Donsbach, 1996), and the political leanings of print outlets are rather distinct. This political bias is said to go back to the roots of German newspapers as party organs, and is more or less expected by the audience: Parties have always had a strong stand in Germany, and although party identification is slowly but steadily declining, one can still observe a parallelism between social (and religious) groups and certain parties. On the other hand, Germany still has a strong public broadcasting system, which is committed by law to civic education and information. And as recent studies have shown, the public television channels are still favored by a majority of voters when it comes to election information. Additionally, there is not much of a difference between the commercial and public channels regarding negative coverage. Rather, the media serve as a neutralizer for increasingly negative press releases from the parties by keeping their own evaluations more balanced despite their partisan leaning (Patterson & Donsbach, 1996).

In other ways, the public service channels have implemented reporting styles that are usually associated more with commercial channels: it has come to a convergence of systems and cultures (Schulz & Zeh, 2006, 2007). One trend in television coverage that causes concern is the tendency towards personalization, strengthened by an increase in strategy frames. Personalization has received a major push with the introduction of U.S.-style televised debates in 2002 which involve the two main candidates only and which seem to have affected media coverage of the campaign also (Reinemann & Wilke, 2007b; Weiss 2005). Strategy frames similarly steer the focus on matters of contest and horse race, in which the two frontrunners have dominance over the candidates of other parties or party programs. And while negativity can be balanced through the professional standards of journalists and partisan bias is deeply rooted in German history and the tradition of a party democracy, personalization is a concept rather alien strange to the German context. A multi-party structure can hardly be boiled down to a duel of two individual contenders, and still the recent developments seem to point in this direction.

But as has been said at the beginning of this chapter, the concern about an "Americanization" of German election communication and coverage is not a new one and has accompanied public and scientific discourse over the last 50 years. Until today the macro-trends, despite following the American role model, are modified and converted to fit into the German political and media context. The same can be expected of new technologies which are advancing fast into the area of campaign communication: Every German party today has a website, as does the first female chancellor Angela Merkel, and in the 2005 election, weblogs made their first appearance in political campaigns (Albrecht & Perschke, 2006). The same developments can be observed in the media landscape, with most national as well as regional and some local newspapers and television and radio channels publishing news on a sometimes hourly basis on their homepages and commenting on candidates and events in their blogs. This makes coverage in general much more rapid and more current, and it will mean heightened effort for candidates and parties in elections to keep up with the new pace of reporting. But it will also mean a new independence from the media: a direct approach to the voters is now possible and can certainly be successful if handled cleverly.

NOTES

1. In Eastern Germany, the Russian allies set up a Communist regime under the leadership of the Socialist Unity Party of Germany (Sozialistische Einheitspartei Deutschland, SED). This regime collapsed in 1989.

2. In Eastern Germany, the Russian allies organized things a little differently: licenses were only given to parties and political organizations so that most press was controlled by the state and the number of newspapers stayed virtually the same throughout the 40 years of Communist rule until German reunification in 1990.

3. All translations are by the authors if not indicated otherwise. More information about the German constitution can be found on the website of the German government, http://www.bundesregierung.de.

4. More information about the German press landscape can be found on the website of the Federal Association of German Newspaper Publishers: http://www.bdzv.de.

5. The press laws of all German federal states can be found at http://www.presserecht.de.

6. Updated information can be found at http://www.ard-werbung.de/mp/publikationen/basisdaten/

7. Updated information can be found at: http://www.ard-werbung.de/mp/publikationen/basisdaten/

8. See also Esser (1999), Schulz & Zeh (2005), Schönbach et al. (1998), Weischenberg et al. (1998).

9. It should be noted that 2002 was actually not the first time voters could watch candidates discuss during campaigns: Since 1972, public television has broadcast "Elefantenrunden" ("mammoth rounds"), relatively open discussion rounds in which most of the candidates or party chairs debate current issues during an election campaign. This approach originated from the adaptation of the U.S. model to the German multi-party context where there are several opposing candidates. But ratings for these "mammoth rounds" declined steadily, and they were cancelled in 1987.

10. Schulz and Zeh (2007) note that although candidates appear in a broadly positive light on German TV, the characteristics that are central to their political roles—leadership qualities, professional competence, as well as credibility and honesty—are mostly negatively rated. These opinions originate mostly from other sources; journalists confine themselves to the judgments of apolitical characteristics or the candidates' position in the race.

11. It has to be said that the Internet was not included in this survey.

REFERENCES

Albrecht, S., & Perschke, R. (2006). *Wahlkampf mit Weblogs—Neue Formen der politischen Kommunikation im Netz* [Election campaigning with blogs—New forms of political communication on the net.]. Diploma thesis, Free University of Berlin.

Brosius, H-B. (1995). *Alltagsrationalitaet in der Nachrichtenrezeption* [Rationality of news reception]. Opladen: Westdeutscher Verlag.

Donsbach, W. (1997). Media thrust in the German Bundestag Election 1994: News values and professional norms in political communication. *Political Communication, 14*(2), 149.

Donsbach, W., & Jandura, O. (2003): Chances and effects of authenticity. Candidates of the German federal election in TV news. *Harvard International Journal of Press/Politics, 8*(1), 49–65.

Donsbach, W., & Patterson, T. (2004). Political news journalists: Partisanship, professionalism, and political roles in five countries. In F. Esser & B. Pfetsch (Eds.), *Comparing political communication. Theories, cases, and challenges* (pp. 251–270). New York: Cambridge University Press.

Donsbach, W., & Weisbach, K. (2005). Kampf um das Meinungsklima. Quellen und Inhalte der Aussagen über den möglichen Wahlausgang [Campaign for the opinion climate: Sources and contents of the statements about the possible election outcomes]. In E. Noelle Neumann, W. Donsbach, H. M. Kepplinger (Eds.), *Wählerstimmungen in der Mediendemokratie: Analysen auf der Basis des Bundestagswahlkampfs 2002* [Voter tendencies in a media democracy: Analyses of the basis of the election campaign for the Bundestag in 2002] (pp. 104–128). Freiburg/München: Karl Alber.

Drück, H. (2004). Germany. In B.-P. Lange & D. Ward (Eds.), *The media and elections. A handbook and comparative study* (pp. 59–77). Mahwah, NJ: Erlbaum.

Esser, F. (1999). Tabloidization of news. A comparative analysis of Anglo-American and German press journalism. *European Journal of Communication, 14*, 291–324.

Esser, F., & D`Angelo (2006). Framing the press and publicity process in U.S., British and German general election campaigns. A comparative study of metacoverage. *Harvard International Journal of Press/ Politics, 11*(13), 44–66.

Esser, F., & De Vreese, C. H. (2007). Comparing young voters' political engagement in the United States and Europe. *American Behavioral Scientist, 50*, 1195–1213.

Geese, S., Zubayr, C., & Gerhard, H. (2005). Berichterstattung zur Bundestagswahl 2005 aus Sicht der Zuschauer [Election reporting on the 2005 Bundestag election from the spectator's viewpoint]. *Media Perspektiven, 12*, 613– 626.

Genz, A., K. Schoenbach, & H. A. Semetko (2001). Amerikanisierung? Politik in den Fernsehnachrichten während der Bundestagswahlkaempfe 1990–1998 [Americanization? Politics in the television news during the Bundestag election campaigns 1990–1998]. In H. D. Klingemann & M. Kaase (Eds.), *Wahlen und Wähler. Analysen aus Anlass der Bundestagswahl 1998* [Elections and voters: Analyses of the results of the 1998 Bundestag election] (pp. 401–414). Wiesbaden, Germany: Westdeutscher Verlag.

Gluchowski, P., & Wilamowitz-Moellendorff, U. (1998). The erosion of social cleavages in Germany. In C. J. Anderson, & C. Zelle (Eds.), *Stability and change in German elections: How electorates merge, converge or collide* (pp. 57–69). Westport, CT: Praeger.

Hagen, L.M. (1993). Opportune witnesses: An analysis of balance in the selection of sources and arguments in the leading German newspapers' coverage of the census issue. *European Journal of Communication, 8*, 317–343.

Hallin, D. C., & Mancini, P. (2004). *Comparing media systems: Three models of media and politics.* Cambridge, CT: Cambridge University Press.

Hofmann, G. (2007). *Die Verschwörung der Journaille zu Berlin. Oder: Der einsame Kampf gegen Meinungsmacher und Meinungsumfrager* [The conspiracy of the Journalists in Berlin: Or the lonely fight against opinion makers and opinion pollsters].Bonn: Bouvier.

Hohlfeld, R. (2006). Bundestagswahlkampf 2005 in den Hauptnachrichtensendungen [The 2005 Bundestag election campaign in the main television newscasts]. *Aus Politik und Zeitgeschichte, 28*, 11–17.

Holtz-Bacha, C. (1999). Mass media and elections: An impressive body of research. In H. B. Brosius & C. Holtz-Bacha (Eds.), *German communication yearbook* (pp. 39–68). Cresskill, NJ: Hampton Press.

Holtz-Bacha, C. (2000). Wahlkampf in Deutschland. Ein Fall bedingter Amerikanisierung [Election campaign in Germany: A case of conditioned Americanization]. In K. Kamps (Ed.), *Trans-atlantik- transportabel?Die Amerikanisierungsthese in der politischen Kommunikation* [Transatlantic-Transportable? The Americanization thesis in political communication] (pp. 43–57). Wiesbaden: Westdeutscher Verlag.

Holtz-Bacha, C. (2003). Bundestagswahlkampf 2002: Ich oder der [The 2002 Bundestag election campaign; Me or him?]. In C. Holtz-Bacha (Ed.), *Die Massenmedien im Wahlkampf: Die Bundestagswahl 2002*[The mass media in election campaign: The 2002 Bundestag election]. Wiesbaden: Westdeutscher Verlag.

Holtz-Bacha, C. (2005). To the advantage of the big parties: TV advertising during the 2002 German national election campaign. *Journal of Political Marketing, 4*(4), 75–84.

Holtz-Bacha, C. (Ed.). (2006). Political advertising in Germany. In L.L. Kaid, & C. Holtz-Bacha (Eds.), *The Sage handbook of political advertising* (pp. 163–180). London: Sage.

Jung, M., & Roth, D. (1998). Wer zu spät kommt, den bestraft der Wähler: Eine Analyse der Bundestagswahl 1998 [The voters punish those who come too late: An analysis of the 1998 Bundestag election]. *Aus Politik und Zeitgeschichte, B52*, 3–13.

Kaase, M. (2000). Germany: A society and media system in transition. In A. Gunther, & A. Mughan (Eds.). *Democracy and the media: A comparative perspective* (pp. 375–402). New York: Cambridge University Press.

Kepplinger, H. M. (1998). *Die Demontage der Politik in der Informationsgesellschaft* [The disassembly of politics in the information society]. Freiburg: Alber.

Kindelmann, K. (1994). *Kanzlerkandidaten in den Medien: Eine Analyse des Wahljahres 1990* [Chancellor candidates in the media: Analysis of the 1990 campaign]. Opladen: Westdeutscher Verlag.

Kleinsteuber, H. J. (2004). Germany. In M. Kelly, G. Mazzoleni, & D. McQuail (Eds.), *The media in Europe* (3rd ed., pp. 78–90). London: Sage

Klingemann, H. D., & Kaase, M. (Eds.) (2001). *Wahlen und Wähler: Analysen aus Anlass der Bundestags-wahl 1998* [Elections and voters: Analyses of the results of the 1998 Bundestag election]. Wiesbaden: Westdeutscher Verlag.

Krüger, U. M. (2006). Fernsehnachrichten bei ARD, ZDF, RTL und Sat.1: Strukturen, Themen und Akteure. [Television news coverage in ARD, ZDF, RTL, and Sat1: Structures, topics and protaganists]. *Media Perspektiven, 2,* 50–74.

Krüger, U. M., Müller-Sachse, K. H., & Zapf-Schramm, T. (2005). Thematisierung der Bundestagswahl 2005 im öffentlich-rechtlichen und privaten Fernsehen [Coverage of the 2005 Bundestag election on public and private television]. *Media Perspektiven, 12,* 598–612.

Noelle-Neumann, E., Donsbach, W., & Kepplinger, H. M. (2005). Wählerstimmungen in der Medien-demokratie [Voter voices in the media democracy]. In E. Noelle-Neumann, W. Donsbach, & H. M. Kepplinger (Eds.), *Wählerstimmungen in der Mediendemokratie: Analysen auf der Basis des Bund-estagswahlkampfs 2002* [Voter tendencies in a media democracy: Analyses of the 2002 Bundestag election] (pp. 9–17). Freiburg/München: Verlag Karl Alber.

Noelle-Neumann, E., & Haumann, W. (1999). Wahlkampf seit 1995. In drei Stufen zum Wahlsieg. In E. No-elle-Neumann, H. M. Kepplinger, & W. Donsbach (Eds.), *Kampa. Meinungsklima und Medienwirkung im Bundestagwahlkampf 1998* (pp. 172–180). Freiburg: Alber.

Noelle-Neumann, E., & Haumann, W. (2005). Pendelbewegungen: Ursachen der Meinungsumschwünge zwischen 1998 und 2002 [Oscillating motions: The causes of public opinion swings between 1998 and 2002]. In E. Noelle-Neumann, W. Donsbach, & H. M. Kepplinger (Eds.), *Wählerstimmungen in der Mediendemokratie: Analysen auf der Basis des Bundestagswahlkampfs 2002* [Voter tendencies in a media democracy. Analyses of the 2002 Bundestag election] (pp. 17–44). Freiburg/München: Verlag Karl Alber.

Patterson, T. E. (1993. *Out of order.* New York: Knopf.

Patterson, T. E., & Donsbach, W. (1996). News decisions: Journalists as partisan actors. *Political Commu-nication, 13,* 455–468.

Pfetsch, B. (1986). Convergence through privatization? Changing media environments and televised politics in Germany. *European Journal of Communication, 11,* 427–451.

Pfetsch, B. (2001). Political communication culture in the US and in Germany. *Harvard International Jour-nal of Press/Politics, 6*(1), 46–67.

Reinemann, C., & Wilke, J. (2007a, July 23-26). It's the debates, stupid: How the introduction of televised debates changed the portrayal of German chancellor candidates in theGerman press, 1949–2005. Paper presented at the 50th Annual Conference of the International Association for Media and Communica-tion Research (IAMCR), Paris.

Reinemann, C., & Wilke, J. (2007b). It's the debates, stupid: How the introduction of televised debates changed the portrayal of German chancellor candidates in the German press, 1949–2005. *Harvard International Journal of Press/Politics, 12*(4), 92–111.

Rössler, P. (2003). Big Pollsters are watching you! Zur Darstellung und Wahrnehmung von Umfragen zur Bundestagswahl 2002 in unterschiedlichen Medien [The rmedia coverage of polls in the 2002 Bund-estag election]. In C. Holtz-Bacha (Ed.), *Die Massenmedien im Wahlkampf: Die Bundestagswahl 2002* [The mass media and election campaigns: The 2002 Bundestag election] (pp. 138–162). Wiesbaden: Westdeutscher Verlag.

Schönbach, K. (1996). The "Americanization" of German election campaigns: Any impact on voters? In D. L. Swanson, & P. Mancini (Eds.), *Politics, media, and modern democracy* (pp. 91–107). Westport, CT: Praeger.

Schönbach, K., & Semetko, H. A. (1994). Medienberichterstattung und Parteienwerbung im Bundestag-swahlkampf 1990. Ergebnisse aus Inhaltsanalyse und Befragung [Media reporting and party advertise-ments in the 1990 Bundestag election campaign: Results from content analysis and surveys]. *Media Perspektiven, 7,* 328–340.

Schönbach, K., Stuerzebecher, D., & Schneider, B. (1998). German journalists in the early 1990s: East and West. In D. Weaver (Ed.), *The global journalist. News people around the world* (pp. 213–228). Cresskill, NJ: Hampton Press.

Schulz, W. (1998). Media changes and the political effects of television. Americanization of the political culture? *Communications, 23,* 83–96.

Schulz, W., Scherer, H., Lutz, B., Kecke, A., & Wagner, H. (1991). Democracy comes to Leipzig, GDR: Political communication in the first free local election after the fall of the Communist regime. *European Journal of Communication, 6,* 391–416.

Schulz, W., & Zeh, R. (2005). The changing election coverage of German television. A content analysis: 1990–2002. *Communications, 30,* 385–407.

Schulz, W., & Zeh, R. (2006). Die Kampagne im Fernsehen-Agens und Indikator des Wandels: Ein Vergleich der Kandidatenerstellung [The campaigns on television: A comparison of the candidate presentations]. In C. Holtz-Bacha (Ed.), *Die Massenmedien im Wahlkampf: Die Bundestagswahl 2005* [The mass media in election campaigns: The 2005 Bundestag election]. Wiesbaden: VS Verlag.

Schulz, W., & Zeh, R. (2007, May). Changing campaign coverage of German television. A comparison of five elections 1990–2005. Paper presented at the 57th annual conference of the International Communication Association (ICA) in San Francisco, USA.

Schulz, W., Zeh, R., & Quiring, O. (2005). Voters in a changing media environment. A data based retrospective on consequences of media change in Germany. *European Journal of communication, 20*(1), 55–88.

Semetko, H. A., & Schönbach, K. (1994). *Germany's "unity" election: Voters and the media.* Cresskill, NJ: Hampton Press.

Semetko, H. A., & Schönbach, K. (2003). News and elections. The German Bundestag campaign in the BILD, 1990–2002. *Harvard International Journal of Press/Politics, 8*(3), 54–69.

Weischenberg, S., Loeffelholz, M., & Scholl, A. (1998). Journalism in Germany. In D. Weaver (Ed.), *The global journalist: News people around the world* (pp. 229–256). Cresskill, NJ: Hampton Press.

Weischenberg, S., Malik, M., & Scholl, A. (2006). *Die Souffleure der Mediengesellschaft. Report über die Journalisten in Deutschland* [The prompters of media society. Reports on German journalists]. Konstanz: UVK.

Weiss, R. (2005). TV-Duelle—im Spiegel des öffentlichen Räsonnements [TV-Duel—in the mirror of open reasons]. In R. Weiss (Ed.), *Zur Kritik der Medienkritik* [Critique of the media criticism]. Düsseldorf: Landesanstalt für Medien.

Wilke, J. (1999). Leitmedien und Zielgruppenorgane [Opinion leading newspapers and niche publications]. In J. Wilke (Ed.), *Mediengeschichte der Bundesrepublik Deutschland* [Media history of the Federal Republic of Germany]. Bonn: Bundeszentrale für politische Bildung.

Wilke, J., & Reinemann, C. (2001). Do the candidates matter? Long-term trends of campaign coverage: A study of the German press since 1949. *European Journal of Communication, 16*(3), 291–314.

19

News Coverage of Elections in the Long Transition of Italian Democracy

Franca Roncarolo

To talk of election news coverage in terms of Italy means reasoning about the peculiar features of a democracy that has undergone both radical changes and extraordinary continuities. After the collapse of the consociational democracy and the dissolution of the traditional party system over the past thirteen years, the Italian political system has experienced the rise and decline of an antipolitical mood, two electoral reforms (soon to become three), and the political career of a media mogul (Berlusconi) who twice came to lead the country without giving up his media empire, but was also twice defeated by a very traditional politician who is not at all at ease on television. Things are no less complex in the field of journalism, where the consequences of an incomplete process of differentiation from politics met the challenges produced by a late and imperfect, but also very rapid and radical, modernization. The result is a hybrid system that shares many features with other mediated democracies but adapts them to a particular context, in which the connection between the political and media spheres has always been close, and where the relationship between "media logic" and "political logic" is still far from reaching equilibrium.

The basic theme of this chapter is that in the meantime Italian election news coverage shows a high degree of mediatization and politicization. It follows the principles of a commercial broadcasting system but maintains a strong focus on political affairs, reserving greater space than in many other mediatized democracies. And while it is less subordinated to parties than in the past, it still has an adversarial orientation in a perspective that is frequently partisan.

THE ITALIAN POLITICAL COMMUNICATION SYSTEM
IN HISTORICAL PERSPECTIVE

A good starting point from which to analyze both changes and continuities of the Italian political communication system is to adapt the periods suggested by Blumler and Kavanagh (1999) or Norris (2000) to the peculiarities of this case, and to focus on the main transformation in the interactions among politics, media, and society that each phase has featured, highlighting the structural reasons that are at the base of the present problems.

The Golden Age of Parties during the Public Television Monopoly

After the Second World War, the very fragmented and highly polarized Italian political system was organized along the lines of a (quasi) consociational democracy (Lijphart, 1999). A proportional electoral law and a multi-party system provided, for a long time, political stability and an effective network to mediate interests, even if not without negative consequences (Mastropaolo & Hopkin, 2001). As usual in the "golden age of parties" (Blumler & Kavanagh, 1999), each major party had a vast web of links with their constituencies and integrated the many direct channels of communication with partisan newspapers.

In this context, the role of the news media was obviously important, but limited by various factors: both internal and external elements made the Italian news media system weaker than in other democracies (Hallin & Mancini, 2004; Mancini, 2005). On the one hand, low newspaper readership and an absence of a developed mass market for cultural consumer goods made television the key in an unbalanced media system (after the first broadcast in 1954, television quickly became popular). On the other hand, this system was never really independent of the political sphere. This was true for the press, which in the absence of a true market mainly developed as a channel of influence. It was even more true for public television, which was the object of both formal control (by a specific Commission) and informal control by the parties, who appointed their followers to top positions and executive boards. As time went by, this control became a form of occupation, which the 1975 reform of RAI (the state broadcasting corporation) institutionalized, "giving" a network to each of the main parties, both majority and opposition.

Despite being so pervasive, though, party control over television was not aimed at exploiting it as a propaganda tool. On the contrary, and similar to other consociational democracies, the aim was to limit partisan politics so as to reduce conflict and protect the political process from the potentially dangerous effects of the media (Marletti & Roncarolo, 2000). Until the early 1960s, RAI did not broadcast any political programs; and even when the first format featuring party representatives was aired, political coverage on television was still carefully restricted in terms of space and form.

Imperfect Modernization and the Crisis of Italian-Style "Particracy"

Two factors ushered in a new phase in the late 1970s: the crisis emerging in the political sphere and the need to modernize the communication market. While parties were progressively and systematically occupying all public spaces, transforming the classic model of party government into the degenerated form of "particracy" (Calise, 1994), the once leading Christian Democrats entered a crisis, which inaugurated a new season both at the institutional level (governments became increasingly unstable) and with regard to the practice of *lottizzazione* (the spoils system, which became even broader and more inclusive). On the other hand, the need to modernize the communication market, which had, until then, been greatly restricted,[1] found a first answer in clause no. 202, whereby in 1976 the Constitutional Court broke the public monopoly of television. Allowing the emergence of private broadcasting, this sentence opened up an important season of economic modernisation, but also triggered contradictory trends that sometimes caused big problems (Marletti, 1993).

Pluralism was the first casualty of the legislative anarchy in which the television system developed.[2] Initially, a huge number of private stations emerged, but three large commercial networks quickly concentrated most resources at the national level (Grasso, 2004). In a short time, the system evolved into a duopoly, in which a public company dominated by political parties shared control of almost the whole national audience on equal terms with Fininvest, the holding company created and run by Berlusconi. The private nature of this company and of other television stations that continued to broadcast at the local level did not prevent them from becoming politically influential. Given the complete absence of rules in the private sector, no broadcaster could survive for long without political alliances.

The effect of commercial networks on politics was also obvious. Needing to appeal to the public and, above all, being free of the rules that obliged public television to discipline its coverage, commercial networks began to introduce innovative formats for electoral programs. Thus, for the first time, paid political advertising was broadcast in the 1979 election (at least at the local level) while 1983 saw the first true "media campaign" with many national ads, talk shows, and debates (Mazzoleni, 1987). Moreover, commercial stations targeted messages to specialized audiences and made room for new content, less abstract and closer to the general public's experience. These changes let citizens experience a more direct (though superficial) approach to politics and politicians. But in the self-referential political phase (Marletti, 1985) that Italian democracy was going through, the potential change in political communication that was triggered by commercial networks was limited by two complementary factors: the structural weakness of a broadcasting system that was very dependent on politics, and the resistance of politicians. While consociational logic prevented journalists from playing the role of watchdog in the political arena, or that of referee in electoral campaigns, politicians were still too unfamiliar with television and too protected from the challenges of political alternation to feel a real need for change. Thus, while exploiting the greater visibility offered by commercial television and airing thousands of spots (Mazzoleni, 1991, p. 152) politicians continued to use television as a channel for inter-elite negotiations, using language more suited to insiders than for a mass audience.

The disjuncture between politicians and the general public widened in the late 1980s. Despite the limited autonomy of the Italian broadcasting system from political parties, the process of differentiation continued to split the media system and formed an intermediate space. Some journalists and many professional communicators developed a more subjective tone in political terms. While continuing to broadcast traditional programs (though with a slightly more personalized tone), on both Fininvest and RAI journalists and anchorpeople began experimenting with a more adversarial approach towards parties (Roncarolo, 2002a). This approach was accentuated in the early 1990s, when the Broadcasting Act required commercial television to broadcast news bulletins, and became widespread during the Tangentopoli scandal (1992–1993), which was extensively covered by all networks. In this climate, many journalists on both public and commercial television voiced a widespread call for a new politics, strongly supporting the Referendum front to the point where it has been suggested they created a "party of the media" (Calise, 1998).

Not surprisingly, as adversarial journalists encountered the effects of the long-term process of erosion of traditional subcultures (Morlino, 1995) and the supply of political representation by emerging crisis entrepreneurs, their coverage of the crisis helped to lay the foundation for an increasingly critical, and finally antipolitical mood (Mastropaolo, 2000). This was a mood that, between 1992 and 1994, turned the parties that had been in government since the Second World War out of politics and opened the door to the political career of Berlusconi.

The Political Communication System after the Collapse of Consociational Democracy

Although commercial television was the key element of change in the media system during the 1980s, its political impact became evident in the 1990s. This was when the most important broadcasting entrepreneur took the field, creating a new party that was very different from any other, and which was much more personal and supported by a professional marketing apparatus. In a very short time it stormed the political arena and showed just how far a leader can go who knows his potential market and, at least rhetorically, can meet the public's needs. Despite his relationship with leading actors of the former political system, in the antipolitical cycle opened by the Tangentopoli scandal (Marletti, 2002), Berlusconi immediately succeeded, setting himself up as leader of a new political season and giving a political voice to the widespread call for change.

Of course, one of the elements that favored the media mogul's success in the political arena was the new quasi-majoritarian electoral law (Katz, 2001). Indeed, being much more voter oriented, the new system benefited those political actors who were skilled at marketing strategies and accustomed to communicating with public opinion, rather than negotiating consent with other political elites. It hardly needs saying that, in the Italian political scene, one actor above all others owned such resources. Not surprisingly, therefore, after a very intensive campaign that exploited all the potentialities of the broadcasting system, in March 1994 Berlusconi's "light organization" won the election, heading a new center-right coalition.

Two elements emerged starkly: first, that the (bipolar and candidate-centered) rationale of the majoritarian electoral law was very suitable for a broadcasting system that, during the previous decade, had become more open to media logic. Second, that despite appearances, a less television-centered season was beginning that was closer to the postmodern model of campaign (Norris 2000). Notwithstanding the strategic role played by television in giving visibility to Berlusconi's newborn party, it was clear that a new, more complex model of campaigning had begun to operate, and that it put marketing expertise at the center.

However, as time went by it became evident that, despite all the changes, many problems remained to be solved in the relationship between media and politics. The main reason was that the Italian political communication system finally had been modernized but without those structural reforms that should have increased the media's autonomy,[3] and that the role of journalists did not receive adequate reflection.

FROM INCREASING ELECTION COVERAGE TO PERMANENT CAMPAIGNING

The many changes seen by the Italian political communication system are documented by various election surveys, and reflected by the changing focus these have had over time. Starting from the early 1980s, for example, scholars at Perugia's *Osservatorio-Archivio della comunicazione politica*[4] have highlighted the cycle of election coverage in the broadcasting system, showing two interesting trends: the different curves of public and commercial television, and election campaigns' tendency to lengthen until they became almost "permanent."

Public and Commercial Television's Attention Curve to the Election

With regard to the first trend, it is worth noting that, while at the beginning of the cycle commercial networks drove the growth process, to the extent that, in 1983, a single channel (Berlusconi's television Canale 5) passed all three public networks combined. After the collapse of the First Republic the roles changed, and RAI took the lead (see Table 19.1).

In 1994, the crisis of the old party system loosened the reins of political control over public television, and eliminated the rule that election coverage could only be broadcast in special election programs. Thus RAI began to do what commercial television had done previously, experimenting with more innovative styles of political coverage and introducing electoral communication into talk shows and information programs. The second factor underlying RAI's leading role was the unintended consequences of the more restrictive rules adopted after the Tangentopoli

TABLE 19.1
Total Election Coverage during the Thirty Days of Election Campaign
(minutes)

Channel	1983			
RAI	1645			
Canale 5	1860			
Rete 4	700			
Italia 1	440			
Total	4645			
Daily average time	154,8			
Channel	1987	1992	1994	1996
RAI	1770	1585	4265	3225
Fininvest	2805	4898	3085	2785
Total time	4575	6483	7350	6010
Daily average time	152,5	216,1	245,0	200,3

Source: Grossi, Mancini & Mazzoleni , 1984, p. 82; Marini & Roncarolo, 1997, p. 61.

scandal, which aimed at reducing the cost of media campaigns.[5] In order to circumvent these rules, which only applied to the 30 days preceding Election Day, Berlusconi anticipated Forza Italia propaganda, running it before the official campaign started. Of course, this new election campaign timing imposed by the center-right coalition leader also pushed the media into changing their schedules. Thus all the networks began broadcasting their electoral programs much earlier than usual, extending the total coverage to the point that, in 1994, it exceeded 19,000 minutes. Although this tendency concerned the entire broadcasting system, unsurprisingly it was particularly marked on Berlusconi's network, which became a kind of megaphone for the leader of Forza Italia and a privileged arena to give visibility to his new product, especially during the pre-campaign phase when there were no rules limiting the election coverage (see Table 19.2).

As research has shown, the strategy of starting campaigning some weeks before the official start was also adopted in the 1996 general election. Once again air-time devoted to covering the election was very high, although, in a less exceptional situation, Mediaset (the former Fininvest) greatly reduced its coverage (Marini & Roncarolo, 1997). But after that the rationale for lengthening the campaign changed and the quantitative dimension of election coverage lost its importance (with the obvious consequence that Italian scholars stopped documenting it).

TABLE 19.2
Total Election Coverage during the Pre-Campaign (minutes)

Channel	1994	1996
RAI	2650	2448
Fininvest – Mediaset	9330	2190
Total pre-campaign	11980	4638
Total (pre-campaign+campaign)	19330	10648

Source: Mancini & Mazzoleni, 1995; Marini & Roncarolo, 1997, p. 63.

The Age of the Permanent Campaign

While initially the habit of beginning campaigning before the official start had been chiefly a way of giving a new political product greater visibility, and a stratagem to circumvent restrictive rules, since the late 1990s it has become a structural feature of a system shifting from contingent practices of long campaigning towards a peculiar version of the original model of the permanent campaign (Blumenthal, 1980). Unlike what happened in the Anglo-Saxon majoritarian democracies, in the Italian case the permanent campaign did not represent the political leadership's attempt to maintain control over a turbulent environment, nor was it directly connected with the dimension of government. It was rather a way for the opposition to influence the climate of opinion (Noelle-Neumann, 1993). Furthermore, it was linked with the emergence of a continuous electoral cycle, where any intermediate election between general elections is used as a test for the majority in government. In other words, it could be said that in the Italian case, permanent campaigning is a strategy aimed more at defeating the majority parties than at strengthening citizens' consent for the government and its agenda.

Needless to say, from the journalistic standpoint this "assault on government," carried out through a permanent campaign that tries to crown the winner when the competition has not yet officially started, is a very good story (Roncarolo, forthcoming). Unsurprisingly, therefore, the transformation of election campaigns into a sort of permanent campaign punctuated by electoral tests has been strengthened by the news media, to which it offers a very suitable product and a new role in the electoral process. Indeed, the creation of a unique electoral cycle that links all tests into a coherent whole multiplies the horse-race effect, thus filling the media's need for suspense, announced winners, and possibly coups de théâtre, as happened in the 2006 election when the expected success of the left risked turning into an astonishing defeat and finally ended as a narrow victory. The increasing number of polls published in the media is indicative of how this process works whenever there is a meaningful enough election campaign (see Table 19.3).

In an apparently paradoxical way, the shift toward permanent campaigning has been associated with a generally decreasing interest in politics, especially on those commercial television channels for which audience is the primary consideration. Even in a very competitive election campaign, as in 2006, Mediaset gave less coverage to the competition not only than RAI but also than the so-called third pole, La7, a small but influential commercial television channel appreciated by the elite, and which aims to build an identity for itself through journalism providing in-depth analysis.

TABLE 19.3
Political Polls in the Italian
Permanent Campaign

Year	Number of polls
2001	148
2002	139
2003	59
2004	227
2005	262
2006	303

Source: Gasperoni, 2007, p. 23.

TABLE 19.4
Time Dedicated to Politics on TV during the 2006 Election Campaign

	Politicians' total speaking time during prime time and evenings (minutes)	Daily average of politicians' time per network (minutes)	Number of days on which one or more politicians appeared on TV programmes (news bulletins excluded)
Rai	8207	29	95
Mediaset	4186	21	66
La7	3175	49	65

Source: Belluati, 2006, p. 289. The data cover the time period January 1st–April 8th.

Of course everything is relative. As Table 19.4 shows, Italian television still devotes a lot of time to politics. During the 2006 election campaign, almost every day on public networks, and two days out of three on commercial television, at least one politician was on the air. The daily average was well below those of the 1990s (Table 19.1),[6] though, and the high concentration of the Mediaset supply in fewer days is typical of the behavior of a partial network that sometimes gives considerable space to politics, but is usually not very interested in it.

NEWS COVERAGE AS THE OUTCOME OF AN INTERACTION

The real point is that Italian political news journalism has been moving along a sort of parabola, whose rising part coincided with the emergence of a more differentiated broadcasting system that challenged the rationale and the equilibrium of the party system.

Journalists first influenced public political discourse when they answered the needs of commercial television by integrating the party-centered style of Italian consociational political communication, which was traditionally mainly oriented towards political issues,[7] with different content. During the first season of mediatization, personal and campaign issues achieved a relevance that, until the emergence of commercial broadcasting, would have been almost unthinkable. However, while consociational democracy was entering its most critical phase, the news coverage of elections became more policy-oriented, to the point that in the 1996 campaign over half (51.1%) of the election news coverage could be classified as policy issues, against about 21% in 1987 (Marini & Roncarolo, 1997, p. 80). This does not mean that a "governing schema" (Patterson, 1993) plays a central role in Italian election coverage. Actually, the shift was partly apparent because, in the Italian context, policy issues are more often quoted than discussed, becoming in the end only symbolic indicators of a more ideological orientation and acting as "cognitive shortcuts." For example, mentioning tax-cutting or social security may be a rhetorical way of reaching conservative voters, feeding their identity, and mobilizing them to vote. Nonetheless, it is undeniable that some important changes did occur, both in candidates' communication and in the media coverage.

The style and contents of political communication changed, first because the new majoritarian electoral context made more space for the political-marketing rationale, which emphasizes the strategic function of programs and stresses the importance of positioning on themes. Of course, they also changed because new politicians entered the field. Although Berlusconi was not so far from the old political class as he claimed, he had totally different experiences from traditional politicians, was much more pragmatic, and was used to being attentive to the public's preferences. Moreover, the contents changed because, in a phase of deep and dramatic changes, the media were swamped by a widespread demand for information that led them to take to the field, interacting with politicians in the agenda-building process, and helping to define election stakes with their thematic frames, although their influence was variable (Marini, 2003; Marini & Roncarolo, 1997).

This point has been examined in several studies, and various interesting elements have emerged; these can be summarized as follows. First, in the context of permanent campaigning, the framing process begins to drive the climate of opinion a long time before the actual electoral contest, and goes through different phases that can influence the dominant mood up until the last moment. Second, the thematic frames selected during this process are the result of a complex interaction, not only involving journalists, but also politicians and stakeholders on the one hand and ordinary citizens on the other. While citizens have only an indirect influence because their preferences and concerns are mainly monitored through opinion polls (which are influenced by the media coverage and political debate), journalists and politicians directly contribute to selecting the frames. Third, being too weak to develop an autonomous process of thematization (Marletti, 1985), but eager to play a more relevant role, Italian political journalism has adopted a strategy that uses news as the starting point for reflexive operations of thematic framing. For example, in the 2001 election campaign events such as robberies and murders began a cycle of attention to the theme of security, while in the 2006 election campaign different facts (ranging from reports by the Italian Institute of Statistics to remarks by the European Central Bank) were interpreted with reference to the more general theme of economic concerns (Mancini & Marini, 2006). Fourth, procedures of agenda setting and framing are easily influenced by politicians and stakeholders who have learnt media logic and know how to use it for their own purposes.

The Influence of Political Actors

The first way of influencing election coverage is to produce media events that are already connected with their own theme (such as "Tax Day" and "Labor Day," respectively organized by center-right and center-left coalitions during the 1996 campaign). The same is true for all those events that effectively communicate a message, as happened when Berlusconi signed his "Contract with the Italian People" on television during the 2001 campaign, or when the Confederation of Italian Industry's management harshly criticized the government's economic policies during its own Convention, at the end of the 2006 election campaign. It is also clear that given the media system's strongly self-referential behavior the more a candidate participates in television programs, the more attention the media system will pay him or her. For example, when in 2006 Berlusconi launched an impressive media offensive, occupying every kind of space (from political talk-shows to football programs), a flood of journalists' comments focused general attention onto him.

Based on the same mechanism, Berlusconi effectively influenced the election coverage by continuously experimenting with new propaganda strategies. Although with a different style and generally speaking on a smaller scale, during recent years the center-left parties have also learned how to drive media coverage and make use of different communication tools.

The strategic use of public opinion polls has been possibly the most important way of influencing both the media agenda and the climate of opinion in the Italian context. As Berlusconi clearly showed, polling data can be used as a key element of a strategy aimed at creating the conditions for actual victory—or at least a significant increase in consent— simply by announcing it. In both 1994 and 2001 he conditioned the electoral competition and the political debate by claiming he was the front-runner and legitimating his statements with data obtained by "private" opinion polls[8] that produced a sizeable bandwagon effect. In the 2006 election campaign, starting from a more difficult situation, he pursued the opposite aim of preventing the full bandwagon effect for his adversaries, and probably obtained a significant underdog effect for himself, besides once more driving the election debate (Pagnoncelli, 2006).

Media Logic and Electoral Laws

If the election news coverage is the outcome of a systematic interaction between journalists and politicians, then this interaction is, from many standpoints, unbalanced. Generally speaking, the Italian political communication system is in the apparently paradoxical situation that, although the media logic has defeated the old rationale of party politics, it has ended up working more in favor of television's commercial needs and politicians' competitive needs than of the needs of journalists and citizens. The 2006 election campaign showed this very clearly. Although in December 2005 Parliament passed a new electoral reform that turned the system back towards a proportional pattern corrected by a majority bonus, neither most politicians nor the media system gave up the greater mediatization and the narrative advantages offered by the majoritarian model of communication. For example, political debate and campaign coverage still continued to focus on leaders, represented the competition through a bipolar scheme, and stressed the decisive character of each vote. With only some exceptions, journalists did not play a really meaningful role this time, either. In a context where citizens could not have any control or influence over who would be elected, because of the blocked lists,[9] they did not document the candidates' profiles. While there was a great debate about leaders' statements, the media provided very little information on which citizens could evaluate the government's past performance and the future programs of two coalitions. On the contrary, they gave a lot of space to behind-the-scenes chronicles and the polling data battle. As in many other mediated democracies, in the Italian context journalists (and the public) have become more used to portraying politics as a strategic game played by actors who pursue their specific aims. It is, however, worth noting that the limited presence of media and political consultants severely restricts this habit. Although this kind of professional is now starting to appear, the long absence of both a true electoral market and an autonomous media system has so far delayed this phenomenon, making spin doctors basically superfluous, but also helping to feed a relationship between journalists and politicians in which the adversarial elements are more political than professional.

JOURNALISTS' ADVERSARIAL ROLE AND TELEVISION BIASES

Besides being the outcome of a differentiation process that opposes two apparatuses with different logics, Italian adversarial journalism must be considered with reference to the traditional politicization and the imperfect modernization of the communication sphere. Lacking the conditions for developing a more autonomous role, Italian journalism has maintained a high degree of politicization, which has developed into two specular models: one more conflictual the other driven by a partisan approach.

The Adversarial Approach

For a long time the conflictual approach was practiced only in the press where, starting in the late 1970s, some newspapers broke the traditional parallelism, interacting with parties as quasi-political actors.[10] Despite television's closer relationship with the political system, it too became more adversarial after the mid-1980s, when some news programs staged the public's dissatisfaction with parties and favored the formation of a new antipolitical mood. Needless to say, tension among journalists and politicians increased in the majoritarian context and with the beginning of Berlusconi's political career. However, it really came to a head during the 2001 election campaign when, after a brief experience as prime minister and a long "crossing of the desert" that began almost immediately after the center-right's defeat in 1996, Berlusconi resolutely marched towards victory. This was a victory that, as many journalists and political adversaries noted, aggravated the unsolved problem of the conflict of interests and, in the meantime, created an enormous concentration of power, giving Berlusconi "control" of a duopoly that shared 95% of the national television audience. Concern over these two issues became associated with the more general crisis of journalism. After having experimented with some political influence during the crisis of consociational democracy, journalism had discovered itself to be basically powerless, being defeated by the majoritarian rationale of politicians, who were asking for a more direct relationship with citizens, and at the same time trapped by the self-referential approach of parties, which had never completely abandoned the logic of the proportional system. The result was the most conflictual election coverage ever (Roncarolo, 2002b). Some journalists who had been leading figures in the previous adversarial seasons openly took the field, while others associated with them followed suit. The anchorman of a satirical RAI program was first, but the journalists who took the field also included some of the Grand Old Men of Italian journalism, in the press as much as on public television. All of them contested Berlusconi, while the center-right coalition sounded a warning that after victory they would take no prisoners, and threatened to fire all journalists on their blacklist. Not surprisingly, the disputes that followed were harsh, but the most negative consequences came after the election: not only because Berlusconi's government really did fire RAI's most critical journalists, but also because the already weak credibility of independent political journalism was further reduced by what many citizens considered journalists' true strategy of taking sides.

The other face of Italian journalism's politicization regards its subordination to the parties. This is a problem that, at present, above all concerns the broadcasting system where the relationship with political parties has remained closer than with the print media.

Forms of Partisanship

In public television the traditional parallelism with the parties in the government was jacked up exponentially after the transition towards a majoritarian system. Significantly, since the first Berlusconi victory the two most important channels have adopted professional routines aimed at guaranteeing the best coverage in news bulletins to the political majority. This goal has been pursued by creating, for example, the "sandwich technique": politicians' statements and comments are edited to give the first and last word—when viewers usually pay most attention—to the government side, while the layer of jam between the two slices of bread is reserved for the opposition. Of course, with this kind of technique the journalist's role has been even further reduced than before, to the point where, especially during the second Berlusconi government, a camera operator would tape politicians' comments without any journalist interviewing them. Things are obviously different in the other journalistic programs—from those that offer in-depth analyses to talk shows—but it is legitimate to think that the unbalanced style of coverage in the news bulletins has important consequences, favoring a more general tendency towards an adversarial approach among journalists who are less prone to accepting the media's subordination to politics, or who simply want to play a more influential role. So it is not surprising that, although in a basically neutral context,[11] there were some clashes between journalists and politicians also in the

TABLE 19.5
Time Devoted to Politics on RAI and Mediaset during Election Campaigns

	1996		2001		2006	
	RAI	*Mediaset*	*RAI*	*Mediaset*	*RAI*	*Mediaset***
Political institutions	*	*	6.9	5.4	1.9	1.5
Centre-right	43.4	45.8	42.5	52.0	49.5	55.8
Centre-left	43.6	42.1	44.7	39.0	47.4	42.6
Others	13	12.1	5.9	3.6	1.1	0.1
Total time (minutes)	268,5	200,9	527,3	389,7	453,9	88,9

* In 1996 Political institutions (President of Republic, Presidents of Chambers, etc.) were aggregated in "Others".
** In 2006 the data about Mediaset referr only to news bulletins and the most important programme of political communication.
Source: Legnante 2006: 434. The table include programmes of political communication and news bulletins.

2006 election campaign, as happened, for example, when, during a live interview with journalist and former television executive Lucia Annunziata, Berlusconi stormed out of the television studio in protest against what he called "one-sidedness." And the fact that, a few months after his election, Prodi complained about Italian journalists because he perceived the media coverage as adverse to him, shows the extent to which the problem is not contingent, nor simply connected to, an ideological bias.

At the same time, from a quantitative standpoint, and especially during election campaigns, RAI's approach is actually quite fair. The same cannot be said for Mediaset (Sani & Legnante, 2001), though. Not only has the Berlusconi-controlled company always favored him, to the extent that the most autonomous Mediaset journalist was removed as editor of the (most-watched) news bulletin that he himself had created thirteen years before, but Mediaset's unbalanced coverage becomes even more evident during election campaigns. In spite of rules prescribing equal access for all parties, Berlusconi's center-right coalition did indeed receive more campaign airtime, especially in 2001 and 2006 (see Table 19.5).

Although the aggregated data conceal the partisan coverage of individual channels,[12] the lack of balance is very evident, and the difference becomes monumental if we focus on Berlusconi and Prodi who, on Mediaset, enjoyed respectively 52% and 17% of the total time devoted to politicians (see www.centrodiascolto.it).

KEY ISSUES ABOUT RULES AND EFFECTS

Two main issues, directly connected with the problem of unbalanced political coverage, are frequently and vigorously debated: the most appropriate regulation of election campaigns, and the effects of propaganda on the public. Both have always been highly controversial issues even though, after the two defeats suffered by Berlusconi, the second has lost some of its most dramatic features.

The issue of regulation came to front stage in the early 1990s after a long failure to appreciate the problems of electronic campaigns, and there it has remained. Although Law 515 tried to fill this gap in December 1993, the problems raised by Berlusconi's campaign in 1994 clearly revealed its limits, highlighting the need for better rules. Starting from Decree no. 83 of 1995, the legislators repeatedly tried to resolve the unbalanced situation of a system in which one candidate was "more equal" than the others. Finally, in 2000, Parliament passed a regulation on equal access and fair coverage—Law no. 28, known as the "par condicio" law—which sought to defend democracy by preventing overexposure in the media (Zaccaria, 2004). Under it, national radio and television are not allowed to sell political advertising either during the election campaign or at any other time (thus taking note of the changes that had occurred with the emergence of the permanent campaign). Vice versa, they must (in the case of public companies) or can (in the case of commercial companies) broadcast *messaggi politici autogestiti*, that is to say parties' or candidates' propaganda messages, which must be long enough to contain political programs or opinions and must be presented in special formats, under several restrictions.[13] With regard to information, during election campaigns radio and television stations must give the same amount of free airtime to each party and candidate. Finally, opinion polls are suspended in the media fifteen days before Election Day.

This law has faced three main kinds of criticism. First, several politicians, above all Berlusconi, denounced the equal access law as unfair because, since it gives the same time to each political party, it damages the rights of the largest ones. Second, local networks, generally with few economic and organizational resources, complained about the difficulties both of offering free coverage and of guaranteeing equal time to all parties (which led to some changes in Law 313/2003). Third, various observers noted that the ban on political advertising even outside election campaigns makes it more difficult to reach citizens whose interest in politics is slight, and risks deepening their lack of interest.

Public Appreciation of Media Coverage and the Effects of Election Camp*aigns*

Despite the limits Law 28/2000 set on political propaganda and the widespread feeling of dissatisfaction with political parties, Italians actually seem more interested in politics and political communication than one might imagine. As research has shown, they get information from the media (especially, but not only, from television), debates with friends and colleagues (aside from relatives), and finally they vote in bigger numbers than in other Western democracies (81.4% in the 2001 and 2006 general elections). Some figures illustrate this clearly. While the number of people who get information about politics from television rose from 62.6% in 1990 to 77.4% in 2001 and to 78% in 2006, those who did not use any of the usual channels (or refused to answer the question) dropped from 15.8 to 6.3% (Legnante, 2006, p. 442). Vice versa, while in 2001 only 0.5% used the Internet as one of their two main sources of political information, during the 2006 election campaign those who visited a website (sometimes or often) grew from about 9% in October 2005 to 20% immediately after the 2006 election (Vaccari, 2006, p. 330). Moreover, both the hyper-regulated debates between center-right and center-left coalition leaders, Berlusconi and Prodi, had very large audiences. The first debate, which occurred after a very long wait,[14] was watched by 52.1% of the population, and even if the audience decreased as the novelty wore off, 42.1% still watched the second debate (Di Giovanni & Palma, 2006, p. 395).

Despite these data, though, it would be wrong to conclude that television is the decisive arena of electoral confrontation in Italy. Of course, in a critical situation such as the 1994 general election, television can play a more strategic role "moving the votes" of citizens who use it to find a new political product, because the party they used to vote for is no longer present on the electoral market (Ricolfi, 1994). Furthermore, there is no doubt that television can be a conclusive tool in the battle to activate those who are undecided whether to vote. Nevertheless, two elements limit the political effects of television in the Italian context.

First, public exposure is extremely selective: from the network a person watches it is easy to predict which coalition he or she will vote for (Grossi, 2000). Since the owner of the three most important commercial television stations became the leader of the center-right coalition, a new cleavage split Italian society, placing the public on two opposite sides. Those who vote for the center-right coalition mainly watch, or anyway prefer, Mediaset networks, while those who vote for the center-left choose RAI channels.

The second element that contributes to limiting television's political influence is Italians' resistance to radically changing their vote: although the enduring ties that used to bind voters to their party with a feeling of belonging have slackened, the Italian electorate still shows a kind of "light fidelity" (Natale, 2002). This feeling, which has probably been fed by Berlusconi's choice of ideological weapons (such as anti-communism) and his dramatizing of the choice, prevents people from "betraying" if not their party at least the coalition, leaving people free at most not to vote. As a consequence, while the campaign may have important effects, reinforcing an existing belief or activating an unwillingness to vote, it seldom succeeds in convincing people to move from one side to the other.

CONCLUSIONS

As we have seen, the Italian political communication system is, by and large, still involved in a complex process of change. Neither the modernization of the media sphere nor the political transition from a consensual to a majoritarian democracy has yet been completed. Political parties still debate about the best electoral law for a segmented (and in some respects fragmented) society that needs more stable and more effective governments, while television has not yet achieved complete autonomy from the political system (even though, from many other standpoints, it has gone a long way along the road to differentiation). Two main consequences come from this peculiar concurrence of mediatization and politicization. On the one hand it has favored the rise of a permanent campaign, which does not help leaders to control the turbulent environment of politics, nor move voters from their "light fidelity" to one political wing or the other, although it probably contributes to keeping the level of electoral participation high. On the other hand, it has made journalists' search for autonomy more difficult. In the absence of adequate reforms of the relationship between politics and television, and of a more reflexive consciousness about the strategic importance of information in a mediated democracy as Italy at present is, the risk is that new flaws (such as an inclination for game frames, and adversarial interpretative journalism) will come to join to the old ones.

NOTES

1. RAI networks could broadcast very little advertising, so the absence of popular newspapers for widespread diffusion of advertising greatly contributed to the development of a modern communication system (Pilati, 1987).
2. No law aimed at regimenting the television system was passed until 1990.
3. While this chapter was being written, the center-left government put forward a bill that will require Mediaset and RAI each to transfer one channel to digital terrestrial television within 15 months of its approval by Parliament. Moreover, in an effort to eliminate the pernicious influence of politics over Italian television, the center-left government has proposed to split RAI into three companies answerable to an independent foundation.
4. Osservatorio is now named Centro interuniversitario di comunicazione politica. See www.unipg.it/cicop/.
5. Law no. 515 imposed various financial and communication restrictions, introducing a distinction between advertising (which was forbidden), propaganda (which was governed by specific rules), and electoral information (which was required to be fair and complete).

6. Of course the two tables are not immediately comparable because during the last 30 days of official campaign the time devoted to candidates is obviously higher, but the rationale of permanent campaigning makes the data about the last 100 days reasonably meaningful.

7. According to the classification of the Osservatorio Archivio della Comunicazione Politica, in Italy political issues regard, for example, the generic themes of ideology, eventual alliances, and relationship among parties and factions, while policy issues concern parties' positions on problems and their policy proposals.

8. Although there is no institutional agency for public opinion research in Italy, like Gallup or Sofres, many pollsters side with one or other political party.

9. As Pasquino (2007) noted, although supported by good reasons (skyrocketing campaign costs, exposure to corrupt dealings, intra-party fighting) the decision to reject the preference vote had dreadful consequences. Indeed, as well as preventing citizens from influencing who would be elected to Parliament, it discouraged candidates from campaigning. So those who were best placed in the list did not campaign because they had no need to, the others because it was useless.

10. The label "quasi-party" was created with reference to *La Repubblica*, the first newspaper that actively participated in the political game, taking the field with its own political preferences (Marletti, 1984).

11. Beyond the fact that the most adversarial journalists had been fired, the 2006 election campaign was less conflictual as regards journalists' approach, because of the widespread disapproval aroused by the open criticism of Berlusconi by some journalists on public television during the 2001 campaign.

12. This is the case of the traditionally left-oriented public channel RAI3 and above all of Rete4, Berlusconi's supporting channel. According to "Centro d'ascolto," a monitoring center, between February 11 and April 7, TG3 broadcast 51.2% of airtime during which politicians were talking to the center-left and 47.6 to the center-right, while TG4 gave 74% to Berlusconi's coalition and only 25.8% to the opposition.

13. For example, these messages cannot break into other programs. The length must be from 1 to 3 minutes on television and from 30 to 90 seconds on the radio.

14. During the 2001 election campaign Berlusconi steadfastly refused to meet the center-left leader in a television debate, while in 2006 Prodi negotiated his participation, obtaining very restrictive regulations over the confrontation.

REFERENCES

Belluati, M. (2006). Mezzogiorno di fuoco. I faccia a faccia tra Prodi e Berlusconi come media event della campagna elettorale TV [High noon: Prodi and Berlusconi face to face as media events of the TV election campaign]. *Comunicazione politica, 7,* 287–309.

Blumenthal, S. (1980). *The permanent campaign.* New York: Simon and Schuster.

Blumler, J., & Kavanagh, D. (1999). The Third Age of political communication: Influences and features. *Political Communication, 16,* 209–230.

Calise, M. (1994). The Italian particracy: Beyond president and parliament. *Political Science Quarterly, 13,* 441–479.

Calise, M. (1998). *La costituzione silenziosa. Geografia dei nuovi poteri* [The silent constitution. Geography of the new powers]. Roma-Bari: Laterza.

Di Giovanni, M., & Palma, A. (2006). Il ruolo della televisione e dell'informazione nella campagna elettorale [The role of television and information in the election campaign]. *Comunicazione politica, 7,* 381–396.

Gasperoni, G. (2007). I sondaggi politici in Italia. Tra arretratezza e diffidenza [Political polls in Italy: Between backwardness and mistrust]. In P. Corbetta & G. Gasperoni (Eds.), *I sondaggi politici nelle democrazie contemporanee* [Political polls in contemporary democracies] (pp. 19-48). Bologna: il Mulino.

Grasso, A. (2004). *Storia della televisione italiana.* [A history of Italian television]. Milano: Garzanti.

Grossi, G. (2000). La televisione a tre dimensioni. Comunicazione mediale e intenzioni di voto nella campagna delle elezioni europee 1999 [Television in three dimensions: Media communication and voting intentions in the 1999 European elections]. *Comunicazione politica, 1,* 205–229.

Grossi, G., Mancini, P., & Mazzoleni, G. (1984). *Giugno 1983: una campagna elettorale* [June 1983: an election campaign]. Torino: Rai/Vpt.

Hallin, D. C., & Mancini, P. (2004). *Comparing media systems: Three models of media and politics.* Cambridge, UK: Cambridge University Press.

Katz, R. S. (2001). Reforming the Italian Electoral Law, 1993. In M. S. Shugartand & M. P. Wattenberg (Eds.), *Mixed-member electoral systems. The best of both worlds?* (pp. 96–122). Oxford: Oxford University Press.

Legnante, G. (2006). Comunicazione, elettori allineati e una campagna di mobilitazione [Communication, aligned electors and a mobilisation campaign]. *Rivista Italiana di Scienza Politica, 36,* 431–453.

Lijphart, A. (1999). *Patterns of democracy: Government forms and performance in twenty-six countries.* New Haven, CT: Yale University Press.

Mancini, P. (2005). *Il sistema fragile* [*The fragile system*]. Roma: Carocci.

Mancini, P., & Marini, R. (2006). Agenda setting, personalizzazione e clima d'opinione nella campagna 2004–2006 [Agenda setting, personalization and climate of opinion in the 2004–2006 election campaign]. *Comunicazione politica, 7,* 259–286.

Mancini, P., & Mazzoleni, G. P. (Eds.) (1995). *I media scendono campo* [The media take to the field]. Roma: Nuova Eri/Rai.

Marini, R. (2003). Tra cronaca e politica: l'agenda dei media in campagna elettorale. [Between news and politics: the media agenda in election campaigns] In P. Mancini (Ed.), *La posta gioco: Temi, personaggi e satira nella campagna elettorale 2001* [The stake. Themes, personalities and satyr in the 2001 election campaign] (pp. 17–44). Roma: Carocci.

Marini, R., & Roncarolo, F. (1997). *I media come arena elettorale:. La campagna 1996 nella tv e sui giornali* [The media as electoral arena: The 1996 campaign on TV and in the newspapers]. Roma: Eri, Rai/Vqpt.

Marletti, C. (1984). *Media e politica* [Media and politics]. Milano: F. Angeli.

Marletti C. (1985). *Prima e dopo. Tematizzazione e comunicazione politica* [Before and after: Theme-setting and political communication]. Torino: Rai/Vpt.

Marletti C. (1993). Media e partiti: La "modernizzazione imperfetta" della comunicazione elettorale in Italia. [Media and political parties: The "imperfect modernization" of Italian electoral information] In P. Mancini (Ed.), *Persone sulla scena. La campagna elettorale 1992 in televisione* [People on the set: The 1992 election campaign on television] (pp. 31–45). Roma: Eri, Rai/Vqpt.

Marletti C. (2002). Il ciclo dell'antipolitica e i risultati delle elezioni del 13 maggio in Italia. Verso un nuovo clima d'opinione? [The cycle of antipolitics and the results of the May 13th elections in Italy: Towards a new climate of opinion?]. *Comunicazione Politica, 3,* 9–30.

Marletti, C., & Roncarolo F. (2000). Media influence in the Italian transition from a consensual to a majoritarian democracy. In R. Gunther & A. Mughan (Eds.), *Democracy and the media: A comparative perspective* (pp. 195–240). New York: Cambridge University Press.

Mastropaolo, A. (2000). *Antipolitica: All'origine della crisi italiana* [Antipolitics: At the origin of the Italian crisis]. Napoli: L'ancora.

Mastropaolo, A., & Hopkin, J. (2001) From patronage to clientelism: Comparing the Italian and Spanish experiences. In S. Piattoni, (Ed.), *Clientelism, interests and democratic representation. The European experience in historical and comparative perspective* (pp. 152–171). Cambridge, UK: Cambridge University Press.

Mazzoleni, G. (1987). Media logic and party logic in campaign coverage: The Italian general election of 1983. *European Journal of Communication, 2,* 81–103.

Mazzoleni, G., (1991). Emergence of the candidate and political marketing: Television and election campaigns in Italy in the 1980s. *Political Communication and Persuasion, 8,* 201–212.

Morlino, L. (1995). Parties and democratic consolidation in Southern Europe. In R. Gunther & N. Diamandouros (Eds.), *The politics of democratic consolidation: Southern Europe in comparative perspective* (pp. 315–388). Baltimore: Johns Hopkins University Press.

Natale, P. (2002). Una fedeltà leggera: i movimenti di voto nella "Seconda Repubblica" [A light fidelity: voting movements in the "Second Republic"]. In R. D'Alimonte, & S. Bartolini (Eds.), *Maggioritario finalmente? La transizione elettorale 1994-2001* [Majoritarianism at last? The electoral transition of 1994-2000] (pp. 283–317). Bologna:.Il Mulino.

Noelle Neumann, E. (1993). *The spiral of silence. Public opinion—Our social skin.* Chicago: University of Chicago Press.

Norris, P. (2000). *A virtuous circle: Political communication in post industrial societies.* Cambridge, UK: Cambridge University Press.

Pagnoncelli, N. (2006). Il sondaggio americano [The American poll]. *Comunicazione politica, 7,* 369–379.

Pasquino, G. (2007). The political context 2001-2006. In J. Newell (Ed.), *The Italian general election of 2006: Romano Prodi's victory.* Manchester: Manchester University Press.

Patterson, T. E. (1993). *Out of order.* New York: Knopf.

Pilati, A. (1987). *Il nuovo sistema dei media* [The new media system]. Milano: Edizioni di Comunità.

Ricolfi, L. (1994). Elezioni e mass media. Quanti voti ha spostato la tv? [Elections and mass media. How many votes did the TV move?]. *Il Mulino, 13,* 1031–1046.

Roncarolo, F. (2002a) A crisis in the mirror. Old and new elements in the change of Italian political communication. In E. Neveu, & R. Kuhn (Eds.), *Political journalism. New challenges, new practices* (pp. 69–91). London: Routledge.

Roncarolo, F. (2002b). Virtual clashes and political games. In J. Newell (Ed.), *Berlusconi's victory: The Italian general election of 2001* (pp. 143–161). Manchester, UK: Manchester University Press.

Roncarolo, F. (forthcoming). "And the winner is…": Competing for votes in the print and broadcast media. In J. Newell (Ed.), *The Italian general election 2006. Romano Prodi's victory.* Manchester: Manchester University Press.

Sani, G., & Legnante, G. (2001). La comunicazione politica in televisione [Political communication on TV]. In G. Sani (Ed.), *Mass media ed elezioni* [Mass media and elections] (pp. 23–72). Bologna: Il Mulino.

Vaccari, C. (2006). La campagna 2006 su Internet: pubblico, siti e agenda [The 2006 campaign on the Internet: users, sites and agendas]. *Comunicazione politica, 7,* 329–341.

Zaccaria, R. (2004). *Diritto dell'informazione e della comunicazione* [The law of information and of communication]. Padova: Cedam.

20

News Coverage of National Elections in Hungary after 1990

Jolán Róka

News coverage of the national election campaigns in Hungary has undergone a radical transformation since the democratic régime change took place in 1990. The mass media played a fundamental role from the very beginning in the democratization process. News coverage of the election campaigns became one of the crucial sources of information about events and candidates in the parliamentary, municipal, and European Parliamentary elections. It was able to influence citizens' ideological, political, and aesthetic views, concepts, and values by using effective marketing tools and appropriate verbal, nonverbal, and visual means of persuasion. Politicians' and political parties' tactics and strategies aimed at the ideological manipulation of the citizens would surely be less effective without their adequate media presentation.

"The mediatization of politics—put in black and white—shows the spread of a communication technique by which politicians try to force the media into an event-following, passive role. Thus, journalists—often despite their intentions—become the means for attempted influencing of the voters' will" (Bajomi-Lázár, 2005b, p. 50). It is more difficult for the media to interpret the voters' will to politicians; the media can accomplish this only when editors find a way to take an active role in political processes.

AN OVERVIEW OF THE HUNGARIAN POLITICAL SYSTEM

Hungarian political traditions are determined by a thousand years of Hungarian statehood. Saint Stephen's concept of statehood and the state provided the framework for Hungarian political culture for a long time before the communist regime and continued following the democratic regime change of 1989 to 1990. Before the political transition the Hungarian political evolution had been characterized by weak democratic, but strong parliamentary traditions for more than a hundred years (Körösényi, Tóth, & Török, 2003).

In the Hungarian political system, the most prominent state and representative organ is its 386-member parliament, the Hungarian National Assembly. Its legal status and functions are regulated by the Constitution. Members of parliament are elected every 4 years following regular election campaign, and the winning party or coalition then nominates the prime minister, who formulates the government program. The head of state is the president of the republic, who is elected by members of parliament for a 5-year period (Gallai & Török, 2003).

Democracy was institutionalized in the Republic of Hungary between 1987 and 1989, as a result of which a multi-tier system came into being, and state power gained a totally new legal frame of operation: the parliamentary democracy. The first democratically elected government began abolishing the centrally planned economy to develop a new market-based economy. "From among the three basic governmental systems found in modern democracies the presidential, the semi-presidential, and the parliamentary—the system formed in Hungary with the democratic transition belongs unambiguously to the last. As we shall see, however, Hungarian parliamentarism in the 1990s is limited and possesses many unusual characteristics" (Körösényi, 1999, p. 147). Among the unusual characteristics of Hungarian parliamentary democracy mentioned by Körösényi are (1) the parliamentary, institution-oriented concept of politics; (2) liberalism as the ruling political concept; (3) nationalism; (4) two versions of the emancipatory-normative concept of politics (institutionalist and anti-institutionalist); (5) a depoliticized concept of the public interest; (6) an antipolitical approach in Hungarian political thought; and (7) a consensus-oriented approach to politics (Körösényi, 1999). Körösényi considers the political parties to be the main actors in Hungarian politics and the formation of public opinion. By the early 1990s, Körösényi (1999) reports that all the parliamentary parties were aligned with one of three camps, the liberal, the national-conservative/Christian, and the socialist. The socialist camp included the Hungarian Socialist Party, the liberal camp the Alliance of Free Democrats, and the Federation of Young Democrats (Fidesz), the national-conservative and Christian camp, the Hungarian Democratic Forum, the Independent Smallholders' Party, and the Christian Democratic People's Party. Later, Fidesz re-aligned with the national-conservative camp. The four most important political parties, which determine the formation of the Hungarian political system, are the Federation of Young Democrats—Hungarian Civic Party (Fidesz-MPP), Hungarian Socialist Party (MSZP), Alliance of Free Democrats (SZDSZ), and the Hungarian Democratic Forum (MDF). The financial base for the parties comes from membership fees, donations, and state subsidy. They all possess a huge executive organization that usually comes together annually or on special occasions (e.g., forming a coalition, leaving a coalition, election of officials). Its main task is to elect party leaders and to decide on the merits of a political case. All four parties also have a "small parliament" that controls the operative leading bodies. All four parties also have an executive body that actually manages the party and determines policy issues. Table 20.1 shows the organizational structures of the parties.

> Politics and media are interdependent in the 21st century. Political parties cannot effectively reach the citizens without the media presenting their program and main representatives. The term "mediatization of politics" refers to this phenomenon. The mediatization of politics originates from the United States in the first half of the 20th century, when American presidents began using the new media (radio, later television) for campaign purposes. Since that time politicians have become media conscious. The modern politician lends color to his message with characteristic phrases, he comes forward with unexpected thoughts in order to seem a charismatic personality. His goal is not only to appear in public, not only to address as many voters as possible in the most convincing way, but to thematize (agenda-set) successfully the political public speech. Politics became media driven: the politician adjusts his communication to the characteristics of modern mass media. (Bajomi-Lázár, 2006, pp. 91–92)

In other words politicians set the political agenda consciously, and the whole political process is directed and manipulated by communication experts: political communication and marketing professionals and spin doctors in the context of infotainment.

Nowadays academic research on political communication and marketing emphasizes that politics is a constructed reality. The citizens rarely have a face-to-face impression of politicians.

TABLE 20.1
The Organizational Structure of the Main Hungarian Parties

Parties	Supreme decision-making forum	Permanent representative body of membership ("small parliament")	Operative leading body	Deputy presidents	Leader
Fidesz-MPP	congress	national committee	national presidency	vice-presidents	president
MDF	parliament	national committee	national presidency	vice-president	President
MSZP	congress	national committee	national presidency	deputy president & vice-presidents	president
SZDSZ	national conference of delegates	national board	governing committee	no	president

Source: Körösényi, Tóth, Török, 2003, p. 203.

Instead, their knowledge about politics and politicians derives from mass media. This knowledge is indirect and mediated.

> In this mediation media play an outstanding role, that offer a forum for the rival political players to make their alternative interpretation of reality, constructions of reality, and messages compete. The winning party of the political competition through media is probably the one that is able to make the voters accept their own concepts as the most authentic. (Körösényi et al., 2003, p. 267)

AN OVERVIEW OF THE HUNGARIAN MEDIA SYSTEM

The Hungarian media system went through a fundamental and rapid transformation after the democratic regime change in 1989. A pluralistic media system came into being, characterized by many participants and intense competition among them. Nowadays thousands of different press organs, radio and television channels, and Internet forums try to satisfy citizens' information needs. The most important question, however, concerns who controls and influences the agenda-setting and the opinion formation processes in Hungary. This analysis of the Hungarian media system is mainly based on the work of Antal and Scherer (2005).

Television has a distinguished time-setting and agenda-setting role in Hungarian society. An average viewer spends more than 4½ hours a day watching TV. The Hungarian audiovisual media are both public and commercial: the public television stations are MTV (Hungarian Television) and Danube Television (Duna TV). MTV has two channels: m1, and m2, which is a satellite channel. Duna TV also has two satellite channels. In the fall of 2006, more than 900,000 adults (i.e., those above the age of 18, who are eligible to vote) chose MTV's Evening News. The most popular public political televised programs are "The Este" (the Evening), which is broadcast every weekday evening and watched by more than 8% of all the adult TV viewers; "Kedd 21" (Tuesday 21) watched by more than 10% of all the adult TV viewers, and "A szólás szabadsága" (Freedom of speech), transmitted on Sunday night and watched by more than 9% of all the adult TV viewers (http://www.hirado.hu/nyomtatas.php?id=154780).

The two most important commercial stations are the Luxemburg based SBS Broadcasting S. A. with 81.5% ownership of the TV2 channel and Bertelsmann AG., the owner of RTL Klub channel. The National Radio and Television Commission (ORTT) decided to provide two of the three terrestrial television frequencies to these commercial television giants in 1997. The program service fee paid for the TV2 (MTM-SBS) and RTL Klub (MRTL) channels is shared partly by the MTV Public Foundation and the Hungária Television Public Foundation, and partly by the Program Service Funds of ORTT.

The Hungarian television market is highly concentrated. This concentration is evidenced by the fact that the owners of RTL Klub and TV2 receive over 36% of the income of the total Hungarian advertising industry, and 90% of the total income from television ads. The fact that the commercial television market is owned by conglomerates also means, however, that a very few companies control program structure and content. TV2 and RTL Klub reach the most valuable age group of the audience from a marketing point of view: viewers between 18 and 49 years old. This conglomerate control has led to a monopoly of the television market and to the tabloidization of program content, and has consequently impeded the growth of competition and freedom of speech. Most of the program topics offered by TV2 and RTL Klub are shallow. Their approach is superficial regarding questions of social discourse, economic information, parliamentary coverage, documentaries, cultural news, and educational or religious programs, but nevertheless the News of RTL Club and the Tények (Facts) of TV2, both starting at 18.30, are nationally the most widely watched evening news programs, while the Evening News of the m1 public channel at 19.00 occupies the third position. In addition to the two main commercial channels there are increasing numbers of small specialized cable channels, such as Film+, Minimax, Cool, Sport, Viasat3, Hallmark, HBO, and Spektrum.

One of the first drastic consequences of the dual media system in Hungary was the radical decrease in the the public television channel MTV1's audience ratings and advertising revenue:

> Relying on the facts, one can conclude, that the formation of the Hungarian media regime shows a tendency towards ceasing the market and content service competition and freedom of speech. In the meantime in contrast to the commercial, tabloid-like television topics, the public information service (that ensures alternatives) could theoretically be more important, but the financing difficulties question the strategic role and the necessary independence of the politically directed public broadcast. (Antal & Scherer, 2005, p. 157)

There are serious concerns, yet to be resolved, about the monopoly of commercial information by the national frequencies. There is still some hope that Hungarian elites will have the power and good judgment to ensure a more free and balanced information flow that can allow competition from smaller market forces, despite the increasing domination of the media market by foreign, profit-driven entities.

The ORTT invited applications for a national commercial radio frequency in 1997. It determined some of the guidelines for the applications; for example, the concessionary fee, providing some public service, news broadcasts, and a preference for Hungarian music. Danubius Radio and Sláger Radio became the winners because they offered the highest concessionary fee. These two commercial radio channels have been the market leaders since 1997 in terms of audience share. Also popular are Juventus Radio, Klub Radio, and Info Radio. There were 147 radio stations in Hungary (6 national, 19 district, 122 local stations) in 2004. The local station has an outstanding role in broadcasting local news; however, there is a significant difference between the Budapest based local radio stations and the "provincial" radio stations. The Budapest radio stations strictly segment their focus group and provide (mainly public-cultural or entertaining-musical) programs corresponding to its interest. In this respect the market leader is the "Chronicle" program of the Kossuth station of Hungarian Public Radio. In contrast to the thematic program structures of the Budapest stations, the provincional ones provide overall content service. In audience share they are ahead of the national stations (Antal & Scherer, 2005, p. 164).

TABLE 20.2
The Number of Sold Copies of Political Daily and Weekly Newspapers

Organs	2000	2001	2002	2003	2004	2005. I.
Magyar Nemzet	67826	68791	98296	80524	75760	74057
Népszava	39851	33494	30207	27991	27270	26432
Magyar Hírlap	36732	33683	37842	32756	28155	0
Népszabadság	204175	197178	193910	173272	163456	157581
168 Óra	37578	40840	46715	35890	33817	33832
Heti Válasz	0	8187	31861	19315	14330	23261
HVG	115274	116130	111980	106243	99104	94750
Magyar Demokrata	0	0	0	46939	39522	39514

Source: Antal & Scherer, 2005, p. 173.

The two most important participants in the Hungarian press market are the Swiss Ringier and the German Axel Springer media conglomerates. Ringier publishes fewer newspapers than Springer, but it is the market leader in publishing sport and political quality papers, and also tabloids. It publishes three of the five most widely read dailies, including *Népszabadság* (People's Freedom), *Blikk*, and *Nemzeti Sport* (National Sport). These newspapers are read by about 1.8 million people daily. Ringier sells about 140 million issues annually in the Hungarian market. Springer dominates the provincial newspaper market. In 2004 it sold about 150 million newspapers. There are some further foreign media companies present in the Hungarian press market, among them Funk Verlag, Sanoma WSOY, Modern Times Group (MTG AB), Westdeutsche Allgemeine Zeitungsverlag GmbH, and the Daily Mail & General Trust Plc.

In the Hungarian media market conglomerates first became involved with the print media, and the first monopolies were formed in the newspaper business. A number of foreign media companies took control of the most profitable papers, and they began dominating advertising revenues as well in the competition for advertisers. Sometimes the entire profit from a given media market leaves Hungary and enriches the holding company abroad. This monopoly process not only has negative economic consequences, but also weakens both the quality of the content and freedom of speech. Table 20.2 clearly shows that sales of national newspapers decrease, at the same time that sales of county papers that provide local news, strengthen. The most popular political quality newspaper is still the *Népszabadság*, but during the last 6 years sales dropped by more than 30%. While sales of the national, quality newspapers decrease, there is a reverse tendency for the tabloids. Their expansion on the press market is spectacular. "In order to moderate the spread of the tabloid press, intellectual, professional groups more and more often express their claim for establishing a subsidy budget, which could provide sources for financing the loss of quality papers, regardless of their political orientation" (Antal & Scherer, 2005, p. 174).

REGULATION OF POLITICAL NEWS COVERAGE DURING ELECTIONS

Hungarian political parties and politicians realized the extraordinary importance of the media in political campaigns as early as in 1990, which in 1993 led to a media war; that is, the never-ending disputes about the lack of media independence and neutrality on the one hand, and the controlling power of the governing parties on the other.

In the Republic of Hungary, TV has gained crucial importance in shaping the political process and it is one of the most politically influential. In 1993, the situation became quite dramatic, as TV had become the target of the parties' political struggle. It was not until 1995 that the parliament passed a law regulating Hungarian television. The Media Law of 1996 regulates the public media (Hungarian Radio, Hungarian Television, Danube Television). The law regulating print media was created ten years earlier, in 1986.

Law No. 1 regarding radio and television broadcasting defines the meaning of political advertising: It is defined as a program that attempts to influence voters; that calls for support by participation in party elections, the party's program, support for its candidate, that appeals for votes; and popularizes a party or movement's name, activity, aims, slogan, emblem, and overall image. In the paragraph about restrictions and bans on advertising, the law decrees:

> In election periods, political advertisements can be broadcast according to the law regarding the election of members of Parliament, local and regional candidates, and mayors. In any other period, political advertisements can only be communicated in connection with a decreed election. It is prohibited to include political advertisements in any programs broadcast to foreign countries. Although another person or institution is sponsoring the political advertisement, this does not decrease either the responsibility or the freedom of the broadcaster, and neither the sponsor nor the broadcaster may change the content or placement of the program because of the ad, just the timing. The broadcaster is not responsible for the content of the political advertisement. A political advertisement must be visually and acoustically separated from other pieces of the program, with a special announcement about its character before and after the broadcast. (Jany, Ilosvai, & Bölcskei, 2000)

Parliamentary elections between 1990 and 2006 were based on the 1989 Act No. 34 regulating the election of members of parliament (1994), enacted by the parliament on October 20, 1989 and also Act C of 1997 on electoral procedure. Act No. 34 contains the regulations concerning suffrage, the electoral system (members of parliament, nomination, determination of election results), and electoral procedures (electoral campaign, polling, electoral bodies, polling wards, registration of voters, publicizing of electoral procedures, legal remedies, by-elections, final provisions). Article 11 in chapter 4 of the act briefly defines the rules regarding the media presentation of the campaign:

> (1) Until the day preceding the election at the latest, the Hungarian Telegraph Agency, Hungarian Radio and Hungarian Television shall carry on an equal footing the electoral announcements of parties putting forward candidates. Each party with a candidate shall be given at least one electoral program free of charge. This same duty shall devolve upon the local studios in their respective area of broadcasting with regard to the electoral programs of candidates. Other advertisements that go toward making a party or any of its candidates more popular can only be broadcast with a clear message declaring such publicity as "Paid Electoral Advertising."

> (2) During the 30 days preceding the election, Hungarian Radio and Hungarian Television shall cover the parties presenting national lists on an equal footing in their news of electoral events and, in their electoral reports, in proportion to the candidates nominated.

> (3) On the last day of the electoral campaigns, Hungarian Radio and Hungarian Television shall broadcast the electoral summary reports prepared by parties presenting national lists, under equal program conditions for parties, for equal lengths of time and without comments (Act No. 34, 1994, p. 25).

The key concepts in the act are equality and proportional media presentations of the parties and the candidates. These principles guide the application of the regulatory system to campaigning (Róka, 2006).

Act C of 1997 on electoral procedure declares that according to the Constitution of the Republic of Hungary, suffrage is equal, voting is direct and secret, the process of elections is democratic. "The aim of this act is that voters, candidates and nominating organizations as well as election bodies may exercise their election related rights on the ground of uniform, clearly arranged and simple rules of procedure, as laid down by law" (Act C of 1997 on electoral procedure).

This Act is applied to the election of members of parliament, members of the European Parliament, the representatives and mayors in local government, and the election of minority municipalities. The election must be called at the latest 72 days before polling day. Some of the basic principles applied in the electoral procedure are: to safeguard the fairness of elections; to ensure voluntary participation in the nomination, election campaign, and voting; and also equality of opportunity among among candidates. These requirements and all the other regulations are enforced and monitored by the National Election Office Hungary.

Act C of 1997 in chapter 6 contains the regulations governing the campaign period. It lasts from the call for the election to midnight on the day before voting. From midnight campaigning must cease. It is also prohibited to publishing the results of opinion polls from 8 days prior to the elections until voting has ended.

Nominating organizations and candidates can produce posters without permission, and they may place them without limitation in certain public places, but they should not cover the posters of other candidates or parties. Radio and television program providers may broadcast political advertisements even handedly for candidates and parties without attaching an explanation or opinion. The same regulation refers to both national and local periodicals and news agencies (see Act C of 1997 on electoral procedure).

HISTORY AND DEVELOPMENT OF POLITICAL NEWS COVEAGE

Before the democratic regime change, the Hungarian print and electronic media functioned under the supervision of the centralized, hierarchic, and bureaucratic political system (Bajomi-Lázár, 2005a, p. 22). The beginning of the new era, or, in other words, the end of a dictatorial media policy, slowly began to form in 1986, when the first commercial radio station, the Danubius Radio, began broadcasting nonideological entertainment programs. That was the year when the first local cable television channels came into being. Law No. 2 regulating print media was put into force, and on the 30th anniversary of the 1956 revolution, the idea of the reburial of Imre Nagy and his fellow martyrs was made public (in a late evening radio program, entitled "Owl", by M. Győrffy) (Bajomi-Lázár, 2005a).

On January 14, 1988 professional journalists openly criticized the totalitarian state's media policy. On May 23 J. Kádár, the leader of the Hungarian Socialist Workers' Party (MSZMP) was relieved of his office, and a new party leader, the moderate reformer K. Grósz, was elected.. On November 2nd the first legally published "alternative" paper, *Hitel* (Credit), appeared. On November 24 the reform communist M. Németh was elected prime minister of Hungary. On March 15, 1989, in front of the headquarters of Hungarian Television, D. Csengery, of the Hungarian Democratic Forum symbolically took control of the institution. Between June and September of 1989 at national roundtable discussions a special committee dealt with the question of the reform of publicity. On August 24 the committee issued a document titled: "Basic Concepts of Unbiased Information" that urged the political independence and neutrality of Hungarian mass media. On June 15 the government eliminated the need to obtain permission before founding a newspaper; it also meant the end of the state monopoly of print media. In 1989, 1,118 new papers were registered. In that year the privatization of print media and the inflow of foreign capital into the media sector began. On July 3 the government announced a frequency moratorium that temporarily froze the distribution of frequencies. On August 19 Nap-TV (the Hungarian word "nap" means sun and also day), the first private television studio began broadcasting. On October 23 the modified constitution came into force; it officially declared freedom of the press. In January 1990 the National Assembly modified the press law of 1986; it also declared freedom of the press and the registration of new papers. In April 1990 the Hungarian Democratic Forum and the Alliance of Free Democrats signed an agreement to confirm the frequency moratorium, and they also expressed the need to keep the two public media and the Hungarian Telegraph Agency (MTI) out of party political battles. They also agreed that the presidents and the vice-presidents of Hungarian Radio and Hungarian Television would be appointed by the president of the republic on the recommendation of the prime minister.

During the years of the democratic regime change political control over the press and electronic media came to an end. The majority of the print media were privatized (Bajomi-Lázár, 2005a). The cultural intelligentsia played an outstanding role in effecting that change because of their prominent position in Hungarian politics.

> The concept of the intelligentsia refers here, however, to a much narrower circle—to the social group that generates ideology and symbols, and that leads culture and public opinion. The proportion of the Parliament filled by the cultural intelligentsia and those working within the liberal professions, at 40%, was exceptionally high by international standards. This new intelligentsia political élite was composed primarily of lawyers, university teachers, scientific researchers, writers, columnists and other intellectuals in the liberal professions. (Körösényi, 1999, p. 95)

Körösényi also emphasizes that the cultural intelligentsia, together with the legal and economic intelligentsia, represented the most influential wing of the new political parties, pressure groups, and the membership of parliament, and they became the most dominant opinion leaders on the national scale.

The press played a particularly crucial role in setting the scene for régime change by the press. From the mid-1980s the press provided an outlet for the reform communist intelligentsia, and from the late 1980s it provided space for the "dissident" opposition intellectuals. An important element of the political influence gained by the intelligentsia in the course of the régime change was the fact that they determined and molded the language and agenda of the democratic transition and of political discourse (Konrád & Szelényi, 1992; Pokol, 1993).

They largely retained this function after the transition. As Körösényi writes:

> Several further factors increased the role of the press and thus the political influence of the media élite.
> 1. One stemmed from the fact that all the parties were established around the same time, during régime change. The weakness of party identities increased the role of the press in the formation of public opinion and party choices.
> 2. The Hungarian press is, however, more than an instrument in the hands of political actors: it has its own independent political role. It does not simply deliver the "message" of politicians and other political actors but, because of the conception of its role, also influences public opinion itself.
> 3. The understanding many among the media élite have of their role is not that of journalists, but rather that of the intelligentsia. A significant number of journalists see their role as similar

to that of the media intelligentsia who are afforded many column inches by the newspapers. They select stories not on the basis of their "news value," but rather according to their personal world-view and political value system and orientation. The media élite is mainly a politically committed—through certainly not homogeneous—actor in Hungarian politics, and through its influence it forms a part of the political élite. The majority of the media élite is left-wing or liberal, while a smaller part is right-wing, nationally oriented, or conservative.

4. A further factor, increasing the political influence of the media élite is the fact that the parties, the intellectuals around them, and the governments themselves try to extend their influence on the media, almost dividing up among themselves the newspapers, radio stations, and television channels.

The fight between certain intellectual groups in the political parties and the media élite for influence over the media led, during the first half of the 1990s, to the so-called media war. During this time, for example, programing—including political news programs—on public-service television and radio were parceled out to the various rival political groups and orientations. Through the establishment of the National Radio and Television Commission (Országos Rádió és Televízió Testület, ORTT), the political control of the parliamentary parties over the public-service media was institutionalized. Both this law and the establishment of two nationwide private television channels in 1997 exercised a balancing influence within the media. (Körösényi, 1999, pp. 95–97)

RESEARCH AND ANALYSIS OF THE CONTENT AND EFFECTS OF ELECTION COVERAGE

The emergence of political communication and political marketing (including the study of political advertising) as a distinct domain of publication, a professional endeavor, and a teaching area goes back to 1990 in Hungary. The first publications were mainly translations of foreign books on political communication and marketing. One of the first published studies on Hungarian political advertising was the analysis of values in party programs by Ágnes Kapitány and Gábor Kapitány (1990). They continued their studies of political programs during the second, third, and fourth democratic elections in 1994, 1998, 2002 (Kapitány & Kapitány, 1994, 1998, 2002a, 2002b).

The goal of their analysis was mainly to answer some questions that the voters were concerned about and that might have had a decisive effect on the outcome of the elections. One of the authors' basic interests was to determine what kinds of values the different parties emphasized (e.g., Europe, nation, property, party image, attitude to the communist past, etc.); what the main differences and similarities were among the parties in that respect (the quantity and quality of the mentioned values); and what sorts of verbal and nonverbal means of communication the parties used to represent those values (e.g., the form of the party program, the political candidates as the performers of the programs, the situation, the background music, the style and language usage). As a result of their analysis an "inventory" of the political values used in the election campaign was prepared that led to the conclusion that the political success of a party lies in the shared values between the party and the voters.

In 1994, 1998, and 2002, Kapitány and Kapitány (1994, 1998, 2002b) performed a similar task in analyzing a sample of the political programs. They were interested in the explicit and implicit values the parties emphasized, the frequency of emphasis, tendencies in the programs, the influencing and modifying role of the different components of the programs, such as music, background, number of participants, their sex, character and style; the symbolic meaning of their values; the means of agenda-setting; parties and cultures; and the differences and similarities between the parties according to the analyzed values. A cluster analysis of the value groups and party groups shed light on some tendencies that could be categorized as key values for political success: the existence of identical values between the party and the citizens.

My own research has led to similar conclusions concerning the success of election campaigns (Róka, 1997). The main objective of my research has been to elaborate the possible interactions between the media agenda and the public agenda in political campaigns in cross-cultural perspective, taking into account the dynamics of agenda-setting and agenda-building in public opinion formation. The basic theoretical paradigm of the study, offered in an article by Gabriel Tarde (1922), was based on the assumption that newspapers impose the majority of their daily topics upon their readers, and thus form the basis of what readers talk about. In doing so, they activate, direct, and nourish first individual, then public, opinion, thus shaping social relationships and acts. After analyzing several election campaigns, I have proposed that the difference between the impact of the media and of political communication on the formation of public opinion is this: Successful media communication must be based on agenda-building; but in political communication, the emphasis must be on agenda-setting.

I also analyzed the verbal and visual aspects of the 1994 Hungarian election campaign (Róka, 1994) and the growing importance of communication technologies on shaping public opinion (Róka, 1999a). In the Hungarian parliamentary elections of 1990 and 1994, I studied the role of political commercials (Róka, 1999b), in the campaigns of 1998 and 2002, marketing strategies (Róka, 2004), in the European Parliament election campaign held in Hungary in 2004, the strategic political marketing implications (Róka, 2005), and the evaluation of political advertising between 1989 and 2004 (Róka, 2006).

Some studies on the Hungarian election campaigns of 1990, 1994, 1998, and 2002, in their general discussions of the campaigns, have referred to TV political ads. For instance, László Kéri (2005), who has evaluated party campaigns (including political programs) since 1990, analyzed the permanent political campaigns between 2002 and 2004. Tóth and Török (2002) analyzed the political agenda of 2001 in respect to all the parliamentary parties with some reference to the prospective political events and changes in 2002. Some papers in the annual *Political Yearbook of Hungary* (18 volumes) also deal with the present and future tendencies of political communication in the era of digital technology (Sándor, Vass, & Tolnai, 2003). The 17th and 18th volumes published an analysis of the political process of 2004 and 2005 with special attention to joining the EU, and also the publication of different public opinion polls, political documents, and press reactions (Sándor, Vass, & Tolnai, 2005). The EP campaign in Hungary attracted the interest of media scholars: Ilonszki, Jáger, and Makkai (2005) gave a thorough analysis of the media presentation of the campaign. Many studies are devoted to the analysis of voters' behavior, the role of media and infocommunication in the information of Hungarian voters on political issues (Angelusz & Tardos, 2005); to the role of Internet in the virtual election campaign of the parties, the functions of on-line political communication, the structure of web pages, the social effect of computer-mediated communication (Kiss & Boda, 2005). In the framework of the European Election Research Project sponsored by the Central-European University an international research team investigated the differences and similarities of parties' and voters' behavior in the EP election of 2004 (Tóka & Bátory, 2006). Political scientists shed light on the changing tendencies of political culture in Hungary, the role of the political élite in that change, the political orientation, attitudes, style, and communication of members of parliament (Simon, 2004); changes in the political and constitutional structure; the dilemma of the political institutional system between 1989 and 2006; the structural and functional tensions of the political system; and global challenges (Gombár et al., 2006). In addition, changes in global civic society and culture, the protests of some Hungarain parties against globalization, the questions of globalization, regionalism, democracy, civic society, and the legal protection were also discussed (Szabó, 2004), along with the mediatization of politics, politicization of the media in the era of globalization (Bayer & Bajomi-Lázár, 2005); and descriptions of the governmental, economic, agricultural, employment, transportation, energy, educational, cultural, juridical, foreign and defence policy of the first year of the Gyucsány government (Gazsó & Stumpf, 2004). Some further studies, along with a summary of international media and press history, discuss the main topics of political communication, theories on the effect of media, media regulation (Bajomi-Lázár, 2006), and also political propaganda in the media, the political ownership of media, and the advertising market in Hungary (Csermely & Sükösd, 2004). Karácsony edited papers on voter behavior, predictions of public opinion polls, tactics, and marketing strategies used in the 2006 parliamentary elections, the outcome of the elections, the percentages of parties in the new parliament, plans and reform of the government (Karácsony, 2006). Angelusz and Tardos (2006) also published an edited book on methodological aspects of election research. The journal *Media Researcher* regularly publishes papers on election campaign communication, political communication, and on media effect studies (Médiakutató, 2005, 2006).

We can conclude then that both the Hungarian political culture and the media culture are controversial. In the discussion of political and election events issue frames are more characteristic of the quality national newspapers and the public electronic media, while game frames are dominant in political infotaiment and tabloidization, and as such they are more typical of commercial electronic media and tabloids. Both descriptive and interpretative journalism have a long tradition in the history of Hungarian media. They show a balanced picture in the quality of public information channels, while interpretative journalism is more dominant in the commercial media sector, as well as political bias.

Heltai, an experienced Hungarian journalist, emphasizes that news coverage essentially is a news contest. The main reason for that is the business competition among the media concerns, the rapid development of communication technology, the permanent stress, the lack of a model to follow, and the combination of decreasing news quality and increasing news quantity.

> The consuming of news ceased to be the privilege of the élite. The number of citizens informed on a basic level became bigger. It also means that the number of active citizens concerning politics fortunately increased. Paradoxically at the same time the lack of information and knowledge of the average reader/viewer also increased. The prestige and authenticity of media decreased.... We consume more news from newspapers, TV, and radio than the European average. Sometimes from the Internet. Simultaneously we have less trust in media, compared to [other] European citizens. All in all we consume news, but rather for entertainment. It is a desperate situation. (Heltai, 2005, p. 16–17)

Nonetheless, researchers have found strong connections between exposure to television news and positive attitudes toward the political system. In Hungary, Voltmer and Schmitt-Beck (2002) discovered that exposure to election news coverage on both public and private television contributes both to general political knowledge levels and to attitudes toward political parties.

THE IMPORTANCE OF OPINION POLLS

Opinion polls are a determining factor, especially during election campaigns, although the informants in most of the cases presume party bias in the results of surveys. As we have mentioned before, 8 days prior to election day, during the campaign silence period, it is prohibited to publish the results of any public opinion polls. Some public opinion research institutes have tried to change this moratorium. The most prominent institutions regularly publish their results in the print and electronic media. In the case of the Gyurcsány scandal, when public trust in the prime minister was shaken, and the possibility of his resignation arose, the importance of public opinion polls increased and they became important in shaping the political process. The public opinion institutions proved a complete fiasco in the 2002 election campaign, but in the 2006 campaign they gained back their credibility because they produced reliable predictions both in the first and second rounds of the parliamentary elections.

There are five prominent public opinion poll institutions in Hungary: Médián, Szonda Ipsos, Századvég, Tárki, and the Hungarian Gallup Organization. Médián was established in 1989 as the first private public opinion poll institute in Hungary. It prepared its first survey about the re-burial of Imre Nagy (prime minister between 1953 and 1955, later from October 23, 1956 until November 4, 1956 during the Hungarian revolution until the Soviet invasion). Médián concentrates its surveys on three thematic issues: (1) market research (the most profitable segment of its activity); (2) social science research (analyzing all the main topics that are part of the public agenda: Internet use, vacation spending habits, the degree of social acceptance of Gyurcsány reform, etc.; (3) political public opinion polls. Its political surveys have a news value in the media because they usually prove to be accurate. It measures the party preferences monthly, more often during election periods, it prepares predictions for the parliamentary, municipal, and European Parliamentary elections, they also, among others, analyzed the polularity of the potential presidents of republic. Its WebAudit system measures the attendance of the biggest home pages daily (http://www.webaudit.hu) (Médián, 2007).

Szonda Ipsos was founded right after the democratic regime change in 1990. It has four main research areas and five infrastructural sections. Its most important areas are market research, media research, and political surveys. It publishes monthly surveys in *Népszabadság* (the most popular quality public newspaper). It also surveys the popularity of parties and politicians. The president and general director of Szonda Ipsos was formerly the aide of Péter Medgyessy, who had to resign in mid-term as prime minister, which accounts for attacks on the company because it was getting a lot of state orders and because of its perceived socialist bias. (http://www.szondaipsos.hu)

Századvég is a community organization, it functions in the form of a foundation; its president was the chancellery minister of the Orbán government between 1998 and 2002. Századvég researches and analyzes public opinion; it also founded an institute for political education in Hungary (Századvég Political School), and has a publishing house (Századvég Kiadó). It measures public feeling regarding political issues between elections, prepares estimates of mandates, and analyzes foreign (mainly German and American) elections. Its prediction for the first round of the 2006 parliamentary election was accurate. It actively expresses its opinion on important political questions, but does not side with any one political party regarding concrete political disputes. It publishes its results on its home page and in the daily press. Left liberal politicians often accuse Századvég of political bias in favor of the Federation of Young Democrats–Hungarian Civic Party (Századvég, 2007).

The Tárki group has four elements: (1) Tárki Social Research Institute Zrt., founded in 1998, is a profit-oriented stock company; (2) the Social Research Informatics Coalition, a non-profit organization, was founded in 1985. It is owned by Tárki Zrt., universities, and research institutes; (3) Tárki Foundation (founded in 1990); (4) Tárki-Data research Kft, the owners of which are private individuals and Tárki Zrt. Its basic principle is to maintain independence from economic and political interest groups. Its main research areas are party preferences and voting willingness. Results of its surveys are published in Magyar Hírlap (Tárki, 2007).

Magyar Gallup Intézet (Hungarian Gallup Institute) belongs to the international research network of the Gallup organization. It has been carrying out surveys in Hungary for more than

10 years. It prepares social and economic surveys, measures party preferences, parliamentary, municipal, and EP elections, as well as mayoral contests. It also measures country image and publishes surveys of Gallup organizations in other countries. Results of Gallup surveys are published in *Népszava*, *Magyar Nemzet*, and on Kossuth Radio, Slager Radio, and on their home page (Magyar Gallup Intézet, 2007).

CONTROVERSAL ISSUES IN ELECTORAL COMMUNICATION

In the Hungarian parliamentary and municipal elections opposing parties attack each other; left-wing parties usually criticize right-wing parties, saying that the right-wing abuses national symbols and wants to monopolize national feeling and such attributes as "civic" and "patriot," and they consider the public as their followers. (This criticism was typical during the 1998 and 2002 election campaigns.) In 2006 the Federation of Young Democrats–Hungarian Civic Party (FIDESZ-MPP) was accused of being demagogic and misusing the issue of Hungarians living beyond the frontiers of Hungary in order to gain more votes.

The right-wing parties have accused the left-wing since 1998 of trying to oust conservative politicians and artists from the media, they are immoral, atheists, do not support the Church and believers, they are against Hungarians living beyond the frontiers of Hungary, and after winning the election they settle accounts with the political opposition. In 2006 the right-wing declared "we will not tolerate a government of liars."

In the 2006 election campaign and soon after it, some unusual and controversial issues emerged. Some of the strategic errors in the campaign of FIDESZ-MPP were due to the use of shallow messages: they tried to convince citizens that they had a lower standard of living than four years earlier (depressive campaign), and promised crucial changes in the next four years, and here the campaign turned positive, using the slogan "Good choice, better life." In the televised debate of the two candidates for prime minister, according to public opinion polls, Viktor Orbán was less convincing than Ferenc Gyurcsány. There were at least three tactical errors that also weakened the position of the FIDESZ-MPP: the "Vizsla case," the "server case," and the "blackmail case," Hungarian *Vizsla* originally was planned to be an independent newspaper by the party. Therefore, it was risky to use the newspaper for negative campaigning. The scandal broke when someone from one of the party offices sent a fax to the editorial office, and the Hungarian Socialist Party (MSZP) made it public. The server case referred to hacking into one of the central computer servers of MSZP; the Fidesz used this case in its campaign; MSZP started a counter-attack that the politicians of FIDESZ-MPP could not handle. In March of 2006 one of the FIDESZ-MPP members of parliament threatened a politician of the Hungarian Democratic Forum, who secretly recorded the conversation, but then made it public. Viktor Orbán commited a further, and the most prominent tactical error, when after the first round of the election, he resigned as the candidate for FIDESZ-MPP prime minister. By resigning he left FIDESZ supporters in a vacuum.

The campaign of the Hungarian Socialist Party both strategically and tactically was one of its most professionally built campaigns. The candidate for prime minister built his image as a talented and rhetorically sophisticated leader, a modern media politician. The campaign had two main messages using two slogans: "Yes" and "No." Yes for Ferenc Gyurcsány, no for Viktor Orbán. Some popular steps also contributed to the strengthening of their position: they reacted at once to floods and bomb attacks. But their main message remained criticism of FIDESZ. Right after winning the parliamentary election, the socialist government announced its "New balance" program, but they failed to expain the necessity of introducing the economic constraints package for the voters and there was a huge difference between campaign promises and post-election reality. That was the moment when FIDESZ began using the expression "lie factory" for the government, and this message became credible as soon as the prime minister's infamous "balatonöszödi" speech for lying before the election came to light. It was a behind-closed-doors speech for the socialist cabinet, but the fact that it became public showed the inevitable problems inside the socialist party. This scandal had several negative and positive consequences: it caused a deep social crisis leading to street demonstrations thoughout the country, the nationwide victory of FIDESZ during the municipial elections in the fall, and the citizens'disappointment in politics and politicians. Hungarian parties (both right-wing and left-wing) commit the same errors each time during their election campaigns. They have to radically change their tactics and strategies if any of them wants to win the parliamentary election in 2010.

To sum up the topic, here is a fragment of the prime minister's speech in Balatonöszöd in May 2006. Ferenc Gyurcsány, the prime inister made public the text of the whole speech on his Internet blog on September 17.

> There is not much choice, because we are f.... Not a little bit, but much. None of the European countries did such a silliness that we did. It might be explained. We evidently lied throughout the last one and a half, two years. It was quite clear, what we said was not true. We are beyond what is possible in this country, we could not imagine earlier that the joint governing of the Hungarian Socialist Party and the liberals could ever do this. In the meantime we actually did not do anything for four years. Nothing. I cannot mention any significant governmental measures that we are proud of, except for bringing the governing back at the end from the shit. (http://www.fn.hu/index.php?action=nyomtat&id=3&cid=143566&layout=no&id=3)

TELEVISION ADVERTISING AND NEW TECHNOLOGIES IMPACT ON ELECTIONS

In the Republic of Hungary the marketing approach to parliamentary election campaigns has been applied since 1998. The switch to the marketing approach meant that politics became business, where success mainly depends on professional communication skills and unique public relations strategies. The final goal is to project the most positive image of the political candidate and the party, and to sell them with the biggest possible profit. The profit is voter support and winning of elections. What are the most widely used tools and channels for gaining the citizens' attention in political campaigns? Since the advent of audiovisual media television plays the most prominent role in political communication and one of the major components of the candidates' campaign are the TV ads and also broadcasts of the candidates' debate. The parties' use of TV ads, regulated by the media law, is not widely discussed by the news media.

Among the new technological advances, the Internet has a potential for becoming very influential. In Hungary the Internet became a part of political skirmishing in 1998, which was completed by some new possibilities provided by the latest advances in telecommunication technology: by prerecorded messages through cable and SMS messages transmitted through mobile phones in 2002 and 2006. The Internet plays a growing role in spreading election information, in collecting donations, and also in activating voters. However, the parliamentary parties' home pages do not reveal how they intend to activate potential "Internet" voters. Thus in the 2006 parliamentary election campaign the parties did not consider it important to let the citizens know about their plans and party programs well before election day—the Hungarian Democratic Forum was an exception. The most informative and well designed home page was prepared by the Alliance of Free Democrats. It included podcasting, interactive interviews, RSS, blog, and introduced the party's candidates for parliament. Blogs as an election campaign tool were also used by the prime minister. Interactive communication possibilities were characteristic only of the home pages of the governing parties and just for the registered users. Both the Hungarian Socialist Party and the Federation of Young Democrates used their home pages for recruiting volunteers, and they also had separate home pages for negative campaigning (http://www.hullamvadasz. hu/index.php3?tanulmany=879&fotip=6).

Kiss and Boda, who carried out a four-year research paroject on political Internet communication, concluded:

> Whether we analyze Hungary or abroad, the accepted political institutes, the parties and governing organs use the world wide web either for political propaganda, or for easing their own job, but almost never for widening the possibilities of intervening in politics. It is very much evident, that the democratic parliamentary model does not decrease by electronic use, it does not prevent it from entering the broad circle of social problems. (2005, p. 234)

They consider the penetration of the Internet into political communication as a strengthening post-parliamentary tendency.

In Hungary 23 different parties have official home pages (out of 144 parties registered by the Supreme Court). The main political parties were able to create effective interactive communication with citizens through the Internet which means that online communication became a new qualitative feature of political participation (though online and offline communication of the separate parties did not differ much strategically, they represented the general conventions, manners, and rules of the given party), but it is not certain yet what online communication contributes to the success of a party. It is even less certain how the Internet might change news coverage of elections, although it certainly will have some effect.

REFERENCES

A kormányfői beszéd teljes szövege [The complete text of the speech of the head of government]. (2006). http://www.fn.hu/index.php?action=nyomtat&id=3&cid=143566&layout=no&id=3.

Act C, 1997 on Electoral Procedure. Retrieved January 1, 2007, from the National Election Office Hungary website: http://www.election.hu/parval2006/en/02/2_0.html

Act No. 34, 1989 on the Election of Members of Parliament. (1994, January). Magyar Közlöny, (7). Retrieved January 1, 2007, from the National Election Office Hungary website: http://www.election.hu/parval2006/en/02/2_0.html

Angelusz, R., & Tardos, R. (2006). *Mérésről mérésre: A választáskutatás módszertani kérdései* [From measurement to measurement: The methodological questions of election research]. Budapest: Demokrácia Kutatások Magyar Központja Közhasznú Alapítvány. Budapesti Corvinus Egyetem Politikatudományi Intézet.

Angelusz, R., & Tardos, R. (2005). *Törések, hálók, hidak* [Breaks, nets, and bridges]. Budapest: Demokrácia Kutatások Magyar Központja Alapítvány.

Antal, Zs., & Scherer, Zs. (2005). Médiapiaci körkép: A monopóliumok kora [A survey of the media market: The age of the monopolies]. In Zs. Antal & T. Gazsó (Ed.), *Magyar médiahelyzet* [Hungarian media situation] (pp. 145–180). Budapest: Századvég.

Bajomi-Lázár, P. (2005a). (Ed.). *Magyar médiatörténet a késő Kádár-kortól az ezredfordulóig* [History of Hungarian media from the late Kádár-era until the turn of millennium]. Budapest: Akadémiai Kiadó.

Bajomi-Lázár, P. (2005b). A politika mediatizálódása és a média politizálódása [The mediatization of politics and the politization of media]. *Médiakutató, 6 (1),* 39–51.

Bajomi-Lázár, P. (2006). *Média és társadalom* [Media and society]. Budapest: Antenna könyvek.

Bayer, J., & Bajomi-Lázár, P. (Ed.) (2005). *Globalizáció, média, politika: A politikai kommunikáció vál-*

tozása a globalizáció korában [Globalization, média, politics: Changes in political communication in the era of globalization]. Budapest: MTA Politikai Tudományok Intézete.

Csermely, Á., & Sükösd, M. (2004). *Propaganda a mai médiában: Írások az internet és a média világából 2004* [Propaganda in today's media: Studies from the world of Internet and media 2004]. Budapest: Média Hungária Könyvek 5.

Ez történt a tévében. MTV: hírműsorok nézettsége az új struktúrában. 2006. október 12 [This happened in television. MTV: the viewing figures in the new structure. October 12, 2006]. http://www.hirado. hu/nyomtatas.php?id=154780.

Félúton. Választási kampány online [Half-way. Election campaign online].(March 1st 2006). http://www. hullamvadasz.hu/index.php3?tanulmany=879&fotip=6

Gallai, S., & Török, G. (2003). *Politika és politikatudomány* [Politics and political science]. Budapest: Aula Kiadó.

Gazsó, T., & Stumpf, I. (2004). A jóléti rendszerváltás csődje. *A Gyurcsány-kormány első éve* [The failure of the welfare political transformation. The first year of the Gyurcsány government]. Budapest: Századvég Kiadó.

Gombár, Cs. Körösényi, A., Lengyel, L., Stumpf, I., & Tölgyessy P. (Ed.). (2006). *Túlterhelt demokrácia. Alkotmányos és kormányzati alapszerkezetünk* [Overloaded Democracy. Our constitutional and governmental basic structure]. Budapest: Századvég Kiadó.

Heltai, P. (2005). A hírverseny terrorja [The terror of the news contest]. In Csermely, Á. (Ed.), *A közszolgálatiság újrafogalmazása a digitális forradalom küszöbén. Írások az internet és a média világából* [Redrafting the public service on the edge of the digital revolution: Papers from the world of Internet and media]. Budapest: Média Hungária Könyvek 7.

Ilonszki, G., Jáger, K., & Makkai, P. (2005). Kampány előtt—kampány után. Képviselők, női képviselők és a média [Before and after the campaign: Members of Parliament, women members of Parliament, media]. *Jel-Kép 3,* 3–21.

Jany, J., Ilosvai, G., & Bölcskei, J. (2000). *Médiajogi kézikönyv* [Handbook of media law]. Budapest: Osiris Kiadó.

Kapitány, Á., & Kapitány, G. (1990). *Értékválasztás. A választási pártműsorok elemzése* [Value choice: The analysis of party election programs]. Budapest: Művelődéskutató Intézet.

Kapitány, Á., & Kapitány, G. (1994). *Értékválasztás. A választási és kampányműsorok szimbolikus és ér-téküzenetei* [Value choice. Symbolic and value messages in campaign programs]. Budapest: Societas.

Kapitány, Á., & Kapitány, G. (1998). *Értékválasztás '98* [Value choice 1998]. Budapest: Új Mandátum Könyvkiadó.

Kapitány, Á., & Kapitány, G. (2002a). *Értékválasztás 2002* [Value choice 2002]. Budapest: Új Mandátum Könyvkiadó.

Kapitány, Á., & Kapitány, G. (2002b*).* A választási kampányműsorok értéküzenetei és szimbólumai [Value messages and symbols in election campaign programs]. *Jel-Kép, 3,* 17–36.

Karácsony, G. (2006). *Parlamenti választás 2006. Elemzések és adatok* [2006 parliamentary election. Analyses and data]. Budapest: Demokrácia Kutatások Magyar Központja. Közhasznú Alapítvány. Budapesti Corvinus Egyetem Politikatudományi   Intézet.

Kéri, L. (2005). *Választástól népszavazásig* [From the campaign to election day]. Budapest: Kossuth kiadó.

Kiss, B., & Boda, Zs. (2005). *Politika az interneten* [Politics on internet]. Budapest: Századvég kiadó.

Konrád, Gy. & Szelényi, I. (1992). *Intellectuals and domination in post-Communist societies* [Értelmiség és dominancia a posztkommunista társadalmakban]. Politikatudományi Szemle, No. 1.

Körösényi, A. (1999). *Government and politics in Hungary*. Budapest: Central European University Press, Osiris.

Körösényi, A., Tóth, Cs., & Török, G. (2003). *A magyar politikai rendszer* [Hungarian political system]. Budapest: Osiris Kiadó.

Magyar Gallup Interzét. (2007). Retrieved June 19, 2007 from: http:/www.gallup.hu

Médiakutató. (2005). *Médiaelméleti folyóirat* [Media researcher. Journal of media theory].*6(*1*)*,

Médiakutató. (2006). *Médiaelméleti folyóirat* [Media researcher. Journal of media theory].*7(*2*)*.

Medián. (2007). Retrieved June 19, 2007 from: http:/www.median.hu

Pokol, B. (1993). Professionalization, intellectuals, politics [Professzionalizálódás, értelmiség, politika]. In B. Pokol (Ed.), *Money and Politics* [Pénz és politika] (pp. 81–90). Budapest, Aula.

Róka, J., (1994, July). Media and elections: The role of visual manipulation in political image-making. Paper presented at the Turbulent Europe: Conflict Identity and Culture Convention, London.

Róka, J. (1997). *Public space: From rumour through conversation to opinion-formation.* Unpublished manuscript. Budapest: Central European University.

Róka, J. (1999a). Do the media reflect or shape public opinion? In B. I. Newman (Ed.), *Handbook of political marketing* (pp. 505–518). Thousand Oaks, CA: Sage.

Róka, J., (1999b). Party broadcasts and effects on Hungarian elections since 1990. In L. L. Kaid (Ed.), *Television and politics in evolving European democracies* (pp. 113–130). Commack, NY: Nova Science.

Róka, J. (2004). Forming political culture and marketing strategies in a central-European setting. *Journal of Political Marketing, 3*(2), 87–108.

Róka, J. (2005). Turnout and its strategic political marketing implications during the 2004 European Parliamentary Election. *Journal of Political Marketing, 4*(2/3), 181–187.

Róka, J. (2006). Political advertising in Hungarian electoral communications. In L. L. Kaid & C. Holtz-Bacha (Ed.), *The Sage handbook of political advertising* (pp. 343–358). Thousand Oaks, CA: Sage.

Sándor, P., Vass, L., Sándor, Á., & Tolnai, Á. (2003). *Magyarország politikai évkönyve* [Political Yearbook of Hungary]. Budapest: Demokrácia Kutatások Magyar Központja Alapítvány.

Sándor, P., Vass, L., Sándor, Á., & Tolnai, Á. (2004). *Magyarország politikai évkönyve* [Political Yearbook of Hungary]. Budapest: Demokrácia Kutatások Magyar Központja Alapítvány.

Sándor, P., Vass, L., Sándor, Á., & Tolnai, Á. (2005). *Magyarország politikai évkönyve* [Political Yearbook of Hungary]. Budapest: Demokrácia Kutatások Magyar Központja Alapítvány.

Sándor, P., Vass, L., & Tolnai, Á. (2006). *Magyarország politikai évkönyve* [Political Yearbook of Hungary]. Budapest: Demokrácia Kutatások Magyar Központja Alapítvány.

Simon, J. (2004). *A politikai kultúra színképei* [The spectrum of political culture]. Budapest: Századvég Kiadó.

Szabó, M. (2004). *Globalizáció, regionalizmus, civil társadalom* [Globalization, regionalism, civic society]. Budapest: Századvég Kiadó.

Századvég. (2007). Retrieved June 19, 2007 from: from: http:/ www.szazadveg.hu

Tárki. (2007). Retrieved June 19, 2007 from http:/ www.tarki.hu.

Tóka, G., & Bátory, Á. (2006). *A 2004. évi európai parlamenti választások. Pártok és szavazói magatartás nemzetközi összehasonlításban* [2004 European parliamentary elections. Parties and voters' behaviour in international comparison]. Budapest: Demokrácia Kutatások Magyar Központja Alapítvány, Budapesti Corvinus Egyetem Politikatudományi Intézet, Századvég Kiadó.

Tóth, Cs., & Török, G. (2002). *Politika és kommunikáció. A magyar politikai napirend témái a 2002-es választások előtt* [Politics and communication. The topics of Hungarian political agenda before the elections of 2002]. Budapest: Századvég Kiadó.

Voltmer, K., & Schmitt-Beck, R. (2002, March). *The mass media and citizens' orientations towards democracy: The experience of six "third-wave" democracies in southern Europe, Eastern Europe and Latin America.* Paper presented to the workshop "Political Communication, the Mass Media, and the Consolidation of New Democracies" at the Joint Sessions of Workshops of the European Consortium for Political Research, Turin, Italy.

21

Election News Coverage in Bulgaria

Lilia Raycheva and Daniela V. Dimitrova

After 45 years of communism, Bulgaria held its first democratic elections in May 1990 following an inter-party coup that had ended totalitarian rule in November 1989. A new Bulgarian Constitution was adopted in 1991. During the following years of transition a normal political environment was gradually established. Among the major achievements during this period were that the country joined NATO in spring 2004 and the European Union in January 2007.

POLITICAL SYSTEM

Political Structure

Under the terms of its Constitution, Bulgaria is a Republic with a Parliamentary system of government. The National Assembly is composed of 240 deputies elected for a term of four years (only the seventh Grand National Assembly of 1990, the first after the democratic changes, consisted of 400 members). Any Bulgarian citizen, who does not hold dual citizenship, who is 21 years of age, who is not under judicial disability, or is not imprisoned, is eligible to run for parliament. Members of Parliament represent not only their constituencies, but also the entire nation (Election Act for Members of Parliament, 2005).

The president is the head of the Republic of Bulgaria. A vice president assists him in his work. The president is elected directly by the people for a term of five years. Every Bulgarian citizen by birth, who is at least 40 years of age, who is eligible to be a member of parliament, and who has lived in the country in the last five years, is eligible to run for president. The last requirement was added in 2001 partly to block any possible attempts on the part of King Simeon II, the Bulgarian monarch in exile who lived in Madrid, Spain, to run for president (Election Act for President and Vice-President, 2006).

The President of the Republic schedules the elections for the National Assembly and for local administrative bodies as well as national referenda decided upon by the National Assembly. The Republic of Bulgaria is divided into municipalities and regions. The municipal council is the local self-administrative body of the municipality. The residents of the respective municipality elect it for a term of four years by a legislatively set order. The mayor is the executive authority of the municipality. The residents or the municipal council elect him or her for a term of four years by a legislatively set order (Local Elections Act, 2005).

The prime minister is the head of government. He is nominated by the president and elected by the National Assembly. The members of the Council of Ministers are nominated by the prime minister and are also elected by the National Assembly. Typically, the party with a parliamentary majority forms a government on its own unless lack of votes requires forming a coalition government. If the leading party is unable to elect a government, the mandate goes to the party with the second number of seats in parliament.

Major Political Parties and National Elections

The transition period of seventeen years witnessed four presidential elections (in 1992, 1996, 2001, and 2006), six parliamentary elections (in 1990, 1991, 1994, 1997, 2001, and 2005), four local elections (in 1991, 1995, 1999, and 2003), and the appointment of ten governments. An encouraging sign is that the last two governments successfully completed their mandates.

The bipolar political model prevailed in the country for more than a decade. The successor of the Bulgarian Communist Party, the Bulgarian Socialist Party (BSP), won the first free election in 1990. An opposition coalition of sixteen political parties, the Union of Democratic Forces (UDF) was formed and won the next national election, but it was replaced in December 1992 by a technocratic government supported by the BSP and the Movement for Rights and Freedoms (MRF), a party representing mainly ethnic Turks. The BSP won the next election in December 1994. The economic crisis of 1996 and 1997, however, led to early elections in April 1997. A center-right coalition led by the UDF came to power. This became the first government after the 1989 political changes to successfully fulfill its mandate of four years.

The next parliamentary election witnessed the success of a newly founded coalition, led by a party created only two months prior to election day by the former Bulgarian king Simeon Saxe-Coburg-Gotha. The Simeon II National Movement (SIINM) won the 2001 election and formed a government with the MRF. Simeon II who had never abdicated as king of Bulgaria was appointed prime minister. During his full-time mandate Bulgaria joined NATO (2004) and signed the EU Accession Treaty (in April 2005). Thus, the bipolar political model was broken.

After the parliamentary elections of 2005 with a turnout of 56%, seven political parties entered Parliament, but none of them was able to reach a majority. Because of the imperfection of the Act for the Election of Members of Parliament, it became possible for the Movement for Rights and Freedoms to fully mobilize the emigrant electorate in Turkey, holding dual citizenship, and to occupy the third position. Its traditional role as a balancing factor in the political arena had been considerably shaken because of the growing national exasperation towards the differentiated ethnic Turkish profile of this party and its aggressive aspirations to control a substantial portion of the pre-accession European Union funding. This popular discontent led some people to support a newly established coalition with a markedly nationalistic character called Attack. Without special campaigning, in less than two months, this new party took 9% of the ballots and won fourth position in Parliament. This surprising result was mainly due to the impact of a television program of the same title anchored by Attack's leader and broadcast on one of the cable TV stations. Even without a clear policy and program, the presence of this party in the exhausted-by-endless-political-fighting Bulgarian society could attract more sympathizers in the future. However, the aggressive approach Attack uses could jeopardize the unique ethnic status quo in the country, one of the notable Bulgarian achievements during the transition period. Although the BSP oriented Coalition for Bulgaria gained most of the vote, the socialists did not get enough seats in Parliament and only after almost two months of heavy negotiations were able to create a governing coalition with the SIINM and the MRF. Socialist party leader Sergei Stanishev became the new prime minister. In addition to the nationalist's Attack coalition, the United

TABLE 21.1
Parties/ Coalitions Elected for Bulgarian National Assembly in June 2005

Party	Valid Votes	% [of Valid Votes]	Seats in Parliament
Coalition for Bulgaria*	1,129,196	30.95%	82
National Movement Simeon II	725,314	19.88%	53
Movement for Rights and Freedoms	467,400	12.81%	34
Attack/Ataka	296,848	8.14%	21
United Democratic Forces**	280,323	7.68%	20
Democrats for Strong Bulgaria	234,788	6.44%	17
Bulgaria People's Union	189,268	5.19%	13
Others	325,040	8.91%	0

Source: IFES Election Guide, http://www.electionguide.org/results.php?ID=144
*In the 2005 election, the Coalition for Bulgaria included the Bulgarian Socialist Party, the Party of Bulgarian Social Democrats, the Political Movement Social Democrats, the Bulgarian Agrarian People's Union Alexander Stambolijski, Civil Union "Roma", Movement for Social Humanism, Green Party of Bulgaria, Communist Party of Bulgaria.
**In 2005, the United Democratic Forces included of the Union of Democratic Forces (SDS), the Democratic Party (DP), the Gergyovden Movement, the Bulgarian Agrarian National Union - United (BZNS-united), and the Roma Movement for an Equal Public Model (MEPM).

Democratic Forces (UtdDF) and the Democrats for a Strong Bulgaria (DSB), both of which were reincarnations of the former UDF, also entered the 2005 Parliament. More details from the last elections are provided in Table 21.1. The next parliamentary elections are scheduled to take place in June 2009.

Besides developing and adopting the new Constitution of the Republic of Bulgaria, the Grand National Assembly completed another important task: on August 1, 1991 it elected a president, Zhelyu Zhelev, the then leader of the Union of Democratic Forces. He was elected after a heated debate, several rounds of dramatic voting, and extensive behind-the-scenes negotiations. He immediately named General Atanas Semerdzhiev (BSP) vice president, which was a forthright manifestation of the willingness for national conciliation. Under the newly adopted Constitution, elections had to be held as soon as possible so as to let the people choose the head of state. Thus, the democratic start in the election of this important institution was also marked.

Since the end of totalitarian rule, four successful presidential elections have been held: in 1992 (Zhelyu Zhelev/Blaga Dimitrova) the Union of Democratic Forces won with 52.85% among 22 nominated pairs; in 1996 (Petar Stoyanov/Todor Kavaldjiev) the Joint Democratic Forces won with 59.73% among 13 nominated pairs, and in 2001 (Georgi Parvanov/Gen. Angel Marin) the Coalition for Bulgaria (close to BSP) won by a close margin (54%) in a second round against the incumbent president Petar Stoyanov (UDF) among 6 nominated pairs. The last Bulgarian presidential election took place in October 2006. Seven pairs of candidates were nominated. The turnout was too low to declare a clear winner so a run-off vote was called between the top two candidates—Georgi Purvanov, incumbent president, and Volen Siderov, leader of the Attack coalition. Purvanov won overwhelmingly with 76% of the vote, becoming the first president of the country after the political changes of 1989 to be elected for a second term. Ahmed Dogan, the leader of the MRF, made a disturbing public statement that the Movement for Rights and Freedoms had secured 509,093 ballots for the acting President (Konstantionov, 2006).

The voting age in Bulgaria is 18. Among a population of about 8 million citizens, 6,477,260 were registered to vote for the 2006 presidential election (Central, 2006). Voter turnout has been on the decline due to increasing voter apathy and cynicism. Apathy has started to displace the initial political euphoria in the society. After the election boom triggered by the political changes

TABLE 21.2
Basic Data for Bulgarian Elections

Elections	No of Political Formations	Voting Activity	Winners	Forms of TV Political Advertising
VII Grand National Assembly (1990)	40 parties/ and coalitions	90.79% (I) 90.60% (II)	BSP47.15% UDF 36.21% BAPU 8.03% MRF 6.02% Zelyo Zelev (UDF), Pres. Atanas Semerdjiev (BSP) Vice-Prezident	Video ads Debates
36-th Parliament (1991)	38 parties and coalitions; 17 independent	84.82%	UDF - 34.35% BSP&coalition - 33.14% MRF - 7.55%	Addresses Video ads Debates
Presidential (1992)	22	75.39% (I) 75.90 (II)	Zelyo Zelev/Blaga Dimitrova(UDF)	Addresses Debate
37-th Parliament (1994)	48 parties and coalitions 8 independent	75.34 %	BSP&coalition – 43.50% UDF – 24.23% BBB-4.7% PU – 6.51% MRF - 5.44%	Video ads Debates
Presidential (1996)	13	63.14 (I) 61.67% (II)	Petar Stoyanov/Todor Kavaldjiev (UDF)	Addresses, Debates, News
38-th Parliament (1997)	39 parties and coalitions 10 independent	62.40 %	JDF 52.26% DL 22.07% ANS 7.60% BEL 5.50% BBB 4.93%	Addresses, Debates, Campaign news
39-th Parliament (2001)	58 Independent 9365	67.03	SIINM - 42.74% CB -17.15% JDF-18.2% MRF - 7.45%	Addresses, Debates, Campaign news
Presidential (2001)	6	41.76% (I) 55.09(II)	Georgi Parvanov/Angel Marin (BSP)	Addresses, Debates, news
40-th Parliament (2005)	22 parties and coalitions 13 independent	55.76%	CB – 33.97% JDF – 8.44% SIINM – 21.83% DSB-7.1% MRF – 14.07% ATTACK – 8.93% BNU – 5.70%	Video ads, Debates, Campaign News
Presidential (2006)	7	44.6%(I) 41.7% (II)	Georgi Parvanov/Angel Marin (BSP)	Addresses, Ads, News, Debates

Source: Raycheva L. 2006, pp. 372-373; www.is-bg.net/cik2005

of 1989, the relative share of people who refused to vote in Bulgaria gradually but unswervingly began to increase and reached half the voting public at the local election of 1999. All the elections since then (parliamentary, presidential, and local) have become a protest vote against the political class. Apparently, Bulgarian voters refused to yield to the mass media and political and sociological propaganda, especially when dished out along negative lines. Thus, they outstripped the politicians, sociologists, and the media in gaining civil self-awareness and behavior.

Data from elections that took place between 1990 and 2006 show voter turnout on the decline, ranging from 91% in the 1990 Grand National Assembly election to 46% in 1995 Local election (Raycheva, 2006). The 2006 Presidential election marked the lowest voter turnout so far—45% for the first round and 42% for the second (Central, 2006). Table 21.2 summarizes these voting patterns. Nevertheless, these voter averages place Bulgaria higher than most other Eastern European countries and many Western European nations during the same period.

Political Outlook

The period of transformation to democracy and a market economy, which started in 1989, has posed significant social challenges to the population in Bulgaria. The transition was slowed down by delayed legislation, aggressive political behavior, and underdeveloped markets. These factors contributed to rapid impoverishment, a high rate of unemployment, and a loss of established social benefits like free healthcare and free education.

Since the turn of the century Bulgaria has begun to improve its legislative, economic, and social situation. Currently, GDP per capita in Bulgaria equals 5,420 Bulgarian Lev (BGN), approximately €2,728. The official average monthly wage is 340 Lev (€175). Bulgaria's population of 7,718,750 is grouped into about 3,000,000 households. It consists of Bulgarians (84%), Turks (9%), Roma (5%), and other ethnic groups (2%). The large majority of the population (84%) professes the Eastern Orthodox faith while 12% are Muslims. The population has decreased by over one million since the last population census prior to the period of transition (1985), mainly due to aging and emigration (National Statistical Institute, 2005).

Since the end of the Cold War Bulgaria has made great progress towards democratization in political life. Significant efforts had been made to establish rules for the organization and financing of pre-election campaigns. However, the long years of one-party dominance were replaced by an ever-expanding host of new political parties, unions, and organizations, which constantly split, regrouped, and united into coalitions, especially on the eve of forthcoming elections. By snatching the opportunity to air the pre-election campaigns, television catalyzed this political reshuffling race.

The main political powers have declared their political niche: socialists on the left, democrats on the right, SIINM in the center, and the ethnic contingent MFR as a viable coalition partner. However, the political declarations for left and right often differ from the political practices. Left-oriented parties may conduct right management policies and vice versa—the right political parties tend to back left political positions. Obviously, the important task for the political class is rather to be in power than to follow clear political principles.

Nevertheless, democratic institutions, civil society, and political campaigning are further developing and growing more mature. In the process of setting up a multiparty political system in Bulgaria, which was a great democratic achievement by itself, all the elections carried out after 1989 played an important part in laying down the basis for political marketing and campaigning in the country.

Telecasts of political commercials and strong press and radio involvement in defining the final choice of the voters began to play a significant role in election campaigns from the very beginning of the democratization of political life. Thus, mass media played a major role in the strong politicization of the Bulgarian population. Journalism frequently distorted the political processes in the country, and yet exerted considerable influence on public opinion (Raycheva, 1999).

MEDIA SYSTEM

Over seventeen years of political, economic, and social upheavals have significantly impacted the development of the mass media system in Bulgaria. Of all institutions, it was the mass media which were the quickest and most flexible to react to the transformation to democracy after November 1989. At the beginning of the transition period, the spirit of the changes was felt for a full year at open meetings and rallies in Sofia. In the areas outside the capital the changes were felt chiefly because of television coverage. That is why the organizers of protest rallies in support of change in the capital made sure they marched past TV headquarters. The media then found themselves fulfilling the dual function of transmitters and catalysts of political change. This dual function was manifested in several critical situations, including: the TV attack against President Petar Mladenov in 1990 that compelled him to resign; the resignation of the BSP Government headed by Andrey Loukanov in 1990; the mass media war launched by the UDF government of Filip Dimitrov, which led to its toppling in 1992; the resignation of the government of Lyuben Berov (under the Movement for Rights and Freedom mandate) in 1994; the withdrawal of the BSP government of Zhan Videnov in 1996; the siege of the House of the National Assembly during a governmental crisis in 1997, which led to a radical power shift; and the forced restructuring of the UDF government of Ivan Kostov in 1999, based on allegations of corruption.

The processes of decentralization, liberalization, and privatization of mass media began spontaneously and in a short time a completely new journalistic landscape was formed in which different patterns of media consumption and new advertising strategies were introduced. While there is no law that regulates the print media in Bulgaria (slander and libel are enacted through the Penal Code), electronic media are regulated under the Radio and Television Act, adopted in 1998, and the Telecommunications Act, adopted the same year. Both of them have been amended frequently. Bulgaria joined the Television without Frontiers Directive (1989) and later ratified the European Union's Convention on Transfrontier Television (1997). Current media regulations have been closely aligned with EU legislation.

The Bulgarian Constitution guarantees freedom of expression for all citizens. Article 40 (1) specifically defends freedom of mass media: "The press and the other mass information media shall be free and shall not be subjected to censorship" (Constitution, 1991).

The transition to a civil society and market economy in Bulgaria involved a number of challenges in mass media development. These included the general insufficiency of financial and technological resources and a lack of professional standards. Media competition stimulated the first dynamic open markets in the country, which established well-developed media consumption patterns. Although the Bulgarian public was offered a highly varied media menu, expectations that the media would aid the processes of democratization in a purposeful and effective manner proved unrealistically high: The media were in need of transformation themselves. Change of property and single-party control was not sufficient for rendering them professional. Although the guild has adopted its Ethical Code of Bulgarian Media (2004), it failed to build the mechanisms for sustaining it and in many cases reacts inadequately to important and publicly significant issues, as well as to a number of professional problems. Deprofessionalization and tabloidization trends accompanied the transformation period. A number of professional journalistic unions were established, but they failed to defend basic professional rights and responsibilities. Similarly to the politicians, former and newly hatched journalists were not ready to shoulder to the full their new role and the subsequent responsibilities of a Fourth Estate in a society under transformation.

The activity of the civil-society structures and professional organizations proved insufficient as well. Prior to the last parliamentary elections of 2005 some of the most renowned public relations agents had publicly pledged not to bribe media in the forthcoming campaign, thus admitting indirectly that during the previous campaigns the media had been rendering political services. Although according to Reporters without Borders third annual report Bulgaria occupies 36th place (among 167 countries in the world) in the freedom of expression index, freedom of speech and independent journalism provided convertible phraseology for many a non-governmental organization disbursing the funds of European and Transatlantic institutions (Third Annual Worldwide Press Freedom Index, 2006). Their activities, though, proved erratic, limited, and ineffective in the long run.

Print Media

Many challenges were encountered in the process of establishing the new press. Prior to the political changes in 1989, the Bulgarian mass media system was centralized, state-owned, and subordinated to the priorities of the party–state governance. The tight ideological control over the mass media was replaced by economic motives. In the post-1989 years many new publications did come and go. Right after the political changes extreme media partisanship developed. Political pluralism fostered the emergence of a multi-party press. Different parties established their own periodicals, giving rise to a new, politically affiliated journalism. Newspapers of the leading political parties became quite popular. Two examples are *Duma*, supported by the Bulgarian Socialist Party, and *Democrazia*, supported by the Union of Democratic Forces. A wide range of highly varied publications quickly took shape: political, popular, quality, topical, and specialized. This brought a decrease in the party press circulation. A special group of publications was established to target foreign information consumers with periodicals issued in English, French, German, Russian, and Turkish. The monopolist position of the state-owned Bulgarian Telegraph Agency (established in 1892) was broken by new private press agencies, such as the Balkan Agency, BGNES, and online agencies.

Currently, the public enjoys a rich media landscape including 423 newspapers (60 dailies) with annual circulation of 310,023 100 and 746 magazines and newsletters with an annual circulation of 13,665,200 (NSI, 2005). The two dailies with the largest circulation are *Trud* (Labor) and *24 Chassa* (24 Hours), as shown in Table 21.3. Both newspapers are owned by the German media group Westdeutsche Allgemeine Zeitung (WAZ).

Electronic Media

In contrast to the turbulent transformation in the print media, the changes in the electronic media were slower, less complete, and lacked general consistency. They started and were carried out in an atmosphere of deregulation; the Radio and Television Act was adopted only in 1998.

The two national institutions that regulate the electronic media are the Council for Electronic Media (CEM) and the Communications Regulation Commission (CRC). They issue radio and TV licenses and register cable and satellite broadcasters. CEM (formerly The National Council for Radio and Television) is the regulatory body that monitors compliance with the Radio and

TABLE 21.3
Top Nine Daily Newspapers in Bulgaria (2004)

Title	Publisher	Circulation (000)	Cover price (Lev)
Dneven Trud	Media Holding	145	0.70
24 Chasa	168 Chasa Ltd.	106	0.70
Standart	Standart News	48	0.50
Maritsa	Maritsa	27	0.50
Noshten Trud	Media Holding	26	0.50
Novinar	Novinar	25	0.50
Sega	Sega AD	15	0.70
Dnevnik	Economedia	14	0.70
Duma	PM Press	11	0.50

Source: World Association of Newspapers, World Press Trends 2006

Television Act, including issues such as advertising, sponsorship, copyright, and protection of minors. The Council also considers complaints by citizens and organizations. CRC (formerly The State Commission of Telecommunications) enforces the Telecommunications Act and manages the radio spectrum.

For a little more than 15 years a highly saturated radio and TV landscape has been evolving. In 2006, there were 215 television and 145 radio channels available in Bulgaria offered by a large number of national, regional and local radio, and terrestrial, cable and satellite, operators. The television market includes three national TV channels: BNT, the public service television broadcaster, and the two commercial television stations bTV, licensed in 2000 and owned by Rupert Murdoch's Balkan News Corporation, and Nova Televisia, licensed in 2002 and owned by the Greek Antenna Group. Two national radio stations exist: BNR, the public service broadcaster and the commercial Darik radio. The programs of these and other channels are additionally distributed by more than 1,800 cable networks and more than 20 nationwide satellite networks. Two telecommunications operators provide a digital package of program services. Radio and television broadcasting on the Internet is rigorously developing. The privately owned radio and TV stations undoubtedly challenged the monopoly of the state-owned TV. Licensing catalyzed this process and, although still in transition, a diverse radio and TV market was established in the country (*Current Developments of Radio and Television Activities in Bulgaria*, 2006).

Recently bTV has taken the lead in audience share from BNT in a country where 98% of households have a television set. According to May 2006 statistics, bTV's weekly national audience of is 86.2%. The corresponding shares for BNT and Nova TV are 80.6%, and 75.6%, respectively (TV Plan TNS, 2006). However, the public service broadcasters enjoy the highest audience credibility: BNT is approved by about 75% of the population and BNR by about 66%. Corresponding shares for the police are 49% and for the army 50% (National Centre for Public Opinion [NCPO], 2006).

Online Media

The advent of new information technologies has strongly influenced the media production cycle. The Internet was officially introduced into Bulgaria in 1997, and its market has expanded at encouraging rates ever since. Access to the Internet is provided mainly via telephone (dial-up) and via cable by specialized providers or as an additional service by the cable television operators. The installation charge is approximately €30, while unlimited access to the Internet may be obtained for a monthly charge of about €20. Satellite Internet is little used. In addition to home and office, the Internet can also be accessed in Internet cafés and in public places with free access to the Net. Overall Internet penetration in Bulgaria, however, remains relatively low: only 17% of Bulgarian households have access to the Internet (NSI, 2004), but the total number of Internet users is 2.2 million (CIA Factbook, 2005).

The use of new technologies is increasingly regarded as the key survival factor in the overcrowded media space. The newspapers with highest circulation maintain online editions, but some of the online versions require payment. News agencies and broadcast media have also entered the online world. In addition, several web-based media exist. A steady tendency for increasing the quantity and the quality of the electronic information and media sites has been observed.

Using the Internet in Bulgaria requires high-tech computer skills and command of a foreign language. This explains why 40 is the age limit for active use of Internet and why Bulgarian online users are generally well educated.

The increasing popularity of the Internet has definitely impacted the media system. However, the online media business model is still problematic. The combination of content sales, subscription fees, and advertising revenues cannot bring sufficient income to assure content variety for attracting bigger audiences. Searching for their identity in the transforming social and market environment, the online and traditional media are serving more eagerly to advertisers rather than audiences. Because of the quicker reaction to breaking news events, online-only media slowly but steadily take over the niches in the breaking news areas, competing successfully with the traditional print media whose main Internet achievement so far has been to place the identical print content online in the form of "shovel ware."

In addition to traditional media and online-only news sites, some citizen-generated content has entered the World Wide Web. The Internet is beginning to be used for "citizens' journalism." Even though this is a relatively new phenomenon, blogs on different social and political issues have multiplied. Another interesting phenomenon is a group of websites designed to facilitate public debate, where members of the public can write a story on a social, political, or economic topic. These articles are published after approval by the site's staff and its most active users. A telling example for that is http://www.newsfactory.org/.

POLITICAL NEWS COVERAGE

Regulations and Trends

Legislation has created a number of normative documents to regulate various aspects of the political parties in pre-election periods. Funding of political parties and election campaigns proved one of the most sensitive and difficult areas for monitoring and regulation. One should certainly allow here for the fact that, from the beginning of democratization, public opinion and expectations have found it difficult to accept the idea of private financing in politics; that is why government institutions were entrusted with the procedures to be followed and overall control of this type of activity. This was especially valid for political canvassing via the national state-owned electronic media where firm rules were instituted and strictly observed. After 1992, with the advent of private radio and TV stations, at first timidly and then more confidently after the parliamentary and presidential elections of 2001, purchase of broadcasting time became possible under the relevant regulations.

Similarly to other democracies, financing of the election campaigns in Bulgaria has been carried out by two major groups of sources: government and non-government funding (Political Parties Act, 2005). According to this law, candidates for elective offices (in the parliamentary, presidential, and local administration elections) have to report publicly before their constituencies and the respective election commissions how they fund their election campaigns (Grand National Assembly Act, 1990).

The Elections Acts and The Radio and Television Act are the main pieces of legislation that apply directly to elections coverage. Article 13 (3) of the Radio and Television Act (1998) states: "Parties and other political organizations shall be entitled to broadcasting time during campaigns before general and presidential elections. The order and conditions for conducting the election campaigns through the BNR and the BNT are set forth in the Election Act" (Radio and TV Act, 1998).

Both The Presidential Election Act and The Election of Members of the National Assembly, Municipal Councillors and Mayors Act provide that

> throughout the election campaign, candidates shall receive equal coverage in the news programmes of the national mass media. The television and radio stations and the cable television operators

owned by natural and legal persons may provide broadcast time for the election campaign of the candidates at equal prices announced in advance. Foreign radio stations broadcasting from the territory of the Republic of Bulgaria shall not provide broadcasting time for election campaigns.

These Acts also specify that

In case of violations of the order for conducting the election campaign by the Bulgarian National Television and the Bulgarian National Radio the candidates concerned may file claims with the Central Elections Commission. The Commission shall examine the petition within 24 hours and issue a decision which will be final.

These acts also stipulate that "Where the broadcast has infringed upon the rights and good name of a candidate, the latter shall have the right to respond in pursuance of Art. 18 of the Radio and Television Act. The request may be submitted to the respective radio or TV operator within 24 hours after the time of the broadcasting."

In spite of some already established traditions as, for instance, the proportional voting system, the existing legislation was further refined in parallel with preparations for every election. The normative documents regulating access to the state-owned national electronic media during canvassing campaigns also underwent some notable changes.

For instance, the 1991 Election of Members of the National Assembly, Municipal Councilors and Mayors Act contained only one article providing right of access to the national mass media for all candidates for member of Parliament, and for all parties and coalitions (An Act for Members of Parliament, Municipality Counselors and Mayors' Elections, 1991, art. 57). The mode of this access was regulated by a decision of the Grand National Assembly. The 1995 Local Elections Act already introduced 13 articles regulating the featuring of political forces in the national media during canvassing campaigns (Local Elections Act, 1995). Problems arising in each pre-election campaign were to be settled by the Central Electoral Commission (CEC) and the Council of Ministers.

It is important to underscore the dynamic nature of these developments. In the 1991 TV election campaign regulations, political advertising was allowed only on the national state-owned TV and was financed exclusively from the state budget. During the 1994 elections possibilities opened for the regional radio and television centers of the state-owned Bulgarian National Radio and Bulgarian National Television to also carry political ads, by observing strict regulations for canvassing of candidates listed in the respective constituencies. Funding again came from the state budget. The order of appearances on the national screen was determined by drawing lots.

CEC introduced another important point in its decision for the 1997 elections: TV and radio stations and cable television stations owned by physical persons and legal entities could assign air time for canvassing of the parties, coalitions, and independent candidates under equal, pre-set conditions and price (Decision of the Central Electoral Commission, 1997).

Since 2001, prior to the Parliamentary election, it has become possible to use the national commercial broadcasters (and not only of the national state-owned operators BNT and BNR) for pre-election purposes. While the rules applied to state-owned television and radio were traditionally strict, private broadcasters were able to avail themselves of the political financial resources. The presidential elections of 2001 marked another so far unique phenomenon in pre-election campaigning in Bulgaria: the use of the Internet for publication of analyses, online polls, and political campaigning. After the local elections in 2003 these trends increased. In already competitive situations some of the commercial broadcasters could afford the luxury of granting free time for political debates, which according to the Elections Acts was not possible for the public stations. The Parliamentary elections of 2005 and the Presidential elections of 2006 witnessed further developments in TV and online coverage.

HISTORY AND DEVELOPMENT OF POLITICAL NEWS COVERAGE

Gross argues that East European media have to go through the following stages: (1) transition from communist media systems; (2) transformation to new media forms, roles, rules, and regulations; and (3) consolidation to media institutions that develop complete autonomy, professional standards, and journalistic independence. In order to reach the third stage, a clear shared understanding of the journalist's professional role is needed (Gross, 2004). Currently at the second phase of development, according to the above cited stages, Bulgarian media have entered but not yet reached a consolidation state. Among the major remaining challenges is the murky relationship between politics and news.

During the first years of transition political parties and politicians tried to control and manipulate the media to serve their own agendas, but this trend waned later. Following the pre-1989 legacy, the Bulgarian news media tend to offer more interpretative rather than descriptive journalism. This applies to political news as well as to other subjects. The framing of politics is a mixture of issue frames and game frames (also called strategy frames) along with the personal opinion of the author of the news story. When political clashes are presented as a competition, there is a danger that it "is likely to create an anti-political climate and an audience of spectators to these gladiatorial political contests, instead of participants in the building of democracy" (Gross, 2003, p. 86).

The Bulgarian news media tend to focus on politicians' personalities, which was especially evident in the case of the former King Simeon II. Politicians who have regular access to media—such as the leader of the Attack coalition Volen Siderov (who anchors a daily TV show) benefit from extra media exposure. With the advent of market research companies, national and specialized surveys on various subjects have become commonplace. Naturally, the media publish the results of political surveys and opinion polls on a regular basis.

Seeking to justify their professional failure to forecast election returns in several elections, many sociologists pointed out the negative last-minute media propaganda by political candidates as the main reason for failed forecasts. Although arousing justifiable curiosity, Bulgarian practices have so far shown that negative campaigning in general repels the voting public and makes it turn either to another political choice or to civic passivity. According to the leading sociological agencies, the campaign wars can explain the low voting activity. It was this active passivity of Bulgarian citizens that led to unexpected elections results.

The question of political bias in the media remains in focus. Politicians from all sides constantly complain that certain media outlets are biased against them. While the news media still mix opinion with fact, egregious cases of political partisanship and bias have decreased since the late 1990s. The tendency is to have less opinionated and improved coverage of politics. However, subtle political pressure still exists. A telling example during the 2006 campaign for the presidential elections was the dismissal of two leading journalists on commercial TV who dared criticize the two major candidates.

The results of a survey conducted among the leading Bulgarian news media show that indeed politics and news have a complex relationship (Media Development Center, 2005). Some respondents reported that it was common for politicians to hire specialized reporters as consultants. Some journalists admitted that they have their own public relations companies or that they work on external projects for different organizations and sometimes for the government. Other journalists said that they had offered advice to politicians on how to improve their public image, election performance, and media relations. These answers pose significant challenges to journalistic independence.

The survey generally showed that "gentle manipulations" exist among the elite media due to editorial, economic, or political pressure (Media Development Center, 2005). Political pressure to air certain stories versus others or to change particular news segments still exists. It is interesting to note also that journalists admit that they may sometimes publish facts without verification, take payment for positive political coverage of a political party or candidate, or withhold pre-election information due to personal biases. As a result, Bulgarian political news coverage is sometimes inaccurate, politicized, and opinionated. As the Media Development Center report (2005) states, there are examples of "violations of at least four basic principles in the Ethical Code [of Bulgarian media]—separating advertising from editorial materials, independence of editorial from commercial policy of the media, separating commentary from news accounts and resistance to political or economic pressure" (Ethical Code, 2004). Specifically, chapter 3 of the Ethical Code, adopted in 2004 by most Bulgarian media, addresses the issue of editorial independence and states as follows:

> 3.1 We shall not be susceptible to political or commercial pressure or influence....
> 3.4 We shall not accept any personal, political or financial inducements that may impact upon our ability to provide the public with accurate information.

Even though Bulgarian media are still subject to economic and political pressures and sometimes mix personal biases and opinions with journalistic reporting, there is a diversity of opinions and plurality in the Bulgarian media today. Although the media since the political changes of 1989 have gained some independence they still lack maturity in regard to their behavior during election campaigns.

POLITICAL ADVERTISING

Bulgarian law regulates political advertising as a form of "pre-election campaign" by political parties and formations and independent candidates. The political campaigns of the leading parties have grown more sophisticated over time. Most of them now hire advertising agencies to help them fine tune their key messages and reach their target audiences. The forms of TV political advertising include addresses, video ads, debates, and campaign news.

The Addresses

An important aspect of the televised parliamentary pre-election campaigns involves the addresses by parliamentary and non-parliamentary organizations and presidential candidates. The campaign is framed usually on the state-owned public service stations with the opening and closing addresses. They are free of charge and frequently represent the only possible vehicle for presentation of the political platform of the small parties with limited funds. The duration of every address is strictly regulated—in practice there is a trend to reduce the length from 10 to 3 minutes. The leader of a political organization usually makes the address. The visual and graphic layout of the recorded addresses is unified for all appearances while the succession of their airing is determined by lots drawn before the CEC. The common disadvantage of these addresses is that, when arranged in blocks (sometimes lasting for several hours because of the numerous political formations), they become a tedious form of political advertising. Thus, instead of fostering the potential voter, they can have an adverse effect. This is the most probable reason why this form of political advertising was not offered during the last parliamentary election campaign of 2005.

The Video Ads

The video ad is the most popular form for political campaigning. The first time it was used was in the 1990 elections for the Grand National Assembly. Though lacking in prior experience, the production teams worked with inspiration and produced some really good political pieces in terms of screen aesthetics. The political organizations later tried to outdo each other in generous offers to famous pop-singers and football players to participate in their political campaigns. Rules of length changed as well, but video ads never exceeded 3 minutes. The quality of the video ads has gradually improved. However, by reason of cost, not all parties and candidates have the opportunity to produce them and to benefit from this type of presentation.

The Debates

Another form of TV political advertising for all election campaigns are the debates, which focus on some of the country's important political, social, and economic issues such as social policy, security, economic reforms, education, and culture. According to the agreed rules, their length varies between 90 and 120 minutes. In all campaigns the number of debates differs, but those organized for the parliamentary formations outnumber those for the non-parliamentary ones.

January 10, 1992 will remain in the history of Bulgarian political life as the date marking the first presidential debate televised "live." The opponents were Dr. Zhelyu Zhelev, the UDF candidate, and Professor Velko Vulkanov, an independent candidate backed by the BSP. The debate was anchored by the long-time journalist Dimitry Ivanov. Both candidates were supposed to have equal time, but the appearance of Professor Vulkanov nevertheless lasted 2.5 times longer than that of Dr. Zhelev.

In the first years of political debating, the discussions were for the most part monologues that presented political platforms in the time frame allotted to each of the participating political organizations. This was especially true for the non-parliamentary organizations where there were so many participants that, practically speaking, there was no time for any real debates to be held. For that reason some political organizations flatly refused to participate. Others only presented their statements in the narrow time slots. Thus this form of TV propaganda turned off many voters who found it boring and tiresome.

The invasion of commercial media in political campaigning since the beginning of the new millennium has broadened the territory for political debates. It also allowed, however, for the major candidates to avoid facing each other in direct debate as happened in the 2006 presidential elections. Then acting President Georgi Purvanov refused to meet his major opponent, Volen Siderov of the Attack coalition, for a televised debate. This strategy proved to be smart for Purvanov who won the second round, though the public was deprived of the major political debate between the candidates.

The Campaign News

Since the 1997 Parliamentary pre-election campaign another form has been added to political advertising practices on state-owned radio and television: campaign news. The goal was to provide more equal representation of the parties and coalitions, especially of those that lacked sufficient intellectual and financial capacity to produce video ads. Strict rules were introduced concerning the number, duration, and the order of broadcasting of campaign news. Particular attention was paid to the observance of the principles of objectivity and equal standing. Usually the duration of the campaign news was fixed at one minute per party or candidate and they were organized in separate pre-election news blocks to be aired after the prime-time news program. The campaign news reports the marches, meetings, concerts, and other events organized by the participating parties, coalitions, and independent candidates. The campaign news segments have an informative rather than a persuasive character.

The inclusion of the private media in the pre-election campaigns allowed for more varied presentations of political actors and events. At the same time it became possible for the commercial electronic media (for the print media it had happened earlier) to take the side of a particular political force. The broadcasting of the "Attack" program on cable television is a case in point. That program became the basis of a new political party of the same name, which won, as mentioned above, the fourth (from seventh) position in the 40th National Assembly and whose leader ranked second in the presidential race of 2006.

As political advertising becomes more sophisticated, so does the Bulgarian voter. The news media also pay regular attention to how political parties build their messages. Media analyses of political strategies and campaign advertising have become common especially in the morning TV programs.

CONCLUSION

During the period of transition to a democratic society and a market economy, political pluralism was established in the country after four decades of one-party rule. Along with the political transformation, all media institutions underwent changes in their management, structure, and professional standards, bringing about, especially in the last decade of the 20th century, a high-level of politicization in Bulgaria.

In line with the regulations, the TV stations (both public and private) carried out fourteen pre-election campaigns: five for parliamentary elections, four for presidential elections, and four for local elections. Thus, in the process of the transformation to democracy the foundations of election news coverage and political advertising were laid down in Bulgaria. Television in particular has the great responsibility of molding public opinion, especially considering the fact that traditionally Bulgarians have the greatest confidence in public television as compared to the other mass media.

Since November 1989, TV political campaigning has made enormous progress. Addresses, videos, debates, and campaign news, aired on both state-owned and commercial television and more recently on the Internet marked the development of political marketing. Political advertising has made its advent. Television became the most important medium for political campaigning. For the first time in Bulgarian history a public debate between the two candidates for president was aired live on television. Campaign news segments were introduced after prime-time TV news programs. However, a lack of advertising strategy is felt in almost all the political formations. Professional inadequacy and bias of some political scientists, sociologists, and media professionals were displayed during the campaigns. Decreased voter turnout due to unfulfilled expectations has been observed.

Finally, content analysis of the political pre-election campaign TV programs shows some interesting tendencies:

1. Only the big political organizations (such as the *BSP*, the *UDF*, the *MRF*, the BAPU, the SIINM, etc.) have the financial and creative resources to produce and participate in all the forms of TV campaigning (videos, addresses, and debates). The smaller organizations have to restrict themselves mainly to addresses and coverage in the campaign news.
2. Gradually, significant progress in terms of creativity has been achieved in producing political advertising spots.
3. Addresses to the electorate proved boring and in the last parliamentary elections of 2005 they were dropped.
4. The debates developed from time-restricted, formal statements and clumsy declarations to more vivid discussions.

Since the turn of the century all the elections (parliamentary, presidential, and local) have been conducted under a competitive media system strategically used for political campaigning. Both campaigns and election returns, however, manifested grave professional problems in the domain of sociology and the media that failed to meet the requirements for unbiased information and predictability of election results. The paradox is that both parliament (2001 and 2005) and president (2001) were elected contrary to sociological forecasts. A steady trend toward low voter turnout has been registered in all the elections.

In the near future Bulgarian politics and media will feel the impact of European Union membership. All major laws have been harmonized to create regulatory conditions very similar to other EU member states. Differences between Eastern and Western European media concerning the application of media ethics and professional standards, particularly in election times, are expected to be overcome. The main question is how long this process will take.

REFERENCES

Act for Members of Parliament, Municipality Counselors and Mayors' Elections. Retrieved January, 2007 from: http://sdp.hit.bg/zinposk.htm.

Bulgaria. (2006). World Association of Newspapers, World Press Trends.

Bulgarian Institute for Legal Development. (BILD). *Bulgarian National Radio and Television Act* (1998). Retrieved December 24, 2006, from http://www.bild.net/legislation/

Central Electoral Commission. *Elections for President and Vice-President of the Republic.* Retrieved January, 2007 from: http//www.cikipvr.org.

CIA World Fact Book: Bulgaria. Retrieved February 15, 2007 from https://www.cia.gov/cia/publications/factbook/geos/bu.html

Constitution of the Republic of Bulgaria.(1991). Retrieved December 24, 2006, from http://www.Parliament.bg/?page=const&lng=en

Current Developments of Radio and Television Activities in Bulgaria. (2006). Sofia, Bulgaria: Council for Electronic Media Bulletin, No 10: 1–2.

Decision of the Central Electoral Commission. (1997). Accessible only in the archive of the Central Electoral Commission.

Election Act for Members of Parliament. Retrieved January 31, 2007 from www.paragraf22.com/pravo/zakoni/zakoni-d/19564.html/

Election Act for President and Vice-President.Retrieved January 31, 2007 from www.paragraf22.com/pravo/zakoni/zakoni-d/75.htm

Ethical Code of Bulgarian Media. (2004). Retrieved December 26, 2006, from http://btv.bg/news/?magic=et_code_en

European Convention on Transfrontier Television. (1989). Retrieved January 31, 2007 from http://conventions.coe.int/Treaty/EN/Treaties/Html/132.htm

Grand National Assembly Act. (1990). Retrieved January 31, 2007 from http://www2.essex.ac.uk/elect/database/legislationAll.asp?country=bulgaria&legislation=bg90

Gross, P. (2003). New relationships: Eastern European media and the post-Communist political world. *Journalism Studies, 4*(1), 79–89.

Gross, P. (2004). Between reality and dream: Eastern European media transition, transformation, consolidation, and integration. *East European Politics and Societies, 18*(1), 110–131.

Konstantinov, M. (2006, December 4). *Dogan is mocking politics.* Mediapool.bg. Retrieved January 31, 2007 from http://www.mediapool.bg/show/?storyid=124055&p=1; http://www.is-bg.net/cik2005

Law of Telecommunications. (2003). Retrieved January 31, 2007 from http://www.crc.bg/v2/eng/index.htm

Local Elections Act. Retrieved September 4, 2005 from http://www.paragraf22.com/pravo/zakoni/zakonid/99.htm

Media Development Center. (2005, October). *Ethics and journalism in Bulgaria.* Retrieved December 24, 2006, from http://www.mediaonline.ba/en/?ID=379

National Center for Public Opinion. (2006). Retrieved January 31, 2007 from http://www.parliament.bg/?page=ns&lng=bg&nsid=9&aid=15

National Statistical Institute. (2004, March). *Survey on information and communication technologies usage in households.* Retrieved December 24, 2006, from http://www.nsi.bg/IKT_e/IKT.htm

National Statistical Institute of Bulgaria Census. (2005). Retrieved January 31, 2007 from http://www.nsi.bg/Census/Census.htm.

National Statistical Institute. (2005). Publishing Activity in 2005. Retrieved January 31, 2007 from http://www.nsi.bg/SocialActivities_e/Culture_e.htm

Political Parties Act. Retrieved January 31, 2007 from www.namrb.org/izbori/Zakoni/ZPP.doc

Raycheva, L. (1999). The impact of television on the democratization processes. In B. Newman (Ed.), *Handbook of political marketing* (pp. 485–505). Thousand Oaks, CA: Sage.

Raycheva, L. (2006). Fifteen years of televised political advertising Developments in Bulgaria. In L. Kaid & C. Holtz-Bacha (Eds.), *The Sage handbook of political advertising* (pp. 359–375). Thousand Oaks, CA: Sage.

Television without Frontiers Directive. (1989). Retrieved January 31, 2007 from http://www.europa.eu.int/eur-lex/en/consleg/pdf/1989/en_1989L0552_do_001.pdf

Third Annual Worldwide Press Freedom Index. (2006). Retrieved January 31, 2007 from http://www.rsf.org/article.php3?id_article=11715; http://www.newsfactory.org/

tns-tvplan.bg Retrieved January, 2007 from: http://www.tns-tvplan.bg.

22

Election Coverage in the Russian Federation

Sarah Oates

The short history of elections, campaigning, and voting in the Russian Federation is a monument to the failure of parties, campaigns, and elections to create a democratic government. One of the greatest experiments in electoral democracy has ended in a society in which political parties and what remains of an elected parliament have almost no political authority. This happened despite the adoption of a modern constitution that appeared to encourage political parties and the free exchange of information in election campaigns. Instead, the legacy of a strong leader continues with an authoritarian president. The president is technically elected by popular vote, but he has consolidated this position primarily through the relentless manipulation of the media system—especially during election campaigns.

The Russian electoral experience from 1993 into the new millennium forces consideration of some key aspects of the role of election coverage in the formation of democracy. Did Russian democracy fail because of poor democratic safeguards in the design of elections? Is one of the key problems the way in which the media has covered the elections? Or has it been a puzzled and confused electorate that has failed to take advantage of the electoral options on offer? Or perhaps Russian democracy failed because of a dearth of support for democratic ideas among the electorate, a difference in values that no amount of careful electoral design could overcome. The answer lies somewhere among these questions, yet the one point that Russia underlines for all polities is that the democratic intentions of electoral design and campaign practices are never *guarantees* that elections can translate voter preferences into a democratic government.

AN OVERVIEW OF THE POLITICAL AND MEDIA SYSTEM IN RUSSIA

The Russian political and media sphere has a democratic design, but authoritarian content that is best understood as a legacy of the Soviet regime. Russia is the largest successor state of the former Union of Soviet Socialist Republics (USSR), which collapsed in 1991 after a failed reactionary coup. The USSR was a repressive state controlled by a narrow circle of elites in the Communist Party of the Soviet Union. Although the Soviet Union was founded on the principles of revolution and workers' rights in the early 20th century, in practice the Soviet Union was run as an authoritarian regime, albeit with relatively socialist principles. A key feature of the state was propaganda, in the sense that the Communist Party felt it crucial to educate and indoctrinate all citizens into the values of the Communist system. As a result, the Soviet Union placed enormous emphasis on its media system, developing newspapers, radio, and television even at times when other efforts at modernization (including running water) were neglected. All mass media were state owned and under direct control of the state bureaucracy. As a result, the Soviet Union had newspapers such as *Pravda* (*Truth*) and *Izvestiya* (*Faith*) with circulation into the tens of millions. Even while many homes still lacked a telephone or running water, virtually all homes were served by television by the early 1990s. Another key factor of the Soviet Union was its emphasis on international security and its role as a nuclear power. The constant confrontation with the United States and its allies meant that Soviet leaders focused on the development of a strong military and a sense of heightened international threat.

The Soviet Union was run by the Communist Party, with decisions made by a small circle of elite leaders in Moscow. Although the word "party" appears in the name of the institution, the CPSU did not function as a political party in the Western sense. Political parties are supposed to translate the wishes of the masses into either delegative or representative parties and leaders. There were regular elections for delegates to Communist Party congresses and a type of Soviet parliament, but there was no real choice in voting. In addition, these congresses and parliaments did nothing more than rubber-stamp decisions by the central leaders until Soviet control started to unravel in the late 1980s. Yet, it was still compulsory for citizens to appear at the ballot places and cast their votes by dutifully ticking the single political choice—the candidate for the Communist Party of the Soviet Union. The entire mechanism of elections was a political showpiece for the Soviet ruling elite.

The Soviet Union appeared to be a monolithic power with strong state control until the mid-1980s. Soviet leaders introduced a policy of "glasnost" (transparency) and "perestroika" (rebuilding) in an attempt to improve the stumbling Soviet economy. However, this limited "transparency" in the mass media soon translated into open criticism of many leaders, as different political factions used the mass media to voice their opinions. Soon, many media outlets were openly questioning the legitimacy of the regime and the system collapsed after a failed, reactionary coup by hard-line Communists.

Immediately after the collapse of the Soviet Union, there were high hopes for an electoral democracy in Russia, although a sizable segment of the 150 million people—particularly those in rural areas, the poor, and the older generation—still supported the notion of state control and the communist party in general. After a period of increasingly fractious government by Russian President Boris Yeltsin and a more socialist Russian legislature, the parliament elected in Soviet times was disbanded by force by the Russian army in October 1993. Yeltsin called for immediate elections and the passage of a new constitution to rule Russia in December 1993.

The new Russian constitution, approved by a narrow majority of the electorate, set up new political institutions for the post-Soviet Russian state. It established the office of the president and a two-chamber parliament called the Federal Assembly. The president retained a large degree of power, most notably the ability of rule by edict as well as the power to dissolve a recalcitrant parliament and call for new elections. The president was to be elected every four years, with a limit of two consecutive terms. The upper house of the parliament (the Council of the Federation) and the lower house (the Duma) had limited power to challenge presidential legislation or to pass legislation of their own. In the 1993 elections, the 198 members of the Council were elected through first-past-the-post ballots in the 89 regions of Russia. The 450 Duma members were elected half through party lists, with 225 seats distributed proportionately to all parties earning more than 5 percent of the national list vote. The other 225 Duma seats were awarded to first-past-the-post winners in the 225 single-member constituencies throughout Russia. The first election was to be held at the same time as the constitutional referendum (in December 1993), with the first parliament to sit for just two years. Then regular parliamentary elections were to be held every four years, unless parliament was dissolved by the president and earlier elections were called (although this had not happened by 2007 in Russia). Due to some unintended consequences and surprising outcomes of early elections, the electoral rules have now shifted. The upper house of the parliament was only elected in 1993; members are now essentially appointed by the president. Starting in December 2007, all of the seats for the Duma are elected via the party list system.

The Russian Media

Just as the political institutions have changed in form, so have the Russian media. In the Soviet system, all media were organs of the state. In Russia, all forms of media ownership are allowed, although there are some limitations on the amount of foreign ownership in media outlets. However, the media sphere in Russia is neither free nor fair. It would appear that Russia is reverting to a Soviet-style relationship, with the media as an actively co-opted player in repressive governance rather than a factor in fostering civil society. It is important to point out that journalists in Russia are struggling with massive barriers to pursuing their profession, including a lack of proper financing, inordinate pressure from officials, and, most worryingly, violence against them that has led to murder in many cases. Russia is one of the deadliest countries in the world for journalists, as measured by international groups such as Reporters Without Borders.[1] The key question about Russian journalists is whether they have fundamentally changed their role in politics from the Soviet era. Under Communist rule, the media were the propaganda wing of the ruling Communist Party of the Soviet Union. Although there were censors, they were not the key factor in the formation of political news. Rather, journalists were well inculcated with the norms of self-censorship, producing news that fit the 'frame' of the Soviet government. In the end of the Soviet period, the introduction of the policy of glasnost (transparency) by Soviet leaders led to an increase in the variety of opinions expressed, but not to a fundamental, permanent change in how post-Soviet journalists perceived their role (Oates, 2006; Pasti, 2005; Voltmer, 2000). They continued to see themselves as political players, rather than political observers in service to the citizens.

It is understandable that journalists who worked as propagandists in the Soviet era might have trouble adjusting to change. However, there is fairly strong evidence that the post-Soviet generation of journalists do not interpret their role as disinterested supporters of civil society (Pasti, 2005; Voltmer, 2000). While the post-Soviet period initially had some variation in opinion, this has become increasingly limited as the Kremlin tolerates less and less opposition to its policies. State-funded media outlets face losing their subsidies if they do not toe the official line. Commercial media outlets that criticize the presidential administration on key issues (such as opposition to the president, corruption, or the war in Chechnya) can lose financial control of their organizations through government sanctions (such as by strict application of tax or finance laws). Even when individual journalists may choose to pursue controversial issues, they will quickly find that cautious editors and publishers will be quick to set limits. Practical issues aside, there is substantial evidence that Russian journalists view themselves more as political players than as political watchdogs or challengers of the political status quo (European Institute for the Media, 1996a, 1996b, 2000a, 2000b; Oates, 2006). They work for their particular political "patron." Viewers, readers, and listeners will be presented with "news" that is essentially propaganda from the point of view of the political patron. As the presidential apparatus has consolidated power in Russia to a large extent, there is now little deviation from the Kremlin line. In particular, this means there is virtually no meaningful news from the current war in Chechnya. Generally, it means that Russian citizens have little ability to meaningfully debate political issues or participate in civic life.

Despite the obvious problems with media coverage, Russians retain a high degree of both trust and interest in their mass media (Oates, 2006). Although they are aware of the bias and omissions on state-run First Channel television, it remains one of the most trusted institutions in the country. In 34 focus groups held in 2000 and 2004, Russian citizens commented that they relied on state-run television in particular for their news.[2] In addition, they exhibited support for the role of television as a political player and social directive, as opposed to a medium that merely attempted to report or interpret events. According to a 2003–2004 survey,[3] 82% of Russians routinely watched national television, compared with 63% who watched local television, 31% who read local newspapers, and 22% who read national newspapers. The survey results showed that television, in addition to its widespread use, is the most likely conduit for political news and information for the Russian public. When asked how often they hear or read about politics in the mass media, 82% of the respondents said they heard about politics either daily or several times a week on television, compared with 46% for radio and 37% for newspapers.

ELECTION CAMPAIGNS IN RUSSIA

How do the political sphere, the media system, and citizen attitudes toward the media affect election campaigns? While there may be a dearth of democracy in Russia, there has been no lack of political parties. Thirteen parties ran on the 1993 ballot, followed by 43 in 1995, 26 in 1999, and 17 in 2003. Most of these parties attracted less than 1% of the vote and appeared on the ballot in only one election. While this is not surprising for tiny parties, it is not only obscure parties that have a poor survival rate in Russia. Just two political parties, the nationalist Liberal Democrats headed by Vladimir Zhirinovsky and the Communist Party of the Russian Federation, have been successful in the Duma's party-list race in all four elections from 1993 to 2003. In addition, Russia's first two presidents—Boris Yeltsin and Vladimir Putin—ran as independents without party affiliation. Due to a weak parliament and lack of a rule of law, political parties have little force or authority in society. This is underlined by the fact that the most popular parties in 1999 and 2003 have been little more than media creations, brought into existence weeks before Duma elections to promote presidential policy and then fading away or even changing name once elected. While there is little inherent political force in parties in Russia, there is also virtually no accountability between the election campaign and the party's role in power.

On paper, the rules for communication in election campaigns would appear to favor a wide dissemination of information in a disinterested manner. All parties and candidates are given free time and free space in the state media (including on the popular and far-reaching "First Channel" on Channel 1). By law, parties and candidates are entitled to equal and fair media coverage. In addition, all political parties and candidates have the right to buy advertising in the mass media. There are spending limits (for example, about $2.4 million per party in the 1999 Duma elections), although they are enforced on a selective basis as there has not been an investigation into the clear diversion of state resources for pro-Kremlin parties. As each party and presidential candidate is given an equal amount of free time in the mass media, including on the prime state television channel, there is a staggering amount of information available. Thus, even the plethora of tiny parties of Russia technically can have the same amount of free time as the big pro-Kremlin parties. This is balanced by the fact that much of the free time is poorly used (and barely watched).[4] In addition, electoral rules were tightened in 1999, when a new law required that parties that did not get at least 2% of the vote would have to reimburse state television and other media outlets for the time used. This effectively shuts out minor parties from using "free" time.

While this would appear to be a relatively equitable system in theory, in practice the rules are generally used to punish or limit the campaigning ability of those out of favor with the Kremlin. In each election, careful studies by the European Institute for the Media and the Organization for Security and Co-operation in Europe have shown marked bias toward the incumbent president or the pro-Kremlin parties on television news (European Institute for the Media, 1996a, 1996b, 2000a, 2000b; OSCE, 2004a, 2004b). As in Soviet times, journalists have continued to serve political masters rather than the interests of the public. As a result, there are distortions, omissions, and even lies broadcast and published about candidates and parties. Those without control of powerful media outlets—particularly state-run television news—are at a serious disadvantage in the campaign. This has become even more marked since the first election of Putin in 2000 and his consolidation of national power. Although some political forces—such as the Communist Party of the Russian Federation and Moscow Mayor Yuri Luzhkov—used to provide political alternatives to the Kremlin, they are no longer independent, meaningful political forces in Russia. As such, coverage of Putin and pro-Putin parties is now sycophantic and broadly reminiscent of Soviet propaganda. Political opposition, even street protests, is either not covered or the participants are vilified on national television. This coverage style is amplified during the campaigns, in which the Kremlin wishes to generate election outcomes that are as positive as possible for pro-government parties.

In addition to guarantees about free and fair elections in the 1993 constitution, there are detailed laws relating to election coverage in the media. The main tenets of the law call for the right of citizens to campaign freely for parties and candidates; equal access to the mass media for all parties and candidates; fair and equal treatment of all parties and candidates; an equal amount of free time or space for all parties and candidates; the rights of parties and candidates to buy broadcast or print advertising; and the dissemination of election results. Although these laws are quite liberal in theory, particularly in terms of the provisions for paid and free time, in practice the system is unfair. Much of this unfairness springs from problems inherent in media coverage of elections, notably enormous differences in financial and other resources of the parties and candidates. For example, most Russian parties and candidates cannot afford to produce professional free-time broadcasts and the results range from mildly amusing amateur productions to unbearably dull talking heads. Those parties that can afford to hire directors and use more sophisticated techniques have been able to make far more effective use of their free time.[5] Obviously, there is the same problem with paid advertising, as most Russian parties simply cannot afford the rates, which were as high as $40,000 a minute on prime-time Channel 1 in 1999.[6] In addition, from the first elections in 1993 to the present, news producers have found themselves deeply frustrated by neophyte politicians with a poor television presence that alienated their audience. Forced by the law to provide a large amount of time to the parties, the state-funded stations found themselves losing viewers during the free-time slots. To make matters worse, parties would often refuse to co-operate in the production of the debates or round-tables, which the law requires should be at least 30% of the free-time content (On Basic Guarantees of Electoral Rights and the Right of Citizens of the Russian Federation, Article 40, Section 2, as amended March 30 1999).[7]

To further complicate matters, the Russian laws on elections continually grow more detailed and unrealistic from a news production point of view. The new law on the Duma elections, signed by President Putin on December 20, 2002, provides examples of these problems. The law, which is more than 100 pages, provides some arguably good principles. For example, it would be beneficial if, as the law states, "Informational materials carried by the mass media or disseminated by other methods shall be objective and accurate and shall not violate the equality of candidates, political parties, electoral blocs" (Article 54, Section 2, Federal Law No.175-FZ, On the Election of Deputies of the State Duma of the Federal Assembly of the Russian Federation). However, the law then carries on from this general principle to overly specific restrictions. The law requires that election items "shall be always presented in the form of separate news items, without any comments" (Article 56, Section 4) and that any description of "possible consequences of the election or non-election of a candidate" is considered overt campaigning (Article 57, Section 3). In addition, news outlets cannot "disseminate information about the activities of a candidate unrelated to his professional activity or duties" without it being considered campaigning (Article 57, Section 5); a person cannot be shown to be endorsing a party or candidate unless there is written consent filed with the election commission (Article 57, Section 8); and a state print outlet must provide no less than 10% of its weekly space to candidates or parties free of charge (Article 61, Section 2). All of these rules would make it almost impossible for journalists to cover an election in a meaningful way. Some of the most detailed rules relate to publishing "informational materials (including such materials which contain reliable information) which may damage the honor, dignity or business reputation of a candidate" (Article 64, Section 6). According to the law, if the mass media organization cannot provide the candidate with an opportunity to broadcast or publish a denial or make an explanation in "defense of his honor, dignity or business reputation" before the end of the campaign, then the media outlet cannot broadcast or publish the information.

Many of these rules are in direct response to the large amount of mud-slinging in Russian elections, a phenomenon that peaked in the 1999 Duma elections. The rule from Article 64, Section 6 on a prohibition on publishing damaging facts is thus linked to the activities of Channel 1 television presenter and analyst Sergei Dorenko, who was notorious for spreading gossip and innuendo without giving his subjects a proper chance of rebuttal in the 1999 elections. Studies also have shown sympathetic coverage of pro-government parties and their leaders on the nightly news, slanting political coverage in the weeks before the elections with excessive, positive reports on these individuals (European Institute for the Media, 1996a, 1996b, 2000a, 2000b; Helvey & Oates, 1997; Oates & Roselle, 2000). Arguably, this has led to the ban on covering those in the elections in non-electoral events and duties. Yet the law is unworkable on two levels. First, it creates such stringent limits on what can be covered in the elections that broadcasters, in particular, are left with virtually no option but to show unedited clips of candidates at rallies and giving speeches. In addition, there is no room for analysis or even an educated discussion. In fact, by 1999, the Russian Central Election Commission was already warning television broadcasters to limit discussions and to present in the most straightforward fashion merely the faces and words of the candidates. This left the voters, faced with dozens of parties and thousands of candidates, even more confused and uninformed.

The practical problems aside, the law bears little resemblance to the Russian media reality. While the parliament and president have chosen to pass a law requiring fairness in election coverage, Russian election coverage continues to be extremely unfair. First, there is an undue amount of coverage, much of it positive, to pro-government parties and candidates (European Institute for the Media 1994-2000; Oates, 2006; OSCE, 2004a, 2004b). Some of this is in terms of the sheer amount of coverage, out of proportion with the initial support for the party. Some parties are virtually ignored or, when mentioned, presented in a more negative sense. The most prominent example of this is the Communist Party of the Russian Federation which, despite being the most consistently popular political party, has received either scant attention or an unfair amount of negative coverage over the elections from 1993 to 2007.

Who is controlling whether a particular candidate or party gains favorable or negative coverage? At one point, different television channels in Russia picked their own candidates and parties to champion. As channels have been forced to shift ownership or shut down altogether, it is clear that positive coverage is reserved for the president and his supporters and negative coverage is for those who can challenge the president. Other politicians, who are deemed too minor to challenge the president's hegemony, are either ignored or covered in a superficial manner. Yet, where does this pattern of coverage originate in Russia and how is it directed? This is a difficult area in which to conduct research. Reporters, editors, and producers are not keen to say that their editorial coverage is "directed" in a Soviet-style fashion. It also is not in their best interest to pass this information on to social science researchers or others if they want to keep their jobs. In addition, it is a point of professional pride. Journalists may genuinely feel that they are reporting political news in a good fashion or at least in a way in which the audience expects it to be covered. Just because they are catering to a taste for *kompromat* (the Russian slang for "compromising materials") and scandal does not mean that their reporting is necessarily flawed. It also is somewhat unfair to single out Russian journalists as failing to meet particular standards, as there is ample evidence of scandal-mongering, mud-slinging, and tabloidization in many media systems. However, it would appear that Russian journalists have a radically different notion of their role in society than their counterparts in countries such as the United States or the United Kingdom. They are clearly functioning as political voices rather than political commentators.

THE HISTORY OF CAMPAIGN NEWS IN RUSSIA:
EXPLAINING DEMOCRATIC FAILURE

The election results of the new Russian Federation are a classic study in the unintended consequences of institutional design. Although Yeltsin and his advisers were clearly interested in promoting a Western-style, market-based economy, the voters also embraced communist and nationalist parties in the 1993 elections. As displacement from the market economy deepened, so did mistrust of Western-style democracy in Russia. By the 1995 elections, the pro-Kremlin, pro-market parties declined further in popularity and the Communist Party of the Russian Federation became the most successful political party in the country. In addition, voting was still relatively strong for nationalist parties, particularly the xenophobic and aggressive Liberal Democrats. Pro-government candidates fared slightly better in the single-member races, but found themselves lacking a majority in the parliament. In addition, Yeltsin faced a particularly difficult electoral battle in 1996. Not only was he suffering from heart disease and a reputation as an alcoholic, the first Russian invasion of Chechnya (1994–1996) was becoming a political quagmire. Yeltsin ran neck-and-neck with Communist contender Gennady Zyuganov in the first round of the 1996 election, but managed a convincing victory in the final elections later that year. Although commercial NTV news had been critical of Yeltsin before the elections, the station dropped this criticism and was supportive of the president—even hiding his heart disease from the public. Station officials explained that this was a tactical political move to avoid the victory of the Communist candidate, who threatened to close all commercial media outlets, but it showed that the commercial media traded journalistic professionalism for political expediency.

The year 1996 marked the last year that the Kremlin feared for its ability to control the electoral outcomes in Russia. Russian politicians learned a great deal from the surprising success of nationalist and communist forces in the 1993 and 1995 Duma elections (Oates, 2006). In particular, the Kremlin and Moscow elites learned to craft party messages that were more socialist and more nationalist in tone. This better reflected the preferences of the electorate than the more pro-market, pro-Western parties supported by the central government in the 1993 and 1995 elections. This could be construed as democratic, in that the pro-government parties were responding to the ideological preferences of the electorate. However, the link between what parties say during campaigns and their actual political behavior once elected is very weak in Russia. As the parliament is relatively weak and fragmented, there is little party cohesion and party accountability for campaign promises. For example, the nationalistic Liberal Democrats and their leader, the outspoken and outrageous Vladimir Zhirinovsky, consistently campaign on promises of confronting the government. However, once in power, the Liberal Democrats often side with the Kremlin. This cycle has repeated itself in several elections. In addition, parties often collapse after the elections. Pro-government parties have changed names several times, often within months or even weeks of an election, making any sort of long-term party accountability impossible.

The Communists, Liberal Democrats, and pro-market Yabloko ("Apple") party are the only Russian parties to consistently succeed in elections, although Yabloko failed to cross the 5% party list barrier in 2003. The other dominant players have been parties created by powerful leaders or institutions, either "parties of personality" or "parties of power." In each election, the Kremlin has promoted a different "party of power" with various leaders to forward its interests. These parties of power have the trappings of fully-fledged political parties, with policy statements and usually with some sort of platform. Yet the foundation of the party is transparent, as the political marketing makes it clear that the party exists to reflect and further the government interests that created, funded, and staffed it. Up to 1999, parties of power created by the Kremlin never managed to maintain their ties with the presidential administration until the next parliamentary election. In 1993, the primary party of power was Russia's Choice, in 1995 it was Our Home is Russia, and in 1999 it was Unity.[8] By 2003, Unity had joined forces with a regional party of power, Fatherland-All Russia, to create the formidable power base of United Russia.

Evidence suggests that the Kremlin has done a better job in each election in creating a political party from scratch, from the selection of leaders to the crafting of the party program to the marketing of the party via television. Although the Kremlin's main party of power received less

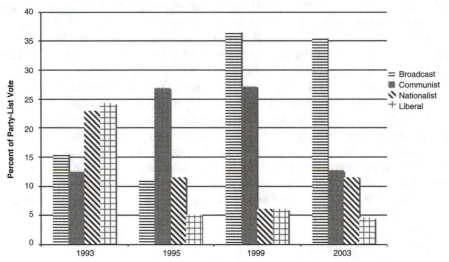

Party type definitions for Chart 1: 1993 — Broadcast: Russia's Choice; Communist: Communist Party of the Russian Federation; Nationalist: Liberal-Democratic Party of Russia; Liberal: Yabloko, Party of Russian Unity and Accord, Democratic Party of Russia, Russian Movement for Democratic Reform. 1995 — Broadcast: Our Home is Russia, Ivan Rybkin Bloc; Communist: Communist Party of the Russian Federation, Working Russia for the Soviet Union; Nationalist: Liberal-Democratic Party of Russia, For the Motherland; Liberal: Yabloko, Democratic Choice of Russia, Party of Russian Unity and Accord. 1999 — Broadcast: Unity, Fatherland-All Russia, Union of Right Forces; Communist: Communist Party of the Russian Federation, Working Russia for the Soviet Union, Stalinist Bloc; Nationalist: Zhirinovsky Bloc (Liberal-Democratic Party of Russia); Liberal: Yabloko. 2003 — Broadcast: United Russia, Fatherland-All Russia, Rodina; Communist: Communist Party of the Russian Federation; Nationalist: Liberal-Democratic Party of Russia; Liberal: Yabloko, Union of Right Forces. While there were other small parties that could have possibly fit within these categories, relatively obscure parties were omitted because there was little information for either the electorate or scholars on their party ideology.

FIGURE 22.1   Election results by party type, Russian Duma elections 1993–2003.

of the party-list vote and fewer single-member constituency seats in 1995 than in 1993, it can be argued that its ability to succeed even when the presidential administration was extremely unpopular showed increasing skill in campaigning. In addition, Unity fared even better as it managed almost to tie for first place in the party-list race with the Communist Party in the 1999 Duma elections, providing a smoother path for Putin's victory in the presidential race a few months later. In 2003, United Russia won the largest party-list vote (38%) of a single party organization in the 12-year history of the Russian Federation. By the 2000 and 2004 presidential elections, state-run television was a loyal supporter of Putin, to the point that Putin did not bother to use his free time. News and analysis programs were promoting him far more effectively.

As noted above, Yabloko, the Liberal-Democratic Party of Russia, and the Communists are the only three parties to have survived over several elections (see Figure 22.1), but support has varied a great deal for the latter two parties. While Yabloko's support had been about 6 to 8% in the elections until it earned just 4.3% in 2003, the nationalist Liberal Democrats in 1993 won about 23% of the party-list vote, then dropped to 6% in 1999 before doubling that in 2003. Support for the Communist Party grew from about 12% in 1993 to about 24% of the party-list vote in 1999, but dropped again to 13% in 2003. All of these parties have fielded candidates in the presidential elections, although only the Communist candidate has ever been a serious contender. Other parties, notably those put forward by the Kremlin, have managed to win seats via the party-list system.

Party success can also be measured by how well the parties perform in the other half of the contest; that is, in the single-member district races that elect half of the 450 Duma seats. Until the 2003 elections, the two electoral methods often balanced each other. For example, although the Liberal Democrats have always managed to win a large or at least reasonable percentage of the party-list vote, the party performs very poorly in single-member districts. Other results have been extremely labile, with the Communists quite strong in the single-member district elections until 2003. In addition, the central party of power did poorly in the single-member districts in 1995 and 1999. The fortunes reversed in 2003, however, when United Russia topped the polls in both the party-list contest and the SMD ballot, with an unprecedented 103 seats through first-past-the-post elections.[9] Combined with its allotment of 120 seats from the party-list elections, United Russia immediately controlled almost half the Duma seats. Much of this success could perhaps be traced to the strong regional support within the original Fatherland-All Russia party, which did extremely well in the single-member districts in 1999 (before joining Unity to form United Russia). The issues of party affiliation and its effect on single-member district are complex and have been analyzed by other scholars (Golosov, 2002; Hale & Orttung, 2003; Hutcheson, 2003; McAllister & White, 2000). For this study, the only convincing evidence in the relationship between the party-list race and single-member district elections lies in the ability of some candidates to use smaller national parties as a springboard for district success. For example, although the Agrarian Party has been unable to win any party-list seats since 1993, single-member candidates have been elected to the Duma in every other election through 2003 while running with the party affiliation.[10]

While arguably the unfair influence of money and power makes PR somewhat undemocratic in the U.S. and Britain, the Russian PR sphere is far more Machiavellian. Although tactics include "white propaganda"—the dissemination of positive information about an organization, party, political candidate, company, etc—far more popular in election campaigns is "black propaganda." This includes planting of negative information, rumors, or even lies about individuals and organizations, usually via journalists who are either bribed or under political influence. This is called "hidden advertising" and is particularly prevalent at election times, as "news" articles or items appear that are actually planted by PR "technologists" as they are known in Russia.

By the 1999 elections, the Russian media, and state-run Channel 1 television in particular, had developed a compelling system of *kompromat*. With *kompromat*, the media provide dodgy "evidence" that a political or business figure has been involved in shady dealings (such as by insinuating a link between the murder of American businessman Paul Tatum and the Moscow mayor standing in opposition to Putin). There is no attempt to make a balanced report or seek a reply from the individual involved. Often, the "evidence" is just quick flashes of financial documents on the television screen or insinuations from the television host on a political chat show (see reports by the European Institute for the Media; Oates, 2006).

What does a Russian election campaign look like to voters via the lens of the mass media? This has evolved from the relatively free and chaotic advertising and news of the first elections in 1993 to a much narrower and arguably more dignified coverage in more recent campaigns. The 1993 campaign generated a relatively large amount of interest, although even in the first contest the inherent biases in the system were apparent. Although all of the 13 parties in the contest received the same amount of free time (in 20-minute slots, which were very long), it was clear that many of the parties lacked political communication skills. The marketing tactics favored long monologues, which were quite difficult to watch. However, nationalist Zhirinovsky made interesting use of his free time, promoting the anti-market, xenophobic, and hawkish policies of his Liberal Democrats with demagogic statements, rash promises, and extreme pronouncements (such as suggesting that all news announcers should look Aryan and saying the United States should give Alaska back to Russia). Zhirinovsky and his party were dismissed as rank outsiders by Yeltsin and his advisers, who were shocked when the Liberal Democrats won 23% of the party-list vote in 1993. In fact, Zhirinovsky and his particular brand of outrageous campaigning has been a fixture in Russian elections from 1993 through 2003 (although his runs for president have never garnered the same level of support). The pro-Kremlin party found that its message supporting capitalism and criticizing the Soviet past was not particularly popular with the voters. Despite receiving an inordinate amount of television news coverage at elections, most of it quite positive, on prime state-run television, pro-Kremlin parties originally performed relatively poorly. In addition, pro-Kremlin parties had significant advantages in the ability to buy advertising (which was no doubt from illegally using state monies to do so) as well as party leaders pulled from the top ranks of the administration.

Pro-Kremlin parties started to do noticeably better in Russian elections in 1999, when there was a distinct change in approach. Although pro-Kremlin parties such as Russia's Choice (1993) and Our Home Is Russia (1995) had relied on media saturation via news coverage, paid advertising, and professionally produced free-time broadcasts, it was not until the party message became more in tune with the electorate that the pro-Kremlin forces were able to sway large numbers of voters. From a somewhat Western, pro-market image that rejected the Soviet past, the pro-Kremlin parties moved steadily toward a more nationalistic message that chimed better with a Soviet, socialist viewpoint. The Kremlin political managers learned from the relatively enduring success of the Liberal Democrats and the Communist Party of the Russian Federation about what party images appealed to the Russian population. This did not signal a fundamental change in the Kremlin's top-down approach to policy, for as noted above campaign messages have little to do with government behavior in Russia. Rather, it allowed the pro-Kremlin forces to exploit the electoral system to gain votes. These votes then legitimized the pro-Kremlin forces both nationally and internationally. The pro-Kremlin parties learned how to play the system to win. In order to tip the balance further, Putin and his allies changed the electoral law after the 2003 Duma elections so that all parliamentary seats are assigned to parties that garner more than 7% of the national party list vote. This allows the Kremlin, which created the most popular party vehicle by 2003 in its United Russia party, to ensure domination of the lower house of the parliament. In addition, the law makes it much more difficult to organize and officially register a political party to run for office.

One way to conceptualize the evolution of campaigning and political power in Russia is to analyze how these "show" parties have come to dominate over parties with at least some degree of ideological coherence in Russia. Parties such as United Russia could be considered "broadcast" parties, in that they are created by the broadcast media via the news, free time, and paid political broadcasting. They have no particular ideology and in fact ideology would get in the way of marketing. They are presented as nationalistic parties for the "good of Russia," with leaders already working in the government. In the 2003 Duma campaign, the main advertising for United Russia featured a set of glowing images of Russia, from street scenes to sweeping landscapes, with either just the sound of the Russian national anthem or a commentary:

> *Each has his own Russia, that you see, that is right next to you, for some it is factories, for some it is fields, your corners, your school, your harvest, the light in the home opposite you.... And if we put it all together, the picture becomes united and we see how great and rich Russia is. We will do everything to build a worthy life for all.* (Translation by author)

Visually, the political advertisements resembled tourism promotions. Verbally, they said nothing of political substance. In terms of music, they linked the party with the state through the stirring, classical tones of the national anthem.

News coverage is clearly and markedly biased in Russia, and this is painfully clear during election campaigns. The heavy bias toward pro-Kremlin forces on state-run Channel 1 used to be balanced, to a degree, by different political biases on other media outlets. However, since Putin's re-election in 2004, there has been markedly little variation in media coverage across all types of media outlets. NTV, the largest commercial television network in Russia, used to be relatively critical of the Kremlin, in particular in its coverage of the first Chechen war (1994–1996). However, the station's ownership was changed after selective enforcement of financial regulations in 2001, and the editorial team was replaced. Since then, NTV has been much less critical of the Kremlin regime.

In the month-long 2003 Duma campaign, an analysis of central news shows showed that the central themes on the flagship news show *Vremya* (*Time*) on the Channel 1 could be described as the efficacy of President Putin; the prominence of top leaders of United Russia and their close political relationship with the president; how the central government would strive to fix problems in the regions; and Russia's role in the international sphere (Oates, 2006). While the coverage on the flagship news program of *Sevodnya* (*Today*) on NTV had less of an emphasis on Putin's administration, it did not challenge it or present political opposition in a serious way. There were differences in the way that the two programs approached the news: *Vremya* had more of an emphasis on the campaign, including news on political parties, while *Sevodnya* had more on crime. However, the quantity of political coverage on *Vremya* is not reflected in quality, as most of the coverage was either essentially propaganda for Putin and the pro-Kremlin parties or negative stories about the Communists. This pattern continued for the 2004 presidential elections, in which *Vremya* became virtually an "infomercial" for Putin. Putin won handily in the first round of the presidential elections in 2004.

THE FUTURE OF RUSSIAN ELECTION CAMPAIGNS

There is little chance that future elections in Russia will bring a greater chance for democracy in the country. Rather, elections now function in the service of the presidential apparatus in Russia.

From a chaotic beginning, Russian parties have been consolidated into a vehicle for elite power. Arguably, political parties also fulfill this function in the West, and campaign practices can often distort rather than realign political power in line with the wishes of the electorate. However, the electorate has become particularly powerless in Russia, as choices have narrowed and there is no realistic alternative to the ruling elites. Nor can communication technology itself address this concern. While the use of the Internet continues to spread in Russia— although relatively slowly when compared with countries such as China—the Internet carries little sense of authority in the country. As there is little chance for grass-root organization and opposition in an increasingly repressive state, political communication cannot counter the authoritarian direction. In the case of Russia, electoral communication is now used to consolidate, rather than challenge, political power.

NOTES

1. See *Journalists Killed in the Line of Duty in the Last 10 Years*, a report from the Committee to Protect Journalists. Available at http://www.cpj.org/killed/Ten_Year_Killed/Intro.html
2. This is from research projects conducted by the author, funded by two grants from the British Economic and Social Research Council (000-22-3133 and 228-25-0048), see Oates (2006) for detailed findings from the focus groups.
3. From a survey of 2,000 respondents across Russia conducted by Russian Research Ltd. from December 21, 2003, to January 16, 2004. These questions were funded by a grant from the British Economic and Social Research Council (Grant 000-22-3133).
4. Officials at RTR (Channel 2) confirmed during an interview with the author in December 1999 that viewership of the free-time political advertising is very low. The state-controlled channels are obligated to carry it. Across 34 focus groups in Russia in 2000 and 2004, this was little recall of, or interest in, free-time party broadcasts.
5. I make this observation based on viewing and studying Russian paid and free-time political advertising over the course of seven elections.
6. Author's interview with Vladimir Evstafiev, head of the Maxima Communication Group, Moscow, December 1999.
7. For example, officials at RTR complained in December 1999 that parties would not cooperate in the production of joint free-time political advertising (information from interviews by the author with RTR First Deputy Editor-in-Chief for the Main Newsroom for the Electronic Mass Media Galina Ivkina and RTR Vesti Company Head of the Department of Special Projects, Sergei Kostornou, December 16, 1999, as part of the 1999 election coverage monitoring mission with the European Institute for the Media, see European Institute for the Media 2000a, 2000b),
8. A review of political party platforms, policy statements, and political advertising by the author has identified these parties as the central "parties of power" created to reflect and carry out the will of the presidential administration. There have been other parties, however, that also have toed the Kremlin line, identified in this research. I have identified these additional parties as the Party of Russian Unity and Accord in 1993, the Ivan Rybkin Bloc in 1995, and the Union of Right Forces in 1999.
9. According to the CEC report on the Duma's formation on February 4, 2004, *Spisik zaregistrirovannykh deputatov gosudarsvennoi Dumy Federal'novo Sobraniya Rossiiskoi Federatsii chetvertovo sozyva*. Online (in Russian). Available at http://gd2003.cikrf.ru/etc/protokol2.doc/
10. It should be pointed out that parties can win the ballot battle, but lose the war in the parliament because parties have relatively little power to force candidates who ran with their party affiliation to join their party grouping in the Duma. Defection is not uncommon (Remington, 2001).

REFERENCES

European Institute for the Media. (1994). *The Russian parliamentary elections: Monitoring of the election coverage of the Russian mass media*. Düsseldorf: European Institute for the Media.

European Institute for the Media. (1996a). *Monitoring the media coverage of the 1995 Russian parliamentary elections*. Düsseldorf: The European Institute for the Media.

European Institute for the Media. (1996b). *Monitoring the media coverage of the 1996 Russian presidential elections*. Düsseldorf: The European Institute for the Media.

European Institute for the Media. (2000a). *Monitoring the media coverage of the December 1999 parliamentary elections in Russia: Final report*. Düsseldorf: European Institute for the Media.

European Institute for the Media. (2000b). *Monitoring the media coverage of the March 2000 presidential elections in Russia*. Düsseldorf: European Institute for the Media.

Golosov, G. V. (2002). Party support or personal resources? Factors of success in the plurality portion of the 1999 national legislative elections in Russia. *Communist and Post-Communist Studies*, *35*(1), 23–38.

Hale, H., & Orttung, R. (2003). The Duma districts: Key to Putin's power. *PONARS Policy Memo*, No. 290, September.

Helvey, L. R., & Oates, S. (1997, August) *Russian television's mixed messages: Parties, candidates and control on Vremya, 1995–1996*. Paper presented at the American Political Science Association Annual Meeting, Washington, D.C.

Hutcheson, D. (2003). *Political parties in the Russian regions*. London: RoutledgeCurzon.

McAllister, I., & White, S. (2000). Split ticket voting in the 1995 Russian Duma elections. *Electoral Studies*, *19*(4), 563–676.

Oates, S. (2006). *Television, democracy and elections in Russia*. London: Routledge.

Oates, S., & Roselle, L. (2000). Russian elections and TV news: Comparison of campaign news on state-controlled and commercial television channels. *Harvard International Journal of Press/Politics, 5*(2), 30–51.

Observation Mission Report (n.d.). Warsaw: Office for Democratic Institutions and Human Rights. Available at http://www.osce.org/item/8051.html

Organisation for Security and Co-operation in Europe/Office for Democratic Institutions and Human Rights (OSCE/ODIHR). (June 2, 2004) *Russian Federation presidential election 14 March 2004 OSCE/ODIHR Election observation mission report*. Warsaw: Office for Democratic Institutions and Human Rights. Available at http://www.osce.org/odihr-elections/14520.html

Organisation for Security and Co-operation in Europe/Office for Democratic Institutions and Human Rights (OSCE/ODIHR). (January 27, 2004) *Russian Federation elections to the State Duma 7 December 2003 OSCE/ODIHR Election*

Pasti, S. (2005). Two generations of contemporary Russian journalists. *European Journal of Communication*, *20*(1), 89–115.

Remington, T. (2001). *The Russian parliament: Institutional evolution in a transitional regime, 1989–1999*. New Haven, CT: Yale University Press.

Voltmer, K. (2000). Constructing political reality in Russia: Izvestiya—Between old and new journalistic practices. *European Journal of Communication*, *15*(4), 469–500.

23

Election Coverage in Mexico: Regulation Meets Crony Capitalism

Chappell Lawson[1]

During the second half of the 1990s, Mexico made the transition from a one-party, autocratic regime to a multiparty electoral democracy (Bruhn et al., 2001; Camp, 1996; Cornelius, 1996; Eisenstadt 2004; Lawson, 2000; Middlebrook, 2004). Mass media play a crucial role in this new democratic system, especially during electoral campaigns (Hughes 2006; Lawson, 2003; Lawson & McCann, 2005). Both broadcasters and publishers devote substantial coverage to candidates and elections, even outside of the official campaign season. Partisan advertising also figures heavily in these contests, especially in presidential races, as political parties receive ample public funds to disseminate their appeals. Candidates from all three of Mexico's main political parties—the conservative National Action Party (PAN), the leftist Party of the Democratic Revolution (PRD), and the once-dominant, ideologically amorphous Institutional Revolutionary Party (PRI)—receive ample attention.

Although Mexicans have access to a range of information sources, from talk-radio programs to the Internet, most citizens get their information from broadcast television. This medium also absorbs the bulk of parties' spending during election season. Broadcast television is in turn dominated by two family-owned networks, Televisa and Televisión Azteca. These firms maintain high technical standards, but they also have a reputation for trading favorable coverage for commercial concessions.

In theory, Mexico boasts a powerful, autonomous regulatory apparatus that oversees campaigns and elections. Constitutional amendments approved in late 2007 will further strengthen this apparatus. Nevertheless, fairly strict regulation of campaigns so far has not fully counteracted the effects of extreme concentration in the media, nor can it preclude collusion between media barons, the government, and conservative political leaders. Consequently, electoral coverage in Mexico exhibits *both* trends toward balance that have characterized reporting since democratization *and* deviations from those trends produced by crony capitalism.

THE MEDIA CONTEXT

As might be expected of a country with more than 100 million inhabitants and a gross domestic product of over $750 billion, Mexico has a well-developed media system. Professional, independent, and ideologically eclectic newspapers are available in the major metropolitan areas of

Mexico City, Guadalajara, Monterrey, and Tijuana, where close to one-third of Mexicans live. These same cities boast at least five television channels, which broadcast at least eight separate "hard news" programs each weekday. Residents of a number of smaller provincial cities—such as Mérida, Hermosillo, Culiacán, and Oaxaca—also have access to high-quality local newspapers and several broadcast television channels. Even the third of the population that lives in rural or semi-rural regions normally receives signals from two television stations and at least one or two radio stations; less than 5% of the population cannot receive broadcast transmissions.

Even these facts understate the diversity of information sources. For instance, Mexicans living in the larger border towns to the north—Tijuana, Mexicali, Juárez, Nuevo Laredo, Reynosa, and Matamoros—can receive signals in their own language from U.S. stations. Upper and middle-class residents across the country have access to new technologies, such as pay-television systems and the Internet. For political junkies, there are roundtable-style television talk shows, nighttime satire programs, and technically sophisticated partisan blogs. As Election Day approaches, citizens everywhere must fend off a visual assault of partisan propaganda—fliers with party logos buried under take-out pizzas, posters hanging from lampposts, billboards overlooking busy thoroughfares, banners strung across town streets, and party symbols carefully stenciled on everything from highway overpasses to roadside rocks. Because elections for local, state, and federal office are not always synchronized, parts of the country have a campaign season almost every year.

Despite the theoretical accessibility of campaign-related communications, low levels of interest in politics tend to restrict the informational diet of most citizens. In October 2005, for instance, 64% of respondents expressed little or no interest in politics ("*poco*" or "*nada*") and 67% reported paying little or no attention to the campaign; even at the end of the race in July 2006, these figures remained 53% and 50% (respectively).[2] Mexicans have significantly fewer "political discussants" than almost every other country in the world where data is available (Baker, 2006). The dearth of interpersonal communication about politics is especially pronounced in rural and semi-rural areas, where the typical resident can name at most one person with whom she discusses politics. Moreover, the greater accessibility of political information during campaigns does not seem to reduce the gap in knowledge between the politically engaged and the politically inert (McCann & Lawson, 2006). Relatively little information thus trickles down to the largely apolitical one-third to one-half of the population. The news that this segment of the public receives during a campaign is the bits they encounter inadvertently: snippets of news on television or radio, images of candidates on posters, and the like.

Another important constraint on information flows is the fact that Mexicans rely extremely heavily on just one of the sources theoretically available to them. Broadcast television is the principal source of information about politics for every demographic group: men and women, poor and rich, educated and uneducated, urbanites and rural dwellers, northerners and southerners, etc. Even those citizens who read newspapers tend to rely primarily on television for current events. The only people for whom television is not the primary source of political information are political junkies and rural residents who cannot afford television sets; that is, the top 5% and bottom 5% of the distribution. In short, no other medium can claim anything approaching the reach and impact of broadcast television.

Equally important as heavy reliance on broadcast television is the fact that the industry is concentrated in two networks: Televisa and Televisión Azteca. Their duopoly is tentacular, in the sense that the great majority of local stations are affiliated with or owned by the networks. Some of these stations generate their own local news programming, and ratings data for local news in the three largest metropolitan centers—Mexico City, Guadajalara, and Monterrey—are two or three times higher than ratings for national news. Nevertheless, centrally developed news programs command much higher ratings than local news elsewhere in the country. In addition, even independent local affiliates generally follow the directives of their corporate headquarters in covering national events, including electoral campaigns (Hughes & Lawson, 2004).

A few figures illustrate the degree of concentration in this crucial medium. In October 2005, approximately 92% of regular television viewers reported receiving their news from programming disseminated by Televisa or Televisión Azteca. Approximately half of respondents got their news from two principal nightly news broadcasts, *Noticiero* ("The Newscast") on Televisa and *Hechos* ("Events") on Televisión Azteca.

After television, the second most widely used information source is radio. Many popular music stations carry news clips that summarize current events, and a number of others feature popular talk-radio programs. Such programs are a crucial source of information for many urban commuters, especially in the famously congested capital city, as well as very poor residents who may not have regular access to television. Ownership in radio is more fragmented and eclectic on television, in part because of there is less expense involved in operating radio stations. Over the last five years, Mexico's federal government has granted some two hundred fifty new concessions, increasing the total number of stations to approximately 1,400. The great majority of these are affiliated with one of twenty networks, but even the top twenty networks combined do not command the same market share in radio as do the top two firms in television.

Print media are even more fragmented than radio, with a large number of dailies and weekly newsmagazines available in the capital. Most other cities have just one or two papers, though Guadalajara and Monterrey have several. The weekly magazine *Proceso* circulates throughout the country, and some other news magazines can also be found in the major cities. As with radio and television, all news-oriented publications devote extensive coverage to campaigns.

One crucial constraint on the role of the print media is their restricted circulation, at least relative to most of Europe and the European-immigrant countries. Reported circulation figures in Mexico are normally inflated, and only a few publications (such as *El Universal*) independently certify their daily production. Daily sales in Mexico probably do not exceed 1.5 million copies per day, and at least one fifth of that figure is composed of tabloids that carry no political content.

A second limitation for the print media is that they are not normally the source of "opinion leadership" or second-stage communication flows. Rather, interpersonal discussions about current events reported in the media tend to be triggered by what is seen on TV. Although some television discussion shows and talk-radio programs follow up on election-related reports in newspapers, and interviews with candidates on radio or television may touch on issues raised by any recent reports in the press, it is far more common for broadcasters to generate their own stories. Television thus retains its primacy in setting public opinion.

CAMPAIGN COVERAGE

Mass media devote a tremendous amount of attention to campaigns. As Table 23.1 shows, Mexican television stations broadcast more than 800 hours of election-related news coverage during the five-month official campaign period in 2006. The main nightly news programs alone ran approximately 1,500 separate stories on the election during the 2006 campaign, collectively totaling close to 5 hours of coverage (Lawson et al., 2007).[3]

Talk-radio programs also lavish attention on politics with daily coverage of campaign events, interviews with leading candidates, and discussions of recent controversies. As Table 23.1 shows, Mexican radio stations collectively broadcast approximately four times the amount of campaign

TABLE 23.1
News Coverage in Mexico's 2006 Federal Elections

All free coverage (seconds)*	PAN	PRI**	PRD/Left**	Main parties
TV	864,723	1,118,701	903,175	2,886,599
Radio	2,965,916	3,604,812	4,682,634	11,253,362
Total	3,830,639	4,723,513	5,585,809	14,139,961
Tone of free coverage	PAN	PRI	PRD/Left	Main parties
TV - % Positive	0.8%	1.0%	0.6%	0.8%
TV - % Neutral	96.7%	96.4%	93.7%	95.6%
TV - % Negative	2.5%	2.7%	5.6%	3.6%
Net positive coverage***	-1.7%	-1.7%	-5.0%	-2.7%
Radio - % Positive	1.4%	1.5%	2.2%	1.8%
Radio - % Neutral	91.8%	88.6%	83.5%	87.3%
Radio - % Negative	6.8%	9.9%	14.3%	10.9%
Net positive coverage***	-5.4%	-8.4%	-12.2%	-9.2%

Notes
*Data cover the period (January 19 to through July 2) for all federal races.
**Both the PRI and the PRD ran in coalition with smaller parties in 2006.
***Net positive coverage = (positive coverage - negative coverage) / total coverage
Sources: Federal Electoral Institute (http://www.ife.org.mx/portal/site/ife/menuitem.52500ee3b4b6fa8f2b2e8170241000a0/
?vgnextoid=4d4b1fa1c91ea010VgnVCM1000002c01000aRCRD); accessed March 20, 2007

coverage in 2006 as did television. For their part, leading newspapers feature more or less continuous front-page coverage of campaigns and extensive commentary on elections. Coverage is candidate-centered, focusing primarily on the races for executive office.

The caliber of campaign coverage varies by outlet. Reporting on the main television networks is slick and visually appealing, with swift handoffs between different reporters. During the 2000 and 2006 election cycles, over 80% of footage on the two main nightly news programs was fresh rather than file; each news item contained on average one new image every five or six seconds (Lawson, 2004, 2007). The quality of coverage in top publications is also very high: newspapers like *Reforma* and *Universal*, for instance, rely on well-trained, uncorrupt reporters who are proficient at fact checking. Journalistic standards at *La Jornada* are lower, however, and they can be close to non-existent in small, provincial publications. The same trends hold in radio: whereas the main talk-radio programs are engaging and informative, programming on local radio stations can also be quite amateur or primitive.

So far, there has been no systematic study of the balance between "horserace" coverage and "substantive" reporting in the Mexican media. On the one hand, mass media are major purveyors of polling data. *Reforma* newspaper maintains a large in-house polling staff that conducted eight large, nationally representative polls between November 1, 2005 and June 23, 2006, as well as a number of small polls.[4] *El Universal* newspaper commissioned eight national polls, *Milenio* five, and *La Jornada* one during that same period. On the other hand, discussion of polling results occupies a rather modest fraction of space in the print media or airtime on television and radio. In this sense, mass media generally do not adopt a "game frame" for election coverage.

At the same time, the traditional distinction between game frames (that is, focusing on who is winning) and "issue frames" (that is, focusing on the substance of policy debates) fails to capture the nature of campaign coverage on television. Rather, most election-related stories on television are "event-driven"; they respond to what candidates do on the campaign trail and what they say about each other. Moreover, to the extent that stories deal with "issues," they focus on candidate traits, criticism of the government's handling of the economy, reports of official mal-feasance, criticism of candidates or parties, and responses to such criticisms.[5] In other words, the "issues" that receive most attention are valence issues rather than positional issues (Stokes, 1963). Television reporting on campaigns is thus distinctly "descriptive" rather than "interpretive" or ideological.

Talk-radio shows, newspapers, and "roundtable" television offer more interpretive frames. Their approaches can vary between "connecting the dots" in a policy sense (such as linking government policies to economic outcomes) to assessing campaign strategy, to offering manifestly partisan opinions. Televisa's political satire program, *El privilegio de mandar* ("The Right to Rule"), offers comic relief at the expense of prominent political figures and jokes mordant enough to rival Jon Stewart's *The Daily Show*.[6]

In terms of tone, news coverage of elections is not gentle toward candidates, but it is not particularly abusive either. First, presidential campaigns afford several opportunities for candidates to speak directly to voters, with rather little "mediation" by anchors or reporters. Ordinary news coverage features lengthy sound bites, in which candidates may speak uninterruptedly for 20 seconds or so (Lawson, 2004). Campaigns also feature lengthy interviews on radio and television with candidates, their spokesmen, and party leaders. Perhaps most importantly, since the first televised debate of 1994, such events have become a key component of races for the presidency, the Head of Government of the Federal District (i.e., Mexico City), and some other state-level offices. These debates generate extensive "post-game" coverage on all media outlets and, in some cases, fodder for television advertisements. Coverage on the main news programs mainly offers highlights and synopses of what candidates said, while talk shows and print media provide more in-depth analysis.

Second, unlike their counterparts in the U.S., Mexican media decline to delve into the private lives of public figures. Mentions of marital problems, sexual orientation, religious faith, and similar topics simply do not appear in newspapers or on TV. Media only seem to turn the spotlight toward candidates' domestic affairs when there appears to be strong suspicion of illicit enrichment by the candidate or members of his family—for instance, when it was revealed that PRI primary contender Arturo Montiel possessed a series of luxury properties or when the PRD-dominated leftist coalition charged that the brother-in-law of PAN candidate Felipe Calderón had engaged in influence-peddling. (The latter accusations proved unsubstantiated.)

Finally, although aural cues are rather negative, visual cues are not (see Graber, 1987). As the data in Table 23.1 show, negative references to candidates outnumber positive ones on radio and television—especially the former (see also Lawson, 2004; Lawson et al. 2007). However, content analysis of television news reveals that images of the candidates on television are almost invariably favorable or neutral. In both 2000 and 2006, for instance, average net positive ratings for all of the three main presidential candidates hovered around +30% (Lawson, 2004; Lawson et al., 2007). Even coverage of the PRI's widely disliked presidential candidate, Roberto Madrazo, was positive in visual terms.

Lest news coverage sound too restrained and professional, it is worth noting that traditional programming coexists with a plethora of "soft news" and "reality news" shows. Even regular news shows have been quite sensationalistic in their coverage of topics like crime (Hallin, 2000; Hughes, 2006; Lawson, 2002). The most notable example of such trends in Mexican television was a series of popular news shows hosted by "Brozo the brooding clown" (Victor Trujillo), which freely mixed news, antics, barbed commentary, and coverage of subjects that other shows might avoid.[7] Such programming was criticized as trivializing politics, but it also encouraged viewers who might not otherwise care enough about politics to watch the news. Mexican politicians are as anxious to appear on such programs as American politicians are to go on Oprah Winfrey.

ADVERTISING AND PARTY STRATEGY

Like news coverage, television advertising for national campaigns has become quite sophisticated since democratization. Several spots in the 2006 campaign—including two prominent attack ads directed at the PRD's presidential candidate, Andrés Manuel López Obrador—approach the status of "classics" (Gisselquist & Lawson, 2006). Notwithstanding these particular spots, content analysis of television advertising during the 2006 presidential race suggests that the ratio of positive to negative advertisements is about two to one; ads aimed at arousing "enthusiasm" likewise dominate those employing scare tactics. Spots very rarely address positional issues, focusing instead on candidates' traits, records in office, promises to particular social groups, and pledges of efficacy in addressing certain valence issues (crime, economic growth, corruption, etc.).

Patterns of paid media coverage also track those of free media in other respects. In terms of volume, parties purchased vast amounts of airtime: more than 43 hours worth of primetime on television for the presidential race alone (see Table 23.2). Total airtime purchased on all radio and television programs in 2006 came to approximately 850 hours.

Parties tend to invest heavily in television relative to other outlets, and in the presidential race relative to legislative contests. As the figures in Table 23.2 suggest, in the 2006 general elections parties spent three times as much on television advertisements as they did on radio, and six times as much as they did on non-broadcast media. Almost two-thirds of spending on the presidential race went to television advertising, against 58% for the Senate campaigns and 48% for the Chamber of Deputy races.

Legislative contests also depend somewhat more on radio: 21% of money in the presidential races went to advertising on that medium, against 25% in Senate races and 28% in races for the lower house. However, the bigger difference lies in the greater investment in street-level politics in races for lower-level office. According to the Mexico 2006 Elite Survey (Bruhn & Greene, 2006, 2007), single-member district candidates for the lower house tended to spend more money on localized propaganda than they did on the mass media. For instance, 75% of candidates from the PRD and the PAN reported spending a majority or a substantial minority of their money on street propaganda; fewer than half made the same claim about the media.[8] Indeed, from the perspective of political operators in Mexico, the main alternative to spending money on television is not spending it on other mass media but rather investing it in old-fashioned canvassing and get-out-the-vote drives. Such efforts are essential for mobilizing urban clientelist networks, residents of certain rural areas, corporatist organizations (such as unions and collective farms), and government employees—groups that still comprise a large percentage of the PRI's base.

For two reasons, Mexico's electoral system does not lend itself to media-intensive campaigns by individual candidates (other than presidential contenders). First, the structure of fundraising tends to centralize power in the hands of the national party leadership. As of 2007, parties were the only organizations allowed to buy airtime for political advertisements during election season, and for this purpose they were provided with copious public funds to dole out as they saw fit.

Constitutional amendments introduced in 2007 will substantially curtail public funding of campaigns. In total, however, the parties will still receive about $100 million per year in off-years to finance their activities; this sum will rise to approximately $130 million for years with midterm elections and $150 million in years with presidential races. Although they will not be allowed

TABLE 23.2
Advertising in Mexico's 2006 Federal Elections

TV advertising (seconds)	PAN	PRI*	PRD/Left*	Main parties
Presidential race	275,309	276,311	319,155	870,775
Deputies races**	48,362	271,027	31,058	350,447
Senate races**	186,097	582,578	53,854	822,529
Generic party spots	295,635	181,889	206,851	684,375
Long duration programs	1,799	0	296,498	298,297
Total TV	**807,202**	**1,311,805**	**907,416**	**3,026,423**
National primetime TV advertising (seconds)	PAN	PRI	PRD/Left	Main parties
Presidential race	68,027	44,355	42,731	155,113
Percent of TV advertising	*24.7%*	*16.1%*	*13.4%*	*17.8%*
Deputies races**	0	580	0	580
Percent of TV advertising	*0.0%*	*0.2%*	*0.0%*	*0.2%*
Senate races**	544	3,150	0	3,694
Percent of TV advertising	*0.3%*	*0.5%*	*0.0%*	*0.4%*
All races	*90,123*	*48,235*	*52,944*	*191,302*
Percent	*11.2%*	*3.7%*	*5.8%*	*6.3%*
Radio advertising (seconds)	PAN	PRI	PRD/Left	Main parties
Presidential race	1,889,295	1,520,659	1,218,434	4,628,388
Deputies races**	277,001	878,325	229,009	1,384,335
Senate races**	573,749	1,418,241	248,008	2,239,998
Generic party spots	1,042,775	701,028	640,521	2,384,324
Long duration programs	25,052	0	0	25,052
Total radio	**3,807,872**	**4,518,253**	**2,335,972**	**10,662,097**

to buy time on television or radio with this money, the parties will also receive substantial free airtime during campaign season. As a result, reliance on television will persist, and central party organizations will continue to dominate campaigning.

Second, although the electoral regime is technically a hybrid, in practice it behaves more like a European-style party-list system. In Mexico's Chamber of Deputies, 300 seats are filled through plurality-winner contests in single-member districts and 200 are selected through party lists, based on a form of proportional representation. In the Senate, each state and the Federal District are represented by three Senators—two from the winning party and one from the party that finishes second in that state. Another 32 Senators, or 25% of the Senate, are selected based on each party's share of the total vote. Because voters cannot alter the order of candidates on the party lists, the national-level party brand name tends to dominate over local or personal considerations. Legislators thus ride on the national party brand, benefiting from its advertising and flourishing or declining with its fortunes.

Data on campaign spending and advertising are collected much less systematically at the state level.[9] However, the patterns that characterize federal politics appear to hold there as well: the lower the level of the office, the greater the reliance on radio and canvassing. Governors, especially in large states, do tend to advertise in mass media, but they also rely heavily on street propaganda, door-to-door efforts, and machine politics. Candidates for lower-level state office, such as mayor and state representative, rarely use television, for which they generally do not have the budget.

The central dynamic in general elections is thus the purchase of large amounts of airtime on television by the main political parties, with individual candidates focusing on lower-cost me-

TABLE 23.2
Continued

Campaign spending (US$)***	PAN	PRI	PRD/Left	Main parties
Presidential race	**$23,439,817**	**$40,440,437**	**$34,873,829**	**$98,754,083**
TV	$11,570,593	$26,817,157	$24,362,500	$62,750,250
Radio	$8,327,243	$4,722,290	$8,164,294	$21,213,827
Other****	$3,541,981	$8,900,990	$2,347,035	$14,790,006
Percent of spending on TV	49%	66%	70%	64%
Deputies races**	**$3,697,322**	**$6,146,205**	**$4,273,788**	**$14,117,316**
TV	$1,043,466	$2,338,001	$3,451,599	$6,833,067
Radio	$1,615,339	$1,659,950	$666,097	$3,941,385
Other	$1,038,517	$2,148,255	$156,092	$3,342,863
Percent of spending on TV	28%	38%	81%	48%
Senate races**	**$8,181,343**	**$10,639,586**	**$10,296,651**	**$29,117,581**
TV	$3,957,707	$4,735,367	$8,093,375	$16,786,449
Radio	$2,302,578	$3,149,133	$1,740,446	$7,192,156
Other***	$1,921,059	$2,755,086	$462,830	$5,138,975
Percent of spending on TV	48%	45%	79%	58%
All races	**$35,318,482**	**$57,226,229**	**$49,444,269**	**$141,988,980**
TV	$16,571,766	$33,890,526	$35,907,474	$86,369,767
Radio	$12,245,160	$9,531,372	$10,570,837	$32,347,368
Other	$6,501,556	$13,804,331	$2,965,958	$23,271,845
Percent of spending on TV	47%	59%	73%	61%

Cost per second	PAN	PRI	PRD/Left	Main parties
Average for all races (TV)	$20.53	$25.84	$39.57	$28.54
Average for all races (radio)	$3.22	$2.11	$4.53	$3.03

Notes

*Both the PRI and the PRD ran in coalition with smaller parties.

**Data are for the official campaign period, from January 19 to June 28. Data on the Senate races cover the period from April 3 to June 28; data for the Chamber of Deputies cover the period from April 19 to June 28. All data are based on unaudited preliminary reports by the parties.

***Exchange rate: 11 pesos per dollar.

****Other expenditures include print, billboards, movie theaters, websites, and general overhead.

Source: Federal Electoral Institute, "Informes especiales de Gastos Aplicados a Campanas Electorales".(http://www.ife.org.mx/portal/site/ife/menuitem.52500ee3b4b6fa8f2b2e8170241000a0/?vgnextoid=4d4b1fa1c91ea010VgnVCM1000002c01000aRCRD); accessed March 20, 2007.

dia and grassroots efforts. For presidential contests, television advertising consumes the bulk of funds. This fact makes regulation of advertising a key issue in campaign coverage.

OWNERSHIP AND BIAS

High-quality, even-handed coverage of national campaigns is a relatively recent phenomenon. Throughout the period of one-party rule, the media generally acted as a cheerleader for the long-ruling PRI. Even after democratization, collusion between media owners and government officials has continued to influence coverage.

For decades, newspapers were beholden to the authoritarian regime. Journalists regularly received bribes from the sources they covered; government officials and PRI politicians purchased inserts disguised as genuine news reports; and overly assertive journalists were harassed by the regime. Starting in the late 1970s and early 1980s, however, a number of outlets began to challenge the regime (Hughes, 2006; Lawson, 2003). By the mid-1990s, independent newspapers of all ideological stripes had sprouted across the country, garnering enough revenue from sales and advertising to free themselves of dependence on the state. Prominent examples include the leftist daily *La Jornada*, the progressive weekly newsmagazine *Proceso*, the *El Financiero* newspaper, the *Reforma* newspaper chain, *El Universal* (which broke its ties with the political establishment in the second half of the 1990s), the Tijuana-based weekly *Zeta*, *Siglo 21* in Guadalajara (and its successor, *Público*), and the conservative daily *El Diario de Yucatán* (Hughes, 2006; Lawson, 2003).

Since the defeat of the PRI in the 2000 presidential race, many of these publications have begun to take sides between the PAN and the PRD (Lawson, 2006). During the 2006 campaign, Mexico's leading independent newspaper *Reforma* and its sister publications (*El Norte* in Monterrey and *Mural* in Guadalajara) took on a thoroughly conservative hue; coverage inclined toward Calderón. Meanwhile, *Proceso* abandoned all pretense of objectivity to become a full-throated advocate for the PRD. Even *El Universal*, based in the PRD stronghold of Mexico City, tilted toward López Obrador, though both it and *Milenio* evinced less of a bias than other outlets. The end result was a more politicized print media system, but one that still represented both left and right.

Trends in radio during the 1980s and 1990s largely paralleled those in print, though in terms of balance they did not go quite as far. Today's talk radio shows trace their origins back more than two decades, when Mexicans fed up with relentlessly pro-establishment coverage on Televisa turned to radio for information about current events (Lawson, 2002). Such shows tend to be conservative, reflecting the preferences of their middle-class audiences. They are not universally so, however, and even the ones with an ideological slant offer competing points of view.

Privately owned independent radio stations outside Mexico City often remain influenced by governors of the states in which they are located. This fact inevitably biases campaign coverage. The effects of such bias on the outcome of national-level elections is miniscule, given the fact that perhaps 10% of Mexicans rely primarily on radio for their information about politics and all three main parties control some states. In sub-national contests, however, the effects of such collusive relationships between business and government may be much larger.[10] In the close relationship between government officials and broadcasters in some locations, radio reflects key features of the television industry.

Mexico's two leading television networks are private family-owned enterprises, with Televisa now having passed from grandfather to father to son. These firms have historically enjoyed extremely close ties to the PRI (Hughes & Lawson, 2004; Lawson, 2002; Molina, 1987; Trejo, 1985, 1988). The late Emilio Azcárraga, father of Televisa's current CEO, declared that he considered his corporation to be "part of the governmental system," that that his employees were "soldiers of the PRI," and that he himself was "the number two PRI supporter in the country" (Fernández & Paxman, 2000; Hughes & Lawson, 2004; Lawson, 2002, p. 30); the "number one" PRI supporter was, of course, the President. Not surprisingly, electoral coverage on Televisa lauded the official party and denigrated the opposition in myriad ways (Acosta & Parra-Rosales, 1994; Arredondo et al., 1991; Bernal & Torreblanca, 1988; Hallin, 2000; Lawson, 2002). For its part, Televisión Azteca was formed in the early 1990s from the state-run Imevisión chain in a privatization process riddled with corruption. News reports later documented the financial links between brother of then-president Carlos Salinas and the new owner of Televisión Azteca (Lawson, 2002). Unsurprisingly, both networks strongly supported the PRI in the 1994 presidential campaign.

Competition between the two networks and democratization in the mid-1990s, however, ultimately led to somewhat greater balance in reporting on elections (De la Selva, 1998; Hughes, 2006; Lawson, 2002, 2003; Trejo, 2001). In addition, as it became clear that the PRI's hold on power was slipping, the networks began to accord opposition parties more favorable coverage.

Finally, reforms in Mexican electoral law ensured that the PAN and the PRD would receive hundreds of millions of dollars in government funding each election season, which made them potentially valuable clients in the eyes of the networks. By 1997, political parties received coverage in proportion to their share of the vote.

Nevertheless, it was still possible to discern the effects of collusion between the networks and the government. In the pivotal 2000 elections, for instance, the tone of coverage of PAN candidate Vicente Fox on Televisa changed markedly against him after it became clear that he might defeat PRI nominee Francisco Labastida (Lawson, 2004; Lawson & McCann 2005). Most observers interpreted this change as a product of pressure on the network by the government and leading figures in the then-ruling party (Lawson, 2004).

Such collusion persisted even after democratization. Mexico's new leaders had little incentive to risk provoking an avalanche of negative coverage by taking on the networks. According to former foreign minister Jorge Castañeda, in 2001, Fox promised Televisa's CEO Emilio Azcárraga-Jean that no third network would be created during his term (Jáquez, 2007).

These trends were confirmed in the middle of the 2006 campaign, with the passage of a new Federal Broadcasting Law.[11] Nicknamed the "Ley Televisa" (Televisa's Law), this remarkable piece of legislation effectively granted the two networks the right to dominate their industry for at least the next two decades, as well as to continue colonizing related industries. The provision for awarding concessions without competitive bidding was later struck down by the Mexican Supreme Court. After President Fox signed the law, coverage of the campaign shifted toward the incumbent party's candidate. More subtle biases also emerged, with Televisa embedding pro-Calderón messages in the dialogue of its hit nighttime soap opera, *La fea más bella* ("The Prettiest of the Ugly").

In some respects, crony capitalism led to the sorts of biases predicted by neo-Marxist models of media behavior (see, for example, Herman & Chomsky, 1988). Nevertheless, the fact that the networks take a mercenary approach toward electoral coverage does not inevitably work to the advantage of conservative parties and the government. Often, incentives cut in different directions. In the run-up to the 2006 presidential election, for instance, owners had to weigh at least the following considerations:

- The potential commercial benefits to be gained from convivial relations with the next president if they "bet" on the ultimate winner and afforded him favorable coverage during the campaign, as well as the danger that a winning candidate could seek to introduce greater competition into broadcasting if he did not feel some sort of debt to the networks.
- The additional advertising revenue that a network could gain from any one party if it accorded that party particularly favorable coverage.
- The tens of millions of dollars in advertising revenue from political parties that the network could earn if it accorded each party fair coverage.
- The possibility that gross bias in favor of any one candidate could alienate some viewers and thus cost the network market share.
- The chance that citizen disgust with bias could trigger demands for greater regulation of television.
- The fact that some candidates were simply more telegenic or provocative than others, and that affording them extra airtime thus made for better television.
- The threat a leftist president might pose to their personal wealth.

Media could draw different conclusions for this set of considerations, and their sense of the best strategy could shift over time. For instance, Televisión Azteca leaned toward López Obrador during the first part of the 2006 presidential race, both because it was betting on him to win the election and because it hoped to secure the bulk of advertising dollars that López Obrador's leftist coalition invested in television.[12] After the race began to narrow and the "Ley Televisa" was signed into law, however, Televisión Azteca's coverage tilted against the left's standard-bearer. As in 2000, such conflicting pressures ultimately failed to produce serious or dramatic biases in news coverage. As the data in Table 23.1 suggest, although coverage of López Obrador was slightly more negative than that of Madrazo and Calderón, he also received more airtime.

The simple fact that news coverage of the campaign ended up roughly balanced, however, does not mean that crony capitalism had no influence on the networks' behavior. As Table 23.2 shows, the ways in which the networks handled the sale of advertising worked against the left in 2006. Simple calculations from the last set of rows in Table 23.2 indicate that López Obrador's PRD-led coalition spent almost twice as much per second as the PAN on TV advertising to buy a decidedly less desirable mix of programming times (that is, less primetime). The most likely explanation is that at least one of the main networks—presumably Televisa—provided time to the PAN at a relative discount.

Article 79-A of the "Ley Televisa" was to have required holders of broadcasting concessions to inform electoral authorities of the amount of airtime purchased by parties and candidates, as well as the revenue they receive from such sales. The manifest purpose of this clause was to make the rates charged for advertising transparent. Because Article 79-A was not scheduled to take effect until January 1, 2007 (that is, after the 2006 election), however, it will be replaced by reforms eliminating paid political advertising altogether—a step that will ensure equity in partisan advertising on television and radio during election campaigns.

REGULATION

Mexico's electoral regime is much closer to the highly "interventionist" French model than it is to the more "liberal" American model. Electoral laws guarantee access to information by citizens and access to the airwaves by political parties. Related articles guarantee parties free use of mail and telegraphic services. Electoral authorities also control the length of campaigns and, in theory, the tone of political discourse. Finally, new reforms to Article 116 of the Constitution will ensure that the same regulatory architecture governs state and local contests. In part because the system is relatively new, however, precisely where Mexico will ultimately fall along this spectrum remains uncertain. Indeed, Mexico's electoral authorities are still translating their relatively broad legal mandates into specific rules, decisions, and precedents. Furthermore, these rules themselves continue to change.

The institution directly responsible for administering the electoral process is the IFE (Eisenstadt, 2004). The Federal Electoral Institute (IFE) is intended to be a wholly autonomous agency. In accordance with the landmark democratic reforms of 1996, its President and eight "Citizen Councilors" are chosen by a vote of two-thirds of the Chamber of Deputies. According to planned constitutional reforms in 2007, the President of the IFE will serve a six-year term and can be re-elected once; the other eight are to serve single, nine-year terms. Replacement of the current IFE leadership, which was chosen simultaneously in 2003, will be staggered in the future to further insulate the body from partisan politics.

This leadership in turn presides over a large bureaucracy of appointees and professional civil servants who select and train poll workers, negotiate with the political parties, supervise the campaign environment, and prepare the official vote tally. Parties must report their campaign expenditures to the IFE, and it has the authority to fine parties that violate spending caps. (Data in Table 23.2 are taken from the preliminary version of reports from the 2006 election.) In 2000, for instance, it fined both the PAN and the PRI for different types of campaign finance violations, leaving them with significantly less money to contest the 2003 election.

Under the reforms of 2007, the IFE will be in charge of allocating public airtime during campaign season. In total, the IFE will have at its disposal 48 minutes of airtime between 6 a.m. and midnight each day; each hour of programming must include two to three minutes of advertising (Article 41, Section III, Part A, Paragraph [a] of the Constitution). Of this time, the IFE is to allocate at least 85% to the political parties according to the same formula that governs their access to public funding. Of this portion, 30% of airtime will be distributed to parties equally and 70% will be based on their share of the vote in the previous election for the lower house of Congress. The IFE will also allocate another 6% of airtime to parties for a combination of five-minute monthly transmissions and twenty-second spots. It can claim for its own purposes 6% of public programming during campaign seasons, with the right to use up to 3% more if it sees fit. In "special circumstances," it can also claim the additional 6% of public airtime that would otherwise be parceled out among the parties. The result is a tightly regulated system for communicating partisan messages on radio and television.

Equally crucial to this system is the fact that no other group is permitted to purchase airtime. The law in force for the 2006 electoral cycle reserved to political parties the "exclusive right" to purchase airtime for messages "oriented toward obtaining votes during electoral campaigns." The constitutional amendments of 2007 will strengthen these provisions, with the intent of closing a loophole private sector groups used to launch controversial "issue advertisements" during the end of the 2006 presidential race. These "issue advertisements," which would have been legal in the U.S. system, did not use the words "vote" or "election," nor did they mention any of the candidates by name. Nevertheless, they echoed themes raised in PAN spots and thus were clearly designed to shape public opinion. The new rules specify explicitly that no person or entity will be allowed to "contract for advertising on radio or television oriented toward influencing citizens' electoral preferences, nor in favor of or against political parties or candidates for elected office" (Part A, Section III of Article 41). Moreover, the IFE will have the power to order the immediate suspension of broadcasts that in its view violate these provisions (Part D, Section III of Article 41).

The IFE also has the authority to rule on the accuracy and tone of political advertisements. During the 2006 race, electoral authorities issued bans on 29 separate spots that were seen as deceptive, defamatory, or simply excessively nasty (Estrada & Poiré, 2007). However, the basis for declaring a particular spot out-of-bounds remained poorly defined, as top officials at the IFE have privately admitted. The new system will retain these provisions, banning any advertisements that "denigrate" institutions or political parties, as well as those that "slander" particular individuals. As with "issue advertising," the reformed provisions of the Constitution explicitly grant the IFE the power to order the immediate suspension of any broadcasts it finds unacceptable.

Exactly how the IFE will choose to exercise these powers remains to be seen. During the 2006 elections, the IFE sometimes favored a highly aggressive regulatory posture. In December 2005, for instance, it declared a month-long "Christmas truce," during which time no campaigning would be allowed; the ostensible motivation for the hiatus was that too much unregulated money was flowing into the political system before the official commencement of the race on January 19. At other times, however, the IFE proved more reticent. For instance, its leadership moved somewhat sluggishly in responding to the "issue advertisements" by private sector groups. Following Calderón's narrow victory, the IFE's inability or unwillingness to act with dispatch became a key element in arguments for annulling the election advanced by López Obrador's legal team. As part of the negotiations that led to the 2007 reforms, IFE President Luis Carlos Ugalde and two other IFE Councilors were replaced. These changes hold out the promise of more consistent rulings by the IFE, as well as restored legitimacy for the institution itself.

One remaining question regarding campaign regulation concerns the tone and content of news coverage. Paragraph 10 of Article 48 of the federal electoral code states that the Executive Director for political parties of the Federal Electoral Institute (IFE) must meet with the IFE's Broadcasting Committee and the Radio and Television Industry Association (CIRT) before the beginning of the campaign season to "suggest" general guidelines for the campaign coverage. The same paragraph also instructs the IFE's Broadcasting Commission to carry out a "sample monitoring" of electoral coverage. (Data in Table 22.1 come from this effort.) However, Mexican law does not explicitly give electoral authorities the right to sanction media organizations for biased or tendentious coverage. As a result, there remains room for bias stemming from collusive relationships between broadcasters and the political leaders.

What Does the Future Hold?

Until recently, a key constraint on Mexican electoral authorities has been their lack of statutory authority to discipline private media, even during official campaign periods. Coupled with the difficulty of measuring bias and preventing collusive arrangements between broadcasters and the government, this debility produced regulatory inconsistency during the 2006 campaign and provoked extensive criticism of the electoral process. In the summer of 2007, however, Mexico's Supreme Court issued several rulings that effectively nullified key provisions of the Ley Televisa. These rulings, as well as the contested outcome of the 2006 election, opened the door for Mexico's Congress to revisit the entire legal architecture governing campaigns. Negotiations between the main parties in Congress ultimately produced a broad electoral reform that further ensures the integrity and authority of Mexican electoral institutions.

These reforms will never enhances perfect equity or consistency in coverage of campaigns, because regulatory changes would not entirely preclude corrupt relationships between media owners and the government, and because election-seeking politicians and powerful media enterprises may find ways to evade even well-crafted regulations. That said, they will push back against the remaining influences of crony capitalism on election coverage. The net result should be to strengthen what is already a well-regulated electoral regime.

NOTES

1. I am grateful to Francisco Flores-Macías, Jesper Strömbäck, and Lynda Lee Kaid for comments on previous versions of this chapter; to Leopoldo Gómez, John Bailey, and Gustavo Flores-Macías for updated ratings data on local television programs; and to Mike Myers for editorial assistance.
2. Data are taken from the Mexico 2006 Panel Study. Principal Investigators in the Mexico 2006 Panel Study include, in alphabetical order: Andy Baker, Kathleen Bruhn, Roderic Camp, Wayne Cornelius, Jorge Domínguez, Kenneth Greene, Joseph Klesner, Chappell Lawson (Principal Investigator), James McCann, Alejandro Moreno (Field Work Coordinator), Alejandro Poiré, and David Shirk. Figures here include only those respondents who participated in both the first and the third wave of the Mexico 2006 Panel Study; levels of political engagement in the general population are even lower. For more information, see: http://web.mit.edu/polisci/research/mexico06/Pres.htm.
3. This figure is based on extrapolations from a content analysis of a random sample of 40 broadcasts of the two main nightly news programs, which uncovered 293 stories whose primary theme was related to the election during January-June of 2006. The average length of each segment was just over 10 seconds; several stories were often strung together in a single newscast.

4. According to Mexican electoral law, polls may not be published in the week before Election Day, which made July 23 the last day of the presidential campaign in which polls could be publicly disseminated.

5. In 2006, Televisa also kept on its website the lengthy responses by presidential candidates to questions about the policy goals and positions on specific issues. These responses effectively constituted the candidates' platforms, which as in the United States were often at some variance with the platforms of their parties.

6. The show, a spin-off from the more general satire program *La parodia* (Parody), ran weekly from January 2005 through the 2006 general elections.

7. Trujillo temporarily retired his green wig and red nose in June 2004 to anchor the program "*El crystal con que se mira* (The Looking Glass) as himself; in that capacity, he broke the scandal that led Montiel to withdraw from the PRI primary.

8. As might be expected, the PAN tends to invest more in media while candidates from the PRD and the PRI rely more on retail politics. In the Mexico 2006 Elite Survey, for instance, 56% of PAN candidates spent heavily on mass media but only 32% of PRD candidates did so.

9. Forthcoming work by Scott Desposato (University of California at San Diego) addresses advertising content at the state level in parts of Mexico.

10. So far, no systematic analysis has been conducted of the effects of radio on local or state-level contests in Mexico.

11. PRD legislators initially supported the Ley Televisa, which would also require the networks to report the rates they charged each party; the PRD correctly suspected that they had been charged higher prices in 2006. PRD leaders later changed their positions and opposed the law. Most PAN and PRI legislators in both houses of Congress favored the law, though some did not.

12. Data are not available on how parties divided their advertising dollars between the two networks, but it appears that the left did invest more heavily in Televisión Azteca than would have been predicted by a strategy of allocating advertising to maximize votes.

REFERENCES

Acosta, M., & Parra-Rosales, L. P. (1994). *Los procesos electorales en medios de comunicación* [Elections in the media]. Mexico City: Academia Mexicana de Derechos Humanos/Universidad Iberoamericana.

Arredondo, P., Fregoso, G., & Trejo, R. (1991) *Así se calló el sistema: comunicación y elecciones en 1988* [What they didn't tell you: Communication and elections in 1988]. Guadalajara: Universidad de Guadalajara.

Baker, A. (2006, December). *Why is voting so regionalized in Mexico: Political discussion and electoral choice in 2006*. Paper presented at the Conference on Mexico's 2006 Presidential Elections at Harvard University, Cambridge, MA.

Bernal, V. M., & Torreblanca, E. (1988). *Espacios de silencio* [Spaces of silence]. Mexico City: Nuestro Tiempo.

Bruhn, K., & Greene, K. F. (2006). *Mexico 2006 Candidate and party elite survey*. Data available online at http://web.mit.edu/polisci/research/mexico06/candsurveytabs1

Bruhn, K., & Greene, K. F. (2007). Elite polarization meets mass moderation in Mexico's 2006 elections. *PS: Political Science and Politics, 40*, 33–38.

Bruhn, K., & Levy, D. C. with Zepadúa, E. (2001). *Mexico: The struggle for democratic development*. Berkeley: University of California Press.

Camp, R. (1996). *Politics in Mexico*. New York: Oxford University Press.

Cornelius, W. (1996). *Mexican politics in transition: The breakdown of a one-party-dominant regime*. La Jolla, CA: Center for U.S.-Mexican Studies/University of California, San Diego.

De la Selva, A. (1998). La televisión en 1997: expansión y lucha de poder. *Revista Mexicana de Comunicación* [Mexican Journal of Communication], *52,* 16–20.

Eisenstadt, T. A. (2004). *Courting democracy in Mexico: Party strategies and electoral institutions*. New York: Cambridge University Press.

Eisenstadt, T. A. (2007). The origins and rationality of the "legal versus legitimate" dichotomy invoked in Mexico's 2006 post-electoral conflict. Symposium, The 2006 Mexican Election and Its Aftermath: The Origins and Rationality of the "Legal versus Legitimate" Dichotomy Invoked in Mexico's 2006 Post-Electoral Conflict. *PS: Political Science and Politics, 40*(1), 39–43.

Estrada, L., & Poiré, A. (2007). The Mexican standoff: Taught to protest, learning to lose. *Journal of Democracy, 18*(2), 77–87.

Fernández, C., & Paxman, A. (2000). *El Tigre. Emilio Azcárraga y su imperio Televisa* [The tiger: Emilio Azcárraga and his Televisa empire]. Mexico, D.F.: Editorial Grijalbo.

Gisselquist, R. M., & Lawson, C. (2006, August). Preliminary findings from content analysis of television spots in Mexico's 2006 presidential campaign. Available at http://web.mit.edu/polisci/research/mexico06/Rp.htm#related

Graber, D. (1987). Kind pictures and harsh words. In K. Schozman (Ed.), *Elections in America* (pp. 115–41). Boston: Unwin-Hyman.

Hallin, D. C. (2000). La Nota Roja: Popular journalism and the transition to democracy in Mexico. In C. Sparks & J. Tullock (Eds.), *Tabloid tales. Global debates over media practices* (pp. 267–282). Lanham, MD: Rowman & Littlefield.

Herman, E. S., & Chomsky, N. (1988). *Manufacturing consent: The political economy of the mass media.* New York: Pantheon Books.

Hughes, S. (2006). *Newsrooms in conflict: Journalism and the democratization of Mexico.* Pittsburg: University of Pittsburg Press.

Hughes, S., & Lawson, C. (2004). Propaganda and crony capitalism: Partisan bias in Mexican television news. *Latin American Research Review, 39*(3), 81–105.

Jáquez, A. (2007). *Doblado en Beijing. Proceso* (1575). Accessed online, January 15, 2007.

Lawson, C. (2000). Mexico's unfinished transition: Democratization and authoritarian enclaves in Mexico. *Estudios Mexicanos/Mexican Studies, 17*, 267–287.

Lawson, C. (2003). *Building the fourth estate: Democratization and the rise of a free press in Mexico.* Berkeley: University of California Press.

Lawson, C. (2004). Television coverage, vote choice, and the 2000 campaign. In J. I. Domínguez & C. Lawson (Eds.), *Mexico's pivotal democratic election: Candidates, voters and the presidential campaign of 2000* (pp. 187–209). Stanford & La Jolla, CA: Stanford University Press/the Center for U.S.-Mexican Studies, University of California at San Diego.

Lawson, C. (2006, November). *Mexico under Calderón: The challenges ahead.* Pacific Council on International Policy Special Report. Available online at http://www.pacificcouncil.org/pdfs/Final%20Report.pdf

Lawson, C. (2007). How did we get here? Mexican democracy after the 2006 elections. In Symposium: The 2006 Mexican Election and Its Aftermath. *PS: Political Science and Politics, 40*(1), 45–48. Available at http://www.apsanet.org/content_39138.cfm

Lawson, C., & McCann, J. A. (2005). Television news, Mexico's 2000 elections, and media effects in emerging democracies. *British Journal of Political Science, 35*, 1–30.

Lawson, C., McCombs, M., & Flores, M. (2007). Content analysis of news coverage of the 2006 Mexican campaign. Dataset.

McCann, J. A., & Lawson, C. (2006). Presidential campaigns and the knowledge gap in three emerging democracies. *Political Research Quarterly, 59*, 13–22.

Middlebrook, K. J. (2004). *The dilemmas of political change in Mexico.* London and La Jolla: Institute of Latin American Studies/University of London/Center for U.S.-Mexican Studies, University of California, San Diego.

Molina, G. (1987). Mexican television news: The imperatives of corporate rationale. *Media, Culture and Society, 9*, 159–187.

Stokes, D. (1963). Spatial models of party competition. *American Political Science Review, 57*, 368–377.

Trejo, R. (Ed.). (1985). *Televisa, el quinto poder* [Televisa, the fifth branch of government]. Mexico City: Claves Latinoamericanas.

Trejo, R. (Ed.). (1988). *Las redes de Televisa* [The Televisa network]. Mexico City: Claves Latinoamericanas.

Trejo, R. (2001). *Mediocracia sin mediaciones: Prensa, televisión y elecciones* [Mediocracy without mediation: Press, television, and elections]. Mexico City: Cal y arena.

24

The Media Coverage of Election Campaigns and Its Effects in Japan

Shinichi Saito and Toshio Takeshita

The relationship between media and politics in Japan has markedly changed in the past several decades. Most notably, the role played by television in politics in general, and election campaigns in particular, has gained unparalleled significance. With the increased importance of television in relation to politics, many notable changes have occurred. For example, Flanagan (1996) contends that "As television has come increasingly to dominate perceptions of politics, it has altered the kinds of issues that dominate the political agenda" (p. 299).[1] Among other issues, this chapter focuses mainly on the role of television in election campaigns and provides an overview of research on media coverage of election campaigns and its influence on the general public in Japan. We begin with a brief overview of the political system and recent political trends in Japan, followed by a brief description of the Japanese media systems in order to provide the background information essential for understanding discussions in the subsequent sections; these will deal with the contents and effects of the news media's election coverage.

THE POLITICAL SYSTEM AND RECENT POLITICAL TRENDS

Japan is a parliamentary democracy within a constitutional monarchy. The Diet is the country's legislative organ; the cabinet is the executive organ; and the law courts are the judicial organ. These three branches of government are separate. The bicameral Diet consists of the Sangi-in (House of Councilors—the Upper House) and the Shugi-in (House of Representatives—the Lower House). The Constitution of Japan, which was promulgated in November 1946, introduced the two-chamber system.

At present, the membership of the House of Representatives is 480 and that of the House of Councilors is 242. Members of both houses are elected by universal adult suffrage. The term of office in the House of Representatives is four years, whereas that in the House of Councilors is six years, with half of its members being elected every third year. While the House of Representatives can be dissolved, the House of Councilors is not subject to dissolution. The electoral system in Japan is currently regulated by the Public Offices Election Law, which was enacted in April 1950. This election law covers local elections as well as elections for National Diet members. The official election campaign periods in Japan are relatively short: 12 days for the House of

Representatives elections (hereafter, "general elections") and 17 days for the House of Councilors and gubernatorial elections.

The 1945 revision of the Election Law for the House of Representatives, which was promulgated in 1889, lowered the minimum age of voters to 20 and that of candidates to 25. The 1945 revision also abolished all discrimination against women in elections, and for the first time, women were granted the right to vote and stand as candidates for elections. The long-standing, multi-seat, medium-sized constituency election system was abolished in January 1994 through a revision of the Public Offices Election Law. The current election system for the House of Representatives is a combination of the single-seat constituency system and a proportional representation of parties. Under the present system, 300 members are elected from single-seat constituencies and 180 from proportional representation constituencies in which the nation is divided into 11 electoral blocs. Voters elect an individual candidate in the single-seat constituencies, and a political party in the proportional representation constituencies. The voters thus cast two ballots.

The House of Councilors Election Law was enacted in February 1947. The 1982 revision of the Public Offices Election Law abolished the nationwide constituency of the House of Councilors election and introduced a system in which the House of Councilors comprises members elected by the proportional representation of parties and constituency voting. Thus, 96 of the 242 members of the House of Councilors are elected by proportional representation from a single nationwide electoral district. (Voters can vote for either an individual candidate or a political party.) The remaining 146 members are elected in 47 prefectural constituencies, each returning two to ten members (voters cast their votes for individual candidates). Similar to the case in the House of Representatives, voters cast two ballots. The minimum age requirement to be a candidate for the House of Councilors is 30 years; that for voters, 20 years.

The Relationship between Television and Politics

For a long period of time, newspapers served as the mainstream political media. However, this situation has undergone a gradual change since the 1980s. While newspapers still play a crucial role in political coverage, television has become the dominant and most influential source of political information for many Japanese citizens in the past two decades. Prime Minister Yasuhiro Nakasone (1982–1987) was probably the first premier who recognized the potential of television in politics (Flanagan, 1991; Krauss, 2002). According to Takase (1999), Nakasone was the first "rhetorical" prime minister in Japanese politics. He was not at the center of the power structure within the Liberal Democratic Party (LDP) as he had only a weak power base. By utilizing television effectively, Nakasone attempted to appeal to public opinion—rather than his fellow Diet members—in order to increase his popularity to help his administration. Nakasone "cultivated his television news image by striking a tall and dignified figure at G-7 meetings and through his 'Ron-Yasu' relationship with Ronald Reagan" (Krauss, 2002, p. 9).

The LDP has governed the country almost continuously since 1955. The one-party dominant system ruled by the LDP, which is referred to as the 1955 regime, lasted until 1993. However, the LDP lost its postwar political dominance for the first time in almost four decades after the general election of July 1993 (see Narita, 2003 for details on Japan's postwar politics). The non-LDP parties (with the exception of the Japanese Communist Party) formed a coalition after the election and launched the Hosokawa administration (1993–1994). Prime Minister Hosokawa achieved success in Nakasone-style televised appearances, and was thus also considered as a premier who made effective usage of television (Krauss, 2002; Takeshita & Ida, in press).

The Hosokawa administration changed the electoral system of the Lower House from a multi-member district system to a combination of a single-member district system and a proportional representation system. This revision of the electoral system paved the way for the two-party system. However, this non-LDP coalition did not last long. The LDP returned to power in June 1994 in an unwieldy alliance with its long-time rival, the Japan Socialist Party (JSP),[2] and the New Party Sakigake, a party of politicians who had defected from the LDP in 1993. The LDP regained a simple majority in the Lower House through defections from the opposition.

Many voters, disillusioned and frustrated with the party process since the collapse of the non-LDP coalition in 1994, gave up all party affiliations and became independents.[3] Political analysts who predict voting behavior argue that the influence of long-term factors such as ideology and party identification has decreased. In contrast, these analysts contend that short-term factors, including politicians' popularity, have gained importance in elections, thus bringing about an unprecedented strengthening of the influence of television on election campaigns.

The administration of former Premier Koizumi, which commenced in 2001—with an approval rating of nearly 80%—and continued until 2006, epitomized the age of telepolitics. Like his predecessors, Nakasone and Hosokawa, Koizumi also attempted to attract media attention and be telegenic in order to garner the public support necessary to compensate for his weak power base within the LDP (Kabashima & Steel, 2007). In fact, he received extensive television coverage not only because he tactically used the medium but also because his style of presentations, often characterized as "one-phrase politics," suited the time-restricted format of television.

In late 2003, the Liberal Party and the Democratic Party of Japan (DPJ) formed an alliance (the DPJ absorbed the Liberal Party) against the LDP. The alliance further increased the possibility of a two-party system. The media framed the 2003 general election as a contest between the LDP and the DPJ for control of the government. As a result, the election turned out to be a choice of government between the LDP and the DPJ; consequently, the smaller parties suffered in the shadows of these two major parties. The 2003 election campaign was also characterized as one of the most policy-oriented campaigns; this is because during the campaign, the DPJ published an itemized policy manifesto and other parties followed suit. Although the LDP won the 2003 parliamentary election, it lost its simple majority. The DPJ, in contrast, made considerable gains.

However, the LDP regained their balance strength in the 2005 general election. After the Upper House rejection of the postal privatization bills in August 2005, Koizumi dared to dissolve the Lower House and scheduled a general election on September 11. He successfully projected the election as being a single-issue referendum on postal reforms, although many LDP members vigorously opposed the postal-reform plan. As pointed out by many critics (Kabashima & Steel, 2007; Nakai, 2007), television undoubtedly played an important role in creating the single-issue referendum. The LDP eventually achieved an absolute majority with 296 seats in the 480-seat chamber; this considerably exceeded any of the analysts' predictions. This landslide was one of the most decisive victories in the party's 50-year history.

For this election, Koizumi delegated more than 30 handpicked candidates—dubbed as the "assassins" by the media (the term was initially used by a politician belonging to the LDP)—to unseat his own party members who rebelled against his postal privatization scheme. This unprecedented incident, coupled with other events such as the unexpected dissolution of the Lower House, led to the creation of the term "Koizumi gekijyo" (Koizumi theater). This dramatic political theater received massive media coverage, even from media outlets that do not usually cover politics, such as sports newspapers or entertainment television programs called "wide shows" (television soft news magazines). The media in general and television in particular were blamed for their coverage that largely focused on the game aspects of the election, such as the assassin vs. rebel drama. Critics also argued that as a result of the media's overemphasis on Koizumi gekijyo, opposition parties and their candidates received insufficient media coverage, which contributed to the LDP's overwhelming victory.

THE JAPANESE MEDIA SYSTEM: NEWSPAPERS AND TELEVISION

Japan has five newspapers with nationwide circulation: *Yomiuri Shimbun, Asahi Shimbun, Mainichi Shimbun, Nihon Keizai Shimbun,* and *Sankei Shimbun.* Japan also has three publications known as block newspapers: *Hokkaido Shimbun, Chunichi Shimbun,* and *Nishinippon Shimbun.* These newspapers are circulated across prefectural boundaries but are not circulated nationally. The national and block newspapers command an oligopolistic market as a whole. In addition, there are many prefectural papers that are distributed and read within each of the 47 prefectures. Most households in metropolitan areas subscribe to one or two national dailies, while readers in the rural areas of Japan prefer local and regional newspapers. Although half of the total revenue of the newspapers was generated through sales, approximately 30% came from advertising in 2006 (Saito, 2000, 2003 for an overview of the media in Japan).

Japan has a dual broadcasting system, consisting of the public broadcaster (Nippon Hoso Kyokai, commonly known as NHK) and commercial broadcasters. Television broadcasting in Japan commenced in February 1953, when NHK went on the air. Nihon TV, the first commercial station, followed in August of the same year. The current state of Japanese broadcasting is the result of a well-balanced competition between NHK and the commercial broadcasters. In addition, the University of the Air Foundation operates one television and one FM channel.[4]

NHK is independent of both government and corporate sponsorship and relies almost entirely on revenue obtained from household reception fees. The commercial broadcasters derive their revenue primarily from advertising and are licensed regional and local broadcasters. Most of the commercial broadcasters are affiliated to one of the five nationwide networks, which are centered on Tokyo's key stations (Nihon TV, Tokyo Broadcasting System, Fuji TV, TV Asahi, and TV Tokyo). Regional commercial stations rely heavily on these networks to supply programs, which account for over 80% of the regional broadcasting time. There are also some independent stations that are not affiliated with networks in metropolitan areas such as Tokyo and Osaka.

In addition to terrestrial broadcasting services, Japan has two types of direct broadcasting satellites (DBS)—the high-powered broadcasting satellite (BS) services and the low-powered communication satellite (CS) services. Statistics from the Ministry of Public Management, Home Affairs, Posts and Telecommunications (MPHPT) indicate that as of December 2004, the penetration rates for households were 25% and 7% for the BS services and the CS services, respectively. Cable television with multiple channels began to develop in the late 1980s. Cable television is also less prevalent than terrestrial broadcasting television, with a penetration rate of 36% in the end of 2004. DBS and cable television services are on the increase, and the number of television channels available to Japanese audiences has been steadily growing. However, traditional media firms are among the main content providers for DBS and cable television services. It is important to note that there are still no television channels specializing in news reporting, such as the U.S. CNN, which can compete with the news programs on terrestial broadcasting stations.

Japan has large media conglomerates owning businesses across different industries and media (Akhavan-Majid, 1990). For example, the Asahi Shimbun group comprises many affiliated companies and collaborating organizations, whose activities cover a wide range of industries and interests. These interests include newspaper publishing and printing, television and radio broadcasting, cultural activities, and advertising. However, a provision (commonly known as the "principle of excluding multiple ownership of the media") in the Essential Standards for Establishing Broadcasting Stations, which prescribes the mandatory provisions for establishing a broadcasting station, prevents a monopoly situation with respect to mass media, and above all, with respect to airwaves. Although the rule allows for some exceptions, and local monopolies do exist in some rural areas, it hinders the development of nationwide media giants.

Press Clubs

Japanese journalism operates under a unique press club system. The Press Club (Kisha Kurabu) is "a nationwide social association with which executives and editors of almost all major Japanese newspapers and broadcasting organizations are affiliated" (Hirose, 1994, p. 63). The origin of press clubs dates back to the last decade of the 19th century, when journalists voluntarily banded together to obtain information from official sources. These clubs play an important role in the news-making process of Japan's major newspapers and broadcasting organizations. Most public institutions, such as the Office of the Prime Minister, the Diet, central government ministries, local government units, the courts, the police, and large corporations, have their own press clubs in their office buildings. The press-club system has been an essential feature of Japanese journalism for many decades, and it facilitates the daily flow of news from sources to news organizations. However, this system has been faced with severe criticism for many years because it discourages meticulousness in journalists and reduces them to the role of mere message carriers, thereby creating uniformity of content.

Policy and Legal Framework for Newspapers and Television

Article 21 of Japan's constitution guarantees freedom of expression, stating that "No censorship shall be maintained, nor shall the secrecy of any means of communication be violated." Further, although Japan has many legal provisions that relate to newspapers, at present, there is no press law that exclusively regulates newspapers. Instead, the Japanese press is governed by the Canon of Journalism, formulated by NSK (the Canon was formulated in 1946, but it was vastly revised in 2000). This moral charter stresses the following: (1) freedom and responsibility, (2) accuracy and fairness, (3) independence and tolerance, (4) respect for human rights, and (5) decency and moderation. With regard to accurate reporting, the canon stipulates that "reporting must be accurate and fair and should never be swayed by the reporter's personal conviction or bias." Therefore, most major newspapers have adopted the so-called "neutrality principle" as their editorial policy. Unlike the Western media's concept of objectivity, the neutrality principle in Japan is more articulate: "The media should not take sides in analytical or editorial articles, but rather assume a conciliatory position. That is why very few newspapers in Japan carry editorial endorsements in election coverage" (Takeshita & Ida, in press).

While broadcasting shares the print media's constitutional guarantee of freedom of speech and expression, it is regulated by the Broadcast and Radio Laws enacted in 1950. The Radio Law deals with technical matters. The Broadcast Law deals with policies that cover the broadcasting system framework and the editorial, management, and operational divisions of programming. The Broadcast Law guarantees freedom of broadcasting. Article 3 states that "broadcast programs shall never be interfered with, or regulated, by any person, except in cases where it is done through invested powers provided by law." However, with regard to the production of domestic broadcast programs, the law requires broadcasters to follow certain directives: (1) to not disturb public security, good morals, and manners; (2) to be politically impartial; (3) to broadcast news without distorting facts; and (4) to clarify the point of issue on controversial matters from as many angles as possible. However, these directives are highly abstract. For example, there is no clear, standard definition for political impartiality. This vagueness in the definition has occasionally aroused heated debates over the issue of television's influence on politics.

With regard to the media and elections, the Public Offices Election Law forbids several acts during election campaigns. For example, door-to-door campaigning is not permitted. Posters and advertising are severely restricted and regulated. The 1969 revision of the Public Offices

Election Law allowed candidates to broadcast their political views, thus enabling television to play an increasingly important role in Japanese politics. However, as Krauss (2002) noted, "a limited number of television and radio spots were allowed each candidate, and all candidates' spots followed the same format" (p. 7). The law currently bans the updating of web pages that carry candidates' opinions and sending e-mail newsletters during election campaigns. However, the debate over lifting the ban on Internet use as a means of conducting election campaigns has acquired momentum.

The Internet and Elections

The estimated number of Internet users has increased explosively over the past several years. According to MPHPT estimates, the number of Internet users has increased from 11.6 million in December 1997 to 47.1 million in December 2000; this number reached 79.5 million at the end of 2005 (including Internet access via cellular phones), signifying a penetration rate of 62.3% (MPHPT, 2006).

With regard to the manner in which people use media during elections, some surveys show that most electorates still depend on the traditional media, and Internet usage for acquiring election information is extremely limited. For example, a survey conducted by the Association for Promoting Fair Elections (*Akarui Senkyo Suishin Kyokai*) soon after the 2003 general election showed that only 0.6% of the respondents stated that the Internet was useful for obtaining election campaign information. By contrast, the respondents chose traditional media, such as official campaign broadcasts (17.6%) and election coverage on television (17.5%) and in newspapers (9.5%) as useful information sources during the election campaign. Similarly, a nationwide public opinion survey conducted by the *Yomiuri Shimbun* after the 2005 general election revealed the restricted use of the Internet as a political information source: Only 2.2% of the respondents regarded the web pages of political parties or candidates as useful information sources when making their voting decisions. In contrast, election coverage by the traditional media, including television and newspapers, was considered to be valuable by approximately 41% of the respondents. Approximately 16% said that television advertisements by campaigning parties helped them in their voting decisions. Thus, the Internet does not supersede traditional news media as a source of information on election campaigns. Probably, there is still some time before the Internet can compete with traditional news media as an important information source of election campaigns.

POLITICAL NEWS COVERAGE IN JAPAN

It can be argued that at present, there are two types of television journalism in Japan: descriptive news (NHK) and interpretive news (many of the news programs on commercial stations). NHK dominated over its commercial counterparts in terms of newscasts until the mid-1980s. Krauss (1996, 2000) has argued that the NHK adopts rigorous neutrality that borders on the anemic, and those who watch the NHK get fact-based news that is quite neutral in terms of competing interests. NHK news emphasizes facts rather than interpretation and gives high priority to the coverage of the national bureaucracy. According to Krauss, NHK news accentuates factual stories when reporting domestic events related to government decisions, proposals, and ceremonies rather than intra-government conflicts and disagreements, thereby legitimating the Japanese state.

However, commercial broadcasting stations have been competing with the NHK in terms of political news since the mid-1980s. *News Station*, which started on TV Asahi in 1985, was the first to change the style of news reporting. For example, the anchor of the news show, Hiroshi Kume, often added his own opinions and comments to political news. Since then, other television stations have also revised their styles of news programs. Consequently, there has been a "news war," in which the news coverage on commercial stations has become increasingly entertainment-oriented, interpretive, and sensational (Otake, 2003; Takase, 1999; Tanaka, 2006). The new types of news programs on commercial broadcasting channels are very different from NHK news, which carries a significantly less amount of critical news and observes the neutrality principle. Since commercial broadcasters derive their revenue primarily from advertising, they must pay more attention to audience ratings. Accordingly, compared to public television, programming by commercial broadcasters tends to focus more on negativity and conflict and deploys various strategies to attract viewers (Krauss, 2000; Otake, 2003; Takase, 1999; Taniguchi, 2002). Tanaka's (2006) qualitative study on news programs revealed the interpretive characteristics of television news on commercial stations.

With the increased popularity of news programs on commercial broadcasting stations, many politicians have expressed concern about the negative influence of those programs on viewers' attitudes toward politics (*Shuin-giin*, 1996). The lawmakers' concerns may partly explain why Tsubaki's remarks caused such a huge controversy in the fall of 1993: Sadayoshi Tsubaki, the then chief of the news bureau at TV Asahi, reportedly boasted about the political power of television news at the National Broadcast Association meeting immediately after the 1993 general election. He stated that while covering the general election, he and his colleagues had sought news stories that would favor the non-LDP camps. As mentioned above, the LDP lost its long-standing political dominance in this general election. Thus, Tsubaki's remarks caused furious indignation among politicians, and consequently, he was forced to resign. However, Tsubaki's remarks later proved to be groundless, and no evidence was found that the news had been biased in favor of the non-LDP parties.

Election Coverage: Issue vs. Strategic Frame

First, it should be noted that while official election campaign periods are relatively short—12 to 17 days—the media election coverage begins several weeks before the official announcement of each election. In the case of elections for the House of Representatives, for example, media coverage of elections virtually begins soon after the dissolution of the Lower House. Although it is sometimes difficult to clearly differentiate between election news coverage and regular political news, it seems fair to say that, roughly speaking, the length of election news coverage lasts for approximately a month.

Media researchers have classified election coverage into two types: policy schema and game schema (Patterson, 1993) or issue frame and strategic frame (Cappella & Jamieson, 1997). Election coverage using a policy schema or an issue frame refers to media coverage that emphasizes policy issues, problems, and solutions. In contrast, election coverage using a game schema or a strategic frame focuses on candidate strategies, win-or-lose aspects of the campaigns, and politicians' selfish interests. Media scholars have argued that while both types of coverage may contribute to heightening voter interest in the election, overemphasis on the game or strategic aspect in the election news coverage can overwhelm the substance of the campaigns and trivialize the most significant opportunity for political participation (Cappella & Jamieson, 1997; Patterson, 1980, 1993). Most American research on election coverage has reported that the media coverage of presidential campaigns mainly focuses on the game or strategic aspect of election campaigns rather than policy issues (Cappella & Jamieson, 1997; Patterson, 1980, 1993).

Although there is little research that focuses on how election news is portrayed in Japan, previous studies have shown that in comparison to the media in the U.S., the Japanese mass media, particularly newspapers, tend to emphasize policy issues more than the game aspect of election. (Note that most Japanese research on election coverage has dealt with the contents of newspapers, partly because newspapers are more accessible to researchers: Japan does not have any television news archives.)

With regard to newspapers, Akuto's (1996) study on the 1979 Tokyo gubernatorial election and the 1986 Machida (a suburban city of Tokyo) mayoral election campaigns revealed that election coverage by Japanese newspapers laid more emphasis on substance than on the game aspect of the elections. Akuto attributed the differences between the American and Japanese reporting styles to the differences in their election systems, primarily the different lengths of the campaign periods. Akuto argued that the election campaign periods in Japan are much shorter than their U.S. counterparts, and the short campaign periods allow more room for substance stories in Japan.

Kono (1998) analyzed the content of news stories on the 1990 general election by two major dailies (*Asahi Shimbun* and *Yomiuri Shimbun*). His analysis revealed that approximately one-third of the news stories in both the papers dealt with "the importance of the election" (i.e., substance coverage). In contrast, the game aspect of the election, such as the election projection, comprised only a small percentage of the reporting (the projection reporting accounted for 13.0% in *Yomiuri Shimbun* and 9.1 % in *Asahi Shimbun*). Thus, there is a general consistency between the findings of Kono and Akuto.

Based on the work of Patterson (1980), Ida (2005) conducted a content analysis of the coverage of three major newspapers on the 2000 and 2003 general elections. Ida categorized the news items into either game reporting or substance reporting. His analysis showed that the ratio of substance reporting in 2003 was larger than the corresponding figure in 2000. He also reported that in *Yomiuri Shimbun*, substance reporting outnumbered game reporting in the 2003 election news coverage: approximately 56% of the news stories were categorized as substance reporting, and 44% of the stories were categorized as game reporting (corresponding figures for the 2000 election coverage were 35.8% and 64.2%, respectively).

With regard to television election coverage, Hagiwara and Fukuda (2001) suggested that television news emphasized the game aspect, whereas newspapers were more likely to emphasize the substance aspect of the campaign. They conducted a content analysis of television news as well as major newspapers to examine the manner in which the media covered the 1999 Tokyo gubernatorial election campaign. Hagiwara and Fukuda reported that television news focused on how the candidates competed with each other, while the newspapers laid more emphasis on covering the policy proposals of the different candidates.

Taniguchi's (2002) content analysis of two major night-time news programs' coverage of the 2000 general election (NHK's *News 10* and TV Asahi's *News Station*) revealed that 76.3% of *News Station's* news items used a strategic frame and 15.3% used an issue frame (8.5% were categorized as other); corresponding figures for *News 10* were 55.6%, 40.3%, and 4.2% respectively. Taniguchi's analysis also revealed that *News Station* tended to depict politicians largely in a negative tone, regardless of the party to which they belonged. Taniguchi also examined the relationship between viewing specific news programs and political cynicism. He concluded that exposure to *News Station* tended to induce political cynicism in viewers; however, this negative influence was not observed for *News 10* newscasts.

Elections and Public Opinion Polls

Major newspapers and television networks regularly report the results of their own opinion polls during the election campaigns. The most important poll in relation to voting behaviors may be the election prediction report. Newspapers have been unrivaled in election projections. On the basis of the results of public opinion polls along with other information gathered by journalists, major newspapers have published their own election prediction reports while the election campaigns were still ongoing (usually several days prior to voting day). They started this practice of announcing projections in the 1950s. Major media firms have conducted large-scale opinion polls using the Random Digit Dialing (or the Random Digital Sampling) method in recent years: for example, the respondents of the poll conducted in September 2005 by *Yomiuri Shimbun* were 155,263 and the corresponding figure for *Asahi Shimbun* was 118,616. Election prediction reporting, which features possible winners or the number of seats each party would gain, arguably comprises the game aspect of election coverage. Many experienced politicians are concerned about the influences induced by these media projections. This issue will be addressed in detail in the next section.

In addition, major media have also conducted sampling surveys that are intended to examine issues considered as important by electorates, their level of interest in the upcoming election, or the party they support; the results are reported in their own newspapers or aired on their own news programs. This type of opinion survey is usually conducted several times during the preliminary and official election campaign periods.

Furthermore, the media also conduct large-scale exit polls (the sample size ranges from 300,000 to 500,000). The exit polls have gained particular importance for television. The final results of the elections are not declared until midnight of the voting day. On voting day, television networks broadcast special reports on each national election during the prime time viewing slot. These reports predict the probable outcome of the elections—that is, the winners or the number of seats each party will gain— based primarily on exit polls. The election special programs, which are characterized by entertainment-oriented reporting, have become the biggest political show on television in recent years, and they enjoy relatively 2

Political Advertising

The Public Offices Election Law banned political advertising on television and in newspapers during election campaigns. Thus, unlike other countries such as the U.S., negative political advertising used to be insignificant in Japan. However, after the 1994 revision of the law, the Ministry of Home Affairs permitted political advertising if it could be regarded as a part of the usual political activities. Thus, in recent years, political advertising, including its negative form, has appeared on television and in newspapers during election campaign periods.

EFFECTS OF ELECTION COVERAGE

Although many studies have been conducted on the effects of the political content of the media in the non-election context, there is only a limited amount of research on the effects of election news coverage in Japan. A limited number of studies on the effects of the media on election news coverage have focused primarily on two major themes: (1) learning from the media concerning issues or candidates (i.e., agenda-setting effects) and (2) influences of projection reports (e.g., bandwagon, underdog, and spiral of silence effects).

Agenda-Setting

Agenda-setting is undoubtedly one of the most influential theories that have attracted the attention of many political communication researchers in Japan (Iwabuchi, 1986; Kobayashi, 1983; Maeda, 1978; Takeshita, 1983). Broadly defined, agenda-setting is regarded as a political process, which has been divided into three distinct research traditions: *media* agenda-setting, *public* agenda-setting, and *policy* agenda-setting (Dearing & Rogers, 1996; Rogers & Dearing, 1988). However, most agenda-setting research in Japan has focused on public agenda-setting, which examines the manner in which the media agenda is transferred to the public agenda. Furthermore, public agenda-setting study can be divided into two distinct types: the hierarchy approach and the longitudinal approaches (Dearing & Rogers, 1996). While longitudinal approaches have drawn the attention of researchers in recent years, the hierarchy approach, initiated by McCombs and Shaw (1972), has dominated agenda-setting studies in Japan.

Agenda-setting studies by Japanese scholars have revealed that agenda-setting effects were subject to a number of social and psychological contingencies that limit its generality. For example, the need for orientation, which is one of the well-known contingent conditions advanced in the U.S. (Weaver, 1980), has proven to be effective in explaining agenda-setting effects in a Japanese setting (Takeshita, 1993). Takeshita also found that agenda-setting effects in Japan appear to be stronger at the perceived community salience level (i.e., respondents' estimation of the issue considered as important by most other people) than at the intrapersonal salience level (i.e., which issue the respondents themselves regarded as important), which is characteristic of Japan (Takeshita, 1993; Takeshita & Takeuchi, 1996).

Takeshita and Mikami (1995) conducted a simultaneous examination of both first- and second-level agenda-setting effects during the 1993 general election. Focusing on the issue of political reform that was overwhelmingly emphasized in the media campaign coverage, they provided evidence supporting the agenda-setting hypothesis at both the general issue level (i.e., political reform) and the sub-issue level (i.e., attributes of political reform). Due to a near-monopoly of the issue of political reform on the news agenda, instead of the usual comparison between the rank order of issues on the media agenda and their ranking on the public agenda, Takeshita and Mikami examined relationships between the level of attentiveness to political news and the degree to which the issue of political reform was salient (first-level) on the one hand, and the degree to which one sub-issue of the reform (then dominant in election news) was salient (second-level) on the other hand, and found statistically significant correlations.

Influences of Election Prediction Reports

Japanese scholars have conducted research on the potential influences of election prediction reports. Compared to other countries, empirical examinations on the influence of election prediction reports on voter preference or voting behavior have been relatively rare in Japan. However, there are some important empirical studies and theoretical arguments that can contribute to this literature. First, it should be noted that while discussing the impacts of the publication of an election prediction, Japanese scholars usually use the generic term "the announcement effects," which include bandwagon and underdog effects. Researchers have divided the announcement effects into two types: *direct announcement effects* and *indirect announcement effects* (Takeshita, 1994). The bandwagon and underdog effects are considered to be direct announcement effects. The indirect announcement effects refer to the influence of election projections by the media on the campaign staff rather than on the voters in general. For example, Kamegaya (1998) suggests that the morale of the campaign staff is boosted when they hear reports that their candidate is fighting a close race. In contrast, the staff's morale is lowered to some extent when the media announces that their candidate will be elected easily. Changes in the level of morale of the campaign staff indirectly impact the general voters' behavior.

Previous studies on the direct announcement effects have produced mixed results, thus rendering research evidence inconclusive. The multi-seat, medium-sized constituency election system that was employed for electing the House of Representatives until 1994—in which multiple candidates from the same political party often stood for an election—was one of the major causes for the difficulty in effectively detecting the possible influences of election prediction reports on voting behavior (Takeshita, 1994). Another possible reason for the inconsistent results may be due to the test methods used in those studies.

Maeda and Kobayashi (1980) concluded that announcement effects might occur as an underdog effect among candidates from the same party under the multiple-member district system. Iwabuchi (1994) also reported similar findings. By contrast, using data from a panel survey conducted in Musashino City, Tokyo, in the 1986 double elections, Ikeda (1988) revealed that the projection of election results had little influence on the respondents' voting intentions, although it had a significant effect on how they perceived the outcome of the race. Ikeda, therefore, doubted the very existence of the announcement effects.

While other relevant studies dealt with the level of the individual election district, Kabashima (1988) examined the existence of announcement effects by focusing on the number of total seats each political party was projected to gain. His analysis revealed that a specific type of voters called "buffer players" was particularly sensitive to the election prediction reports. The buffer players referred to voters who allowed the LDP to hold office, and at the same time, wanted to maintain a balance between the power of the government and that of its opposition, thus keeping the LDP competitive and responsive to the voters' needs. According to Kabashima's analysis (1988), approximately 23% of the buffer players voted for opposition parties or abstained from voting after they were exposed to media projections reporting the LDP's expected overwhelming victory. Such buffer players, who demonstrate announcement effects, are therefore considered as strategic voters.[6]

All the empirical studies on the announcement effects reviewed above were conducted under the multi-seat, medium-sized constituency election system.[7] Empirical investigation into the announcement effects under the current election system is yet to be conducted. Thus, research should continue to investigate the possible influence that media projection reports have on voters' preferences and voting behaviors.

Spiral of Silence

The spiral of silence theory (Noelle–Neumann, 1974, 1984) has attracted a considerable amount of attention among communication and public opinion researchers in Japan. This is probably because "the conformist or consensus-oriented image of the public, on which the spiral of silence process is based, correlates with some Japanese cultural traits" (Takeshita & Ida, in press). However, the results of follow-up studies on the spiral of silence hypothesis, conducted by Japanese scholars, have shown mixed findings. While some studies have provided evidence supporting the spiral of silence hypothesis (Tokinoya, 1996), many other studies conducted in Japan have failed to support it. For example, a study by Iwabuchi (1989), who examined the hypothesis with regard to issues, such as the privatization of JNR and the introduction of a sales tax, did not support the hypothesis. Ikeda (1989) also failed to prove the spiral of silence hypothesis in a study conducted during the 1986 double elections. Furthermore, contrary to the prediction of the theory, Kobayashi (1990) found that the respondents in the minority position were more willing than those in the majority position to express their opinions. Tokinoya's (1989) study produced mixed results: his data supported the hypothesis for some topics but not for others, suggesting that the topics may be a contingent condition for the spiral of silence hypothesis. Focusing on the issue of whether Japan should join the permanent UN Security Council members, Yasuno (2006) found only partial evidence supporting the spiral of silence hypothesis and emphasized the necessity of considering the strength and direction of opinions as contingent conditions while testing the hypothesis.

CONCLUSIONS

As discussed in this chapter, the role of television in Japanese politics has gained unparalleled significance. As many political analysts have pointed out, we are undoubtedly living in the age of telepolitics. Combined with other factors, the emergence of the new type of news and information programs on commercial stations in the mid-1980s may have acted as a trigger for Japanese tele-politics. With regard to the news programs that are characterized by an entertainment-oriented and interpretive style of reporting, many Japanese scholars have alleged that packaging politics as entertainment could demean and foster cynicism about politics (Otake, 2003; Takase, 1999; Taniguchi, 2002). The interpretive style of news reporting and the overemphasis on the negative and conflicting aspects of politics in newscasts, which have gained prominence in recent years in Japan, could induce "videomalaise" (Robinson, 1976). However, some scholars have argued that these television news shows might help the audience to gain information about complicated political issues and contribute toward enhancing their knowledge. With regard to the U.S. and some European countries, Norris (2000) has claimed that news media exert a positive impact on democracy. The controversy over the possible impact of television news on political attitudes and voting behaviors has not yet been settled. Future research should evaluate the net effects of the positive and negative influences of television news on politics.

Krauss (2002) argues that two significant changes have been occurring in the Japanese political scene: (1) the prime minister's image has deviated from that of his party and (2) prime ministers with distinguished media images attain far higher cabinet ratings. Krauss interpreted these phenomena as "the beginnings of the 'presidentialization' of the prime minister's role" (Krauss, 2002, p. 10), which refers to the increasing importance of the personalization of the prime minister's role toward voters. As Kabashima and Imai (2001) demonstrated, the image of the prime minister can have a marked impact on a voter's choice of party in the proportional representation constituency. Under these circumstances, the media strategy adopted by political leaders should inevitably become increasingly ingenious. This is clearly evident in the 2005 general election led by former Prime Minister Koizumi. One of the most notable tactics in the Koizumi administration was its effective use of non-traditional political media to convey its message to the general public (Hoshi & Osaka, 2006; Kabashima & Steel, 2007; Uesugi, 2006).[8] The degree of effectiveness with which political leaders can handle non-traditional as well as traditional political media has probably become one of the decisive factors for them to survive in the age of telepolitics.

As previously noted, Koizumi succeeded in creating the single-issue referendum on postal reforms in the 2005 general election, despite the opposition parties' emphasis on other important issues, such as pension reform or foreign policy. From the perspective of the agenda-setting theory, this election raised an important question about who actually set the public agenda: Was it the media? Or was it their news sources (political elites) who set the public agenda through setting the media agenda? To what extent did the media play an independent role in setting the public agenda? Takeshita and Ida (in press) contend that "mainstream media are likely to convey only the news items obtained from the press clubs, following the neutrality principle. As a result, the media often passively relay the agenda of the sources, reflecting the interests of the elite and imposing them on the general public." Media scholars need to address the issue of who sets the public as well as media's agenda in the age of telepolitics.

Finally, with regard to the role of the Internet in election campaigns, it can be said that the use of this medium is still limited, partly because the Public Offices Election Law currently bans updating web pages that carry candidates' opinions and sending e-mail newsletters during election campaigns. However, the prohibition of Internet use as a means of conducting election campaigns will probably be abolished in the foreseeable future. Thus, the role of the Internet may gain increasing importance. The manner in which the Internet affects communication behavior during election campaigns would be a crucial research question for future studies.

NOTES

1. According to Flanagan, position issues such as the role of the emperor, Japan's alignment with the U.S., the conflict between the conservatives' growth-at-any-cost economic policies, and growing concerns about pollution, which deeply divided electorates along a conservative–progressive split, dominated political debate in the 1950s and 1960s. However, the media has down-played position issues, and instead, valence issues (e.g., against crime or corruption) have dominated political debates since the 1970s. This shift of the political debate from position issues to valence issues has contributed to a transformation of electoral decisions into referenda on the quality of the incumbent regime's performance (Flanagan, 1996).
2. In 1996, the party name was changed from JSP to Social Democratic Party (SDP).
3. Data from nationwide public opinion surveys conducted by the NHK every fifth year, for example, reveal that the percentage of unaffiliated voters has increased remarkably after 1994: 31.6% in 1973, 32.2% in 1983, 37.8% in 1988, 40.7% in 1993, 52.3% in 1998, and 56.9% in 2003 (NHK Broadcasting Culture Research Institute, 2004).
4. The University of the Air Foundation is the only state-funded broadcaster in Japan.
5. In countries such as the U.S., where numerous time zones exist, the impact of media reporting on early election returns based on exit polls should be a big concern because such reporting may disenfranchise voters who have not yet cast their votes. However, the reporting of election returns in that sense is insignificant in Japan, which covers only one time zone.
6. With regard to the underdog effects, Marsh (1984) suggested that these effects may be due to a desire to reduce the margin of victory for the winner. According to Marsh, "the reasons could be rational, for example, not wanting the party to win by too big a majority for fear of what overconfident parties are likely to do" (p. 567). Thus, a similar kind of strategic voting may be observed in other countries, although the buffer player is a by-product of the long-standing LDP-dominant system of the 1955 regime (Kabashima, 1988).
7. Previous studies indicate that the extent of the announcement effects, even if they exist, is modest. Furthermore, some researchers have contended that the bandwagon and underdog effects may cancel each other out, thus making the influence of media projections on voting intentions negligible. However, using Gerbner and his associates' metaphor (Gerbner et al., 1986, 2002), we should note that even these small effects should not be ignored because a shift of even a few degrees in average temperature can cause significant climate changes; for example, the ice age or global warming. Thus, sometimes, even small effects have significant consequences.
8. Koizumi also began the cabinet e-mail newsletters service in June 2001. His e-zine had nearly 2.3 million subscribers at peak times.

REFERENCES

Akhavan-Majid, R. (1990). The press as an elite power group in Japan. *Journalism Quarterly, 67,* 1006–1014.

Akuto, H. (1996). Media in electoral campaigning in Japan and the United States. In S. J. Pharr & E. Krauss (Eds.), *Media and politics in Japan* (pp. 313–337). Honolulu: University of Hawaii Press.

Cappella, J. N., & Jamieson, K. H. (1997). *Spiral of cynicism: The press and the public good.* New York: Oxford University Press.

Dearing, J. W., & Rogers, E. M. (1996). *Agenda-setting.* Thousand Oaks, CA: Sage.

Flanagan, S. C. (1996). Media exposure and the quality of political participation in Japan. In S. J. Pharr & E. Krauss (Eds.), *Media and politics in Japan* (pp. 277–312). Honolulu: University of Hawaii Press.

Gerbner, G., Gross, L., Morgan, M., & Signorielli, N. (1986). Living with television: The dynamics of the cultivation process. In J. Bryant & D. Zillmann (Eds.), *Perspectives on media effects* (pp. 17–48). Hillsdale, NJ: Erlbaum.

Gerbner, G., Gross, L., Morgan, M., Signorielli, N., & Shanahan, J. (2002). Growing up with television: Cultivation processes. In J. Bryant and D. Zillmann (Eds.), *Media effects: Advances in theory and research: A second edition* (pp. 43–68). Hillsdale, NJ: Erlbaum.

Hagiwara, S., & Fukuda, M. (2001). Terebi ni okeru senkyo-hodo: 1999nen Tokyo-tochiji-senkyo wo jirei toshite [Television coverage of election campaigns: The case of the 1999 Tokyo governor's election]. In S. Hagiwara (Ed.), *Henyo suru media to nyusu-hodo* [Changing media and news reporting] (pp. 115–143). Tokyo: Maruzen.

Hirose, H. (1994). The press club system in Japan: Its past, present and future. *Keio Communication Review, 16,* 63–75.

Hoshi, H., & Osaka, I. (2006). *Terebi seiji* [Television politics]. Tokyo: Asahi Shimbun.

Ida, M. (2005). Manifesuto-senkyo to senkyo hodo: Sandaishi no naiyo-bunseki [The impact of manifesto on the coverage of general election in Japan: A content analysis of major newspapers]. *Seikei Ronso, 73*(5/6), 181–199. (Tokyo: Meiji University).

Ikeda, K. (1988). Tohyo-ito keisei-katei niokeru sho-yoin [Factors affecting voting decision-making processes]. In University of Tokyo Institute of Journalism & Communication Studies (Ed.), *Senkyo-hodo to tohyo-kodo* [Election coverage and voting behavior] (pp.239–274). Tokyo: University of Tokyo Press.

Ikeda, K. (1989). "Spiral of silence" hypothesis and voting intention: A test in the 1986 Japanese national election. *Keio Communication Review, 10,* 51–62.

Iwabuchi, Y. (1986). Masu-media no joho to soten-sentaku [Mass media information and issue choice]. In H. Horie & M. Uemura (Eds.), *Tohyo-kodo to seiji ishiki* [Voting behavior and political awareness] (pp. 181–195). Tokyo: Keio-Tsushin.

Iwabuchi, Y. (1989). Seijiteki soten to yoron keisei katei [Political issues and public opinion processes]. *Seigakuin Daigaku Ronso, 2,* 55–79.

Iwabuchi, Y. (1994). Yosoku hodo to anaunsumento kouka [Mass media and announcements effects]. *Seikei Kenkyu, 30*(4), 153–173.

Kabashima, I. (1988). *Seiji sanka* [Political participation]. Tokyo: University of Tokyo Press.

Kabashima, I., & Imai, R. (2001). Nisennen sosenkyo [The 2000 general election], *Senkyo Kenkyu, 16,* 5–17.

Kabashima, I., & Steel, G. (2007). The Koizumi revolution. *PS: Political Science & Politics, 40,* 79–84.

Kamegaya, M. (1998). Anaunsumento-koka no "Kansetsu-koka" no jissho ni kansuru kokoromi [Indirect "announcement-effects" of electoral poll results]. *Senkyo Kenkyu, 13,* 110–119.

Kobayashi, Y. (1983). Joho to masu media [Information and mass media]. In N. Tomita & N. Okazawa (Eds.), *Joho to demokurashi* [Information and democracy] (pp. 167–193). Tokyo: Gakuyo-Shobo.

Kobayashi, Y. (1990). Masu media to seiji ishiki [Mass media and political attitudes in Japan]. *Leviathan, 7,* 97–114.

Kono, T. (1998). 1990 nen syuinsen ni kansuru houdo no naiyo bunnseki [Content analysis of newspaper coverage on the 1990 general election]. In R. Shiratori, N. Sakaue, & T. Kono (Eds.), *90 nendai shoto no seiji choryu to senkyo* [The political trend and elections in the early 1990s] (pp. 153–177). Tokyo: Shin-hyoron.

Krauss, E. S. (1996). Portraying the state: NHK television news and politics. In S. J. Pharr & E. Krauss (Eds.), *Media and politics in Japan* (pp. 89–129). Honolulu: University of Hawaii Press.

Krauss, E. S. (2000). *Broadcasting politics in Japan: NHK and television news.* Ithaca, NY: Cornell University Press.

Krauss, E. S. (2002). The media's role in a changing Japanese electorate. *Asian Program Special Report, 101,* 6–12. (Woodrow Wilson International Center for Scholars).

Maeda, T. (1978). Kodokushi to seiji-ishiki [Newspaper reading and political consciousness]. *Hogaku-Kenkyu, 51,* 311–338. Tokyo: Keio University.

Maeda, T., & Kobayashi, Y. (1980). The announcement-effects of election predictions. *Keio Communication Review, 1,* 41–59.

Marsh, C. (1984). Do polls affect what people think? In C. F. Turner and E.Marthin (Eds.), *Surveying subjective phenomena* (Vol. 2, pp. 565–-591). New York: Russell Sage Foundation.

McCombs, M. E., & Shaw, D. L. (1972). The agenda-setting function of mass media. *Public Opinion Quarterly, 36,* 176–187.

Ministry of Public Management, Home Affairs, and Posts and Telecommunications (MPHPT). (2006). *Information and communications in Japan: White paper 2006* (in Japanese). Tokyo: Gyousei.

Nakai, K. (2007). Seiji ni honro sareta senkyo houdo [Election coverage trifled with by politics]. *Senkyo Kenkyu, 22,* 25–35.

Narita, N. (2003). *Changing Japanese politics.* Tokyo: Foreign Press Center.

NHK Broadcasting Culture Research Institute (2004). *Gendai-nihonjin no ishiki-kozo* [The structure of the modern Japanese consciousness]. Tokyo: NHK.

Noelle-Neumann, E. (1974). The spiral of silence: A theory of public opinion. *Journal of Communication, 24*(1), 43–51.

Noelle-Neumann, E. (1984). *The spiral of silence: Public opinion—Our social skin.* Chicago: University of Chicago Press.

Norris, P. (2000). *A virtuous circle: Political communications in postindustrial societies.* Cambridge, UK: Cambridge University Press.

Otake, H. (2003). *Nihongata popurizumu* [Japanese style populism]. Tokyo: Chuo-kouronsha.

Patterson, T. E. (1980). *The mass media election: How Americans choose their president.* New York: Praeger.

Patterson, T. E. (1993). *Out of order.* New York: Knopf.

Robinson, M. J. (1976). Public affairs television and the growth of political malaise: The case of "the Selling of the Pentagon." *American Political Science Review, 70*(2), 409–432.

Rogers, E. M., & Dearing, J. W. (1988). Agenda-setting research: Where has it been? Where is it going? In J. Anderson (Ed.), *Communication yearbook 11* (pp. 555–594). Newbury Park, CA: Sage.

Saito, S. (2000). Japan. In S. A. Gunaratne (Ed.), *Handbook of the media in Asia: An overview.* (pp. 561–585). New Delhi: Sage.

Saito, S. (2003) Japan. In H. Rao (Ed.), *News media & new media: The Asia-Pacific Internet handbook—Episode V* (pp. 312–327). Singapore: Eastern Universities Press.

Shuin-giin no media hyoka [How lower house members look at the media] (1996, April 4). *The Yomiuri Shimbun,* p. 2.

Takase, J. (1999). *Joho to seiji* [Information and politics]. Tokyo: Shin-Hyoron.

Takeshita, T. (1983). Media gidai-settei kasetsu no jisshoteki kento [An empirical examination of media agenda-settign hypothesis]. *Shimbun-kenkyujo Kiyo, 31,* 101–143.

Takeshita, T. (1993). Agenda-setting effects of the press in a Japanese local election. *Studies of Broadcasting, 29,* 193–216.

Takeshita, T. (1994). Masu media to anaunsumento kouka [the mass media and the announcements effects]. In N. Kurita (Ed.), *Seiji shinrigaku rinyuaru* [Political psychology renewal] (pp. 115–136). Tokyo: Gakubunsha.

Takeshita, T. (1997). Exploring the media's roles in defining reality: From issue-agenda setting to attribute-agenda setting. In M. McCombs, D. L. Shaw, & D. Weaver (Eds.), *Communication and democracy: Exploring the intellectual frontiers in agenda-setting theory* (pp.15–27). Mahwah, NJ: Erlbaum.

Takeshita, T. & Ida, M. (in press). Political communication in Japan. In L. Willnat & A. J. Aw (Eds.), *Political communication in Asia*. New York: Routledge.

Takeshita, T. & Mikami, S. (1995). How did mass media influence the voters' choice in the 1993 general election in Japan? A study of agenda-setting. *Keio Communication Review, 17*, 27–41.

Takeshita, T. & Takeuchi, I. (1996). Media agenda setting in a local election: The Japanese case. In S. J. Pharr & E. S. Krauss (Eds.), *Media and politics in Japan* (pp. 339–351). Honolulu: University of Hawaii Press.

Tanaka, T. (2006). Popyuraka suru nyusu to media popurizumu [Popularized news and media populism]. In M. Ito (Ed.), *Terebi nyusu no syakaigako gaku* [Sociology of television news] (pp. 128–149). Kyoto: Sekai shiso sha

Taniguchi, M. (2002). Masu media [Mass media]. In A. Fukuda & M. Taniguchi (Eds.), *Demokurashi no seijigaku* [Politics of democracy] (pp. 269–286). Tokyo: University of Tokyo Press.

Tokinoya, H. (1989). Testing the spiral of silence theory in East Asia. *Keio Communication Review, 10*, 35–49.

Tokinoya, H. (1996). A study on the spiral of silence theory in Japan. *Keio Communication Review, 18*, 33–45.

Uesugi, T. (2006). *Koizumi no shori media no haiboku* [The victory of Koizumi, the defeat of the media]. Tokyo: Soshisya.

Weaver, D. H. (1980). Audience need for orientation and media effects. *Communication Research, 7*, 361–376.

Yasuno, S. (2006). *Jusoteki na yoron keisei katei* [Stratified process of public opinion formation]. Tokyo: University of Tokyo Press.

IV

ELECTION NEWS COVERAGE
IN A COMPARATIVE PERSPECTIVE

25

News Coverage of EU Parliamentary Elections

Michaela Maier and Jürgen Maier

THE POLITICAL SYSTEM AND VOTING IN THE EUROPEAN UNION

The history of the European Union goes back to 1951 when Belgium, France, Italy, Luxembourg, the Netherlands, and West Germany founded the European Coal and Steel Community (ECSC). After centuries of military conflicts in Europe, the foundation of the ECSC was mainly driven by the idea of ensuring peace in Europe. To do so, the ECSC controlled the most important raw materials of the war industry. The work of the ECSC was considered very successful, so the six member states decided to further promote economic and political integration. As a consequence, in 1957 the European Economic Community (EEC) as well as the European Atomic Energy Community (EURATOM) were founded. In 1967, the respective ECSC, EEC, and EURATOM parliaments were merged into one European Parliament, serving what is now called the European Union (EU; since 1993).

The European integration process has accelerated tremendously during the last four decades. Most visibly, a significant number of European countries have joined the EU ("horizontal integration"; for a distinction of the different dimensions of European integration see, Schimmelfennig & Rittberger, 2005). Currently, the EU is comprised of 27 member states (including 10 post-communist countries) with a total of 490 million people; another seven countries are interested in membership. In addition, the cooperation of the EU member states has been extended to more and more policy fields ("sectoral integration"). Besides economic issues, the EU is now dealing with questions of international and homeland security, educational, cultural, environmental, energy, or transport policy, for example. Finally, the members of the EU have transferred more and more responsibilities to the EU institutions, which issue rulings that are binding for all member states ("vertical integration"). The institutional design of the EU follows the idea of a parliamentary democracy separating executive (Council of Ministers, European Commission), legislative (European Parliament), and judicial power (European Court of Justice). Looking at the distribution of power between these institutions, it is obvious that the impact of the European Parliament (EP) on the EU decision-making process has increased considerably since its foundation in 1952.

In the first years after the foundation of the EP, its members were delegated by the national parliaments of the member states. The first direct elections to the EP were held in 1979 and have been conducted every five years since then. Although there is still no uniform European voting system, the 2002 EP Elections Act defines three general rules. First, as in 1999, the voting system of EP elections has to be of an essentially proportional nature. As a consequence, the voting systems of British, French, and German national elections differ significantly from the voting procedure applied in EP elections. Second, if they wish, member states may set an electoral threshold of up to 5% as a requirement for representation in the European Parliament. In 2004, in eight countries (e.g., France, Germany) there was a 5% hurdle, meaning that if the parties gathered less than 5% of the votes they were not represented in the EP. In Austria and Sweden the threshold was 4%, and in Greece it was 3%. Third, the 2002 EP Elections Act set a four-day election period running from Thursday to the following Sunday. In 2004, most of the countries preferred to vote on Sunday, but some member states (e.g., Netherlands, UK) chose another election day within the election period. Italy as well as the Czech Republic decided to open the polling stations for two days in a row. Within this framework of general rules, all member states conform with national provisions taking the country-specific situation into account: In all countries one must be 18 years old to be entitled to vote. The minimum age to stand for election varies between 18 (e.g., Germany, Netherlands, Spain) and 25 years (Italy). Some countries have legal provisions assuring equal access of male and female candidates to elective offices. Voting in Belgium, Greece, and Luxembourg is compulsory. Absentee ballots were unrestricted only in Germany, Denmark, and the Netherlands; most of the countries provide this service only to citizens living abroad. Most of the member countries form single constituencies; only a minority of states had multiple constituencies (e.g., Belgium, Italy, UK). Some EU countries only allow voting of closed party lists; about one half of the member states apply a system in which voters may choose their preferred candidates from different lists. Ireland and Malta use the single transferable vote system. Swedish voters are allowed to strike out listed candidates and to add new names (for an overview of the different electoral regulations see, e.g., European Parliament, 2004).

The most striking observation about European voting behavior is that European elections are usually seen as "second-order" elections (Reif, 1997; Reif & Schmitt, 1980). As a consequence, turnout is low in almost all member states. In addition, participation in EP elections has decreased substantially during the last decades: The average turnout dropped from 63% in 1979 to 45.5% in 2004.[1] In 2004, in some of the new member states less than a third of the eligible voters showed up on election day (Maier & Tenscher, 2006; Steinbrecher & Huber, 2006). In addition, those citizens casting their vote often use EP elections for a referendum about the work of the current national government (also see Kevin, 2003). As a rule, parties belonging to the national governments lose votes in EP elections. In contrast, smaller parties as well as parties that are against the European integration process are often successful in European elections (e.g., 2004 in Belgium, the Czech Republic, Poland, Sweden, and the UK).

MEDIA SYSTEMS, USE, AND REGULATION OF ELECTION COVERAGE THROUGHOUT THE EU

Until the 1980s, most European countries only had a publicly funded broadcasting system, but by the 1999 EP elections a dual broadcasting system with private and public stations existed in almost all EU member states (Banducci & Semetko, 2003; Brants & de Bens, 2000; McQuail, 2004; Siune & Hultén, 1998).[2] Since the introduction of private television and radio channels, fears have been expressed that political content would be marginalized in favor of entertainment topics (for an overview see Brants, 1998); this has been discussed in the theoretical framework of the so-called convergence thesis (Schatz, Immer, & Marcinkowski, 1989) in most European countries. In fact, numerous findings indicate that the formats and content of both the public and private broadcasting subsystems are becoming more and more similar. However, the results of national studies, which have to be consulted because comparative analyses are lacking, suggest that private TV stations have made attempts to fulfil more professional standards, although the public channels, which have the legal obligation to provide political information, still offer a significantly greater amount of such information to viewers (Brants & de Bens, 2000; Holtz-Bacha & Norris, 2001; Kevin, 2003; Maier, 2002; Pfetsch, 1996).

In most European countries more than 70% of the adult citizens watch TV on a daily basis. The estimated average viewing time is 3.5 hours which means an increase of half an hour per day during the last 10 years. At the same time, since the 1990s daily newspapers in Europe have been subject to a process of steady decline of their circulation rates and shrinking ranges since more and more media are competing for the temporal and financial resources of their potential readership. Furthermore, the very low rates of newspaper readership among 14- to 19-year-olds is a further indicator of the critical situation of European newspapers (e.g., for Germany, the range is about 50% in comparison with more than 80% in the group of over age 50; see BDZV, 2004, p. 30; Lauf, 2001).

De Vreese, Banducci, Semetko, and Boomgaarden (2006) argue that the structural developments of the news market are important because they determine citizens' opportunities to access political news. Indeed, empirical findings show that newspapers give more space than broadcast media to political news and especially news about the European Union because space is not so limited and production costs are not so high. There also exist significant differences between different types of media outlets: Broadsheet newspapers publish more political information than boulevard papers, and private TV stations tend to provide less political information than public broadcasters, which is especially the case for European issues (e.g., Medien Tenor, 2006; Peter & de Vreese, 2004; Peter, Lauf, & Semetko, 2004; Pfetsch, 1996).

At the same time, for most European citizens, media coverage is the only source of information about the European Union and its institutions. Since the first EP elections research has shown that citizens experience politics on the European level and European elections even more than national politics mainly through mass media (Blumler, 1983a). For example, Norris (2000) found that only 3% of the public had direct contact with EU-institutions within the last three months before the survey, while three-quarters were able to recall information on the EU which they had gotten from the media. Overall, 60% named television as their most important source of information on the EU, 41% daily newspapers, and 24% the radio (Norris, 2000, p. 209). It is the assumption underlying all research on the content and impact of election coverage that the information carried by the media provides citizens with the information they need to make their decisions about parties and candidates and that media coverage has an influence on their attitude formation and their voting decision and perhaps even on long-term attitudes (also see de Vreese, Lauf, & Peter, 2007).

Noting this important role of the news media at the time of elections the Committee of Ministers in 1999 released a recommendation (Nr. R [99] 15) to the EU member states regarding the media coverage of election campaigns. While preparing that recommendation the "intergovernmental group of specialists on media in a pan-European perspective (MM-S-EP)" had found that media coverage in some member states was handled by regulatory intervention, while other countries relied on self-regulation or even left the field unregulated. The expert group came to the conclusion that regarding the equal treatment of political parties by the media, general shortcomings existed within the EU and they decided to prepare a recommendation for the member states "as guidance to journalists, politicians and courts" in order "to ensure a minimum of democratic election standards" (Committee of Ministers, 1999, p. 2). In this recommendation the experts tried to find the right balance between the general principle of freedom of expression, the respect for freedom of the media, including their self-regulation, and the "fundamental principle of fair, balanced and impartial coverage" (p. 3). The public service broadcasters (but also private TV stations) are held especially responsible for ensuring fair and thorough election coverage so that the pluralistic expression of opinions is facilitated during electoral campaigns. The recommendation also states that national laws can allow free airtime for political parties as well as paid advertising, but it stresses that all political contenders should be treated in an "equal and non-discriminatory manner" (p. 3). When publishing the results of opinion polls, the media should be required to name the persons or organizations that paid for the poll and conducted it, and also indicate sample size and time as well as the margin of error. In addition the experts suggest that the member states might want to consider prohibiting the "dissemination of partisan electoral messages" (p. 4) on the day before the vote. The recommendation ends with the proposal that the individual countries should find measures to implement the principles of fairness, balance, and impartiality within their national media law. For examples of such national laws see individual country chapters in this book.

HISTORY AND DEVELOPMENT OF EU ELECTION COVERAGE

Although the 2004 election was already the sixth direct election to the EP, de Vreese et al. (2006) remarked that "Structured knowledge about the media's coverage of European elections is only emerging." Indeed, after the first EP election had evoked a considerable amount of research activities, academic interest seems to have faded, and the results at hand for EP elections can by no means keep up with the extensive research conducted on the occasion of national elections. There is a lack especially in the field of comparative research. Comparative content analyses of the media coverage in all EU member states exist only for the 1979, 1999, and 2004 EP elections (Blumler, 1983b; de Vreese et al., 2006; Peter, Lauf, & Semetko, 2004). In addition, a handful of national studies exist. Because of differences in the media analyzed (e.g., television vs. print media), the period of the campaign examined, as well as the coding procedures applied, the longitudinal comparability of results is limited. From an analytical point of view, the findings of these studies can be divided into three categories: First, the amount of media coverage on EP elections, second, the content, and third, the tone of this coverage.

Amount of Media Coverage of EP Elections

In the first direct EP election in June 1979 about 100 million voters from nine countries were called to the ballot box in order to take part in what would be "a revolutionary event" in the eyes of those who had striven for years to achieve the goal of direct elections (Blumler & Thoveron, 1983, p. 3). Although the media coverage of the first European election was generally less intensive than for national elections, Kelly and Siune (1983, pp. 43) showed that a considerable amount of information about the upcoming election was aired on television (party broadcasts, discussions, special election programs, newscasts, etc.). In all countries, the coverage increased as election day came closer, but there was quite some difference in campaign coverage among EC member states. The "heaviest" coverage occurred in Denmark, the Netherlands, Germany, and France with in total of about 1,000 minutes devoted to the election. The least coverage was provided in Ireland and Luxembourg (401 and 371 minutes respectively; Kelly & Siune, 1983, p. 43). The differences in campaign coverage could be traced back to two factors: First, the total amount of coverage depended on the duration of the campaign in the respective country, which varied from one week in Italy to six weeks in the Netherlands and Germany. Second, the attention TV paid to the 1979 EP election depended on the decisions of TV producers as to how much time should be allotted to the upcoming events and in which format they would broadcast the information.

That there are significant differences between single countries in reference to the degree of mass media reporting on EP elections is also one of the major findings of Leroy and Siune (1994), who compared the TV coverage for the EP elections in 1979, 1984, and 1989 for Belgium and Denmark. As a reason for these differences they point to the different history and development of the national media systems as well as to different traditions of media coverage. A second finding of their study is that the attention media paid to EP elections has further decreased since 1979, a result which is also confirmed for the public TV channels in Germany between 1979 and 1989 (Reiser, 1994). Retrospectively, several researchers come to the conclusion that the novelty of the first EP election had attracted more media attention than any of the following elections, which "did not have any unique qualities" (also see de Vreese, Lauf, & Peter, 2007; Leroy & Siune, 1994, p. 53; van der Eijk, 2000). According to Leroy and Siune (1994), in Denmark as well as in Belgium three quarters of the televised election coverage was broadcast by public and only one quarter by commercial TV stations.

Whereas information on the media coverage of the 1994 EP election is completely lacking, in 1999 a research team around Holli Semetko, Edmund Lauf, and Claes de Vreese took up the research of Blumler's (1983b) study on the first EP election. As most European citizens regularly name television as their preferred source of information about the EU (Peter, Lauf, & Semetko, 2004), they content analyzed the TV coverage in all 15 EU member states[3] during the last two weeks before the election. Again, one of the major research findings was that the amount of TV news coverage about the EU varied considerably among the member countries: While in most Mediterranean and Scandinavian countries, as well as in Austria, the election coverage accounted for 13% and more of all political coverage, in Belgium, Germany, Ireland, the Netherlands, Spain, and the UK the share was not higher than 6% (see also Banducci & Semetko, 2003; Kevin, 2003; Lauf & Peter, 2004; for Germany see also Brettschneider & Rettich, 2005). Using multivariate regressions, Peter, Lauf, and Semetko (2004) identified the polarization of elite opinion as the most important variable explaining cross-national differences in the amount of EP election coverage. Again, public outlets broadcast more news on the EP elections than private channels. In addition, the level of media coverage also depended on contextual variables: The less satisfied the citizens were with domestic democracy, the more media attention the elections on the supranational level drew. De Vreese, Lauf, and Peter (2007) found that the existence of an anti-EU party (and thus the polarization of elite opinions toward European integration) was a strong predictor for the share of coverage, and that the more polarized the national elite opinion on the EU was, the more coverage the election received. In contrast to this, the position of the EP election in the cycle of national elections was insignificant; the authors did not find any evidence that the coverage of European elections was higher if national elections were approaching.

On the occasion of the 2004 EP election the research team around Semetko and de Vreese conducted a content analysis similar to their 1999 study, now also taking into account the news coverage of three national newspapers (two quality papers and one tabloid) in addition to the two most important public and private TV newscasts in all 25 member countries of the EU during the last two weeks before the elections (de Vreese et al., 2006). They found that approximately 10% of the media reports dealt with EU topics; which is, for example in Germany, not a higher degree of coverage than in years without EP elections (Brettschneider & Rettich, 2005).[4] De Vreese et al. (2006) reported that the amount of media coverage was slightly higher in the 10 "new" countries which had joined the EU in May 2004 than in the 15 "old" member states (10.4 versus 9.2%). The fact that the election in the new member states generally drew more media attention than in the old member states is at least partially in line with the result from the 1999 analysis that the news factor novelty seems to be relevant for journalistic selectivity in the context of the EU elections (Peter, Lauf, & Semetko, 2004). On average, 80% of the media reports were specifically devoted to the elections; for Germany Brettschneider and Rettich (2005) found that this share was only about 25%. Compared to previous elections, the overall visibility of the election had increased (De Vreese et al., 2006). This holds especially true for the television coverage in the old EU member countries, whereas the coverage in the national newspapers had increased in some and decreased in other old EU states (Berganza & Beroiz, 2006; de Vreese et al., 2006; Nord & Strömbäck, 2006). In some other old EU countries like Germany, the share of reports on EP elections did not change substantially (Brettschneider & Rettich, 2005; Wilke & Reinemann, 2005; however, Zeh & Holtz-Bacha, 2005, came to contrary conclusions). The finding that public TV stations and quality newspapers paid more attention to the election than private channels and tabloid papers could also be confirmed for the old as well as the new member states (Berganza & Beroiz, 2006; Brettschneider & Rettich, 2005; Demertzis, 2006, p. 285; De Vreese et al., 2006; Gerstlé, Magni-Berton, & Piar, 2006).

Content of Media Coverage on EP Elections

According to Siune (1983), the "Europeanness" of the media coverage on the first direct election of the EP was ambiguous. On the one hand, journalists or national politicians were the predominant communicators in most countries. On the other hand, a great share of the media reports focused on specific European issues (e.g. economy, agriculture, energy; in total 38%) and activities connected with the European campaign (party matters and alliances; in total 27%), whereas European ideological themes (17%) and EC institutions (13%) received significantly less attention.

In contrast, for the 1989 EP election in Denmark and Belgium Leroy and Siune (1994) found that the media coverage focused on domestic issues (e.g., 54% in Belgium and 72% in Denmark). In Germany, the share of non-European issues in media coverage varied between 35% for quality newspapers and 44% for public television channels (Reiser, 1994; the domestic focus of the EP election coverage was also true for 1994, see Paterson, Lees, & Green, 1996). In addition, Reiser (1994) found that all media outlets emphasized negativism and conflict more than the parties did in their campaigns. In Belgium, Denmark as well as in Germany, the most important media topic was the election itself. Nevertheless, Leroy and Siune (1994) reported only weak attempts by the media to develop a public discourse on European integration, to inform citizens about the functioning of the Parliament, and to discuss the current issues which the European political elites were dealing with.

The results for the 1999 EP election fit this picture. Peter, Lauf, and Semetko (2004) found that in most EC member countries, the share of news on EU-related topics other than the election was higher and was also presented more prominently in terms of length, placement, and presentational effort. De Vreese, Lauf, and Peter (2007) found that only 7% of the actors mentioned in TV reports on the European elections were EU-level actors, while 83% were domestic actors. At the same time only 4% of the quotes in the reports on the EP elections came from EU actors, while 89% were quotes from domestic actors. The representation of EU actors in the media significantly declined with the number of previous EP elections. The authors interpreted this effect on the background of the theory of news values (Galtung & Ruge, 1965; Maier, 2003; Schulz, 1976) and stated that the novelty of the EP election in a country had a positive effect on the reporting on EU representatives. In addition, with regard to the locations where the news took place, they found out that 85% of the news was reported from the country where the news program was broadcast—a fact which was seen as a further indication of the low Europeanness of the election media coverage (de Vreese, Lauf, & Peter, 2007). This overall result is supported by Kevin (2001, p. 35) who on the basis of a content analysis from media outlets in France, Germany, Ireland, Italy, the Netherlands, Spain, Sweden, and the UK came to the conclusion that the 1999 EP election had been "a national event with by and large national party candidates and a focus on national issues" (see also Kevin, 2003, pp. 79; Mather, 2001; Paterson & Green, 2001). However, she also points out that the degree of Europeanness differed in the single countries. In some of the EU member states there were notable efforts to approach the election from a European perspective; for example, by publishing election guides, outlines of party programs, reports on the campaigns, activities which especially took place in the French and Swedish press. In contrast, the cross-national finding that a major part of media reports focused on predictions of low turnout must be considered counterproductive. De Vreese (2003) argued that such predictions might turn into a self-fulfilling prophecy because the greatest impact of media reporting occurs when the message is homogenous, such as in this case of pessimistic forecast of voter turnout.

In 2004 again the news coverage focused more on domestic political issues in the member countries than on EU-related topics (Demertzis, 2006; de Vreese et al., 2006; Gerstlé et al., 2006; Kaid et al., 2005; Kopáček, 2006; Simon, 2006; Zeh & Holtz-Bacha, 2005). Even though more EU actors were featured in the news in 2004 than in 1999, in most of the countries they were outnumbered by domestic or national politicians and institutions (Brettschneider & Rettich, 2005; de Vreese et al., 2006; Demertzis, 2006). In addition, in most countries the media framed the campaign as a game or a horse race by, for example, providing results from public opinion polls or discussing campaign strategies. Only in a few countries did the majority of the media reports predominantly deal with specific issues (Berganza & Beroiz, 2006; Gerstlé et al., 2006; Kaid et al., 2005; Nord & Strömbäck, 2006). Zeh and Holtz-Bacha (2005) reported for Germany that public broadcasters usually referred to EU institutions or the EU integration process but only to a small degree to the election itself (Zeh & Holtz-Bacha, 2005, p. 263). In contrast, they characterized the coverage of private TV stations as "ordinary reports on foreign countries" almost without any reference to the EU. Moreover, private broadcasting stations emphasized human interest topics such as major sports events (Zeh & Holtz-Bacha, 2005, p. 257; for a contrary result for France see Gerstlé et al., 2006). Findings from Greece and Hungary indicated that the press focused on European issues more than TV did and made a greater effort to explain the institutional structures as well as political processes of the EU (Demertzis, 2006; Simon, 2006).

Tone of Media Coverage on EP Elections

Except for the UK, which traditionally has mixed feelings about the EU (Kevin, 2001), the tone of the reports on the 1979 EP election was generally neutral. This was especially the case for journalists' evaluative remarks, while politicians in general were more positive than negative (Siune, 1983). Siune (1983) concluded that the media coverage on the first direct election of the EP was, with the exception of France, often an unpersonalized affair with hardly any controversy, conflict, evaluation, or attack.

For 2004, de Vreese et al. (2006) were able to reconfirm the results of the 1979 EP election: The tone of the election coverage was predominantly neutral. Only evaluative statements about the EU and its representatives were rather negative (see also Kaid et al., 2005). This holds true especially for the old member countries (for Germany, see also Brettschneider & Rettich, 2005; for a comparison of Germany and the UK see Nehlig, 2005), while in the new member states the tone of the election coverage depended on the media outlet: Quality newspapers and television generally chose a positive tone, while tabloid papers tended to be rather negative (de Vreese et al., 2006; for the Czech Republic see Kopáček, 2006).

AWARENESS AND EFFECTS OF EU ELECTION COVERAGE

Compared to the research on the amount, the content, and the tone of EP election coverage, the situation concerning research on the impact of this coverage on political cognitions, political attitudes, and political behavior of European citizens is even less satisfactory: Hardly any studies exist on the influence of media reporting on political orientations in the context of EP elections. This is an astonishing fact because the same as in international politics it is not possible to experience European politics first-hand either (Page & Shapiro, 1992). Therefore, the pictures of Europe in the voters' heads strongly depend on the coverage of the mass media (see, e.g., Brettschneider, Maier, & Maier, 2003). As a consequence, news coverage on European issues should have a stronger impact on citizens than in the case of domestic politics (Norris, 2000). According to Zaller's (1992) two-sided information flow hypothesis, one condition for this interrelation is, of course, that citizens are exposed to media coverage with a consistent evaluative (i.e., predominantly positive or predominantly negative) direction to a considerable degree (also see de Vreese & Boomgarden, 2006). Thus, this section of the paper deals with two aspects: First, are voters really aware of media coverage on EP elections? And second, what is the effect of media coverage on political orientations and behavior?

Awareness of Media Coverage on EP Elections

Although there are concerns about the small amount of media coverage on the EU as well as on EP elections, empirical studies show that voters are reached by this media reporting. This was especially true for the first direct election in 1979, where all in all the hope was fulfilled that "European awareness would spread beyond the confines of cosmopolitan elites into the ranks of mass public" (Blumler, 1979, p. 508). The most important source of information was television; between 44 (Northern Ireland) and 77% of the European citizens (Germany) were exposed to a TV program about the election (Thoveron, 1983). Men were across the board more exposed to TV news than women, older voters more than younger voters, and members of upper social classes more than workers (Cayrol, 1983). In contrast, exposure to newspaper reports on the EP elections occurred less frequently and varied from 24% (Belgium) to 48% (Germany; see Thoveron, 1983).

Ten years later, exposure to the EP election campaign had decreased in most of the member states (Cayrol, 1991). The lowest exposure rate in the context of the 1989 EP election campaign was measured in Belgium (13% with "regular exposure"), where in addition the decrease of reported contact with televised campaign information was the steepest (minus 16 percentage points). In contrast, in Germany exposure was higher than in all other countries (50%) and had increased substantially during the last decade (plus 14 percentage points). Nevertheless, TV was still the most important information source in all countries (Cayrol, 1991, p. 21). Once again, the socio-political profile of campaign awareness observed in 1979 reappeared in almost all states (Cayrol, 1991, p. 22; Scherer, 1995; Schulz & Blumler, 1994).

In 2004, campaign awareness had increased again with 89% of the citizens in both the old and the new EU member states reporting that they heard things concerning the electoral campaign on television or on the radio. Sixty-five percent (67% in the old and 57% in the new EU countries) read about the electoral campaign in the newspapers (European Commission, 2004, p. 30). The exposure to press reports on the election varied substantially among countries: While in Austria, Ireland, Luxembourg, and Finland between 80 and 90% of the people had read about the upcoming event in the newspaper, this share was below 50% in Portugal, Poland, and Greece (European Commission, 2004). As in former studies, the voter's media exposure was related to his or her social background. In general, male, middle-aged, and highly educated voters, residents of metropolitan areas as well as white collar workers showed the highest awareness of press reports on the EP election (European Commission, 2004). In addition, a German study showed that the Internet was not an important source of information. Whereas 93% were exposed to TV reports and 83% read in the newspaper about the EP election campaign, only 11% received information from the Internet (Wüst & Roth, 2005). However, data from Spain indicated that merely being exposed to information does not necessarily mean that one has acquired knowledge on the subject and felt well informed about the EU and the upcoming election; 42% of the citizens in 1999 and 62% in 2004 felt they were little or not at all informed about EU issues (Berganza & Beroiz, 2006).

Effects of Media Coverage on EP Elections

The possible effects of media coverage on voters are manifold. On the one hand, there are possible effects on political cognitions, political attitudes, and political behavior. On the other hand, information transmitted by the media can have a mobilizing, reinforcing, or converting effect on political orientations (see, e.g., Lazarsfeld, Berelson, & Gaudet, 1944). Especially because the coverage of EP election by TV, press, radio, and recently also the Internet does not focus solely on the same topic (such as the election itself), but refers to more general European issues as well as to domestic policies, possible media effects can vary in direction and magnitude. In addition, it is hard to separate media effects from the impact of other campaign messages like those from the political parties and their candidates, associations, churches, public opinion research institutes, and interpersonal communication between voters.

So far, research on the impact of media coverage of EP elections has addressed only a few aspects of this "network of effects." Most of the studies concentrated on the relationship between media coverage, respective media reception, and turnout. Blumler (1983a) showed for the first direct EP election that campaign exposure had a significant positive impact on turnout in almost all countries—especially for those voters who were very interested in the campaign (Blumler, 1983a). A closer look at the impact of campaign exposure made clear that the most important force was television. Exposure to newspapers was only relevant in Denmark (Blumler, 1983a). However, Schönbach (1983a) found only weak effects of media reception on turnout in Germany. Using a panel survey, the only relevant effect he reported was that voters with low campaign interest were more likely to vote if they frequently read press reports in their local newspaper. In contrast, there was no impact of media reception on already involved voters. In addition, exposure to TV or weekly journals did not have any effects. For the 1989 EP election Cayrol (1991) found that nonvoters were exposed to campaign information provided by press and TV to a much smaller degree than voters. Further, abstainers felt that television allocated "too much time" to the EP campaign and that the coverage did not show "where my party stands" to any great extent. In addition, the content and the format of the TV reports were not very appealing: About one fifth of both voters and nonvoters evaluated the coverage as "boring." For the 1999 EP election, Banducci and Semetko (2003) reported a low positive correlation between the visibility of the EP election campaign in the media and turnout at the aggregate level. However, Schönbach and Lauf (2002) found little evidence that television reporting helped improve turnout by "trapping," especially citizens with low political interest while they watched TV. They found that it was more newspapers and interpersonal conversation which influenced less involved citizens to turn out and vote. For the 2004 EP elections, Weßels (2005) as well as the European Commission (2004) showed that media reception was strongly correlated with turnout. The difference in turnout between citizens who had contact with mass media and those who did not was an average 18 percentage points (European Commission, 2004). Weßels (2005) showed using a different analysis that this difference was much larger for citizens from new EU member states than for citizens from old EU countries (34 vs. 20 percentage points). For France, Gerstlé, Magni-Berton, and Pier (2006) found that low media consumption and the perception that the media had paid too little attention to the EU were very important determinants of abstention.[5] These results point in one direction: The more effort was put into EP election campaigns and the more visible the upcoming election was in the media, the more citizens were reached by the campaign and willing to participate in the election (also see Banducci & Semetko, 2003; Blondel, Sinnott, & Svensson, 1998; Tenscher, 2005). In contrast to this finding, results from a local German study on the 2004 EP election indicated that the consumption of mass media did not help citizens to reduce their uncertainties about their participation and their voting decision (Schneider & Rössler, 2005). In line with the work of McGraw, Hasecke, and Conger (2003), Schneider and Rössler (2005) argued that a high level of information does not automatically increase the level of certainty.

Regarding the relationship between consumption of media reports related to EP elections and political cognitions and attitudes, the number of empirical studies is likewise very small. This is astonishing because recent research on general attitudes toward the EU, specific policy fields of the EU, or EU-related events, such as the introduction of the Euro or the discussion about the European Constitutional Treaty, considered the impact of political communication (e.g., Brettschneider, Maier, & Maier, 2003; Dalton & Duvall, 1986; de Vreese & Boomgarden, 2006; Maier, Brettschneider, & Maier, 2003; Norris, 2000; Peter, 2003; Semetko, van der Brug, & Valkenburg, 2003). Schönbach's (1983b) analysis of the 1979 EP election showed that British, Dutch, and German voters significantly increased their knowledge during the campaign (see also Schönbach, 1983a). However, the impact of mass media on knowledge was in general low. In addition, no overall pattern emerged (Schönbach, 1983b): In the Netherlands, television was more important than press reports. In Germany, the opposite was the case. Additional analyses demonstrated that the impact of media on political cognitions depended rather on the awareness of the voters than on the type of media which was used (Schönbach, 1983a). In the UK both factors were equally important. In contrast to this, Blumler (1983a) demonstrated that in almost all analyzed countries, the level of issue awareness was significantly influenced by the reception of mass media. Generally speaking, television had the most important impact. Exposure to radio made a difference for issue awareness in France and Ireland; an effect of newspaper reading occurred only in Germany. Regarding the impact of media information provided during an EP election campaign on political attitudes, Schönbach (1983a) found that, on the one hand, the support for an increasingly vertical integration in Germany did not change substantially. On the other hand, the preferred speed of integration was higher at the end of the campaign than at the beginning. The reception of television as well as of newspapers led all in all to significantly more positive attitudes toward EU integration.

SUMMARY AND DISCUSSION

"Studies of political phenomena and in particular those of the electoral process cannot ignore communication" (Cayrol, 1991, p. 17). This is especially true for EP elections and EU referenda where the mass media—television, the press, radio, and most recently the Internet—are suspected of having a much higher influence on voters' cognitions and attitudes as well as on their political behavior than in national elections. To uncover this relationship social science as well as communication research has to focus on two aspects: First, it seems to be necessary to close the gap of structured knowledge on the media's coverage of EP elections. Second, voters' reception of media coverage and their individual belief systems need to be systematically linked.

Concerning the first aspect, the most seminal insights come from comparative studies on the 1979, the 1999, and the 2004 EP elections; the latter provide data for longitudinal analyses. In addition, a number of national studies supply more detailed information on country-specific aspects of the media coverage of EP elections. Although the amount of media coverage on EP elections differs substantially between the EU member states, in general media attention is much lower for EP than for national "first-order" elections (e.g., de Vreese, 2001a; de Vreese, Lauf, & Peter, 2007). In addition, EP elections get even less media coverage than other major EU events like the EU-summits which take place twice a year (de Vreese, 2001b). Some scholars provide evidence that, especially in the old member states, the amount of media coverage has decreased since 1979. This is, of course, quite astonishing considering the fact that the power of the EP has significantly increased during the last decades. In addition, media reports on EP elections predominantly address domestic issues, show and quote domestic actors, and take place at domestic locations; only in a few countries do journalists make notable efforts to convey to citizens an understanding of the EU and its institutions. If the EU, its institutions, representatives, policies, or future goals are the subject of discussion, the tone of the coverage tends to be negative. Furthermore, there are major differences in the amount, the reflectance, the Europeanness, and the tone of the coverage between public and private TV channels. The all in all more appropriate work of public TV stations points in the direction that they generally seem to understand the coverage of EP elections as a feature of their informational duty. Still, there are some serious doubts whether media coverage of the EP elections enabled voters to make an informed decision about the future of Europe.

Some authors conclude that the well-known democratic deficit of the EU, reflected by a lack of popular support for the idea of European integration as well as for the EU institutions, critical perceptions of the legitimacy of the EU, and low levels of voter participation (e.g., Eichenberg & Dalton, 1993), is also a communication deficit: "According to this view, EU institutions have been unsuccessful in shaping European identity and promoting the connection between citizens and EU institutions via the media" (de Vreese et al., 2006, p. 479). This is especially true for the development of a European public sphere, which was already expected to happen after the first direct election in 1979 (Blumler, 1979). A European public sphere, which means a common public debate on a common European news agenda, requires corresponding media coverage in member countries with a shared point of reference, a common discourse which frames particular issues as mutual European problems (Risse & Van de Steeg, 2003; see also Schlesinger, 1995), as well as news on European issues which have "to become a significant part of the every-day news-consuming habits of European audiences, [and] entail that those living within the EU have begun to think of their citizenship, in part at least, as transcending the level of the member nation-states" (Schlesinger & Kevin, 2000, p. 228). The weakness of the media's EU and EP election coverage cannot be exclusively explained by journalistic criteria of news selection or the general conditions of how the media work. At least in part, the media's agenda is not independent from the political agenda, which is strongly influenced by parties and politicians. The latter apparently still do not take EP elections seriously, as shown, for example, by the content of campaign advertisements, which are dominated by domestic issues; and in addition there are the deplorable attempts to create one European campaign instead of multiple national election campaigns. Therefore, EP election campaigns are not only second-order elections for the media but also for politicians. For most of the latter, European elections are, in other words, "as exciting as kissing your sister" as the Swedish Prime Minister Göran Persson pointed out in the context of the 2004 EP election (Nord & Strömbäck, 2006, p. 191).

In sum, research focusing on media coverage seems to be a good way of approaching the issues, especially when we consider the fact that Blumler's (1983b) comprehensive comparative approach was revived for the 1999 and 2004 EP elections. Obviously, a series of content analyses, which enables the longitudinal and comparative analysis of media coverage of EP elections, is highly valuable for the scientific community and hopefully path-breaking for the development of research in this field. Of course, there is still room for improvement. First, only the most important public and private TV stations as well as the major quality newspapers and tabloids have been content analyzed so far. For television this might be an appropriate strategy. For the press, this strategy might be suboptimal, because it excludes local newspapers which probably are the most important type of newspaper in all European countries. In addition, in order to be able to make a reliable statement about the general media tenor in a country, it would be desirable to have a broader database to avoid overestimating particular cases and variations. Furthermore, analysis of communication through the Internet should be given more attention. For example, Kevin (2001) has already stated that Internet versions of media outlets provide the unique opportunity to follow links to previous reports and other material concerning facts, events, and actors involved in the process of European integration and the election campaign; at the same time it is less restricted to the national level. Second, the time period covered in these studies is very short. To map the dynamics of media coverage on EP elections, a significant extension to, say the last four weeks of the campaign is desirable. Third, to explain cross-national differences of the amount, the content, and the tone of media coverage, contextual information (e.g., the political system, the voting system, the media system, the general public's opinion on the EU, elite public opinion, relevant political or economic events) seems to be very important. Recently, de Vreese (2003) added some of these aspects to the data of content analyses and began to take into account contextual variables by analyzing cross-country differences in media coverage. But to be able to value journalistic efforts, to add a European perspective to the media agenda which might not become obvious in a merely quantitative study, it might be necessary to combine quantitative and qualitative analyses (as demonstrated by Kevin, 2001).

Concerning media reception and media effects, only a few studies exist. Most of them provide information on voters' awareness of EP elections and the sources of information they use. The main results are that voters have contact with media reports on EP elections—especially with those provided by TV. As for the media coverage, huge cross-national differences exist for the level of media reception, too. In terms of effects, some studies analyze associations between media awareness and participation in EP elections. In general, the finding is a weak but positive relationship. In addition, a couple of studies indicate that voters learn much about European issues in the course of an EP election campaign. In contrast, empirical work on the impact of election coverage on political attitudes as well as on voting behavior has curiosity value with results that can hardly be generalized.

In sum, the previous research on media effects leaves more questions than answers. Several strategies appear useful to close this gap. First, analyses at the aggregate level should be considered more closely. There are two ways to realize this: On the one hand, there are still deficits in connecting the media's agenda with the agenda of political parties. On the other hand, statistical analyses of the relationship between the different aspects of media coverage captured in comparative media content analyses (i.e., the amount of coverage, different dimensions of content, and the tone of the coverage for different TV stations, newspapers, radio stations, and websites) and different aspects of public opinion and electoral behavior would be helpful to identify those variables which are relevant in explaining cross-national differences in, for example, turnout. If, in addition, these associations are controlled for other relevant explanatory variables, we could move forward in the direction of a macro-level theory of media influence on public attitudes and collective behavior in the context of EP elections. Of course, aggregate level data is connected with a specific problem in statistical inference: Statistical associations between media coverage, public opinion, and electoral behavior on the aggregate level are not a sufficient indicator for an effect of mass media on individual political attitudes and political behavior. Drawing such conclusions might be an ecological fallacy (e.g., King, 1997). As a consequence, to identify individual level associations (and to safeguard macro theories at the micro level) we need data on the individual level. Thus, a second promising strategy would be to link survey data with content analyses. This, of course, requires measures of media exposure in public opinion polls. The more precise these measures are (i.e., distinguish between the frequency of exposure to different TV stations, newspapers, etc.), the more precisely we can determine for each individual what the amount, the content, and the tone of the received media information was, and the more reliable will be the estimation of media effects on attitudes and behavior. Of course, panel data is almost always more valuable than cross-sectional data because it spares us the classic "chicken-and-egg" question whether media coverage or public opinion comes first. Third, strictly speaking, panel and especially cross-sectional data cannot prove causal relationships. To be absolutely sure, we need data from experimental designs. In this context, not only laboratory experiments will be useful but also online experiments.

As de Vreese (2001b, p. 301) pointed out, the EU, especially when it comes to elections, is a communicative challenge for political actors as well as the mass media. Politicians, who seek support for the European political system and for their decisions, have to "offer information about European integration in a manner that fits the format of important information sources such as television news" (see also Anderson & McLeod, 2004). The media is invoked "to report adequately about complex political and economic matters that rank among the most significant changes in Europe since World War II." The results so far are rather disappointing: On the one hand, public support for the EU is at best lukewarm, the turnout rates at EP elections are declining, the "permissive consensus" (Lindberg & Scheingold, 1970) between citizens and elites (who themselves give the impression that Europe is of minor importance) about Project Europe seems to be lost. On the other hand, Europe in general does not get a whole lot of media attention (e.g., de Vreese, 2001b; Norris, 2000). Citizens' contemptuousness seems to be a consistent consequence (Norris, 2000, p. 203):

> European citizens cannot be expected to care much about European elections, to feel connected to MEPs, or to know much about their rights within the EU if there is minimal news coverage of the European Parliament debates in Strasbourg, if major initiatives concerning aid for the Balkans, monetary union, and employment programs go unreported in the press, and if the coverage that is widely available is generally hostile towards European Community institutions and policies.

Even though this interrelation between media coverage and public opinion about Europe seems to be likely, we unfortunately still do not know for sure if it is true. To answer this important question, we need more structured, cross-nationally, and longitudinally comparable data about the media coverage of the EU and especially of EP elections, which can be linked to survey and experimental data. Of course, some efforts have been made during the last years. But a long road still lies ahead.

NOTES

1. Holtz-Bacha (2005, p. 7) noted in her summary on mass media and EP elections from a German perspective that the number of member states with compulsory voting has declined since 1979. She argued that *ceteris paribus* the abolishment of this law would have had a negative effect on the overall turnout rate anyway.

2. With the launch of the Irish private channel TV 3 in 1998 almost all European countries had dualized their broadcasting systems, with the exception of Switzerland where no private full-service stations exist but only private special interest programs (e.g., news, music, sports; see IP, 2005) and Luxembourg which has traditionally had only private television.

3. In the analysis of television news Luxembourg had to be excluded due to technical problems (De Vreese, Lauf, & Peter, 2007, note 2).

4. Outside Europe, the media coverage of the 2004 EP election was almost nonexistent (Williams & Kaid, 2006).

5. In addition, there was also a small but significant negative effect of media consumption on vote for a protest party (Gerstlé, Magni-Berton, & Piar, 2006, p. 343).

REFERENCES

Anderson, P., & McLeod, A. (2004). The great non-communicator. The mass communication deficit of the European parliament and its press directorate. *Journal of Common Market Studies, 5,* 897–917.

Banducci, S., & Semetko, H. (2003). Media and mobilization in the 1999 European parliamentary election. In M. Bond (Ed.), *Europe, parliament and the media* (pp. 189–203). London: The Federal Trust for Education & Research.

Berganza, R., & Beroiz, J. (2006). The influence of the March 11th Madrid bombings on the 2004 European campaign in Spain: An analysis of television news. In M. Maier & J. Tenscher (Eds.), *Campaigning in Europe—Campaigning for Europe: Political parties, campaigns, mass media and the European parliament elections 2004* (pp. 261–275). Münster: Lit.

Blondel, J., Sinnott, R., & Svensson, P. (1998). *People and parliament in the European Union: Participation, democracy, and legitimacy.* Oxford: Clarendon Press.

Blumler, J. G. (1979). Communication in the European elections: The case of British broadcasting. *Government and Opposition, 14,* 508–530.

Blumler, J. G. (1983a). Communication and turnout. In J. G. Blumler (Ed.), *Communicating to voters: Television in the first European parliamentary elections* (pp. 181–209). London: Sage.

Blumler, J. G. (Ed.). (1983b). *Communicating to voters: Television in the first European parliamentary elections.* London: Sage.

Blumler, J. G., & Thoveron, G. (1983). Analysing a unique election: Themes and concepts. In J. G. Blumler (Ed.), *Communicating to voters: Television in the first European parliamentary elections* (pp. 3–24). London: Sage.

Brants, K. (1998). Who's afraid of infotainment. *European Journal of Communication, 3,* 315–335.

Brants, K., & de Bens, E. (2000). The status of TV broadcasting in Europe. In J. Wieten, G. Murdock, & P. Dahlgren (Eds.), *Television across Europe: A comparative introduction* (pp. 7–22). Newbury Park: Sage.

Brettschneider, F., Maier, M., & Maier, J. (2003). From D-Mark to Euro: The impact of mass media on public opinion Germany. *German Politics, 12,* 45-64.

Brettschneider, F., & Rettich, M. (2005). Europa—(k)ein Thema für die Medien [Europe—no theme for the media]. In J. Tenscher (Ed.), *Wahl-Kampf um Europa: Analysen aus Anlass der Wahlen zum Europäischen Parliament 2004* [Election campaign in Europe: Analysis of the Vote for the European Parliament 2004] (pp. 136–156). Wiesbaden: Verlag für Sozialwissenschaften.

Bundesverband Deutscher Zeitungsverleger (BDZV). (2004). *BDZV-Jahrespressekonferenz 2004: Die wichtigsten Zahlen auf einen Blick* [BDZV-Annual Press Conference 2004. The most important things in one look]. Berlin.

Cayrol, R. (1983). Media use and campaign evaluations: Social and political stratification of the European electorate. In J. G. Blumler (Ed.), *Communicating to voters. Television in the first European parliamentary elections* (pp. 163–180). London: Sage.

Cayrol, R. (1991). European elections and the pre-electoral period: Media use and campaign evaluations. *European Journal of Political Research, 19,* 17–29.

Committee of Ministers (1999). *Recommendation No. R (99) 15 of the Committee of Ministers to member States on measures concerning media coverage of election campaigns.*

Dalton, R. J., & Duvall, R. (1986). The political environment and foreign policy opinions: British attitudes towards European integration 1972–79. *British Journal of Political Science, 16,* 113–134.

Demertzis, N. (2006). Europe on the agenda? The Greek case. In M. Maier & J. Tenscher (Eds.), *Campaigning in Europe— Campaigning for Europe: Political parties, campaigns, mass media and the European parliament elections 2004* (pp. 277–293). Münster: Lit.

de Vreese, C. H. (2001a). Election coverage. New directions for public broadcasting. The Netherlands and beyond. *European Journal of Communication, 16,* 155–180.

de Vreese, C. H. (2001b). Europe in the news: A cross-national comparative study of the news coverage of the key EU events. *European Union Politics, 2,* 283–307.

de Vreese, C. H. (2003). Television reporting of second-order elections. *Journalism Studies, 4,* 183–198.

de Vreese, C. H., Banducci, S. A., Semetko, H. A., & Boomgaarden, H. G. (2006). The news coverage of the 2004 European parliamentary election campaign in 24 countries. *European Union Politics, 7,* 477–504.

de Vreese, C. H., & Boomgaarden, H. G. (2006). Media effects on public opinion about the enlargement of the European Union. *Journal of Common Market Studies, 44,* 419–436.

de Vreese, C. H., Lauf, E., & Peter, J. (2007). The media and European parliament elections: Second-rate coverage of a second-order event? To be published in W. van der Brug & C. van der Eijk (Eds.), *European elections and domestic politics. Lessons from the past and scenarios for the future.*

Eichenberg, R. C., & Dalton, R. J. (1993). Europeans and the European community: The dynamics of public support for European integration. *International Organization, 47,* 507–534.

European Commission. (2004). *Flash Eurobarometer 162: Post European Elections 2004 Survey–Analytical Report.* Retrieved January 29, 2007, from http://ec.europa.eu/public_opinion/flash/FL162en.pdf.

European Parliament. (2004). *Citizens—Go to the polls!* Retrieved February 4, 2004, from http://www.europarl.europa.eu/highlights/en/101.html

Galtung, J., & Ruge, M. H. (1965). The structure of foreign news. The Congo, Cuba and Cyprus crises in four Norwegian newspapers. *Journals of Peace Research, 2,* 64–91.

Gerstlé, J., Magni-Berton, R., & Piar, C. (2006). Media coverage and voting in the European parliamentary election in France 2004. In M. Maier & J. Tenscher (Eds.), *Campaigning in Europe—Campaigning for Europe: Political parties, campaigns, mass media and the European parliament elections 2004* (pp. 339–352). Münster: Lit.

Holtz-Bacha, C. (2005). Massenmedien und Europawahlen: Low key campaigns—Low key response [Mass media and European elections: Low key campaigns—low key response]. In C. Holtz-Bacha (Ed.), *Europawahl 2004. Die Massenmedien im Europawahlkampf* [European Election 2004: The mass media in the European campaign] (pp. 7–34). Wiesbaden: Verlag für Sozialwissenschaften.

Holtz-Bacha, C., & Norris, P. (2001). To entertain, inform, and educate: Still the role of public television. *Political Communication, 18,* 123–140.

IP International Marketing Committee. (2005). *Television 2005: International key facts.* Paris: IP Network.

Kaid, L. L., Postelnicu, M., Landreville, K., Williams, A. P., Hostrup-Larsen, C., Urriste, S., Fernandes, J., Yun, H.-J., & Bagley, D. (2005). Kampagnen im neuen Europa: Die Darstellung der Europawahl 2004 in den Medien [Campaigning in the new Europe: The presentation of the 2004 European election in the media]. In C. Holtz-Bacha (Ed.), *Europawahl 2004: Die Massenmedien im Europawahlkampf* [European Election 2004: The mass media in the European campaign] (pp. 228–251). Wiesbaden: Verlag für Sozialwissenschaften.

Kelly, M., & Siune, K. (1983). Television campaign structures. In J. G. Blumler (Ed.), *Communicating to voters: Television in the first European parliamentary elections* (pp. 41–64). London: Sage.

Kevin, D. (2001). Coverage of the European parliament elections of 1999: National public spheres and European debates. *Javnost—The Public, 8,* 21–38.

Kevin, D. (2003). *Europe in the media. A comparison of reporting, representation, and rhetoric in national media systems in Europe.* Mahwah, NJ: Erlbaum.

King, G. (1997). *A solution to the ecological inference problem: Reconstructing individual behavior from aggregate data.* Princeton, NJ: Princeton University Press.

Kopáček, P. (2006). More or less Europe: Media coverage of European parliamentary elections in the Czech Republic. In M. Maier & J. Tenscher (Eds.), *Campaigning in Europe—Campaigning for Europe: Political parties, campaigns, mass media and the European parliament elections 2004* (pp. 219–236). Münster: Lit.

Lauf, E. (2001). Research note. The vanishing young reader: Sociodemographic determinants of newspaper use as a source of political information in Europe 1980–98. *European Journal of Communication, 16,* 233–243.

Lauf, E., & Peter, J. (2004). EU-Repräsentanten in Fernsehnachrichten: Eine Analyse ihrer Präsenz in 13 EU-Mitgliedsstaaten vor der Europawahl 1999 [EU-Representation in television news: An analysis of presence in 13 EU Member States in the 1999 European election]. In L. M. Hagen (Ed.), *Europäische Union und mediale Öffentlichkeit. Theoretische Perspektiven und empirische Befunde zur Rolle der Medien im europäischen Einigungsprozess* [The European Union and media openness: Theoretical perspectives and empirical Findings on the role of the media in European Unification Process] (pp. 162–177), Köln: Halem.

Lazarsfeld, P. F., Berelson, B., & Gaudet, H. (1944). *The people's choice: How the voter makes up his mind in a presidential campaign.* New York: Duell, Sloan, and Pearce.

Leroy, P., & Siune, K. (1994). The role of television in European elections: The cases of Belgium and Denmark. *European Journal of Communication, 9,* 47–69.

Lindberg, L. N., & Scheingold, S. A. (1970). *Europe's would-be polity: Patterns of change in the European Community.* Englewood Cliffs: Prentice-Hall.

Maier, J., Brettschneider, F., & Maier, M. (2003). Medienberichterstattung, Mediennutzung und die Bevölkerungseinstellungen zum Euro in Ost- und Westdeutschland [Media coverage, media use and public attitudes toward the Euro in East and West Germany]. In F. Brettschneider, J. W. van Deth, & E. Roller (Eds.), *Europäische Integration in der öffentlichen Meinung* [European integration in public opinion] (pp. 213–233). Opladen: Leske & Budrich.

Maier, M. (2002). *Zur Konvergenz des Fernsehens in Deutschland: Ergebnisse qualitativer und repräsentativer Zuschauerbefragungen* [On convergence in German television: Discussion of qualitative and representative audience questions]. Konstanz: UVK.

Maier, M. (2003). Nachrichtenfaktoren: Stand der Forschung [News factors: Conditions of the research]. In G. Ruhrmann, J. Woelke, M. Maier, & N. Diehlmann (Eds.), *Der Wert von Nachrichten im deutschen Fernsehen* [The Importance of news in German television] (pp. 27–50). Opladen: Leske & Budrich.

Maier, M., & Tenscher, J. (Eds.). (2006). *Campaigning in Europe—Campaigning for Europe: Political parties, campaigns, mass media and the European parliament elections 2004.* Münster: Lit.

Mather, J. (2001). The United Kingdom. In J. Lodge (Ed.), *The 1999 elections to the European parliament* (pp. 214–228). New York: Palgrave.

McGraw, K. M., Hasecke, E., & Conger, K. (2003). Ambivalence, uncertainty, and processes of candidate evaluation. *Political Psychology, 24,* 421–448.

McQuail, D. (2004). Introduction. In M. Kelly, G. Mazzoleni, & D. McQuail (Eds.), *The media in Europe: The euromedia handbook* (pp. 1–3). London: Sage.

Medien Tenor. (2006). Business as usual: The media image of the EU in Germany and abroad, 2003–2005. *Media Tenor Journal, 1,* 10–13.

Nehlig, S. (2005). Berichterstattung über den Europawahlkampf 2004 im deutsch-englischen Vergleich [Reporting on the 2004 European campaign in German-English Comparison]. In C. Holtz-Bacha (Ed.), *Europawahl 2004. Die Massenmedien im Europawahlkampf* [European Election 2004: The mass media in the European campaign] (pp. 197–277). Wiesbaden: Verlag für Sozialwissenschaften.

Nord, L. W., & Strömbäck, J. (2006). Game is the name of the frame: European parliamentary elections in Swedish Media 1995-2004. In M. Maier & J. Tenscher (Eds.), *Campaigning in Europe—Campaigning for Europe: Political parties, campaigns, mass media and the European parliament elections 2004* (pp. 191–205). Münster: Lit.

Norris, P. (2000). *A virtuous circle: Political communication in post-industrial societies.* New York: Cambridge University Press.

Page, B. I., & Shapiro, R. Y. (1992). *The rational public: Fifty years of trends in American policy preferences.* Chicago: Chicago University Press.

Paterson, W. E., & Green, S. (2001). Germany. In J. Lodge (Ed.), *The 1999 elections to the European parliament* (pp. 72–88). New York: Palgrave.

Paterson, W. E., Lees, C., & Green, S. (1996). The Federal Republic of Germany. In J. Lodge (Ed.), *The 1994 elections of the European parliament* (pp. 66–83). London: Pinter.

Peter, J. (2003). Konsonanz 30 Jahre später: Eine international vergleichende Studie zum Einfluss konsonanter Berichterstattung auf Meinungen zur europäischen Integration [Consistency 30 years later: An international comparitive study of the influence of consistent reporting and opinons about European integration]. *Publizistik, 48,* 190–208.

Peter, J., & de Vreese, C. H. (2004). In search of Europe: A cross-national comparative study of the European Union in national television news. *Harvard Journal of Press/Politics, 4,* 3–24.

Peter, J., Lauf, E., & Semetko, H. (2004). Television coverage of the 1999 European parliamentary elections. *Political Communication, 21,* 415–433.

Pfetsch, B. (1996). Convergence though privatization? Changing media environments and televised politics in Germany. *European Journal of Communication, 8,* 427–451.

Reif, K., & Schmitt, H. (1980). Nine second-order national elections: A conceptual framework for the analysis of European election results. *European Journal of Political Research, 8,* 3–44.

Reif, K. (1997). European elections as member state second-order elections revisited. *European Journal of Political Research, 31,* 115–124.

Reiser, S. (1994). *Parteienkampagne und Medienberichterstattung im Europa-Wahlkampf 1989: Eine Untersuchung zu Dependenz und Autonomieverlust im Verhältnis von Massenmedien und Politik* [Party campaigns and media reporting in the 1989 European elections: An investigation of the dependence and loss of autonomy in the relationship between mass media and politics]. Konstanz: UVK.

Risse, T., & Van de Steeg, M. (2003). An emerging European public sphere? Empirical evidence and theoretical clarifications. Unpublished paper. Retrieved March 6, 2007, from http://web.fu-berlin.de/atasp/texte/030624_europeanpublicsphere.pdf.

Schatz, H., Immer, N., & Marcinkowski, F. (1989). Der Vielfalt eine Chance? [A chance for variety?] *Rundfunk und Fernsehen, 37,* 5-24.

Scherer, H. (1995). Kommunikationskanäle der Europawahl 1989. Eine international vergleichende Studie [Communication channels in the 1989 European election: An international comparative study]. In L. Erbring (Ed.), *Kommunikationsraum Europa* [European Communication area] (pp. 203–222). Konstanz: UVK/Oelschläger.

Schlesinger, P. (1995). Europeanisation and the media: National identity and the public sphere. *Arena Working Paper, 7,* 1–33.

Schlesinger, P., & Kevin, D. (2000). Can the European Union become a sphere of publics? In E. O. Eriksen & J. E. Fossum (Eds.), *Democracy in the European Union: Integration though deliberation* (pp. 206–229). London: Routledge.

Schimmelfennig, F., & Rittberger, B. (2005). Theories of European integration: Assumptions and hypotheses. In J. Richardson (Ed.), *European Union: Power and policy-making* (pp. 73–95). London: Routledge.

Schneider, D., & Rössler, P. (2005). Der unentschlossene Europawähler: Die Bedeutung von Mediennutzung und Erwartungen an den Wahlausgang für Unentschlossenheit oder Unsicherheit im individuellen Wahlentscheidungsprozess [The undecided European voter: The meaning of media use and expectations of the outcome for undecidedness or uncertainty in the individual election decision process]. In C. Holtz-Bacha (Ed.), *Europawahl 2004: Die Massenmedien im Europawahlkampf* [2004 European elections: The mass media in the European campaign] (pp. 270–306). Wiesbaden: Verlag für Sozialwissenschaften.

Schönbach, K. (1983a). *Das unterschätzte Medium: Politische Wirkungen von Presse und Fernsehen im Vergleich* [The underestimated medium: Comparison of the Importance of the press and television]. München: Saur.

Schönbach, K. (1983b). What and how voters learned. In J. G. Blumler (Ed.), *Communicating to voters: Television in the first European parliamentary elections* (pp. 299–318). London: Sage.

Schönbach, K., & Lauf, E. (2002). The trap effect of television and its competitors. *Communication Research, 5,* 564–583.

Schulz, W. (1976). *Die Konstruktion von Realität in den Nachrichtenmedien: Analyse der aktuellen Berichterstattung* [The construction of realiaty in the news media: Analyses of actual reporting]. Freiburg: Alber.

Schulz, W., & Blumler, J. G. (1994). Die Bedeutung der Kampagnen für das Europa-Engagement der Bürger: Eine Mehr-Ebenen-Analyse. [The meaning of the campaign for the European involvement of citizens: A multi-level analysis.] In. O. Niedermayer & H. Schmitt (Eds.), *Wahlen und Europäische Einigung* [Voters and the European ageement] (pp. 199–223). Opladen: Westdeutscher Verlag.

Semetko, H., van der Brug, W., & Valkenburg, P. (2003). The influence of political events on attitudes towards the European Union. *British Journal of Political Science, 33,* 621–634.

Simon, Á. (2006). Two Hungaries? European parliamentary elections and their media coverage in Hungary. In M. Maier & J. Tenscher (Eds.), *Campaigning in Europe—Campaigning for Europe: Political parties, campaigns, mass media and the European parliament Elections 2004* (pp. 237–250). Münster: Lit.

Siune, K. (1983). The campaigns on television: What was said and who said it. In J. G. Blumler (Ed.), *Communicating to voters. Television in the first European parliamentary elections* (pp. 223–240). London: Sage.

Siune, K., & Hultén, O. (1998): Does public broadcasting have a future. In D. McQuail & K. Siune (Eds.), *Media policy: Convergence, concentration and commerce* (pp. 23–37). London: Sage.

Steinbrecher, M., & Huber, S. (2006). European elections' turnout from 1979 to 2004. In M. Maier & J. Tenscher (Eds.), *Campaigning in Europe—Campaigning for Europe* (pp. 15–30). Münster: Lit.

Tenscher, J. (2005). Wahl-Kampf um Europa: Eine Einführung [Election campaign in Europe: An Introduction]. In J. Tenscher (Ed.), *Wahl-Kampf um Europa: Analysen aus der Wahlen zum Europäischen Parlament* [Election campaign in Europe: Analyses of the voting for European parliament] (pp. 7–28). Wiesbaden: Verlag für Sozialwissenschaften.

Thoveron, G. (1983). How European received the campaign: Similarities and differences of national response. In J. G. Blumler (Ed.), *Communicating to voters: Television in the first European parliamentary elections* (pp. 142–162). London: Sage.

van der Eijk, C. (2000). Why some people vote and others do not. In H. Agné, C. van der Eijk, B. Laffan, B. Lejon, P. Norris, H. Schmitt, & R. Sinnott (Eds.), *Citizen participation in European politics* (pp. 13–55). Stockholm: Elanders Gotab.

Weßels, B. (2005). Europawahlen: Wählermobilisierung und europäische Integration [European elections: Election mobilization and European integration]. In J. Tenscher (Ed.), *Wahl-Kampf um Europa: Analysen zum Anlass der Wahlen zum Europäischen Parlament 2004* [Campaigning for Europe: Analyses on the 2004 European Parliamentary elections] (pp. 86–104). Wiesbaden: Verlag für Sozialwissenschaften.

Wilke, J., & Reinemann, C. (2005). Auch in der Presse immer eine Nebenwahl? Die Berichterstattung über die Europawahlen 1979–2004 und die Bundestagswahlen 1980-2002 im Vergleich [Also a second-order election for the press? The coverage of the European election 1979 to 2004 and the national elections 1980 to 2002 in comparison]. In C. Holtz-Bacha (Ed.), *Europawahl 2004. Die Massenmedien im Europawahlkampf* [The 2004 European election: The mass media in the European election campaign] (pp. 153–173). Wiesbaden: Verlag für Sozialwissenschaften.

Williams, A. P., & Kaid, L. L. (2006). Media framing of the European parliamentary elections: A view from the United States. In M. Maier & J. Tenscher (Eds.), *Campaigning in Europe—Campaigning for Europe: Political parties, campaigns, mass media and the European parliament Elections 2004* (pp. 295–304). Münster: Lit.

Wüst, A., & Roth, D. (2005). Parteien, Programme und Wahlverhalten [Parties, party programs and voting behavior]. In J. Tenscher (Ed.), *Wahl-Kampf um Europa. Analysen zum Anlass der Wahlen zum Europäischen Parlament 2004* [Campaigning for Europe: Analyses on the 2004 European Parliamentary elections] (pp. 56–85). Wiesbaden: Verlag für Sozialwissenschaften.

Zaller, J. R. (1992). *The nature and origins of mass opinion.* New York: Cambridge University Press.

Zeh, R., & Holtz-Bacha, C. (2005). Die Europawahl in den Hauptabendnachrichten des Fernsehens [The coverage of the European election in the major TV newscasts]. In C. Holtz-Bacha (Ed.), *Europawahl 2004: Die Massenmedien im Europawahlkampf* [2004 European election: The mass media in the European campaign] (pp. 252–269). Wiesbaden: Verlag für Sozialwissenschaften.

26

Election News Coverage Around the World: A Comparative Perspective

Lynda Lee Kaid and Jesper Strömbäck

The preceding chapters provide compelling evidence that modern elections are indeed mediated events, experienced by politicians and parties and by their public audiences through a lens that reflects differences in political systems and media alignments around the world. In the initial framework chapter of this volume, we described the assumptions of the mediatization of politics. The analyses provided for each country discussed in the chapters that followed our framework establish clearly that these assumptions have generally been met for most of the countries covered. Mediated communication clearly dominates the channels of information and persuasion in these countries, and most exhibit media systems that are, at least in part, independent of government control. There is certainly no lack of evidence that the third phase of mediatization has arrived as most parties and candidates in most countries have not hesitated to adapt their campaign styles to *media logic*. How well this media logic has become internalized and integrated into the political systems is perhaps less clear in every situation and country. Nonetheless, we suggest that the trend is clearly in this direction, and thus, we use the elements of these assumptions in this concluding chapter to organize, illustrate, and compare news coverage of elections around the world.

THE DOMINANCE OF MEDIATED COMMUNICATION IN ELECTIONS

Every chapter about every country in this volume makes it clear that communication is a central and guiding element of the modern electoral process. No modern system of government can function without continuing and comprehensive means for transferring information to its publics. In modern democracies, mass media provide the mechanism for this transfer.

Certainly, our commitment to this aspect of the democratic process is based on the belief that access to fair and accurate information is an underpinning of the democratic process. Without the free flow of such information, citizens cannot assess their choices and make decisions that ensure the continuation of a free and open society.

In almost every case, our contributing authors suggest that it is television that is the dominant channel for commuication between government, candidates, and those whose votes and policy compliance they seek. Table 26.1 outlines the dominant media for election coverage in the chapters covered here. In almost all countries, television is the dominant medium, although more so in some countries than in others. For example, in Sweden newspapers remain very important, whereas in the United States, television is significantly more important than newspapers, particularly with respect to the influence over public opinion. There appears to be only one exception in Table 26.2, and that is South Africa, where radio penetration is still higher and more accessible than television.

MEDIA AND ELECTORAL SYSTEMS

The second aspect of our framework posits the importance of a media independent of government control. The intertwining of media and government is often complex, and there are many variations in this relationship among the countries in this volume.

Overall, throughout the world, the Freedom House (2007) in its annual ranking of press freedom in individual countries considers 38% of the countries in the world to have free press systems, including the United States, most of Western and Eastern Europe, Japan, Australia, and Israel. Another third (38%) have press systems that are ranked as "not free"; only Russia fits this list among the countries in this volume. Finally, about 30%, including Brazil, Bulgaria, Serbia, India, and Mexico, are considered to have "partly free" press sytems. These ratings are shown in

TABLE 26.1
Electoral and Media Systems

Country	(Direct) Presidential. Elections held	Electoral System *	Press Freedom**
United States	Yes	Majority vote	Free
Australia	No	Majority vote	Free
Brazil	Yes	Proportional representation	Partly Free
Britain	No	Majority vote	Free
Bulgaria	Yes	Proportional representation	Partly Free
Canada	No	Majority vote	Free
France	Yes	Majority vote	Free
Germany	No	Combination	Free
Greece	No	Proportional representation	Free
Hungary	No	Combinaton	Free
India	No	Combination	Partly Free
Israel	No	Proportional representation	Free
Italy	No	Proportional representation	Free
Japan	No	Combination	Free
Mexico	Yes	Combination	Partly Free
Netherlands	No	Proportional representation	Free
Poland	Yes	Proportional representation	Free
Russia	Yes	Combination	Not Free
Serbia	No	Proportional	Partly Free
South Africa	No	Proportional representation	Free
Spain	No	Proportional representation	Free
Sweden	No	Proportional	Free
European Union	No	Proportional	Free

* With respect to the lower house of parliament.
**Based on press ratings of Freedom House (2007)

Table 26.1 which also illustrates the type of electoral system in each country. This information on electoral system structures does not seem to suggest any relationship between political system structure and level of press freedom. Most countries, regardless of press freedom level, have proportional (or combination) electoral systems for voting, and in every case, except the United States, the political party is the major player in the national election system. About one-third of the countries directly elect a president; the remainder either have no president (relying solely on a prime minister in a parliamentary system) or the president is chosen by the national assembly.

The more direct relationship between electoral systems and media systems is discussed in many of the individual chapters. In almost every country similar historical patterns of media development can be seen. For instance, newspapers and other print media were originally the major mouthpieces of parties and governments, but as technology modernized and newspapers were supplanted by electronic media, newspaper influence has generally declined in election campaigns. Concurrently, there has been a decline in the ties between newspapers and political parties (Lange & Ward, 2004), often spurred by increasing commercialization within the media sphere. This is particularly true with regards to countries that belong to the liberal and the democratic corporatist models of media and politics, whereas countries that form part of the polarized pluralist model differ in the sense that the media in those countries are more subordinated to the party-political system (Hallin & Mancini, 2004).

Unquestionably, there is less and less direct involvement of government in the media's actual coverage patterns. As Table 26.2 indicates, however, there are still many attempts to insist on or to regulate "fair and balanced" treatment of political candidates or parties. These attempts take many forms. For instance, some countries (for example, Canada, Italy, Japan, South Africa) merely state in their constitutions or other regulatory edicts that coverage of candidates and parties should be fair, equitable, balanced, equal, or impartial. France, however, takes a much more deliberate approach, requiring precise balance in print and broadcast media coverage and engaging in elaborate monitoring activities to measure and report coverage allocation among parties. Spain requires neutral coverage of all parties and mandates that reporting on parties be in proportion to their vote totals in the previous election. However, Spain does not engage in meticulous monitoring of these requirements. Some countries, like Germany, also prohibit appearances by candidates on entertainment shows prior to elections. Thus, in Germany a candidate could not appear on an entertainment-oriented talk show, as Bill Clinton did in 1992 when he played his saxaphone on the Arsenio Hall show, or as John Edwards did, when he announced his formal candidacy for president on Comedy Central's *The Daily Show*.

At the far end of the regulatory spectrum is the situation in Russia. As Sarah Oates explains in chapter 22, the amount of detailed and stringent regulation of news coverage contained in the Russian media regulations create a quagmire for journalists, making it difficult to develop meaningful coverage strategies.

Another aspect of regulation of news coverage relates to the coverage of opinion polls. Again, there is substantial variation among countries. Some countries (the United States, Australia, Brazil, Britain, Bulgaria, India, Israel, Japan, the Netherlands, and Sweden) have no restrictions at all on the release of opinion polls in the media (see Table 26.2). A few countries do not prohibit the release of polling results but require that the media carefully disclose the methodology used in the poll (Germany, Serbia, Canada). However, many countries impose restrictions on publication of polling results. France, Greece, and Mexico require no poll reporting one week before the election, while Canada prohibits announcement of poll results on election day, Poland insists on no poll reports the day before the election, and Russia requires a 3-day moratorium on poll results before election day. More stringent is Italy's prohibition of poll announcements within 15 days of the election.

TABLE 26.2
Characteristics of Election Coverage

Country	Dominant medium	Regulation of election news coverage	Restrict polls	Type of coverage*
United States	TV	No	No	Horserace
Australia	TV	Yes	No	Horserace
Brazil	TV	Yes	No	Horserace/strategy
Britain	TV	Requires accuracy and balance	None on election day	Strategy
Bulgaria	TV	Requires equal treatment of cands. and parties	No	Mixture of issue and game frame
Canada	TV	Must be fair and equitable	Prohibited on election day; publishe method	Horserace
France	TV	Extreme balance requirements monitored	Yes	Strategy
Germany	TV	No appearance in entertainment shows	No but must specify representativeness	High percentage of strategy/game/horserace
Greece	TV	Yes; time allocated among parties	Banned one week before election	Candidate image more than issues
Hungary	TV	Carry on equal footing in the news	Polls forbidden 8 days before election	Not available
India	TV	Yes	No	Not available
Israel	TV	Prohibit election propaganda during last 60 days, except for time given party spots	No	Balance issue and game frames; game frame usually dominant
Italy	TV	Must have balanced coverage	No polls 15 days before election	Not available
Japan	TV	Directives call for impartiality; no side taking	No	Issues in newspapers; game frame and negativity in TV
Mexico	TV	No	Polls not published one week before election	Candidates; not game frame or issues
Netherlands	TV	No	No	Substantaive issues
Poland	TV	No	Election silence—no polls day before the election	Horse race (polls)
Russia	TV	Yes	Yes	Not available
Serbia	TV	Requires objective, fair, equal	Poll reports must give methods	Not available
South Africa	Radio	Yes; required to give equal treatment to parties	Polls cannot be published during last 6 weeks	Emphasis on polls and horserace
Spain	TV	Neutral coverage and reporting; proportional acc. to previous vote totals	Prohibited 5 days before election; provide methodological details	Mixed
Sweden	TV	Should be impartial on TV, but no detailed regulations.	No	Issues more than game frame in newspapers and public tv but game frame more in commercial tv and tabloids

*Interpret with caution; definitions and approaches vary.

MEDIA LOGIC AND ELECTION COVERAGE

The adoption of *media logic* in campaign coverage is also clear in most countries. Table 26.2 shows that almost all of the countries discussed in this volume have developed media coverage systems where "horserace" coverage is prominent or even dominant. This means that the news media have adopted coverage habits that favor reports of campaign strategy, polling, and "game frames" over analysis of substantive policy issues. Identified several decades ago as a feature of the U.S. system (chapters 2 and 3), the tendency to focus on who is ahead and who is behind, on poll results, and on the campaign itself, rather than on substantive issues has been described as typical in almost every electoral system where it has been investigated.

The fact that it has become more common for the media in different countries around the world to cover elections as if they are mainly a kind of horserace does not mean, however, that this tendency is equally strong across countries. Thus, a few exceptions to the dominance of the horserace coverage model can be found in the chapters in this volume, as shown in Table 26.2. For instance, the Netherlands has retained a concentration on issues in its news coverage of elections. Several countries illustrate a medium distinction in media logic characteristics. For instance, election coverage in newspapers in Sweden and Japan is characterized by, comparatively speaking, rather substantive issue coverage, whereas election coverage on television in these two countries is dominated by the "game frame" and horserace coverage. Bulgaria and Mexico report media coverage that is more oriented toward emphasizing the candidates' personalities than the horserace, although still at the expense of substantive issue coverage. In addition, most evidence suggests that although horserace coverage is common in all countries, it is more common in the United States than in most other countries (Strömbäck & Dimitrova, 2006; Strömbäck & Shehata, 2007; Strömbäck & Aalberg, 2008). This might, as suggested by chapter 1, be due to the commercial character of the U.S. media system in combination with the majoritarian electoral system which always produces clear winners and losers in each electoral district and each election.

Another aspect of media logic can sometimes be the tendency of the media to present politics and political leaders in a negative light. Some observers suggest that this is a natural outcome of the fact that journalists often perceive their role as one of a "watchdog" over government. Such a role carries an assumed obligation for the journalist to criticize and to investigate, to approach government and government figures from a skeptical viewpoint. This stance can lead to critical or negative coverage, although investigative journalism does not need to equal negative or critical news coverage. In many countries there is not yet sufficient empirical research on the content of election news coverage to identify definite trends. However, the focus on negative coverage is definitely obvious in the United States. In chapter 3 Stephen Farnsworth and Robert Lichter discuss this trend in negative coverage on network television news. Frank Esser and Katherina Hemmer (chapter 18) have also found this negativity trend to be characteristic of German press coverage, although they argue that the German media have often lagged behind in adopting a "watchdog" function over politics. Tamir Shaefer, Gabriel Weimann, and Yariv Tsfati (chapter 13) have also reported negative coverage of candidates and parties in Israel, totalling as much as 60% negative news in the 2003 election.

Bias in Election Coverage

The possibility that the media exhibit bias, particularly for or against political parties or party candidates, is an enduring and controversial concern about news coverage of elections. If voters must rely on the media for most of their information in making electoral choices, then the objectivity or impartiality of that information is an important presumption of democratic systems. This is particularly true in systems where internal pluralism is the rule (i.e., many viewpoints expressed within each medium), while it is less important in systems where external pluralism predominates (i.e., many different media expressing or giving voice to different viewpoints). Nevertheless, almost every election cycle in almost every country inevitably brings some accusations of partisan media bias, and the research in our volume does not attempt to report on or to adjudicate such speculation. Very few countries have sufficient empirical evidence on this question to come to any over-arching conclusions. At the same time, the distinction between partisan bias and structural bias is important to keep in mind. If the media in a particular country cover an election in a way that favors one or several parties over one or several other parties, it does not necessarily prove that the media is politically biased. It could also be due to the journalistic norms in combination with the particular circumstances of news production (Graber, 2006). Only if there is a systematic tendency for the media to favor or disfavor certain parties or politicians over several elections is there strong evidence suggesting partisan bias.

The distinction between partisan and structural bias notwithstanding, researchers in the United States have done more concentrated empirical work on the question of partisan bias than have scholars in probably any other country. The first empirical research studies on television news bias were done in the 1970s and generally concluded that there was little identifiable partisan bias in the coverage of national networks ABC, CBS, and NBC (Frank, 1973; Hofstetter, 1976). This is also the general direction of research findings across several media outlets and years outlined by Mira Sotirovic and Jack McLeod in chapter 2. However, looking only at national network news, Stephen Farnsworth and Robert Lichter (chapter 3) have identified coverage imbalances that favored Democratic candidates in several recent U.S. elections. They conclude: "In sum, a general pattern of negativism on network news has coincided with an intermittent tendency toward more favorable press for Democrats than Republicans. In four of the past nine elections for which exhaustive systematic content analysis data are available (1980, 1988, 1998, and 2000), both sides received mainly negative notices. In the other five (1984, 1992, 1994, 1996, and 2004), Democrats fared substantially better on the evening news programs than did Republicans" p. 53). The issue is controversial, though, illustrating both the difficulty of studying media bias and the suggestion in chapter 1, that the issue of media bias is likely to be more hotly debated in countries which form part of the liberal model, simply because partisan bias is not considered as legitimate in such countries.

Many developing democracies have had difficulties in breaking the hold of ruling governments on media outlets in situations where government control of the media went hand-in-hand with control of the national government. Sarah Oates (chapter 22) makes it clear that Russia's political system still suffers from extensive government domination that severely constrains, if not prohibits, objectivity during elections. Lars Willnat and Annette Aw (chapter 8) discovered that media coverage of elections in India is often biased toward the ruling party. Similar bias toward the ruling government have also been observed in Mexico (chapter 23): "All told, television coverage of campaigns has two faces. On the one hand, reporting is technically expert, serious, and at first glance non-partisan. On the other hand, the relationships between broadcasters and the government can produce biases that are not readily apparent in content analysis of campaign coverage." In South Africa (chapter 17) the national broadcasting system has come under fire for giving more media attention to the ruling party.

More severe problems have been identified in emerging democracies in East Europe. In chapter 21 Lilia Raycheva and Daniela Dimitrova express optimism that tendencies toward media bias in Bulgaria have decreased as the media and political system have developed and matured. However, serious problems remain: "It is interesting to note also that journalists admit that they may sometimes publish facts without verification, take payment for positive political coverage of a political party or candidate, or withhold pre-election information due to personal biases. As a result, Bulgarian political news coverage is sometimes inaccurate, politicized, and opinionated." Poland's problems may be similar but less severe. In Poland researchers report that content analyses of newspapers, magazines, and television news support "the claim that the mass media are in the main free and independent." Nonetheless, some bias was apparent, usually in favor of established parties: "The public broadcasters often did not accept the principles of objectivity, factuality, and impartiality. The presentations of parties and candidates were in many cases not neutral and balanced."

Effects of Media Coverage of Elections

Questions about the effects of media coverage of elections remain of great concern to scholars and political observers. If one accepts the underlying premise that the media in democratic societies should function as both objective conveyors of information to create an informed electorate and watchdogs of government to illuminate and deter corruption, then evaluation of these effects is a critical undertaking. While we would not suggest that definitive answers are available, in the United States such questions are routinely asked, and strong research traditions exist to attempt evaluations. There is strong evidence that American media are successful in setting the public's agenda about issues (McCombs, 2004) as well as in framing politics (Iyengar, 1991; Reese, Gandy & Grant, 2001), and that the media do succeed in transferring some political knowledge to citizens (Drew & Weaver, 2006; Norris, 2000).

The summaries by Mira Sotirovic and Jack McLeod in chapter 2 and Stephen Farnsworth and Robert Lichter in chapter 3 concur in this view of news media effectiveness in the United States. Sotirovic and McLeod conclude: "Almost 90% of the public in the last presidential election indicated that they feel they learned enough about the candidates and the issues to make informed choices. Despite all the popular and academic criticism of media performance and the low public esteem of press conduct in campaigns, both subjective estimates and evidence we presented in this chapter indicate that the coverage of campaigns contributes to learning." Elisabeth Gidengil is also optimistic about the results of news exposure in Canada, concluding in chapter 4 that news coverage may have strong learning effects on issues. In Israel, despite trends toward personalization and negativity, Tamir Shaefer, Gabriel Weimann, and Yariv Tsfati (chapter 13) report that several studies on the effectiveness of news media coverage on the vote have yielded support for agenda setting and priming effects, as well as intention to vote.

Scammell and Semetko also note some agenda-setting effects from news coverage in Britain (chapter 5) and to the mixed effects of exposure on knowledge gain. More interesting are the findings in Britain that favorable coverage of a party in the news media can translate into powerful support at the polls, whereas negative coverage has much less effect.

In Spain the extent of media exposure to information about the Madrid train bombings in 2004 has been traced directly to the likelihood of blaming the government for the attacks (chapter 11). In contrast, researchers in South Africa (chapter 17) document strong discrepencies between the issues covered by the media and the issue concerns of the public. They report findings that issues stressed by the media were of importance to only 2% of South Africa's voters.

Public vs. Commercial Television News

One difference between the United States news media coverage and that of many other countries is the significant role played by public television systems. In the United States, public television has very low viewership and thus plays a, relatively speaking, minor role in the news coverage of elections. Outside the United States public broadcasting has retained significance even where private commercial broadcasting has gained strong footholds. To be sure, the effects of public broadcasting dominance is not the same in every country, and it is important to recognize the difference between public service broadcasting in solid democracies and in weaker transforming democracies. For instance, the BBC in Britain has retained its separation from the government and parties and has a reputation for objectivity and neutrality, as has Sveriges Radio and Sveriges Television in Sweden. On the other hand, as discussed in chapter 22, Russian public television has been less successful in this regard.

In some countries there are marked differnces in the outcomes of exposure to election news on public versus commercial television (Voltmer & Schmitt-Beck, 2002). For instance, NHK (the public channel) in Japan maintains a neutral and objective reporting style while commercial broadcasters have adopted more dramatic styles characterized by negativity (chapter 24). In Sweden these differences between public and private commercial media translate into differences in effects for citizens. Those who read newspapers frequently and are exposed to public television news tend to be more knowledgeable about campaign issues; but this is not true of those who primarily rely on commercial television news.

METHODOLOGICAL ISSUES IN COMPARATIVE RESEARCH ON ELECTION NEWS

The chapters in this volume has shown that impressive efforts are undertaken to study the content of election news in various countries around the world. Compared to the amount of research devoted to the content of election news, there is, however, less research on the antecedents and the effects of election news coverage. Moreover, it is rather obvious that although most election news researchers rely on a similar body of research, there is not much empirical coordination taking place across borders. For example, in many but not all countries there is empirical research on the extent to which the media frame politics as issues versus as a strategic game, and in several but not all countries there is research on the degree of negativity and tendencies towards personalization of political news coverage. However, even when scholars in different countries study the same phenomena, they tend to use different operationalizations and coding instructions. Stated differently, there do not seem to be any standardized instruments and coding instructions. The unfortunate end result is that it is often difficult to compare the election news coverage across borders, and although the terminology used is often similar, the extent to which the empirical results are comparable is often uncertain. In this context it is thus important to note the need for further research comparing election news across countries with the exact same methodology, operationalizations, and definitions. From this perspective, one of the main challenges for further research on election news is to develop standardized instruments and coding instructions that can be used by various scholars around the world.

CONCLUSIONS

There is unquestionably a great deal that we do know about the content and effects of news coverage of elections, but also a great deal we do not know. The contributors to this volume have helped to advance our understanding of these complex concerns by aggregating and summarizing some of what we do know, but they also point to what we need to consider in the future in order to advance our understanding and knowledge about election news coverage, its antecedents, content, and effects.

For example, we still do not know very much about the factors that influence the development of media systems and especially the intertwining of media and political system outcomes. Some of the countries discussed in this volume appear to illustrate an "Americanization" process, whether as mere description or as attribution of blame. There seems to be some agreement that the characteristics labeled as "Americanization" can often also be categorized as "professionalization." Plasser (2000) has outlined and discussed these factors and applied them to many countries. In this volume, Bogusława Dobek-Ostrowska and Bartłomiej Łódzki (chapter 14) describe this process in Poland as one of reliance on campaign consultants and media coverage of opinion polling and strategy. Jolán Róka describes Hungary's political and media system evolution similarly: campaigns are more professionalized, increasingly a marketing and business enterprise (chapter 20).

Many countries, including Japan, South Africa, and Germany, suggest that these developments have also led to a "personalization" of the election process. Such situations are often accompanied by a weakening of the political parties. However, it is not clear exactly how such developments, or how the conduct and the professionalization of political campaigning more generally, influence the news media coverage of elections.

However, there is also evidence that television plays an important role in helping to mold democratic societies around the world and that exposure to television can have a positive effect on citizen adoption of democratic values (Voltmer & Schmitt-Beck, 2002). After studying media's contribution to democratic culture in several East European and Latin American countries, Voltmer and Schmitt-Beck (2002) concluded: "Given that almost no other media are relevant in a positive way for this very basic orientation in any of the six countries, it seems no exaggeration to state that as far as mass media are concerned public television bears the potential to be the single most important factor of democratic consolidation" (p. 28). Such conclusions provide fuel for a more optimistic view of the impact of future election news coverage. At the same time, accounts from established democracies often reach negative conclusions with respect to the influence of the media in general, and television in particular, on the quality of democratic and electoral processes. This suggests that the role of the election news coverage might be fundamentally different in established and transforming democracies, in addition to the differences in the role of the media and the election news coverage that can be traced back to different political and electoral systems.

In addition, it is critical to note that researchers are only beginning to explore the impact that the World Wide Web is having on elections and election news coverage, and the evolution of democratic societies. In the United States we already know that attention to Internet news is an important predictor of voter learning of candidate issue positions (Drew & Weaver, 2006).

As Mira Sotirovic and Jack McLeod (chapter 2) suggest, in the future news organizations are likely to conform to the news styles they believe young citizens (their most lucrative market) want. That will mean more Internet, more interactive formats, blogs, and personality-driven formats like *The Daily Show*. In Poland, for instance, the spread of Internet campaigning has already led to more personalization (more candidate pictures, blogs, Internet chats with the candidates). In Hungary and Bulgaria the Internet is expanding rapidly as a mechanism for political involvement and news dissemination. In many other countries, however, the pace of Internet involvement in political processes is much slower. Mauro Porto suggests that the slow advance of technological innovations, partially a result of social inequalities, in Brazil accounts for the low penetration of Internet capabilities.

What is especially intriguing is the dynamics between, on the one hand, the level of Internet penetration, and, on the other, the importance of the Internet in electoral or political processes. In some countries, Internet penetration in general is low, explaining the minor importance of the Internet in political processes. In other countries, Internet penetration is high, and the importance of the Internet in politics is great. However, there are also some countries, for example Sweden and Canada, where the role of the Internet in political processes is limited, despite high Internet penetration. This suggests that high Internet penetration is a necessary, although not sufficient, condition for this new medium to develop into an important medium with respect to election campaigning and the dissemination of electorally relevant information.

To sum up, research on the content of election news coverage is important from a democratic perspective because modern politics has become mediated and increasingly mediatized. Such research is also rather common in democracies around the world, and as witnessed by the chapters in this book, there are some rather similar trends across borders. Among these are the interest in opinion polls, the tendency to frame politics as a strategic game or as a horserace rather than as issues, a more or less strong focus on negative news, and signs that interpretative journalism and personalized news coverage have become more common. However, there is less research on the antecedents and the effects of election news coverage, and a paucity of truly comparative research using the same definitions and methodological instruments. To the extent that research on the effects of election news coverage exists in various countries, it does show, however, that the way the news media cover elections is influential.

From our perspective the implication is clear: Due to the importance of election news coverage in democracies around the world, there is a need for more, and more coordinated, comparative research on the antecedents, content, and effects of election news. From that perspective, we hope that this book will serve as a useful springboard for further efforts to develop comparative and coordinated research on election news across borders. Only by more coordinated and comparative research on election news will it be possible to further our understanding of the antecedents of the content of election news and how it is shaped by factors such as the political system, the media system and the degree of commercialism, the electoral system, the conduct of political campaigning, and people's behavior as voters and media consumers.

REFERENCES

Drew, D., & Weaver, D. (2006). Voter learning in the 2004 presidential election: Did the media matter? *Journalism and Mass Communication Quarterly, 83*(1), 25–43.

Frank, R. S. (1973). *Message dimensions of television news.* Lexington, MA: Lexington Books.

Freedom House (2007*). Global press freedom 2007: Growing threats to media independence.* Washington, D.C.: Freedom House. Retrieved September 8, 2007, from: http://www.freedomhouse.org/uploads/fop/2007/pfscharts.pdf

Graber, D. A. (2006). *Mass media & American politics* (7th ed.). Washington, D.C.: CQ Press.

Hallin, D. C., & Mancini, P. (2004). *Comparing media systems: Three models of media and politics.* New York: Cambridge University Press.

Hofstetter, C.R. (1976). *Bias in the news.* Columbus, OH: Ohio State University Press.

Iyengar, S. (1991). *Is anyone responsible? How television frames political issues.* Chicago: University of Chicago Press.

Lange, B-P., & Ward, D. (Ed.) (2004). *The media and elections: A handbook and comparative study.* Mahwah, NJ: Erlbaum.

McCombs, M. (2004). *Setting the agenda: The mass media and public opinion.* Cambridge, UK: Polity Press.

Norris, P. (2000). *A virtuous circle: Political communications in postindustrial societies*. Cambridge, UK: Cambridge University Press.

Plasser, F. (2000). American campaign techniques worldwide. *The Harvard International Journal of Press/ Politics, 5*(4), 33–54.

Reese, S. D., Gandy Jr, O. H., & Grant, A. E. (Eds.). (2001). *Framing public life: Perspectives on media and our understanding of the social world*. Mahwah, NJ: Erlbaum.

Strömbäck, J., & Aalberg, T. (2008). Election news coverage in democratic corporatist countries: A comparative study of Sweden and Norway. *Scandinavian Political Studies, 31*(1), 91–106.

Strömbäck, J., & Dimitrova, D. V. (2006). Political and media systems matter: A comparison of election news coverage in Sweden and the United States. *The Harvard International Journal of Press/Politics, 11*(4), 131–147.

Strömbäck, J. & Shehata, A. (2007). Structural biases in British and Swedish election news coverage. *Journalism Studies, 8*(5), 798–812.

Voltmer, K., & Schmitt-Beck, R. (2002, March). *The mass media and citizens' orientations towards democracy: The experience of six "third-wave" democracies in southern Europe, Eastern Europe and Latin America*. Paper presented to the workshop "Political Communication, the Mass Media, and the Consolidation of New Democracies" at the Joint Sessions of Workshops of the European Consortium for Political Research, Turin, Italy.

Index